The Great Educators

The Great

Readings for

Professional-Technical Series

Nelson-Hall Company nh Chicago

Educators

Leaders in Education

Hugh C. Black
University of California
Davis

Kenneth V. Lottich
University of Montana
Missoula

Donald S. Seckinger
University of Wyoming
Laramie

ISBN: 0-911012-48-6

Library of Congress Catalog Card Number: 72-88717

Copyright © 1972 by Hugh C. Black, Kenneth V. Lottich, and Donald S. Seckinger

Manufactured in the United States of America

Whatsoever things are good, whatsoever things are true, whatsoever things are lovely, whatsoever things are of good report, if there be any virtue, if there be any knowledge . . . think on these things.

Phillippians 4:8

There is a bit of Aristotle I always like to quote. He says it is a definition of happiness. It is that, but I think it is also what education should strive for: "the exercise of vital powers along lines of excellence, in a life affording them scope."

Edith Hamilton

Contents

Preface   xv

Part One: What It Is All About—The Questions

Overview   3

1   **The Need to Uneducate?**   5
Frederico Fellini ● *Playboy* Interview

2   **"The System"—One Kind of Education**   9
Ross Finney
(From *A Sociological Philosophy of Education*)

3   **What Kind of People Are We?**   11
Haynes Johnson ● Kent State's Fifth Victim; Opa Locka:
A Town Full of Hatred

4   **Leadership?**   16
Barbara W. Tuchman
(From "The Missing Element: Moral Courage")

5   **How Can the Whole People Be Best Educated?**   21
The Subject of Education and Its General Necessity
Edward Everett: Superior and Popular Education
Calvin O. Davis: The Rewards of Teaching
Edward Everett: The Importance of Education in a Republic
Basic Beliefs Expressed by Founding Fathers and Early Leaders
in Political Documents in the United States
George Washington: Speech to Both Houses of
Congress
George Washington: Farewell Address
Northwest Ordinance
Mirabeau Buonoparte Lamar: Message of the President
(of Texas) to Both Houses
Thomas Jefferson: Letter to Colonel Yancy
Thomas Jefferson: Letter to Governor Tyler
James Madison: Letter to W. T. Barry
James Monroe: Letter to the Governor of Virginia
John Adams: Thoughts on Government
John Jay: Letter to Dr. Benjamin Rush
Thomas Jefferson: Letter to George Wythe
Emma Lazarus: Words chiseled in base of the Statue of
Liberty
Edward Everett: Superior and Popular Education

6   **Can We Meet the Challenge Today?**   34
Arnold Toynbee ● Education: The Long View

Part Two: Possible Insights from Education among Primitive
    Peoples and the First Large Ancient Civilizations

Overview   41
7 Formal Value Inculcation in Simpler Societies   44
    Donald S. Seckinger • Education in Primitive and Modern
    Societies: A Comparison
8 A Hypothesis and World View of Meaning   48
    Susanne K. Langer • Symbolic Transformation
9 Man and His Fetishes—Primitive   61
    Barbara Ward • Shrunken Heads—and Shrunken Minds
10 Man and His Fetishes—Modern?   67
    Andrew Kopkind • The Power of Prayer
11 The Egyptian Way and the Way of the East   68
    Hugh C. Black • Man's Ways with Ideas
    Edith Hamilton • (From The Greek Way)

Part Three: Possibilities from Our Graeco-Roman Heritage

Overview   81
12 The Light of Experience through History   84
    Arnold Toynbee • ("Preface to the Second Edition," Greek
    Civilization and Character)
13 The Ever-Present Past   86
    Edith Hamilton • The Lessons of the Past: Adventures of
    the Mind 11
14 The Educational Ideal of the Man of Action and the Man of   95
    Wisdom
    Stringfellow Barr
    (From The Will of Zeus)
15 Spartan Education and Life—The Totalitarian Pattern   104
    (From Plutarch, "Lycurgus," The Lives of the Noble
    Grecians and Romans)
16 Athenian Education and Life—A Democratic Way   113
    Thucydides • The Funeral Speech of Pericles
    Plato's Summary of Athenian Education—Old Greek
    Period
    (From Protagoras)
17 Isocrates (436-338 B.C.). Whom, Then, Do I Call Educated?   120
    (From Panathenaicus)
18 Socrates (469?-399 B.C.)   121
    On Virtue
    (From Plato, Meno)
    The Accusations against Socrates
    (From Plato, Apology)

Contents

The Midwife of Knowledge
(From Plato, *Theaetetus*)

19 Plato (428/7-348/7 B.C.)   133
Education in the *Republic*

20 Aristotle (384-322 B.C.)   163
(From *Nichomachean Ethics*)

21 The New Greek Education of the Alexandrian Age (c. 338-30
B.C.)   180
(The Euphebic Oath)

22 The Roman Family (as Seen by an Early American Sociologist)   181
Mosiah Hall
(From *A Practical Sociology*)

23 Oratory—The Contrast between the New and Old Education   186
Publius Cornelius Tacitus (55-c. 120 A.D.)
(From *A Dialogue on Oratory*)

24 Oratory as the Aim of Education   191
Marcus Tullius Cicero (106-43 B.C.)
(From *De Oratore*)

25 Marcus Fabius Quintilianus (c. 35-c. 95 A.D.) on Education   195
(From *Institutio Oratoria*)

Part Four: Some Possibilities from Our Judeo-Christian Heritage

Overview   231
26 The Contribution of the Hebrews to Culture: Ethical
Monotheism   234
The Transition from Yahweh (God of Power, Battles) to
God (a Universal God)
Anthropomorphism
Tribal Monolatry with Polytheistic Elements
The Eighth Century Prophets: Amos, Micah, Hosea,
and Isaiah
The Fall of Samaria (722/21 B.C.)
King Josiah's Reform (621 B.C.) and Monoyahwism
Jeremiah and Ethical Monotheism
The Exile (598/87, 587/86-538 B.C.), the Problem, and
New Prophets
The Post-Exilic Period
Jesus of Nazareth
The Sermon on the Plain (Sermon on the Mount in
Matthew 5-7)
St. Paul

27 Christianity: The Counter-Culture   264
Radoslav A. Tsanoff
(From *The Great Philosophers*)

28 **Conflict: Christianity as Seen by Romans**   268
    Minicius Felix
      (From *The Octavius*)
29 **The "Counter-Culture": Christian Living**   273
    Tertullian
      (From *Apology*)
30 **Beliefs and Opinions in Conflict**   278
      (From the *Address of Tatian to the Greeks*)
31 **The "Counter-Culture": Family Up-Bringing**   286
    Hugh C. Black ● St. John Chrysostum (347?-407) and
    Raising Up an Athlete for Christ
32 **The "Counter-Culture": Catechumenal Instruction**   292
    Hugh C. Black ● The Priest and Church between Man and
      God
    How the Catechumens Are to Be Instructed
      (From *The Apostolical Constitutions*)
33 **The "Counter-Culture": Christian Schooling**   296
    St. Basil (330-379 A.D.)
      (From the *Address to Young Men on the Right Use of
        Greek Literature*)
    St. Augustine (354-430 A.D.)
      (From *The Confessions of St. Augustine* and *On Christian
        Doctrine*)
34 **Monasticism**   316
    The Rule of St. Benedict
35 **Triumph for the "Counter-Culture"**   321
    The Alliance of Church and State: Precursors of Scholasticism
      and Universities
      Charlemagne (742-814): Biographical Sketch
      *Rhabanus Maurus (b. about 766 A.D.): Education of the
        Clergy*
36 **Feudalism and the Guild System in Medieval Education**   330
    Elmer Harrison Wilds and Kenneth V. Lottich
      (From *The Foundations of Modern Logic*)
37 **The Renaissance. Erasmus (1466-1536)**   340
    The Treatise of Erasmus *De Ratione Studii,* that is, Upon
      the Right Method of Instruction, 1511
    The Treatise *De Pueris statim ac liberaliter instituendis,*
      Addressed to William, Duke of Cleves, 1529
38 **The Reformation. Martin Luther (1483-1546)**   382
      (From the *Letter to the Mayors and Aldermen of All the
        Cities of Germany in Behalf of Christian Schools*)
39 **Christianity and Problems of the Nineteenth Century**   392
    Orestes A. Brownson, "Concerning the Transcendental

Philosophy of the Germans, and of Cousins, and Its Influence
on Opinion in this Country")

40 Christianity and Problems of Today 397
Ronnie Dugger
(From Dark Star—Hiroshima Reconsidered in the Life
of Claude Eatherly of Lincoln Park, Texas)

Part Five: Precursors of the Contemporary in Educational Theory

Overview 403
41 Francis Bacon (1561-1626). Developments in Logic 409
Induction and Scientific Method
Barriers to Truth. Francis Bacon's Idols
42 John Amos Comenius (1592-1670). A Unified Approach 416
(From The Great Didactic)
43 John Locke (1632-1704). A Dual System 429
Locke's Proposals for Reform of the Poor Law
The Education of the Gentry
44 Jean Jacques Rousseau (1712-1778). Paradox 452
The Social Contract
Emile
45 Johann Heinrich Pestalozzi (1746-1827) 474
The Conditions Against Which Pestalozzi Led a Reform
(From an address by Adolph Diesterweg)
Pestalozzi's Ideas. Selections from His Writings
Pestalozzi and Today
(Hugh C. Black, "Pestalozzi and the Education of the
Disadvantaged")
46 Friedrich Wilhelm Froebel (1782-1852) 496
(From The Education of Man)
47 Johann Friedrich Herbart (1776-1841) 503
(From the Brief Encyclopedia of Practical Philosophy and
the Science of Education)
48 Herbert Spencer (1820-1903) 517
What Knowledge Is of Most Worth?
(Chapter I in Education: Intellectual, Moral, and Physical)
49 Horace Mann (1796-1859) 557
(From The Massachusetts System of Common Schools)
50 William T. Harris (1835-1909). The Conservator 577
(From Merle Curti, The Social Ideas of American
Educators)
51 Francis W. Parker (1837-1902) 603
(From Notes of Talks on Teaching)

52 John Dewey (1859-1952)   613
        A New Scientific Formulation of the Nature of Experience
        Based upon Biology and a Change in Psychology
        (From *Reconstruction in Philosophy*)
        The Core of Dewey's Way of Thinking
            (From Edwin A. Burtt, "The Core of Dewey's Way of
            Thinking")
        Criteria for Determining an Educative Experience: Continuity
        and Interaction
            (Hugh C. Black, "The Learning-Product and the Learning-
            Process Theories of Education: An Attempted
            Synthesis")
        What Is Educationally Vital: The Formation of a Disciplined
        Logical Ability to Think
            (Chapter 6 in John Dewey, *How We Think*)
53 The Continuing Controversy over Education   632
        William C. Bagley
            ("An Essentialist's Platform for the Advancement of
            American Education")

        Part Six: The Contemporary Scene. Will We Make It?

        Overview   651
54 Synthesis Based on Analysis?   654
        Hugh C. Black ● A Four-Fold Classification of Educational
        Theories
55 Linguistic Analysis?   668
        Jonas F. Soltis ● Analysis and Anomalies in Philosophy of
        Education
56 Existentialism?   684
        M. I. Berger ● Existential Criticism in Educational Theory:
        A Subjective View of a Serious Business
57 The Problem of Recovering an Inclusive View of Life and the
    Universe   691
        Edwin A. Burtt ● The Philosophy of Man as an All-Embracing
        Philosophy
58 The Problem of Violence   703
        Arthur Schlesinger, Jr. ● Existential Politics and the Cult of
        Violence
59 The Problem of the Political State   715
        Hans J. Morgenthau ● Reflections on the End of the Republic
60 Problems of Finance   724
        James M. Cronin ● School Finance in the Seventies: The
        Prospect for Reform

Contents xiii

61 **Problems of Curriculum** 728
    Arthur W. Foshay • How Fare the Disciplines?

62 **Problems of the Disadvantaged** 736
    Robert J. Havighurst • Curriculum for the Disadvantaged

63 **Controversy in Higher Education** 743
    José A. Argüelles • The Believe-In—An Aquarian Age
      Ritual
    Marjorie Grene • Believe-In—What?—A Reply to José
      Argüelles
    José A. Argüelles • Towards a New University Model—A
      Response to Professor Grene

64 **What Shall the Schools Do?** 764
    Donald S. Seckinger • Freedom and Responsibility in
      Education
    Donald S. Seckinger • Initiative Learning
    Hugh C. Black • A Missing Chord in Educational Theory

  Index of Names 780

Preface

Yes, you are included when we say "For Leaders in Education," for that phrase includes everyone from teachers to students, and from administrative personnel to concerned and puzzled citizens. In our society, we are the people who are responsible for education—all of us. We exercise our responsibilities when we vote for school board members; when we vote school bonds and pay taxes; when we vote on candidates for our legislatures who will pass laws affecting education and who will appoint or approve regents and trustees of state colleges and universities; when we take part in parent-teacher meetings and town meetings; and when we talk about the school program or system. In these many ways we determine our educational program, we express our values, and we contribute—for good or ill—to the present and to the future.

We thus share a common concern and interest: the subject of "education." About it, we have in common at least one certainty: everyone is an authority. Each of us knows what should be done, and we are liberal in expressing what is wrong with our schools, teachers, and pupils. But in our saner moments, when we stop to think, we realize that our opinions and beliefs about this subject of education differ. Hence we also share with each other uncertainties about education, especially today when a considerable number of us advocate change on the assumption that any change will be for the better and without any conception of what might truly be "better." These materials are intended for those of us who are just possibly ready to turn to discussions of what truly matters and to be about that business which Plato saw long ago as our uniquely human adventure in ideas. We act on the judgment he put into the mouth of Socrates (in the classic *Apology*): "Only the examined life is worth living."

Discussion seems to be what our university students of the day seem to want, whether young or old, on or off campus. So many rebellious students are no longer content with the old ways which they say pass for "education." So many turn a deaf ear to their professors, to college courses, to lectures, and to customary ways of introducing the young to the perennial questions and wisdoms of mankind about man, and life, and education. To those of such bent this compilation of readings should prove appealing, for the compilers had them very much in mind and came close to titling the work *Readings for Discussion*.

While not limited by any means to students in these courses, our materials for discussion are mainly intended to supplement courses treating such subjects as introduction to education, foundations of education, social foundations of education, educational sociology, and history and philosophy of education. We hope teachers of these education courses will find the readings a versatile assemblage lending themselves to combinations and approaches limited only by the creativity of the instructors. Especially do our students preparing to become teachers need this kind of lively, dynamic dialectic of ideas to challenge them to see new possibilities for teachers of today's children.

Other seekers of wisdom about education in addition to activist discussants should find these selections appealing. For here appear original, first-hand sources with which the student may work in his attempt to analyze them and then to synthesize his own position. To facilitate this objective we have included, on occasion, articles which are not original sources but which pull together salient features of a development.

To both types of students—the activist discussants and the workers with first-hand sources—the compilers suggest the wisdom of supplementing our collection of readings with at least one of the standard textbooks in the history and philosophy of education. On the assumption that the reader will actually so bestir himself, the compilers have deliberately omitted much of the usual editorial addenda. Our view is that the survey and the source book of readings must go together, so complex are the problems of education. In effect, we are advocating the approach used by Ellwood P. Cubberley (in 1920 through Houghton-Mifflin Company of Boston) in supplementing his textbook in the history of education with his *Readings in the History of Education.* We urge our readers, then, to supplement these readings with the knowledge available from one of the standard textbooks in the history and foundations of education.

An introductory section of readings catches us up in the dynamic dialectic which the discussion of education can be and starts us off with present interests and problems. The order of succeeding selections is chronological, beginning with the earliest periods and coming forward to the present. A reading may have been selected as an original source which the standard survey texts only mention or cite briefly. Or it may be a particularly excellent summary of a development the reader needs to grasp as a whole. Or the reading may carry forward one of the discussion questions at the end of a chapter in a survey text, inspiring a discussion that makes the historical materials extremely relevant to our times and immediate problems. Whichever of these purposes the reading may serve, it should be provocative and lead to live education for live students.

H. C. B.; K. V. L.; D. S. S.

PART ONE
WHAT IT IS ALL ABOUT —
THE QUESTIONS

Overview

That the subject of education is deserving of more than a "Mickey Mouse" consideration becomes apparent from these first readings, which acquaint us with the crucial questions about which we shall seek wisdom as we turn to the various possibilities for answers in other parts of the book. For these are complex matters, the pursuit of which leads us to the most basic issues of our lives and our values. The quest after our individual answers will demand our keenest intelligence and send us ranging over many other fields of knowledge.

We begin our discussion in education with the present and a theme already expressed in the arts: Should not our main concern be to uneducate rather than educate? Frederico Fellini has fascinated modern audiences with such film productions as *8½* and *Juliet of the Spirits*. Our first reading, from a *Playboy* interview, reveals to us what Fellini considers the common theme linking his films. If he finds the concepts inculcated through education to be worthless and useless baggage he wants off his back, perhaps we should consider, discuss, and argue the quality and worthiness of education today. For that, we have good precedent in the United States. That argument has characterized twentieth-century education!

Our reply to Fellini and to any other discussant of education will depend upon our particular answer to the fundamental question of this book: What is education? Although published in 1928, Ross Finney's description of "the system" sounds very much like that of a radical critic in the 1970s. It reveals another concept of education held by many and another part of our continuing controversies over education. For traditionalists and their radical critics, whether in 1928, 1938, 1948, 1958, or 1968, have opposing answers in their theories or philosophies of education. These initial readings, then, present contrasting extremes in their views of education. Oversimplified or overgeneralized, these views reflect most of our thinking about what education ought to be. They should challenge us to explore further our knowledge about education, to become aware of other possibilities, and to formulate our own best notion of what education needs to be. This is important because whatever our specific answer may be, it determines so very much in human lives in our society.

Especially in a democratic society is one's view of education crucial. Some have thought that our education is related to the kind of people we are and the kind of living we enjoy or suffer. Our next readings raise searching questions about people in the United States and where we are today. Then we are invited to think specifically about education in a democracy. Since each generation usually has to think through for itself what kind of education is best in a democracy, certain "self-evident" truths or beliefs by early leaders are presented as vital material for debate and discussion. But our answers to the educational questions in a democratic society also have to be relevant to the world of today. The selection of excerpts from Arnold Toynbee's article "Education: The Long View" should bring home to us all the challenging tasks we face today when we take "education" seriously. And that is a far cry from "Mickey Mouse" consideration.

Part One is a challenge to seek individual answers to the questions of what education is all about. The question, What is education? must be answered. In this way we develop our theory or philosophy or view of education. The question, How can the whole people in a democratic society be best educated? must be answered as adequately as possible by a people who intend to be their own rulers. When these questions are asked with respect to formal educational efforts and to schooling, we face more specific questions. What is the ideal teacher-pupil relationship—the focus for our educational efforts? If the teacher is indeed the expert at supplying the guidance, control, and direction needed by the immature student, what is he to teach? How? To what end or purpose? To develop what kind of person? In what kind of society? In what kind of world? So, if we truly engage in educational discussions, we are challenged to think through the problems of aims and purposes and objectives, of curriculum, of method, and of all the manifold problems of school and society. These are the questions education is all about.

1
The Need to Uneducate?

Frederico Fellini
Playboy Interview

From "Playboy Interview: Frederico Fellini" — a candid conversation with the protean creator of such trail-blazing cinematic allegories as *La Straca*, *La Dolce Vita*, and *8½*, in *Playboy*, 13 (No. 2, February, 1966): 55-66. (Reprinted with the permission of *Playboy*, © 1966, 1972 by *Playboy*.)

Playboy: Still, if we confine ourselves to the original impulse that inspired them, is there a common theme linking your films?

Fellini: My work can't be anything other than a testimony of what I am looking for in life. It is a mirror of my searching.

Playboy: Searching for what?

Fellini: For myself freed. In this respect, I think there is no cleavage or difference of content or style in all my films. From first to last, I have struggled to free myself—always from the past, from the education laid upon me as a child. That is what I'm seeking, though through different characters and with a changing tempo and images.

Playboy: In what sense do you want to escape your past?

Fellini: I became burdened in childhood with useless baggage that I now want off my back. I want to *un*educate myself of these worthless concepts, so that I may return to a virginal personality—to a rebirth of real intent and of real self. Then I won't be lost in a collective whole that fits nobody because it's made to fit *everybody*. Wherever I go, from the corner of my eye I see young people moving in groups, like schools of fish. When I was young, we all moved in separate directions. Are we developing a society like ants, in blocs and colonies? This is one of the things I fear more than anything else. I loathe collectivity. Man's greatness and nobility consist in standing *free* of the mass. How he extricates himself from it is his own personal problem and private struggle. This is what my films describe.

Playboy: Can you give us an actual example from one of your films?

Fellini: In *8½*, society's norms and rules imprisoned Guido in his boyhood with a sense of guilt and frustration. From childhood many of us are conditioned by a similar education. Then, growing up, we find ourselves in profound conflict—a conflict created by having been taught to idealize our lives, to pursue aesthetic and ethical ideals of absolute good or evil. This imposes impossible standards and unattainable aspirations that can only impede the spontaneous growth of a normal human being, and may conceivably destroy him. You must have experienced this yourself. There arrives a moment in life when you discover that what you've been told at home, in school or in church is simply not true. You discover that it binds your authentic self, your instinct, your true growth. And this opens up a schism, creates a conflict that must eventually be resolved—or succumbed to. In all forms of neurosis there is this clash between certain forms of idealization in a moral sense and a contrary aesthetic form. It all started with the Greeks when they enshrined a classical standard of physical beauty. A man who did not correspond to that type of beauty felt himself excluded, inferior, an outsider. Then came Christianity, which established an ethical beauty. This doubled man's problems by creating the dual possibility that he was neither beautiful as a Greek god nor holy as a Catholic one. Inevitably, you were guilty of either nonbeauty or unsaintliness, and probably both. So you lived in disgrace: Man did not love you, nor did God; thus you remained outside of life.

Playboy: And today?

Fellini: In a modified form, this same ethic-aesthetic still prevails, and there is no escape from it through mere denial, though many have tried. You *can* escape very simply, however: by realizing that if you are not beautiful, it's all right anyway; and if you're not a saint, that's all right, too—because reality is not ideality. But this self-acceptance can occur only when you've grasped one fundamental fact of life: that the only thing which exists is yourself, your true individual self in depth, which wants to grow spontaneously, but which is fettered by inoperative lies, myths and fantasies proposing an unattainable morality or sanctity or perfection—all of it brainwashed into us during our defenseless childhood.

Playboy: Once you've liberated yourself from the past, what then?

Fellini: Then you are free to live in the present, and not seek cowardly flight toward the past—or toward the future, either.

Playboy: In what way toward the future?

Fellini: I mean that we must cease projecting ourselves into the future as though it were plannable, foreseeable, tangible, controllable —it's not; or as though it were a dimension existing outside and beyond ourselves. We must learn to deal with matters as they are, not as we hope or fear they may eventuate. We must cope with them as they exist now, today, at this moment. We must awaken to the fact that the future is already *here*, to be lived in the present. In short, wake up and live!

Playboy: Though most of your protagonists, at the end of their spiritual odysseys, do learn to live with themselves as they are and with life as it is, some interpreters have seen their awakening as little more than a fatalistic resignation to the human condition.

Fellini: No, no! Not a fatalistic resignation, but an *affirmative acceptance* of life, a burgeoning of *love* for life. The return of Guido to life in *8½* is not a defeat. Rather, it is the return of a victor. When he finally realizes that he will never be able to resolve his problems, only to *live* with them—when he realizes that life itself is a continuous refutation of resolution—he experiences an exhilarating resurgence of energy, a return of profound religious sentiment. "I have faith," he says, "that I am inserted into a design of Providence whose end I don't and can't and will never comprehend—and wouldn't want to even if I could. There's nothing for me to do but pass through this panorama of joy and pain—with all my energy, all my enthusiasm, all my love, accepting it for what it is, without expecting an explanation that does not concern me, that does not involve me, that I am not called upon to give." He is at peace with himself at last—free to accept himself as he is, not as he wished he were or might have been. That is the optimistic finale to *8½*.

Playboy: Doesn't *Juliet of the Spirits* have essentially the same moral?

Fellini: Essentially, yes—only carried along another, deeper plane, with more decadent undertones, and told in a less realistic way. *Juliet* touches on myths within human psychology; its images, therefore, are those of a fable. But it treats of a profound human reality: the institution of marriage, and the need within it for individual liberation. It's the portrait of an Italian woman, conditioned by our modern society, yet a product of misshapen religious training and ancient dogmas—like the one about getting married and living happily ever after. When she grows up and finds it hasn't come true, she can neither face nor understand it; and so she escapes into a private world of remembered yesterdays and mythical tomorrows. Whatever she does is influenced by her childhood, which she recaptures in other-worldly visions; and by the future, which she brings to life in bizarre and lively fantasies. The present exists for her only in the electronic unreality of television commercials. She is finally awakened from these visions by a grim reality: the desertion of her husband; but this fulfillment of her worst fear becomes the most positive episode of her life, for it forces her to find herself, to seek her free identity as an individual. And this gives her the insight to realize that all the fears—the phantoms that

lived around her—were monsters of her own creation, bred of misshapen education and misread religion. She realizes that the spirits
have been necessary, even useful, and deserve to be thanked; and the
moment she thanks them, she no longer fears and hates them, and they
turn into positive, pleasant beings.

Playboy: Is there some specific message in this for all of us?

Fellini: A lesson—a lesson we must all learn—as *Juliet* finally
did: that marriage, if it is to survive, must be treated as the *beginning,*
not as the happy ending; that it's something you have to work at; but
that it's also not the alpha and omega of human existence; and that
it must not be something you accept from the outside, like an inviolate
taboo, never to be shattered. Why not admit it? Marriage as an
institution needs re-examining. We live with too many nonfunctioning
ideologies. Modern man needs richer relationships.

2
"The System" —
One Kind of Education?

Ross L. Finney

From Ross L. Finney, *A Sociological Philosophy of Education* (New York, The Macmillan Company, 1928), pp. 366-368.

The reader is invited to believe that in college one of the most serious obstacles to real education is our system of credits, with the roll calls, examinations, marks, distribution curves, honor points, espionage and other accessories that the credits system involves.

For of sincere intellectual interest this system is a negative motivation in several ways.[1] In the first place it gives rise to an elaborate technique upon the student's part for "getting by"; that is, of getting what the school asks him to want, namely, credits, with the least possible effort. It puts a premium on easy courses. It creates files of old questions, outlines, notes, and other pointers, that are passed on from upper to lower classmen. It inspires the art of flattering, cajoling, and otherwise manipulating the professors. It often causes those who get low grades to hate their teachers, which is a frame of mind quite unconducive of learning from them. It sets up in students a fear of showing any sign of disagreement with a teacher—one of its most stultifying effects. And it motivates all cheating. In the second place it stresses the kind of subject matter that might be called "cramable," as against the kind that is really the most educative. The students go through textbooks, library references, and lecture notes looking for memorizable items of the kind that lend themselves to examination questions, without much regard for their relative significance. And the so-called objective tests make this worse instead of better. Some of the most important results of education cannot be measured; and the measurement of results tends always to discourage the most viable teaching on that account. In the third place, the system—in connection with organized courses, sequences, and majors—tends to repress the spontaneous interests of stufents, and force them into prescribed grooves. If the student strikes a lead of special interest he too often must abandon it, because of the pressure of

[1] For this insidious disease of the intellect Dean H. W. Holmes has invented the term *credititis*. See *Atlantic Monthly*,

prescribed assignments, to which the imminent examinations force him to give attention. Scarcely anything can be more deadening to real intellectual interest. Closely related to this is the subconscious intention that students often develop during the dry course of forgetting it all as soon as the examination is over.

. . . Students take courses because they are required, or because they are in a sequence or major, or because they just happen to fit into a schedule. . . . But worst of all, the system tends to absolve the school itself of responsibility for selling knowledge to the students on its intrinsic merits. If they were not taking courses for the sake of earning credits, more need would be felt for explaining to them the real value of the subject matter, and of discarding subject matter that in reality has but little value, if any at all.

During fifteen or twenty years' experience in college teaching one will have overheard innumerable eager conversations in the corridors about examinations, marks, and the like; but it is the rarest of experiences to hear a group of students talking about subject matter itself as of intrinsic interest. It is easy for system-blinded faculty members to blame that attitude to the frivolous mindedness of students; but it is at least as reasonable to blame it to the system. The students are showing interest at exactly the spot where the system motivates their interest. A system that threw the students back upon the intrinsic merits of the subject matter itself might tend to eliminate those students who were incapable of developing any honest interest in it; and it might encourage those who did have such capacity.

3
What Kind of People Are We?

Haynes Johnson

Kent State's Fifth Victim; Opa-Locka: A Town Full of Hatred

The Sacramento (California) *Bee*, Sunday March 28, 1971, Section P. Copyright, 1971, Washington Post. Reprinted with permission. Los Angeles Times/Washington Post News Service.

Opa-Locka, Fla.—When Mary Vecchio came home from Kent State last spring in her flowered miniskirt and sandals held together by tape, she broke down and cried. "I'm so glad to be home," she said, as she embraced her father. It was "the most wonderful thing."

The scene of that tearful airport reunion—Mary, the gangling big-eyed girl with the long dark hair, angular face, and high cheekbones, surrounded by her emotional family, brothers, sisters, mother, father —was recorded by an army of newspaper photographers and television cameramen. The happy ending to an American tragedy. Mary Vecchio, the "mystery coed" whose look of horror as she knelt over a slain student had been captured by a photographer to become a symbol of national protest, was home.

She wasn't even a coed, it turned out. Just a 14-year-old who had run away from home and turned up, by chance, on the Kent State campus the day the Guardsmen fired into the crowd of students, killing four of them. Her parents had seen that picture and identified her. Now, at the airport, it was over.

'Ruined' by Tragedy

Two weeks ago, Mary Vecchio, now 15, was committed for a six-month period to a juvenile home south of Miami. She had run away again. The Kent State aftermath, her lawyer says, "has ruined her. You can't put that kind of load on a 14-year-old girl and expect her to take it. And if

11

you want to be sociological about it, the family unit for all practical purposes has been destroyed."

He was referring to the climate at home to which Mary returned: Parents who refused to let their children see Mary; the insults in the community; the attitude of the high school principal who initially suspended her ("the youngsters didn't want to have anything to do with her—and I was proud of them," he says); the policemen who harassed Mary, her parents and lawyer contend, picking her up four times on charges ranging from loitering to sniffing transmission fluid (none of the charges stood up in court: Mary has never been convicted of a crime); the restriction imposed by the youth curfew ordinance of Opa-Locka coupled with the restrictions of her own parents; the exploiters who manufactured and sold T-shirts and 6-foot posters showing Mary kneeling over the dead student's body, all without the Vecchios' permission; the monthly proceedings before the juvenile judge because Mary had been placed on probation after she ran away; the transfer to a new school, where she encountered new problems because of her notoriety; the testimony she had to give before the Kent State grand jury—and the FBI—and the state's attorney; the charges by the then-governor of Florida, Claude Kirk, made over statewide television, implying that Mary was part of a Communist plot; and the torrent of mail—obscene, abusive, vicious hate mail—that poured into the Vecchio household from throughout America.

Symbol of Youth

Perhaps above all, it was the attitude of people that made Mary Vecchio a symbol of all American problems of wayward youth, student protests, violence, anti-Americanism."

In a sense, she has become the fifth victim of Kent State.

The letters alone were enough to leave lasting scars. Mary's mother, Claire, a heavy-set woman with coal black hair and dark eyes, keeps them in a box in her bedroom. "I still get shocked," she said, opening the box and taking out the letters, "because I don't believe in bad language myself."

"Look at that," she said, pulling out a newspaper clipping.

It showed pictures of the four slain students, along with one of Mary. Her face had been X-ed out in red ink. Across the top was written: "It's too bad you weren't shot." Mrs. Vecchio shook her head and said: "Can you imagine her looking at that?"

Others, opened at random, read:

"We are wondering why you still worry about your daughter, being she slept with all those hippies that are all diseased. We have no doubt she'll wind up being one of the biggest whores and prostitutes."

"The pictures in all the magazines in this country and abroad of you receiving with welcome arms your daughter is really a farce. If you wanted to find her, you could have. There are ways."

"We believe she should be placed in a juvenile home where she would not cause any trouble on campuses across the country. . . ."

It was signed: "A taxpayer of Ohio."

"Some young people here know what she is—a dirty, foul, syphilitic whore."

"If she is ever seen in Ohio again she will be shot."

"Keep your hoodlum daughter in Florida where she belongs. What you need is a good beating with a strap, beating until you bleed good red blood. Your parents should have left you where you were! You don't deserve to be associated with decent people."

"Mary: You dirty tramp. It's too bad it wasn't you that was shot."

"I am a veteran, I done my hitch. . . . The soldiers hang your picture up and spit on it. See how you stand with the Army? You should do the world a favor and kill yourself."

One from Pleasantville, N.Y., began "Dear Mary Ann," the way she was identified in the press, although her parents call her "Mary," and said:

"You hippie Communist bitch!

"Did you enjoy sleeping with all those dope fiends and Negroes when you were in Ohio? The deaths of the Kent State four are on the conscience of yourself and other rabble rousers like you.

"Congratulations."

Threats In Mail

The Vecchios themselves received threatening letters. "Even I got letters saying they were going to get me for raising such a radical into the world," Mrs. Vecchio says. "There was one letter that said they were going to come here and abolish the whole family, like the Sharon Tate thing. The FBI still has that one."

Mary, she says, has now changed completely.

"She was the happiest child, the friendliest person you ever saw," her mother said. "When she smiled she made you happy. They said in her school it was like the sunshine coming in. And that laugh! When you heard that laugh, you had to laugh.

"But Mary is so different now. She is so nervous. She can't even talk about it. And they're still calling her a Communist. Even her relatives say they're ashamed of her."

Others who know Mary well see different aspects of change. Her father, Frank, a 49-year-old maintenance man for the Dade County Port Authority, says: "Mary don't care for nothing in the world. Nothing. Years ago, she had love for life, love for her family, love for the baby, but now she doesn't have anything to live for. She's not the same girl. Nowhere the same."

Phillip Vitello, a Coral Gables lawyer who represents Mary, describes Mary in different terms. "The story's even worse than it seems," he says. "It's affected her mind to a tremendous degree. She's become more withdrawn. She refuses to relate to anybody. Now, she won't even talk to me or to her parents or to the judge."

Frank Vecchio calls himself one of Opa-Locka's pioneers. "This was the most wonderful town you could live in," he says. But as for now: "I don't even want to walk in this town."

Vecchio is bitter. "No matter where Mary went, in a restaurant or anywhere, she was harassed," he says. "She was told she was not welcome."

Labeled Communists

One night after Mary came home, he and Mary and the Vecchios' youngest child, a 3-year-old girl, went to a restaurant in Opa-Locka. As soon as they walked in, the manager recognized them.

"He said that she wasn't a decent person, nothing but a Communist," Vecchio says. "He said, 'You and your whole family are Communists, and I don't have to serve any Communists.'"

An argument developed. The manager called police. Vecchio was arrested on charges of public profanity (he denies cursing) and paid $61 in court costs when the case came up.

Vecchio also claims Mary was harassed by police and by the school principal. After Opa-Locka police picked up Mary four times, the Vecchios filed a million-dollar suit against the department, charging Mary's civil rights were being violated. That suit is still pending.

Police Chief Herb Chastain will not talk about the Vecchio case.

Mary's former principal at Westview Junior High denies he treated the girl any differently from any other student. He describes what happened this way:

"When she came back, the youngsters did not accept her. She was very unhappy at our school. She was a truant. She was a disciplinary problem. She used profanity. She was a disturbing influence within the classroom, so we suspended her. She tried to get attention in the manner of her conduct.

"I disciplined her every time she did something wrong. I tried to make her a better girl. She kept misbehaving and I punished her — and

I would do it again. The influence she could have on the other students wasn't good. All I can judge her on is the conduct that she exhibited in the classroom.

"To be frank with you, I never wanted her back in my school, but I had to take her."

While the reasons are unclear, there is no question that parents told their children to stay away from Mary Vecchio after she came back to Opa-Locka. "The word was out that Mary was a bad influence," her father says.

Mary's final act of rebellion a few weeks ago grew out of an inconsequential incident. She wanted to go to a rock concert on a Saturday night, and her parents said no. Mary went anyway. She did not return home.

In Youth Home

"We waited Sunday and we waited Monday. So Tuesday we reported her missing to police," her mother says. A few days later Mary was picked up in a girl friend's apartment. She was taken before a juvenile court proceeding because she had violated her probation.

"When Judge Weaver asked her why she had run away, Mary simply said 'to go to a rock concert,'" her lawyer says.

Mary was committed to the Kendall Youth Home south of Miami. There, the judge, her parents, and her lawyer hope, she will receive counseling and training.

4
Leadership?
Barbara W. Tuchman

By Barbara W. Tuchman. Excerpts from "The Missing Element: Moral Courage," *In Search of Leaders*, American Association for Higher Education, *Current Issues in Higher Education—1967*, G. Kerry Smith, editor (National Education Association, 1201 Sixteenth Street, N.W., Washington, D. C., 20036, 1967), pp. 3-9.

What I want to say is concerned less with leadership than with its absence, that is, with the evasion of leadership. Not in the physical sense, for we have, if anything, a superabundance of leaders—hundreds of Pied Pipers, or would-be Pied Pipers, running about, ready and anxious to lead the population. They are scurrying around, collecting consensus, gathering as wide an acceptance as possible. But what they are *not* doing, very notably, is standing still and saying, "*This* is what I believe. This I will do and that I will not do. This is my code of behavior and that is outside it. This is excellent and that is trash." There is an abdication of moral leadership in the sense of a general unwillingness to state standards.

Of all the ills that our poor criticized, analyzed, sociologized society is heir to, the focal one, it seems to me, from which so much of our uneasiness and confusion derive, is the absence of standards. We are too unsure of ourselves to assert them, to stick by them, or if necessary, in the case of persons who occupy positions of authority, to impose them. We seem to be afflicted by a widespread and eroding reluctance to take any stand on any values, moral, behavioral, or aesthetic.

Everyone is afraid to call anything wrong, or vulgar, or fraudulent, or just bad taste or bad manners. . . .

Our time is one of disillusion in our species and a resulting lack of self-confidence—for good historical reasons. Man's recent record has not been reassuring. After engaging in the Great War with all its mud and blood and ravaged ground, its disease, destruction, and death, we allowed ourselves a bare twenty years before going at it all over again. And the second time was accompanied by an episode of man's inhumanity to man of such enormity that its implications for all of us have not yet, I think, been fully measured. A historian has recently stated that for such a phenomenon as the planned and nearly accomplished extermination of a people to take place, one of three preconditions necessary was public indifference.

16

Since then the human species has been busy overbreeding, polluting the air, destroying the balance of nature, and bungling in a variety of directions so that it is no wonder we have begun to doubt man's capacity for good judgment. It is hardly surprising that the self-confidence of the nineteenth century and its belief in human progress has been dissipated. "Every great civilization," said Secretary Gardner last year, "has been characterized by confidence in itself." At mid-twentieth century, the supply is low. As a result, we tend to shy away from all judgments. We hesitate to label anything wrong, and therefore hesitate to require the individual to bear moral responsibility for his acts.

We have become afraid to fix blame. Murderers and rapists and muggers and persons who beat up old men and engage in other forms of assault are not guilty; society is guilty; society has wronged them; society beats its breast and says *mea culpa*—it is our fault, not the wrongdoer's. The wrongdoer, poor fellow, could not help himself.

I find this very puzzling because I always ask myself, in these cases, what about the many neighbors of the wrongdoer, equally poor, equally disadvantaged, equally sufferers from society's neglect, who nevertheless maintain certain standards of social behavior, who do *not* commit crimes, who do not murder for money or rape for kicks. How does it happen that they know the difference between right and wrong, and how long will they abide by the difference if the leaders and opinion-makers and pacesetters continue to shy away from bringing home responsibility to the delinquent?

Admittedly, the reluctance to condemn stems partly from a worthy instinct—*tout comprendre, c'est tout pardonner*—and from a rejection of what was often the hypocrisy of Victorian moral standards. True, there was a large component of hypocrisy in nineteenth-century morality. Since the advent of Freud, we know more, we understand more about human behavior, we are more reluctant to cast the first stone—to condemn—which is a good thing; but the pendulum has swung to the point where we are now afraid to place moral responsibility at all. Society, that large amorphous, nonspecific scapegoat, must carry the burden for each of us, relieving us of guilt. We have become so indoctrinated by the terrors lurking in the dark corridors of the guilt complex that guilt has acquired a very bad name. Yet a little guilt is not a dangerous thing; it has a certain social utility.

When it comes to guilt, a respected writer—respected in some circles—has told us, as her considered verdict on the Nazi program, that evil is banal—a word that means something so ordinary that you are not bothered by it; the dictionary definition is "commonplace and hackneyed." Somehow that conclusion does not seem adequate or even apt. *Of course*, evil is commonplace; *of course*, we all partake of it. Does that mean that we must withhold disapproval, and that when evil appears in dangerous degree or vicious form we must not condemn but only understand? That may be very Christian in intent, but in reality it is an escape from the necessity of exercising judgment— which exercise, I believe, is a prime function of leadership.

What it requires is courage—just a little, not very much—the courage to be independent and stand up for the standard of values one believes in. That kind of courage is the quality most conspicuously missing, I think, in current life. I don't mean the courage to protest and walk around with picket signs or boo Secretary McNamara which, though it may stem from the right instinct, is a group thing that does not require any very stout spirit. I did it myself for Sacco and Vanzetti when I was about twelve and picketed in some now forgotten labor dispute when I was a freshman and even got arrested. There is nothing to that; if you don't do that sort of thing when you are eighteen, then there is something wrong with you. I mean, rather, a kind of lonely moral courage, the quality that attracted me to that odd character, Czar Reed, and to Lord Salisbury, neither of whom cared a rap for the opinion of the public or would have altered his conduct a hair to adapt to it. It is the quality someone said of Lord Palmerston was his "you-be-damnedness." That is the mood we need a little more of.

Standards of taste, as well as morality, need continued reaffirmation to stay alive, as liberty needs eternal vigilance. To recognize and to proclaim the difference between the good and the shoddy, the true and the fake, as well as between right and wrong, or what we believe at a given time to be right and wrong, is the obligation, I think, of persons who presume to lead, or are thrust into leadership, or hold positions of authority. That includes—whether they asked for it or not—all educators and even, I regret to say, writers.

For educators it has become increasingly the habit in the difficult circumstances of college administration today to find out what the students want in the matter of curriculum and deportment and then give it to them. This seems to me another form of abdication, another example of the prevailing reluctance to state a standard and expect, not to say require, performance in accord with it. The permissiveness, the yielding of decision to the student, does not—from what I can tell—promote responsibility in the young so much as uneasiness and a kind of anger at *not* being told what is expected of them, a resentment of their elders' unwillingness to take a position. Recently a student psychiatric patient of the Harvard Health Services was quoted by the director, Dr. Dana Farnsworth, as complaining, "My parents never tell me what to do. They never stop me from doing anything." That is the unheard wail, I think, extended beyond parents to the general absence of a guiding, reassuring pattern, which is behind much of society's current uneasiness.

It is human nature to want patterns and standards and a structure of behavior. A pattern to conform to is a kind of shelter. You see it in kindergarten and primary school, at least in those schools where the children when leaving the classroom are required to fall into line. When the teacher gives the signal, they fall in with alacrity; they know where they belong and they instinctively like to *be* where they belong. They like the feeling of being in line.

Most people need a structure, not only to fall into but to fall out of. The rebel with a cause is better off than the one without. At least he knows what he is *"agin."* He is not lost. He does not suffer from an identity crisis. It occurs to me that much of the student protest now may be a testing of authority, a search for that line to fall out of, and when it isn't there students become angrier because they feel more lost, more abandoned than ever. In the late turmoil at Berkeley, at least as regards the filthy speech demonstration, there was a missed opportunity, I think (however great my respect for Clark Kerr) for a hearty, emphatic, and unmistakable "No!" backed up by sanctions. Why? Because the act, even if intended as a demonstration of principle, was in this case, like any indecent exposure, simply offensive, and what is offensive to the greater part of society is anti-social, and what is anti-social, so long as we live in social groups and not each of us on his own island, must be curtailed, like Peeping Toms or obscene telephone calls, as a public nuisance. The issue is really not complicated or difficult but, if we would only look at it with more self-confidence, quite simple.

. . . The recent excitement only shows how easily we succumb, when reliable patterns or codes of conduct are absent, to a confusion of values.

A similar confusion exists, I think, with regard to the omnipresent pornography that surrounds us like smog. . . .

. . . If one looks around at the movies, especially the movie advertisements, and the novels and the pulp magazines glorifying perversion and the paperbacks that make de Sade available to school children, one does not get the impression that in the 1960's we are being stifled in the Puritan grip of Anthony Comstock. Here again, leaders—in this case authors and critics—seem too unsure of values or too afraid of being unpopular to stand up and assert the perfectly obvious difference between smut and free speech, or to say "Such and such is offensive and can be harmful." Happily, there are signs of awakening. . . .

In the realm of art, no less important than morals, the abdication of judgment is almost a disease. . . . If they know better, why do they allow themselves to do worse? As leaders in their field of endeavor, they should have been setting standards of beauty and creative design, not debasing them.

One finds the same peculiarities in the visual arts. Non-art, as its practitioners describe it—the blob school, the all-black canvases, the paper cut-outs and Campbell soup tins and plastic hamburgers and pieces of old carpet—is treated as art, not only by dealers whose motive is understandable (they have discovered that shock value sells); not only by a gullible pseudocultural section of the public who are not interested in art but in being "in" and wouldn't, to quote an old joke, know a Renoir from a Jaguar; but also, which I find mystifying, by the museums and the critics. I am sure they know the difference between the genuine and the hoax. But not trusting their own judgment, they seem afraid to say no to anything, for fear, I suppose, of making a mistake and turning down what may be next decade's Matisse.

For the museums to exhibit the plastic hamburgers and twists of scrap iron is one thing, but for them to *buy* them for their permanent collection puts an imprimatur on what is fraudulent. Museum curators, too, are leaders who have an obligation to distinguish—I will not say the good from the bad in art because that is an elusive and subjective matter dependent on the eye of the time—but at least honest expression from phony. Most of what fills the galleries on Madison Avenue is simply stuff designed to take advantage of current fads and does not come from an artist's vision or an honest creative impulse. The dealers know it; the critics know it; the purveyors themselves know it; the public suspects it; but no one dares say it because that would be committing oneself to a standard of values and even, heaven forbid, exposing oneself to being called square.

In the fairy story, it required a child to cry out that the Emperor was naked. Let us not leave that task to the children. It should be the task of leaders to recognize and state the truth as they see it. It is their task not to be afraid of absolutes.

If the educated man is not willing to express standards, if he cannot show that he has them and applies them, what then is education for? Its purpose, I take it, is to form the civilized man, whom I would define as the person capable of the informed exercise of judgment, taste, and values. If at maturity he is not willing to express judgment on matters of policy or taste or morals, if at fifty he does not believe that he has acquired more wisdom and informed experience than is possessed by the student at twenty, then he is saying in effect that education has been a failure.

5
How Can the Whole People Be Best Educated?

The Subject of Education and Its General Necessity

Edward Everett

Superior and Popular Education

An address delivered before the Adelphic Union Society of Williams College, on Commencement Day, 16th August 1837, Edward Everett, "Superior and Popular Education," *Orations and Speeches on Various Occasions*, 11th ed. (Boston: Little, Brown, and Company, 1887), II, pp. 207-208.

I know it [the subject of education] is a worn theme; as old as the first dawnings of imparted knowledge in the infancy of the world, and familiar to the contemplation of every succeeding age, even to the present time. But it still remains, for us, a topic of unabated and ever-urgent interest. Although it is a subject on which philosophers of every age have largely discoursed, so far from being exhausted, it probably never presented itself to the human mind under so many new and important aspects as at the present day, and I may add, in these United States. I may safely appeal to every person who hears me, and who is in the habit of reflecting at all on the character of the age in which we live, whether, next to what directly concerns the eternal welfare of man, there is any subject which he deems of more vital importance than the great problem, how the whole people can be best educated. If the answer of the patriot and statesman to this appeal were doubtful, I might still more safely inquire of every considerate parent who hears me, whether the education of his children, their education for time and eternity, (for, as far as human means are concerned, these objects are intimately connected) is not among the things which are first, last, and most anxiously upon his mind.

21

Calvin O. Davis

The Rewards of Teaching

Calvin O. Davis, "The Rewards of Teaching," *School and Society*, L (November 25, 1939), p. 692.

Without education there would be no such thing as civilization, but merely raw naturalism. . . . Education is the one indispensable element of human civilized existence; and without teachers there would be little if any education. Schools are therefore the world's best insurance policy and society's most profitable investment. Without their contributions free government, the safety of life and property and in short the very means necessary to the pursuit of happiness would be wanting. Without education all the great professions, such as law, medicine, engineering, journalism and the like, would be impossible; all modern art and science would be non-existent; all cultural advances of the civilized world would disappear. Surely therefore the very nature and needs of the contemporary world make the teacher an indispensable member of society. Hence the student whose highest ambition is to reorder social service to his age and generation can find no wider field in which to play his part than that of the profession of teaching.

Education in a Democracy

Edward Everett

The Importance of Education in a Republic

Op. cit., II, 316-321, 323, remarks at a county common school convention, held at Taunton, Massachusetts on the 10th October, 1838, when a resolution was under consideration which asserted the connection between public intelligence and a republican form of government." (p. 313):

. . . But on the system established in the United States, where the people are not only in theory the source of power, but in practice are actually called upon, constantly, to take an efficient part in constituting and administering the government, it is plain that education is universally and indispensably necessary, to enable them to exercise their rights and perform their duties. This will be put beyond question by considering a few particulars.

I. The first duty, in a popular government, is that which is attached to the elective franchise; though I fear it is too little regarded in this light. It is not merely the right, but it is the duty, of the citizen, by the exercise of the right of suffrage, to take a part, at periods recurring after short intervals, in organizing the government. This duty cannot be discharged with rectitude, unless it be discharged with intelligence; and it becomes the duty of the citizen to make up his own mind on all the great questions which arise in administering the government. How numerous and important these questions are, I need not say. Since you and I, Mr. President, have been of years to observe the march of affairs, the people of the United States have been called to make up a practical judgment on the following, among other great questions—the *protective policy*, that is, on the legislation necessary to introduce and establish an infant branch of manufactures; a question, however easily disposed of by theorists, on both sides, of infinite practical difficulty; on *internal improvement*, that is, the construction of public works of communication between the various parts of the country, at the expense of the general government; on the *circulating medium*, and how far the currency, which is the representative of value, must have intrinsic value itself; on the *different families of the human race* existing in the country and the rights and duties which result from their relation to each other; on the *relations* of the country with *foreign* powers, in reference to colonial trade, disputed boundaries, and indemnification for wrongs and spoliations; on the disposal of the *public domain*, and its bearings on the progress of population and of republican government in the mighty west; on the nature of our political system, as consisting in the harmonious *adjustment of the federal and state governments*. I have named only a part of the questions which, within the last twenty years, have been, some of them constantly, before the community—the turning-points of municipal, state, and national elections. The good citizen, who is not willing to be the slave of a party because he is a member of it, must make up his mind for himself on all those great questions, or he cannot exercise the right of suffrage with intelligence and independence. As the majority of the people are well or ill informed on these subjects, the public policy of the country will be guided by wisdom and truth, or the reverse.

I do not mean that it is necessary that every citizen should receive an education which would enable him to argue all these questions, at length, in a deliberative or popular assembly; but, while it is his right and his duty to give effect to his judgment at the polls, and while the constitution necessarily gives as much weight to the vote of the uninformed and ignorant as to that of the well-instructed and intelligent citizen, it is plain that the avenues to information should be as wide and numerous as possible; and that the utmost practicable extension should be given to a system of education which will confer on every citizen the capacity of deriving knowledge, with readiness and accuracy, from books and documents. The whole energy of the state should be directed to multiply the numbers of those capable of forming an independent and rational judgment of their own, and to diminish as much as possible the numbers of the opposite class, who, being blinded by ignorance, are at the mercy of any one who has an interest and the skill to delude them.

II. But the exercise of the elective franchise is only the beginning of the duties of the citizen. The constitution makes it the right, the laws make it the duty, of all citizens, within certain ages, to bear arms. It may sound strange to connect this duty with the subject of education. I hope no practical demonstration of the connection of the topics will ever arise among us. But this right and this duty, lightly esteemed in quiet times, may become of fearful import. Arms are placed in the hands of the citizen for the most important purposes; not for parade and holiday display, but to defend his country against violence from abroad; to maintain the supremacy of the laws; to preserve the peace of the community. Heaven grant that the day may be far distant when our citizens shall be called to wield them for either purpose. But if the experience of the past warrant an anticipation of the future, the time may come when this duty, also, is to be performed. It will not then be a matter of indifference whether the honor and peace of the community are committed to an ignorant and benighted multitude, like those which swell the ranks of the mercenary standing armies of Europe, or to an educated and intelligent population, whose powers of reflection have been strengthened by exercise, and who are able to discriminate between constitutional liberty and arbitrary power on the one hand, and anarchy on the other.

III. There are other civil duties to be performed, for which education furnishes a still more direct and appropriate preparation. The law of the land calls the citizen to take a part in the administration of justice. Twelve men are placed in the jury box, to decide on the numberless questions which arise in the community — questions of character, of property, and of life. The jury passes on your fortune and your reputation; pronounces whether you live or die. Go into the courts; are they light matters which those twelve men are to decide? Look in the anxious faces of those whose estates, whose good name, whose all, is at stake, hanging on the intelligence of those twelve men, or any one of them. What assurance is there, but that which comes from our schools, that these men will understand and do their duty? Those little boys, now sporting in the streets, or conning their tasks in our town schools, in a few short years will be summoned, in their turns, to discharge this important trust. Can we deem it a matter of indifference whether or not their minds have been early accustomed to follow a train of thoughts or a statement of facts? Did not the secretary give us, this morning, from his own experience, the instance of a witness who, in a case of slander, where every thing turned on his testimony, first swore that what he saw, he saw through one window, and then through another, and then through a door? Woe to the community, where the degree of stolidity and ignorance, necessary to constitute such a witness, abound; and where it must appear, not only on the stand, but in the jury box. It appears to me a most imperative duty, on the part of a state which calls its citizens to discharge this momentous office, to do all in its power to qualify them for it by a general system of education. Is it said, there is learned counsel to argue and explain the cause to a jury, however ignorant? But there is counsel on both sides; the jury must decide after hearing them both. But the court will instruct the jury. No doubt, as far as the law is concerned; but the court's instructions are addressed to minds supposed to be capable of following out an argument, estimating evidence, and making up an independent opinion. I do not say that there are not some minds to whom the best opportunities of education would not impart the requisite qualifications of an intelligent juror. But I may appeal to every professional character and magistrate in this convention that, in an important case, if he were to be called on to select a jury on which he could place full reliance, he would select men of good common sense, who had received a good common education.

IV. But I have not yet named all the civil duties for which education is needed, as the preparatory discipline. The various official trusts in society are to be filled, from a commission of the peace to the place of chief justice; from a constable up to the President of the United States. The sphere of duty of some of these functionaries is narrow; of others, large and inexpressibly responsible; of none, insignificant. Taken together, they make up the administration of free government — the greatest merely temporal interest of civilized man. There are three courses, between which we must choose. We must have officers unqualified for their duties; or we must educate a privileged class, to monopolize the honors and emoluments of place; or we must establish such a system of general education, as will furnish a supply of well-informed, intelligent, and respectable citizens, in every part of the country and in every walk of life, capable of discharging the trusts which the people may devolve upon them. The topic is of great compass, but I cannot dwell upon it. It is superfluous to say which of the three courses is most congenial with the spirit of republicanism.

V. I have thus far spoken of those reasons for promoting common school education, which spring from the nature of our government.

There are others, derived from the condition of our country. Individual enterprise is everywhere stimulated; the paths of adventure are opened; the boundless west prevents the older settlements from being over-stocked, and gives scope for an unexampled development of energy. Education is wanted, to enlighten and direct those active, moving powers. Without it, much wild vigor will be exerted in vain. Energy alone is not enough; it must be turned to feasible objects, and worked by sound principles.

Again, this spirit of enterprise runs naturally towards the acquisi-tion of wealth. In this I find no matter of reproach; only let it not be a merely Carthaginian prosperity. Let a taste for reading and reflection be cultivated, as well as property acquired. Let us give our children the keys of knowledge, as well as an establishment in business. Let them, in youth, form habits and tastes which will remain with them in after-life, in old age, and furnish rational entertainment at all times. When we collect the little circle, at the family board and at the fireside, in our long winter evenings, let us be able to talk of subjects of interest and importance—the productions and institutions of our own and foreign countries; the history of our venerated fathers; the wonders of the material universe; the experience of our race; great moral interests and duties—subjects surely as important as dollars and cents. Let us, from early years, teach our children to rise above the dust beneath their feet, to the consideration of the great spiritual concerns of immortal natures. A mere bookworm is a worthless character; but a mere money-getter is no better.

It is a great mistake, to suppose that it is necessary to be a profes-sional man, in order to have leisure to indulge a taste for reading. Far otherwise. I believe the mechanic, the engineer, the husbandman, the trader, have quite as much leisure as the average of men in the learned professions. I know some men, busily engaged in these different callings of active life, whose minds are well stored with various useful knowledge acquired from books. There would be more such men, if education in our common schools were, as it well might be, of a higher order; and if common school libraries, well furnished, were introduced into every district, as I trust, in due time, they will be. . . .

No leisure, Mr. President, for reading? Is there a man in the com-munity, of an intelligent mind, and with any, the least, tincture of improvement, derived from education, who, when coming, at nightfall, from his labor, (I care not how hard or humble,) if told that, beneath his roof, he would find Shakespeare, or Milton, or Scott, or Irving, or Channing, seated in actual presence by his fireside, and waiting to converse with him, would talk of wanting leisure, or of fatigue?

Basic Beliefs
Expressed by Founding Fathers
and Early Leaders
in Political Documents
of the United States

George Washington (1732-1799), First President

Jared Sparks (ed.), *The Writings of George Washington* (Boston: Ferdinand Andrews, Publisher, 1840), XII.

Speech to both Houses of Congress, January 8, 1790
(1st Congress, 2d Session)

Nor am I less persuaded, that you will agree with me in opinion, that there is nothing which can better deserve your patronage than the promotion of science and literature. Knowledge is in every country the surest basis of public happiness. In one, in which the measures of government receive their impression so immediately from the sense of the community, as in ours, it is proportionably essential. To the security of a free constitution it contributes in various ways; by convincing those who are intrusted with the public administration, that every valuable end of government is best answered by the enlightened confidence of the people; and by teaching the people themselves to know, and to value their own rights; to discern and provide against invasions of them; to distinguish between oppression and the necessary exercise of lawful authority, between burthens proceeding from a disregard to their convenience and those resulting from the inevitable exigencies of society; to discriminate the spirit of liberty from that of licentiousness, cherishing the first, avoiding the last, and uniting a speedy but temperate vigilance against encroachments, with an inviolable respect to the laws. (pp. 9-10)

Farewell Address, September 19, 1796
To the People of the United States:

Of all the dispositions and habits, which lead to political prosperity, Religion and Morality are indispensable supports. . . .

It is substantially true, that virtue or morality is a necessary spring of popular government. The rule, indeed, extends with more or less force to every species of free government. Who, that is a sincere friend to it, can look with indifference upon attempts to shake the foundation of the fabric?

Promote, then, as an object of primary importance, institutions for the general diffusion of knowledge. In proportion as the structure of a government gives force to public opinion, it is essential that public opinion should be enlightened. (p. 227)

Northwest Ordinance of 1787

Religion, morality, and knowledge being necessary to good government and the happiness of mankind, schools and the means of education shall forever be encouraged.

Mirabeau Buonaparte Lamar (1798-1895), Second President of the Republic of Texas (1838-1841) and considered "The Father of Education in Texas," in Message of the President [of the Republic of Texas] to Both Houses, December 21 [20th?], 1838, eleven or twelve days after his inauguration

> Journal of the House of Representatives of the Republic of Texas. Regular Session of Third Congress, Nov. 5, 1838. Thursday, December 20th, 1838. By Order of the Secretary of State. (Houston: Intelligencer Office— S. Whiting, Printer, 1839), pp. 168, 169, 170.

If we desire to establish a Republican Government upon a broad and permanent basis, it will become our duty to adopt a comprehensive and well regulated system of mental and moral culture. Education is a subject in which every citizen and especially every parent feels a deep and lively concern. It is one in which no jarring interests are involved, and no acrimonious political feelings excited; for its benefits are so universal that all parties can cordially unite in advancing it. It is admitted by all, that a cultivated mind is the guardian genius of democracy and, while guided and controlled by virtue, is the noblest attribute of man. It is the only dictator that freemen acknowledge, and the only security that freemen desire. The influence of education. . . . Without its aid, how perilous and insufficient would be the deliberations of a Government like ours? How ignoble and useless its legislation for all the purposes of happiness? How fragile and insecure its liberties? . . . And peace would be joyless, because its train would be unattended by that civilization and refinement which alone can give zest to social and domestic enjoyments, and how shall we protect our rights if we do not comprehend them? And can we comprehend them unless we acquire a knowledge of the past and present condition of things, and practice the habit of enlightened reflection. Cultivation is as necessary to the supply of rich intellectual and moral fruits, as are the labors of the husbandman to bring forth the valuable productions of the earth. . . . To patronize the general diffusion of knowledge, industry and charity, has been near the heart of the good and wise of all nations, while the ambitious and the ignorant would fain have threatened a policy so pure and laudable. . . . Let me therefore urge it upon you, gentlemen, not to postpone the matter too long. The present is a propitious moment to lay the foundation of a great moral and intellectual edifice, which will in after ages be hailed as the chief ornament and blessing of Texas."

Thomas Jefferson (1743-1826), Third President
Letter to Colonel Charles Yancy from Monticello, January 6, 1816

Paul Leicester Ford (ed.), *The Writings of Thomas Jefferson* (New York and London: G. P. Putnam's Sonns, 1899), X, p. 4.

If a nation expects to be ignorant and free, in a state of civilization, it expects what never was and never will be. The functionaries of every government have propensities to command at will the liberty and property of their constituents. There is no safe deposit for these but with the people themselves; nor can they be safe with them without information. Where the press is free, and every man able to read, all is safe.

Letter to Governor Tyler from Monticello, May 26, 1810

H. A. Washington (ed.), *The Writings of Thomas Jefferson* (Washington, D.C.: Taylor & Maury, 1853), V, p. 525.

I have indeed two great measures at heart, without which no republic can maintain itself in strength. 1. That of general education, to enable every man to judge for himself what will secure or endanger his freedom. 2. To divide every county into hundreds, of such size that all the children of each will be within reach of a central school in it.

James Madison (1751-1836), Fourth President
Letter to W. T. Barry, August 4, 1822

Gaillard Hunt (ed.), *The Writings of James Madison* (New York and London: G. P. Putnam's Sons, 1910), IX, p. 103.

A popular Government, without popular information, or the means of acquiring it, is but a Prologue to a Farce or a Tragedy; or, perhaps both. Knowledge will forever govern ignorance: And a people who mean to be their own Governors, must arm themselves with the power which knowledge gives.

James Monroe (1758-1831), Fifth President
Letter to the Governor of Virginia from London, England, November 29, 1803

Stanislaus Murray Hamilton (ed.), *The Writings of James Monroe* (New York and London: G. P. Putnam's Sons, 1900), IV, pp. 109-110.

It is an opinion which I have long entertained, on which every day's experience and observation tends to confirm, that however free our political institutions may be in the commencement, liberty cannot long be preserved unless the society in every district, in all its members, possesses that portion of useful knowledge which is necessary to qualify them to discharge with credit and effect, those great duties of citizens on which free Government rests. The responsibility of public servants, however well provided for by the Constitution, becomes vain and useless if the people in general are not competent judges, in the course of the administration, of all the questions which it involves. If it was wise, manly and patriotic in us to establish a free Government, it is equally incumbent on us to attend to the necessary means of its preservation.

John Adams (1735-1826), Second President

"Thoughts on Government," in Charles Francis Adams (ed.), *The Works of John Adams* (Boston: Charles C. Little and James Brown, 1851), IV, p. 199.

Laws for the liberal education of youth, especially of the lower class of people, are so extremely wise and useful, that, to a humane and generous mind, no expense for this purpose would be thought extravagant.

John Jay (1745-1829), First Chief Justice

Letter to Dr. Benjamin Rush from New York, March 24, 1785

Henry P. Johnston (ed.) *The Correspondence and Public Papers of John Jay* (New York and London: G. P. Putnam's Sons, 1891), Ill, p. 139.

I consider knowledge to be the soul of a republic, and as the weak and the wicked are generally in alliance, as much care should be taken to diminish the number of the former as of the latter. Education is the way to do this, and nothing should be left undone to afford all ranks of people the means of obtaining a proper degree of it at a cheap and easy rate.

Thomas Jefferson

Letter to George Wythe from Paris, August 13, 1786

H. A. Washington (ed.), *op. cit.*, II, pp. 7-8.

I think by far the most important bill in our whole code, is that for the diffusion of knowledge among the people. No other sure foundation can be devised, for the preservation of freedom and happiness. If anybody thinks that kings, nobles, or priests are good conservators of the public happiness, send him here. It is the best school in the universe to cure him of that folly. He will see here, with his own eyes, that these descriptions of men are an abandoned confederacy against the happiness of the mass of the people. The omnipotence of their effect cannot be better proved, than in this country particularly, where, notwithstanding the finest soil upon earth, the finest climate under heaven, and a people of the most benevolent, the most gay and amiable character of which the human form is susceptible; where such a people, I say, surrounded by so many blessings from nature, are loaded with misery, by kings, nobles, and priests, and by them alone. Preach, my dear Sir, a crusade against ignorance; establish and improve the law for educating the common people. Let our countrymen know, that the people alone can protect us against these evils, and that the tax which will be paid for this purpose, is not more than the thousandth part of what will be paid to kings, priests and nobles, who will rise up among us if we leave the people in ignorance.

Emma Lazarus

Words chisled in the base of the Statue of Liberty

Give me your tired, your poor,
Your huddled masses yearning to breathe free,

The wretched refuse of your teeming shore.
Send these, the homeless, tempest-tost to me;
I lift my lamp beside the golden door.

Edward Everett
Superior and Popular Education

Adelphic Union Society address, *op. cit.*

. . . there are two offices to be performed by education, of harmonious character and tendency, but of different sphere and mode of operation. One regards the discipline and training of mind to the highest point of intellectual excellence, and the other regards the diffusion of useful knowledge among the community at large, and the consequent elevation of the general character. (p. 212)

The province of education, in which we may all labor, and in which the effects to be immediately hoped for stand in some assignable proportion to the means employed, is the improvement of the minds of the mass of the people. (p. 224)

It is at once melancholy and fearful to reflect how much intellect is daily perishing from inaction, or worse than perishing from the false direction given it in the morning of life. (p. 224)

". . . I fear there exists even here, a woful waste of mental power, through neglect of education. Taking our population as a whole, I fear that there is not nearly time enough passed at school; that many of those employed in the business of instruction are incompetent to the work; and that our best teachers are not sufficiently furnished with literary apparatus, particularly with school libraries. If these defects could be supplied, I believe a few years would witness a wonderful effect upon the community; that an impulse, not easily conceived beforehand, would be given to individual and social character.

"I am strongly convinced that it behoves our ancient commonwealth to look anxiously to this subject, if she wishes to maintain her honorable standing in this union of states. . . .

". . . I think this matter must be looked to. If the all-important duty of training the young is intrusted to the cheapest hand that can be hired to do the work — to one who is barely able to pass a nominal examination, by a committee sometimes more ignorant than himself, in the *modicum* of learning prescribed by law; and slender as the privilege of such instruction is, if it be enjoyed by our children but for ten or twelve weeks in the year, as is the case in too many towns in the commonwealth, it is plain to see that they are deprived of the best part of their birthright. . . . I cannot but think that a majority of the citizens of Massachusetts, of all pursuits and callings, might, without the least detriment to their interests, send their children steadily to a good school seven months in the year, and more or less of the time the other five. Without detriment, did I say? Nay, with incalculable advantage to their children, to themselves, and to the state.

"It would be more rational to talk about not affording seedcorn than to talk about not affording our children as much of their time as is necessary for their education. What! shall a man plant his field, and allow his child's intellect to run to weeds? It would be as wise to eat up all the wheat, and sow the husks and the chaff for next year's crop, as, on a principle of thrift, to sow ignorance and its attendant helplessness and prejudices in your children's minds, and expect to reap an honorable and a happy manhood. . . .

"Our governments, as well as individuals, have, I must needs say, a duty to discharge to the cause of education. Something has been done — by some of the state governments much as been done — for this cause; but too much, I fear, remains undone." (pp. 225-228)

6
Can We Meet
the Challenge Today?

Arnold Toynbee

Education: The Long View

Excerpts from Arnold Toynbee, "Education: The Long View," *Saturday Review*, XLIII (No. 47, November 19, 1960): 60-62, 76-81. Copyright Saturday Review, Inc.

. . . During these first 5,000 years of the history of civilization, one of the most characteristic, and most ugly, features of this new way of life has been the monopoly of its amenities, spiritual as well as material, by a small minority of the members of societies in process of civilization. This blot on the scutcheon of civilization during its first phase has not been due solely to the selfishness of the ruling minority. Even if all the members of this group had succeeded in rising above their natural human egotism and had tried with all their might to share their cultural heritage with the unprivileged majority of their fellow human beings, they would have been defeated, before the Industrial Revolution, by the smallness of the economic surplus remaining in hand after the satisfaction of elementary economic needs. This revolution started in the Western World about two hundred years ago and, since then, has been increasing in momentum and communicating itself from the Western peoples to the rest of mankind.

In a pre-industrial agricultural economy, in which human and animal muscle power has not been reinforced by mechanical power, all but a small minority of the members of society are condemned to live as a peasantry whose puny production cannot provide amenities beyond such common necessities as food, clothing, and shelter for more than a small minority. This injustice was made intolerable by the appearance in the world of higher religions that divined and proclaimed the infinite spiritual values of every human soul, irrespective of the social class in which it has been placed by the accident of birth. An injustice that has long since been intolerable has now been made unnecessary by the Industrial Revolution, which has brought it within our economic power at last to provide the amenities of civilization for mankind in the mass—always supposing that we do not use the new power generated by the progress of technology for the self-destruction of the human race.

Our present Industrial Revolution is, of course, only one in a long series of technological advances; but it is perhaps the first since the invention of agriculture that has been potent enough to provide appreciable social and cultural benefits for all members of a society that has made it. . . . Our present-day Industrial Revolution is the first that has opened up the prospect of providing the material means for raising the standard of living of the world's vast peasantry above the neolithic level that was attained round the rim of the Fertile Crescent during the age preceding the dawn of civilization there. This present possibility of bringing the benefits of civilization to the whole of the great un-privileged majority of the human race carries with it a moral command to execute the act of justice that is now at last within our power. This is the new requirement with which mankind, and consequently the ancient human institution of education, is confronted today. The educational problems involved are of the same order of magnitude as the requirement itself.

One problem is presented by the unalterable and inescapable fact that a human being has a strictly limited capacity. . . . On the other hand, human knowledge is cumulative in science and technology. In the humanities as well, knowledge tends to accumulate within the time spans of particular civilizations and higher religions, and sometimes outlives the disintegration and disappearance of these social matrices of humane culture. This accumulation of culture confronts the givers and receivers of formal education with a Psyche's task of ever-increasing difficulty; and this difficulty confronts all individuals alike, in every civilization and in every social class.

. . . "The proper study of mankind is man" because man's dealings with himself and with his human neighbors are the part of man's business in which he has been conspicuously unsuccessful thus far; and the penalty for failure here becomes heavier, the greater the power over non-human nature that the advance of natural science places in man's hands for him to wield, in his perversity, against himself. The need for balancing an education in natural science and technology with an education in the humanities has been recognized . . .

Meanwhile, the ocean of knowledge has grown to an immeasurable size, not only in natural science but in the humanities as well. . . .

. . . The peoples of the world cannot learn to understand each other if they confine their attention to the present surface of life and ignore the historical depths. We cannot truly know a person, a people, a civilization, or a religion without knowing something about its history; and here, by yet another route we are again brought face to face with the problem created by the inordinate increase in the quantity of our knowledge.

Today our knowledge of the past is increasing at an unprecedented rate, and this at both ends of its ever lengthening vista. The archeologists are making history by exhuming buried and forgotten civilizations as fast as the politicians are making it by taking new action for contemporary historians to study. The public records produced in the United Kingdom during the Second World War, which lasted less than six years, are said to equal in quantity all the surviving records produced previously by the United Kingdom and its component states, the kingdoms of England and Scotland. The wartime records of one single government department in London would extend, it is said, for seventeen miles if the files were stacked on edge and placed in a row as tightly as they could be packed. The records of archeological excavations are also formidably extensive; and, in between, our knowledge of comparatively well-known periods in the histories of the civilizations and the religions has been increased and, in the process, transformed by the study of previously unknown or neglected documents and by the reinterpretation of previously familiar ones.

This immense and growing mass of knowledge about man and his non-human environment daunts the minds that are exposed to it and throws them on the defensive. In self-defense we are tempted to ask ourselves again whether our institutions for formal education cannot simply reject the greater part of this formidable load, or, short of that, divide it up into packages that can be distributed among different pairs of shoulders without risk of breaking any backs. The reply to this cry of distress has to be in the negative: *"Homo sum, humani nihil a me alienum puto"* ("I am a human being, so I cannot be indifferent to anything that has to do with human life and human nature"). Every man, woman, and child alive today is living in a world in which mankind is faced with the extreme choice between learning to live together as one family and committing genocide on a planetary scale. Neither the human race nor any living member of it can afford to ignore the present human situation. We must cope with it if we are not to destroy ourselves; in order to cope with it we must understand it; and trying to understand it commits each and all of us to making some acquaintance with at least three vast realms of knowledge: a knowledge of non-human nature; a knowledge of human nature; and a knowledge of the characters and histories of the local and temporary cultures—some relatively primitive, others relatively advanced—that man has created and transmitted and modified and discarded in the course of the ages that have passed since his pre-human ancestors became human. Formal education's minimum task has thus become a big undertaking in our day; and every child will have a strenuous course of formal as well as informal education to run in order to grow up into being an effective citizen of our new world.

How, then, are our educational institutions to convey this overwhelmingly massive heritage of knowledge to a puny and ephemeral human mind? The task would be an intimidating one even if we could confine it to the education of the privileged heirs of the Western cultural tradition. These, if anyone, should be receptive to an education of this comprehensive kind; for it is they who have called into existence the world-wide social framework within which the whole human race is now living. This has started as a Western framework (though, no doubt, it will turn into a very different one); and the privileged minority in the Western society has played the chief part in giving it its present shape. Thus they, if anyone, ought to feel at home in it. Yet how hard it is, today, to educate even this favored minority to cope with what is its own heritage! And before we have seen our way to solving even this limited educational problem, we have to plunge on into the still more difficult problems of educating the unprivileged majority of Westerners and the huge non-Western majority of the human race, for whom the present Western framework of their life is something alien and uncongenial. Clearly this educational task is a tremendous one. Yet we cannot afford to shy away from it or to exclude any part of the human race from its scope. We have to help mankind to educate itself against the danger of its destroying itself; and this is a duty that we dare not repudiate.

PART TWO

POSSIBLE INSIGHTS FROM EDUCATION AMONG PRIMITIVE PEOPLES AND THE FIRST LARGE ANCIENT CIVILIZATIONS

Overview

Questing after better understanding of life, mankind, and the essential educational issues outlined in Part One, we pursue wisdom. Edith Hamilton wrote that "wisdom . . . in the last analysis is the art of living, hardly to be attained except through long experience."[1] No one of us will live long enough to gain through direct experience the insights necessary for fully civilized living. But we do have the possibility of devoting our energies to those mental pursuits about which William Ellery Channing declared, in his public lectures in Boston in 1838: "It is not to brute force, to physical strength so much as to art, to skill, to intellectual and moral energy, that men owe their mastery over the world. It is mind which has conquered matter."[2] We can seek knowledge of the racial experience of living which we find in books.

> It is chiefly through books that we enjoy intercourse with superior minds, and these invaluable means of communication are in the reach of all. In the best books, great men talk to us, give us their most precious thoughts, and pour their souls into ours. God be thanked for books. They are the voices of the distant and the dead, and make us heirs of the spiritual life of past ages. Books are the true levellers. They give to all, who will faithfully use them, the society, the spiritual presence, of the best and greatest of our race. No matter how poor I am; no matter though the prosperous of my own time will not enter my obscure dwelling; if the sacred writers will enter and take up their abode under my roof, if Milton will cross my threshold to sing to me of Paradise, and Shakespeare to open to me the worlds of imagination and the workings of the human heart, and Franklin to enrich me with his practical wisdom, I shall not pine for want of intellectual companionship, and I may become a cultivated man though excluded from what is called the best society in the place where I live.[3]

But there have been so many experiences, and there are so many books, writings, and articles. We can be drowned in the "ocean of

---

[1] *Spokesmen for God—The Great Teachers of the Old Testament* (New York: W. W. Norton & Company, Inc., 1949, Norton Library N169), p. 102.

[2] As quoted in Gabriel Compayré, *History of Pedagogy*, 2nd ed. (Boston: D. C. Heath and Company, 1886), p. 564.

[3] *Ibid.*, pp. 564-565.

knowledge" Toynbee has called to our attention. What to do? Our approach shall be to do in education as in life: continuously to look for possibilities. Somewhat arbitrary though our classifications may be, we shall look to different periods in the experience of living and educating, selecting from each period a few sources which best indicate to us possibilities about life and education today.

Study of the first two periods entails the study of education among primitive peoples and in the first large ancient civilizations. Each subject comprises a vast specialized body of knowledge and materials continuously being worked over and added to by colleagues in anthropology, history, and education. Scarcely can our selections do justice to the myriad sources for discovering insights into education. What we have done is to select only a few which might (1) incite the reader to further exploration, or (2) offer precious insights into our selves, our lives, and education today as exciting materials for discussion, or (3) serve both purposes.

Chapter 7, Donald S. Seckinger's "Education in Primitive and Modern Societies: A Comparison," serves both purposes well. Summarizing some representative findings in anthropology, he philosophizes about culture in ways which should incite us to further knowledge and more intense debates. From primitive education he cites significant characteristics bearing on our own great problem of cultural reconciliation. Behind Seckinger's lines there seems to lie a concern that voluntary American democracy at the grass roots is in trouble. Out of the needs and expectations he finds in today's students, he frames a challenge to us to gain a better understanding of common social processes. With respect to education and schooling, we in our complex society today debate and argue the matters at issue between the generations — the question of standards and their acquisition and inculcation, as Barbara W. Tuchman has outlined in her article in Part One. Seckinger challenges us to bridge gaps and seek "a common faith, a common sense of shared humanity which might reunite us with the organic origins of civilization." Surely these materials will stimulate our debates and discussions as we seek better perspectives about proper education today.

Philosophy as yet another field of knowledge fruitful for the student of education becomes apparent in Chapter 8, "Symbolic Transformation," the first chapter of Susanne K. Langer's *Philosophy in a New Key—A Study in the Symbolism of Reason, Rite, and Art.* Mrs. Langer's new world view into human mentality and her hypothesis concerning meaning and what lies behind those human experiences expressed in language, ritual, myth, and music — all that is the product of twentieth-century thinking. It is included here in the early period of man's story and the development of culture because it belongs with the story of man's leap from mere *homo sapiens* to Man and culture and civilization. It is well, we think, to have this concept of the human mind as a transformer presented here for testing and debate as the reader begins to work his way through the story of the human career.

The study of the past is fascinating in itself and may well be studied with no other purpose than to understand. But we live today in a very complex world with complex problems, problems requiring as much understanding and insight as we can muster. The remaining readings in Part Two have been selected because they are both enjoyable as fascinating reading and helpful to us in understanding ourselves. Chapters 9 and 10 should be read together, for Andrew Kopkind's "The Power of Prayer" — a dramatic account of the Presidential Prayer Breakfast — is a telling example of the thesis proposed by Barbara Ward in Chapter 9: "Knowledge of cause and effect in nature has freed man from one form of superstition. But he has yet to overcome his trust in fetishes in his personal and political life." Perhaps we need to look at ourselves with the vision afforded by a look at primitive peoples.

Also contributing to our perspective would be the experiences of the ancient Chinese, Hindus, Persians, Babylonians, Assyrians, and Egyptians. Of these first ancient civilizations we have selected the Egyptian and present Hugh C. Black's sample of some lows and highs in the story of culture and civilization to stimulate us to further debate about "Man's Ways with Ideas." A brief selection from Edith Hamilton's *The Greek Way* summarizes for us the way of the ancient East and points to a different way we shall trace in Part Three when we turn to the Graeco-Roman part of our heritage and that great leap beyond the pragmatic and empirical to the intellectual and spiritual.

7
Formal Value Inculcation in Simpler Societies

Donald S. Seckinger

Education in Primitive and Modern Societies: A Comparison

In primitive societies, enculturation appears to be far more efficient, effective, and thorough in comparison to what takes place in contemporary social settings. We might say that two principles of education are carried through in primitive societies; learning-by-doing in real life situations and systematic ideological conditioning.

Living and learning are not separated, either in the informal modes of indulgent child rearing or the more formal stages of value inculcation which take place at puberty. As a growing child, the prospective citizen of the primitive society participates in the common activities of the extended family and community. Children share in the simpler work tasks of the home and village and imitate adult roles in their play. Adults take a common responsibility for the encouragement and correction of the young.

The child is part of the real world of the tribe in the sense of participating as a helper in activities related to physical survival, and especially the domestic side of these activities, such as food gathering and preparation and the repair of items of clothing and shelter. He does not, however, participate in the arts and crafts, the mysteries and rituals, the hunting and the brewing of potions, or the sharing of tribal secrets, until undergoing the ordeal of formal value inculcation. Then, and only then, does he become a fully responsible social being.

The most striking feature of education in primitive societies, in our modern view, is the elaborate formalization of ideological or citizenship training. I call this training in the sense of being a very rigid, dogmatic, no-nonsense conditioning carried out with great exactitude, in great detail, and with no deviations allowed. One might say this is education in terms of its broad goals of cultural allegiance, but the means used are characterized by a ruthless and fanatical intensity.

One example of formal value inculcation comes from the Tiwi tribes of North Australia, as described by the Australian-Canadian anthropologist C. W. M. Hart. At puberty or shortly after, arrangements are made for the boy to be "abducted" by senior cross-cousins from "the other side of the tribe" whom he has never seen. The adults play their assigned roles, and the terrified boy is subjected to an elaborate and extended brainwashing:

> . . . what is actually being taught in the initiation schools is the whole value system of the culture, its myths, its religion, its philosophy, its justification of its own entity as a culture. Primitive society clearly values these things, values them so much that it cannot leave them to individual families to pass on to the young.[1]

No society can entrust its cultural heritage to informal agencies only. The ideological-mythological component of that heritage, certainly, demands a formal, systematic, clearly defined institutionalization.

For those of us standing outside of primitive societies as observers, it may seem illogical that ideology and mythology should be so carefully passed on from one generation to another when the tribe usually exists on the edge of physical survival. Yet if we stop to consider, it may well be the myths of a people which keep them alive. If one believes that certain rituals will eventually yield a result in the hunt, for example, he will drive himself to his outermost physical limits to run down the quarry.

Thus, it is necessary that the youth be totally immersed in his citizenship training, down to the last detail. One common feature, as indicated, is the use of strangers, cross-cousins, or "outsiders" from "the other side of the tribe" or related tribes. Failing this, as Hart points out, it is necessary to "mask" members of one's own tribe, to create the desired effect.[2]

Although advanced training in arts and crafts is sometimes also accomplished by formal means, by far the most significant feature of primitive education in primitive societies is the fact that when such

---

[1] C. W. M. Hart, "Contrasts between Prepubertal and Postpubertal Education," in George D. Spindler, ed., *Education and Culture* (New York: Holt, Rinehart and Winston, 1963), p. 419.

[2] *Ibid.*, p. 418. See especially Footnote 2. Dr. Margaret Mead pointed out this feature in connection with the Arapesh, whose social structure precludes "strangers" from participation.

societies go to the trouble to conduct formal schooling, it is mainly for the purpose of formal value inculcation. The thoroughness of this training for citizenship is possible only in the presence of a clearly defined system of values, a vision of what a person ought to be in his relations to the body politic. This vision, unfortunately, is conspicuously absent in the complex industrial democracies of the modern world.

How ridiculously brutal and simplistic it would seem to a modern youth, for example, to have to attend such an institution as the Mano tribe's West African "Bush School." Charles describes the establishment of this school, which is an *ad hoc* affair conducted over a period of a few months, in contrast to the Tiwi initiation classes, which run for two years. The purpose, however, is essentially the same. As he takes it, from the anthropologist G. W. Harley:

> There was no stated time at which the school would be conducted. The usual procedure was to wait until there were enough boys coming of age to make a school session worth the trouble and expense. Also, it was considered desirable to have a son of the chief in each class to become its alumni leader later. Several years could elapse between sessions. . . . The time being agreed upon, a special campsite in the jungle was cleared to serve as the campus. Huts were constructed for the officials and the initiates (students). . . . The initiation began at the raffia curtain. Passage through (or sometimes over) the raffia curtain symbolized death. The boy was dead. A new man would emerge from the camp at the end of the school session[3]

The elements of mystery appear as the boys bid farewell to their families and pass through the curtain to a place which has now been made sacred by the religious leaders of the tribe. They are sworn to secrecy, isolated from the outside world, and, in extreme cases, given the death penalty for attempted escape. If a boy dies while at school he is not mourned, for he was considered to have died at the raffia curtain. Those who "graduate" take new names, which will be theirs in the new life of adulthood.

We would be hard pressed to find the equivalents in symbolism, ritual, and myth in the modern world. Compare, for example, the terror of the youth in primitive society when the wise men tell him he will literally die if his lessons are not properly learned, to the routine recitation of the pledge of allegiance to the flag in our modern schools, or the ritual observance of national holidays. In terms of influencing

---

[3] M. R. Charles, *A Preface to Education* (New York: The Macmillan Co., 1965), p. 47.

student behavior our contemporary incantations in the direction of democratic citizenship seem feeble indeed.

This is not to advocate a new miracle cult in our schools, or to promote some kind of "Americanism" by means of heightened propaganda campaigns. I do not believe the alternative to formal value inculcation in primitive societies can be found in scientific brainwashing and thought control. Tendencies for this already exist in the management of news and the pervasive character of mass media. Propagandistic means do not work in a democracy. They are either too feeble, and become the targets of skepticism and debunking, or if they are made effective, then our social system is no longer a representative reflection of the wishes of its people.

Is there a viable alternative? I would suggest a few possibilities along these lines. Our problem of citizenship education, if democracy is to survive in a world filled with cultural conflicts and hostilities, is essentially a matter of bridging gaps. Industrialization continues to separate us from ourselves, to divide productive labor from creative living and learning. Many students as well as teachers have resigned themselves, as this is written in the early 1970's, to the inevitable discontinuity between high and popular culture, between the adult world and the world of youth, and between majority and minority interests.

We lack a common faith, a common sense of shared humanity which might reunite us with the organic origins of civilization. Our schools could make a start at reunification by allowing greater student participation in decision-making at earlier ages, if we as teachers were willing to take the risks involved and if students themselves were willing to undergo the consequences. But even this would not be enough. In my view, the polarization of conflicting interest groups in our complex industrial democracy cannot be reconciled through formal schooling alone. Nothing less than the moral reorientation of communities, families, churches, and civic organizations, from the local level up, can heal our culture.

I suppose that to you, our students, you, who are our hope for the future of civilization, this is asking a great deal. Perhaps it is seeking the impossible dream. Yet, if you do not make a moral commitment to inform yourself and your peers, and to act in your local communities in helping relationships, then we are surely lost. The light that shone so briefly in ancient Athens, and which we all take so much for granted, will in this generation go out. This is the choice we are all making now, on behalf of all the generations to come.

8
A Hypothesis and World View of Meaning

Susanne K. Langer

Symbolic Transformation

Susanne K. Langer, "Symbolic Transformation," *Philosophy in a New Key—A Study in the Symbolism of Reason, Rite, and Art*, 2nd ed. (Cambridge, Mass.: Harvard University Press, 1951; from the Fifteenth Printing, Mentor Paperback MT635, New York: The New American Library, Inc.), chapter 2, pp. 35-54.

The vitality and energies of the imagination do not operate at will; they are fountains, not machinery.

D. G. James, *Skepticism and Poetry.*

A changed approach to the theory of knowledge naturally has its effect upon psychology, too. As long as sense was supposed to be the chief factor in knowledge, psychologists took a prime interest in the organs that were the windows of the mind, and in the details of their functioning; other things were accorded a sketchier and sometimes vaguer treatment. If scientists demanded, and philosophers dutifully admitted, that all true belief must be based on sense-evidence, then the activity of the mind had to be conceived purely as a matter of recording and combining; then intelligence had to be a product of impression, memory, and association. But now, an epistemological insight has uncovered a more potent, howbeit more difficult, factor in scientific procedure—the use of symbols to attain, as well as to organize, belief. Of course, this alters our conception of intelligence at a stroke. Not higher sensitivity, not longer memory or even quicker association sets man so far above other animals that he can regard them as denizens of a lower world: no, it is the power of using symbols — the power of *speech*—that makes him lord of the earth. So our interest in the mind has shifted more and more from the acquisition of experience, the domain of sense, to the *uses* of sense-data, the realm of conception and expression.

The importance of symbol-using, once admitted, soon becomes

48

paramount in the study of intelligence. It has lent a new orientation especially to genetic psychology, which traces the growth of the mind; for this growth is paralleled, in large measure, by the observable uses of language, from the first words in infancy to the complete self-expression of maturity, and perhaps the relapse into meaningless verbiage that accompanies senile decline. Such researches have even been extended from the development of individuals to the evolution of mental traits in nations and races. There is an increasing *rapprochement* between philology and psychology—between the science of language and the science of what we do with language. The recent literature of psychogenetics bears ample witness to the central position which symbol-using, or language in its most general sense, holds in our conception of human mentality. Frank Lorimer's *The Growth of Reason* bears the sub-title: "A Study of the Role of Verbal Activity in the Growth and Structure of the Human Mind." Grace De Laguna's *Speech: Its Function and Development* treats the acquisition of language as not only indicative of the growth of concepts, but as the principal agent in this evolution. Much the same view is held by Professor A. D. Ritchie, who remarks, in *The Natural History of the Mind*: "As far as thought is concerned, and at all levels of thought, it [mental life] is a symbolic process. It is mental not because the symbols are immaterial, for they are often material, perhaps always material, but because they are symbols. . . . The essential act of thought is symbolization."[1] There is, I think, more depth in this statement than its author realized; had he been aware of it, the proposition would have occurred earlier in the book, and given the whole work a somewhat novel turn. As it is, he goes on to an excellent account of sign-using and sign-making, which stand forth clearly as the essential means of intellection.

Quotations could be multiplied almost indefinitely, from an imposing list of sources—from John Dewey and Bertrand Russell, from Brunschwicg and Piaget and Head, Köhler and Koffka, Carnap, Delacroix, Ribot, Cassirer, Whitehead—from philosophers, psychologists, neurologists, and anthropologists—to substantiate the claim that symbolism is the recognized key to that mental life which is characteristically human and above the level of sheer animality. Symbol and meaning make man's world far more than sensation; Miss Helen Keller, bereft of sight and hearing, or even a person like the late Laura Bridgman, with the single sense of touch, is capable of living in a wider and richer world than a dog or an ape with all his senses alert.

Genetic psychology grew out of the study of animals, children, and savages, both from a physiological and from a behavioristic angle. Its

[1] Pages 278-279.

fundamental standpoint is that the responses of an organism to the environment are adaptive, and are dictated by that organism's *needs*. Such needs may be variously conceived; one school reduces them all to one basic requirement, such as keeping the metabolic balance, persisting in an ideal status;[2] others distinguish as elementary more specific aims—e.g., nutrition, parturition, defense—or even such differentiated cravings as physical comfort, companionship, self-assertion, security, play.[3] The tenor of these primary concepts is suggested largely by the investigator's starting point. A biologist tends to postulate only the obvious needs of a clam or even an infusorian; an animal-psychologist generalizes somewhat less, for he makes distinctions that are relevant, say, to a white rat, but hardly to a clam. An observer of childhood conceives the cardinal interests on a still higher level. But through the whole hierarchy of genetic studies there runs a feeling of continuity, a tendency to identify the "real" or "ultimate" motive conditions of human action with the needs of primitive life, to trace all wants and aims of mankind to some initial protoplasmic response. This dominant principle is the most important thing that the evolutionist school has bestowed upon psychology—the assumption, sometimes avowed, more often tacit, that *"Nihil est in homine quod non prius in amoeba erat."*

When students of mental evolution discovered how great a role in science is played by symbols, they were not slow to exploit that valuable insight. The acquisition of so decisive a tool must certainly be regarded as one of the great landmarks in human progress, probably the starting point of all genuinely intellectual growth. Since symbol-using appears at a late stage, it is presumably a highly integrated form of simpler animal activities. It must spring from biological needs, and justify itself as a practical asset. Man's conquest of the world undoubtedly rests on the supreme development of his brain, which allows him to synthesize, delay, and modify his reactions by the interpolation of *symbols* in the gaps and confusions of direct experience, and by means of "verbal signs" to add the experiences of other people to his own.

There is a profound difference between using symbols and merely using signs. The use of signs is the very first manifestation of mind. It arises as early in biological history as the famous "conditioned reflex," by which a concomitant of a stimulus takes over the stimulus-function. The concomitant becomes a *sign* of the condition to which the reaction is really appropriate. This is the real beginning of mentality, for here is the birthplace of *error*, and therewith of truth. If truth and error are

[2] Cf. Eugenio Rignano, *The Psychology of Reasoning* (1927).

[3] Cf. William James, *The Principles of Psychology* (1899; first published in 1890), II, 348.

to be attributed only to belief, then we must recognize in the earliest misuse of signs, in the inappropriate conditioned reflex, not error, but some prototype of error. We might call it *mistake*. Every piano player, every typist, knows that the hand can make mistakes where consciousness entertains no error. However, whether we speak of truth and error, or of their respective prototypes, whether we regard the creature liable to them as conscious or preconscious, or dispense with such terms altogether, the use of signs is certainly a *mental* function. It is the beginning of intelligence. As soon as sensations function as signs of conditions in the surrounding world, the animal receiving them is moved to exploit or avoid those conditions. The sound of a gong or a whistle, itself entirely unrelated to the process of eating, causes a dog to expect food, if in past experience this sound has always preceded dinner; it is a sign, not a part, of his food. Or, the smell of a cigarette, in itself not necessarily displeasing, tells a wild animal that there is danger, and drives it into hiding. The growth of this sign-language runs parallel with the physical development of sense organs and synaptic nerve-structure. It consists in the transmission of *sense messages* to muscles and glands—to the organs of eating, mating, flight and defense—and obviously functions in the interest of the elementary biological requirements: self-preservation, growth, procreation, the preservation of the species.

Even animal mentality, therefore, is built up on a primitive semantic; it is the poser of learning, by trial and error, that certain phenomena in the world are signs of certain others, existing or about to exist; adaptation to an environment is its purpose, and hence the measure of its success. The environment may be very narrow, as it is for the mole, whose world is a back yard, or it may be as wide as an eagle's range and as complicated as a monkey's jungle preserve. That depends on the variety of *signals* a creature can receive, the variety of combinations of them to which he can react, and the fixity or adjustability of his responses. Obviously, if he has very fixed reactions, he cannot adapt himself to a varied or transient environment; if he cannot easily combine and integrate several activities, then the occurrence of more than one stimulus at a time will throw him into confusion; if he be poor in sensory organs—deaf, or blind, hard-shelled, or otherwise limited—he cannot receive many signals to begin with.

Man's superiority in the race for self-preservation was first ascribed to his wider range of signals, his greater power of integrating reflexes, his quicker learning by trial and error; but a little reflection brought a much more fundamental trait to light, namely his peculiar use of "signs." Man, unlike all other animals, uses "signs" not only to *indicate* things, but also to *represent* them. To a clever dog, the name of a person is a signal that the person is present; you say the name, he pricks up his ears and looks for its object. If you say "dinner," he becomes restive, expecting food. You cannot make any communication to him that is not taken as a signal of something immediately forthcoming. His mind is a simple and direct *transmitter* of messages from the world to his motor centers. With man it is different. We use certain "signs" among ourselves that do not point to anything in our actual surroundings. Most of our words are not signs in the sense of signals. They are used to talk *about* things, not to direct our eyes and ears and noses toward them. Instead of announcers of things, they are reminders. They have been called "substitute signs," for in our present experience they take the place of things that we have perceived in the past, or even things that we can merely imagine by combining memories, things that *might* be in past or future experience. Of course such *signs* do not usually serve as vicarious stimuli to actions that would be appropriate to their meanings; where the objects are quite normally not present, that would result in a complete chaos of behavior. They serve, rather, to let us develop a characteristic attitude toward objects *in absentia*, which is called "thinking of" or "referring to" what is not here. "Signs" used in this capacity are not *symptoms* of things, but *symbols*.

The development of language is the history of the gradual accumulation and elaboration of verbal symbols. By means of this phenomenon, man's whole behavior-pattern has undergone an immense change from the simple biological scheme, and his mentality has expanded to such a degree that it is no longer comparable to the minds of animals. Instead of a direct transmitter of coded signals, we have a system that has sometimes been likened to a telephone-exchange,[4] wherein messages may be relayed, stored up if a line is busy, answered by proxy, perhaps sent over a line that did not exist when they were first given, *noted down and kept* if the desired number gives no answer. Words are the plugs in this super-switchboard; they connect impressions and let them function together; sometimes they cause lines to become crossed in funny or disastrous ways.

This view of mentality, of its growth through trial and error, its apparently complicated but essentially simple aims—namely, to advance the persistence, growth, and procreation of the organism, and to produce, and provide for, its progeny—brings the troublesome concept of Mind into line with other basic ideas of biology. Man is doing in his elaborate way just what the mouse in his simplicity is doing, and what the unconscious or semiconscious jellyfish is performing

[4] The simile of the telephone-exchange has been used by Leonard Troland in *The Mystery of Mind* (1926), p. 100 ff.

after its own chemical fashion. The ideal of *"Nihil est in homine . . ."* is supported by living example. The speech line between man and beast is minimized by the recognition that speech is primarily an instrument of social control, just like the cries of animals, but has acquired a representative function, allowing a much greater degree of cooperation among individuals, and the focusing of personal attention on absent objects. The passage from the sign-function of a word to its symbolic function is gradual, a result of social organization, an instrument that proves indispensable once it is discovered, and develops through successful use.

If the theoretic position here attributed to students of genetic psychology requires any affidavit, we can find it in the words of a psychologist, in Frank Lorimer's *The Growth of Reason*:

> The apes described by Köhler," he says, "certainly have quite elaborate 'ape-ways' into which a newcomer is gradually acculturated, including among other patterns ways of using available instruments for reaching and climbing, a sort of rhythmic play or dance, and types of murmurs, wails and rejoicings. . . .
>
> It is not surprising that still more intelligent animals should have developed much more definite and elaborate 'animal ways,' including techniques of tool-uses and specific mechanisms of vocal social control, which gradually developed into the 'folk-ways' of the modern anthropologist. . . .
>
> Vocal acts are originally involved in the intellectual correlation of behaviour just as other physiological processes are. During the whole course of meaningless vocal chatter, vocal processes gradually accumulate intensity and dominance in behaviour. . . . Specific vocables become dominant *foci* of fixed reactions to various situations and the instruments of specific social adjustments. . . . The gradual differentiation and expansion of the social functions of vocal activity, among a race of animals characterized by increasingly complex nervous systems, is the fundamental principle of the historic trend of *vocal* activity to *verbal* activity, and the emergence of language.[5]

An interpretation of observed facts that adjusts them to a general scientific outlook, a theory that bridges what used to appear as a *saltus naturae*, a logical explanation displacing a shamefaced resort to miracle, has so much to recommend it that one hates to challenge it on any

[5] Pages 76-77.

count. But the best ideas are also the ones most worth reflecting on. At first glance it seems as though the genetic conception of language, which regards the power of symbol-using as the latest and highest device of practical intelligence, an added instrument for gaining animal ends, must be the key to all essential features of human mentality. It makes rationality plausible, and shows at once the relationship of man and brute, and the gulf between them as a fairly simple phenomenon.

The difficulty of the theory arises when we consider how people with synaptic switchboards between their sense organs and their muscles should use their verbal symbols to make the telephone-exchange work most efficiently. Obviously the only proper use of the words which "plug in" the many complicated wires is the denotation of *facts*. Such facts may be concrete and personal, or they may be highly general and universal; but they should be chosen for the sake of orientation in the world for better living, for more advantageous practice. It is easy to see how *errors* might arise, just as they occur in overt action; the white rat in a maze makes mistakes, and so does the trout who bites at a feather-and-silk fly. In so complicated an organ as the human cortex, a confusion of messages or of responses would be even more likely than in the reflex arcs of rodents or fish. But, of course, the mistakes should be subject to quick correction by the world's punishments; behavior should, on the whole, be rational and realistic. Any other response must be chalked up as failure, as a miscarriage of biological purposes.

There are, indeed, philosophical and scientific thinkers who have accepted the biogenetic theory of mind on its great merits, and drawn just the conclusions indicated above. They have looked at the way men really use their power of symbolic thinking, the responses they actually make, and have been forced to admit that the cortical telephone-exchange does business in most extraordinary ways. The results of their candid observations are such books as W. B. Pitkin's *Short Introduction to the History of Human Stupidity*, Charles Richet's *L'homme Stupide* (which deals not with men generally regarded as stupid, but with the impractical customs and beliefs of aliens, and the folly of religious convictions), and Stuart Chase's *The Tyranny of Words*. To contemplate the unbelievable folly of which symbol-using animals are capable is very disgusting or very amusing, according to our mood; but philosophically it is, above all, confounding, How can an instrument develop in the interests of better practice, and survive, if it harbors so many dangers for the creature possessed of it? How can language increase a man's efficiency if it puts him at a biological disadvantage beside his cat?

Mr. Chase, watching his cat Hobie Baker, reflects:

Hobie can never learn to talk. He can learn to respond to

my talk, as he responds to other signs. . . . He can utter cries indicating pain, pleasure, excitement. He can announce that he wants to go out of doors. . . . But he cannot master words and language. This in some respects is fortunate for Hobie, for he will not suffer from hallucinations provoked by bad language. He will remain a realist all his life. . . . He is certainly able to think after a fashion, interpreting signs in the light of past experience, deliberately deciding his course of action, the survival value of which is high.

Instead of words, Hobie sometimes uses a crude gesture language. We know that he has a nervous system corresponding to that of man, with messages coming into the receptors in skin, ear and eye and going over the wires to the cortex, where memories are duly filed for reference. There are fewer switchboards in his cortex than in mine, which may be one of the reasons why he cannot learn to talk. . . .

Meaning comes to Hobie as it comes to me, through past experience. . . .

Generally speaking, animals tend to learn cumulatively through experience. The old elephant is the wisest of the herd. This selective process does not always operate in the case of human beings. The old are sometimes wise, but more often they are stuffed above the average with superstitions, misconceptions, and irrational dogmas. One may hazard the guess that erroneous identifications in human beings are pickled and preserved in words, and so not subject to the constant check of the environment, as in the case of cats and elephants. . . .

I find Hobie a useful exhibit along this difficult trail of semantics. What 'meaning' connotes to him is often so clear and simple that I have no trouble in following it. I come from a like evolutionary matrix. 'Meaning' to me has like roots, and a like mechanism of apprehension. I have a six-cylinder brain and he has a one-lunger, but they operate on like principles.

. . . Most children do not long maintain Hobie Baker's realistic appraisal of the environment. Verbal identifications and confused abstractions begin at a tender age. . . . Language is no more than crudely acquired before children begin to suffer from it, and to misinterpret the world by reason of it.[6]

A cat with a "stalking-instinct," or other special equipment, who could never learn to use that asset properly, but was forever stalking

[6] Stuart Chase, *The Tyranny of Words* (1938), pp. 46-56.

chairs or elephants, would scarcely rise in animal estate by virtue of his talent. Men who can use symbols to facilitate their practical responses, but use them constantly to confuse and inhibit, warp and misadapt their actions, *and gain no other end by their symbolic devices*, have no prospect of inheriting the earth. Such an "instinct" would have no chance to develop by any process of successful exercise. The error-quotient is too great. The commonly recognized biological needs—food and shelter, security, sexual satisfaction, and the safety of young ones—are probably better assuaged by the realistic activities, the meows and gestures, of Hobie Baker than by the verbal imagination and reflection of his master. The cat's world is not falsified by the beliefs and poetic figments that language creates, nor his behavior unbalanced by the bootless rites and sacrifices that characterize religion, art, and other vagaries of a word-mongering mind. In fact, his vital purposes are so well served without the intervention of these vast mental constructions, these flourishes and embellishments of the cerebral switchboard, that it is hard to see why such an overcomplication of the central exchange was ever permitted, in man's "higher centers," to block the routes from sensory to motor organs and garble all the messages.

The dilemma for philosophy is bad enough to make one reconsider the genetic hypothesis that underlies it. If our basic needs were really just those of lower creatures much refined, we should have evolved a more realistic language than in fact we have. If the mind were essentially a recorder and transmitter, typified by the simile of the telephone-exchange, we should act very differently from the way we actually do. Certainly no "learning-process" has caused man to believe in magic; yet "word-magic" is a common practice among primitive peoples, and so is vicarious treatment—burning in effigy, etc.—where the proxy is plainly a mere symbol of the desired victim. Another strange, universal phenomenon is ritual. It is obviously symbolic, except where it is aimed at concrete results, and then it may be regarded as a communal form of magic. Now, all magical and ritual practices are hopelessly inappropriate to the preservation and increase of life. My cat would turn up his nose and his tail at them. To regard them as mistaken attempts to control nature, as a result of wrong synapses, or "crossed wires," in the brain, seems to me to leave the most rational of animals too deep in the slough of error. If a savage in his ignorance of physics tries to make a mountain open its caverns by dancing round it, we must admit with shame that no rat in a psychologist's maze would try such patently ineffectual methods of opening a door. Nor should such experiments be carried on, in the face of failure, for thousands of years; even morons should learn more quickly than that.

Another item in human behavior is our serious attitude toward art. Genetic psychology usually regards art as a form of play, a luxury product of the mind. This is not only a scientific theory, it is a common-sense view; we *play an instrument, we act a play*. Yet like many common-sense doctrines, it is probably false. Great artists are rarely recruited from the leisure class, and it is only in careless speech that we denote music or tragedy as our "hobby"; we do not really class them with tennis or bridge. We condemn as barbarous people who destroy works of art, even under the stress of war—blame them for ruining the Parthenon, when only a recent, sentimental generation has learned to blame them for ruining the homes that surrounded the sanctuary of Beauty! Why should the world wail over the loss of a play product, and look with its old callousness on the destruction of so much that dire labor has produced? It seems a poor economy of nature that men will suffer and starve for the sake of play, when play is supposed to be the abundance of their strength after their needs are satisfied. Yet artists as a class are so ready to sacrifice wealth and comfort and even health to their trade, that a lean and hollow look has become an indispensable feature in the popular conception of genius.

There is a third factor in human life that challenges the utilitarian doctrine of symbolism. That is the constant, ineffectual process of *dreaming* during sleep. The activity of the mind seems to go on all the time, like that of the heart and lungs and viscera; but during sleep it serves no practical purpose. That dream-material is symbolic is a fairly established fact. And symbols are supposed to have evolved from the advantageous use of *signs*. They are representative signs, that help to retain things for later reference, for comparing, planning, and generally for purposive thinking. Yet the symbolism of dreams performs no such acquired function. At best it presents us with the things we do *not* want to think about, the things which stand in the way of practical living. Why should the mind produce symbols that do not direct the dreamer's activities, that only mix up the present with unsuitable past experiences?

There are several theories of dream, notably, of course, the Freudian interpretation. But those which—like Freud's—regard it as more than excess mental energy or visceral disturbance do not fit the scientific picture of the mind's growth and function at all. A mind whose semantic powers are evolved from the functioning of the motor arc should *only think*; any vagaries of association are "mistakes." If our viscera made as many mistakes in sleep as the brain, we should all die of indigestion after our first nursing. It may be replied that the mistakes of dream are harmless, since they have no motor terminals, though they enter into waking life as memories, and we have to learn to discount them. But why does the central switchboard not rest when there is no need of making connections? Why should the plugs be popped in and out, and set the whole system wildly ringing, only to end with a universal "Excuse it, please"?

The love of magic, the high development of ritual, the seriousness of art, and the characteristic activity of dreams, are rather large factors to leave out of account in constructing a theory of mind. Obviously the mind is doing something else, or at least something more, than just connecting experiential items. It is not functioning simply in the interest of those biological needs which genetic psychology recognizes. Yet it is a natural organ, and presumably does nothing that is not relevant to the total behavior, the response to nature that constitutes human life. The moral of this long critique is, therefore, *to reconsider the inventory of human needs*, which scientists have established on a basis of animal psychology, and somewhat hastily set up as the measure of a man. An unrecorded motive might well account for many an unexplained action. I propose, therefore, to try a new general principle: to conceive the mind, still as an organ in the service of primary needs, but of *characteristically human needs*; instead of assuming that the human mind tries to do the same things as a cat's mind, but by the use of a special talent which miscarries four times out of five, I shall assume that the human mind is *trying to do something else*; and that the cat does not act humanly *because he does not need to*. This difference in fundamental needs, I believe, determines the difference of function which sets man so far apart from all his zoölogical brethren; and the recognition of it is the key to those paradoxes in the philosophy of mind which our too consistently zoölogical model of human intelligence has engendered.

It is generally conceded that men have certain "higher" aims and desires than animals; but what these are, and in what sense they are "higher," may still be mooted without any universal agreement. There are essentially two schools of opinion: one which considers man the highest animal, and his supreme desires as products of his supreme mind; and another which regards him as the lowest spirit, and his unique longings as a manifestation of his otherworldly admixture. To the naturalists, the difference between physical and mental interests, between organismic will and moral will, between hungry meows and harvest prayers, or between faith in the mother cat and faith in a heavenly father, is a difference of complexity, abstractness, articulateness, in short: a difference of degree. To the religious interpreters it seems a radical distinction, a difference, in each case, of kind and cause. The moral sentiments especially are deemed a sign of the ultimate godhead in man; likewise the power of prayer, which is regarded as a gift, not a native and natural power like laughter, tears, language, and song. The Ancient Mariner, when suddenly he could pray, had not merely found his speech; he had received grace, he was given back the divine status from which he had fallen. According to the religious conception, man is at most half-brother to the beast. No matter how many of his traits may be identified as simian features, there is that in him yet which springs from a different source and is forever unzoölogical. This view is the antithesis of the naturalistic; it breaks the structure of genetic psychology in principle. For, the study of psychogenesis has grown up on exactly the opposite creed—that man is a true-blooded, full-franchised denizen of the animal kingdom, without any alien ancestors, *and therefore has no features or functions which animals do not share in some degree.*

That man is an animal I certainly believe; and also, that he has no supernatural essence, "soul" or "entelechy" or "mind-stuff," enclosed in his skin. He is an organism, his substance is chemical, and what he does, suffers, or knows, is just what this sort of chemical structure may do, suffer, or know. When the structure goes to pieces, it never does, suffers, or knows anything again. If we ask how physical objects, chemically analysable, can be conscious, how ideas can occur to them, we are talking ambiguously; for the conception of "physical object" is a conception of chemical substance *not* biologically organized. What causes this tremendous organization of substances, is one of the things the tremendous organisms do not know; but with their organization, suffering and impulse and awareness arise. It is really no harder to imagine that a chemically active body wills, knows, thinks, and feels, than that an invisible, intangible something does so, "animates" the body without physical agency, and "inhabits" it without being in any *place*.

Now this is a mere declaration of faith, preliminary to a confession of heresy. The heresy is this: that I believe there is a primary need in man, which other creatures probably do not have, and which actuates all his apparently unzoölogical aims, his wistful fancies, his consciousness of value, his utterly impractical enthusiasms, and his awareness of a "Beyond" filled with holiness. Despite the fact that this need gives rise to almost everything that we commonly assign to the "higher" life, it is not itself a "higher" form of some "lower" need; it is quite essential, imperious, and general, and may be called "high" only in the sense that it belongs exclusively (I think) to a very complex and perhaps recent genus. It may be satisfied in crude, primitive ways or in conscious and refined ways, so it has its own hierarchy of "higher" and lower," elementary and derivative forms.

This basic need, which certainly is obvious only in man, is the *need of symbolization.* The symbol-making function is one of man's primary activities, like eating, looking, or moving about. It is the fundamental process of his mind, and goes on all the time. Sometimes we are aware of it, sometimes we merely find its results, and realize that certain experiences have passed through our brains and have been digested there.

9
Man and His Fetishes — Primitive

Barbara Ward
Shrunken Heads and Shrunken Minds

By Barbara Ward, well-known British author and lecturer who has traveled and lived in Africa, *The New York Times Magazine*, November 9, 1958, pp. 14, 85, 88, 90. © by The New York Times Company. Reprinted by permission.

Knowledge of cause and effect in nature has freed man from one form of superstition. But he has yet to overcome his trust in fetishes in his personal and political life.

No one can travel far in Africa—or indeed in any area of tribal society—without becoming aware of how large a part the fetish plays in men's affairs. In almost any village, the visitor will notice an enclosure set apart behind a high hedge. If he peers inside—he will not be encouraged to do so—he will see strange objects hanging from branches or simply lying about. They may look like bones wrapped in rags, the foot of an animal, beads and a shrunken monkey's head. But there is no doubt what they are—the guardian fetishes of the village.

The simplest way to describe a fetish is to say that it is a focus of magical power. It is a lever through which a man can, by the proper actions and formulas, influence the unseen and incomprehensible forces which determine his destiny. The force of his will and his desire operating through this power center compels the cooperation of whatever it is that lies hidden beyond.

As such, of course, the fetish can be put to as many uses as there are human desires. African markets have their fetish stalls. Among the bright pyramids of local fruit, the gaudy rolls of textiles and the wild variety of tinware, glassware, hardware, shoeware and general gadgetry, there is always a stand where magic is laid out like vegetables in a supermarket. Neat divisions separate the love philters from the pebbles which guard against the evil eye or the sand which, sprinkled on the doorstep, turns back the plague.

Fetishes enter into grave political decisions. In some countries a politician may return to discuss affairs with his local fetish priest as an American Congressman goes off to keep in touch with the grassroots.

And fetishes have, at times, literally the power of life and death. A few months ago, in the Northern Territories of Australia, an aboriginal woman stumbled into a government dispensary carrying her sick child. She explained it was being "sung to death" by the tribe.

Not long after, another aborigine was taken by stretcher in a state of semiparalysis to a Darwin hospital. There was no discernible cause for his illness, but the members of his community were willing him to die. No doubt, after a ceremonial gathering of the tribe, the fetish priest had danced with a bone in his shoe and at last had "pointed the bone" at the wretched man. Thereafter—had it not been for outside intervention—he would have been doomed. Even in Darwin it took him months to recover.

Most terrible of all are the fetishes that demand human sacrifice. Since the most precious thing in the world is the lifeblood of the human species, it is not difficult to believe that in extreme emergency the dark, baffling powers which order destiny demand the sacrifice of man's highest good—life itself.

When British troops approached the city of Benin in Nigeria a century ago, the nearer they came the more frantic became the sacrifices. When at last the city fell, the horrified soldiers marched to the palace between lines of crucified slaves, and in the central court the fetish place was black with encrusted blood and piled with the bones of murdered men.

In theory, at least, there is no mystery about the potency of fetishes. It is compounded of two things:

On the one hand, most societies at the tribal level have only a very rudimentary knowledge of physical cause and effect. If you do not know how something works, there is nothing essentially incredible in the idea that a fetish might make it work better.

On the other hand, the human psyche has enormous latent powers of self-conviction and, once convinced, can operate with a potency impossible to the skeptical, the cynical, the indifferent or the half-persuaded.

It is hard for Western man, after a century or so of scientific indoctrination, to imagine himself back in the twilight of tribal ignorance. Even if the ultimate energy of the universe remains a mystery, most of its proximate activities are penetrable and controllable. If a river floods, modern man does not blame the anger of the weather gods, but the lack of dams, levees and afforestation—or of Congressional appropriations. And so he does not turn to a fetish to appease the gods and stop the flooding—possibly by drowning a man cere-monially in the river. He gets to work on his Senator—and not to drown him, either.

Equally, this widespread knowledge of how things in fact work has altered the whole level of Western credulity. The Australian aborigine was in danger of death because the psychic energies of all his group, willing him to die, fused with his conviction that they had the power to kill him. Modern man knows that looks do not kill, however uncomfortable social ostracism can be. And since he does not believe people can will him to death, they cannot do so. The most they can do is to give him a nervous breakdown—which, heaven knows, is unpleasant enough.

Nowhere, in fact, has the liberation from fear wrought by science worked more strongly than in the field of sickness. We may not have the complete answer to physical health but one specter at least is banished—that our child's fever is caused by the ill will of the man next door. Knowledge of the human body, of its functioning, of the parts played by viruses and infections, this perhaps more than any other branch of science has packed away the philters and the amulets, the stones and charms against the evil eye, the whole paraphernalia of magical protection against a malice which existed in imagination only, but was no less potent on that account.

This is a great liberation—none the less great for being taken largely for granted. But before modern Western man falls into a posture of self-congratulation on his release from the credulity of his ancestors, he had better be certain that all trace of the fetish approach has been banished from his world. The question is not simply whether trivial superstitions have survived—dislike of the number thirteen or determination to avoid walking under ladders. The problem is a deeper one. If the essence of the fetish system is to manipulate people's psychic energies and to direct them toward specific ends, there are surely some areas of Western life where the fetish system is still in full swing.

Compare, for instance, the case of the lovelorn girl in tribal and in modern society. Back in the African bush she talks over her plight with her friends and they tell her that such and such a fetish priest has a particular potion which, drunk at the full moon, will make her perfectly irresistible. Off she goes, gets her potion, drinks it and, so great is her new confidence, she may well become irresistible. There certainly is a sense in which people are as glamorous as they think they are, and a love philter, implicitly believed in, is a powerful reinforcement.

The modern girl does not, of course, depend upon a potion. She relies upon the scents and creams that our modern fetish priests, the advertisers, assure her will bring the loved one to her arms. "I owe all this to X's bath salts" parallels the working of the fetish in tribal society.

The strength of the fetish lies in the fact that behind the normal aims of most societies—to marry, to have children, to live as comfortably as possible, to be well regarded by one's neighbors—there can be mobilized so much emotional force, so much tension, anxiety, desire and determination that the remedy put forward becomes, as it were, charged with the energies of the person seeking it.

The fetish priest plays on the welling-up of these emotional and irrational drives and, even though the charms he offers—the ground chalk or the bone smeared with grease or the bottle of river water—are perfectly neutral, there is often enough belief about to give them some efficacy. Anyway, they always *might* work and people driven by love or envy or ambition are not going to pass up the chance.

In modern society the irrational impulses are still there in spite of the centuries of reason and science that lie behind us. The grosser superstitions may have faded out, but more and more the aim is not simply to offer to supply a known want but to set in motion the underlying forces of instinct and unreason which perfectly reasonable wants can still generate.

It is not enough for a breakfast food to have a pleasant taste and to contain a balanced supply of protein and vitamins. It must also have the power to invigorate a young executive into securing a promotion. The extra dimension of magic must be added on. It is almost as though a whole new system of fetishes had come in through the back door of modern materialistic rationalist society.

But may not modern man, while admitting his addiction to a whole range of tribal magic, claim that he has at least advanced beyond the most terrible of the ancient obsessions?

Nowhere, he may say, do you see the continuance of such horrors as the Aztec belief that, since the life of the sun could be nourished only with human blood, battles must be fought and prisoners captured so that the priests could carve out their living hearts with sharpened obsidian knives in Montezuma's bloody capital. Surely the doors of knowledge have been opened wide and great gusts of reality and understanding—of the solar system, of the processes of nature, of climate and weather and harvesting—have swept away the hideous altars and the systematic shedding of blood.

But wars are still fought and blood is still shed in our own century. Can we be sure that the fetish system is so entirely banished and that the violent forces of unreason have beaten so complete a retreat? It is barely twenty years since Hitler turned German "blood and soil" into a dark god in whose name millions of men and women were massacred.

Today, there is a disturbing resemblance between the reasoning of the Aztecs and the reasoning of Mr. Khrushchev.

If you believe that the destiny of society and the fate of man depend upon nourishing the life of the sun, there is no limit to what you will do to keep the sun supplied. Within the false premises the reasoning is perfectly logical and cogent. Similarly, since Mr. Khrushchev believes that communism is the destiny of humanity, he is justified— within his own logic—in demanding any sacrifice to bring it about.

In some ways the Aztecs' attitude is more rational. Earthly existence and hence happiness do depend upon the sun. No sane man—after Hungary—can argue that they depend upon the achievement of communism. But the means are equally aberrant. The sun is not nourished with blood. The millennium of brotherhood is not advanced by lying, cheating, hating, distorting, deporting, murdering and going at regular intervals to the brink of war.

In democratic societies this wholesale lunacy is less likely. After all, the basic assumption of democratic politics—which is that there are likely to be two sides to most questions—is essentially rational. Methods of trial and error and experiment, respect for your opponents' honesty and good intentions, concern for the electors' concrete needs and difficulties—all these are inherent in the democratic process and add up to an atmosphere unfavorable to the wilder forms of magic.

Democracies produce their demogogues—the one-track men who see salvation in bimetalism or damnation in this or that racial minority —but stable democracies are able to make the distinction between rational leadership and political fetishism. The Mosleys, the McCarthys cannot go on as Hitler did, to put the whole of society under the spell of their malign myths.

But before we democrats end on a high note of self-congratulation it is well to remember that there can be a passive as well as an active reliance upon magic.

One of the roles of the fetish priest is to safeguard old ways and to give magical sanctions to the fact of inertia. Magic not only paints the bright prospects of certain actions. It also warns against the frightful consequences of other, usually more unorthodox, courses. To go on as before, to believe that all is well, that the fathers of the tribe know best and that innovation will bring disaster—this, too, is part of the heritage of a magical society and it would take a bold analysis of the West today to decide that this passive fetishism has entirely disappeared.

After elections won with the slogans of "peace and prosperity" or "Tory freedom pays" or "leave it to Adenauer," after campaigns based upon the charismatic and tranquilizing qualities of party leaders, it is possible to feel an uneasy doubt whether the reason that is democracy's proudest claim has been especially active in recent years.

Perhaps in a stable world the mild politics of inertia would do no positive harm. But our world is one in which one-third of humanity is subjected to the myths and demonologies of communism. It is a world in which the rising flood of populations threatens within a few decades to sweep away all the familiar landmarks. Above all, it is a world in which a single miscalculation can turn the globe into a spinning fireball. In such a world, to base politics on the idea of the cozy life is as magical as to try to stem a flood by throwing in a baby.

In short, the rule of reason and the discernment of cause and effect which have liberated modern man from the worst superstitions of the old fetish system still have work to do. We discern cause and effect in external physical phenomena. We no longer use blood sacrifice to help the crops, or human victims to improve the climate. But we are much less adept at discerning cause and effect in the ambitions and stresses of our personal or political lives.

Rationally, we do not believe that the extra fins on the back of the car affect our standing in the world. Rationally, we know that only the utmost energy, intelligence, foresight and sustained effort can steer the free society through the shoals of our infinitely dangerous world. But reason has to operate in an environment bemused by commercialized emotions and specious political promises.

Perhaps it is just as hard for us to stay sane and balanced in this atmosphere as it is for tribal man to understand the orderly physical laws of cause and effect. He is in a prison of ignorance. Perhaps we are in one, too. The difference is that we know he can get out of his. Can we be so confident about ourselves?

10
Man and His Fetishes — Modern?

Andrew Kopkind

The Power of Prayer

By Andrew Kopkind in *The New Republic*, 152 (No. 10, Issue 2624, March 6, 1965): 19, 20. Reprinted by permission of The New Republic, © 1965, Harrison-Blaine of New Jersey, Inc.

More things are wrought by prayer than this world ever dreams of, and if any doubt it, they should look in on a Presidential Prayer Breakfast. . . .

. . . The Presidential Prayer Breakfast, and its sister meeting, the Congressional Wives Prayer Breakfast, represent the highest expression of official religious sentiment. The year's hard work—stamping "Pray for Peace" on envelopes and shouting "under God" loudly in the Pledge of Allegiance—finds its natural climax in the reaffirmation of national prayerfulness by the President and his First Lady, in witness before members of the Cabinet, the Supreme Court, Congress, the Diplomatic Corps, the active and retired Military, Industry, Science, Labor, Education.

There may have been some among the 1,300 men and 700 women at the breakfasts this year who were unable to comprehend the relationship between all that prayer and the U.S. government, which after all is constitutionally prohibited from promoting any religion.

11
The Egyptian Way
and the Way of the East

Hugh C. Black

Man's Ways with Ideas

Attempting a panorama of modern civilization under the significant title *Whither Mankind*, a 1928 book describes the so human condition of most of us. "Few people," it said, "are really interested in matters beyond their immediate concerns, or have any intellectual interest at all." Absorbed in their own problems of livelihood, sex, and pleasure, most people "lead a parochial existence. They read little beyond the innately interesting things, and avoid real mental exertion. They forget readily the fragments of culture which reached them in school and which bob up now and then in newspaper and magazine." Whether we sample man's career today or way back in ancient Egyptian times when he began to mix "civilized" behavior with his "savagery," the story is revealing. Complex and difficult to unfold, the story is much the same: not always one of unmistakable "progress"; most often a tending of mankind upward and downward. In the ups and downs of his career, man's life seems to have been a contest and struggle between elements in his nature, his society, and times in which choices have been made sending him and his society either on the upward slope of achievement or on the downward slope of the degrading, the degenerate. For himself and for others (his family, his neighbors and community, his state and nation, his world) the risks have been great and the stakes high. Throughout man's career there have loomed possibilities (greater perhaps at certain periods than others because of the cultural capital afforded through better education) for the fruition of human capacities (and the perfecting of man's ideal nature) or for its opposite.

We may interpret this pessimistically. I have done so previously [in a 1955 article: "Values, Philosophy, and Education," *Progressive Education*, 32 (1955): 109-116] in saying that I am shocked by the reaction of the American people to those values which a few—past and present—declare, cherish, prize, esteem; to values worthy of realization in the lives of all. Today, I said in the past, we Americans fail to

68

establish the optimum conditions necessary for the realization of these values. In fact, we apparently outstrip ourselves in constructing road blocks, barriers to the realization of values, some of which we remain unaware of, but many of which we at least give lipservice to. One may argue well that there seems to be an innate perversity at work in the universe urging us to take the easy way out, to follow the whim of the moment and the immediate desire, to follow the herd, or to refuse to "break the cake of custom," in short: "to do that which will destroy what really matters in life, and to crush in its incipient stages the life that ought to be."

Against the view that our human condition is usually to destroy that which we ought to cherish is a more optimistic account. For this account of man's ways with ideas we may turn to L. T. Hobhouse in sociology [*Morals in Evolution*, 4th ed. (New York: Henry Holt & Co., 1925)], to James H. Breasted in Egyptology and history [*The Dawn of Conscience* (New York: Charles Scribner's Sons, 1933, 1950) who quotes Emerson's *Essay on Politics*: "We think our civilization near its meridian, but we are yet only at the cock-crowing and the morning star. In our barbarous society the influence of character is in its infancy."], to T. H. Green in the philosophy of Idealism [*Prolegomena to Ethics* (Oxford, At the Clarendon Press, 3rd edition, 1890)], or to L. G. Collingwood [*The Idea of Nature* (New York, Oxford University Press, Galaxy paperback, 1960)]. This is a belief that in history we can find man's attempt to find a positive answer to the question of "what in particular it is that man has it in him to become." This rests on a supposition of "a free or self-objectifying spiritual agency in human history." Through exercise of his capacity to reason, to reflect on his human experiences, man can grasp some ideal of his rights and duties and some vision of the potentialities and capacities of humanity. Amid the confusing mass of conceptions from lower, animistic, materialistic, conservative, magic practices there is always the possibility that men individually and in groups can perceive through such confusions and obscurity some outline of a higher principle, goal, or ideal of the best life. There is hope for insight into the full development of the human spirit in character, in conduct, and in conscience and the possibility of ever fuller achievement of a better being for the individual and a better life in society. Man's own human accomplishments and achievements give testimony to his salvation's lying in the cultivation of the best within himself and his self-denying to serve others as himself, to recognize more fully an "I" relationship to "Thou" and a "Thou" relationship to "I." Though not perfectly nor ever absolutely known, there are human excellencies and virtues to give guidance and direction.

The story of man's ways with ideas, his discovery in the human experiencing of life what man can do and should become is vital to discussions of education today when judgments should be made regarding quality education for all. For education is the bridge between the gap of man's real situation (his so human condition previously described) and the insights into his ideal wisdom and what his career ought to be. This insight into the connection between education and ideas was clearly perceived and put for us so well by the philosopher Whitehead when he declared in his 1916 presidential address to the Mathematical Association of England: "What education has to impart is an intimate sense for the power of ideas, for the beauty of ideas, and for the structure of ideas, together with a particular body of knowledge which has peculiar reference to the life of the being possessing it." This power of conscious thought and responsible behavior has generally been recognized to be man's most distinguishing characteristic. Whether mankind goes anywhere significant, especially in a democratic society such as ours, may very well rest upon the similar dictum of Pascal: thought makes the whole dignity of man, and the endeavor to think well is the basic morality. My thesis here is that its achievement depends partly on the quality of education.

Education enhances the life of individuals and betters our society to the extent more persons give "better" directions to their lives through grasp of "better" visions of what man's capacities and potentialities are and what we might become. This is made possible through reflection on the social experience of mankind, communication between generations of the virtues and excellencies generally recognized, and the attainment of these more fully. This entails knowledge of man's capacities as revealed in his "peak" and his "sink" experiences of life. Hence education involves social experiences resulting in persons who have intelligences (insights or wisdom) about life. But those social experiences we call education should also result in persons of character and conscience. Individual persons may attain a dignity worthy of man's capacities as he makes choices, judgments, and preferences in terms of worthy ideals. Conscience and character, society and education go together; for the social process is involved. Conscience, for example, is more than the individual's sense or principle for making moral judgments about his conduct and behavior. Derived from *con* (together) and *scire* (to know), "conscience" signifies something known or held in common with others. "Conscience is a standard of life, an ideal of conduct that the individual implicitly agrees with others to maintain and chooses himself to observe. It is a rule or code of conduct imposed by the group and accepted as binding by the individual." Leaders in education, then, must be cognizant of man's ideas about conscience in the interest of better character.

The history of Egypt is recommended as a rich source of this knowledge, for it is representative of the first large civilizations of antiquity. Here may be found a fascinating chapter in man's ways with ideas; for if we can trust James H. Breasted as a guide, we can see *The Dawn of Conscience,* an evolution of a sense of moral responsibility, and a recognition of distinctions between right and wrong, good and bad, the approved and the disapproved. Out of early mankind's social relationships beginning in the family arose indications of a higher social, moral, industrial, political, and religious life. By turning to those backgrounds of our heritage we may begin to take part in and seek to understand the great "conversation" which education is.

That "great conversation" began in the primeval forests, but it picked up mightily when man entered the social arena of living in large numbers along the rich river valleys and started his adventure of ideas about how to live well when living in society, in mutual relationships with others under common expectations. Out of these human interactions and reflections upon his experiences man began to evolve civilization, the art of how to live. Here he began his adventure in forming the basic institutions of the family, social classes, government, religion, and industrial organization. The story takes a great leap forward when we turn later to the Greek genius where, according to Sir Richard Livingstone, we may see what man may achieve at his best when he is free from such barriers as politics and religion. There neither politics nor religion stood in the way of man's seeing things as they are, of finding truth or falling into error, of seeing life steadily and as a whole. In Greece, he said, "man was not sacrificed to his god or his country." In Egypt, the story is one of mixed politics and religion, of man's ideas about himself, his country, his gods *and* his sacrifices. From the study of both Egyptian and Greek cultures we begin to raise the crucial questions of our times about man's ways with ideas. Especially should we raise the questions of our doing better now than mankind has done in the past. For is not man's way with ideas usually that of giving way to the apathy of the moment, the drag of inertia, the pressures of tradition and custom and power and might? The "best" we know is often left far behind in what has been called "cultural lag." We are influenced most often not by ideas or knowledge or the intellect, but we settle for our immediate interests and concerns and are the kind of persons reflecting the character and conscience described in the 1928 book I mentioned in the beginning: "Few people have any intellectual interest at all." Difficult it may be from the conflicting accounts of the historians and Egyptologists to ascertain genuine knowledge and truths about the questions we raise even about Egyptian man and our racial childhood. Yet we can get some glimpses of highs and lows, of point and counter-point, in man's achievements as we begin what the philosopher Whitehead titled the *Adventures of Ideas* and he continued to portray for us in *Science in the Modern World* and *Process and Reality*. Small though our sample here shall be perhaps it is enough to indicate the fun of finding some mountaintop views of what man can do and what he might become through better education or the depths to which he can slide when he fails in knowledge of possibilities and true education.

Late in his long career as educational historian and philosopher, my teacher, Frederick Eby, expressed well what recently one of my own students called to my attention:

> The truth of the matter is, education is a gradual initiation into life, the revealing of the nature and significance of life to the young. It is the observing and imitating of how men lived and are living. It gives concrete pictures of personalities who have experienced the highest values of human existence. It is an examination of the kind of life that is most worth living. Education assists the young to observe widely, analyze, and compare the various kinds and qualities of life so as to select those of greatest promise.

For this educative purpose, I commend to any leader in education today the Egyptian experience as he may make it out from a variety of sources. Here I sample from a few to indicate the beckoning adventure of lows and highs.

In the March 1960 issue of *Holiday* magazine (Volume 27, pp. 62 ff.), Aubrey Menen affords us popular insights in his account of "A Visit to Ancient Egypt." He returned from Egypt impressed with what he saw and the stern facts which tell us of the civilization built up there and its lessons for us. For example, in Cairo he was impressed with a colossal statue thirty-two feet high carved from a single block of stone and perfectly preserved for three thousand one hundred and eighty-five years after the death of Ramses II, the Egyptian Pharaoh who had it carved out of what the Egyptologist Cyril Aldred described in 1968 as the "egomania that made him the most bombastic of all the divine Pharaohs." An adept learner himself from his earlier advertising agency job, Menen attributed to Rameses II the wish not to be forgotten and the wish to impress upon his own and future generations his wealth, power, and beauty. The lesson for us to see is the power of advertising: that high-class advertising, a work of art done (in terms of today's Madison Avenue approach) as a prestige job, pays. Moreover, other gigantic toys littering Egypt, such as the Great Pyramid of Cheops [Khufu's Great Pyramid of Gizeh], Menen found, are less tastefully done. Vulgar and banal "as an electric sign in Times Square," they teach the same lesson he was taught in the advertising agency: advertising pays, as it always does, "and the brasher it is the better." In visiting Thebes, he noted the two cities, one for the living and the other for the dead. He felt that the Egyptians valued more highly the city of the dead and that they were more like children than adults. He would probably agree that if the Greeks were the adolescents of the human race, then the Egyptians were the children of it. For, his article tells us, they exhibited the directness of children, settling such profound problems as that of life after death in the simplest way. Life after death, they saw, as just like life before it. Their heaven was purely materialistic, devoid of anything spiritual. They practiced the advertising agency precept: "There is no idea so silly that you cannot persuade a great number of people to believe it is true." Their priests— the professional persuaders of their day—sold the people the idea that religion was purely a matter of giving sumptuous gifts to the innumerable and unimportant gods, the costly presents being received by the powerful and elite priesthood. In religion this left no feeling, he felt, of solemnity, no sense of mystery. It portrays life at its materialistic, pragmatic level.

Fascinating it is to turn from such a popular magazine writer of our day as Menen and seek to discover the difficult-to-ascertain knowledge of the past from the historians and Egyptologists. Along with the classic works of James H. Breasted and later products of the Oriental Institute of the University of Chicago are more recent studies. These include Christiane Desroches-Noblecourt's *Tutankhamen: Life and Death of a Pharaoh* (Paperback, abridged ed., Garden City, New York: Doubleday & Company, Ind., 1965) and Cyril Aldred, *Akhenaten: Pharaoh of Egypt—A New Study* (Lengerich, Germany: Thames and Hudson, Ltd., 1968) with its especially helpful epilogue "Akhenaten and the Historians," pp. 257-260. Such studies enlighten us further about man's ways with ideas.

We begin with the king of Dynasty XIX, Ramses II, who ruled from 1304-1237 B. C. and whose "prestige job" colossal statue so impressed the modern traveler Menen. Evidently he was an ambitious and aggressive Ramsesides of a new dynasty who had been left a strong, united, and prosperous state by Har-em-hab, who in a long reign from 1349-1319 B. C. had dealt successfully with material conditions attributed to a predecessor in Dynasty XVIII: Akhenaten (Amenophis IV), 1378-1362 B. C. Held by Breasted to be the first individual, the world's first idealist, and the first attainer of monotheism, Akhenaten's great ideas had come to nothing or very little. In later times he was referred to as "that criminal of Akhet-Aten" (Tell el-Amarna) and was considered one of the "heretic" kings, an innovator of religious ideas, intolerant of the customary gods whose temples he closed and so disorganized the machinery of the bureaucratic government that Harem-hab had to contend with dissatisfaction and lawlessness at home and increasing pressure from the Hittites abroad.

Developing out of the past, the religious ideas of the heretic king, Akhenaten, resulted in a new spirit in art. Earlier barriers had confined artistic expression. Akhenaten's new spirit did away with such barriers in art, and there was a striving after realism, truth, and individualism which sometimes in its extreme manifestations inclined toward the unusual (and perhaps contained the seeds of its own later destruction?). Probably the masses paid only sight attention to the innovations in religion and in art. For Akhenaten's attempt to institute all these fine ideas of the reason in the world of politics, practice, and people ran head-on into the beliefs and opinions of the people. The cake of custom for them was the Osirian faith, concern for continuation of a material life in the hereafter through priestly ritual and magic. Like other peoples of the first ancient large civilizations, the Egyptian people were directed by their belief in magic, "by a faith in the supernatural that generally worked for a beneficent end by giving them a confidence and discipline which enabled the odds of adversity to be overcome." All was in vain, morale was shattered when the people felt that the gods had withdrawn from them their favors. Akhenaten's experiment was intolerant of most of the Osirian beliefs. Probably toward the end of his reign after the death of Smenkh-ka-Re, Akhenaten sent forth his edicts destroying the statues of Amun of Thebes and vindictively proscribed the other cults of Egypt which he had largely ignored in the first five years of his reign. He even gave orders for erasing the plural form for the word 'god' wherever it might be found, a denial of the existence of the other, customary gods of the people in support of Aten. Whatever Akhenaten's achievement in the realm of ideas—whether he lead in the direction of monotheism, failing to achieve essential monotheism and stopping short with henotheism or Monophysitism—the results described (perhaps in overdrawn terms) by his successor Tut-ankh-Amun in the great Restoration Stela he erected at Karnak in his fourth regnal year are revealing:

> . . . the temples from one end of the land to the other had fallen into ruin; their shrines were desolate and had become wilder-nesses overgrown with weeds; their sanctuaries were as though they had never been; their precincts were trodden path. The land was in confusion for the gods had forsaken this land. If (an army) were sent to Asia to widen the frontiers of Egypt, it met with no success. If one prayed to a god to ask things of

him, he did not come. If one supplicated a goddess, likewise
she did not come either. Their hearts were enfeebled so that
what had been made was destroyed.

The recovery measures to restore morale and order among the people
included a restoration of such former gods as the Theban Amun, of
the old sanctuaries and temples, a re-directing of the treasures to the
more orthodox priesthood, and a restoration of the machinery of the
bureaucracy so essential to the well-being of the national state.

To what avail the great innovations, the ideas of an Akhenaten
blazing new trails toward man's higher mental and spiritual potentialities? A part of the reality lies in Tut-ankh-Amun's policy of return
to orthodoxy, a rescinding of the proscription of the other gods, and a
quiet dropping of the worship of the Sun God Aten. In the hindsight
of some who came afterward, Akhenaten's heresy was a prime error
which had brought Egypt ill-luck and misfortune. It was an unfortunate
interlude best forgotten. And Ramses II did his best to do just that. Even
though a divine ruler, he exhibited his so human qualities. A totalitarian
enhances his rule and promotes his own self best by belittling his
predecessors. So he instituted the procedures to efface all memorials to
Akhenaten: advertising one's self is to be preferred to knowledge and
truth and spirit!

Ideas of justice and fair-play and fair-dealing, to what avail in
mankind's dealing with ideas and ideals, of spirit and intellect? Perhaps
very little as against the realities of might and power, as this account
indicates. Yet even here there is the germ of what might yet be. For
no one succeeded in covering up entirely the great germ of Akhenaten's
great hymn to Aten which still thrills anyone disposed to look into
it and to benefit from its later sprouting forth in the 104th Psalm of
another part of our tradition. At this point in our knowledge who can
say to what extent these human experiences contributed to what came
later in the human career?

Out of a later part of our heritage came these words from Proverbs
8: 1-11:

> Does not wisdom call,
>   does not understanding raise her voice?
> On the heights beside the way,
>   in the paths she takes her stand;
> Beside the gates in front of the town,
>   at the entrance of the portals she cries aloud:
> "To you, O men, I call,
>   and my cry is to the sons of men.
> O simple ones, learn prudence;

O foolish men, pay attention.
Hear, for I will speak noble things,
    and from my lips will come what is right;
For my mouth will utter truth;
    wickedness is an abomination to my lips.
All the words of my mouth are righteous;
    there is nothing twisted or crooked in them.
They are all straight to him who understands
    and right to those who find knowledge.
Take my instruction instead of silver,
    and knowledge rather than choice gold;
For wisdom is better than jewels,
    and all that you may desire cannot compare with her.

In writing about "Man" under the topic of "The Hebrews" in H. and H. A. Frankfort (and others), *The Intellectual Adventure of Ancient Man: An Essay on Speculative Thought in the Ancient Near East* (Chicago: University of Chicago Press, 1946, Fourth Impression, 1957), William A. Irwin very fittingly for our close put it like this:

> Wisdom we first saw as a human attainment, then as a cosmic quality immanent in the world and in human life. Here we discover the nexus of the two. In poetic terminology, she stands in the busiest concourse of human affairs, wherever man may be, and there accosts all and sundry. Receive instruction; choose the better things of life; final satisfaction cannot be found in material things but only in the uncharted region vaquely known as the spiritual realities of life. This pervasive, immanent quality of life and the world has been ever active in human life, individual and collective, in leading, persuading, and inducing men to higher and better things. Through this function of the divine wisdom immanent in man the whole long story has come about of our groping progress from our brute ancestry, our slow attainment of civilization, and our unceasing outreach for ever better things in thought and practice.
>
> Here, then, is the ultimate nature of man.

Selection from Edith Hamilton, *The Greek Way* (New York: W. W. Norton & Company, Inc., 1930), pp. 38-39.

[Edith Hamilton, a grand scholar of our Graeco-Roman heritage, quotes Aristotle's "so characteristically Greek words."]

Since then reason is divine in comparison with man's whole

nature, the life according to reason must be divine in comparison with (usual) human life. Nor ought we to pay regard to those who exhort us that as men we ought to think human things and keep our eyes upon mortality: nay, as far as may be, we should endeavor to rise to that which is immortal, and live in conformity with that which is best, in us. Now, what is characteristic of any nature is that which is best for it and gives most joy. Such to man is the life according to reason, since it is this that makes him man.

[And then she writes her comparison in these words.]

Love of reason and of life, delight in the use of the mind and body, distinguished the Greek way. The Egyptian way and the way of the East had led through suffering and by the abnegation of the intellect to the supremacy of the spirit. . . . What marked the Greeks off from Egypt and India was not an inferior degree of spirituality but a superior degree of mentality. Great mind and great spirit combined in them. The spiritual world was not to them another world from the natural world. It was the same world as that known to the mind. Beauty and rationality were both manifested in it. . . . Reason and feeling were not antagonistic. The truth of poetry and the truth of science were both true.

PART THREE
POSSIBILITIES FROM OUR GRAECO-ROMAN HERITAGE

Overview

That part of our cultural heritage to which we turn next for wisdom about life and education today offers much to any age undergoing a basic shift in thinking, values, and actions. Like us, our Greek and Roman ancestors felt concern for the great ideas and ideals on which depended their very lives and freedoms. They, too, searched for new and stable foundations of living. Although they did not experience change on as large a scale or at as accelerating a pace as we, they also lived in terror about what was happening to individuals, to a society, and even to civilization itself. Today many ask the question, "Who am I?" Part of the answer, some of us reply, lies in recognizing that we are "human beings" who must discover what it means to be human. The Greeks give us a great start, for humanism is the Greek contribution to culture.

As we debate what ideals education should pursue in that deliberate moulding of human character which Werner Jaeger said education should be,[1] we can profit by learning what those who went before us discovered—as did our more immediate predecessors of the Renaissance. For the Graeco-Roman debates about what the ideals of education should be first defined most of the basic positions which we take today in our debates over education in a period of crisis, conflict, and chaos. Today, for example, one generation battles another, sometimes in terms of concern for truth versus persuasion through modern media of communication. But that controversy is as old as the classics presented here, where we may witness the dramatic contest between philosophers who sought wisdom about the fundamental nature of truth, goodness, and beauty and rhetoricians who trained orators to be effective in practical life through the arts of eloquence and the skills of persuasion!

We can learn from the Greeks and Romans, for their experiences and insights represent for us the vast step forward suggested by Edith Hamilton in the last chapter. This step forward in man's story represents the discovery of something more fundamental than fire, or gunpowder, or electricity. Sir Richard Livingstone described it as "a new outlook, a new attitude to life, in which possibilities of endless development are contained, a tiny seed which is the parent of a forest, a stone flung

---

[1] *Paideia: the Ideals of Greek Culture*, translated from the second German edition by Gilbert Highet (New York: Oxford University Press, 1939), p. xxii.

into the waters whose ripple is carried to their remotest shores. . . . once the step forward is taken, the world is changed forever."[2]

Today we seem to need what the Greeks and Romans gave us, especially in the centuries between 600 B.C. and 400 B.C. in Greece: the spirit of reason—as Livingstone puts it, "the desire to see things as they are . . . to follow the argument where it leads." We agree with Livingstone that that spirit was incarnate in Socrates and that an acquaintance with Socrates should be part of any liberal education. Socrates exemplifies the best of this part of our heritage. In Part Four we shall turn to our Judeo-Christian heritage to catch a glimpse of another event and a truly great man who exemplifies another spirit: Jesus of Nazareth. Livingstone believed the world has never been the same since the two great events of Socrates and Jesus. We wonder if he is correct in his assessment of the effects of the Greek event:

> It seems at times . . . that it has made little difference, that men have not even begun to learn its lesson, and that intolerance, prejudice and unreason are still unchallenged. But it is not so. The leaven has been hid in the measure of meal and is working towards the leavening of the whole, though its action is slow, and though perhaps to the end there may be lumps of dough that it will never reach. Even to-day the achievements of reason are more impressive than its failures.[3]

That we may profit from the light which history discloses about living, that there is an ever-present past from which we can learn—these are precious beliefs which two scholars, Arnold Toynbee and Edith Hamilton, share with us in Chapters 12 and 13, which constitute a preface to the Greek section of Part Three. To any generation which shuns the past as irrelevant, such beliefs should be grist for debate, as are the remaining readings, which are grouped according to the main periods customarily designated by historians of education.

Chapter 14 takes us to the Homeric Period for acquaintance with the educational ideal of the man of action and the man of wisdom, as interpreted so well for us by Stringfellow Barr from Homer's classics. In the Old Greek Period we get a view of two contrasting ways of life and two different approaches to education. Chapter 15 from Plutarch's *Lives* summarizes the totalitarian pattern of Spartan education and life; Chapter 16, Thucydides' "Funeral Speech of Pericles" and Plato's summary of Athenian education in *Protagoras*, present the contrasting

---

[2] *Portrait of Socrates* (New York and Oxford: Oxford University Press, 1938), p. v.

[3] *Ibid.*, p. vi.

democratic pattern in Athens. Chapters 17 through 20 represent classics from the monumental transitional period beginning with the Age of Pericles, a period of fruition and change more meaningful than any other for our study. Philosophy and education come to the fore in this period. For out of the socioeconomic and sociopolitical events of those changing times arose the need to answer the problems of education. But, as indicated precisely in the reading from *Meno* in Chapter 18, the problems of education cannot be answered until we have first grappled with the basic issues of life treated by philosophy: the nature of reality, knowledge, truth, goodness, and beauty. So this becomes a period of "greats": of Isocrates, Socrates, Plato, and Aristotle and of such Sophists as Protagoras, Gorgias, Hippias, and Prodicus. It is a time of controversy over the perennial issues of man. It is here, we suggest, that our modern high school graduate should turn to find "relevancy," especially if he is the person one university English teacher reports him to be:

> If his intellectual performance or his careless judgments
> on complex questions are challenged, the student is fond of
> observing that 'one opinion is as good as another,' or 'everyone
> is entitled to his own opinion.' And these responses are uttered
> with no particular arrogance; rather they are pleasantly said
> as though they were universally accepted truths.[4]

What fun he would have with the contest of such noble men as Socrates, Plato, and Aristotle against the Sophists! Also "relevant" is the insight the Hellenistic Era yields about the practices men institute after a period of theory. Space permits only the brief example of the Ephebic Oath in Chapter 21 to represent this period, the subject of much recent scholarship by our colleagues in the classics.

Chapters 22, 23, and 24 introduce us to the ancient Romans and the contrast between earlier Roman life and education and the later period of Greek influence, in which oratory won out over philosophy. We conclude with the classic statements of Quintilian, with whom any educated person should be familiar if he is to understand the practices common in schools from the Renaissance to the present. Many who prefer practical insights into teaching over the more theoretical aspects of education will find delight in the modernity of this ancient Roman!

[4] Leo J. Hertzel, "More Money, More Learning?" *New Republic*, March 6, 1961, p.11.

12
The Light of Experience through History

Arnold J. Toynbee

Arnold J. Toynbee, "Preface to the Second Edition," *Greek Civilization and Character: The Self-Revelation of Ancient Greek Society* (Boston: The Beacon Press, 1950), pp. xvii-xviii. Reprinted by permission of The Beacon Press, publisher.

More than a quarter of a century has now passed since I translated the passages assembled in this volume and wrote the introduction, and during these intervening twenty-six years the waters of our own Western history have rolled on with a gathering impetus. A second world war has followed the first, and in A. D. 1950 we can perhaps see whither we are heading rather more clearly than we could in A. D. 1924. At any rate, there is a more vivid and more widespread realization in our Western world today than there was then of the historical truth that we are living through a time of decision, and that the choices which we are having to make in our generation are momentous. We are aware that it is all-important for us to choose right, and that our chances of success depend largely on our ability to make right estimates of the alternative courses before us. What light have we that we can project upon the darkness of the future? We have the precious light of experience, which has always been Mankind's guide to action in public, as in private, affairs. No sensible person, of course, has ever imagined that a mechanical application of past experience to present problems will grind out automatic solutions of these. Experience gives us enigmatic hints, not blue-printed instructions. Yet these hints are invaluable, since they are the only light on the future that we can bring to bear; and, where the future that is in question is a society's, not an individual's, the experience of other societies has the same significance for us as the experience of our contemporaries and our elders in the ordering of our personal lives.

The experience of the Hellenic society—the Greco-Roman world—is particularly illuminating from this point of view, because the Greeks' and Romans' experience is now over—their world is now dead—and, in consequence, we know the plot of that play from beginning to end, in sharp contrast to our ignorance of what lies before ourselves in a play which is still being acted, and in which we living actors have all the time to improvise our parts.

For this reason, Greek and Roman history is perpetually gaining in interest for us as it is receding in time. Every passing year of our own history that makes Greek and Roman history chronologically more remote brings it closer to us psychologically. If there is any key to the riddle of our destiny, that key lies here, I believe; and, believing this, I find the fascination of Greek and Roman history always growing greater for me as I live through one decade after another of the formidable contemporary history of the Modern world.

13
The Ever-Present Past

Edith Hamilton

The Lessons of the Past: Adventures of the Mind 11

Edith Hamilton, "Adventures of the Mind 11," *The Saturday Evening Post*, 231 (No. 13, September 27, 1958): 25, 114–117.

Is there an ever-present past? Are there permanent truths which are forever important for the present? Today we are facing a future more strange and untried than any other generation has faced. The new world Columbus opened seems small indeed beside the illimitable distances of space before us, and the possibilities of destruction are immeasurably greater than ever. In such a position can we afford to spend time on the past? That is the question I am often asked. Am I urging the study of the Greeks and Romans and their civilizations for the atomic age?

Yes; that is just what I am doing. I urge it without qualifications. We have a great civilization to save—or to lose. The greatest civilization before ours was the Greek. They challenge us and we need the challenge. They, too, lived in a dangerous world. They were a little, highly civilized people, the only civilized people in the west, surrounded by barbarous tribes and with the greatest Asiatic power, Persia, always threatening them. In the end they succumbed, but the reason they did was not that the enemies outside were so strong, but that their own strength, their spiritual strength, had given way. While they had it they kept Greece unconquered and they left behind a record in art and thought which in all the centuries of human effort since has not been surpassed.

The point which I want to make is not that their taste was superior to ours, not that the Parthenon was their idea of church architecture nor that Sophocles was the great drawing card in the theaters nor any of the familiar comparisons between fifth-century Athens and twentieth-century America, but that Socrates found on every street corner and in every Athenian equivalent of the baseball field people who were caught up by his questions into the world of thought. To be able to be caught up into the world of thought—that is to be educated.

How is that great aim to be reached? For years we have eagerly discussed ways and means of education and the discussion still goes on. William James once said that there were two subjects which if mentioned made other conversation stop and directed all eyes to the speaker. Religion was one and education the other. Today Russia seems to come first, but education is still emphatically the second. In spite of all the articles we read and all the speeches we listen to about it, we want to know more; we feel deeply its importance.

There is today a clearly visible trend toward making it the aim of education to defeat the Russians. That would be a sure way to defeat education. Genuine education is possible only when people realize that it has to do with persons, not with movements.

When I read educational articles it often seems to me that this important side of the matter, the purely personal side, is not emphasized enough; the fact that it is so much more agreeable and interesting to be an educated person than not. The sheer pleasure of being educated does not seem to be stressed. Once long ago I was talking with Prof. Basil L. Gildersleeve of Johns Hopkins University, the greatest Greek scholar our country has produced. He was an old man and he had been honored everywhere, in Europe as well as in America. He was just back from a celebration held for him in Oxford. I asked him what compliment received in his long life had pleased him most. The question amused him and he laughed over it, but he thought too. Finally he said, "I believe it was when one of my students said, 'Professor, you have so much fun with your own mind.'" Robert Louis Stevenson said that a man ought to be able to spend two or three hours waiting for a train at a little country station when he was all alone and had nothing to read, and not be bored for a moment.

What is the education which can do this? What is the furniture which makes the only place belonging absolutely to each one of us, the world within, a place where we like to go? I wish I could answer that question. I wish I could produce a perfect decorator's design warranted to make any interior lovely and interesting and stimulating; but, even if I could, sooner or later we would certainly try different designs. My point is only that while we must and should change the furniture, we ought to throw away old furniture very cautiously. It may turn out to be irreplaceable. A great deal was thrown away in the last generation or so, long enough ago to show some of the results.hFurniture which had for centuries been foremost, we lightly, in a few years, discarded. The classics almost vanished from our field of education. That was a great change. Along with it came another. There is a marked difference between the writers of the past and the writers of today who have been educated without benefit of Greek and Latin. Is this a matter of cause and effect? People will decide for themselves, but I do not think anyone will question the statement that clear thinking is not the characteristic which distinguishes our literature today. We are more and more caught up by the unintelligible. People like it. This argues an inability to think, or, almost as bad, a disinclination to think.

Neither disposition marked the Greeks. They had a passion for thinking things out, and they loved unclouded clarity of statement as well as of thought. The Romans did, too, in their degree. They were able to put an idea into an astonishingly small number of words without losing a particle of intelligibility. It is only of late, with a generation which has never had to deal with a Latin sentence, that we are being submerged in a flood of words, words, words. It has been said that Lincoln at Gettysburg today would have begun in some such fashion as this: "Eight and seven-tenths decades ago the pioneer workers in this continental area implemented a new group based on an ideology of free boundaries and initial equality," and might easily have ended, "That political supervision of the integrated units, for the integrated units, by the integrated units, shall not become null and void on the superficial area of this planet." Along with the banishment of the classics, gobblede-gook has come upon us—and the appalling size of the Congressional Record, and the overburdened mail service.

Just what the teaching in the schools was which laid the founda-tion of the Greek civilization we do not know in detail; the result we do know. Greek children were taught, Plato said, to "love what is beautiful and hate what is ugly." When they grew up their very pots and pans had to be pleasant to look at. It was part of their training to hate clumsiness and awkwardness; they loved grace and practiced it. "Our children," Plato said, "will be influenced for good by every sight and sound of beauty, breathing in, as it were, a pure breeze blowing to them from a good land."

All the same, the Athenians were not, as they showed Socrates when he talked to them, preoccupied with enjoying lovely things. The children were taught to think. Plato demanded a stiff examination, especially in mathematics, for entrance to his Academy. The Athenians were a thinking people. Today the scientists are bearing away the prize for thought. Well, a Greek said that the earth went around the sun sixteen centuries before Copernicus thought of it. A Greek said if you sailed out of Spain and kept to one latitude, you would come at last to land, seventeen hundred years before Columbus did it. Darwin said, "We are mere schoolboys in scientific thinking compared to old

Aristotle." And the Greeks did not have a great legacy from the past as our scientists have; they thought science out from the beginning.

The same is true of politics. They thought that out, too, from the beginning, and they gave all the boys a training to fit them to be thinking citizens of a free state that had come into being through thought.

Basic to all the Greek achievement was freedom. The Athenians were the only free people in the world. In the great empires of antiquity—Egypt, Babylon, Assyria, Persia—splendid though they were, with riches beyond reckoning and immense power, freedom was unknown. The idea of it never dawned in any of them. It was born in Greece, a poor little country, but with it able to remain unconquered no matter what manpower and what wealth were arrayed against her. At Marathon and at Salamis overwhelming numbers of Persians had been defeated by small Greek forces. It had been proved that one free man was superior to many submissively obedient subjects of a tyrant. Athens was the leader in that amazing victory, and to the Athenians freedom was their dearest possession. Demosthenes said that they would not think it worth their while to live if they could not do so as free men, and years later a great teacher said, "Athenians, if you deprive them of their liberty, will die."

Athens was also at its height an almost perfect democracy—that is, for men. There was no part in it for women or foreigners or slaves, but as far as the men were concerned it was more democratic than we are. The governing body was the Assembly, of which all citizens over eighteen were members. The Council of Five Hundred which prepared business for the Assembly and, if requested, carried out what had been decided there, was made up of citizens who were chosen by lot. The same was true of the juries. Minor officials also were chosen by lot. The chief magistrates and the highest officers in the army were elected by the Assembly. Pericles was a general, very popular, who acted for a long time as if he were head of the state, but he had to be elected every year. Freedom of speech was the right the Athenians prized most and there has never been another state as free in that respect. When toward the end of the terrible Peloponnesian War the victorious Spartans were advancing upon Athens, Aristophanes caricatured in the theater the leading Athenian generals and showed them up as cowards, and even then as the Assembly opened, the herald asked, "Does anyone wish to speak?"

There was complete political equality. It was a government of the people, by the people, for the people. An unregenerate old aristocrat in the early fourth century, B. C. writes: "If you *must* have a democracy, Athens is the perfect example. I object to it because it is based on the welfare of the lower, not the better, classes. In Athens the people who row the vessels and do the work, have the advantage. It is their prosperity that is important." All the same, making the city beautiful was important too, as were also the great performances in the theater. If, as Plato says, the Assembly was chiefly made up of cobblers and carpenters and smiths and farmers and retail-business men, they approved the construction of the Parthenon and the other buildings on the Acropolis, and they crowded the theater when the great tragedies were played. Not only did all free men share in the government; the love of the beautiful and the desire to have a part in creating it were shared by the many, not by a mere chosen few. That has happened in no state except Athens.

But those free Greeks owned slaves. What kind of freedom was that? The question would have been incomprehensible to the ancient world. There had always been slaves; they were a first necessity. The way of life everywhere was based upon them. They were taken for granted; no one ever gave them a thought. The very best Greek minds, the thinkers who discovered freedom and the solar system, had never an idea that slavery was evil. It is true that the greatest thinker of them all, Plato, was made uncomfortable by it. He said that slaves were often good, trustworthy, doing more for a man than his own family would, but he did not follow his thought through. The glory of being the first one to condemn it belongs to a man of the generation before Plato, the poet Euripides. He called it, "That thing of evil," and in several of his tragedies showed its evil for all to see. A few centuries later the great Greek school of the Stoics denounced it. Greece first saw it for what it is. But the world went on in the same way. The Bible accepts it without comment. Two thousand years after the Stoics, less than a hundred years ago, the American Republic accepted it.

Athens treated her slaves well. A visitor to the city in the early fourth century, B. C., wrote: "It is illegal here to deal a slave a blow. In the street he won't step aside to let you pass. Indeed you can't tell a slave by his dress; he looks like all the rest. They can go to the theater too. Really, the Athenians have established a kind of equality between slaves and free men." They were never a possible source of danger to the state as they were in Rome. There were no terrible slave wars and uprisings in Athens. In Rome, crucifixion was called "the slave's punishment." The Athenians did not practice crucifixion, and had no so-called slave's punishment. They were not afraid of their slaves.

In Athens' great prime Athenians were free. No one told them what they must do or what they should think—no church or political party or powerful private interests or labor unions. Greek schools had no donors of endowments they must pay attention to, no government financial backing which must be made secure by acting as the government wanted. To be sure, the result was that they had to take full responsibility, but that is always the price for full freedom. The Athenians were a strong people, they could pay the price. They were a thinking people; they knew what freedom means. They knew—not that they were free because their country was free, but that their country was free because they were free.

A reflective Roman traveling in Greece in the second century A. D. said, "None ever throve under democracy save the Athenians; *they* had sane self-control and were law-abiding." He spoke truly. That is what Athenian education aimed at, to produce men who would be able to maintain a self-governed state because they were themselves self-governed, self-controlled, self-reliant. Plato speaks of "the education in excellence which makes men long to be perfect citizens, knowing both how to rule and be ruled." "We do not allow absorption in our own affairs to interfere with participation in the city's; we yield to none in independence of spirit and complete self-reliance, but we regard him who holds aloof from public affairs as useless." They called the useless man a "private" citizen, *idiotes*, from which our word "idiot" comes.

They had risen to freedom and to ennoblement from what Gilbert Murray calls "effortless barbarism"; they saw it all around them; they hated its filth and fierceness; nothing effortless was among the good things they wanted. Plato said, "Hard is the good," and a poet hundreds of years before Plato said,

> Before the gates of Excellence the high gods have placed sweat.
> Long is the road thereto and steep and rough at the first,
> But when the height is won, then is there ease.

When or why the Greeks set themselves to travel on that road we do not know, but it led them away from habits and customs accepted everywhere that kept men down to barbaric filth and fierceness. It led them far. One example is enough to show the way they took. It was the custom—during how many millenniums, who can say?—for a victor to erect a trophy, a monument of his victory. In Egypt, where stone was plentiful, it would be a slab engraved with his glories. Farther east, where the sand took over, it might be a great heap of severed heads, quite permanent objects; bones last a long time. But in Greece, though a man could erect a trophy, it must be made of wood and it could never be repaired. Even as the victor set it up he would see in his mind how soon it would decay and sink into ruin, and there it must be left. The Greeks in their onward pressing along the steep and rough road had learned a great deal. They knew the victor might be the vanquished next time. There should be no permanent records of the manifestly impermanent. They had learned a great deal.

An old Greek inscription states that the aim of mankind should be "to tame the savageness of man and make gentle the life of the world." Aristotle said that the city was built first for safety, but then that men might discover the good life and lead it. So the Athenians did according to Pericles. Pericles said that Athens stood for freedom and for thought and for beauty, but in the Greek way, within limits, without exaggeration. The Athenians loved beauty, he said, but with simplicity; they did not like the extravagances of luxury. They loved the things of the mind, but they did not shrink from hardship. Thought did not cause them to hesitate, it clarified the road to action. If they had riches they did not make a show of them, and no one was ashamed of being poor if he was useful. They were free because of willing obedience to law, not only the written, but still more the unwritten, kindness and compassion and unselfishness and the many qualities which cannot be enforced, which depend on a man's free choice, but without which men cannot live together.

If ever there is to be a truly good and great and enduring republic it must be along these lines. We need the challenge of the city that thought them out, wherein for centuries one genius after another grew up. Geniuses are not produced by spending money. We need the challenge of the way the Greeks were educated. They fixed their eyes on the individual. We contemplate millions. What we have undertaken in this matter of education has dawned upon us only lately. We are trying to do what has never been attempted before, never in the history of the world—educate all the young in a nation of 170 millions; a magnificent idea, but we are beginning to realize what are the problems and what may be the results of mass production of education. So far, we do not seem appalled at the prospect of exactly the same kind of education being applied to all the school children from the Atlantic to the Pacific, but there is an uneasiness in the air, a realization that the individual is growing less easy to find; an idea, perhaps, of what standardization might become when the units are not machines, but human beings.

Here is where we can go back to the Greeks with profit. The Athenians in their dangerous world needed to be a nation of independent men who could take responsibility, and they taught their children accordingly. They thought about every boy. Someday he would be a citizen of Athens, responsible for her safety and her glory, "each one," Pericles said, "fitted to meet life's chances and changes with the utmost versatility and grace." To them education was by its very nature an individual matter. To be properly educated a boy had to be taught music; he learned to play a musical instrument. He had to learn poetry, a great deal of it, and recite it—and there were a number of musical instruments and many poets; though, to be sure, Homer was the great textbook.

That kind of education is not geared to mass production. It does not produce people who instinctively go the same way. That is how Athenian children lived and learned while our millions learn the same lessons and spend hours before television sets looking at exactly the same thing at exactly the same time. For one reason and another we are more and more ignoring differences, if not trying to obliterate them. We seem headed toward a standardization of the mind, what Goethe called "the deadly commonplace that fetters us all." That was not the Greek way.

The picture of the Age of Pericles drawn by the historian Thucydides, one of the greatest historians the world has known, is of a state made up of people who are self-reliant individuals, not echoes or copies, who want to be let alone to do their own work, but who are also closely bound together by a great aim, the commonweal, each one so in love with his country—Pericles' own words—that he wants most of all to use himself in her service. Only an ideal? Ideals have enormous power. They stamp an age. They lift life up when they are lofty; they drag down and make decadent when they are low—and then, by that strange fact, the survival of the fittest, those that are low fade away and are forgotten. The Greek ideals have had a power of persistent life for twenty-five hundred years.

Is it rational that now when the young people may have to face problems harder than we face, is it reasonable that with the atomic age before them, at this time we are giving up the study of how the Greeks and Romans prevailed magnificently in a barbaric world; the study, too, of how that triumph ended, how a slackness and softness finally came over them to their ruin? In the end, more than they wanted freedom, they wanted security, a comfortable life, and they lost all—security and comfort and freedom.

Is not that a challenge to us? Is it not true that into our education have come a slackness and softness? Is hard effort prominent? The world of thought can be entered in no other way. Are we not growing slack and soft in our political life: When the Athenians finally wanted not to give to the state, but the state to give to them, when the freedom they wished most for was freedom from responsibility, then Athens ceased to be free and was never free again. Is not that a challenge?

Cicero said, "To be ignorant of the past is to remain a child."

Santayana said, "A nation that does not know history is fated to repeat it." The Greeks can help us, help us as no other people can, to see how freedom is won and how it is lost. Above all, to see in clearest light what freedom is. The first nation in the world to be free sends a ringing call down through the centuries to all who would be free. Greece rose to the very height, not because she was big, she was very small; not because she was rich, she was very poor; not even because she was wonderfully gifted. So doubtless were others in the great empires of the ancient world who have gone their way leaving little for us. She rose because there was in the Greeks the greatest spirit that moves in humanity, the spirit that sets men free.

Plato put into words what that spirit is. "Freedom," he says, "is no matter of laws and constitutions; only he is free who realizes the divine order within himself, the true standard by which a man can steer and measure himself." True standards, ideals that lift life up, marked the way of the Greeks. Therefore their light has never been extinguished.

"The time for extracting a lesson from history is ever at hand for them who are wise." Demosthenes.

14
The Educational Ideal of the Man of Action and the Man of Wisdom
Stringfellow Barr

Excerpts from Stringfellow Barr, *The Will of Zeus—A History of Greece from the Origins of Hellenic Culture to the Death of Alexander* (Philadelphia and New York: J. B. Lippincott Company, 1961), pp. 4-5, 27-28, 16-17, 18, 20-26.

Hellenic culture was born not only out of the meager soil of Greece and the island-studded Aegean Sea, but also out of myth—out of myths that dealt with gods and men and with commerce between them, out of myths put in the mouths of minstrels by a Muse, the goddess daughter of Zeus, father of gods and men alike. And of all the myths that engendered that culture out of soil and sea, two were by all odds the most powerful: the myth of Achilles' wrath, which Homer sang in his epic poem, the *Iliad*, and the myth of Odysseus' questing voyage, which the same poet sang in his epic, the *Odyssey*. Both myths were acts: they were verbs, not nouns or adjectives. In the world of Achilles he and his fellow Achaeans acted in battle, and their Trojan opponents acted also. Even the gods participated in the confused struggle on the plains of Troy, some on one side, some on the other: in this myth, the *Iliad*, even the gods acted. This thrust and energy perhaps accounted for the fact that Hellenic culture, which did not wholly create either *Iliad* or *Odyssey*, was nevertheless in large part created by them. . . .

Neither of these epic myths is history; or they are history so transmuted into poetry that the historian has had to retransmute them, so far as he could, before he could trust them.

The tales of Achilles' ruinous wrath and of Odysseus' restless quest were not only mighty poems for bards to sing at the feasts of chieftain-kings and their nobles. They were the collected memories of a people who had gone to earth beneath the onslaught of the Dorian tribes—the Mycenaean people, who had achieved a coarsened version of the elegant life of ancient Crete, of its Minoan sea power, its Minoan law and order. The *Iliad* and the *Odyssey* and the lesser epics of the Homeric Cycle, like the legends of Theseus, king of Athens; of Perseus, who reigned in Tiryns, who slew the Gorgon Medusa, and who founded Mycenae itself; of King Minos of Crete and his wife's monstrous son, the Minotaur, shut up in the Labyrinth to feed on human victims; of Oedipus, prince of Corinth, who in ignorance slew his father and married his mother and ruled Thebes; of Jason and his Argonauts, who sailed to the Black Sea in search of the Golden Fleece, and of Medea, the barbarian queen Jason brought back from his voyage; all these oral legends served the early Greeks as history. But it was a history that had been half forgotten and that had been transmuted into poetry, so that the history of many centuries of Minoan culture, of Mycenaean power, of Achaean and Dorian invaders from the north, of the struggle between the invaders' Olympic gods and the local gods of the settled population the invaders overran, of the great Achaean crusade to Troy, and of the political disintegration and military disorder that followed the coming of the Dorians—this history became scrambled, jumbled, like the geological strata of the Grecian land itself, folded by volcanic action, eroded by later rivers, partly drowned in the sea, with only a peak emerging here and there as an island. . . .

Achilles' wrath against Agamemnon, his grief over the death of Patroclus, his slaying of Hector, the grief he shared with Priam, and the understanding born of grief all happened in the last year of the siege of Troy. When the minstrels sang the *Iliad,* the song made clear that Achilles would not survive the city's fall.

But Odysseus, the hero of the *Odyssey,* having survived the war, spent ten years in wandering about the Mediterranean in quest of his home. Both men acted. Both men were warrior-kings who fought at Troy. Both men sought immortal fame. Both men enlisted the aid of the immortal gods. But even in the *Iliad* Odysseus is "wise Odysseus"; the epithet "wise" is never once affixed to Achilles' glorious name. He is godlike Achilles, but not godlike in wisdom. And though Achilles was forced by catastrophe to a kind of understanding at last, Odysseus from the start deliberately and continuously sought to understand. He sought to know. He longed to know the unfamiliar, mysterious, and terrible reaches of the cruel sea. He longed to see strange cities and converse with strange men. It is true he was trying to get home, that he was king of Ithaca and that therefore home was Ithaca; but his restless mind kept diverting him. He loved Ithaca, but he kept looking for a home which Ithaca could but reflect. He loved his queen, Penelope, yet he lay with a goddess, the nymph Calypso, who was even more beautiful, and immortal as well. Achilles' world was war, its glory and horror, the lust of battle, the pride of victory, the thrill of the nearness of death, the fear that unloosened the knees of men, and the song the minstrel would one day sing. Odysseus' world was the unknown sea, exploration, discovery, search, learning. The ordeals he underwent were the ordeals of a learner, and the goddess who guided his voyage was the goddess of wisdom, Athena.

. . . And like countless other sailors Odysseus both hated the sea and loved it. The sea was salt and barren and unharvested—though the Greek would one day learn to harvest it—and Odysseus yearned to die, in his longing to see his native land or only to see the smoke that curled up from its dwellings. There were times, as in his rescue from the sea on the shores of Phaeacia, when he could sink down in the reeds of a river to kiss the earth, the giver of grain. And yet this barren sea that gave no grain beckoned him; bore him to strange places where he could learn the world beyond beloved Ithaca; in short, taught him. Taught him, and therefore changed him: when at last he reached the shores of Ithaca itself, he knew it not after his long absence, for about him the goddess of wisdom herself had shed a mist. Under her guidance Odysseus entered his kingdom. But he entered it disguised as a beggar, and therefore saw an Ithaca he had never before seen.

Though Odysseus returned to his kingdom as a beggar, he never ceased to be an Achaean warrior-chieftain, capable of indignant wrath. He was as ruthless as Achilles when the hour had come to slay the suitors in his own Great Hall and to punish their insolence. Had not his grandfather chosen a name for him, when he was but a baby, that suggested "Child of Wrath"? But he knew the limitations of wrath, too. . . .

He could experience wrath, and he also desired glory. When the Cyclops, Polyphenus, the one-eyed cannibal giant, had shut up in his cave both Odysseus and his comrades and had begun to devour those comrades, Odysseus by his own statement devised evil in the deep of his heart, "if in any way I might take vengeance on him, and Athene grant me glory."[13] When he had blinded the Cyclops and his ships were slipping silently out to sea from the shore where the blind giant raged, Odysseus endangered his own life and the lives of all his comrades by a triumphant boast worthy of Achilles himself. He called back to shore exultantly:

Cyclops, if any one of mortal men shall ask thee about the shameful blinding of thine eye, say that Odysseus, the sacker of cities, blinded it, even the son of Laertes, whose home is in Ithaca.[14]

[13] Homer: *Odyssey*, IX, 316-17. Loeb.
[14] *Ibid.*, IX, 502-5.

It was then that the blinded Cyclops successfully prayed to his father, the sea god Poseidon, to delay Odysseus' return to Ithaca.

But throughout most of his voyage Odysseus was busy less with either vengeance or glory than with solutions to hard and dangerous problems and with learning; and it was a Phaeacian challenger to athletic contests, not the Odysseus he challenged, who made the very Achaean assertion that "there is no greater glory for a man so long as he lives than that which he achieves by his own hands and his feet."[15] Odysseus' greatest glory was achieved by seeking and learning.

. . . But neither the immortality of the gods on the one hand nor the brutishness of animals on the other could ensnare him: he steered between them as surely as he steered between Scylla and Charybodis.

He remained, throughout, the wise Odysseus; Odysseus of many wiles; Odysseus, the wise and crafty-minded; Odysseus, the peer of the gods in counsel; neither immortal like the gods, nor yet sunk in animality; and the goddess who guided him homeward against the vengeance of the wrathful Poseidon's treacherous sea was Athena, goddess of wisdom. It was this same Athena who assured his son [Telemachus] that Odysseus "will contrive a way to return, for he is a man of many devices."[21] But she never ceased to supplement his unusual wisdom with her own divine wisdom. Part of his own wisdom, indeed, consisted in scrupulously following hers. His reward was to see many cities and to learn the minds of many men. As for the immortality of fame, there were more ways to win fame than by muscle and brawn and the long-sword of gleaming bronze and the willingness to die. Could a bronze sword, backed with muscle, outwit the treacherous sea? Human intelligence was better and more godlike than brute force. That was why Odysseus could boast to his gentle host, the king of the Phaeacians: "I am Odysseus, son of Laertes, who am known among men for all manner of wiles, and my fame reaches unto heaven."[22] Fame was a perquisite of wisdom, even among the immortal gods, perhaps especially among the immortal gods.

True, the wisdom Odysseus displayed was primarily a practical wisdom, a shrewdness, a cunning. But the gods favored that, too; or certainly some of them did. Old Autolycus, the maternal grandfather of Odysseus, who had chosen to name him Man of Wrath, had, according to Homer, "excelled all men in thievery,"[23] thanks to the god

---

[15] *Ibid.*, VIII, 147-48.
[21] *Ibid.*, I, 205.
[22] *Ibid.*, IX, 19-20.
[23] *Ibid.*, XIX, 395-96.

Hermes, who understood the art well. It was this shrewdness, this cunning, that enabled Odysseus to escape the countless dangers of a Mediterranean world filled with magic, like the wand and potions of Circe and like Hermes' herb to counteract those potions: "Moly, the gods call it."[24] It was the wisdom, too, of his wife, Penelope, and the wisdom of his son, Telemachus, guided by Athena, that laid the groundwork for Odysseus' return and triumph. Athena had endowed Penelope not only with that most valuable of women's skills in Homeric society, a knowledge of fair handiwork, but also "an understanding heart, and wiles."[25] She knew how to weave a web that would serve as shroud for Odysseus' aging father, but she also knew how to unravel it at night and delay its completion and therefore how to postpone her choice of suitors in case her true lord might yet return.

Although Odysseus left eleven of his twelve ships safely behind, he insisted on taking his own ship and its crew to the land of the Cyclopes. He wanted to learn who these Cyclopes were, whether they were cruel, and wild, and unjust, or whether they loved strangers and feared the gods in their thoughts.[26] And even after it became clear that he and his crew were in danger, even after his comrades had besought him to leave, he waited at Polyphemus' cave "to the end that I might see the man himself, and whether he would give me gifts of entertainment."[27] When he was forced to pass the man-devouring, sweetly singing Sirens, he took Circe's advice. He stopped the ears of his crew against that overpowering song, but he had them lash him to the mast with ears unstopped, that with delight he might listen to the voice of the two Sirens.[28] And he was richly rewarded, for the Sirens, according at least to their own boast, "know all things that come to pass upon the fruitful earth."[29] Odysseus wanted to know all too, not merely for immediate practical reasons, but because it is the nature of man to desire knowledge. His voyage had the practical aim of getting himself and his comrades back to the Ithaca they had left behind them twenty long years before. But Odysseus converted a return trip into an exploration; into a kind of education; into an intellectual, not a merely physical, adventure.

The cost of standing in battle, shield to shield, beside Achilles was high; but so was the cost of exploration in Odysseus' ship. There

24 *Ibid.*, X, 305.

25 *Ibid.*, II, 117-18.

26 *Ibid.*, IX, 174-76.

27 *Ibid.*, IX, 229.

28 *Ibid.*, XII, 49-52.

29 *Ibid.*, XII, 191.

were those men whom the Cyclops had devoured in his blood-spattered cave. There were those others who had, at least temporarily, been turned by Circe into swine. There were the ghastly narrows between Scylla and Charybdis, and these must be followed through. Odysseus knew in advance that, rowed they never so swiftly, the six-headed monster Scylla would yet have time to seize six of his crew. Yet, if the men were warned of this, they might stop rowing at the crucial moment and huddle together in the hold, and then there would be more than six men lost. So he approached the strait, with that special kind of heavy-heartedness that the leader is often forced to bear alone. When the monster struck, the six victims "cried aloud, calling upon me by name for that last time in anguish of heart."[30] While she devoured them, they stretched out their hands toward him in their awful death struggle, and, "Most piteous did mine eyes behold that thing of all that I bore while I explored the paths of the sea."[31] The passage between Scylla and Charybdis was, of course, inevitable; but the blood-smeared cave of the Cyclops was not. And when, later, one of Odysseus' followers called him "reckless Odysseus" and recalled that it was "through this man's folly"[32] that those men too had perished, Odysseus must have learned, or learned again, what the restless mind of the thinker could cost those he loved, and could cost the thinker, too.

Part of his wisdom lay in his love of law and justice, and part in his obedience to the gods. For he was a civilized man, . . . Zeus himself spoke to Athena of "godlike Odysseus, who is beyond all mortals in wisdom, and beyond all has paid sacrifice to the immortal gods."[35]

Achilles had frequently prayed, to get the gods to help him work his unexamined will. But Odysseus knew what Achilles did not: that, since the gods understood more than men, it was possible to get from them a more godlike kind of aid: they could help a man not only to slay his enemies; not only to outwit them; but to understand and to know. It was this that made his odyssey a wise man's pilgrimage and a learning of the human condition. Wisdom brought him a sense of proportion that Achilles lacked, and so this seaman's yarn was suffused with a humor which the *Illiad*, with all its power and majesty, conspicuously lacked.

In the world of Achilles human courage, even the lionlike courage of Achilles himself, was not adequate to the human problem. Something,

---

[30] *Ibid.*, XII, 249-50.
[31] *Ibid.*, XII, 258-59.
[32] *Ibid.*, X, 436-37.
[35] *Ibid.*, I, 65-7.

wisdom could do: it was crafty Odysseus' ruse of the wooden horse, filled with Achaean warriors, that at last brought Troy low. But the sack of Troy brought to Odysseus himself a second ten years of trial and made him a man of many sorrows. For in his world human wisdom, even his many devices, were not adequate to the human predicament either. At Troy Odysseus shared the fame of wisdom with ancient Nestor, king of Pylos; and it was later, at Pylos, that Nestor's own son informed a visiting stranger that all men had need of the gods.[40] . . .

Nestor's son merely voiced what every wise man knew: that all men had need of the gods. But this still left difficulties. Beyond the hundred and one daily rituals that kept this terrible need fresh in men's minds, there still were difficulties, even for those wise enough, as Odysseus himself was clearly wise enough, to know that there were things they did not know. Not even the gods knew everything, or they could not have deceived each other. That they knew more than men and that they appeared to men and advised them, seemed certain. But it was troubling that, in those direct encounters of the divine and human, the god was almost always disguised, usually as some human friend of the human party to the encounter. At the conclusion of such an encounter, the god might turn into a sea eagle or some other bird and fly off: Athena repeatedly withdrew in this fashion from the human world of Odysseus. Human witness was uncertain: Athena appeared to Odysseus in the hut of his swineherd, Eumaeus; but Telemachus was there and "did not see her before him, or notice her; for in no wise do the gods appear in manifest presence to all."[41] Yet Telemachus was not blind to gods, as witness the fact that a moment later, when Athena had beckoned Odysseus from the hut, had touched him with a golden wand, and had transfigured him, his dear son marveled, and, seized with fear, turned his eyes aside, lest it should be a god."[42] And Odysseus reassured him:

> Be sure I am no god; why dost thou liken me to the immortals?
> Nay, I am thy father, for whose sake thou dost with groaning
> endure many griefs and submittest to the violence of men.[43]

But Telemachus, who had "not noticed" Athena, reasoned that only a god could transform himself from an aged beggar into this handsome, kingly man. This sort of transfiguration of man by god happened repeatedly, both in Odysseus' world and in that of Achilles.

[40] *Ibid.,* III, 48.
[41] *Ibid.,* XVI, 160-61.
[42] *Ibid.,* XVI, 178-79.
[43] *Ibid.,* XIV, 187-89.

A god could put courage in an Achilles or wisdom in an Odysseus. Did not Athena herself "put strength and courage"[44] in Telemachus's heart when he dreaded going among the unfriendly wooers of his mother, to the extent even of making him a "godlike man"[45]? But in urging the voyage to Pylos, she promised that she, or some god, would put wisdom in his mind. Telemachus shrank from encountering Nestor, renowned for his wise words, since he himself was "as yet all unversed in subtle speech."[46] Her answer told something of the relation of gods and men: "Telemachus, somewhat thou of thyself devise in thy breast, and somewhat heaven [*daimōn*]|too will prompt thee."[47] If Telemachus sounded childishly timid, yet in his world men were keenly aware of the mysterious work of what Homer repeatedly called "wingéd words," those symbols that conveyed invisible thoughts from the mysterious recesses of one human mind to the mysterious recesses of another.

Often the gods communicated to men by dreams. But could a dream be trusted? Penelope told Odysseus, her still-disguised husband, that her absent lord had appeared to her in a dream and had foretold his return. But when Odysseus urged her to accept the dream as true, she replied sadly: "Stranger, dreams are baffling and unclear of meaning, and in no wise do they find fulfillment in all things for men."[48] Some dreams were true and some were false, and how could Penelope tell which class her dream belonged to? As a matter of fact, although Penelope presumably did not know it, Zeus had sent a dream to Agamemnon at Troy precisely in order to deceive him into fighting and losing.

Wingéd words, dreams, and gods disguised as men were heard or seen by some bystanders and not by others. Could the human mind be sure of any of them, in its doomed effort to understand its world? Yet some wingéd words seemed to fly straight, from mind to mind; Penelope herself admitted that some dreams came true; and some men had been certain they encountered a god. Should words, then, "remain unwingéd"[49]—that is, should men keep silence? And cease to search their dreams for meaning? And believe the god they were sure they saw was probably but a man? After all, Odysseus, who spoke wingéd words, and urged belief in a dream, and walked and talked with gods— even Odysseus admitted that "Nothing feebler does earth nurture than

---

[44] *Ibid.*, I, 320-21.
[45] *Ibid.*, I, 324.
[46] *Ibid.*, III, 23.
[47] *Ibid.*, III, 26-7.
[48] *Ibid.*, XIX, 560-61.
[49] *Ibid.*, XIX, 29; XVII, 57.

man, of all things that on earth are breathing and moving."[50] For just this reason he made use of prayer, of signs and tokens, and of words. After the events in the *Odyssey* had all occurred, and Odysseus had understood his kingdom in a new way, and his wife, and his son, did he obey the injunction Tiresias gave him beneath the earth in the House of Hades? Did he reaffirm his belief in the invisible world of the gods that penetrated his own? Did he reaffirm his faith in the power of things to serve as symbols, in the power of his world to have meaning, even to be transfigured?

Tiresias ordered him, when the suitors had been slain, to take a shapely oar and strike inland until he came to men who had never heard of the sea, or of ships, or of the oars that serve ships as wings. And this should be a sign to him: when a wayfarer should mistake the oar on Odysseus' shoulder for a fan with which to winnow grain, then Odysseus should erect the oar in the earth and sacrifice to the god of the sea, Poseidon. Later, after a long and prosperous life, death would come to Odysseus—from the sea. Tiresias, of course, was a prophet, with more faith in symbols than most men dared to hold.

[50] *Ibid.*, XVIII, 130-31.

15
Spartan Education and Life—
The Totalitarian Pattern

Plutarch, Selections from "Lycurgus," *The Lives of the Noble Grecians and Romans,* translated by John Dryden and revised by Arthur Hugh Clough (New York: The Modern Library—Giant G-5), pp. 59-69, *passim.*

In order to achieve the good education of their youth (which, as I said before, he thought the most important and noblest work of a lawgiver), he [Lycurgus] went so far back as to take into consideration their very conception and birth, by regulating their marriages. For Aristotle is wrong in saying, that, after he had tried all ways to reduce the women to more modesty and sobriety, he was at last forced to leave them as they were, because that in the absence of their husbands, who spent the best part of their lives in the wars, their wives, whom they were obliged to leave absolute mistresses at home, took great liberties and assumed the superiority; and were treated with overmuch respect and called by the title of lady or queen. The truth is, he took in their case, also, all the care that was possible; he ordered the maidens to exercise themselves with wrestling, running, throwing the quoit, and casting the dart, to the end that the fruit they conceived might, in strong and healthy bodies, take firmer root and find better growth, and withal that they, with this greater vigour, might be the more able to undergo the pains of child-bearing. And to the end he might take away their overgreat tenderness and fear of exposure to the air, and all acquired womanishness, he ordered that the young women should go naked in the processions, as well as the young men, and dance, too, in that condition, at certain solemn feasts, singing certain songs, whilst the young men stood around, seeing and hearing them. On these occasions they now and then made, by jests, a befitting reflection upon those who had misbehaved themselves in the wars; and again sang encomiums upon those who had done any gallant action, and by these means inspired the younger sort with an emulation of their glory. Those that were thus commended went away proud, elated, and gratified with their honour among the maidens; and those who were rallied were as sensibly touched with it as if they had been formally reprimanded; and so much the more, because the kings and the elders, as well as the rest of the city, saw and heard all that passed. Nor was there anything shameful in this nakedness of the young women; modesty attended them, and all wantonness was excluded. It taught them simplicity and a care for good health, and gave them some taste of higher feelings, admitted as they thus were to the field of noble action and glory. Hence it was natural for them to think and speak as Gorgo, for example, the wife of Leonidas, is said to have done, when some foreign lady, as it would seem, told her that the women of Lacedaemon were the only women in the world who could rule men; "With good reason," she said, "for we are the only women who bring forth men."

These public processions of the maidens, and their appearing naked in their exercises and dancings, were incitements to marriage, operating upon the young with the rigour and certainty, as Plato says, of love, if not of mathematics. . . .

In their marriages, the husband carried off his bride by a sort of force; nor were their brides ever small and of tender years, but in their full bloom and ripeness. After this, she who superintended the wedding comes and clips the hair of the bride close round her head, dresses her up in man's clothes, and leaves her upon a mattress in the dark; afterwards comes the bridegroom, in his everyday clothes, sober and composed, as having supped at the common table, and, entering privately into the room where the bride lies, unties her virgin zone, and takes her to himself; and, after staying some time together, he returns composedly to his own apartment, to sleep as usual with the other young men. And so he continues to do, spending his days, and, indeed, his nights, with them, visiting his bride in fear and shame, and with circumspection, when he thought he should not be observed; she, also, on her part, using her wit to help and find favourable opportunities for their meeting, when company was out of the way. In this manner they lived a long time, insomuch that they sometimes had children by their wives before ever they saw their faces by daylight. Their interviews, being thus difficult and rare, served not only for continual exercise of their self-control, but brought them together with their bodies healthy and vigorous, and their affections fresh and lively, unsated and undulled by easy access and long continuance with each other; while their partings were always early enough to leave behind unextinguished in each of them some remaining fire of longing and mutual delight. After guarding marriage with this modesty and reserve, he was equally careful to banish empty and womanish jealousy. For this object, excluding all licentious disorders, he made it, nevertheless, honourable for men to give the use of their wives to those whom they should think fit, that so they might have children by them; ridiculing those in whose opinion such favours are so unfit for participation as to fight and shed blood and go to war about it. Lycurgus allowed a man who was advanced in years and had a young wife to recommend some virtuous and approved young man, that she might have a child by him, who might inherit the good qualities of the father, and be a son to himself. On the other side, an honest man who had love for a married woman upon account of her modesty and the well-favouredness of her children, might, without formality, beg her company of her husband, that he might raise, as it were, from this plot of good ground, worthy and well-allied children for himself. And indeed, Lycurgus was of a persuasion that children were not so much the property of their parents as of the whole commonwealth, and, therefore, would not have his citizens begot by the first-comers, but by the best men that could be found; the laws of other nations seemed to him very absurd and inconsistent, where people would be so solicitous for their dogs and horses as to exert interest and to pay money to procure fine breeding, and yet kept their wives shut up, to be made mothers only by themselves, who might be foolish, infirm, or diseased; as if it were not apparent that children of a bad breed would prove their bad qualities first upon those who kept and were rearing them, and well-born children, in like manner, their good qualities. These regulations, founded on natural and social grounds, were certainly so far from that scandalous liberty which was afterwards charged upon their women, that they knew not what adultery meant. . . .

Nor was it in the power of the father to dispose of the child as he thought fit; he was obliged to carry it before certain triers at a place called Lesche; these were some of the elders of the tribe to which the child belonged; their business it was carefully to view the infant, and, if they found it stout and well made, they gave order for its rearing, and allotted to it one of the nine thousand shares of land above mentioned for its maintenance, but, if they found it puny and ill-shaped, ordered it to be taken to what is called the Apothetae, a sort of chasm under Taygetus; as thinking it neither for the good of the child itself, nor for the public interest, that it should be brought up, if it did not, from the very outset, appear made to be healthy and vigorous. Upon the same account, the women did not bathe the new-born children with water, as is the custom in all other countries, but with wine, to prove the temper and complexion of their bodies; from a notion they had that epileptic and weakly children faint and waste away upon their being thus bathed, while, on the contrary, those of a strong and vigorous habit acquire firmness and get a temper by it, like steel. There was much care and art, too, used by the nurses; they had no swaddling bands; the children grew up free and unconstrained in limb and form, and not dainty and fanciful about their food; not afraid in the dark, or of being left alone; and without peevishness, or ill-humour, or crying. Upon this account Spartan nurses were often bought up, or hired by people of other countries; and it is recorded that she who suckled Alcibiades was a Spartan; who, however, if fortunate in his nurse, was not so in his preceptor; his guardian, Pericles, as Plato tells us, chose a servant for that office called Zopyrus, no better than any common slave.

Lycurgus was of another mind; he would not have masters bought out of the market for his young Spartans, nor such as should sell their pains; nor was it lawful, indeed, for the father himself to breed up the children after his own fancy; but as soon as they were seven years old they were to be enrolled in certain companies and classes, where they all lived under the same order and discipline, doing their exercises and taking their play together. Of these, he who showed the most conduct and courage was made captain; they had their eyes always upon him, obeyed his orders, and underwent patiently whatsoever punishment he inflicted; so that the whole course of their education was one continued exercise of a ready and perfect obedience. The old men, too, were spectators of their performances, and often raised quarrels and disputes among them, to have a good opportunity of finding out their different characters, and of seeing which would be valiant, which a coward, when they should come to more dangerous encounters. Reading and writing they gave them, just enough to serve their turn; their chief care was to make them good subjects, and to teach them to endure pain and conquer in battle. To this end, as they grew in years, their discipline was proportionately increased; their heads were close-clipped, they were accustomed to go barefoot, and for the most part to play naked.

After they were twelve years old, they were no longer allowed to wear any undergarments, they had one coat to serve them a year; their bodies were hard and dry, with but little acquaintance of baths and unguents; these human indulgences they were allowed only on some few particular days in the year. They lodged together in little bands upon beds made of the rushes which grew by the banks of the river Eurotas, which they were to break off with their hands without a knife; if it were winter, they mingled some thistle-down with their rushes, which it was thought had the property of giving warmth. By the time they were come to this age there was not any of the more hopeful boys who had not a lover to bear him company. The old men, too, had an eye upon them, coming often to the grounds to hear and see them contend either in wit or strength with one another, and this as seriously and with as much concern as if they were their fathers, their tutors, or their magistrates; so that there scarcely was any time or place without some one present to put them in mind of their duty, and punish them if they had neglected it.

Besides all this, there was always one of the best and honestest men in the city appointed to undertake the charge and governance of them; he again arranged them into their several bands, and set over each of them for their captain the most temperate and boldest of those they called Irens, who were usually twenty years old, two years out of the boys; and the oldest of the boys, again, were Mell-Irens, as much as to say, who would shortly be men. This young man, therefore, was their captain when they fought and their master at home, using them for the offices of his house; sending the eldest of them to fetch wood, and the weaker and less able to gather salads and herbs, and these they must either go without or steal; which they did by creeping into the gardens, or conveying themselves cunningly and closely into the eating-houses; if they were taken in the fact, they were whipped without mercy, for thieving so ill and awkwardly. They stole, too, all other meat they could lay their hands on, looking out and watching all opportunities, when people were asleep or more careless than usual. If they were caught, they were not only punished with whipping, but hunger, too, being reduced to their ordinary allowance, which was but very slender, and so contrived on purpose, that they might set about to help themselves, and be forced to exercise their energy and address. This was the principal design of their hard fare; there was another not inconsiderable, that they might grow taller; for the vital spirits, not being overburdened and oppressed by too great a quantity of nourishment, which necessarily discharges itself into thickness and breadth, do, by their natural lightness, rise; and the body, giving and yielding because it is pliant, grows in height. The same thing seems, also, to conduce to beauty of shape; a dry and lean habit is a better subject for nature's configuration, which the gross and over-fed are too heavy to submit to properly. Just as we find that women who take physic whilst they are with child, bear leaner and smaller but better-shaped and prettier children; the material they come of having been more pliable and easily moulded. The reason, however, I leave others to determine.

To return from whence we have digressed. So seriously did the Lacedaemonian children go about their stealing, that a youth, having stolen a young fox and hid it under his coat, suffered it to tear out his very bowels with its teeth and claws and died upon the place, rather than let it be seen. What is practised to this very day in Lacedaemon is enough to gain credit to this story, for I myself have seen several of the youths endure whipping to death at the foot of the altar of Diana surnamed Orthia.

The Iren, or under-master, used to stay a little with them after supper, and one of them he bade to sing a song, to another he put a question which required an advised and deliberate answer; for example, Who was the best man in the city? What he thought of such an action of such a man? They used them thus early to pass a right judgment upon persons and things, and to inform themselves of the abilities or defects of their countrymen. If they had not an answer ready to the question, Who was a good or who an ill-reputed citizen, they were looked upon as of a dull and careless disposition, and to have little or no sense of virtue and honour; besides this, they were to give a good reason for what they said, and in as few words and as comprehensive as might be; he that failed of this, or answered not to the purpose, had his thumb bit by the master. Sometimes the Iren did this in the presence of the old men and magistrates, that they might see whether he punished them justly and in due measure or not, and when he did amiss, they would not reprove him before the boys, but, when they were gone, he was called to an account and underwent correction, if he had run far into either of the extremes of indulgence or severity.

Their lovers and favourers, too, had a share in the young boy's honour or disgrace; and there goes a story that one of them was fined by the magistrate, because the lad whom he loved cried out effeminately as he was fighting. And though this sort of love was so approved among them, that the most virtuous matrons would make professions of it to young girls, yet rivalry did not exist, and if several men's fancies met in one person, it was rather the beginning of an intimate friendship, whilst they all jointly conspired to render the object of their affection as accomplished as possible.

They taught them, also, to speak with a natural and graceful raillery, and to comprehend much matter of thought in few words. For Lycurgus, who ordered, as we saw, that a great piece of money should be but of an inconsiderable value, on the contrary would allow no discourse to be current which did not contain in few words a great deal of useful and curious sense; children in Sparta, by a habit of long silence, came to give just and sententious answers; for, indeed, as loose and incontinent livers are seldom fathers of many children, so loose and incontinent talkers seldom originate many sensible words. King Agis, when some Athenian laughed at their short swords, and said that the jugglers on the stage swallowed them with ease, answered him. "We find them long enough to reach our enemies with;" and as their swords were short and sharp, so, it seems to me, were their sayings. They reach the point and arrest the attention of the hearers better than any. Lycurgus himself seems to have been short and sententious, if we may trust the anecdotes of him. . . .

We may see their character, too, in their very jests. For they did not throw them out at random, but the very wit of them was grounded upon something or other worth thinking about. For instance, one, being asked to go hear a man who exactly counterfeited the voice of a nightingale, answered, "Sir, I have heard the nightingale itself." Another, having read the following inscription upon a tomb—

Seeking to quench a cruel tyranny,
They, at Selinus, did in battle die,

said, it served them right; for instead of trying to quench the tyranny, they should have let it burn out. A lad, being offered some game-cocks that would die upon the spot, said that he cared not for cocks that would die, but for such that would live and kill others. Another, seeing people easing themselves on seats, said, "God forbid I should sit where I could not get up to salute my elders." In short, their answers were so sententious and pertinent, that one said well that intellectual much more truly than athletic exercise was the Spartan characteristic.

Nor was their instruction in music and verse less carefully attended to than their habits of grace and good-breeding in conversation. And their very songs had a life and spirit in them that inflamed and possessed men's minds with an enthusiasm and ardour for action; the style of them was plain and without affectation; the subject always serious and moral; most usually, it was in praise of such men as had died in defence of their country, or in derision of those that had been cowards; the former they declared happy and glorified; the life of the latter they described as most miserable and abject. There were also vaunts of what they would do, and boasts of what they had done, varying with the various ages, as, for example, they had three choirs in their solemn festivals, the first of the old men, the second of the young men, and the last of the children; the old men began thus:—

We once were young, and brave, and strong;

the young men answered them, singing:—

And we're so now, come on and try;

the children came last and said:—

But we'll be strongest by and by.

Indeed, if we will take the pains to consider their compositions, some of which were still extant in our days, and the airs on the flute to which they marched when going to battle, we shall find that Terpander and Pindar had reason to say that musing and valour were allied. The first says of Lacedaemon—

The spear and song in her do meet,
And Justice walks about her street;

And Pindar—

Councils of wise elders here,
And the young men's conquering spear,
And dance, and song, and joy appear;

both describing the Spartans as no less musical than warlike; in the words of one of their own poets—

> With the iron stern and sharp,
> Comes the playing on the harp.

For, indeed, before they engaged in battle, the king first did sacrifice to the Muses, in all likelihood to put them in mind of the manner of their education, and of the judgment that would be passed upon their actions, and thereby to animate them to the performance of exploits that should deserve a record. At such times, too, the Lacedaemonians abated a little the severity of their manners in favour of their young men, suffering them to curl and adorn their hair, and to have costly arms and fine clothes; and were well pleased to see them, like proud horses, neighing and pressing to the course. And, therefore, as soon as they came to be well-grown, they took a great deal of care of their hair, to have it parted and trimmed, especially against a day of battle, pursuant to a saying recorded of their lawgiver, that a large head of hair added beauty to a good face, and terror to an ugly one.

. . . Their discipline continued still after they were full-grown men. No one was allowed to live after his own fancy; but the city was a sort of camp, in which every man had his share of provisions and business set out, and looked upon himself not so much born to serve his own ends as the interest of his country. Therefore if they were commanded nothing else, they went to see the boys perform their exercises, to teach them something useful or to learn it themselves of those who knew better. And indeed one of the greatest and highest blessings Lycurgus procured his people was the abundance of leisure which proceeded from his forbidding to them the exercise of any mean and mechanical trade. Of the money-making that depends on troublesome going about and seeing people and doing business, they had no need at all in a state where wealth obtained no honour or respect. The Helots tilled their ground for them, and paid them yearly in kind the appointed quantity, without any trouble of theirs. To this purpose there goes a story of a Lacedaemonian who, happening to be at Athens when the courts were sitting, was told of a citizen that had been fined for living an idle life, and was being escorted home in much distress of mind by his condoling friends; the Lacedaemonian was much surprised at it and desired his friend to show him the man who was condemned for living like a freeman. So much beneath them did they esteem the frivolous devotion of time and attention to the mechanical arts and to money-making.

It need not be said that upon the prohibition of gold and silver, all lawsuits immediately ceased, for there was now neither avarice nor poverty amongst them, but equality, where every one's wants were supplied, and independence, because those wants were so small. All their time, except when they were in the field, was taken up by the choral dances and the festivals, in hunting, and in attendance on the exercise-grounds and the places of public conversation. Those who were under thirty years of age were not allowed to go into the market-place, but had the necessaries of their family supplied by the care of their relations and lovers; nor was it for the credit of elderly men to be seen too often in the market-place; it was esteemed more suitable for them to frequent the exercise-grounds and places of conversation, where they spent their leisure rationally in conversation, not on money-making and market-prices, but for the most part in passing judgment on some action worth considering; extolling the good, and censuring those who were otherwise, and that in a light and sportive manner, conveying, without too much gravity, lessons of advice and improvement. Nor was Lycurgus himself unduly austere; it was he who dedicated, says Sosibius, the little statue of Laughter. Mirth, introduced seasonably at their suppers and places of common entertainment, was to serve as a sort of sweetmeat to accompany their strict and hard life. To conclude, he bred up his citizens in such a way that they neither would nor could live by themselves; they were to make themselves one with the public good, and, clustering like bees around their commander, be by their zeal and public spirit carried all but out of themselves, and devoted wholly to their country. What their sentiments were will better appear by a few of their sayings. Paedaretus, not being admitted into the list of the three hundred, returned home with a joyful face, well pleased to find that there were in Sparta three hundred better men than himself. And Polycratidas, being sent with some others ambassador to the lieutenants of the king of Persia being asked by them whether they came in a private or in a public character, answered, "In a public, if we succeed; if not, in a private character." Argileonis, asking some who came from Amphipolis if her son Brasidas died courageously and as became a Spartan, on their beginning to praise him to a high degree, and saying there was not such another left in Sparta, answered, "Do not say so; Brasidas was a good and brave man, but there are in Sparta many better than he."

16
Athenian Education and Life— A Democratic Way

Thucydides

The Funeral Speech of Pericles

Thucydides, "The Funeral Speech of Pericles," Book II, 36-47, in *Thucydides*, translated by Benjamin Jowett, 2d ed., revised (Oxford: The Clarendon Press; London: Oxford University Press, 1900), I, pp. 127-135. Reprinted by permission of The Clarendon Press, Oxford.

I will speak first of our ancestors, for it is right and seemly that now, when we are lamenting the dead, a tribute should be paid to their memory. There has never been a time when they did not inhabit this land, which by their valour they have handed down from generation to generation, and we have received from them a free state. But if they were worthy of praise, still more were our fathers, who added to their inheritance, and after many a struggle transmitted to us their sons this great empire. And we ourselves assembled here to-day, who are still most of us in the vigour of life, have carried the work of improvement further, and have richly endowed our city with all things, so that she is sufficient for herself both in peace and war. Of the military exploits by which our various possessions were acquired, or of the energy with which we or our fathers drove back the tide of war, Hellenic or Barbarian, I will not speak; for the tale would be long and is familiar to you. But before I praise the dead, I should like to point out by what principles of action we rose to power, and under what institutions and through what manner of life our empire became great. For I conceive that such thoughts are not unsuited to the occasion, and that this numerous assembly of citizens and strangers may profitably listen to them.

Our form of government does not enter into rivalry with the institutions of others. We do not copy our neighbours, but are an example to them. It is true that we are called a democracy, for the administration is in the hands of the many and not of the few. But while the law secures equal justice to all alike in their private disputes, the claim of excellence is also recognised; and when a citizen is in any way distinguished, he is preferred to the public service, not as a matter of privilege, but as the reward of merit. Neither is poverty a bar, but a man may benefit his country whatever be the obscurity of his condition. There is no exclusiveness in our public life, and in our private inter-course we are not suspicious of one another, nor angry with our neighbour if he does what he likes; we do not put on sour looks at him which, though harmless, are not pleasant. While we are thus uncon-strained in our private intercourse, a spirit of reverence pervades our public acts; we are prevented from doing wrong by respect for the authorities and for the laws, having an especial regard to those which are ordained for the protection of the injured as well as to those unwritten laws which bring upon the transgressor of them the reproba-tion of the general sentiment.

And we have not forgotten to provide for our weary spirits many relaxations from toil; we have regular games and sacrifices throughout the year; our homes are beautiful and elegant; and the delight which we daily feel in all these things helps to banish melancholy. Because of the greatness of our city the fruits of the whole earth flow in upon us; so that we enjoy the goods of other countries as freely as of our own.

Then, again, our military training is in many respects superior to that of our adversaries. Our city is thrown open to the world, and we never expel a foreigner or prevent him from seeing or learning anything of which the secret if revealed to an enemy might profit him. We rely not upon management or trickery, but upon our own hearts and hands. And in the matter of education, whereas they from early youth are always undergoing laborious exercises which are to make them brave, we live at ease, and yet are equally ready to face the perils which they face. And here is the proof. The Lacedaemonians come into Attica not by themselves, but with their whole confederacy fol-lowing; we go alone into a neighbour's country; and although our opponents are fighting for their homes and we on a foreign soil, we have seldom any difficulty in overcoming them. Our enemies have never yet felt our united strength; the care of a navy divides our attention, and on land we are obliged to send our own citizens everywhere. But they, if they meet and defeat a part of our army, are as proud as if they had routed us all, and when defeated they pretend to have been vanquished by us all.

If then we prefer to meet danger with a light heart but without laborious training, and with a courage which is gained by habit and not enforced by law, are we not greatly the gainers? Since we do not anticipate the pain, although, when the hour comes, we can be as brave as those who never allow themselves to rest; and thus too our city is equally admirable in peace and in war. For we are lovers of the beautiful, yet simple in our tastes, and we cultivate the mind without loss of manliness. Wealth we employ, not for talk and ostentation, but when there is a real use for it. To avow poverty with us is no disgrace; the true disgrace is in doing nothing to avoid it. An Athenian citizen does not neglect the state because he takes care of his own household; and even those of us who are engaged in business have a very fair idea of politics. We alone regard a man who takes no interest in public affairs, not as a harmless, but as a useless character; and if few of us are originators, we are all sound judges of a policy. The great impediment to action is, in our opinion, not discussion, but the want of that knowledge which is gained by discussion preparatory to action. For we have a peculiar power of thinking before we act and of acting too, whereas other men are courageous from ignorance but hesitate upon reflection. And they are surely to be esteemed the bravest spirits who, having the clearest sense both of the pains and pleasures of life, do not on that account shrink from danger. In doing good, again, we are unlike others; we make our friends by conferring, not by receiving favours. Now he who confers a favour is the firmer friend, because he would fain by kindness keep alive the memory of an obligation; but the recipient is colder in his feelings, because he knows that in requiting another's generosity he will not be winning gratitude but only paying a debt. We alone do good to our neighbours not upon a calculation of interest, but in the confidence of freedom and in a frank and fearless spirit. To sum up: I say that Athens is the school of Hellas, and that the individual Athenian in his own person seems to have the power of adapting himself to the most varied forms of action with the utmost versatility and grace. This is no passing and idle word, but truth and fact; and the assertion is verified by the position to which these qualities have raised the state. For in the hour of trial Athens alone among her contemporaries is superior to the report of her. No enemy who comes against her is indignant at the reverses which he sustains at the hands of such a city; no subject complains that his masters are unworthy of him. And we shall assuredly not be without witnesses; there are mighty monuments of our power which will make us the wonder of this and of succeeding ages; we shall not need the praises of Homer or of any other panegyrist whose poetry may please for the moment, although his representation of the facts will not bear the light of day. For we have compelled every land and every sea to open a path for our valour, and have everywhere planted eternal memorials of our friendship and of our enmity. Such is the city for whose sake these men nobly fought and died; they could not bear the thought that she might be taken from them; and every one of us who survive should gladly toil on her behalf.

I have dwelt upon the greatness of Athens because I want to show you that we are contending for a higher prize than those who enjoy none of these privileges, and to establish by manifest proof the merit of these men whom I am now commemorating. Their loftiest praise has been already spoken. For in magnifying the city I have magnified them, and men like them whose virtues made her glorious. And of how few Hellenes can it be said as of them, that their deeds when weighed in the balance have been found equal to their fame! Methinks that a death such as theirs has been gives the true measure of a man's worth; it may be the first revelation of his virtues, but is at any rate their final seal. For even those who come short in other ways may justly plead the valour with which they have fought for their country; they have blotted out the evil with the good, and have benefited the state more by their public services than they have injured her by their private actions. None of these men were enervated by wealth or hesitated to resign the pleasures of life; none of them put off the evil day in the hope, natural to poverty, that a man, though poor, may one day become rich. But, deeming that the punishment of their enemies was sweeter than any of these things, and that they could fall in no nobler cause, they determined at the hazard of their lives to be honourably avenged, and to leave the rest. They resigned to hope their unknown chance of happiness; but in the face of death they resolved to rely upon themselves alone. And when the moment came they were minded to resist and suffer, rather than to fly and save their lives; they ran away from the word of dishonour, but on the battle-field their feet stood fast, and in an instant, at the height of their fortune, they passed away from the scene, not of their fear, but of their glory.

Such was the end of these men; they were worthy of Athens, and the living need not desire to have a more heroic spirit, although they may pray for a less fatal issue. The value of such a spirit is not to be expressed in words. Any one can discourse to you for ever about the advantages of a brave defence, which you know already. But instead of listening to him I would have you day by day fix your eyes upon the greatness of Athens, until you become filled with the love of her; and when you are impressed by the spectacle of her glory, reflect that this empire has been acquired by men who knew their duty and had the courage to do it, who in the hour of conflict had the fear of dishonour always present to them, and who, if ever they failed in an enterprise, would not allow their virtues to be lost to their country, but freely gave their lives to her as the fairest offering which they could present at her feast. The sacrifice which they collectively made was individually repaid to them; for they received again each one for himself a praise which grows not old, and the noblest of all sepulchres—I speak not of that in which their remains are laid, but of that in which their glory survives, and is proclaimed always and on every fitting occasion both in word and deed. For the whole earth is the sepulchre of famous men; not only are they commemorated by columns and inscriptions in their own country, but in foreign lands there dwells also an unwritten memorial of them, graven not on stone but in the hearts of men. Make them your examples, and, esteeming courage to be freedom and freedom to be happiness, do not weigh too nicely the perils of war. The unfortunate who has no hope of a change for the better has less reason to throw away his life than the prosperous who, if he survive, is always liable to a change for the worse, and to whom any accidental fall makes the most serious difference. To a man of spirit, cowardice and disaster coming together are far more bitter than death striking him unperceived at a time when he is full of courage and animated by the general hope.

Wherefore I do not now commiserate the parents of the dead who stand here; I would rather comfort them. You know that your life has been passed amid manifold vicissitudes; and that they may be deemed fortunate who have gained most honour, whether an honourable death like theirs, or an honourable sorrow like yours, and whose days have been so ordered that the term of their happiness is likewise the term of their life. I know how hard it is to make you feel this, when the good fortune of others will too often remind you of the gladness which once lightened your hearts. And sorrow is felt at the want of those blessings, not which a man never knew, but which were a part of his life before they were taken from him. Some of you are of an age at which they may hope to have other children, and they ought to bear their sorrow better; not only will the children who may hereafter be born make them forget their own lost ones, but the city will be doubly a gainer. She will not be left desolate, and she will be safer. For a man's counsel cannot have equal weight or worth, when he alone has no children to risk in the general danger. To those of you who have passed their prime, I say: "Congratulate yourselves that you have been happy during the greater part of your days; remember that your life of sorrow will not last long, and be comforted by the glory of those who are gone. For the love of honour alone is ever young, and not riches, as some say, but honour is the delight of men when they are old and useless."

To you who are the sons and brothers of the departed, I see that the struggle to emulate them will be an arduous one. For all men praise the dead, and, however pre-eminent your virtue may be, hardly will you be thought, I do not say to equal, but even to approach them. The living have their rivals and detractors, but when a man is out of the way, the honour and good-will which he receives is unalloyed. And,

if I am to speak of womanly virtues to those of you who will henceforth be widows, let me sum them up in one short admonition: To a
woman not to show more weakness than is natural to her sex is a great
glory, and not to be talked about for good or for evil among men.

I have paid the required tribute, in obedience to the law, making use
of such fitting words as I had. The tribute of deeds has been paid in
part; for the dead have been honourably interred, and it remains only
that their children should be maintained at the public charge until
they are grown up: this is the solid prize with which, as with a garland,
Athens crowns her sons living and dead, after a struggle like theirs.
For where the rewards of virtue are greatest, there the noblest citizens
are enlisted in the service of the state. And now, when you have duly
lamented, every one his own dead, you may depart.

Such was the order of the funeral celebrated in this winter, with
the end of which ended the first year of the Peloponnesian War.

Plato's Summary of Athenian Education— Old Greek Period

Plato, *Protagoras*, 325-326, in *The Dialogues of Plato*, translated into
English with analyses and introductions by B. Jowett in five volumes,
3rd ed. (London: Oxford University Press, 1892), pp. 146-148. Reprinted
by permission of The Clarendon Press, Oxford.

Education and admonition commence in the first years of childhood,
and last to the very end of life. Mother and nurse and father and tutor
are vying with one another about the improvement of the child as soon
as ever he is able to understand what is being said to him: he cannot
say or do anything without their setting forth to him that this is just
and that is unjust; this is honourable, that is dishonourable; this is
holy, that is unholy; do this and abstain from that. And if he obeys,
well and good; if not, he is straightened by threats and blows, like a
piece of bent or warped wood. At a later stage they send him to
teachers, and enjoin them to see to his manners even more than to his
reading and music; and the teachers do as they are desired. And when
the boy has learned his letters and is beginning to understand what is
written, as before he understood only what was spoken, they put into

his hands the works of great poets, which he reads sitting on a bench at school; in these are contained many admonitions, and many tales, and praises, and encomia of ancient famous men, which he is required to learn by heart, in order that he may imitate or emulate them and desire to become like them. Then, again, the teachers of the lyre take similar care that their young disciple is temperate and gets into no mischief; and when they have taught him the use of the lyre, they introduce him to the poems of other excellent poets, who are the lyric poets; and these they set to music, and make their harmonies and rhythms quite familiar to the children's souls, in order that they may learn to be more gentle, and harmonious, and rhythmical, and so fitted for speech and action; for the life of man in every part has need of harmony and rhythm. Then they send them to the master of gymnastic, in order that their bodies may better minister to the virtuous mind, and that they may not be compelled through bodily weakness to play the coward in war or on any other occasion. This is what is done by those who have the means, and those who have the means are the rich; their children begin to go to school soonest and leave off latest. When they have done with masters, the State again compels them to learn the laws, and live after the pattern which they furnish, and not after their own fancies; and just as in learning to write, the writing-master first draws lines with a style for the use of the young beginner, and gives him the tablet and makes him follow the lines, so the city draws the laws, which were the invention of good lawgivers living in the olden time; these are given to the young man, in order to guide him in his conduct whether he is commanding or obeying; and he who transgresses them is to be corrected, or, in other words, called to account, which is a term used not only in your country, but also in many others, seeing that justice calls men to account. Now when there is all this care about virtue private and public, why, Socrates, do you still wonder and doubt whether virtue can be taught? Cease to wonder, for the opposite would be far more surprising.

17
Isocrates (436-338 B.C.)
Whom, Then, Do I Call Educated?

Iscorates, *Panathenaicus*, 28-33, in *Isocrates*, with an English translation by George Norlin, The Loeb Classical Library (Cambridge, Massachusetts: Harvard University Press, 1929), II, pp. 391-393.

Whom, then, do I call educated. . . ? First, those who manage well the circumstances which they encounter day by day, and who possess a judgement which is accurate in meeting occasions as they arise and rarely misses the expedient course of action; next, those who are decent and honourable in their intercourse with all with whom they associate, tolerating easily and good-naturedly what is unpleasant or offensive in others and being themselves as agreeable and reasonable to their associates as it is possible to be; furthermore, those who hold their pleasures always under control and are not unduly overcome by their misfortunes, bearing up under them bravely and in a manner worthy of our common nature; finally, and most important of all, those who are not spoiled by successes and do not desert their true selves and become arrogant, but hold their ground steadfastly as intelligent men, not rejoicing in the good things which have come to them through chance rather than in those which through their own nature and intelligence are theirs from their birth. Those who have a character which is in accord, not with one of these things, but with all of them—these, I contend, are wise and complete men, possessed of all the virtues.

These then are the views which I hold regarding educated men.

18
Socrates (469?-399 B.C.)
On Virtue

Plato, *Meno*, 71-72, in *The Dialogues of Plato, op. cit.*, II, pp. 28-29, 31.

Meno. Can you tell me, Socrates, whether virtue is acquired by teaching or by practice; or if neither by teaching nor practice, then whether it comes to man by nature, or in what other way?

Socrates. . . . I am certain that if you were to ask any Athenian whether virtue was natural or acquired, he would laugh in your face, and say: "Stranger, you have far too good an opinion of me, if you think that I can answer your question. For I literally do not know what virtue is, and much less whether it is acquired by teaching or not." And I myself, Meno, living as I do in this region of poverty, am as poor as the rest of the world; and I confess with shame that I know literally nothing about virtue; and when I do not know the 'quid' of anything how can I know the 'quale'? . . .

Men. . . . But are you in earnest, Socrates, in saying that you do not know what virtue is? And am I to carry back this report of you to Thessaly?

Soc. Not only that, my dear boy, but you may say further that I have never known of any one else who did, in my judgment.

Men. Then you have never met Gorgias when he was at Athens?

Soc. Yes, I have.

Men. And did you not think that he knew?

Soc. I have not a good memory, Meno, and therefore I cannot now tell what I thought of him at the time. And I dare say that he did know, and that you know what he said: please, therefore, to remind me of what he said; or, if you would rather, tell me your own view; for I suspect that you and he think much alike.

Men. Very true.

Soc. Then as he is not here, never mind him, and do you tell me: By the gods, Meno, be generous, and tell me what you say that virtue is; for I shall be truly delighted to find that I have been mistaken, and that you and Gorgias do really have this knowledge; although I have been just saying that I have never found anybody who had.

Men. There will be no difficulty, Socrates, in answering your question. Let us take first the virtue of a man—he should know how to administer the state, and in the administration of it to benefit his friends and harm his enemies; and he must also be careful not to suffer harm himself. A woman's virtue, if you wish to know about that, may also be easily described: her duty is to order her house, and keep what is indoors, and obey her husband. Every age, every condition of life, young or old, male or female, bond or free, has a different virtue: there are virtues numberless, and no lack of definitions of them; for virtue is relative to the actions and ages of each of us in all that we do. And the same may be said of vice, Socrates.[1]

Soc. How fortunate I am, Meno! When I ask you for one virtue, you present me with a swarm of them,[2] which are in your keeping. Suppose that I carry on the figure of the swarm, and ask of you, What is the nature of the bee? and you answer that there are many kinds of bees, and I reply: But do bees differ as bees, because there are many and different kinds of them; or are they not rather to be distinguished by some other quality, as for example beauty, size, or shape? How would you answer me?

Men. I should answer that bees do not differ from one another, as bees.

Soc. And if I went on to say: That is what I desire to know, Meno; tell me what is the quality in which they do not differ, but are all alike; —would you be able to answer?

Men. I should.

Soc. And so of the virtues, however many and different they may be, they have all a common nature which makes them virtues; and on this he who would answer the question, "What is virtue?" would do well to have his eye fixed: Do you understand?

Men. I am beginning to understand; but. . . .

Men. Why, Socrates, even now I am not able to follow you in the attempt to get at one common notion of virtue as of other things.

Soc. No wonder; but I will try to get nearer if I can, for you know that all things have a common notion. . . .

The Accusations against Socrates

Plato, *Apology*, 17-20, 22-24, 26-28, in *The Dialogues of Plato, op. cit.*, II, pp. 109-112, 115-116, 118-121.

. . . If I defend myself in my accustomed manner, and you hear me using

[1] Cp. Arist. *Pol.* i, 13, §10.
[2] Cp. *Theaet.* 146 D.

the words which I have been in the habit of using in the Agora, at the tables of the money-changers, or anywhere else, I would ask you not to be surprised, and not to interrupt me on this account. For I am more than seventy years of age, and appearing now for the first time in a court of law, I am quite a stranger to the language of the place; and therefore I would have you regard me as if I were really a stranger, whom you would excuse if he spoke in his native tongue, and after the fashion of his country:—Am I making an unfair request of you? Never mind the manner, which may or may not be good; but think only of the truth of my words, and give heed to that: let the speaker speak truly and the judge decide justly. . . .

I will begin at the beginning, and ask what is the accusation which has given rise to the slander of me, and in fact has encouraged Meletus to prefer this charge against me. Well, what do the slanderers say? They shall be my prosecutors, and I will sum up their words in an affidavit: "Socrates is an evil-doer, and a curious person, who searches into things under the earth and in heaven, and he makes the worse appear the better cause; and he teaches the aforesaid doctrines to others." Such is the nature of the accusation. . . . But the simple truth is, O Athenians, that I have nothing to do with physical speculations. . . .

As little foundation is there for the report that I am a teacher, and take money; this accusation has no more truth in it than the other. Although, if a man were really able to instruct mankind, to receive money for giving instruction would, in my opinion, be an honour to him. There is Gorgias of Leontium, and Prodicus of Ceos, and Hippias of Elis, who go the round of the cities, and are able to persuade the young men to leave their own citizens by whom they might be taught for nothing, and come to them whom they not only pay, but are thankful if they may be allowed to pay them. . . . Happy is Evenus, I said to myself, if he really has this wisdom [of human and political virtue] and teaches at such a moderate charge [five minae]. Had I the same, I should have been very proud and conceited; but the truth is that I have no knowledge of the kind.

I dare say, Athenians, that some one among you will reply, "Yes, Socrates, but what is the origin of these accusations which are brought against you; there must have been something strange which you have been doing? All these rumours and this talk about you would never have arisen if you had been like other men: tell us, then, what is the cause of them, for we should be sorry to judge hastily of you." Now I regard this as a fair challenge, and I will endeavour to explain to you the reason why I am called wise and have such an evil fame. . . .

This inquisition [of politicans, philosophers, poets, and artisans to find out the meaning of the Delphian oracle that Socrates was the wisest of men] has led to my having many enemies of the worst and most dangerous kind, and has given occasion also to many calumnies. And I am called wise, for my hearers always imagine that I myself possess the wisdom which I find wanting in others: but the truth is, O men of Athens, that God only is wise; and by his answer he intends to show that the wisdom of men is worth little or nothing; he is not speaking of Socrates, he is only using my name by way of illustration, as if he said, He, O men, is the wisest, who, like Socrates, knows that his wisdom is in truth worth nothing. And so I go about the world, obedient to the god, and search and make enquiry into the wisdom of any one, whether citizen or stranger, who appears to be wise; and if he is not wise; and my occupation quite absorbs me, and I have no time to give either to any public matter of interest or to any concern of my own, but I am in utter poverty by reason of my devotion to the god.

There is another thing:—young men of the richer classes, who have not much to do, come about me of their own accord; they like to hear the pretenders examined, and they often imitate me, and proceed to examine others; there are plenty of persons, as they quickly discover, who think that they know something, but really know little or nothing; and then those who are examined by them instead of being angry with themselves are angry with me: This confounded Socrates, they say; this villainous misleader of youth!—and then if somebody asks them, Why, what evil does he practise or teach? they do not know, and cannot tell; but in order that they may not appear to be at a loss, they repeat the ready-made charges which are used against all philosophers about teaching things up in the clouds and under the earth, and having no gods, and making the worse appear the better cause; for they do not like to confess that their pretence of knowledge has been detected—which is the truth; and as they are numerous and ambitious and energetic, and are drawn up in battle array and have persuasive tongues, they have filled your ears with their loud and inveterate calumnies. And this is the reason why my three accusers, Meletus and Anytus and Lycon, have set upon me; Meletus, who has a quarrel with me on behalf of the poets; Anytus, on behalf of the craftsmen and politicians; Lycon, on behalf of the rhetoricians: and as I said at the beginning, I cannot expect to get rid of such a mass of calumny all in a moment. And this, O men of Athens, is the truth and the whole truth; I have concealed nothing, I have dissembled nothing. And yet, I know that my plainness of speech makes them hate me, and what is their hatred but a proof that I am speaking the truth?—Hence has arisen the prejudice against me; and this is the reason of it, as you will find out either in this or in any future enquiry.

I have said enough in my defence against the first class of my accusers; I turn to the second class. They are headed by Meletus, that good man and true lover of his country, as he calls himself. Against these, too, I must try to make a defence:—Let their affidavit be read: it contains something of this kind: It says that Socrates is a doer of evil, who corrupts the youth; and who does not believe in the gods of the state, but has other new divinities of his own. Such is the charge; . . .

It will be very clear to you, Athenians, as I was saying, that Meletus has no care at all, great or small, about the matter. But still I should like to know, Meletus, in what I am affirmed to corrupt the young. I suppose you mean, as I infer from your indictment, that I teach them not to acknowledge the gods which the state acknowledges, but some other new divinities or spiritual agencies in their stead. These are the lessons by which I corrupt the youth, as you say.

Yes, that I say emphatically.

Then, by the gods, Meletus, of whom we are speaking, tell me and the court, in somewhat plainer terms, what you mean! for I do not as yet understand whether you affirm that I teach other men to acknowledge some gods, and therefore that I do believe in gods, and am not an entire atheist—this you do not lay to my charge,—but only you say that they are not the same gods which the city recognizes—the charge is that they are different gods. Or, do you mean that I am an atheist simply, and a teacher of atheism?

I mean the latter—that you are a complete atheist.

. . . For he certainly does appear to me to contradict himself in the indictment as much as if he said that Socrates is guilty of not believing in the gods, and yet of believing in them—but this is not like a person who is in earnest.

I should like you, O men of Athens, to join me in examining what I conceive to be his inconsistency; and do you, Meletus, answer. And I must remind the audience of my request that they would not make a disturbance if I speak in my accustomed manner: . . .

. . . Such nonsense, Meletus, could only have been intended by you to make trial of me. You have put this into the indictment because you had nothing real of which to accuse me. But no one who has a particle of understanding will ever be convinced by you that the same men can believe in divine and superhuman things, and yet not believe that there are gods and demigods and heroes.

I have said enough in answer to the charge of Meletus: any elaborate defence is unnecessary; but I know only too well how many are the enmities which I have incurred, and this is what will be my destruction if I am destroyed;—not Meletus, nor yet Anytus, but the envy and detraction of the world, which has been the death of many good men, and will probably be the death of many more; there is no danger of my being the last of them.

Some one will say: And are you not ashamed, Socrates, of a course of life which is likely to bring you to an untimely end? To him I may fairly answer: There you are mistaken: a man who is good for anything ought not to calculate the chance of living or dying; he ought only to consider whether in doing anything he is doing right or wrong—acting the part of a good man or of a bad. . . .

. . .—if you say to me, Socrates, this time we will not mind Anytus, and you shall be let off, but upon one condition, that you are not to enquire and speculate in this way any more, and that if you are caught doing so again you shall die;—if this was the condition on which you let me go, I should reply: Men of Athens, I honour and love you; but I shall obey God rather than you, and while I have life and strength I shall never cease from the practice and teaching of philosophy, exhorting any one whom I meet and saying to him after my manner: You, my friend,—a citizen of the great and mighty and wise city of Athens,—are you not ashamed of heaping up the greatest amount of money and honour and reputation, and caring so little about wisdom and truth and the greatest improvement of the soul, which you never regard or heed at all? . . . For know that this is the command of God; and I believe that no greater good has ever happened in the state than my service to the God. For I do nothing but go about persuading you all, old and young alike, not to take thought for your persons or your properties, but first and chiefly to care about the greatest improvement of the soul. I tell you that virtue is not given by money, but that from virtue comes money and every other good of man, public as well as private. This is my teaching, and if this is the doctrine which corrupts the youth, I am a mischievous person. But if any one says that this is not my teaching, he is speaking an untruth. Wherefore, O men of Athens, I say to you, do as Anytus bids or not as Anytus bids, and either acquit me or not; but whichever you do, understand that I shall never alter my ways, not even if I have to die many times.

. . . I would have you know, that if you kill such an one as I am, you will injure yourselves more than you will injure me. . . .

And now, Athenians, I am not going to argue for my own sake, as you may think, but for yours, that you may not sin against the God by condemning me, who am his gift to you. For if you kill me you will not easily find a successor to me, who, if I may use such a ludicrous figure of speech, am a sort of gadfly, given to the state by God; and the state is a great and noble steed who is tardy in his motions owing to his very size, and requires to be stirred into life. I am that gadfly which God has attached to the state, and all day long and in all places am always fastening upon you, arousing and persuading and reproaching you. You will not easily find another like me, and therefore I would advise you to spare me. I dare say that you may feel out of temper (like a person who is suddenly awakened from sleep), and you think that you might easily strike me dead as Anytus advises, and then you would sleep on for the remainder of your lives, unless God in his care of you sent you another gadfly. When I say that I am given to you by God, the proof of my mission is this:—if I had been like other men, I should not have neglected all my own concerns or patiently seen the neglect of them during all these years, and have been doing yours, coming to you individually like a father or elder brother, exhorting you to regard virtue; such conduct, I say, would be unlike human nature. If I had gained anything, or if my exhortations had been paid, there would have been some sense in my doing so; but now, as you will perceive, not even the impudence of my accusers dares to say that I have ever exacted or sought pay of any one; of that they have no witness. And I have a sufficient witness to the truth of what I say — my poverty.

. . . I have been always the same in all my actions, public as well as private, and never have I yielded any base compliance to those who are slanderously termed my disciples, not that I have any regular disciples. But if any one likes to come and hear me while I am pursuing my mission, whether he be young or old, he is not excluded. Nor do I converse only with those who pay; but any one, whether he be rich or poor, may ask and answer me and listen to my words; and whether he turns out to be a bad man or a good one, neither result can be justly imputed to me; for I never taught or professed to teach him anything. And if anyone says that he has ever learned or heard anything from me in private which all the world has not heard, let me tell you that he is lying.

. . . and if I say again that daily to discourse about virtue, and of those other things about which you hear me examining myself and others, is the greatest good of man, and that the unexamined life is not worth living, you are still less likely to believe me. Yet I say what is true, although a thing of which it is hard for me to persuade you. . . .
. . . The difficulty, my friends, is not to avoid death, but to avoid unrighteousness; for that runs faster than death. I am old and move slowly, and the slower runner has overtaken me, and my accusers are keen and quick, and the faster runner, who is unrighteousness, has overtaken them. And now I depart hence condemned by you to suffer the penalty of death,—they too go their ways condemned by the truth to suffer the penalty of villainy and wrong; and I must abide by my

award—let them abide by theirs. I suppose that these things may be regarded as fated,—and I think that they are well.

. . . Me you have killed because you wanted to escape the accuser, and not to give an account of your lives. . . . If you think that by killing men you can prevent some one from censuring your evil lives, you are mistaken; that is not a way of escape which is either possible or honourable; the easiest and noblest way is not to be disabling others, but to be improving yourselves. . . .

Wherefore, O judges, be of good cheer about death, and know of a certainty, that no evil can happen to a good man, either in life or after death. He and his are not neglected by the gods; nor has his own approaching end happened by mere chance. . . .

Still I have a favour to ask of them ["my condemners, my accusers"]. When my sons ["three in number, one almost a man, hand two others who are still young"—one of whom is a child in his mother's arms] are grown up, I would ask you, O my friends, to punish them; and I would have you trouble them, as I have troubled you, if they seem to care about riches, or anything, more than about virtue; or if they pretend to be something when they are really nothing,—then reprove them, as I have reproved you, for not caring about that for which they ought to care, and thinking that they are something when they are really nothing. And if you do this, both I and my sons will have received justice at your hands.

The hour of departure has arrived, and we go our ways—I to die, and you to live. Which is better God only knows.

The Midwife of Knowledge

Plato, *Theaetetus*, 148-152, in *The Dialogues of Plato, op. cit.,* IV, pp. 201-205.

Soc. Well, then, be of good cheer; do not say that Theodorus was mistaken about you, but do your best to ascertain the true nature of knowledge, as well as of other things.

Theaet. I am eager enough, Socrates, if that would bring to light the truth.

Soc. Come, you made a good beginning just now; let your own answer about roots be your model, and as you comprehended them all in one class, try and bring the many sorts of knowledge under one definition.

Theaet. I can assure you, Socrates, that I have tried very often, when the report of questions asked by you was brought to me; but I can neither persuade myself that I have a satisfactory answer to give, nor hear of any one who answers as you would have him; and I cannot shake off a feeling of anxiety.

Soc. These are the pangs of labour, my dear Theaetetus; you have something within you which you are bringing to the birth.

Theaet. I do not know, Socrates; I only say what I feel.

Soc. And have you never heard, simpleton, that I am the son of a midwife, brave and burly, whose name was Phaenarete?

Theaet. Yes, I have.

Soc. And that I myself practise midwifery?

Theaet. No, never.

Soc. Let me tell you that I do though, my friend: but you must not reveal the secret, as the world in general have not found me out; and therefore they only say of me, that I am the strangest of mortals and drive men to their wits' end. Did you ever hear that too?

Theaet. Yes.

Soc. Shall I tell you the reason?

Theaet. By all means.

Soc. Bear in mind the whole business of the midwives, and then you will see my meaning better:—No woman, as you are probably aware, who is still able to conceive and bear, attends other women, but only those who are past bearing.

Theaet. Yes, I know.

Soc. The reason of this is said to be that Artemis—the goddess of childbirth—is not a mother, and she honours those who are like herself; but she could not allow the barren to be midwives, because human nature cannot know the mystery of an art without experience; and therefore she assigned this office to those who are too old to bear.

Theaet. I dare say.

Soc. And I dare say too, or rather I am absolutely certain, that the midwives know better than others who is pregnant and who is not?

Theaet. Very true.

Soc. And by the use of potions and incantations they are able to arouse the pangs and to soothe them at will; they can make those bear who have a difficulty in bearing, and if they think fit they can smother the embryo in the womb.

Theaet. They can.

Soc. Did you ever remark that they are also most cunning match-makers, and have a thorough knowledge of what unions are likely to produce a brave brood?

Theaet. No, never.

Soc. Then let me tell you that this is their greatest pride, more than cutting the umbilical cord. And if you reflect, you will see that the same art which cultivates and gathers in the fruits of the earth, will be most likely to know in what soils the several plants or seeds should be deposited.

Theaet. Yes, the same art.

Soc. And do you suppose that with women the case is otherwise?

Theaet. I should think not.

Soc. Certainly not; but midwives are respectable women who have a character to lose, and they avoid this department of their profession, because they are afraid of being called procuresses, which is a name given to those who join together man and woman in an unlawful and unscientific way; and yet the true midwife is also the true and only matchmaker.

Theaet. Clearly.

Soc. Such are the midwives, whose task is a very important one, but not so important as mine; for women do not bring into the world at one time real children, and at another time counterfeits which are with difficulty distinguished from them; if they did, then the discernment of the true and false birth would be the crowning achievement of the art of midwifery—you would think so?

Theaet. Indeed I should

Soc. Well, my art of midwifery is in most respects like theirs; but differs, in that I attend men and not women, and I look after their souls when they are in labour, and not after their bodies: and the triumph of my art is in thoroughly examining whether the thought which the mind of the young man brings forth is a false idol or a noble and true birth. And like the midwives, I am barren, and the reproach which is often made against me, that I ask questions of others and have not the wit to answer them myself, is very just—the reason is, that the god compels me to be a midwife, but does not allow me to bring forth. And therefore I am not myself at all wise, nor have I anything to show which is the invention or birth of my own soul, but those who converse with me profit. Some of them appear dull enough at first, but afterwards, as our acquaintance ripens, if the god is gracious to them, they all make astonishing progress; and this is in the opinion of others as well as in their own. It is quite clear that they never learned anything from me; the many fine discoveries to which they cling are of their own making. But to me and the god they owe their delivery. And the proof of my words is, that many of them in their ignorance, either in their self-conceit despising me, or falling under the influence of others,[1] have gone away too soon; and have not only lost the children of whom I had previously delivered them by an ill bringing up, but have stifled whatever else

---

[1] Reading with the Bodleian ms.

they had in them by evil communications, being fonder of lies and shams than of the truth; and they have at last ended by seeing themselves, as others see them, to be great fools. Aristeides, the son of Lysimachus, is one of them, and there are many others. The truants often return to me, and beg that I would consort with them again—they are ready to go to me on their knees—and then, if my familiar allows, which is not always the case, I receive them, and they begin to grow again. Dire are the pangs which my art is able to arouse and to allay in those who consort with me, just like the pangs of women in childbirth; night and day they are full of perplexity and travail which is even worse than that of the women. So much for them. And there are others, Theaetetus, who come to me apparently having nothing in them; and as I know that they have no need of my art, I coax them into marrying some one, and by the grace of God I can generally tell who is likely to do them good. Many of them I have given away to Prodicus, and many to other inspired sages. I tell you this long story, friend Theaetetus, because I suspect, as indeed you seem to think yourself, that you are in labour—great with some conception. Come then to me, who am a midwife's son and myself a midwife, and do your best to answer the questions which I will ask you. And if I abstract and expose your first-born, because I discover upon inspection that the conception which you have formed is a vain shadow, do not quarrel with me on that account, as the manner of women is when their first children are taken from them. For I have actually known some who were ready to bite me when I deprived them of a darling folly; they did not perceive that I acted from goodwill, not knowing that no god is the enemy of man— that was not within the range of their ideas; neither am I their enemy in all this, but it would be wrong for me to admit falsehood, or to stifle the truth. Once more, then, Theaetetus, I repeat my old question, "What is knowledge?"—and do not say that you cannot tell; but quit yourself like a man, and by the help of God you will be able to tell.

Theaet. At any rate, Socrates, after such an exhortation I should be ashamed of not trying to do my best. Now he who knows perceives what he knows, and, as far as I can see at present, knowledge is perception.

Soc. Bravely said, boy; that is the way in which you should express your opinion. And now, let us examine together this conception of yours, and see whether it is a true birth or a mere wind-egg:—You say that knowledge is perception?

Theaet. Yes.

Soc. Well, you have delivered yourself of a very important doctrine about knowledge; it is indeed the opinion of Protagoras, who has another way of expressing it. Man, he says, is the measure of all things, of the existence of things that are, and of the non-existence of things that are not:—You have read him?

Theaet. O yes, again and again.

Soc. Does he not say that things are to you such as they appear to you, and to me such as they appear to me, and that you and I are men?

Theaet. Yes, he says so.

Soc. A wise man is not likely to talk nonsense. Let us try to understand him. . . .

19
Plato (428/7-348/7 B.C.)
Education in the *Republic*

Selections from Plato's *Republic* in *The Dialogues of Plato, op. cit.*, III, pp. 208-229. Introduction, Summary to VI, 508 and Epilogue by Hugh C. Black. Stephanus pagination numbers have been inserted at the beginning of the nearest paragraph. Because of this there may be a one-page inaccuracy in some instances.

When Plato has Socrates say: ". . . as concerning justice, what is it? . . ." (I, 331), he introduces us to the eternal questions of a quest which is as much ours as his. The result is a classic of European literature, a treatise which begins with political problems, leads to ethics, and makes education central. "Plato saw," observed Sir Richard Livingstone (*Plato & Modern Education*, Macmillan, 1944, p. 28), "that the fate of any political scheme depended on the character of those who worked it, that characters were not born but made, and that they are made through education; but only through an education which leads up to the vision that he called the Idea of the Good and which is never far from it." We may agree or not with Livingstone's belief that "The main difference between Plato's conception of education and our own is that his concern was to impart values, ours is to impart knowledge and teach people to think" (*Ibid.*, p. 32). But in this outline of how things might be in the ideal scheme of the *Republic*, Plato states the questions which we are challenged to answer. For we also quest after "that which sheds light on all things" that we may have a pattern by which to order our lives both individual and social. And that is what the *Republic* is about.

In *Euthyphro* Plato had Socrates say:

> I want to know what is the idea of piety which makes all pious actions pious . . . explain to me what is this idea, that I may have it to turn to, and to use as a standard whereby to judge your actions and those of other men, and be able to say that whatever action resembles it is pious, and whatever does not, is not pious (6 d, e).

In the *Republic* Plato inquires into the nature of "absolute justice and into the character of the perfectly just, and into injustice and the perfectly unjust, that we might have an ideal." He has Socrates say:

> We were to look at these in order that we might judge of our own happiness and unhappiness according to the standard

133

which they exhibited and the degree in which we resembled them, but not with any view of showing that they could exist in fact (V, 472).

This is the ideal of knowing the nature of justice and injustice so that "the meaning of acting unjustly and being unjust, or, again, of acting justly, will also be perfectly clear" (IV, 444). Although the actual falls short of the truth and ideals may never be fully realized, the attempt to achieve this knowledge is the way to create an ideal of a perfect state and a perfect life.

This quest begins with the diversities of current opinion about justice in Book I. The elderly Cephalus sees justice as nothing more than "to speak the truth and to pay your debts" (I, 331); Polemarchus, as "the art which gives good to friends and evil to enemies" (I, 332); and Thrasymachus, as "the interest of the stronger" (I, 338). The dialogue turns to a consideration of Thrasymachus' statement that "the life of the unjust is more advantageous than that of the just" (I, 347), and Book I ends with Socrates saying: "And the result of the whole discussion has been that I know nothing at all. For I know not what justice is, and therefore I am not likely to know whether it is or is not a virtue, nor can I say whether the just man is happy or unhappy." Book II turns the inquiry to the subject of justice in the state and in the individual which continues through Book IV. What is the true principle by which our individual and community lives should be ordered if we are to live best? In discovering and setting forth this principle and the ideal form society should take, Plato outlines an educational scheme which he later criticizes as insufficient, modifies somewhat, and advances into a different scheme set forth in Books V, VI, and VII. In the latter, according to Richard Lewis Nettleship (*The Theory of Education in the Republic of Plato*, Chicago, University of Chicago Press, 1906, p. 93), "the question for Plato becomes that of 'What is the education by which the human mind may be brought nearer to that truth which is at once the keystone of knowledge and the pole star of conduct?'" The ideally best condition of individual and social life arises from a right education described in Books V, VI, and VII in which the best elements rule in a harmonious cooperation for the good of the whole. In the remaining third section, especially Books VIII and IX, Plato describes "the descent" of man and state when this aristocratic system goes awry under the bad influences of environment and the lower nature takes over the higher. That is the over-all structure of the *Republic*.

In Book II Plato seeks to discover the nature of justice by looking for it in the larger unit of the state as an aid in locating it in the smaller setting of the individual. According to Plato, the basis for the evolution of a state lies in the fact that no individual is self-sufficing. Each individual is born with innate differences by which he is peculiarly fitted for a particular occupation in life. All individuals are alike in that we have many needs, but each individual is different from all others and is best fitted by nature to do only one thing, to satisfy best only one need. When several individuals come together in one place to help satisfy the needs of each other, a state evolves. In Plato's words:

> A State, I said, arises, as I conceive, out of the needs of mankind; no one is self-sufficing, but all of us have many wants. . . . Then, as we have many wants, and many persons are needed to supply them, one takes a helper for one purpose and another for another; and when these partners and helpers are gathered together in one habitation the body of inhabitants is termed a State (II, 369).

Specialization, then, is one characteristic of the state. This follows for the reason that

> . . . all things are produced more plentifully and easily and of a better quality when one man does one thing which is natural to him and does it at the right time, and leaves other things (II, 370).

From this Plato concludes that the society of the ideal state will be composed of several classes or orders. Those of the lower order, such as farmers, artisans, and traders, will perform their function of satisfying the economic needs of the entire state. Those of the second order, the Auxiliaries or warriors, will perform the necessary function of maintaining internal order, of subordinating and controlling the lower class, and of warding off invasion from without. Those of the higher order, Guardians or philosopher rulers, the eldest and best, will perform their proper function of governing. In such a state everything would be ordered with a view to the good of the whole; there we would most likely find justice and happiness for the community as a whole (IV, 420).

Foreseeing that his ideal society might be inundated by certain waves and that the aim for the good of all might be destroyed by the temptation of private interests, Plato abolished private property and families for the warrior class, provided for equal responsibility of women with men in sharing public duties, and established co-education.

In such a society, it might be asked, what is civic or popular virtue or righteousness? Wherein consist the wisdom, courage, temperance, and justice of the individuals composing the state in their capacity as citizens? According to Plato, wisdom consists in the prudent and wise leadership of the few who take the lead and govern the rest without thought for some particular interest but with thought "for the best possible conduct of the state as a whole in its internal and external relations." Courage consists in the conviction, inculcated by lawfully established education, about the sort of things which may rightly be feared. Said Plato:

> The city will be courageous in virtue of a portion of herself which preserves under all circumstances that opinion about the nature of things to be feared and not to be feared in which our legislator educated them; and this is what you term courage (IV, 429).

Temperance consists in a control of pleasures and desires, in society's mastery of itself, in the desires of the inferior multitude being controlled by the desires and wisdom of the superior few. It is a kind of harmony which pervades and unites all the parts of the whole, a kind of orderliness in which there is control of the lower by the higher. Justice consists in each one doing his own proper work. When each of the three classes of society keeps to its own proper business in the commonwealth and does its own work, that is justice and what makes a just society.

Since the community is the individual "writ large," similar qualities of righteousness may be found in the individual. Just as the state contains three orders to hold it together, so, too, does the soul contain three elements: the rational, the appetitive, and the "spirited" ("the natural auxiliary of reason, when not corrupted by bad upbringing"). The individual in whom these several qualities of his nature do their own work will be just.

> And ought not the rational principle, which is wise, and has the care of the whole soul, to rule, and the passionate or spirited principle to be the subject and ally? . . .
>
> Both together will they not be the best defenders of the whole soul and the whole body against attacks from without; the one counselling, and the other fighting under his leader, and courageously executing his commands and counsels?
>
> True.
>
> And he is to be deemed courageous whose spirit retains in pleasure and in pain the commands of reason about what he ought or ought not to fear?
>
> Right, he replied.
>
> And him we call wise who has in him that little part which rules, and which proclaims these commands; that part

too being supposed to have a knowledge of what is for the interest of each of the three parts and of the whole?

Assuredly.

And would you not say that he is temperate who has these same elements in friendly harmony, in whom the one ruling principle of reason, and the two subject ones of spirit and desire are equally agreed that reason ought to rule, and do not rebel?

Certainly, he said, . . . (IV, 442).

Such is Plato's analysis of the human soul, of personality, of the ideal virtues which should be the product of education. Its relevance to leaders in education has been best expressed long ago when Nettleship (*op. cit.*, p. 26) wrote:

. . . whatever we may think of his analysis of the soul in its details, we shall hardly escape the conclusion that some such analysis is an indispensable condition of a really rational theory of education; in other words, that neither a state nor an individual can undertake to educate in a systematic way unless they start with some idea, not only of what they wish to teach, nor only of the type of character which they wish to produce, but also of the living being to which the matter to be taught is relative, and upon which the given character is to be impressed.

About that, Plato is specific and clear:

But in reality justice was such as we were describing, being concerned however, not with the outward man, but with the inward, which is the true self and concernment of man: for the just man does not permit the several elements within him to interfere with one another, or any of them to do the work of others,—he sets in order his own inner life, and is his own master and his own law, and at peace with himself; and when he has bound together the three principles within him, which may be compared to the higher, lower, and middle notes of the scale, and the intermediate intervals—when he has bound all these together, and is no longer many, but has become one entirely temperate and perfectly adjusted nature, then he proceeds to act, if he has to act, whether in a matter of property, or in the treatment of the body, or in some affair of politics or private business; always thinking and calling that which preserves and co-operates with this harmonious condition, just and good action, and the knowledge which presides over it, wisdom, and that which at any time impairs this condition, he will call unjust action, and the opinion which presides over it ignorance (IV, 443, Jowett).

Plato's notion of injustice, the opposite of justice, might well be noted here; for it also is useful to us in understanding later parts of the *Republic* which describe "the descent" of man and of society.

> Must not injustice be a strife which arises among the three principles—a meddlesomeness, and interference, and rising up of a part of the soul against the whole, an assertion of unlawful authority, which is made by a rebellious subject against a true prince, of whom he is the natural vassal,—what is all this confusion and delusion but injustice, and intemperance and cowardice and ignorance, and every form of vice? Exactly so (IV, 444).

With Plato, the ideal for the individual is that of virtue "the health and beauty and well-being of the soul" (IV, 444) rather than vice ("the disease and weakness and deformity" of the soul). The impelling demand is the creation of justice by instituting order in the parts of the soul to effect the well-being of the individual. Moreover, education and nurture become "the one great principle" (IV, 423) for establishing the harmony and order requisite to the good state, the good society. The aim is to develop good individuals who are efficient in their citizenship and strive to realize the good of the whole, the public welfare.

It is important then to begin early with character education in the form of ideal religious and moral presentations through literature. If the future citizens are to be "men who reverence God and are like God as far as it is possible for man to be so" (II, 383, Nettleship, p. 39), "to honour the gods and their parents, and to value friendship with one another" (III, 386, Jowett), then habitually the youth should have placed before their minds "the true nature of God and of what is most godlike in man" (Nettleship, p. 31). If the moral ideals of man's "whole duty to man" is honor to parents, love of fellow-citizens, courage, truthfulness, and self-control (Nettleship, p. 39), the poets must trace them out in the lives and actions of national heroes and great men and these only, not the calumnies of popular literature, be presented to the young. Obviously then the education in "music for the soul" which Plato places before "gymnastic for the body" entails censorship and control.

> And shall we just carelessly allow children to hear any casual tales which may be devised by casual persons, and to receive into their minds ideas for the most part the very opposite of

those which we should wish them to have when they are grown up?

We cannot.

Then the first thing will be to establish a censorship of the writers of fiction, and let the censors receive any tale of fiction which is good, and reject the bad; and we will desire mothers and nurses to tell their children the authorised ones only. Let them fashion the mind with such tales, even more fondly than they mould the body with their hands; but most of those which are now in use must be discarded (II, 377).

The process of this educational plan has been summarized in these words:

The child is to be bred up in the belief that beings greater and better than himself have behaved in a certain way, and his natural impulse to imitate is thus to be utilized in forming his own character (Nettleship, p. 32).

The objective, according to the same scholar, is to lay a foundation of character "which will not have to be cut away as years go on, but will invite and sustain the superstructure of manhood" (Nettleship, p. 31). Impress most deeply on the minds of children those ideas we should wish them to retain when they are grown up. This process entails exposure through a deliberate process of education and nurture, a superintendence over the young by the elders, even, as we have quoted, a censorship. Plato advocates a musical education which properly should infuse a spirit of order and develop the "true love" of beauty. And Plato "demanded an art which should not merely stimulate, but should also discipline, the feelings; which should not follow but lead them; which should chasten their disorder and brace their indolence by making them move in the delicate lines of proportion and beauty, and respond to the quiet emphasis of harmony and rhythm. For the balance and symmetry which are essential to good artistic work are also, he conceived, essential to true artistic feeling. Love is the typical feeling awakened by sensuous beauty, and the genuine love of genuine beauty is incompatible with ungoverned emotion" (Nettleship, pp. 63-64). As Plato himself put it:

We would not have our guardians grow up amid images of moral deformity, as in some noxious pasture, and there browse and feed upon many a baneful herb and flower day by day, little by little, until they silently gather a festering mass of corruption in their own soul. Let our artists rather be those who are gifted to discern the true nature of the beautiful and graceful; then will our youth dwell in a land of health, amid fair sights and sounds, and receive the good in everything; and beauty, the effluence of fair works shall flow into the eye and ear, like a health-giving breeze from a purer region, and insensibly draw the soul from earliest years into likeness and sympathy with the beauty of reason.

There can be no nobler training than that, he replied.

And therefore, I said, Glaucon, musical training is a more potent instrument than any other, because rhythm and harmony find their way into the inward places of the soul, on which they mightily fasten, imparting grace, and making the soul of him who is rightly educated graceful, or of him who is ill-educated ungraceful; and also because he who has received this true education of the inner being will most shrewdly perceive omissions or faults in art and nature, and with a true taste, while he praises and rejoices over and receives into his soul the good, and becomes noble and good, he will justly blame and hate the bad, now in the days of his youth, even before he is able to know the reason why; and when reason comes he will recognise and salute the friend with whom his education has made him long familiar (III, 401-402, Jowett).

The education in music and gymnastic is intended to establish in youngsters the habit of order. This shall constitute in them a *principle* of growth and make unnecessary attention to the small things which some schoolmen and parents put first in importance: as Plato states it, such details as ". . . when the young are to be silent before their elders; how they are to show respect to them by standing and making them sit; what honor is due to parents; what garments or shoes are to be worn; the mode of dressing the hair; deportment and manners in general" (IV, 425, Jowett).

Plato then turns to a second system of education which gives us an even more significant standard for education: that of understanding, of *knowledge* (of beauty and goodness), a vision of education as "the genuine study of the laws of nature and the world." This is the dynamic questing after ideals through knowledge, the pursuit and travail expressed in the words:

It is in the nature of the real lover of learning to be ever struggling up to being, and not to abide among the manifold and limited objects of opinion; he will go on his way, and the edge of his love will not grow dull nor its force abate, until he has got hold of the nature of being with that part of his soul to which it belongs so to do, and that is the part which is akin to being; with this he will draw near, and mingle being with being, and beget intelligence and truth, and find knowledge and true life and nourishment, and then, and not till then, he will cease from his travail (VI, 490 a-b, as translated by Nettleship, *op. cit.*, p. 24).

Plato's new insight into education is that well-being depends upon knowledge of the good which will yield understanding of the moral and physical order and harmony of the universe. This requires a specially selected student and a new kind of education:

Who is to do this questing? Not the many, but the few who may be turned to catch the vision of the good (like the sun) by taking "the longer road" through the four stages of cognition (the line)—a progression from unenlightenment of the mind to enlightenment and knowledge of the good illustrated in the allegory of the cave or den. Thus does the well-being of all and the realization of the ideal society depend upon the startling demand that philosophers become kings:

> *Until philosophers are kings, or the kings and princes of this world have the spirit and power of philosophy, and political greatness and wisdom meet in one, and those commoner natures who pursue either to the exclusion of the other are compelled to stand aside, cities will never have rest from their evils,—no, nor the human race, as I believe,—and then only will this our State have a possibility of life and behold the light of day* (V, 473, Jowett).

He it is who is called properly to seek the highest knowledge of all which is higher than justice and the other virtues: the idea of good. About this, there is a diversity of opinion: some holding that it is pleasure; others, that it is knowledge. We turn now to Plato's notions of it as he has Socrates discourse about sight, the eye, and the sun.

Plato, The Republic, *vi, 508-VII, 526*

VI, 508: Noble, then, is the bond which links together sight and visibility, and great beyond other bonds by no small difference of nature; for light is their bond, and light is no ignoble thing?

Nay, he said, the reverse of ignoble.

And which, I said, of the gods in heaven would you say was the lord of this element? Whose is that light which makes the eye to see perfectly and the visible to appear?

You mean the sun, as you and all mankind say.

May not the relation of sight to this deity be described as follows?

How?

Neither sight nor the eye in which sight resides is the sun?

No.

Yet of all the organs of sense the eye is the most like the sun?

By far the most like.

And the power which the eye possesses is a sort of effluence which is dispensed from the sun?

Exactly.

Then the sun is not sight, but the author of sight who is recognised by sight?

True, he said.

And this is he whom I call the child of the good, whom the good begat in his own likeness, to be in the visible world in relation to sight and the things of sight, what the good is in the intellectual world in relation to mind and the things of mind:

Will you be a little more explicit? he said.

Why, you know, I said, that the eyes, when a person directs them towards objects on which the light of day is no longer shining, but the moon and stars only, see dimly, and are nearly blind; they seem to have no clearness of vision in them?

Very true.

But when they are directed towards objects on which the sun shines, they see clearly and there is sight in them?

Certainly.

And the soul is like the eye: when resting upon that on which truth and being shine, the soul perceives and understands, and is radiant with intelligence; but when turned towards the twilight of becoming and perishing, then she has opinion only, and goes blinking about, and is first of one opinion and then of another, and seems to have no intelligence?

Just so.

509: Now, that which imparts truth to the known and the power of knowing to the knower is what I would have you term the idea of good, and this you will deem to be the cause of science,[1] and of truth in so far as the latter becomes the subject of knowledge; beautiful too, as are both truth and knowledge, you will be right in esteeming this other nature as more beautiful than either; and, as in the previous instance, light and sight may be truly said to be like the sun, and yet not to be the sun, so in this other sphere, science and truth may be deemed to be like the good, but not the good; the good has a place of honour yet higher.

[1] Reading διανοοῦ.

What a wonder of beauty that must be, he said, which is the author of science and truth, and yet surpasses them in beauty; for you surely cannot mean to say that pleasure is the good?

God forbid, I replied; but may I ask you to consider the image in another point of view?

In what point of view?

You would say, would you not, that the sun is not only the author of visibility in all visible things, but of generation and nourishment and growth, though he himself is not generation?

Certainly.

In like manner the good may be said to be not only the author of knowledge to all things known, but of their being and essence, and yet the good is not essence, but far exceeds essence in dignity and power.

Glaucon said, with a ludicrous earnestness: By the light of heaven, how amazing!

Yes, I said, there is a great deal more.

Then omit nothing, however slight.

I will do my best, I said; but I should think that a great deal will have to be omitted.

I hope not, he said.

You have to imagine, then, that there are two ruling powers, and that one of them is set over the intellectual world, the other over the visible. I do not say heaven, lest you should fancy that I am playing upon the name ($οὐραγός$, $ὁρατός$). May I suppose that you have this distinction of the visible and intelligible fixed in your mind?

I have.

510: Now take a line which has been cut into two unequal[1] parts, and divide each of them again in the same proportion, and suppose the two main divisions to answer, one to the visible and the other to the intelligible, and then compare the subdivisions in respect of their clearness and want of clearness, and you will find that the first section in the sphere of the visible consists of images. And by images I mean, in the first place, shadows, and in the second place, reflections in water and in solid, smooth and polished bodies and the like: Do you understand?

Yes, I understand.

Imagine, now, the other section, of which this is only the resemblance, to include the animals which we see, and everything that grows or is made.

Very good.

Would you not admit that both the sections of this division have

[1] Reading $ἄνισα$

different degrees of truth, and that the copy is to the original as the sphere of opinion is to the sphere of knowledge?

Most undoubtedly.

Next proceed to consider the manner in which the sphere of the intellectual is to be divided.

In what manner?

Thus:—There are two subdivisions, in the lower of which the soul uses the figures given by the former division as images; the enquiry can only be hypothetical, and instead of going upwards to a principle descends to the other end; in the higher of the two, the soul passes out of hypotheses, and goes up to a principle which is above hypotheses, making no use of images[2] as in the former case, but proceeding only in and through the ideas themselves.

I do not quite understand your meaning, he said.

Then I will try again; you will understand me better when I have made some preliminary remarks. You are aware that students of geometry, arithmetic, and the kindred sciences assume the odd and the even and the figures and three kinds of angles and the like in their several branches of science; these are their hypotheses, which they and every body are supposed to know, and therefore they do not deign to give any account of them either to themselves or others; but they begin with them, and go on until they arrive at last, and in a consistent manner, at their conclusion?

Yes, he said, I know.

And do you not know also that although they make use of the visible forms and reason about them, they are thinking not of these, but of the ideals which they resemble; not of the figures which they draw, but of the absolute square and the absolute diameter, and so on—the forms which they draw or make, and which they have shadows and reflections in water of their own, are converted by them into images, but they are really seeking to behold the things themselves which can only be seen with the eye of the mind?

That is true.

511: And of this kind I spoke as the intelligible, although in the search after it the soul is compelled to use hypotheses; not ascending to a first principle, because she is unable to rise above the region of hypothesis, but employing the objects of which the shadows below are resemblances in their turn as images, they having in relation to the shadows and reflections of them a greater distinctness, and therefore a higher value.

I understand, he said, that you are speaking of the province of geometry and the sister arts.

[2] Reading ὧνπερ ἐκεῖνο εἰκόνων.

And when I speak of the other division of the intelligible, you will understand me to speak of that other sort of knowledge which reason herself attains by the power of dialectic, using the hypotheses not as first principles, but only as hypotheses—that is to say, as steps and points of departure into a world which is above hypotheses, in order that she may soar beyond them to the first principle of the whole; and clinging to this and then to that which depends on this, by successive steps she descends again without the aid of any sensible object, from ideas, through ideas, and in ideas she ends.

I understand you, he replied; not perfectly, for you seem to me to be describing a task which is really tremendous; but, at any rate, I understand you to say that knowledge and being, which the science of dialectic contemplates, are clearer than the notions of the arts, as they are termed, which proceed from hypotheses only: these are also contemplated by the understanding, and not by the senses: yet, because they start from hypotheses and do not ascend to a principle, those who contemplate them appear to you not to exercise the higher reason upon them, although when a first principle is added to them they are cognizable by the higher reason. And the habit which is concerned with geometry and the cognate sciences I suppose that you would term understanding and not reason, as being intermediate between opinion and reason.

You have quite conceived my meaning, I said; and now, corresponding to these four divisions, let there be four faculties in the soul—reason answering to the highest, understanding to the second, faith (or conviction) to the third, and perception of shadows to the last—and let there be a scale of them, and let us suppose that the several faculties have clearness in the same degree that their objects have truth.

I understand, he replied, and give my assent, and accept your arrangement.

VII, Steph., 514: And now, I said, let me show in a figure how far our nature is enlightened or unenlightened:—Behold! human beings living in an underground den which has a mouth open towards the light and reaching all along the den; here they have been from their childhood, and have their legs and necks chained so that they cannot move, and can only see before them, being prevented by the chains from turning round their heads. Above and behind them a fire is blazing at a distance, and between the fire and the prisoners there is a raised way; and you will see, if you look, a low wall built along the way, like the screen which marionette players have in front of them, over which they show the puppets.

I see.

515: And do you see, I said, men passing along the wall carrying all sorts of vessels, and statues and figures of animals made of wood and stone and various materials, which appear over the wall? Some of them are talking, others silent.

You have shown me a strange image, and they are strange prisoners.

Like ourselves, I replied; and they see only their own shadows, or the shadows of one another, which the fire throws on the opposite wall of the cave?

True, he said; how could they see anything but the shadows if they were never allowed to move their heads?

And of the objects which are being carried in like manner they would only see the shadows?

Yes, he said.

And if they were able to converse with one another, would they not suppose that they were naming what was actually before them?[1]

Very true.

And suppose further that the prison had an echo which came from the other side, would they not be sure to fancy when one of the passers-by spoke that the voice which they heard came from the passing shadow?

No question, he replied.

To them, I said, the truth would be literally nothing but the shadows of the images.

That is certain.

And now look again, and see what will naturally follow if the prisoners are released and disabused of their error. At first, when any of them is liberated and compelled suddenly to stand up and turn his neck round and walk and look towards the light, he will suffer sharp pains; the glare will distress him, and he will be unable to see the realities of which in his former state he had seen the shadows; and then conceive some one saying to him, that what he saw before was an illusion, but that now, when he is approaching nearer to being and his eye is turned towards more real existence, he has a clearer vision,—what will be his reply? And you may further imagine that his instructor is pointing to the objects as they pass and requiring him to name them,— will he not be perplexed? Will he not fancy that the shadows which he formerly saw are truer than the objects which are now shown to him?

Far truer.

And if he is compelled to look straight at the light, will he not have a pain in his eyes which will make him turn away to take refuge in the objects of vision which he can see, and which he will conceive to be in reality clearer than the things which are now being shown to him?

[1] Reading παρόντα.

True, he said.

516: And suppose once more, that he is reluctantly dragged up a steep and rugged ascent, and held fast until he is forced into the presence of the sun himself, is he not likely to be pained and irritated? When he approaches the light his eyes will be dazzled, and he will not be able to see anything at all of what are now called realities.

Not all in a moment, he said.

He will require to grow accustomed to the sight of the upper world. And first he will see the shadows best, next the reflections of men and other objects in the water, and then the objects themselves; then he will gaze upon the light of the moon and the stars and the spangled heaven; and he will see the sky and the stars by night better than the sun or the light of the sun by day?

Certainly.

Last of all he will be able to see the sun, and not mere reflections of him in the water, but he will see him in his own proper place, and not in another; and he will contemplate him as he is.

Certainly.

He will then proceed to argue that this is he who gives the season and the years, and is the guardian of all that is in the visible world, and in a certain way the cause of all things which he and his fellows have been accustomed to behold?

Clearly, he said, he would first see the sun and then reason about him.

And when he remembered his old habitation, and the wisdom of the den and his fellow-prisoners, do you not suppose that he would felicitate himself on the change, and pity them?

Certainly, he would.

And if they were in the habit of conferring honours among themselves on those who were quickest to observe the passing shadows and to remark which of them went before, and which followed after, and which were together; and who were therefore best able to draw conclusions as to the future, do you think that he would care for such honours and glories, or envy the possessors of them? Would he not say with Homer,

"Better to be the poor servant of a poor master," and to endure anything, rather than think as they do and live after their manner?

Yes, he said, I think that he would rather suffer anything than entertain these false notions and live in this miserable manner.

Imagine once more, I said, such an one coming suddenly out of the sun to be replaced in his old situation; would he not be certain to have his eyes full of darkness?

To be sure, he said.

517: And if there were a contest, and he had to compete in measuring the shadows with the prisoners who had never moved out of the den, while his sight was still weak, and before his eyes had become steady (and the time which would be needed to acquire this new habit of sight might be very considerable), would he not be ridiculous? Men would say of him that up he went and down he came without his eyes; and that it was better not even to think of ascending; and if any one tried to loose another and lead him up to the light, let them only catch the offender, and they would put him to death.

No question, he said.

This entire allegory, I said, you may now append, dear Glaucon, to the previous argument; the prison-house is the world of sight, the light of the fire is the sun, and you will not misapprehend me if you interpret the journey upwards to be the ascent of the soul into the intellectual world according to my poor belief, which, at your desire, I have expressed—whether rightly or wrongly God knows. But whether true or false, my opinion is that in the world of knowledge the idea of good appears last of all, and is seen only with an effort; and, when seen, is also inferred to be the universal author of all things beautiful and right, parent of light and of the lord of light in this visible world, and the immediate source of reason and truth in the intellectual; and that this is the power upon which he who would act rationally either in public or private life must have his eye fixed.

I agree, he said, as far as I am able to understand you.

Moreover, I said, you must not wonder that those who attain to this beatific vision are unwilling to descend to human affairs; for their souls are ever hastening into the upper world where they desire to dwell; which desire of theirs is very natural, if our allegory may be trusted.

Yes, very natural.

And is there anything surprising in one who passes from divine contemplations to the evil state of man, misbehaving himself in a ridiculous manner; if, while his eyes are blinking and before he has become accustomed to the surrounding darkness, he is compelled to fight in courts of law, or in other places, about the images or the shadows of images of justice, and is endeavouring to meet the conceptions of those who have never yet seen absolute justice?

Anything but surprising, he replied.

518: Any one who has common sense will remember that the bewilderments of the eyes are of two kinds, and arise from two causes, either from coming out of the light or from going into the light, which is true of the mind's eye, quite as much as of the bodily eye; and he who remembers this when he sees any one whose vision is perplexed and weak, will not be too ready to laugh; he will first ask whether that soul of man has come out of the brighter life, and is unable to see because unaccustomed to the dark, or having turned from darkness to the day is dazzled by excess of light. And he will count the one happy in his condition and state of being, and he will pity the other; or, if he have a mind to laugh at the soul which comes from below into the light, there will be more reason in this than in the laugh which greets him who returns from above out of the light into the den.

That, he said, is a very just distinction.

But then, if I am right, certain professors of education must be wrong when they say that they can put a knowledge into the soul which was not there before, like sight into blind eyes.

They undoubtedly say this, he replied.

Whereas, our argument shows that the power and capacity of learning exists in the soul already; and that just as the eye was unable to turn from darkness to light without the whole body, so too the instrument of knowledge can only by the movement of the whole soul be turned from the world of becoming into that of being, and learn by degrees to endure the sight of being, and of the brightest and best of being, or in other words, of the good.

Very true.

And must there not be some art which will effect conversion in the easiest and quickest manner; not implanting the faculty of sight, for that exists already, but has been turned in the wrong direction, and is looking away from the truth?

Yes, he said, such an art may be presumed.

519: And whereas the other so-called virtues of the soul seem to be akin to bodily qualities, for even when they are not originally innate they can be implanted later by habit and exercise, the virtue of wisdom more than anything else contains a divine element which always remains, and by this conversion is rendered useful and profitable; or, on the other hand, hurtful and useless. Did you never observe the narrow intelligence flashing from the keen eye of a clever rogue—how eager he is, how clearly his paltry soul sees the way to his end; he is the reverse of blind, but his keen eye-sight is forced into the service of evil, and he is mischievous in proportion to his cleverness?

Very true, he said.

But what if there had been a circumcision of such natures in the days of their youth; and they had been severed from those sensual pleasures, such as eating and drinking, which, like leaden weights, were attached to them at their birth, and which drag them down and turn the vision of their souls upon the things that are below—if, I say, they had been released from these impediments and turned in the opposite direction, the very same faculty in them would have seen the truth as keenly as they see what their eyes are turned to now.

Very likely.

Yes, I said; and there is another thing which is likely, or rather a necessary inference from what has preceded, that neither the uneducated and uninformed of the truth, nor yet those who never make an end of their education, will be able ministers of State; not the former, because they have no single aim of duty which is the rule of all their actions, private as well as public; nor the latter, because they will not act at all except upon compulsion, fancying that they are already dwelling apart in the islands of the blest.

Very true, he replied.

Then, I said, the business of us who are the founders of the State will be to compel the best minds to attain that knowledge which we have already shown to be the greatest of all—they must continue to ascend until they arrive at the good; but when they have ascended and seen enough we must not allow them to do as they do now.

What do you mean?

I mean that they remain in the upper world: but this must not be allowed; they must be made to descend again among the prisoners in the den, and partake of their labours and honours, whether they are worth having or not.

But is not this unjust? he said; ought we to give them a worse life, when they might have a better?

520: You have again forgotten, my friend, I said, the intention of the legislator, who did not aim at making any one class in the State happy above the rest; the happiness was to be in the whole State, and he held the citizens together by persuasion and necessity, making them benefactors of the State, and therefore benefactors of one another; to this end he created them, not to please themselves, but to be his instruments in binding up the State.

True, he said, I had forgotten.

Observe, Glaucon, that there will be no injustice in compelling our philosophers to have a care and providence of others; we shall explain to them that in other States, men of their class are not obliged to share in the toils of politics: and this is reasonable, for they grow up at their own sweet will, and the government would rather not have them. Being self-taught, they cannot be expected to show any gratitude for a culture which they have never received. But we have brought you into the world to be rulers of the hive, kings of yourselves and of the other citizens, and have educated you far better and more perfectly than they have been educated, and you are better able to share in the double duty. Wherefore each of you, when his turn comes, must go down to the general underground abode, and get the habit of seeing in the dark. When you have acquired the habit, you will see ten thousand times better than the inhabitants of the den, and you will know what the several images are, and what they represent, because you have seen the beautiful and just and good in their truth. And thus our State, which is also yours, will be a reality, and not a dream only, and will be administered in a spirit unlike that of other States, in which men fight with one another about shadows only and are distracted in the struggle for power, which in their eyes is a great good. Whereas the truth is that the State in which the rulers are most reluctant to govern is always the best and most quietly governed, and the State in which they are most eager, the worst.

Quite true, he replied.

And will our pupils, when they hear this, refuse to take their turn at the toils of State, when they are allowed to spend the greater part of their time with one another in the heavenly light?

Impossible, he answered; for they are just men, and the commands which we impose upon them are just; there can be no doubt that every one of them will take office as a stern necessity, and not after the fashion of our present rulers of State.

521: Yes, my friend, I said; and there lies the point. You must contrive for your future rulers another and a better life than that of a ruler, and then you may have a well-ordered State; for only in the State which offers this, will they rule who are truly rich, not in silver and gold, but in virtue and wisdom, which are the true blessings of life. Whereas if they go to the administration of public affairs, poor and hungering after their own private advantage, thinking that hence they are to snatch the chief good, order there can never be; for they will be fighting about office, and the civil and domestic broils which thus arise will be the ruin of the rulers themselves and of the whole State.

Most true, he replied.

And the only life which looks down upon the life of political ambition is that of true philosophy. Do you know of any other?

Indeed, I do not, he said.

And those who govern ought not to be lovers of the task? For, if they are, there will be rival lovers, and they will fight.

No question.

Who then are those whom we shall compel to be guardians? Surely they will be the men who are wisest about affairs of State, and by whom the State is best administered, and who at the same time have other honours and another and a better life than that of politics?

They are the men, and I will choose them, he replied.

And now shall we consider in what way such guardians will be produced, and how they are to be brought from darkness to light,—as some are said to have ascended from the world below to the gods?

By all means, he replied.

The process, I said, is not the turning over of an oyster-shell,[2] but the turning round of a soul passing from a day which is little better than night to the true day of being, that is, the ascent from below,[3] which we affirm to be true philosophy?

Quite so.

And should we not enquire what sort of knowledge has the power of effecting such a change?

Certainly.

What sort of knowledge is there which would draw the soul from becoming to being? And another consideration has just occurred to me: You will remember that our young men are to be warrior athletes?

Yes, that was said.

Then this new kind of knowledge must have an additional quality?

What quality?

Usefulness in war.

Yes, if possible.

There were two parts in our former scheme of education, were there not?

Just so.

There was gymnastic which presided over the growth and decay of the body, and may therefore be regarded as having to do with generation and corruption?

True.

522: Then that is not the knowledge which we are seeking to discover?

No.

But what do you say of music, which also entered to a certain extent into our former scheme?

Music, he said, as you will remember, was the counterpart of gymnastic, and trained the guardians by the influences of habit, by harmony making them harmonious, by rhythm rhythmical, but not giving them science; and the words, whether fabulous or possibly true, had kindred elements of rhythm and harmony in them. But in music there was nothing which tended to that good which you are now seeking.

You are most accurate, I said, in your recollection; in music there certainly was nothing of the kind. But what branch of knowledge is there, my dear Glaucon, which is of the desired nature; since all the useful arts were reckoned mean by us?

Undoubtedly; and yet if music and gymnastic are excluded, and the arts are also excluded, what remains?

Well, I said, there may be nothing left of our special subjects;

---

[2] In allusion to a game in which two parties fled or pursued according as an oyster-shell which was thrown into the air fell with the dark or light side uppermost.

[3] Reading οὖσαν ἐπάνοδν

and then we shall have to take something which is not special, but of universal application.

What may that be?

A something which all arts and sciences and intelligences use in common, and which every one first has to learn among the elements of education.

What is that?

The little matter of distinguishing one, two, and three—in a word, number and calculation:—do not all arts and sciences necessarily partake of them?

Yes.

Then the art of war partakes of them?

To be sure.

Then Palamedes, whenever he appears in tragedy, proves Agamemnon ridiculously unfit to be a general. Did you never remark how he declares that he had invented number, and had numbered the ships and set in array the ranks of the army at Troy; which implies that they had never been numbered before, and Agamemnon must be supposed literally to have been incapable of counting his own feet—how could he if he was ignorant of number? And if that is true, what sort of general must he have been?

I should say a very strange one, if this was as you say.

Can we deny that a warrior should have a knowledge of arithmetic?

Certainly he should, if he is to have the smallest understanding of military tactics, or indeed, I should rather say, if he is to be a man at all.

I should like to know whether you have the same notion which I have of this study?

What is your notion?

523: It appears to me to be a study of the kind which we are seeking, and which leads naturally to reflection, but never to have been rightly used; for the true use of it is simply to draw the soul towards being.

Will you explain your meaning? he said.

I will try, I said; and I wish you would share the enquiry with me, and say "yes" or "no" when I attempt to distinguish in my own mind what branches of knowledge have this attracting power, in order that we may have clearer proof that arithmetic is, as I suspect, one of them.

Explain, he said.

I mean to say that objects of sense are of two kinds; some of them do not invite thought because the sense is an adequate judge of them; while in the case of other objects sense is so untrustworthy that further enquiry is imperatively demanded.

You are clearly referring, he said, to the manner in which the senses are imposed upon by distance, and by painting in light and shade.

No, I said, that is not at all my meaning.

Then what is your meaning?

When speaking of uninviting objects, I mean those which do not pass from one sensation to the opposite; inviting objects are those which do; in this latter case the sense coming upon the object, whether at a distance or near, gives no more vivid idea of anything in particular than of its opposite. An illustration will make my meaning clearer:—here are three fingers—a little finger, a second finger, and a middle finger.

Very good.

You may suppose that they are seen quite close: And here comes the point.

What is it?

Each of them equally appears a finger, whether seen in the middle or at the extremity, whether white or black, or thick or thin—it makes no difference; a finger is a finger all the same. In these cases a man is not compelled to ask of thought the question, what is a finger? for the sight never intimates to the mind that a finger is other than a finger.

True.

And therefore, I said, as we might expect, there is nothing here which invites or excites intelligence.

There is not, he said.

524: But is this equally true of the greatness and smallness of the fingers? Can sight adequately perceive them? and is no difference made by the circumstance that one of the fingers is in the middle and another at the extremity? And in like manner does the touch adequately perceive the qualities of thickness or thinness, of softness or hardness? And so of the other senses; do they give perfect intimations of such matters? Is not their mode of operation on this wise—the sense which is concerned also with the quality of softness, and only intimates to the soul that the same thing is felt to be both hard and soft?

You are quite right, he said.

And must not the soul be perplexed at this intimation which the sense gives of a hard which is also soft? What, again, is the meaning of light and heavy, if that which is light is also heavy, and that which is heavy, light?

Yes, he said, these intimations which the soul receives are very curious and require to be explained.

Yes, I said, and in these perplexities the soul naturally summons to her aid calculation and intelligence, that she may see whether the several objects announced to her are one or two.

True.

And if they turn out to be two, is not each of them one and different?

Certainly.

And if each is one, and both are two, she will conceive the two as in a state of division, for if they were undivided they could only be conceived of as one?

True.

The eye certainly did see both small and great, but only in a confused manner; they were not distinguished.

Yes.

Whereas the thinking mind, intending to light up the chaos, was compelled to reverse the process, and look at small and great as separate and not confused.

Very true.

Was not this the beginning of the enquiry "What is great?" and "What is small?"

Exactly so.

And thus arose the distinction of the visible and the intelligible.

Most true.

This was what I meant when I spoke of impressions which invited the intellect, or the reverse—those which are simultaneous with opposite impressions, invite thoughts; those which are not simultaneous do not.

I understand, he said, and agree with you.

And to which class do unity and number belong?

I do not know, he replied.

525: Think a little and you will see that what has preceded will supply the answer; for if simple unity could be adequately perceived by the sight or by any other sense, then, as we were saying in the case of the finger, there would be nothing to attract towards being; but when there is some contradiction always present, and one is the reverse of one and involves the conception of plurality, then thought begins to be aroused within us, and the soul perplexed and wanting to arrive at a decision asks "What is absolute unity?" This is the way in which the study of the one has a power of drawing and converting the mind to the contemplation of true being.

And surely, he said, this occurs notably in the case of one; for we see the same thing to be both one and infinite in multitude?

Yes, I said; and this being true of one must be equally true of all number?

Certainly.

And all arithmetic and calculation have to do with number?

Yes.

And they appear to lead the mind towards truth?

Yes, in a very remarkable manner.

Then this is knowledge of the kind for which we are seeking, having a double use, military and philosophical; for the man of war must learn the art of number or he will not know how to array his troops, and the philosopher also, because he has to rise out of the sea of change and lay hold of true being, and therefore he must be an arithmetician.

That is true.

And our guardian is both warrior and philosopher?

Certainly.

Then this is a kind of knowledge which legislation may fitly prescribe; and we must endeavor to persuade those who are to be the principal men of our State to go and learn arithmetic, not as amateurs, but they must carry on the study until they see the nature of numbers with the mind only; nor again, like merchants or retail-traders, with a view to buying or selling, but for the sake of their military use, and of the soul herself; and because this will be the easiest way for her to pass from becoming to truth and being.

That is excellent, he said.

Yes, I said, and now having spoken of it, I must add how charming the science is! and in how many ways it conduces to our desired end, if pursued in the spirit of a philosopher, and not of a shopkeeper!

How do you mean?

I mean, as I was saying, that arithmetic has a very great and elevating effect, compelling the soul to reason about abstract number, and rebelling against the introduction of visible or tangible objects into the argument. You know how steadily the masters of the art repel and ridicule any one who attempts to divide absolute unity when he is calculating, and if you divide, they multiply,[4] taking care that one shall continue one and not become lost in fractions.

That is very true.

526: Now, suppose a person were to say to them: O my friends, what are these wonderful numbers about which you are reasoning, in which, as you say, there is a unity such as you demand, and each unit is equal, invariable, indivisible,—what would they answer?

They would answer, as I should conceive, that they were speaking of those numbers which can only be realised in thought.

Then you see that this knowledge may be truly called necessary,

---

[4] Meaning either (1) that they integrate the number because they deny the possibility of fractions; or (2) that division is regarded by them as a process of multiplication, for the fractions of one continue to be units.

necessitating as it clearly does the use of the pure intelligence in the attainment of pure truth?

Yes; that is a marked characteristic of it.

And have you further observed, that those who have a natural talent for calculation are generally quick at every other kind of knowledge; and even the dull, if they have had an arithmetical training, although they may derive no other advantage from it, always become much quicker than they would otherwise have been.

Very true, he said.

And indeed, you will not easily find a more difficult study, and not many as difficult.

You will not.

And, for all these reasons, arithmetic is a kind of knowledge in which the best natures should be trained, and which must not be given up.

I agree.

Let this then be made one of our subjects of education. And next, shall we enquire whether the kindred science also concerns us?

Epiloque

In his scheme of higher education Plato places after arithmetic the study of plane and solid geometry, astronomy, and harmonics as those sciences we may summarize as "mathematics" and which lead to the culminating study of dialectic.

In the study of geometry Plato would pay attention to those greater and more advanced parts which compel the soul "to make more easy the vision of the idea of the good" and to "turn the gaze towards that place, where is the full perfection of being, which she ought, by all means, to behold" (VII, 526). Knowledge rather than practice is the real objective of the whole science of geometry: the kind which will "draw the soul towards truth and create the spirit of philosophy." But Plato recognizes the value of the secondary "side-effects" of the study of geometry: the practical value (a) to the general in pitching a camp, taking up a position, or directing war and marching manoeuvres, (b) to caring for the practical necessities of daily life, and (c) to anyone in developing quickness of apprehension. The right order is plane geometry first, followed by the study of solids.

Astronomy, the study of solids in motion and revolution, is next in order and the fourth subject in Plato's curriculum. Here the right way is not to observe the "spangled heavens." At most, this approach might yield an appreciation of the exquisiteness of the heavenly workmanship and the beauty in patterns. But the stars are material objects sharing with the visible world their imperfections. Their study through observations will not yield exact knowledge, for the motions of the sun, moon, and stars are relative speeds. Rather the genuine study of astronomy is to let the heavens alone and by means of applying reason and thought to problems, as in geometry, proceed toward the ideal: abstract relations of velocities expressed in numbers and in perfect figures. Astronomy, to Plato, is a branch of pure mathematics.

The study of harmonics with a view to the beautiful and good is next to be studied. Again, as in the previous subjects, Plato wishes to go beyond the present stage of the science. Customarily students of harmony waste their time in measuring audible concords and sounds one against another. Ideally, they should rise to a higher level of formulating problems and investigating which numbers are inherently consonant and which are not, and for what reasons. Harmonics is to be studied as a means to the knowledge of beauty and goodness.

If the ideal ever becomes a reality (VII, 534), the selected few who are to become rulers must have reason in them and undergo "such an education as will enable them to attain the greatest skill in asking and answering questions." Dialectic, the coping-stone of the sciences and set over them, is this final subject in Plato's scheme for higher intellectual preparation. Only one who has been a disciple of the previous sciences —mathematics—can attain to the power of the dialectician: the power to elevate "the highest principle in the soul to the contemplation of that which is best in existence," to attain a conception of what each thing is in its own nature, in its essence. The arts in general are concerned with the desires or opinions of men or are cultivated for production and construction. The mathematical sciences give some apprehension of true being, but they only dream about being and fail to see reality because they use hypotheses which are unexamined and do not know their own first principle.

> Then dialectic, and dialectic alone, goes directly to the first principle and is the only science which does away with hypotheses in order to make her ground secure; the eye of the soul, which is literally buried in an outlandish slough, is by her gentle aid lifted upwards; and she uses as handmaids and helpers in the work of conversion, the sciences which we have been discussing (VII, 533).

This study leads to the kind of person who is

> able to abstract and define rationally the idea of the good, and unless he can run the gauntlet of all objections, and is ready to disprove them, not by appeals to opinion, but to absolute

truth, never faltering at any step of the argument—unless he can do all this, you would say that he knows neither the idea of good nor any other good; he apprehends only a shadow, if anything at all, which is given by opinion and not by science; —dreaming and slumbering in this life, before he is well awake here, . . . (VII, 534).

A detailed account of the method of dialectic which we so much desire to have, Plato refuses to give us, just as he similarly refuses to define for us the Good. His *Letter VII*, 341c, reveals that Plato would never commit these deepest thoughts to writing. He believed their apprehension could only come as a revelation after a long intellectual training and "a close companionship" when, suddenly, "like a blaze kindled by a leaping spark, it is generated in the soul and at once becomes self-sustaining." (L. A. Post translation) Perhaps the best insight we have is the opinion of Francis M. Cornford (*The Republic of Plato*, New York, Oxford University Press, 1945, p. 251):

In this field the Forms will be studied by the method of question and answer which Plato inherited from Socrates, the respondent putting forward his 'hypothetical' attempts at definition, the questioner demanding an 'account' of his meaning and subjecting his suggestions to examination and refutation (elenchus) and so leading him on to amend them. Such a procedure, covering the whole field of moral conceptions, would ideally lead up to a perfect vision of the nature of Goodness itself.

In summarizing Plato's "second" education all that remains is to outline the program of studies indicating the order:

To 17 or 18. This is the period of childhood in which instruction in mathematics is offered. Plato informs us: ". . . calculation and geometry and all the other elements of instruction, which are a preparation for dialectic, should be presented to the mind in childhood" (VII, 536). This education is not to be forced on the child; for (a) "a freeman ought not to be a slave in the acquisition of knowledge of any kind" and (b) "knowledge which is acquired under compulsion obtains no hold on the mind." Whether the music and gymnastic of the first education is to be continued here as a part of the second education is not made clear, although Cornford declares with seeming certitude: "the early training in literature and music and in elementary mathematics will be carried on" (*op. cit.*, p. 256).

From 17 or 18 to 20. This is to be a period of "necessary gymnastics"—of intense physical training which leaves little time for study. (Cornford, *ibid.*, includes "military training" with physical training here, but I can find no specific mention of it either in his translation nor in that of Jowett nor of Paul Shorey.)

From 20 to 30. For those selected from the youth of 20 years of age, this is to be a period for the synoptic study of mathematics (arithmetic, plane geometry, solid geometry, astronomy, and harmonics). In their earlier education these "sciences" had been taught "without any order"; that is, as separate, unrelated subjects of the curriculum. During this period of ten years, from 20 to 30, a select few will begin to see "the natural relationship of them to one another and to true being." This is a start toward seeing things in their connectedness, the distinctive task of the dialectician.

From 30 to 35. After a further selection, five years are to be given to the study of dialectic—the attempt to see all branches of learning synoptically, as one connected whole. This is the subject of study which stands as the coping-stone of the whole structure. It is a search for the first principles of morality.

From 35 to 50. This is the period in which the philosopher-ruler candidate is sent down again "into the den and compelled to hold any military or other office which young men are qualified to hold: in this way they will get their experience of life, and there will be an opportunity of trying whether, when they are drawn all manner of ways by temptation, they will stand firm or flinch."

After 50. After distinguishing themselves in every action of their lives and in every branch of knowledge come into their own, those who have reached 50 years of age enter a period

> at which they must raise the eye of the soul to the universal light which lightens all things, and behold the absolute good; for that is the pattern according to which they are to order the State and the lives of individuals, and the remainder of their own lives also; making philosophy their chief pursuit, but, when their turn comes, toiling also at politics and ruling for the public good, not as though they were performing some heroic action, but simply as a matter of duty; and when they have brought up in each generation others like themselves and left them in their place to be governors of the State, then they will depart to the Islands of the Blest and dwell there; . . . (VII, 540).

Thus does Plato answer the question of how the ideal state might come into being: by producing through right education the philosophic statesman and giving him a free hand to remould society. What remains in the *Republic* (after this seeming aside) is to describe "the descent" of society and the individual (Books VIII-IX) and end with reflections on immortality and the rewards of justice (Book X). Amid such rich resources for the political scientist, two insights may best be pointed to here for leaders in education today. The first is a warning description of conditions when the insatiable desire of wealth creates a demand for democracy and the insatiable desire of freedom creates a demand for tyranny so that this kind of anarchy results:

> . . . the father grows accustomed to descend to the level of his sons and to fear them, and the son is on a level with his father, he having no respect or reverence for either of his parents; and this is his freedom, and the metic is equal with the citizen and the citizen with the metic, and the stranger is quite as good as either. . . .
>
> And these are not the only evils. . . . In such a state of society the master fears and flatters his scholars, and the scholars despise their masters and tutors; young and old are all alike; and the young man is on a level with the old, and is ready to compete with him in word or deed; and old men condescend to the young and are full of pleasantry and gaiety; they are loth to be thought morose and authoritative, and therefore they adopt the manners of the young (VIII, 562).

The other is a specific recommendation (in line with the earlier comment at VI, 497, that "Hard is the good"):

> Let each one of us leave every other kind of knowledge and seek and follow one thing only, if peradventure he may be able to learn and may find some one who will make him able to learn and discern between good and evil, and so to choose always and everywhere the better life as he has opportunity. He should consider the bearing of all these things which have been mentioned severally and collectively upon virtue; he should know what the effect of beauty is when combined with poverty or wealth in a particular soul, and what are the good and evil consequences of noble and humble birth, of private and public station, of strength and weakness, of cleverness and dullness, and of all the natural and acquired gifts of the soul, and the operation of them when conjoined; he will then look at the nature of the soul, and from the consideration of all these qualities he will be able to determine which is the better and which is the worse; and so he will choose, giving the name of evil to the life which will make his soul more just; all else he will disregard. For we have seen and know that this is the

best choice both in life and after death. A man must take with him into the world below an adamantine faith in truth and right, that there too he may be undazzled by the desire of wealth or the other allurements of evil, lest, coming upon tyrannies and similar villainies, he do irremediable wrongs to others and suffer yet worse himself; but let him know how to choose the mean and avoid the extremes on either side, as far as possible, not only in this life but in all that which is to come. For this is the way of happiness" (X, 618-619).

20
Aristotle (384-322 B.C.)

Aristotle, *Nichomachean Ethics*, translated by James E. C. Welldon; selections from Books I and II (New York: Walter J. Black, Inc., 1943), pp. 87-101, 101-113.

From Book I

Every art and every scientific inquiry, and similarly every action and purpose, may be said to aim at some good. Hence the good has been well defined as that at which all things aim. But it is clear that there is a difference in ends; for the ends are sometimes activities, and sometimes results beyond the mere activities. Where there are ends beyond the action, the results are naturally superior to the action.

As there are various actions, arts, and sciences, it follows that the ends are also various. Thus health is the end of medical art, a ship of shipbuilding, victory of strategy, and wealth of economies. It often happens that a number of such arts or sciences combine for a single enterprise. . . . In all these cases, the ends of the master arts or sciences, whatever they may be, are more desirable than those of the subordinate arts or sciences, as it is for the sake of the former that the latter are pursued. It makes no difference to the argument whether the activities themselves are the ends of action, or something beyond the activities, as in the above-mentioned sciences.

If it is true that in the sphere of action there is some end which we wish for its own sake, and for the sake of which we wish everything else, and if we do not desire everything for the sake of something else (for, if that is so, the process will go on *ad infinitum*, and our desire will be idle and futile), clearly this end will be good and the supreme good. Does it not follow then that the knowledge of this good is of great importance for the conduct of life? Like archers who have a mark at which to aim, shall we not have a better chance of attaining what we want? If this is so, we must endeavor to comprehend, at least in outline, what this good is, and what science or faculty make it its object.

It would seem that this is the most authoritative science. Such a kind is evidently the political, for it is that which determines what sciences are necessary in states, and what kinds should be studied, and how far they should be studied by each class of inhabitant. We see too that even the faculties held in highest esteem, such as strategy, economics, and rhetoric, are subordinate to it. Then since politics makes use of the other sciences and also rules what people may do and what they may not do, it follows that its end will comprehend the ends of the other sciences, and will therefore be the good of mankind. For even if the good of an individual is identical with the good of a state, yet the good of the state is evidently greater and more perfect to attain or to preserve. For though the good of an individual by himself is something worth working for, to ensure the good of a nation or a state is nobler and more divine.

These then are the objects at which the present inquiry aims, and it is in a sense a political inquiry . . .

As every science and undertaking aims at some good, what is in our view the good at which political science aims, and what is the highest of all practical goods? As to its name there is, I may say, a general agreement. The masses and the cultured classes agree in calling it happiness, and conceive that "to live well" or "to do well" is the same thing as "to be happy." But as to what happiness is they do not agree, nor do the masses give the same account of it as the philosophers. The former take it to be something visible and palpable, such as pleasure, wealth, or honor; different people, however, give different definitions of it, and often even the same man gives different definitions at different times. When he is ill, it is health, when he is poor, it is wealth; if he is conscious of his own ignorance, he envies people who use grand language above his own comprehension. Some philosophers, on the other hand, have held that, besides these various goods, there is an absolute good which is the cause of goodness in them all. [Editor's Note: Plato, for example.] It would perhaps be a waste of time to examine all these opinions; it will be enough to examine such as are most popular or as seem to be more or less reasonable. . . .

Men's conception of the good or of happiness may be read in the lives they lead. Ordinary or vulgar people conceive it to be a pleasure, and accordingly choose a life of enjoyment. For there are, we may say, three conspicuous types of life, the sensual, the political, and, thirdly, the life of thought. Now the mass of men present an absolutely slavish appearance, choosing the life of brute beasts, but they have ground for so doing because so many persons in authority share the tastes of Sardanapalus [Editor's Note: The personification of gross luxury and extravagance, being an ancient Assyrian despot.] Cultivated and energetic people, on the other hand, identify happiness with honor, as honor is the general end of political life. But this seems too superficial an idea for our present purpose; for honor depends more upon the people who pay it than upon the person to whom it is paid, and the good we feel is something which is proper to a man himself and cannot be easily taken away from him. Men too appear to seek honor in order to be assured of their own goodness. Accordingly, they seek it at the hands of the sage and of those who know them well, and they seek it on the ground of their virtue; clearly then, in their judgment at any rate, virtue is better than honor. Perhaps then we might look on virtue rather than honor as the end of political life. Yet even this idea appears not quite complete; for a man may possess virtue and yet be asleep or inactive throughout life, and not only so, but he may experience the greatest calamities and misfortunes. Yet no one would call such a life a life of happiness, unless he were maintaining a paradox. But we need not dwell further on this subject, since it is sufficiently discussed in popular philosophical treatises. The third life is the life of thought, which we will discuss later.

The life of money making is a life of constraint; and wealth is obviously not the good of which we are in quest; for it is useful merely as a means to something else. It would be more reasonable to take the things mentioned before—sensual pleasure, honor, and virtue—as ends than wealth, since they are things desired on their own account. Yet these too are evidently not ends, although much argument has been employed to show that they are. . . .

. . . We call that which is sought after for its own sake more final than that which is sought after as a means to something else; we call that which is never desired as a means to something else more final than things that are desired both for themselves and as means to something else. Therefore, we call absolutely final that which is always desired for itself and never as a means to something else. Now happiness more than anything else answers to this description. For happiness we always desire for its own sake and never as a means to something else, whereas honor, pleasure, intelligence, and every virtue we desire partly for their own sakes (for we should desire them independently of what might result from them), but partly also as a means to happiness, because we suppose they will prove instruments of happiness. Happiness, on the other hand, nobody desires for the sake of these things, nor indeed as a means to anything else at all.

If we start from the point of view of self-sufficiency, we reach the same conclusion; for we assume that the final good is self-sufficient. By self-sufficiency we do not mean that a person leads a solitary life all by himself, but that he has parents, children, wife and friends and fellow citizens in general, as man is naturally a social being. Yet here it is necessary to set some limit; for if the circle must be extended to include ancestors, descendents, and friends' friends, it will go on indefinitely. Leaving this point, however, for future investigation, we call the self-sufficient that which, taken even by itself, makes life desirable and wanting nothing at all; and this is what we mean by happiness.

Again, we think happiness the most desirable of all things, and that not merely as one good thing among others. If it were only that, the addition of the smallest more good would increase its desirableness; for the addition would make an increase of goods, and the greater of two goods is always the more desirable. Happiness is something final and self-sufficient and the end of all action. . . .

Perhaps, however, it seems a commonplace to say that happiness is the supreme good; what is wanted is to define its nature a little more clearly. The best way of arriving at such a definition will probably be to ascertain the function of man. For, as with a flute player, a sculptor, or any artist, or in fact anybody who has a special function or activity, his goodness and excellence seem to lie in his function, so it would seem to be with man, if indeed he has a special function. Can it be said that, while a carpenter and a cobbler have special functions and activities, man, unlike them, is naturally functionless? Or, as the eye, the hand, the foot, and similarly each part of the body has a special function, so may man be regarded as having a special function apart from all these? What, then, can this function be? It is not life; for life is apparently something that man shares with plants; and we are looking for something peculiar to him. We must exclude therefore the life of nutrition and growth. There is next what may be called the life of sensation. But this too, apparently, is shared by man with horses, cattle, and all other animals. There remains what I may call the active life of the rational part of man's being. Now this rational part is twofold; one part is rational in the sense of being obedient to reason, and the other in the sense of possessing and exercising reason and intelligence. The active life too may be conceived of in two ways, either as a state of character, or as an activity; but we mean by it the life of activity, as this seems to be the truer form of the conception.

The function of man then is activity of soul in accordance with reason, or not apart from reason. Now, the function of a man of a certain kind, and of a man who is good of that kind—for example, of a harpist and a good harpist—are in our view the same in kind. This is true of all people of all kinds without exception, the superior excellence being only an addition to the function; for it is the function of a harpist to play the harp, and of a good harpist to play the harp well. This being so, if we define the function of man as a kind of life, and this life as an activity of the soul or a course of action in accordance with reason, and if the function of a good man is such activity of a good and noble kind, and if everything is well done when it is done in accordance with its proper excellence, it follows that the good of man is activity of soul in accordance with virtue, or, if there are more virtues than one, in accordance with the best and most complete virtue. But we must add the words "in a complete life." For as one swallow or one day does not make a spring, so one day or a short time does not make a man blessed or happy. . . .

. . . But there is plainly a considerable difference between calling the supreme good possession or use, a state of mind, or an activity. For a state of mind may exist without producing anything good—for example, if a person is asleep, or in any other way inert. Not so with an activity, since activity implies acting and acting well. As in the Olympic games it is not the most beautiful and strongest who receive the crown but those who actually enter the combat, for from those come the victors, so it is those who act that win rightly what is noble and good in life.

Their life too is pleasant in itself. For pleasure is a state of mind, and whatever a man is fond of is pleasant to him . . . Now most men find a sense of discord in their pleasures, because their pleasures are not all naturally pleasant. But the lovers of nobleness take pleasure in what is naturally pleasant, and virtuous acts are naturally pleasant. Such acts then are pleasant both to these persons and in themselves. Nor does the life of such persons need more pleasure attached to it as a sort of charm; it possesses pleasure in itself. For, it may be added, a man who does not delight in noble acts is not good; as nobody would call a man just who did not enjoy just action, or liberal who did not enjoy liberal action, and so on. If this is so, it follows that acts of virtue are pleasant in themselves. They are also good and noble, and good and noble in the highest degree, for the judgment of the virtuous man on them is right, and his judgment is as we have described. Happiness then is the best and noblest and pleasantest thing in the world; nor is there any such difference between these things as the inscription at Delos suggests:

Justice is noblest, health is best,
To gain one's wish is pleasantest.

For they all are characteristics of the best activities, and happiness, we hold, is the same as these or as one and the noblest of these.

Still it is clear, as we said, that happiness requires the addition of external goods; for it is impossible, or at least difficult, to do noble deeds with no outside means. For many things can be done only through the aid of friends or wealth or political power; and there are some things the lack of which spoils our felicity, such as good birth, wholesome children, and personal beauty. For a man who is extremely ugly in appearance or low born or solitary and childless can hardly be happy; perhaps still less so, if he has exceedingly bad children or friends, or has had good children or friends and lost them by death. As we said, then, happiness seems to need prosperity of this kind in addition to virtue. For this reason some persons identify happiness with good fortune, though others do so with virtue. . . .

The question is consequently raised whether happiness is something that can be learned or acquired by habit or training of some kind, or whether it comes by some divine dispensation, or even by chance.

Now if there is anything in the world that is a gift of the gods to men, it is reasonable to take happiness as a divine gift, and especially divine as it is the best of human things. This point, however, is perhaps more appropriate to another investigation than the present. But even if happiness is not sent by the gods but is the result of goodness and of learning or training of some kind, it is apparently one of the most divine things in the world; for that which is the prize and end of goodness would seem the best good and in its nature godlike and blessed. It may also be widely extended; for all persons who are not morally deformed may share in it by a process of study and care. And if it is better that happiness should come in this way than by chance, we may reasonably suppose that it does so come, since the order of things in Nature is the best possible, as it is in art and in causation generally, and most of all in the highest kind of causation. And to leave what is greatest and noblest to chance would be altogether unworthy. The definition of happiness itself helps to clear up the question; for happiness we have defined as a kind of virtuous activity of the soul. . . .

It is reasonable then not to call an ox or a horse or any other animal happy; for none of them is capable of sharing in this activity. For the same reason no child can be happy, since the youth of a child keeps him for the time being from such activity; if a child is ever called happy, the ground of felicitation is his promise, rather than his actual performance. For happiness demands, as we said, a complete virtue and a complete life. And there are all sorts of changes and chances in life, and the most prosperous of men may in his old age fall into extreme calamities, as Priam did in the heroic legends. [Editor's Note: Priam, King of Troy, in Homer's *Iliad*.] And a person who has experienced such chances and died a miserable death, nobody calls happy. . . .

. . . If it is right to wait for the end, and only when the end has come, to call a man happy, not for being happy then (after death) but for having been so before, surely it is an extraordinary thing that, at the time when he is happy, we should not speak the truth about him, because we are unwilling to call the living happy in view of the changes to which they are liable, and because we have formed an idea of happiness as something permanent and exempt from the possibility of change, while every man is liable to many turns of fortune's wheel. Unquestionably, if we follow the changes of fortune, we shall often call the same person happy at one time and miserable at another, making the happy man out as "a sort of chameleon with no stability." But to follow the changes of fortune cannot be right. It is not on these that good or evil depends; they are necessary accompaniments to human life, as we said; but it is a man's virtuous activities that constitute his happiness and their opposites that constitute his misery.

The difficulty we have now discussed proves again the correctness of our definition. For there is no human function so constant as virtuous activities; they seem to be more permanent than the sciences themselves. Among these activities too the most noble are the most permanent, and it is of them that the life of happiness chiefly and most continuously consists. This is apparently the reason why they are not likely to be forgotten. The element of durability then which is required will be found in the happy man, and he will preserve his happiness through life; for always or chiefly he will pursue such actions and thoughts as accord with virtue; nor will anyone bear the chances of life so nobly, with such a perfect composure, as he who is truly good and "foursquare without a flaw." . . . Nobility shines out when a person bears with calmness the weight of accumulated misfortunes, not from insensibility but from dignity and greatness of spirit.

Then if activities determine the quality of life, as we said, no happy man can become miserable; for he will never do what is hateful and mean. For our idea of the truly good and wise man is that he bears all the chances of life with dignity and always does what is best in the circumstances. . . . If this is so, the happy man can never become miserable. I do not say that he will be fortunate if he meets such chances of life as Priam. Yet he will not be variable or constantly changing, for he will not be moved from his happiness easily or by ordinary misfortunes, but only by great and numerous ones; nor after them (great misfortunes) will he quickly regain his happiness. If he regains it at all, it will be only over a long and complete period of time and after great and notable achievement.

We may safely then define a happy man as one who is active in accord with perfect virtue and adequately furnished with external goods, not for some chance period of time but for his whole lifetime. But perhaps we ought to add that he should always live so and die as he has lived. It is not given us to foresee the future, but we take happiness as an end, altogether final and complete; and, this being so, we shall call people happy during their lifetime if they possess and continue to possess these characteristics—yet happy only so far as men are happy.

Inasmuch as happiness is an activity of soul in accordance with perfect virtue, we must now consider virtue, as this will perhaps be the best way of studying happiness. . . . Clearly it is human virtue we have to consider; for the good of which we are in search is, as we said, human good, and the happiness, human happiness. By human virtue or excellence we mean not that of the body, but that of the soul, and by happiness we mean an activity of the soul.

There are some facts concerning the soul which are adequately stated in popular discourses, and these we may rightly accept. It is said, for example, that the soul has two parts, one irrational and the other rational. Whether these parts are separate like the parts of the body or like anything divisible, or whether they are theoretically distinct but in fact inseparable, like the convex and concave in the circumference of a circle, is of no importance to the present inquiry.

Of the irrational part of the soul one part is shared by man with all living things, and vegetative; I mean the part which is the cause of nutrition and growth. For we may assume such a faculty of the soul to exist in all young things that take food, even in embryos, and the same faculty to exist in things full grown, since it is more reasonable to suppose it is the same faculty than something different. Manifestly the virtue or excellence of this faculty is not peculiarly human but is shared by man with all living things; this part or faculty seems especially active in sleep, whereas goodness and badness never show so little as in sleep. Hence the saying that during half their lives there is no difference between the happy and the unhappy. And this is only natural; for sleep is an inactivity of the soul as regards its goodness or badness, except in so far as certain impulses affect it slightly and make the dreams of good men better than those of ordinary people. Enough, however, on this point; we shall now leave the faculty of nutrition, as it has by its nature no part in human goodness.

There is, we think, another natural element of the soul which is irrational and yet in a sense partakes of reason. For in continent and incontinent persons we praise their reason, and that part of their soul which possesses reason, because it counsels them aright and directs them to the best conduct. But we know there is in them also another element naturally opposed to reason that fights and contends against reason. Just as paralyzed parts of the body, when we try to move them to the right, pull in a contrary direction to the left, so it is with the soul; the impulses of incontinent people run counter to reason. But while in the body we see the part which pulls awry, in the soul we do not see it. We may, however, suppose with equal certainty that in the soul too there is something alien to reason, which opposes and thwarts it. The sense in which it is distinct from other things is unimportant. But it too partakes of reason, as we said; at all events, in a continent person it obeys reason, and in a temperate and brave man it is probably still more obedient, for in him it is absolutely harmonious with reason.

It appears then that the irrational part of the soul is twofold; for the vegetative faculty does not participate at all in reason, but the element of appetite and desire in general shares in it, in so far as it is submissive and obedient to reason. It is so in the sense in which we speak of "paying attention" to a father or to friends, but not in the sense in which we speak of "paying attention" to mathematics. All advice, reproof, and exhortation are witness that this irrational part of the soul is in a sense subject to influence by reason. And if we say that this part participates in reason, then as a part possessing reason, it will be twofold, one element possessing reason absolutely and in itself, the other listening to it as a child listens to its father.

Virtue too may be divided to correspond to this difference. For we call some virtues intellectual and others moral. Wisdom, intelligence, and prudence are intellectual; liberality and temperance moral. In describing a person's moral character we do not say that he is wise or intelligent but that he is gentle or temperate. A wise man, however, we praise for his mentality, and such mentality as deserves praise we call virtuous.

From Book II

Virtue then is twofold, partly intellectual and partly moral, and intellectual virtue is originated and fostered mainly by teaching; it demands therefore experience and time. Moral virtue on the other hand is the outcome of habit, and accordingly its name, *ethike*, is derived by a slight variation from *ethos*, habit. From this fact it is clear that moral virtue is not implanted in us by nature; for nothing that exists by nature can be transformed by habit. Thus a stone, that naturally tends to fall downwards, cannot be habituated or trained to rise upwards, even if we tried to train it by throwing it up ten thousand times. Nor again can fire be trained to sink downwards, nor anything else that follows one natural law be habituated or trained to follow another. It is neither by nature then nor in defiance of nature that virtues grow in us. Nature gives us the capacity to receive them, and that capacity is perfected by habit.

Again, if we take the various natural powers which belong to us, we first possess the proper faculties and afterwards display the activities. It is obviously so with the senses. Not by seeing frequently or hearing frequently do we acquire the sense of seeing or hearing; on the contrary, because we have the senses we make use of them; we do not get them by making use of them. But the virtues we get by first practicing them, as we do in the arts. For it is by doing what we ought to do when we study the arts that we learn the arts themselves; we become builders by building and harpists by playing the harp. Similarly, it is by doing just acts that we become just, by doing temperate acts that we become temperate, by doing brave acts that we become brave. The experience of states confirms this statement, for it is by training in good habits that lawmakers make the citizens good. This is the object all lawmakers have at heart; if they do not succeed in it, they fail of their purpose; and it makes the distinction between a good constitution and a bad one.

Again, the causes and means by which any virtue is produced and destroyed are the same; and equally so in any art. For it is by playing the harp that both good and bad harpists are produced; and the case of builders and others is similar, for it is by building well that they become good builders and by building badly that they become bad builders. If it were not so, there would be no need of anybody to teach them; they would all be born good or bad in their several crafts. The case of the virtues is the same. It is by our actions in dealings between man and man that we become either just or unjust. It is by our actions in the face of danger and by our training ourselves to fear or to courage that we become either cowardly or courageous. It is much the same with our appetites and angry passions. People become temperate and gentle, others licentious and passionate, by behaving in one or the other way in particular circumstances. In a word, moral states are the results of activities like the states themselves. It is our duty therefore to keep a certain character in our activities, since our moral states depend on the differences in our activities. So the difference between one and another training in habits in our childhood is not a light matter, but important, or rather, all-important. . . .

Our present study is not, like other studies, purely theoretical in intention; for the object of our inquiry is not to know what virtue is but how to become good, and that is the sole benefit of it. We must, therefore, consider the right way of performing actions, for it is acts, as we have said, that determine the character of the resulting moral states.

That we should act in accordance with right reason is a common general principle, which may here be taken for granted. The nature of right reason, and its relation to the virtues generally, will be discussed later. But first of all it must be admitted that all reasoning on matters of conduct must be like a sketch in outline; it cannot be scientifically exact. We began by laying down the principle that the kind of reasoning demanded in any subject must be such as the subject matter itself allows; and questions of conduct and expediency no more admit of hard and fast rules than questions of health.

If this is true of general reasoning on ethics, still more true is it that scientific exactitude is impossible in treating of particular ethical cases. They do not fall under any art or law, but the actors themselves have always to take account of circumstances, as much as in medicine or navigation. Still, although such is the nature of our present argument, we must try to make the best of it.

The first point to be observed is that in the matters we are now considering deficiency and excess are both fatal. It is so, we see, in questions of health and strength. (We must judge of what we cannot see by the evidence of what we do see.) Too much or too little gymnastic exercise is fatal to strength. Similarly, too much or too little meat and drink is fatal to health, whereas a suitable amount produces, increases, and sustains it. It is the same with temperance, courage, and other moral virtues. A person who avoids and is afraid of everything and faces nothing becomes a coward; a person who is not afraid of anything but is ready to face everything becomes foolhardy. Similarly, he who enjoys every pleasure and abstains from none is licentious; he who refuses all pleasures, like a boor, is an insensible sort of person. For temperance and courage are destroyed by excess and deficiency but preserved by the mean.

Again, not only are the causes and agencies of production, increase, and destruction in moral states the same, but the field of their activity is the same also. It is so in other more obvious instances, as, for example, strength; for strength is produced by taking a great deal of food and undergoing a great deal of exertion, and it is the strong man who is able to take most food and undergo most exertion. So too with the virtues. By abstaining from pleasures we become temperate, and, when we have become temperate, we are best able to abstain from them. So again with courage; it is by training ourselves to despise and face terrifying things that we become brave, and when we have become brave, we shall be best able to face them.

The pleasure or pain which accompanies actions may be regarded as a test of a person's moral state. He who abstains from physical pleasures and feels pleasure in so doing is temperate; but he who feels pain at so doing is licentious. He who faces dangers with pleasure, or at least without pain, is brave; but he who feels pain at facing them is a coward. For moral virtue is concerned with pleasures and pains. It is pleasure which makes us do what is base, and pain which makes us abstain from doing what is noble. Hence the importance of having a certain training from very early days, as Plato says, so that we may feel pleasure and pain at the right objects; for this is true education. . . .

But we may be asked what we mean by saying that people must become just by doing what is just and temperate by doing what is temperate. For, it will be said, if they do what is just and temperate they are already just and temperate themselves, in the same way as, if they practice grammar and music, they are grammarians and musicians.

But is this true even in the case of the arts? For a person may speak grammatically either by chance or at the suggestion of somebody else; hence he will not be a grammarian unless he not only speaks grammatically but does so in a grammatical manner, that is, because of the grammatical knowledge which he possesses.

There is a point of difference too between the arts and the virtues. The productions of art have their excellence in themselves. It is enough then that, when they are produced, they themselves should possess a certain character. But acts in accordance with virtue are not justly or temperately performed simply because they are in themselves just or temperate. The doer at the time of performing them must satisfy certain conditions; in the first place, he must know what he is doing; secondly, he must deliberately choose to do it and do it for its own sake; and thirdly, he must do it as part of his own firm and immutable character. If it be a question of art, these conditions, except only the condition of knowledge, are not raised; but if it be a question of virtue, mere knowledge is of little or no avail; it is the other conditions, which are the results of frequently performing just and temperate acts, that are not slightly but all-important. Accordingly, deeds are called just and temperate when they are such as a just and temperate person would do; and a just and temperate person is not merely one who does these deeds but one who does them in the spirit of the just and the temperate.

It may fairly be said then that a just man becomes just by doing what is just, and a temperate man becomes temperate by doing what is temperate, and if a man did not so act, he would not have much chance of becoming good. But most people, instead of acting, take refuge in theorizing; they imagine that they are philosophers and that philosophy will make them virtuous; in fact, they behave like people who listen attentively to their doctors but never do anything that their doctors tell them. But a healthy state of the soul will no more be produced by this kind of philosophizing than a healthy state of the body by this kind of medical treatment. . . .

We have next to consider the nature of virtue. Now, as the properties of the soul are three, namely, emotions, faculties, and moral states, it follows that virtue must be one of the three. By emotions I mean desire, anger, fear, pride, envy, joy, love, hatred, regret, ambition, pity—in a word, whatever feeling is attended by pleasure or pain. I call those faculties through which we are said to be capable of experiencing these emotions, for instance, capable of getting angry or being pained or feeling pity. And I call those moral states through which we are well or ill disposed in our emotions, ill disposed, for instance, in anger, if our anger be too violent or too feeble, and well disposed, if it be rightly moderate; and similarly in our other emotions.

Now neither the virtues nor the vices are emotions; for we are not called good or bad for our emotions but for our virtues or vices. We are not praised or blamed simply for being angry, but only for being angry in a certain way; but we are praised or blamed for our virtues or vices. Again, whereas we are angry or afraid without deliberate purpose, the virtues are matters of deliberate purpose, or require deliberate purpose. Moreover, we are said to be moved by our emotions, but by our virtues or vices we are not said to be moved but to have a certain disposition.

For these reasons the virtues are not faculties. For we are not called either good or bad, nor are we praised or blamed for having simple capacity for emotion. Also while Nature gives us our faculties, it is not Nature that makes us good or bad; but this point we have already discussed. If then the virtues are neither emotions nor faculties, all that remains is that they must be moral states. . . .

The nature of virtue has been now described in kind. But it is not enough to say merely that virtue is a moral state; we must also describe the character of that moral state.

We may assert then that every virtue or excellence puts into good condition that of which it is a virtue or excellence, and enables it to perform its work well. Thus excellence in the eye makes the eye good and its function good, for by excellence in the eye we see well. Similarly, excellence of the horse makes the horse excellent himself and good at racing, at carrying its rider and at facing the enemy. If then this rule is universally true, the virtue or excellence of a man will be such a moral state as makes a man good and able to perform his proper function well. How this will be the case we have already explained, but another way of making it clear will be to study the nature or character of virtue.

Now of everything, whether it be continuous or divisible, it is possible to take a greater, a smaller, or an equal amount, and this either in terms of the thing itself or in relation to ourselves, the equal being a mean between too much and too little. By the mean in terms of the thing itself, I understand that which is equally distinct from both its extremes, which is one and the same for every man. By the mean relative to ourselves, I understand that which is neither too much nor too little for us; but this is not one nor the same for everybody. Thus if 10 be too much and 2 too little, we take 6 as a mean in terms of the thing itself; for 6 is as much greater than 2 as it is less than 10, and this is a mean in arithmetical proportion. But the mean considered relatively to ourselves may not be ascertained in that way. It does not follow that if 10 pounds of meat is too much and 2 too little for a man to eat, the trainer will order him 6 pounds, since this also may be too much or too little for him who is to take it; it will be too little, for example, for Milo [Editor's Note: a famous wrestler] but too much for a beginner in gymnastics. The same with running and wrestling; the right amount will vary with the individual. This being so, the skillful in any art avoids alike excess and deficiency; he seeks and chooses the mean, not the absolute mean, but the mean considered relatively to himself.

Every art then does its work well, if it regards the mean and judges the works it produces by the mean. For this reason we often say of successful works of art that it is impossible to take anything from them or to add anything to them, which implies that excess or deficiency is fatal to excellence but that the mean state ensures it. Good artists too, as we say, have an eye to the mean in their works. Now virtue, like Nature herself, is more accurate and better than any art; virtue, therefore, will aim at the mean. I speak of moral virtue, since it is moral virtue which is concerned with emotions and action, and it is in these we have excess and deficiency and the mean. Thus it is possible to go too far, or not far enough in fear, pride, desire, anger, pity, and pleasure and pain generally, and the excess and the deficiency are alike wrong; but to feel these emotions at the right times, for the right objects, towards the right persons, for the right motives, and in the right manner, is the mean or the best good, which signifies virtue. Similarly, there may be excess, deficiency, or the mean, in acts. Virtue is concerned with both emotions and actions, wherein excess is an error and deficiency a fault, while the mean is successful and praised, and success and praise are both characteristics of virtue.

It appears then that virtue is a kind of mean because it aims at the mean.

On the other hand, there are many different ways of going wrong; for evil is in its nature infinite, to use the Pythagorean phrase, but good is finite and there is only one possible way of going right. So the former is easy and the latter is difficult; it is easy to miss the mark but difficult to hit it. And so by our reasoning excess and deficiency are characteristics of vice and the mean is a characteristic of virtue.

For good is simple, evil manifold.

. . . Virtue then is a state of deliberate moral purpose, consisting in a mean relative to ourselves, the mean being determined by reason, or as a prudent man would determine it. It is a mean, firstly, as lying between two vices, the vice of excess on the one hand, and the vice of deficiency on the other, and, secondly, because, whereas the vices either fall short of or go beyond what is right in emotion and action, virtue discovers and chooses the mean. Accordingly, virtue, if regarded in its essence or theoretical definition, is a mean, though, if regarded from the point of view of what is best and most excellent, it is an extreme.

But not every action or every emotion admits of a mean. There are some whose very name implies wickedness, as, for example, malice, shamelessness, and envy among the emotions, and adultery, theft, and murder among the actions. All these and others like them are marked as intrinsically wicked, not merely the excesses or deficiencies of them. It is never possible then to be right in them; they are always sinful. Right or wrong in such acts as adultery does not depend on our committing it with the right woman, at the right time, or in the right manner; on the contrary, it is wrong to do it at all. It would be equally false to suppose that there can be a mean or an excess or deficiency in unjust, cowardly or licentious conduct; for, if that were so, it would be a mean of excess and deficiency, an excess of excess and a deficiency of deficiency. But as in temperance and courage there can be no excess or deficiency, because the mean there is in a sense an extreme, so too in these other cases there cannot be a mean or an excess or a deficiency, but however the acts are done, they are wrong. For in general an excess or deficiency does not have a mean, nor a mean an excess or deficiency. . . .

There are then three dispositions, two being vices, namely, excess and deficiency, and one virtue, which is the mean between them; and they are all in a sense mutually opposed. The extremes are opposed both to the mean and to each other, and the mean is opposed to the extremes. For as the equal if compared with the less is greater, but if compared with the greater is less, so the mean state, whether in emotion or action, if compared with deficiency is excessive, but if compared with excess is deficient. Thus the brave man appears foolhardy. Similarly, the temperate man appears licentious compared with the insensible man but insensible compared with the licentious; and the liberal man appears extravagant compared with the stingy man but stingy compared with the spendthrift. The result is that the extremes each denounce the mean as belonging to the other extreme; the coward calls the brave man foolhardy, and the foolhardy man calls him cowardly; and so on in other cases.

But while there is mutual opposition between the extremes and the mean, there is greater opposition between the two extremes than between extreme and the mean; for they are further removed from each other than from the mean, as the great is further from the small and the small from the great than either from the equal. Again, while some extremes show some likeness to the mean, as foolhardiness to courage and extravagance to liberality, there is the greatest possible dissimilarity between extremes. But things furthest removed from each other are called opposites; hence the further things are removed, the greater is the opposition between them.

In some cases it is deficiency and in others excess which is more opposed to the mean. Thus it is not foolhardiness, an excess, but cowardice, a deficiency, which is more opposed to courage, nor is it insensibility, a deficiency, but licentiousness, an excess, which is more opposed to temperance. There are two reasons why this should be so. One lies in the nature of the matter itself; for when one of two extremes is nearer and more like the mean, it is not this extreme but its opposite that we chiefly contrast with the mean. For instance, as foolhardiness seems more like and nearer to courage than cowardice, it is cowardice that we chiefly contrast with courage; for things further removed from the mean seem to be more opposite to it. This reason lies in the nature of the matter itself; there is a second which lies in our own nature. The things to which we ourselves are naturally more inclined we think more opposed to the mean. Thus we are ourselves naturally more inclined to pleasures than to their opposites, and are more prone therefore to self-indulgence than to moderation. Accordingly we speak of those things in which we are more likely to run to great lengths as more opposed to the mean. Hence licentiousness, which is an excess, seems more opposed to temperance than insensibility.

We have now sufficiently shown that moral virtue is a mean, and in what sense it is so; that it is a mean as lying between two vices, a vice of excess on the one side and a vice of deficiency on the other, and as aiming at the mean in emotion and action.

That is why it is so hard to be good; for it is always hard to find the mean in anything; it is not everyone but only a man of science who can find the mean or center of a circle. So too anybody can get angry— that is easy—and anybody can give or spend money, but to give it to the right person, to give the right amount of it, at the right time, for the right cause and in the right way, this is not what anybody can do, nor is it easy. That is why goodness is rare and praiseworthy and noble. One then who aims at a mean must begin by departing from the extreme that is more contrary to the mean; he must act in the spirit of Calypso's advice, "Far from this spray and swell hold thou thy ship," (Odyssey) for of the two extremes one is more wrong than the other. As it is difficult to hit the mean exactly, we should take the second best course, as the saying is, and choose the lesser of two evils. This we shall best do in the way described, that is, steering clear of the evil which is further from the mean. We must also note the weaknesses to which we are ourselves particularly prone, since different natures tend in different ways; and we may ascertain what our tendency is by observing our feelings of pleasure and pain. Then we must drag ourselves away towards the opposite extreme; for by pulling ourselves as far as possible from what is wrong we shall arrive at the mean, as we do when we pull a crooked stick straight.

In all cases we must especially be on our guard against the pleasant, or pleasure, for we are not impartial judges of pleasure. Hence our attitude towards pleasure must be like that of the elders of the people in the *Iliad* towards Helen, and we must constantly apply the words they use; for if we dismiss pleasure as they dismissed Helen, we shall be less likely to go wrong. By action of this kind, to put it summarily, we shall best succeed in hitting the mean.

Undoubtedly this is a difficult task, especially in individual cases. It is not easy to determine the right manner, objects, occasion and duration of anger. Sometimes we praise people who are deficient in anger, and call them gentle, and at other times we praise people who exhibit a fierce temper as high spirited. It is not however a man who deviates a little from goodness, but one who deviates a great deal, whether on the side of excess or of deficiency, that is blamed; for he is sure to call attention to himself. It is not easy to decide in theory how far and to what extent a man may go before he becomes blameworthy, but neither is it easy to define in theory anything else in the region of the senses; such things depend on circumstances, and our judgment of them depends on our perception.

So much then is plain, that the mean is everywhere praiseworthy, but that we ought to aim at one time towards an excess and at another towards a deficiency; for thus shall we most easily hit the mean, or in other words reach excellence.

21
The New Greek Education of the Alexandrian Age (c. 338-30 B.C.)

The Euphebic Oath in the Euphebic Training instituted about 335 B.C. Translation on p. 499 of Greek text on p. 498 derived from Pollux, *Onomasticon*, viii, 105, and Stobaeus, *Florilegium*, xliii, 48, in John Wilson Taylor, "The Athenian Euphebic Oath," *Classical Journal*, XIII (No. 7, April, 1918), pp. 495-501. See also Clarence A. Forbes, *Greek Physical Education* (New York: D. Appleton-Century Co., 1929), pp. 109-178, oath on p. 149.

I will never bring reproach upon my hallowed arms nor will I desert the comrade at whose side I stand, but I will defend our altars and our hearths, single-handed or supported by many. My native land I will not leave a diminished heritage but greater and better than when I received it. I will obey whoever is in authority and submit to the established laws and all others which the people shall harmoniously enact. If anyone tries to overthrow the constitution or disobeys it, I will not permit him, but will come to its defense single-handed or with the support of all. I will honor the religion of my fathers. Let the gods be my witnesses, Agraulus, Enyalius, Ares, Zeus, Thallo, Auxo, Hegemone.

22
The Roman Family (as Seen by an Early American Sociologist)

Mosiah Hall

Reprinted by permission of Charles Scribner's Sons from *A Practical Sociology*, pages 37-44, by Mosiah Hall (1918).

Mr. Pessimo. I've just looked up my Roman history, Optime, and I feel sure that a clear-cut picture of the Roman family will cause you to revise your notion of ancient family life, and force you to admit its superiority over the modern family.

Mr. Optime. I am glad to admit that the early Roman household was the most favorable type of the patriarchal family known to history, and that it embraced many admirable qualities which the modern home would do well to emulate.

Mr. P. In contrast with the loosely organized home of to-day the Roman family was highly unified. Members of the modern family have an exaggerated idea of equality with the disposition to assert their rights and so weaken the family unity; as soon as the children become self-supporting they throw off parental authority and shift for themselves. In the Roman family all authority resided in the oldest male head, who was the priest of the family ancestor-worship, and in him was vested all legal rights as well as the sole ownership of family property. This organization preserved the unity of the family and gave to it a permanency which is painfully lacking in the modern home. Think of the contrast, Optime. This family organization persisted for half a thousand years. Our family life changes with our fancy and in accordance with the prevailing style.

Mr. O. You do well to praise the Roman family, Pessimo, but you must not allow your enthusiasm to blind you to its defects. You must not forget that many influences besides that of the home entered into Roman civilization, and that each of these contributed something to the strength and unity of family life.

Mr. P. I do not quite follow you. To my way of thinking, the Roman family itself was the centre of all activity, and from it radiated all the virtues that made for Roman civilization.

Mr. O. It would be more nearly true to say that the nature of Roman civilization determined the family organization, since, as you know, a part is never equal to the whole. Therefore, the Roman family cannot be understood until we know what factors entered into Roman life. Undoubtedly the family organization embraced more factors of that life than did any other part; hence, the family constituted the most important factor of Roman civilization.

Mr. P. And the modern home is weak, then, because it is the centre of so few of the activities of civilization?

Mr. O. You are improving wonderfully, Pessimo.

Mr. P. The Roman family was truly a centre of energy, it embraced religious worship, education, legal practice, and industrial activity. The family ideals were stern, simple, and wholesome, but to my mind the authority possessed by the head of the family was the secret of family strength and unity.

Mr. O. Be careful, Pessimo, you're wandering again from the straight and narrow path.

Mr. P. Yes, we never could agree on the question of authority. I'm convinced, however, that the stern discipline and the perfect obedience exacted of both wife and children were responsible chiefly for the superiority of the Roman family. Writers claim that divorce and family desertion were practically unknown, and that the older children were never known to break away from the family relationship.

Mr. O. The fact is, Pessimo, that this authority was too absolute, and it prevented the development of initiative and self-control on the part of the women. We shall see that during the days of Imperial Rome, when women obtained their freedom, they were so unaccustomed to its exercise that they abused it most shamefully. Listen to the words of the great censor, Cato: "The husband is the judge of his wife. If she has committed a fault, he punishes her; if she is caught in adultery, he kills her; but if she catches him she would not dare lay a finger upon him, and indeed, she has no right." No, Pessimo, you must look to other things than authority for the high moral qualities of Roman life.

Mr. P. What factors, for example?

Mr. O. One was the profound respect accorded the Roman matron. James Bryce declares: "One can hardly imagine a more absolute subjection of one person to another who was, nevertheless, not only free but respected and influential, as we know that the wife in old Rome was." When the young bride was lifted over the threshold of her husband's home, she turned and faced him with the solemn words, "Where thou are lord I am lady"—and this was no idle boast. Unlike the Greek wife, she ruled over her household. She occupied the central room (atrium) of the house, and here she spun and weaved and directed the labors of her household. She was guardian of the family honor; she shared with her husband in the education of her children, and officiated beside him as priestess in the family worship. In opposition to Oriental custom, she was permitted her personal freedom, and when she walked abroad, robed in the *stola maternalis*, men made way for her as she passed as a mark of respect for a matron of Rome. The state erected a statue to the memory of the Roman matron, Cornelia.

Mr. P. We cannot agree in this matter, Optime. In my opinion the high virtues of the Roman matron were due more to her obedience to authority than to the exercise of this freedom.

Mr. O. This also must be noted: A large proportion of the people were farmers, who owned and tilled their own land. This prevented the concentration of population in cities, where, as is well known, the tendency is toward social vice and degeneracy.

Mr. P. Yes, that's a good point.

Mr. O. Furthermore, during the early centuries of Roman history there was an urgent need of a rapid increase in population, especially for soldiers to protect the commonwealth. This necessity placed a premium on children, particularly males, and made child-bearing praiseworthy.

Mr. P. It sounds reasonable.

Mr. O. That accounted largely for the fact that the early Romans disapproved celibacy, and that prostitution and divorce were infrequent. Do you know, Pessimo, that divorce is four times as great in modern childless homes as it is among families having children?

Mr. P. Where are you leading me, Optime?

Mr. O. At an early period, also, Rome evinced a genius for jurisprudence. The enactment of the *Laws of the Twelve Tables* marked an epoch in the world's history; thereafter law and order were destined slowly to replace force, and justice to take the place of license. The Tables, together with other laws and codes that followed, earned for Rome the proud title of lawgiver to the nations. Do you not agree, Pessimo, that much of the stability of Roman family life was due to these laws?

Mr. P. There seems no escape from that conclusion.

Mr. O. Then you will admit further that the superiority of the Roman family was due to many related factors, and that the question of authority was probably not very important after all.

Mr. P. I'm not so certain of that. The explanation must be given as to why this high ideal of Roman life did not persist and save the empire from decay and final destruction. Probably the disintegration of one factor only was a sufficient cause. You may be forced to acknowledge, after all, that the trouble was precipitated, if not actually caused, by the breaking down of the authority of the home and the consequent freeing of the women, who thereupon became degenerate and licentious.

Mr. O. State your fears more clearly.

Mr. P. During the Imperial days of Rome the sacred ceremony of marriage, known as *manus*, was broken down and almost disappeared; the form known as *usus*, which was "marriage by consent," gradually took its place. This resulted in the abolition of the authority of the husband over the household, and left the Roman matron "to all intents and purposes a free agent, controlling her own actions, and to some extent her property." You must know, Optime, that this change marked the beginning of the downfall of Rome.

Mr. O. The change in the marriage ceremony, Pessimo, was not in itself injurious, because out of it arose the highest ideal of the marriage relationship known to the ancient world. To quote Goodsell: "Before noting the abuses which crept into family life in the days of the Empire it would be well to recognize the worthy ideal of marriage which prevailed during the late Republic." That the ideal was not realized in many instances does not impugn its high and honorable character. This conception of marriage made the wife the equal of her husband, and recognized her right to the full and free development of her powers as an individual having responsibilities and privileges. James Bryce defined the free Roman marriage as "a partnership in the whole of life, a sharing of rights both sacred and secular."

Mr. P. To what, then, do you attribute Roman degeneracy?

Mr. O. After Rome reached her ideal of world conquest and "sat upon her seven hills and ruled the world," she was unable to project any other ideal worthy of her mighty ambition. She, therefore, settled down to enjoy her ill-gotten wealth. Rich Romans bought or seized most of the small farms to add to their country estates, slaves did most of the labor, and consequently a large group of landless men flocked to the cities. One writer remarks: "Such conditions do not furnish favorable soil for the growth of healthy ideals of civic or of family life. Men and women alike were infected with the dry rot of selfishness and a frenzied pleasure-seeking." Soon they came to look upon the earlier, almost religious, conception of family duties as troublesome and out of date; in consequence concubinage and prostitution grew rapidly, and "in time the vices of the men infected the women" and produced what the poet Juvenal described as "the cruelest and most wanton women of antiquity."

Mr. P. On the contrary, this sexual immorality and resulting degeneracy must have been due to the equality and liberty of action granted the women. So lax became the sex relationship and so shameful the prevalence of divorce that one writer mentions as the boast of a certain woman that she "counted her years by the number of husbands she had had." St. Jerome states that he had seen a man in Rome living with his twenty-first wife, and this man was her twenty-second husband. It is said "men changed their wives as their garments." Now, Optime, I submit that this is sufficient proof that women cannot safely be granted equality and freedom, and that a strong central authority is needed at the head of the household. Here you have the actual results of the emancipation of women which you so warmly champion. I hope you will not be so anxious now to repeat the experiment.

Mr. O. Oh, Pessimo, you are hopeless! You forever "place the cart before the horse." Your charge is directly refuted by Goodsell, who declares: "It cannot be too emphatically pointed out that the evils characteristic of sex relations and family life in the Roman Empire were signs of the general social and moral degeneracy of the times, rather than the direct outcome of the increased liberty accorded women."

When a nation becomes morally decadent every institution of society is affected. Marriage and sex relationship suffer first of all. Fully a dozen factors contributed to cause the destruction of Roman civilization; one of these was sexual immorality. To attribute the downfall to one factor alone—the immorality of women—is sheer perversity. This insult to womanhood is one of the historic slanders of the ages which the quickened conscience and chivalry of the present should hasten to repudiate.

23
Oratory—the Contrast between the New and Old Education

Publius Cornelius Tacitus (55-c. 120 A.D.)

Selections from *A Dialogue on Oratory*, 28, 29, 30, 31, 32, 34 and 35, in Tacitus, *Dialogus Aricola and Germania*, translated with introduction and notes by W. Hamilton Fyfe (Oxford: Clarendon Press, 1908), pp. 29-38. Reprinted by permission of the Clarendon Press, Oxford.

[Messala speaking to Maternus "with that old-world freedom which in these degenerate days is even farther from us than their eloquence."] ... Everybody knows why oratory and all the other arts have degenerated from their former glory. The cause is not a dearth of students, but rather the indolence of our young men, the indifference of their parents, the ignorance of the professed teachers, and the general neglect of the old-world morality. These evils, originating in Rome, gradually permeated Italy, and are now finding their way into the provinces. Well, you know your own homes best, so I will confine myself to these native Roman vices which infect our sons in their very cradles, and grow upon them more and more every year. But first I must say a word about our ancestors' strict methods of training, by which they formed their sons' characters. In the old days every Roman's son, born in wedlock, was reared not in the lodgings of some hired nurse, but at his mother's knee and under her sheltering care. Her function was to keep house and devote herself to her children. She could have no higher praise. However, they also selected a relative, some lady of ripe years and reliable character, to whose charge all the children of the family could be safely entrusted. In her presence they could say nothing disgraceful and do nothing dishonourable. She not only controlled their studies and school exercises, but her modest piety also had a refining influence upon their leisure hours and childish recreations. It was thus, we read, that Cornelia the mother of the Gracchi, Aurelia the mother of Caesar, and

Atia the mother of Augustus, presided over their boys' early education and brought them up to be leaders of men. And what was the result of this strict training? The young man grew up frank and honest, untainted by any moral blemish, and was ready to devote himself at once, heart and soul, to some honourable calling. Whatever his inclination—whether towards the army or the law or the art of public speaking—he gave his whole attention to his profession and probed its possibilities to the full.

But in these days our babies are handed over to some Greek servant-girl, while one of the men-servants—often a low scoundrel unfit for any important charge—is told off at random to help her. From his tenderest years the child's untaught mind is filled with these nurses' superstitious tales. Throughout the household no one feels any scruples about anything he may do or say in the presence of the young master. Nay, even parents do not train their boys in honesty and modest behaviour, but let them grow up insubordinate and saucy, till they gradually lose all sense of shame and all respect for themselves and for other people. Then there is a peculiar Roman failing with which our children seem to be imbued at birth—I mean the passion for the theatre and for looking on at athletic contests. When a man's mind is filled with such interests, there is little room left for intellectual pursuits. Yet how many people are there who talk of anything else at home? What else do you hear young men discussing, if you go into a lecture-room and listen to their conversation? Why even the masters talk more on these subjects to their classes than on any other, for they attract pupils not by strict discipline or by proved ability but by obsequious behaviour and seductive flattery.

30. I pass by the question of elementary education, though there too great negligence is shown. Far too little labour is spent on the study of literature and of history, or in acquiring knowledge of science or of philosophy or of politics. Everybody seeks out the people they call "rhetoricians." . . . The real orator is one who can speak on any conceivable matter in a style that is noble, brilliant, and convincing, and can at the same time do justice to his subject, gain his object, and delight his hearers.

31. Such was the firm belief of those ancient orators, and they understood what was needed to this end: not to practise exercises in the schools of rhetoric, not merely to train the voice and vocal organs in imaginary disputes without the remotest bearing on real life, but rather to fill the mind with those studies which seek to determine the nature of virtue and vice, of honesty and meanness, of justice and injustice. They provide the raw material of oratory. For in court we chiefly dilate upon justice, in debates we treat of expediency, and in eulogies we

speak of moral goodness: often, too, we blend all three subjects together. Now a man's treatment of these subjects cannot be full and varied and brilliant unless he has studied human character, and has learnt the nature of virtue and of wickedness and of those qualities which cannot be ranked as either good or bad. Such knowledge is the source of the orator's power. He can more easily excite or soothe the jury's anger if he knows what anger is; and he can more readily move them to pity if he understands the nature of pity and the emotions by which it is aroused. If a speaker has been trained in such subjects as these, no matter whether he has to speak before jurors who are hostile or biased or jealous or sulky or nervous, he will be able to feel the pulse of his audience, and, with all his well-stocked outfit ready for use, he can adapt his speech to suit their temper and give them in each case the treatment which their character demands. . . .

32. . . . There is no true orator, and has never been one, who has not come into court equipped with varied learning, just as a soldier goes to battle equipped with all his arms. Our modern speakers are so indifferent in this respect that you can detect in their speeches the abominable errors of modern colloquial speech. They are ignorant of the law, they pay no heed to the resolutions of the senate, they even scoff at the statutes of the land, and have a positive horror of the study of philosophy and its conclusions. They are content with a few narrow platitudes. They have degraded oratory. Once she was the queen of all the arts, and filled our minds with a stately retinue of liberal studies: but now they have dethroned her, docked and shorn her of her retinue, her glory, and almost of all her natural dignity, until oratory is studied like the meanest trade. This I conceive to be the prime reason why we have fallen so far below the standard of the ancient orators. . . .

34. Well, in the old days, when a youth who was being educated for the bar had obtained at home a sound moral training and some liberal culture, his father or some other relative took him to one of the orators who held a leading position in the country. The boy was then attached to him and followed him everywhere, attending at all his speeches whether in the law-courts or at public meetings; even witnessing his sharp encounters with opponents, and listening to his denunciations. Thus he learnt to fight, as it were, upon the field of battle. The young men soon gained great experience, self-confidence, and good judgment, carrying on their studies, as they did, in the full light of day amid the actual contests of the courts, where no one can contradict himself or say anything stupid without incurring the judge's disapproval, an onslaught from his adversary, and sharp criticism even from the counsel on his own side. So they quickly picked

up a real and unaffected eloquence: and although they were attached to one speaker, still they had frequent opportunities of hearing all the great pleaders of the day both in civil and in criminal cases. Besides, in seeing many different audiences they became familiar with people's very diverse tastes, and soon learnt to detect what found favour with each type of audience and what was displeasing. By this means they secured the very best kind of teacher, one who could show them the real nature of eloquence, and not its counterfeit presentment: they secured rivals and opponents who fought them in real earnest with the button off their foils; and audiences always large and always different, composed of critics both favourable and hostile, so that neither the merits nor the demerits of their speeches passed unnoticed. A really great and lasting reputation must, as you know, be earned among the opposition benches as well as on one's own side: indeed, its growth there is less fitful and more likely to last. Under this system of education the young man, whom we are describing, became the pupil of the great speakers, heard speeches in the forum and attended cases in court. He gained experience from the efforts of others, got to know the law by hearing it cited every day, became familiar with the look of a jury, and learned the vagaries of the popular taste. Thus, whatever case he ultimately came to undertake, whether for the prosecution or for the defence, he was at once able to deal with it by his own unaided efforts. L. Crassus, at the age of eighteen, prosecuted C. Carbo; Caesar was twenty-one when he prosecuted Dolabella, Asinius Pollio twenty-two when he attacked Cato; and Calvus was very little older when he wrote those speeches against Vatinius which we still read to-day with admiration.

35. In these days we take our sons to the schools kept by the people who call themselves "rhetoricians." These schools first came into existence a little before Cicero's time, and found little favour with our forefathers, as one may gather from the fact, which Cicero relates, that the censors Crassus and Domitius ordered them to be closed, calling them "schools of misbehaviour." Well, as I say, we take them to schools where it is hard to tell whether the surroundings or the schoolfellows or the studies do the more harm to their characters. For a boy learns no respect in a place where every one is as ignorant as himself: he gains no profit from his schoolfellows, since they are all boys or young men together, and care neither what their speeches are like nor what is thought of them. Even the exercises he does generally frustrate their own object. For, as you know, the rhetoricians usually deal with two kinds of subject, "deliberative" and "forensic" speeches. The former are, it is true, entrusted to the younger pupils as being the easier and demanding less ability, but "forensic" speeches are the task of the

stronger students, and, really, they are the most absurd and unreal compositions. Their subject having no bearing upon real life, it necessarily follows that their style is bombastic and unreal. Thus they come to discuss in the longest possible words the due reward of tyrannicide, the alternatives open to the victim of a rape, the cure for an epidemic, the morality of incest, and all the other subjects which are debated daily in the schools, but never, or hardly ever, in real life. . . .

24
Oratory as
the Aim of Education

Marcus Tullius Cicero
(106-43 B.C.)

De Oratore, I, iv. 13-vi. 21; viii. 29-35, in Cicero De Oratore with an English translation by E. W. Sutton and H. Rackham, The Loeb Classical Library (Cambridge, Massachusetts: Harvard University Press, 1942), I, pp. 11, 13, 15, 17, 23, 25, 27.

13, iv; . . . in this city of our own assuredly no studies have ever had a more vigorous life than those having to do with the art of speaking.

14: For as soon as our world-empire had been established, and an enduring peace had assured us leisure, there was hardly a youth, athirst for fame, who did not deem it his duty to strive with might and main after eloquence. At first indeed, in their complete ignorance of method, since they thought there was no definite course of training or any rules of art, they used to attain what skill they could by means of their natural ability and of reflection. But later, having heard the Greek orators, gained acquaintance with their literature and called in Greek teachers, our people were fired with a really incredible enthusiasm for eloquence. *15:* The importance, variety, and frequency of current suits of all sorts aroused them so effectually, that, to the learning which each man had acquired by his own efforts, plenty of practice was added, as being better than the maxims of all the masters. In those days too, as at present, the prizes open to this study were supreme, in the way of popularity, wealth, and reputation alike. As for ability again—there are many things to show it—our fellow-countrymen have far excelled the men of every other race. *16:* And considering all this, who would not rightly marvel that, in all the long record of ages, times, and states, so small a number of orators is to be found?

But the truth is that this oratory is a greater thing, and has its sources in more arts and branches of study, than people suppose.

V: For, where the number of students is very great, the supply of masters of the very best, the quality of natural ability outstanding, the variety of issues unlimited, the prizes open to eloquence exceedingly splendid, what else could anyone think to be the cause, unless it be the really incredible vastness and difficulty of the subject? *17:* To begin with, a knowledge of very many matters must be grasped, without which oratory is but an empty and ridiculous swirl of verbiage: and the distinctive style has to be formed, not only by the choice of words, but also by the arrangement of the same; and all the mental emotions, with which nature has endowed the human race, are to be intimately understood, because it is in calming or kindling the feelings of the audience that the full power and science of oratory are to be brought into play. To this there should be added a certain humour, flashes of wit, the culture befitting a gentleman, and readiness and terseness alike in repelling and in delivering the attack, the whole being combined with a delicate charm and urbanity. *18:* Further, the complete history of the past and a store of precedents must be retained in the memory, nor may a knowledge of statute law and our national law in general be omitted. And why should I go on to describe the speaker's delivery? That needs to be controlled by bodily carriage, gesture, play of features and changing intonation of voice; and how important that is wholly by itself, the actor's trivial art and the stage proclaim; for there, although all are labouring to regulate the expression, the voice, and the movements of the body, everyone knows how few actors there are, or ever have been, whom we could bear to watch! What need to speak of that universal treasure-house the memory? Unless this faculty be placed in charge of the ideas and phrases which have been thought out and well weighed, even though as conceived by the orator they were of the highest excellence, we know that they will all be wasted.

19: Let us therefore cease to wonder what may be the cause of the rarity of orators, since oratory is the result of a whole number of things, in any one of which to succeed is a great achievement, and let us rather exhort our children, and the others whose fame and repute are dear to us, to form a true understanding of the greatness of their task, and not to believe that they can gain their coveted object by reliance on the rules or teachers or methods of practice employed by everybody, but to rest assured that they can do this by the help of certain other means.

20, VI: And indeed in my opinion, no man can be an orator complete in all points of merit, who has not attained a knowledge of all important subjects and arts. For it is from knowledge that oratory must derive its beauty and fullness, and unless there is such knowledge, well-grasped and comprehended by the speaker, there must be something empty and almost childish in the utterance. . . .

29, VIII: In that place, as Cotta was fond of relating, Crassus introduced a conversation on the pursuit of oratory, with a view to relieving all minds from the discourse of the day before. *30:* He began by saying that Sulpicius and Cotta seemed not to need exhortation from him but rather commendation, seeing that thus early they had acquired such skill as not merely to be ranked above their equals in age, but to be comparable with their elders. "Moreover," he continued, "there is to my mind no more excellent thing, than the power, by means of oratory, to get a hold on assemblies of men, win their good will, direct their inclinations wherever the speaker wishes, or divert them from whatever he wishes. In every free nation, and most of all communities which have attained the enjoyment of peace and tranquility, this one art has always flourished above the rest and ever reigned supreme. 31: For what is so marvellous as that, out of the innumerable company of mankind, a single being should arise, who either alone or with a few others can make effective a faculty bestowed by nature upon every man? Or what so pleasing to the understanding and the ear as a speech adorned and polished with wise reflections and dignified language? Or what achievement so mighty and glorious as that the impulses of the crowd, the consciences of the judges, the austerity of the Senate, should suffer transformation through the eloquence of one man? 32: What function again is so kingly, so worthy of the free, so generous, as to bring help to the suppliant, to raise up those that are cast down, to bestow security, to set free from peril, to maintain men in their civil rights? What too is so indispensable as to have always in your grasp weapons wherewith you can defend yourself, or challenge the wicked man, or when provoked take your revenge?

"Nay more (not to have you for ever contemplating public affairs, the bench, the platform, and the Senate-house), what in hours of ease can be a pleasanter thing or one more characteristic of culture, than discourse that is graceful and nowhere uninstructed? For the one point in which we have our very greatest advantage over the brute creation is that we hold converse one with another, and can reproduce our thought in word. 33: Who therefore would not rightly admire this faculty, and deem it his duty to exert himself to the utmost in this field, that by so doing he may surpass men themselves in that particular respect wherein chiefly men are superior to animals? To come, however, at length to the highest achievements of eloquence, what other power could have been strong enough either to gather scattered humanity into one place, or to lead it out of its brutish existence in the wilderness up to our present condition of civilization as men and citizens, or, after the establishment of social communities, to give shape to laws, tribunals, and civic rights? 34: And not to pursue any further instances—wellnigh countless as they are—I will conclude the whole matter in a few words, for my assertion is this: that the wise control of the complete orator is that which chiefly upholds not only his own dignity, but the safety of countless individuals and of the entire State. Go forward therefore, my young friends, in your present course, and bend your energies to that study which engages you, that so it may be in your power to become a glory to yourselves, a source of service to your friends, and profitable members of the Republic."

25
Marcus Fabius Quintilianus (c. 35-c. 95 A.D.) on Education

Selections from *Quintilian on Education Being a Translation of Selected Passages from the* Institutio Oratoria *with an Introductory Essay on Quintilian, his Environment and his Theory of Education* by William M. Smail (Oxford: Clarendon Press, 1938). Reprinted by permission of the Clarendon Press, Oxford).

Book I—Introduction

9. It is the perfect orator that we are training and he cannot even exist unless he is a good man. We therefore demand in him not only exceptional powers of eloquence but also every mental excellence.

10. Nor indeed would I admit that the principles which underlie an upright and honourable life should be left to the philosophers, as some have thought; for the ideal citizen, fitted to take his share in the management of public and private affairs, able to govern cities by his wise counsels, to establish them upon a sure foundation of good laws and to improve them by the administration of impartial justice, is assuredly none other than the orator.

11. Wherefore, admitting that I will make use of certain principles which are to be found in the books of the philosophers, I would none the less maintain that they truly and rightfully belong to our sphere and have a direct bearing on the Art of Oratory.

12. Or if it be found that we have to talk continually of justice, bravery, temperance, and the other virtues to such an extent that scarcely a single case can be found which does not involve some question of this kind, and if all these themes have to be set forth by means of constructive reasoning and lucid exposition, will it be doubted that wherever intellectual power and ready eloquence are demanded, there is the peculiar province of the orator?

13. These qualities, as Cicero very clearly shows, were not only joined by nature but also associated in practice, so that originally the same men were considered both wise and eloquent. Then this twofold study was divided and through lack of art it comes about that the arts appeared to be distinct. For as soon as the tongue became a source of gain, and men began to make an evil use of the good gift of eloquence,

those who were considered fluent speakers abandoned the care of morals;

14. And being thus cast off it fell a prey, so to speak, to the feebler intellects. Then certain men, despising the toilsome pursuit of eloquence, fell back upon the moulding of the human mind and the establishment of laws to regulate the life of man; and thus they kept what was indeed the nobler part, if a division were possible, but assumed a totally unwarranted title by claiming for themselves alone the name of "lovers of wisdom." For neither the greatest generals nor those who played the most prominent parts in the weightiest counsels and in the administration of the Commonwealth dared to advance so preposterous a claim. They preferred to do the noblest deeds rather than to profess them.

15. I would willingly concede that many of the old professors of philosophy taught things honourable and lived in accordance with their own precepts. But in these our times the name has often cloaked great vices. In such cases philosophers did not make it the object of their labour through goodness and devotion to be considered "lovers of wisdom" but sought rather to make a long face, a mournful manner, and an unusual garb conceal the worst depravity of morals.

16. Those topics which are claimed by the philosophers as exclusively their own are handled by every one of us continually. Who, unless he be the most depraved of men, does not speak of what is just, right, and good? What man even amongst our bumpkins does not make some inquiry into the causes of natural phenomena? while the proper use of words and their different meanings ought to be the common concern of all who care aught for human speech.

17. Yet all these matters will be best understood and exemplified by the orator. And, if a perfect orator had ever existed, the precepts of human excellence would not now be sought in the schools of the philosophers. As things are, it is sometimes necessary to refer to those authors who have seized upon what I have called the deserted portion of the art of oratory (and the better portion to boot), and as it were to reclaim our own, not that we may use their discoveries but in order to show that they have appropriated what is not theirs.

18. Let us then define the orator as a man who can truly be called wise, perfect not only in character (for in my opinion, though some think differently, that is not enough) but also in knowledge and every sort of eloquence.

19. Such a man perhaps has never yet existed. But that is no reason why we should not strive towards the highest ideal, as was done by the ancients for the most part. For, although they considered that so far no wise man had been discovered, they none the less wrote down the precepts whereby wisdom might be attained.

20. Assuredly there is such a thing as perfect eloquence nor does the nature of the human intellect forbid its realization. And even if it never were attained, still those who strive towards the highest will reach greater heights than those who despair at the outset of ever reaching their ideal and stop short at the lowest levels. . . .

Book I, Chapter II
The Method of Primary Instruction

1. When his son is born, let the father first of all conceive the highest hopes concerning him, for so he will become more careful from the start.

There is no foundation in fact for the complaint that to very few is given the power of understanding what is taught them but that the majority waste both time and labour through slowness of intellect.

On the contrary, you can find many who are clever at puzzling things out and quick at learning. Indeed such aptitude is natural to man, and just as birds are born to fly, horses to run, and wild beasts to show fierceness, so our peculiar gift is mental activity and cleverness and for that reason the origin of mind is held to be divine.

2. But dullness and lack of aptitude for learning are no more in accordance with man's nature than are bodily abnormalities and deformity; they occur but seldom and the proof of it is this, that most men form high hopes of their sons; but when, as these sons grow older, such hopes fade away, clearly it is not nature that is at fault but human care.

"Still, one man does surpass another in natural ability."

3. Granted; but even so he will accomplish more or less; for no one is found who has not profited at all by study.

Let him who has grasped this fact, as soon as he becomes a father, devote the keenest possible attention to the promise of the budding orator.

4. Before all things else, let the speech of his nurses be correct. Chrysippus wished them, if it were possible, to be educated women, but at any rate he desired the best available to be selected. And of course in the case of nurses account must first be taken of moral character; still let them also speak correctly.

5. Theirs are the voices the child will hear first, theirs the words he will try to reproduce. And we are naturally most tenacious of what we learned while our minds were still unformed: as the flavour imparted to vessels when they are new remains in them and the colours of woollen stuffs wherewith their original whiteness has been transformed cannot be washed out.

And further those very impressions which are less desirable are the more enduring. Good things are easily changed for the worse, but when will you turn vices into virtues? Do not then allow the boy, even in infancy, to become familiar with a way of speaking which has afterwards to be unlearned.

6. In the parents I would fain have as much education as is possible. Nor do I refer to the fathers only. . . .

7. Those who have not themselves enjoyed the benefits of education must not devote less care to the proper instruction of their children, and their own deficiencies (in learning) should make them the more careful in all other particulars.

Of the slave companions amongst whom the object of these high hopes is to be reared, the same may be said as of the nurses.

8. In the case of *paedagogi* (attendants) this further point should be insisted upon, that they be either thoroughly educated—and this I should like to be the first consideration—or else aware of their lack of education. Nothing is worse than those who have made some little progress beyond the first elements and on the strength of this are filled with a false idea of their own knowledge. . . .

9. Their deficiencies too often harm the morals of the young.

10. If any one thinks that I am demanding a great deal, let him consider that it is an orator that is being trained: a difficult task even when nothing has failed us in moulding him; and further that other greater difficulties remain: for he must also have unceasing application, teachers of outstanding merit, and a wide range of studies.

11. And so the best principles must be laid down; if they prove irksome to any one, their failure lies with the man and not with the system of instruction. However, if our future orator is not so fortunate as to have such nurses, companions, and attendants as I should most like him to have, at any rate let there be some one person constantly by his side, some one not unskilled in speaking, to correct at once any blunders in speech made by these others in the presence of his charge and so to prevent such blunders from taking root in his mind. Provided always it be understood that my former recommendations indicate the sound plan, and that this is only a palliative.

12. I prefer that a boy should start with the Greek language: first because he will pick up Latin, which is in common use, whether we wish it or no, and second because he should be instructed first in Greek studies from which ours derive their origin.

13. Yet I would not have such slavish adherence to this principle as to compel the boy to speak and study Greek only, for a considerable time, as is usually the custom. For in this way arise countless faults of pronunciation, through the corrupting influence of foreign sounds and

faults of speech also to which Greek forms of expression cling through constant familiarity, persisting tenaciously even in the speaking of a different language.

14. Latin therefore should follow at no great interval and before long the two languages should advance together. Thus it will come to pass that when we begin to give equal attention to both languages neither one will hurt the other.

15. Some have thought that children under seven years of age should not be taught letters because that is the earliest age at which such studies can be understood and such toil endured. Until the time of Aristophanes the grammarian, it was a common tradition that Hesiod held this view. Aristophanes was the first to deny to that poet the *Hypothekai* (Suggestions) in which this view is found.

16. But other writers too, including Eratosthenes, have preached the same doctrine. A better view is that held by those who like Chrysippus would have some instruction for every stage of the child's life. Chrysippus, though assigning the first three years to nurses, lays it down that even they should mould the child's mind by the best training possible.

17. But why should an age which is already dealing with morals have no dealings with letters? I am well aware that, in the whole space of time of which I am speaking, scarcely as much is achieved as can be bestowed by a single year when the child is older, yet it seems to me that our opponents have here spared the teacher rather than the pupil.

18. How will they be better employed, in any case, from the time when they can speak? For they must do something. Or why should we despise this gain, however small it may be, in the period prior to the seventh year? Assuredly, no matter how small the contribution of those earlier years, yet the child will learn greater things in that year which would otherwise have been devoted to the lesser.

19. And this gain, carried forward through the years, adds to the total, and time thus saved in infancy is an acquisition to youth.

Let the same rule be laid down for the years that follow so that the pupil may not be late in beginning to learn what every one has to learn. Let us not then lose the earliest years—the less so since the rudiments of letters depend on memory alone: and memory not only exists in small children but is also most tenacious at that stage.

20. Nor am I so ignorant of the capacities of different ages as to think that we should straightway place a grievous burden upon tender minds and remorselessly exact close application. For one thing especially must be guarded against, viz. lest one who cannot yet love studies come to hate them and even after the passing of childhood's years shrink from a bitter task once undergone.

Let this first instruction be in the form of play; let the pupil be asked questions and praised for his answers, let him never rejoice in ignorance of anything; sometimes, when he will not learn, let another be taught of whom he may be jealous; let him compete sometimes with others and quite often think himself victorious: let him also be excited by rewards, which at that age are eagerly sought after.

21. These are trivial matters we are expounding, we who profess to have the training of an orator. But even studies have their infancy and as the rearing of bodies, destined ere long to be of the stoutest, starts with milk and the cradle, so he who was to be the most eloquent of men once uttered an infant's wail and made the first attempts at speech with halting tongue and found difficulty in distinguishing the forms of the letters. And whilst a knowledge of certain things is not sufficient in itself, it is not therefore unnecessary to possess it.

22. But, if no one blames a father who considers these things worthy of attention in his own son's case, why should one be blamed for bringing to public notice things he would be right in doing in the privacy of his own home? It is the more necessary to do so, since younger minds take in smaller things more readily and as human bodies cannot be moulded to certain flexions of the limbs save when they are tender, so with men's minds, strength itself when it comes makes them more unyielding in most respects.

23. Would Philip King of Macedon have chosen that the first rudiments of letters should be imparted to his son Alexander by Aristotle the greatest philosopher of the day, or would the latter have undertaken the task, save in the belief that the first elements in our studies are best handled by the best teachers and that these elements have an important bearing on the final result?

24. Let us pretend then that it is Alexander who is committed to our charge, placed on my lap, a child worthy of infinite care (though every man thinks that of his own child). Am I then to be ashamed to point out even in the very rudiments of instruction certain shortcuts to the end in view?

For example, I certainly do not approve of what I see to be common practice, viz. that children should learn the names and order of the letters before their forms.

25. This (practice) hinders the recognition of the letters since the child soon ceases to attend to their shapes and simply follows his memory which outstrips his observation. And so teachers even when they seem to have fixed the letters firmly enough in the minds of their pupils in the straightforward order in which they are at first usually written, hark back again and by varying the arrangement introduce confusion until their pupils know the letters by their appearance and not by their sequence. Thus, as in the case of persons, so in the case of letters they will best be taught appearance and name together.

26. But what is a hindrance in the case of letters will do no harm with syllables.

Further, I approve of a practice devised to stimulate the child to learn, viz. that of giving him ivory letters to play with and anything else that can be proved to add to the child's pleasure, which it may be a delight to him to handle, look at, and name.

27. When the child begins to trace the outlines of the letters it will be useful to have them cut out on a board, in as beautiful a script as possible, so that his pen may be guided along them as if in furrows. Thus he will not go wrong as in writing on waxen tablets (for he will be confined within the edges on either side and will therefore be unable to deviate from his model), and by tracing definite outlines with greater speed and frequency he will develop the proper muscles and will not require the helping hand of a teacher placed upon his own.

28. Important, too, in this connection is a matter which is often apt to be neglected by educated people, I mean care in writing neatly and quickly. For since writing itself is the most essential thing in our studies and the one thing from which alone springs true and deeply rooted proficiency, a slow pen hinders thought and a badly formed and slovenly hand cannot be deciphered.

This involves the labour of dictating what has to be written over again.

29. Wherefore always and everywhere, but especially in private and familiar letters, it will be a source of pleasure to have given attention even to this small matter.

30. There is no short cut to the learning of syllables. They must all be learnt by heart; nor, as is frequently the case, should the more difficult be postponed till they are dealt with in writing words.

31. Nay, more—we must not even trust unduly to a first learning by heart. It will be found more profitable to go back and spend much time in driving them home, and in reading, too, not to hurry on to continuous or quick reading until a clear and unhesitating joining of the letters has been attained without at any rate any pausing for thought. Then with these syllables let words be formed and so let the pupil begin to weave sentences together.

32. It is incredible how reading is retarded by undue haste. This gives rise to hesitation, stumbling, and repetition on the part of pupils who venture beyond their powers, and then when they go astray, lack confidence even in what they already know.

33. Let reading, then, be first of all confident, then connected, and for a long time let it be slow till by practice correctness and speed are achieved together.

34. For to keep looking to the right, as is always taught, and to see ahead are matters not only of theory but also of practice, since the

reader has to pronounce what comes first while he looks at what follows, and most difficult of all, the attention of the mind has to be divided so that one thing is done with the voice, another with the eyes.

When the child begins to write words in the ordinary course it will be worth while to see that he does not waste his labour on common words chosen haphazard.

35. For whilst engaged on something else, he will from the very first be able to learn the meaning ofsmore recondite terms to which the Greeks give the name γλῶσσαι , and on the threshold of his studies to master something which otherwise will demand its own special time for study.

Since we are still dwelling on matters of slight importance, I would urge that lines set as models for copying should not convey idle sentiments but some useful instruction.

36. Recollections of such maxims remain with a man till he is old and when impressed upon a mind still unformed will even aid in building character. The sayings of famous men, too, and chosen passages, especially from the poets (for the youthful mind finds greater pleasure in learning poetry), may be learnt by heart as a relaxation. A good memory is a prime essential in oratory, as I shall explain in due course, and memory is best strengthened and nourished by exercise. Moreover, in those years of which we are now speaking, still incapable of producing anything original, memory is practically the only mental power which can profit by a teacher's care.

37. To give freedom of speech and clearness of pronunciation it will be found useful to demand from pupils of this age that they roll forth as quickly as possible words and lines of studied difficulty, made up of a series of clashing syllables and as it were broken in sound: in Greek these are called χαλινοί (bridles or bits). Such practice is a trifling thing to speak of, but if it be neglected, many faults of speech not removed in early years remain for life through force of evil habit, which cannot afterwards be corrected.

Book I, Chapter 2
The Comparative Merits of Private and Public Education

1. But now let our young pupil begin gradually to grow and to leave his mother's lap and begin serious studies. The most important question now is whether it is better to keep the student in the privacy of his own home or to hand him over to a large school and to what may be termed public instructors.

2. The latter course, I observe, has won the approval not only of those who have moulded the manners of most famous states but also

of the most eminent authorities on education. It must, however, be admitted that some disagree with this wellnigh universal practice on grounds of private opinion. Two considerations in particular appear to weigh with these critics. The first is that it is safer on moral grounds to avoid a throng of youths whose age is peculiarly prone to vicious practices, whence it is claimed—and I would the claim were false—that evil consequences have frequently arisen.

The second consideration is this, that no matter who the future teacher is, it seems likely that if he has but one pupil he will devote his time more freely to him than if he has to share that time amongst several.

3. The former plea is by far the more important. For if it were admitted that schools, whilst affording better instruction, do harm to morals, I should judge the principles of right living of more importance than those of the noblest oratory. But to my mind the two things are inseparably bound up together.

For I hold that a man cannot be a true orator without being a good man too, nor do I wish to see the two dissociated even if it be possible.

I shall therefore deal with this point before taking up the other.

4. It is thought that in schools morals are corrupted.

Now it is perfectly true that this does happen sometimes, but it happens in the home also: and of that we have countless instances, just as we have countless instances of the maintenance in both places of a spotless reputation. It is the natural disposition of the boy and the care taken of him which make all the difference. Given a mind inclined towards things evil, given carelessness in the moulding and guarding of the boy's purity in early years, and it will be found that seclusion offers just as good an opportunity for evil practices. For a private tutor may be a scoundrel, and intercourse with wicked slaves is no safer than intercourse with immoral youths of free birth.

5. But if the boy's natural disposition is good and if the parents are not sunk in blind and careless sloth, it is possible to choose the noblest instructors (and that is the foremost consideration with wise parents) and a system of instruction of the strictest kind, and at the same time to place at the boy's side some friend of weighty character or some faithful freedman whose constant companionship may even reclaim those of whom the parents were afraid.

6. It were an easy task to demolish fears on that score. Would that we did not ourselves corrupt the morals of our children! Even in earliest infancy we spoil them by our indulgence. The soft way in which we bring them up, calling it kindness, saps all strength of mind and body. What will the child not covet when he is a grown man, if he

creeps about in purple? Before he is pronouncing his first words, he knows what "cook" means and cries for oysters. We train their palates before we train their speech.

7. They grow up lolling in litters and if they ever touch the ground, it is clinging to supporting hands on either side. We take delight in their naughty sayings: words that would not be tolerated even in our pet boys from Alexandria we hail with laughter and kisses.

Nor is it strange that our children should utter such words, for we teach them ourselves, they hear them from us.

8. They see our courtesans, and our boy favourites. Every banquet makes lewd songs re-echo through the house. Shameful sights are revealed to our children's eyes. Thus is bred familiarity, till such things become quite natural. The poor victims learn these vicious lessons ere they know them to be vicious, and then, dissolute and weak, instead of picking up these evil things at school, they take them thither with them.

9. But, it will be urged, in the matter of studies a single teacher will have more time to give, if he has but a single pupil. Now, in the first place there is nothing to hinder this single private pupil, whoever he may be, from being identical with the pupil taught at school.

But even if it were impossible to combine public and private instruction, I should have preferred the light of an honourable assembly to the darkness of solitude. For all the best teachers delight in crowded classrooms and consider themselves worthy of a still larger audience.

10. But less able teachers as a rule, from a consciousness of their own failings, are content to stick to single pupils and to perform what is in a way the duty of a *paedogogus* (attendant).

11. Supposing, however, that through power or wealth or friendship a parent can secure a splendid, nay an unrivalled, teacher to instruct his son in his own home, still that teacher is not going to spend the whole day upon one pupil. Can the attention of any pupil be so continuously on the stretch, without growing weary, as the eyes do by constant gazing at a single object? And there is this special consideration, that study calls for far more solitary application than actual instruction.

12. The teacher does not stand beside the pupil when he is writing or learning things by heart or thinking—indeed, when one is doing any of these things any one's interposition is a hindrance. Reading, too, does not in every case and all the time require guidance or interpretation. For when could one become acquainted with the countless authors to be studied? The time devoted to instruction, then, is but a small fraction in which the work is marshalled, so to speak, for the whole day.

13. Accordingly instruction can be given to several pupils in succession even in cases where individual attention is required.

But much instruction can be conveyed by the voice of one teacher to all his pupils simultaneously. I say nothing of the analyses and declamations of the rhetoricians, for however great the audience each individual hearer will carry off the whole thing with him.

14. The voice of the teacher, then, is not like a banquet where there is less for each in proportion as more partake of it, but rather resembles the sun shedding upon all alike the same amount of light and heat. So, too, if a professor of literature expounds the principles of speaking or unravels knotty points of interpretation, explains historical problems or interprets poetry, all his audience will be instructed at one and the same time.

15. But, it will be said, for correction and for preparation numbers are a hindrance. Suppose that is true (is there anything at all that gives absolute satisfaction?), we shall in a moment weigh that disadvantage against the advantages of public instruction. Some one else will urge, "Yes, but I do not wish a boy to be sent to a place where he will be neglected." Now, you will find that a good teacher does not burden himself with a greater number of pupils than he can manage. Further, we must be careful above all things else to secure the intimate friendship of such a master, so that in teaching he may not simply be guided by a sense of duty, but also by affection for his pupil. In this way we shall never be mere units in a throng.

16. Again, no master who has the slightest tinge of culture will fail to give special encouragement, for his own glory's sake as well as for his pupil's, to any one in whom he discovers application and aptitude.

Supposing, then, that large schools are to be avoided (and even that I do not admit, in cases where a teacher is popular by reason of his excellence), still that does not mean that all schools are to be shunned. For it is one thing to avoid them, another to choose amongst them.

17. And now, if I have demolished the objections to public instruction, I shall proceed to state my own views on the matter.

18. First and foremost, let the future orator, whose life is to be spent in great assemblies and in the blaze of public life, become accustomed from his earliest years to face men unabashed and not grow pale by living in solitude and so to say in the cloister's shade. The mind requires constant stimulus and excitement, but in such retirement it either flags and rusts as it were in the gloom or else becomes swollen with empty self-conceit. For one who does not match himself with others must needs overrate his own powers.

19. Then when he must display the fruits of his study, he gropes about in broad daylight and finds everything new and strange, as is natural with one who has learnt in solitude what has to be done amidst a throng.

20. I pass over the friendships formed at school. They last in

undiminished strength through life, and are sealed with a kind of religious sanction. For to be initiated into the same studies is as sacred a bond as to be initiated into the same mysteries of religion.

Where will our pupil pick up what is known as "common sense," if he has avoided society? For the gregarious instinct belongs not merely to human beings but even to dumb animals.

21. Further, at home he can only learn what he himself is taught, but at school what is taught to others also. Every day he will hear many things approved, many things corrected; he will profit by another's sloth rebuked, another's industry commended. Words of praise will stir him to emulation.

22. He will think it disgraceful to be surpassed by pupils of his age, and a fine thing to have beaten his seniors. All these things stimulate the mind, and though ambition may in itself be a vice, none the less it is frequently the source of virtues.

23. There is one useful method known to me, which was employed by my own teachers. They arranged us in classes, determining the order of speaking according to the ability of the pupils. Thus as each boy appeared to excel in proficiency he stood higher in the order of declamation.

24. Tests of progress were held from time to time, and to earn promotion was a great prize with us, whilst to be head of the class was by far the most coveted honour.

The class order was not decided once for all. Each month gave the vanquished a fresh opportunity to do battle. Thus those who held high places through previous success did not relax their efforts, and shame stirred the less successful to strive to wipe out their disgrace.

25. So far as I can form a conjecture, I would maintain that this rivalry did far more to kindle our zeal for oratorical studies than the exhortations of teachers, the care of *paedogogi* (attendants), and the wishes of our parents.

26. Amongst more advanced students of literature, then, rivalry stimulates progress. In the case of beginners and those whose minds are still unformed, imitation of their fellow pupils is more pleasant than attempts to imitate the master, for the reason that it is easier. Those who are learning the rudiments will scarcely dare aspire to hopes of achieving what they look upon as the very highest eloquence. They will rather fasten upon what is nearer to them, just as vines twining round trees, cling first to the lower branches before they reach the tops.

27. So true is this principle that even the master himself (if indeed he will set usefulness before vainglory) must make it his business, in dealing with minds still unformed, not to start by over-

loading the feeble intellects of his pupils, but to control his own powers and come down to the level of their understanding.

28. For just as narrow-necked jars spill a flood of liquid poured over them, whereas they fill up when it flows in gradually or even drop by drop, so we must observe carefully the capacity of youthful minds. For that which is too difficult for their understanding will not find entrance to the boys' minds which, if we may put it so, have too narrow an opening for its reception.

29. It is useful, then, for the pupil to have those whom he may seek first to imitate, then to surpass. In this way hopes of yet higher achievement will gradually be formed.

There is this further consideration, that teachers themselves cannot in the presence of single pupils feel the same mental stimulus and exhilaration in speaking as they do when inspired by the large audiences a school affords.

30. The most important factor in eloquence is a certain state of mind. The orator's mind must be roused, it must form images of objects and, in a sense, be transformed into the nature of the things of which he speaks. Further, the nobler and the loftier the mind of the orator, the more powerful the springs, if I may say so, of its action. And so it feeds upon applause, it expands in its whirling flight, it glories in the consciousness of great achievement.

31. On the other hand, the orator feels a kind of silent disdain in lowering to the instruction of a single pupil the noble power of eloquence won by such mighty labour. He feels ashamed to rise above the level of ordinary conversation. And, indeed, let any one imagine the style of one declaiming, or the voice, gesture, and pronunciation of a pleader, the animation in short of both mind and body, the effort, to speak of nothing else, and the fatigue involved—all before an audience of one! Would such an orator not seem to be affected with something very like madness? There would be no such thing as eloquence amongst men, if we only spoke with one man at a time.

Book I, Chapter 3
Methods of Discerning Ability in the Young and of Handling Them

1. The skilled teacher, when a pupil is entrusted to his care, will first of all seek to discover his ability and natural disposition. A good memory is the chief indication of ability in a pupil and its excellence lies in two things, ease in acquiring knowledge and accuracy in retaining it. Next comes the faculty of imitation, for that also is characteristic of a teachable nature, i. e. provided that the pupil reproduces what he is taught and not

a person's appearance, for example, and gait and any unfortunate peculiarity he may have.

3. My ideal pupil will readily acquire the knowledge presented to him and some things, too, he will elicit by questions: yet he will follow his master rather than seek to outrun him. Such precocity of intellect seldom, if ever, attains to full fruition.

6. When the teacher has noticed the points I have mentioned, let him next observe how the mind of his pupil is to be handled. Some boys are lazy unless you urge them on, some do not brook commands, some are restrained by fear, some dispirited by it, some are fashioned by long-continued application, some make greater progress through spurts of hard work. Mine be the pupil who kindles at a word of praise, who glories in distinction, who weeps at defeat.

7. He must be nourished with hopes of success, he will feel the sting of reproof, desire for glory will spur him on: in such a pupil I shall never be afraid of idleness.

8. Some relaxation, however, must be given to all, not only because there is no single thing which can endure unceasing toil, and even inanimate and lifeless objects, to be able to preserve their energy, relax as it were in alternating periods of rest, but also because zeal for learning depends upon inclination, a thing which cannot be forced.

9. Thus pupils refreshed and restored by recreation bring more energy to their studies and a keener mind, whereas the mind as a rule refuses tasks imposed by harsh compulsion.

13. From the beginning, then, the boy must be exhorted never to show selfishness or dishonesty or lack of self-control, and Virgil's precept is ever to be kept in mind: "So powerful are habits formed in tender age."

14. As for corporal punishment, though it is a recognized practice and though Chrysippus does not object to it, I am altogether opposed to it, first because it is disgusting, fit only for slaves and undoubtedly an insult (as appears, if you change the age of the victim): in the next place, because a pupil whose mind so ill befits a free man's son as not to be corrected by reproof, will remain obdurate even in face of blows— like the vilest of slaves: and finally because such chastisement will be quite unnecessary if there is some one ever present to supervise the boy's studies with diligence.

15. As things are, it seems usually to happen that the carelessness of *paedagogi* is amended by the pupils being punished for doing what is wrong instead of being compelled to do what is right.

Then again, if you coerce the young child by means of blows, how would you deal with the grown youth who cannot thus be driven by fear and has more important things to learn?

16. Remember too that, when children are beaten, many unseemly cries, of which they will afterwards be ashamed, often escape them in their grief or fear, and the shame of this breaks and humiliates the spirit and makes them, sick at heart, shun the very light of day.

17. Now if, in choosing guardians and teachers, too little care has been taken to select those of sterling moral character, I am ashamed to mention the shameful practices for which men make this right of corporal punishment an excuse, and the opportunity sometimes afforded to others too by the terror of it in the wretched child's mind. I shall not dwell upon this topic: what is understood (by the reader) is already more than enough. Suffice it to say this: no one ought to have undue liberty in dealing with an age that is still feeble and helpless in face of ill treatment.

18. I shall now begin to speak of the branches of study necessary in the training of a pupil who is to be moulded into a potential orator, and explain which of them should be begun at the different stages in his education.

Book I, Chapter 4—Grammar

1. When a boy has learned to read and write with ease, he must come first of all under the care of the grammarians. It matters not whether I speak of the Greek or of the Latin grammarian, though I prefer the Greek to have precedence; but both pursue the same method.

2. The range of instruction which these teachers profess to cover may be divided very briefly into two parts, the art of speaking correctly (i. e. grammar in the modern sense) and the interpretation of the poets. But within its recesses the subject includes more than appears on the surface.

3. For with speaking is also joined the theory of writing, and the interpretation of the poets is preceded by correct reading, whilst the art of criticism is associated with both. Indeed the old grammarians employed that art in the most drastic fashion. Not only did they make free to mark lines with the stigma of a censor, so to speak, and to remove as changelings from an author's family books which in their opinion had been falsely ascribed to him, but they also formed a canon to which they admitted some authors while excluding others.

4. Further, it is not enough to have read the poets: all manner of writings must be ransacked not only for the subject-matter but also for words, which often gain their authority from the writers who use

them. Then again grammar cannot be complete without a study of music, since it has to pronounce on questions of metre and rhythm; nor could it make the poets intelligible without a knowledge of astronomy, for, to take a single instance, in indicating the seasons of the year they constantly refer to the rising and setting of constellations. Again a knowledge of philosophy is essential to grammar, not only because of the countless passages in almost every poem derived from the most intimate and subtle mysteries of natural science, but also for the sake of Empedocles in Greek, and Varro and Lucretius in Latin, literature: writers who have embodied the teaching of philosophy in their verse.

5. And yet again there is need of no slight eloquence to enable grammar to pronounce with accuracy and fluency upon the various subjects I have mentioned.

For these reasons we have no sympathy with critics who decry the study of grammar on the ground that it is trivial and dry. Unless the foundations of the future orator have been well and truly laid by this study, all the learning you build upon them will fall to the ground. It is a branch of knowledge which is necessary in youth and pleasant in old age, a sweet companion in retirement, the only one in the whole range of studies which has in it more usefulness than empty show.

6. Let no one then despise the elements of grammar as trivial things, not because it is a difficult task to distinguish consonants from vowels and to subdivide them into semi-vowels and mutes, but because those who enter the inner shrine, as it were, of this sanctuary will come into the presence of many mysteries fitted not merely to sharpen the wits of boys but to give scope for the exercise of the profoundest erudition and knowledge.

Book I, Chapter 8—Grammar (continued)

1. It remains to deal with Reading. To instruct a pupil in this subject as to where he should check his breathing, where he should mark the pause in a line, where the sense of a sentence is completed and where it begins, when the voice should be raised or lowered, how the voice should be modulated in each case and what is the requisite degree of slowness or of speed, of animation or of gentleness—all these are things which can only be demonstrated to pupils in actual practice.

2. There is, therefore, only one general principle which I would lay down here to enable my pupil to do all these things correctly, viz. let him *understand* what he is reading. Moreover, his reading should be above all things manly and dignified, with a certain degree of sweetness: not indeed like the reading of prose, because it is poetry he is reading and the poets themselves bear witness that they are singers, yet not

degraded to a careless singsong or to that effeminate and affected drawl which is the fashion nowadays, a mannerism most fittingly rebuked, as we read, by Gaius Caesar while he was still a boy, in these words: "If you are singing, you are singing badly; and if you are reading, you are singing."

3. Further, I would not have my pupil indulge in impersonations after the manner of the comic stage, as some teachers advocate, yet I do wish that there should be a certain modulation of the voice, whereby such passages may be distinguished from those in which the poet speaks in his own person.

4. In general, much careful training is required to secure above all things else that tender minds, which will retain a deep impression of whatever is presented to them when they are still unformed and ignorant, may learn not merely what is eloquent, but far rather what is morally good.

5. And therefore it is an eminently sound practice to begin reading with Homer and Virgil, though maturer judgement is required for a full understanding of their merits. But for that there is time enough, for they will be read more than once. Meanwhile, let the pupil's mind soar to the sublime levels of epic song, and draw the breath of inspiration from the majesty of its theme and become imbued with its noble sentiments.

6. Tragedies are useful and the lyric poets nourish the youthful mind provided always that you select not only suitable authors but also suitable passages from their works. For there is much loose morality among the Greek lyrists, nor would I choose to expound Horace in certain passages.

Elegies, at any rate those on erotic themes, and poems in hendeca-syllabics, the short metre of Sotadean verse (a type of poetry which a teacher should never even mention) should be kept out of the course of reading if possible or, if not, they should be reserved for an age of greater strength and maturity.

7. Comedy may contribute in a most useful way to eloquence, for it runs through the whole gamut of character and emotion, but of its use in the education of our pupils I shall speak a little later in the proper place. When once their moral character is firmly established it will deserve a prominent place in their studies. . . .

Book I, Chapter 12
Can Boys Be Taught A Number of Subjects at the Same Time?

1. The question is often asked, whether, granting that these things should be learned, they can all be taught and acquired at one and the

same time. This some deny, holding that the mind is confused and wearied by many subjects of diverse import, for which there is neither mental nor bodily strength nor sufficient time; holding, too, that, no matter how true it is that pupils of maturer age can endure the toil, the years of childhood should not be burdened.

2. These critics, however, do not realize the strength of the human mind, which is so swift and agile, so all-embracing, if I may say so, in its outlook that it cannot limit itself to a single object, but directs its energy to several, not merely on the same day but at the same moment of time.

3. Is it not the case that performers on the harp attend at the same time to the music they have to remember, to the sound of the voice, and to its countless modulations, while with the right hand they run over certain strings and with the left strike others, stop, or release them? The foot, too, is not idle, but maintains the regular beat of the music, and all these things are done simultaneously.

4. Again, do not we pleaders, when we are called suddenly, say certain things while we are thinking of others to follow, attending at the same time to the selection of arguments, the choice of words, arrangement, gesture, delivery, facial expression, and movements of the body? And if these in all their diversity are, as it were, the product of a single effort, why should we not divide our hours of study among a number of different subjects? Especially as change of occupation in itself refreshes and restores the mind, while, on the other hand, it is considerably more difficult to concentrate for long upon a single task. Thus reading affords a respite from writing and the monotony of reading is relieved by changes of subject.

5. However much we have done already, yet we are in a measure fresh for what we are starting upon. Who could help being jaded, if he had to listen all day long to one teacher of a subject—no matter what? He will be refreshed by change just as, in the case of food, variety refreshes the stomach and nourishes us without that distaste which monotony of diet must arouse.

6. Or else let those critics show me an alternative method of learning. Are we to devote ourselves entirely to the grammarian, then to the teacher of geometry, dropping now what we learnt before? Are we then to pass on to the music master, our previous studies forgotten? And when we study Latin literature, are we to ignore Greek? In a word, are we to do nothing but what we took up last?

7. Why do we not give the same advice to farmers, bidding them not to grow vines, olives, and orchard trees at the same time, not to tend meadowlands, stock, gardens, beehives, and poultry? Why do we ourselves assign each day a certain time to business in the forum, so

much to the needs of friends, so much to family responsibilities, so much to exercise, and so much to pleasure? Any one of these things would weary us if pursued uninterruptedly. So much easier is it to do many things than to do one for a long time.

8. There is, indeed, no need to fear that boys will find it difficult to endure the toil of study. For no age is less susceptible to fatigue. This may perhaps be surprising, but you can prove it by experiment: the mind is more receptive before it sets hard.

9. This is clearly proved by the fact that within two years of a child's being able to form words correctly he speaks practically the whole language without any one urging him on. Yet for how many years do our imported slaves wrestle with the Latin language?

If you start teaching reading to an adult, you may appreciate the reason for describing those who excel in their own arts as $\pi\alpha\iota\lambda o\mu\alpha\theta\epsilon\iota\sigma$ (i.e. taught young).

10. Again, a boy's nature is better fitted to endure toil than a young man's. Clearly, just as the bodies of young children take less harm than would an adult's from their constant falling on the ground, their creeping on hands and knees, and, later on, their constant games and running about all day long, because they are light and no burden to themselves, so their minds, too, I suppose, because they move with less effort and apply themselves to study without forcing their own initiative, simply allowing themselves to be moulded passively, do not feel the same measure of fatigue.

11. Moreover, in accordance with the general adaptability of youth, they follow their teachers without question and do not measure the progress already made, and indeed they are as yet without any sort of critical judgement as regards their work. Further, as we have often found, the senses are less affected by hard work than by hard thinking.

12. But there will never be more time for study (than in childhood), because at that age all progress depends upon what is heard from teachers. When the pupil goes apart to write, when he creates and composes something himself, then he will have either no time or no inclination to begin these studies.

13. Therefore, seeing that the grammarian cannot and ought not to take up the whole day, to what other studies shall we by preference assign these odds and ends of time?

14. I have no desire that our pupil should be wholly absorbed in these pursuits: he need not play or set songs to music, nor need he go into the most subtle intricacies of geometry. It is not a comic actor in his delivery or a dancer in his gestures that I am fashioning. Yet even if I were to demand complete proficiency there would still be time.

For the age of learning is long and I am not speaking of dullards.

15. Finally, why was Plato pre-eminent in all these things which, as I think, ought to be studied by the future orator? Because he was not content with the training which Athens could give or with that of the Pythagoreans which he had sailed to Italy to seek, but also visited the priests of Egypt and mastered all their mysterious lore.

16. We make the plea of difficulty a cloak for our own laziness. For we have no love of work, nor is eloquence sought after in itself as being honourable and the purest of all things, but we gird ourselves for base purposes and for the amassing of ignoble wealth.

17. Many a man may speak in the forum without the training I have sketched and pocket his fee, but may he be less wealthy than the base huckster and may the auctioneer make more out of the use of his voice. I would not even wish my book to be read by one who calculates what this training will bring him in.

18. But he who by a measure of divine inspiration has formed in his mind a true vision of eloquence, who sets before his eyes what a great poet calls "oratory, queen of the world," and who seeks his reward not in the fees his cases bring him in but in his own mind in the joy of contemplation and of knowledge, a lasting reward that is not the sport of fortune—such a man will easily persuade himself to spend upon geometry and music the hours that are wasted (by others) on shows, on games in the campus, on dice, on idle talk, to say nothing of sleep and long-drawn-out banquets, realizing as he will do how much more real enjoyment he will have in these studies than in such boorish forms of pleasure. For heaven has bestowed upon many this blessing, that they find their greatest pleasures in the noblest things.

19. But we have ourselves been carried away by this sweet delight. So much for the studies wherein the boy must be grounded before he passes on to higher things. The next book will make a fresh start, and pass to the duties of the teacher of rhetoric.

Book II, Chapter 2
The Character and Responsibilities of the Teacher

1. When the boy has reached in his studies a degree of advancement which enables him to grasp what we have indicated as the first steps in rhetorical instruction, he must be handed over to the teachers of that art. It is of especial importance that the moral character of these teachers should be considered.

2. I am led to emphasize this point here, not because I attach no importance to the matter in the case of other teachers, too (witness what I said in the preceding book), but because the very age of the pupils makes it more necessary to mention it.

3. Pupils are transferred to the school of rhetoric when they are practically grown up, and they continue there when they are young men; accordingly, we must at this stage exercise even greater care that the stainless character of the teacher may preserve their more tender years from harm and that the weight of his authority may deter their bolder age from excess.

4. It is not enough that he should himself show rigid self-control, he must also by the strictness of his discipline control the behaviour of the pupils who gather round him. Let him, then, above all things adopt the attitude of a parent toward his pupils and consider that he is taking the place of those who entrust their children to him.

5. He must have no vices himself and tolerate none in his pupils. Let him be stern but not melancholy, friendly but not familiar, lest in the one case he incur dislike, in the other contempt. He must constantly dwell upon the honourable and the good; for the more he admonishes his pupils the less he will require to punish them. He must never lose his temper, yet he will not pass over what deserves correction; he must be simple in his teaching, able to endure hard toil, persevering rather than exacting.

6. He must answer questions readily and put questions himself to those who do not ask them. In praising the recitations of his pupils he must not be either niggardly or extravagant, for in the former case he will arouse a distaste for toil, in the latter a spirit of self-complacency.

7. In correcting faults he will not be harsh and never abusive; for many are driven away from the studies they have entered upon by the fact that some teachers find fault as though they hated the offender.

8. Every day he must himself recite something, nay, many things, that his hearers can carry away with them. For though he may supply them with abundant material for imitation from the books they are reading, yet what is termed the living voice gives richer nourishment, especially if it be the voice of a teacher whom pupils, provided they are rightly trained, both love and respect. It is wellnigh impossible to say how much more readily we imitate those for whom we have a liking.

9. The common custom of allowing boys to stand up and shout their applause is not at all a proper one. Young people, when they are listening to others, ought to express their feelings in a modest fashion. Thus the pupil will rely upon the judgement of his teacher and believe that he has recited well when he wins the teacher's approval.

10. The vicious practice which nowadays goes by the name of politeness, whereby everything good or bad is praised in turn, is not only unseemly and more worthy of the theatre than of the stern discipline of a school, but also a deadly foe to real study. For care and toil seem superfluous when praise awaits no matter what effusion.

11. The audience, then, just as much as the reciter should keep

their eyes upon the teacher's face: for thus what is good will be distinguished from what is bad, and if writing gives fluency, listening gives the power of judgement.

12. As it is, the boys lean forward girt for the fray and at every period not merely rise but even dart out of their places and shout their applause with unseemly din. The compliment is a mutual one, and this is the reward of the reciter. The result is pride and vain self-conceit, so much so that, puffed up by this tumultuous demonstration on the part of their fellow students, they feel aggrieved if the master is not also lavish in his praise.

13. Teachers, too, should insist upon attention and modest behaviour in those who listen to their declamations: for the master ought not to speak to suit the taste of his pupils, but vice versa. Nay, he should, if possible, pay careful attention and observe what each pupil praises and how he praises it, and rejoice that his good points win approval not more for his own sake than for the sake of those who duly appreciate them.

14. I do not approve of boys and young men sitting together. For though such a teacher as ought to be in charge of their studies and their morals can maintain proper discipline even among grown youths, yet the weaker should be kept apart from the stronger and not merely the charge but even the suspicion of immorality avoided.

15. These points I thought ought to be noted briefly. As for grosser vices, I do not think it necessary even to warn the teacher that both he and his school should be free from them. And if there is any one who in choosing a teacher for his son does not avoid manifest evil, let him be assured that through this omission all the other rules which we are trying to lay down for the guidance of youth are rendered null and void.

Book II, Chapter 3
Should We Employ the Best Teacher to Instruct Beginners?

1. We ought not to pass over in silence the view of those who, even when they consider boys ready for the school of rhetoric, think they ought not to be handed over right away to the most distinguished teacher, but keep them for a while with the less eminent teachers, on the ground that a master of mediocre talent is more suited for the task of imparting instruction in the arts, since he is easier to understand and imitate and less inclined to be intolerant of the drudgery of elementary teaching.

2. I do not think it would take long to prove how much better it is to be grounded in the best principles, and how difficult it is to eradicate

faults that have once taken firm root: it means that a double load is placed upon the shoulders of the next teacher, and to undo faulty teaching is harder than to teach aright.

3. That is why the famous musician Timotheus is said to have been in the habit of demanding double fees from those who had been under other teachers as compared with those who came to him entirely untaught. The view to which I have just referred is at fault in two respects. In the first place, these people imagine that inferior teachers are good enough in the meantime, and are content because they can put up with any sort of mental food;

4. and though such carelessness is in itself worthy of censure, it would none the less be endurable if such instructors merely fell short in quantity and not in quality. The second misapprehension is a commoner one: people think that those who possess richer gifts of eloquence do not condescend to elementary instruction, partly because they have a distaste for the drudgery of the lower studies and partly because they cannot teach them.

5. For myself, I do not consider one who will not descend to these levels a teacher at all, and I maintain that the best orator, if he will, is best able to impart such instruction. First, because it is reasonable to expect that one who surpasses all others in eloquence has also the best understanding of those elements through which eloquence is attained;

6. second, because in teaching method is all important, and the most learned men possess it in the highest degree; and lastly, because no one is great in the higher branches of a subject if he lacks a sound foundation in the elements. Unless perchance Phidias made a matchless Jove, but another artist would have executed the detailed ornamentation of the work better than he, or an orator will not know how to pronounce words, or an eminent physician be unable to cure trifling ailments.

7. What, then? Is there no higher eloquence too great for the feeble minds of boys to understand? There is indeed: but our eloquent instructor will have to be wise as well, and know the principles of teaching, coming down to the level of his pupil, as a swift walker, if he happens to be walking with a child, gives him his hand and shortens his stride, and does not go too fast for his small companion.

8. Moreover, it is usually the case that the instruction of the most learned is easier to understand and far more lucid. The first virtue of eloquence is clearness, and the weaker a man's talent the more he strives to raise himself and to puff himself out, as those who are of small stature rise on tiptoe and as weak men bluster.

9. Those whose style is pompous, vicious, high-sounding, and full of other forms of affectation suffer, as I think, not from excess of strength but rather of weakness, like bodies swollen not with health but

with disease, or weary travellers ever straying from the straight road. Thus the worse a man's eloquence the less easy he will be to follow.

10. I have not forgotten that in the preceding book, while maintaining that learning at school is better than instruction in the home, I said that in the elementary stages, when but little progress has been made, pupils are more easily fired to imitate their fellow-pupils because such emulation is easier: a point which some may take as though it meant that I am now contradicting my earlier view. Far from it.

11. It is the best possible reason for handing over a boy to the best teachers that with them the pupils, being better taught, will either say what is worth imitating or will be corrected at once, if they make a mistake. But the ignorant teacher will perhaps even give his approval to what is faulty and through his judgement upon it commend it to his hearers.

12. The teacher, then, should be outstanding alike in eloquence and moral character, able like Phoenix in Homer to teach his pupils both how to speak and how to act.

Book XII, Chapter 1
The Orator Must Be A Good Man

1. Let our ideal orator, then, conform to the definition of Marcus Cato, "a good man, skilled in speaking." In any case let him be what Cato put first and what is by nature the more important and the greater thing, viz. a good man. And that not only for this reason that if the power of speech were enlisted in the service of wickedness there would be nothing more harmful to public and private interests than eloquence, and we ourselves who have done our best to contribute something towards skill in speaking would have done mankind grievous disservice in fashioning these weapons not for a soldier but for a brigand.

2. Why do I speak of myself? Even Nature, in respect of that peculiar gift which as it appears she has bestowed on man, distinguishing him thereby from other animals, would prove to be no true parent but a step-mother, if she intended fluency of speech to be the accomplice of crime, the betrayer of innocence, the enemy of truth. For it were better that men be born dumb and lack all power of reasoning than that they should employ the gifts of Providence for mutual destruction.

3. Nay, my judgement in this matter goes farther. Not only do I assert that the orator ought to be a good man, I say that no one will be an orator unless he is a good man. Surely you cannot admit discernment in those, who, when faced with a choice between good and evil, prefer to follow the baser course, or foresight in men who through their own actions expose themselves, at an unexpected turn of events,

to the gravest penalties not infrequently of the law and always of a guilty conscience.

4. And if it is not only a saying amongst wise men but also a matter of common belief that no one but a fool is wicked, surely the orator will never be a fool. A further point is this, that the mind cannot concentrate even upon the pursuit of the noblest ideal unless it be free from all vice: first, because the same breast cannot harbour both good and evil, and it is no more possible for the same mind to think the best and the worst thoughts at the same time than it is for a man to be at once good and bad.

5. In the next place for this reason also, that a mind which is absorbed in such an ideal must be free from all other interests, even those that are without blame. For thus, and thus only, free and entire, with nothing to hinder or distract it, it will fix its single gaze upon the object of its quest.

6. If too much care given to estates, over-anxious devotion to money-making, the pleasure of the chase, and days devoted to public spectacles all encroach seriously upon our studies (for time is lost to one thing that is given to another), what think you will be the effects of greed, avarice, and envy, whose lawless fancies disturb even men's slumbers and the dreams of sleep?

7. Nothing is so burdened, so changeable, so torn and distracted by countless varied passions as is the evil mind. When it is plotting guile it is harassed by hope, anxiety, and toil: when it has accomplished its evil purpose it is tormented by uneasiness, remorse, and dread of all manner of penalties. What room is there amid such distractions for letters or any noble accomplishment? No more assuredly than there is for corn on ground cumbered with thorns and brambles.

8. Come, is not temperance essential if we are to endure the toil of study? What hope, then, is there in lust and luxury? Does not love of praise spur us on more than aught else in our literary pursuits? But do we think that bad men care for praise? Moreover, it is obvious that the major portion of a speech consists in discussing what is just and good. Will an evil and unjust man speak of these things in a way that befits their dignity?

9. Finally, to dismiss the greater part of this inquiry, let us grant what is really impossible, that the best man and the worst have the same natural ability, the same application, the same training—which will prove the better speaker? Surely he who is also the better man. The same man, then, will never be at once evil and a perfect orator. For nothing is perfect that is surpassed by something else.

10. Still, that we may not seem in Socratic fashion, to frame answers to suit ourselves, let it be granted that there is some one so

blindly set against the truth as to venture to maintain that the bad man endowed with the same ability, application, and training as the good man will be just as good an orator as he. Let us prove the folly of this opponent, too.

11. Surely no one will doubt this, that the purpose of any speech is to make the case put forward seem true and righteous to the jury? Now which will succeed more easily in the task of persuasion, the good man or the bad? The good man, of course, will usually say what is true and righteous.

12. But even if on occasion at the call of duty (a thing which may happen, as I shall show presently) he tries to present a false case, he will of necessity be listened to with greater confidence. In the case of bad men, owing to their contempt for what men think and their ignorance of what is right, even the pretence of truth and righteousness breaks down at times. And so they make unreasonable claims and shameless statements.

13. These are backed up with unseemly obstinacy and fruitless toil in the pursuit of ends which certainly cannot be achieved. For just as in their lives, so in their cases, their hopes are insatiate. It often happens that even when they speak the truth they are not believed, and to have a man of such character to plead a case condemns it right away.

14. Now I must meet the objections which I can see launched at me by wellnigh universal consent. Was Demosthenes, then, not an orator? Yet we have it on record that he was a bad man. Was Cicero no orator? Yet many have found fault with his moral character also. What am I to do? I must face the storm of indignation my answer will arouse, but I must first soothe the feelings of my audience.

15. It does not seem to me that Demosthenes is so deserving of bitter obloquy that I should credit all the charges heaped upon him by his enemies, when I read his splendid public utterances and the noble story of his death;

16. nor do I see that Marcus Tullius at any point in his career lacked the true spirit of a loyal citizen. The proof lies in his glorious achievements as consul, his blameless conduct as provincial governor, his refusal to act upon the board for the partition of Campania, his constancy during those calamitous civil wars which fell within his lifetime, a constancy unmoved by hope or fear and never wavering in allegiance to the righteous cause of the republic.

17. Some think he lacked courage: to them he has himself made an excellent reply, that he was "timid not in enduring dangers but in striving to avoid them." And this he proved by the very manner of his death, which he met with unwavering fortitude.

18. But if these men did lack the highest virtue, to those who ask

me if they were orators I shall reply in the manner of the Stoics when they are asked if Zeno was a wise man or Cleanthes or Chrysippus, "these were indeed great men and worthy of all reverence, yet they did not reach the full perfection of man's nature."

19. Even Pythagoras did not choose to be called wise like those who went before him, but rather a seeker after wisdom. Still following the ordinary practice in speaking, I have often said, and shall say again, that Cicero was a perfect orator, just as in ordinary speech we call our friends good and prudent, terms which properly apply only to the perfectly wise man. But when I have to speak exactly and in strict conformity with truth, I shall still be in search of that perfect orator whom Cicero himself was seeking.

20. I admit that he stands upon the very pinnacle of eloquence, and can scarcely imagine any possible addition that would improve his oratory, but rather might perchance discover passages which I may think he would ultimately have removed; that, indeed, is pretty much the verdict of expert critics, viz. that he had countless excellences and also some defects, and he himself bears witness that he pruned much of his youthful exuberance. Yet since he never claimed for himself the name of wisdom, albeit fully conscious of his merits and, since he could have spoken better had longer life been granted him and a more tranquil age in which to compose his speeches, we should not do him an injustice in believing that he did not reach the very highest point, though no one has come nearer to it.

21. If I felt otherwise, I might defend this position with greater force and freedom. Or while Marcus Antonius asserted that he never saw an eloquent speaker (which is far less than the perfect orator) and even Marcus Tullius himself had not yet discovered him and only pictured and imagined him, can I dare to deny that in the vast eternity of time to come something may be found more perfect than aught that has been hitherto?

22. I pass by those who fail to do justice to Cicero and Demosthenes, even in the sphere of eloquence: yet Cicero himself does not think Demosthenes quite perfect, saying that he sometimes nods, nor does Cicero seem perfect either to Brutus and Calvus, who actually censure faults in his composition in letters addressed to Cicero himself, or to the two Asinii, who in several passages make quite bitter attacks upon his style.

23. Suppose we grant, though nature by no means allows it, that there has been found a bad man who is supremely eloquent: even so I will refuse him the name of orator, just as I cannot concede the name of brave man to all who have shown themselves prompt in action, for bravery has no meaning apart from virtue.

24. Does not he who is called in to plead cases require an integrity which no greed can corrupt, no influence seduce, no fear overawe? Shall we then bestow the sacred name of orator upon a traitor, a renegade, a sham defender? Nay, if even advocates of moderate ability profit by possessing what is commonly styled goodness, why should not the perfect orator, who never has existed but yet may exist, be perfect, as well in moral character as in eloquence?

25. It is no mere forensic hack that we are training, no hireling voice, no plodding advocate, to call him by no harsher name, such as is commonly styled *causidicus* (pleader); no, it is a man endowed with genius, one whose training has embraced the whole circle of the liberal arts, a gift of heaven to earth such as no age has ever seen, peerless and perfect in every aspect, a man of noble thought and noble speech.

26. For such a man how small a field will there be in the protection of the innocent, the conviction of the wicked, or in the championing of truth against falsehood in trivial suits involving money? In such tasks, too, no doubt he will show himself supreme, but his genius will shine forth more brightly in greater ones, when a senate's policy has to be guided or a people's folly checked.

27. Was it not such a man that Virgil seems to have imagined, assigning him the task of soothing the populace when stones and fire-brands are already flying?

If then some grave and pious man appear
They hush their noise and lend a listening ear.

We have then before all else a good man; after this he will add "skilled in speaking":

He soothes with sober words their angry mood
And quenches their innate desire for blood.

(Dryden's *Virgil*.)

28. In war, too, will not this same man whom we are training, if the soldiers are to be heartened for the fray, in his address draw upon the inmost truths of philosophy? For how, when men are entering into battle, can all those fears of toil, of pain, of death itself, be banished from their minds unless they are replaced by love of country, courage, and the living image of the good?

29. And these he will best bring home who has first taught them to himself. Hypocrisy betrays itself no matter how it be concealed, nor can there be a fluency of utterance which will not halt and hesitate if word and thought chime not together. Now a bad man must say one thing and think another.

30. Good men will never be at a loss for noble speech and sterling subject-matter (for they will be wise as well), and even if their speech

lacks showy trappings it is by its own nature sufficiently adorned and no righteous utterance is lacking in eloquence.

31. Wherefore let our youth, nay all of us of every age (for it is never too late for noble aspirations), strive with all our minds towards this goal and labour at this task; it may be our good fortune to succeed. For if nature does not forbid the existence of a good man, and of one skilled in speaking, why should not some one combine these in himself? And why should not each man hope that he will be the one to do so?

Book XII, Chapter 2
The Orator Must Know How Character Is Formed

1. The orator, then, is a good man and such a man cannot be conceived without moral excellence; moral excellence, though it derives certain impulses from nature, must yet be perfected by training. Before all else the orator must in his studies cultivate morality, and he must deal with all subjects that touch upon the honourable and the just, for without these no one can be either a good man or skilled in speaking.

2. Unless perchance we agree with those who think that morals come by nature and are in no way helped by training; as though forsooth the very meanest handicraft admittedly requires a teacher, but virtue, the gift whereby man might approach most nearly to the gods, has come to us unsought and without effort simply because we have been born. Will that man be temperate who does not know what temperance is?

3. Or that man brave who has not by earnest thought driven from him the fear of pain, of death, of punishment hereafter? Or that man just who has not examined justice and goodness and never studied in some learned work the laws common by nature to all men and also those set up amid individual people and nations? How trifling must they consider that which they regard as so easy!

4. But I leave this point, which no one with the slightest tinge of culture will, I think, dispute. I pass on to the next consideration, which is that no one will be skilled enough even in speaking who has not plumbed the depths of man's nature and formed his own moral character by study and reflection.

5. Lucius Crassus is right in saying, in the third book of Cicero's *De Oratore*, that everything that is said about equity, justice, truth, goodness, and their opposites, belongs to the orator's province, and that philosophers when they champion these with the force of eloquence are using the weapons of rhetoric, not their own. Yet he also admits that these must now be sought from philosophy, apparently because he thinks that philosophy is more fully in possession of them.

6. Hence, also, follows what Cicero maintains in several of his

books and letters, viz. that fluency in speaking is derived from the deepest springs of wisdom and that accordingly the same men were for a time the teachers of morality and of eloquence.

Now this plea of mine does not mean that I desire the orator to be a philosopher, for no other group of men have withdrawn themselves more completely from the duties of citizenship and all the responsibilities of the orator.

7. What philosopher has ever attended the law courts with assiduity or won fame in popular assemblies? Which of them has taken part in the administration of the state, the main subject of the teaching of most of them? Nay, I would have my pupil a wise man of the Roman type showing himself truly a useful citizen, not by disputation behind closed doors but by practical experience and exertion.

8. But the study of philosophy, abandoned by those who have betaken themselves to eloquence, no longer occupies its proper sphere, here in the open spaces of the forum, but has withdrawn first into the porticoes and wrestling schools and then into the lecture theaters. So that what the orator must have, and cannot get from the teachers of eloquence, he must of course seek from those with whom it has remained, by careful study of the authors who give instruction concerning virtue; and thus the life of the orator may be linked with a knowledge of things both human and divine.

9. How much greater and more beautiful would these things appear if the teachers of them could also discourse upon them with surpassing eloquence! Would that the day might come when some such perfect orator as we desire would win back this art which is now hated because of the insolent presumption and vice of those who corrupt its excellences and, as it were, reconquer it and restore it to the domain of eloquence.

10. Philosophy is divided into three parts, viz. natural philosophy, ethics, and dialectic (logic), and by which of these is it not associated with the work of the orator?

Taking them in the reverse order there can be no question about the last (dialectic) which is wholly concerned with words, seeing that it is the business of orators to know the exact meaning of each term, to clear up ambiguities, to disentangle confused statements, to judge of truth and falsehood, to prove or to refute what you will.

11. Dialectic, however, is not to be employed with the same subtlety and precision in pleading as in philosophical disputation, because the orator is bound not only to convince his hearers but also to move and to delight them, and for this he has need of a certain degree of energy and strength and charm of manner; even as the current is stronger in rivers that flow between high banks with a

great whirling flood than in shallow streams which even pebbles can obstruct.

12. Just as teachers of wrestling do not instruct their pupils in the various throws, as they call them, with the idea that those who have learned them should employ them all in the actual wrestling contest (for more depends on weight and steadiness and wind), but in order that they may have a reserve upon which to draw for one throw or the other, as opportunity offers;

13. So with this part of philosophy, dialectic, or if we prefer to call it so, the art of disputation: it is often useful in making limitations, inclusions, and distinctions, and in the solving of ambiguities by differentiation and division, as well as in leading an adversary on and getting him into difficulties. At the same time, if it takes entire control of a contest in the forum it will hinder the effectiveness of better methods and, by its very subtlety, will throw away the strength of the case in splitting it up to its own minuteness.

14. Thus you will find some who are wonderfully skillful in disputation, but who, when they cease hairsplitting, are not equal to the weight of a serious piece of pleading, like certain small animals which are swift in movement in a confined space but are easy to catch in the open.

15. Next, the moral part of philosophy, which is called ethics, of a surety is entirely within the orator's province. Amid the endless variety of cases, as we have shown in earlier books, in which some points are sought out by conjecture, others are settled by definition, others are barred by law or removed to another court, others are proved by deductive reasoning or collide with each other or are split up because of legal ambiguity, in all of them hardly one can be mentioned which does not involve some discussion of equity and goodness, whilst we are all aware that very many turn entirely upon some question of morality.

16. In deliberative oratory again, what method of exhortation is there apart from the question of honour? And what of the third division of oratory, which includes the duty of assigning praise and blame? Surely it is concerned with the discussion of right and wrong.

17. Will the orator not dilate upon justice, courage, temperance, self-control, and dutiful affection? Our ideally good man, who not merely knows these virtues as words and names, and has not merely heard them to repeat them with his lips, but who has taken them to his bosom and thinks in accordance with them, will have no difficulty in pondering them and will speak truly that which he knows.

18. Since every general question is wider in range than any question concerning particulars, because the part is contained in the

whole and the universal is not added to the particular, assuredly no one will doubt that general questions are especially associated with philosophical studies.

19. Now there are many points which require to be made clear by brief and appropriate definitions (hence the class of cases where the question at issue is spoken of as one of definition); must not the orator be equipped for this task, too, by those who have made a special study of it? Nay, does not every question of equity turn either on the exact use of words, or the discussion of what justice is, or the discovery of a motive? And of these some fall within the province of logic and some of ethics.

20. Oratory, then, if it be truly oratory, is by its nature intermingled with all these questions of philosophy, whilst mere fluency that lacks this training must go astray, having either no guides or guides that are deceitful.

Natural philosophy offers wider scope than any other branch for the practice of eloquence because one must speak of things divine in a loftier strain than of things human; it also embraces the whole department of ethics, without which, as we have shown, oratory is impossible.

21. If the universe is controlled by divine guidance, surely the state will have to be managed by good men. If our minds are of divine origin, surely we are bound to cling to virtue and not be slaves to the pleasures of an earthly body. Will the orator not touch constantly upon these themes? Will he not be bound to speak at length concerning omens and oracles and in fact everything of a religious nature, such questions being frequently the subjects of the senator's most serious debates—I mean if he is going to be as we wish him, a true citizen as well as an orator? How can we even imagine eloquence in a man who is ignorant of the highest of things?

22. If common sense did not support my views, yet surely we should be convinced by examples. Take the case of Pericles. His eloquence, though no specimens of it have survived, is said to have been characterized by a power almost too great to be believed. Such is the testimony of the historians and of the old writers of comedy, the most free-spoken of men. And he is recorded to have been a pupil of Anaxagoras the natural philosopher. Similarly Demosthenes, greatest of all the Greek orators, is said to have studied under Plato.

23. Marcus Tullius of course often tells us that he owed more to the walks of the Academy than to the lecture-rooms of the teachers of rhetoric. Nor would his eloquence have gushed forth in so mighty a stream had he limited his genius to the forum and not let it range freely to the farthest bounds of the universe.

There now arises a further question: which school of philosophers is most useful for eloquence? There are not many which can contest the palm in this respect.

24. First Epicurus puts himself out of the running, for he bids his followers fly from all scientific training as fast as ever they can go. Aristippus, who places the supreme good in bodily pleasures, does not urge us to endure such toil. What share can Pyrrhon have in our pursuits? He cannot be sure of the existence of the jury he is to address, of the prisoner whom he is to defend, of the senate before whom he is to state his views.

25. Some regard the Academy as most useful because the practice of arguing on both sides of a question resembles most nearly the preliminary exercises for pleading in the forum. As a proof they add the fact that this school has produced very eminent orators. The Peripatetics also boast of their achievements in the field of oratory. They practically invented the exercise of speaking on general questions for the sake of practice.

The Stoics, whilst they must admit that their teachers have lacked richness and splendour in eloquence, maintain none the less that they are unexcelled in strictness of demonstration and subtlety of reasoning.

26. Such are the rival claims of the philosophers. As though bound by an oath or forbidden by some religious scruple, they think it a sin to depart from the tenets they have once embraced. But an orator has no need to swear allegiance to any sect.

27. For his is a greater and a nobler task, I mean that for which he is a candidate, if he is going to win praises for the perfection both of his life and of his eloquence. Accordingly he will set before himself as models all the most eloquent speakers and for the moulding of his character he will pick out the noblest precepts and follow the straight path towards virtue. He will use every kind of training, but will devote himself most to the highest and the noblest.

28. What richer topic for a weighty and eloquent speech can be found than virtue, the state, providence, the origin of mind, friendship? These are subjects to which mind and speech rise together, viz. what is truly good, what soothes fear, checks evil desires, raises us above common prejudice, and proves our minds divine.

29. Not only the dictates of philosophy, but still more the noble deeds of history, must be known and pondered well. And assuredly nowhere will you find a richer store than in the records of the Roman people.

30. Will the lessons of courage, justice, honour, self-control, simplicity, contempt for pain and death, be taught by any better than

by such heroes as Fabricius, Curius, Regulus, Decius, Mucius, and countless others? As the Greeks excel in precepts, so the Romans excel in examples, which is better far.

31. Nor will our orator rest content with a knowledge of these only (without imitating them), for he will not be satisfied to regard the immediate present and to-day alone, but will consider the whole range of men's remembrance in the days to come as the field for an honourable life and the arena in which fame is to be won. And from such sources let him drink deep draughts of justice, let him win courage and sincerity to adorn his pleadings in the forum and his speeches in the Senate. For he will not be a perfect orator unless he has the knowledge and the courage to speak out honestly what he believes.

PART FOUR
SOME POSSIBILITIES FROM OUR JUDEO-CHRISTIAN HERITAGE

Overview

"In the beginning was the Word," wrote the author of the Gospel of John in opening his account. "In the beginning was the Situation," said Sir Richard Livingstone about John Dewey. These two statements set before us the perennial argument over education which each generation in our century has struggled with. Out of our Judeo-Christian heritage, "Solomon, son of David, king of Israel," speaks to us in the first chapter of Proverbs, to the end that "men may know wisdom and instruction, understand words of insight, receive instruction in wise dealing, righteousness, justice, and equity; that prudence may be given to the simple, knowledge and discretion to the youth—the wise man also may hear and increase in learning, and the man of understanding acquire skill." He intones: "The fear of the LORD is the beginning of knowledge; fools despise wisdom and instruction" and warns his son against enticers who say to a youth, "Come with us," counseling him instead: "My son, do not walk in the way with them, hold back your foot from their paths." The sage goes on to deplore the predicament of his time: "Wisdom cries aloud in the street; in the markets she raises her voice; on the top of the walls she cries out; at the entrance of the city gates she speaks: 'How long, O simple ones, will you love being simple? How long will scoffers delight in their scoffing and fools hate knowledge? . . . I also will laugh at your calamity; I will mock when panic strikes you, when panic strikes you like a storm and your calamity comes like a whirlwind, when distress and anguish come upon you.'"

Laid out for us here is the problem of our own time, when a generation is torn between two tendencies: formal education and informal education. Formal schooling is identified with the older generation and relies on "the Word" about the wisdom of living, based on the experiences of others and distilled into books, which can be acquired only through mastery of the skills of abstract, symbolic learning. Formal education always runs the risk of becoming disassociated from "real" persons living "real" lives in the world of their own times. Informal education is identified with the younger generation, which displays little respect for the past or the wisdom of the older generation and seeks to discover its own answers about how to live through the act of living itself, through individual acts of vital living, through not obeying the injunction to "hold back your foot from their paths." The readings of Part Four have been selected to add wisdom about living and schooling when these two tendencies clash. Dewey at least was right in thinking that the central problem of philosophy of education is to maintain a balance between these two contending elements of education: formal and informal.

If we would acquire wisdom about living and were agreed that "The fear of the LORD is the beginning of wisdom," we would need to understand what is meant by "the LORD." In this question of what God is like we must come to terms with "the Word" out of our tradition. The readings of Part Four, then, begin with the fascinating story of a dynamic social heritage, in which the student may trace the story of the transition from belief in Yahweh, a god of power and battles, to God, a universal God. This is the main story that the Bible tells, the foundation for three of the world's great religions, and constitutes the main Judeo-Christian contribution to culture and civilization: the ideal of striving to realize a society of justice and righteousness and a spirit of love and brotherhood. Instead of telling this story of "the Word," of this dynamic achievement of the knowledge of one God (said by some scholars to be one of the finest accomplishments of the human spirit), we let the student "discover" the story himself as he works through the subheads that lead from "Anthropomorphism" to "Jesus of Nazareth." He can then ponder for himself the interpretation given "Christianity" by Paul and the later development of a heritage both rich and confusing. What does "being a Christian" really mean? Here are source materials.

Education, so some of us believe, has to do with people and their lives and the direction to be given human lives. Into this perennial struggle to make sense and meaning out of our lives, to discover, if we can, the purposes of it and what it is all about, there enter different accounts of "the Word." Prominent in the past (and also very much in the foreground nowadays) are those who would find guidance in a non-Christian view of life and values. Today, unless we follow the Stoic part of the Graeco-Roman tradition, we might follow the direction of "letting go." In an earlier time this was one part of the non-Christian view of life. Opposed to it is the view, stressed in Christianity, of "not letting go." Sometimes this struggle is put in terms of reconciling the rational and emotional sides of our nature. Sometimes it is spoken of as the demand in our time for both understanding and compassion. The contending values are set forth extremely well by Radoslav A. Tsanoff in Chapter 27, and one may even read into those struggles of an earlier day the making of a counter-culture (Chapters 28, 29, and 30). Along with a view of life usually goes a view of education. Consequently, in comparing the non-Christian and Christian views of life, the remaining readings should prove helpful. Chapter 31 gives a picture of Christian family upbringing; Chapter 32, of church instruction; and Chapter 33, of the attitude and practices of "Christians" toward non-Christian literature and schools.

During the Middle Ages different "educations" went with the different ways of life of the classes of society of that time. Chapter 34 indicates something about the education and life of monks living in monasteries—a way of life known as monasticism. Chapter 35 is rooted in the triumph of the "counter-culture" of Christianity and indicates something about the life of clergy under the "Schoolmen" in universities, a way of life known as Scholasticism. Chapter 36 presents the way of life and education of the warrior class under chivalry and feudalism and of the burgher class under the guild system.

Much space has been given to humanism as represented by Erasmus in Chapter 37, for humanism brings out the best in educational lore, if one takes seriously the view that life and education begin with "the Word" and thus entail books, and schools, and teachers, and formal schooling. Even in our own day formal schooling could profit from the insights, experiences, and wisdom expressed by Erasmus. When the reader couples this understanding and wisdom with that gained from Chapter 38, the plea Martin Luther made to the mayors and aldermen of the cities of Germany in behalf of Christian schools, he has acquired the basic background for understanding life and education in Europe and America.

We conclude with Chapters 39 and 40, which jump ahead to anticipate problems faced in much later days by those who wondered about life and its responsibilities. How shall we reconcile, if we can, our feelings and our intellect? Perry Miller's anthology, *The Transcendentalists*, has traditionally made students keenly aware of this continuing problem fought out in the pages of American literature. We dip briefly into those pages to let Orestes Brownson stimulate us with the spirit of transcendentalism. Ronnie Dugger's summary in Chapter 40 of his study of a man who helped trigger an atomic bomb over Hiroshima brings home to each of us our individual responsibility for life, education, and human welfare amidst forces and pressures that stagger the imagination. Here in Part Four of our book is tremendous food for thought for leaders in education.

26
The Contribution of the Hebrews to Culture: Ethical Monotheism

The Transition from Yahweh (God of Power, Battles) to God (a Universal God)

The Bible text in this publication is from the Revised Standard Version of the Bible, copyrighted 1946 and 1952 by the Division of Christian Education of the National Council of the Churches of Christ in the U.S.A. and used by permission.

Anthropomorphism

And they heard the sound of the LORD GOD walking in the garden in the cool of the day, and the man and his wife hid themselves from the presence of the LORD GOD among the trees of the garden. (Genesis 3:8.)

Then Noah built an altar to the LORD, and took of every clean animal and of every clean bird, and offered burnt offerings on the altar. And when the LORD smelled the pleasing odor, the LORD said in his heart, "I will never again curse the ground because of man, for the imagination of man's heart is evil from his youth; neither will I ever again destroy every living creature as I have done. While the earth remains, seedtime and harvest, cold and heat, summer and winter, day and night, shall not cease." (Genesis 8:20-22.)

And the LORD appeared to him [Abraham] by the oaks of Mamre, as he sat at the door of his tent in the heat of the day. He lifted up his eyes and looked, and behold, three men stood in front of him. When he saw them, he ran from the tent door to meet them, and bowed himself to the earth, and said, "My lord, if I have found favor in your sight, do not pass by your servant. Let a little water be brought, and wash your feet, and rest yourselves under the tree, while I fetch a morsel of bread, that you may refresh yourselves, and after that you may pass on—since you have come to your servant." So they said, "Do as you have said." And Abraham hastened into the tent to Sarah, and said, "Make ready quickly three measures of fine meal, knead it, and make cakes." And Abraham ran to the herd, and took a calf, tender and good, and gave it to the servant, who hastened to prepare it. Then he took curds, and milk, and the calf which he had prepared, and set it before them; and he stood by them under the tree while they ate.

They said to him, "Where is Sarah your wife?" And he said, "She is in the tent." He said, "I will surely return to you in the spring, and Sarah your wife shall have a son." And Sarah was listening at the tent door behind him. Now Abraham and Sarah were old, advanced in age; it had ceased to be with Sarah after the manner of women. So Sarah laughed to herself, saying, "After I have grown old, and my husband is old, shall I have pleasure?" The LORD said to Abraham, "Why did Sarah laugh, and say, 'Shall I indeed bear a child, now that I am old?' Is anything too hard for the LORD? At the appointed time I will return to you, in the spring, and Sarah shall have a son." But Sarah denied, saying, "I did not laugh"; for she was afraid. He said, "No, but you did laugh."

Then the men set out from there, and they looked toward Sodom; and Abraham went with them to set them on their way. The LORD said, "Shall I hide from Abraham what I am about to do, seeing that Abraham shall become a great and mighty nation, and all the nations of the earth shall bless themselves by him? No, for I have chosen him, that he may charge his children and his household after him to keep the way of the LORD by doing righteousness and justice; so that the LORD may bring to Abraham what he has promised him." Then the LORD said, "Because the outcry against Sodom and Gomorrah is great and their sin is very grave, I will go down to see whether they have done altogether according to the outcry which has come to me; and if not, I will know."

So the men turned from there, and went toward Sodom; but Abraham still stood before the LORD. Then Abraham drew near, and said, "Wilt thou indeed destroy the righteous with the wicked? Suppose there are fifty righteous within the city; wilt thou then destroy the place and not spare it for the fifty righteous who are in it? Far be it from thee to do such a thing, to slay the righteous with the wicked, so that the righteous fare as the wicked! Far be that from thee! Shall not the Judge of all the earth do right?" And the LORD said, "If I find at Sodom fifty righteous in the city, I will spare the whole place for their sake." Abraham answered, "Behold, I have taken upon myself to speak to the Lord, I who am but dust and ashes. Suppose five of the fifty righteous are lacking? Wilt thou destroy the whole city for lack of five? And he said, "I will not destroy it if I find forty-five there." Again he spoke to him, and said, "Suppose forty are found there." He answered, "For the sake of forty I will not do it." Then he said, "Oh let not the Lord be angry, and I will speak. Suppose thirty are found there." He answered, "I will not do it, if I find thirty there." He said, "Behold, I have taken upon myself to speak to the Lord. Suppose twenty are found there." He answered, "For the sake of twenty I will not destroy it." Then he said, "Oh let not the Lord be angry, and I will speak again but this once. Suppose ten are found there." He answered, "For the sake of ten I will not destroy it." And the LORD went his way, when he had finished speaking to Abraham; and Abraham returned to his place. (Genesis 18.)

Tribal Monolatry with Polytheistic Elements

Then Moses and the people of Israel sang this song to the LORD, saying,

> I will sing to the LORD, for he has triumphed gloriously;
> the horse and his rider he has thrown into the sea.
> The LORD is my strength and my song,
> and he has become my salvation;
> this is my God, and I will praise him,
> my father's God, and I will exalt him.
> The LORD is a man of war; the LORD is his name.
>
> Pharaoh's chariots and his host he cast into the sea;
> and his picked officers are sunk in the Red Sea.
> The floods cover them;
> they went down into the depths like a stone.
> Thy right hand, O LORD, glorious in power,
> thy right hand, O LORD, shatters the enemy.
> In the greatness of thy majesty thou overthrowest thy adversaries;
> thou sendest forth thy fury, it consumes them like stubble.
> At the blast of thy nostrils the waters piled up,
> the floods stood up in a heap;
> the deeps congealed in the heart of the sea.
> The enemy said, 'I will pursue, I will overtake,
> I will divide the spoil, my desire shall have its fill of them.
> I will draw my sword, my hand shall destroy them.'
> Thou didst blow with thy wind, the sea covered them;
> they sank as lead in the mighty waters.
>
> Who is like thee, O LORD, among the gods?

Who is like thee, majestic in holiness,
terrible in glorious deeds, doing wonders?
Thou didst stretch out thy right hand,
the earth swallowed them.

Thou hast led in thy steadfast love
the people whom thou hast redeemed.
thou hast guided them by thy strength to thy holy abode.
The peoples have heard, they tremble;
pangs have seized on the inhabitants of Philistia.
Now are the chiefs of Edom dismayed;
the leaders of Moab, trembling seizes them;
all the inhabitants of Canaan have melted away.
Terror and dread fall upon them;
because of the greatness of thy arm, they are as still as a stone,
till thy people, O LORD, pass by,
till the people pass by whom thou hast purchased.
Thou wilt bring them in, and plant them on thy own mountain,
the place, O LORD, which thou hast made for thy abode,
the sanctuary, O LORD, which thy hands have established.
The LORD will reign for ever and ever.

For when the horses of Pharaoh with his chariots and his horsemen went into the sea, the LORD brought back the waters of the sea upon them; but the people of Israel walked on dry ground in the midst of the sea. Then Miriam, the prophetess, the sister of Aaron, took a timbrel in her hand; and all the women went out after her with timbrels and dancing.

And Miriam sang to them:

Sing to the LORD, for he has triumphed gloriously;
the horse and his rider he has thrown into the sea.

Then Moses led Israel onward from the Red Sea, and they went into the wilderness of Shur; they went three days in the wilderness and found no water. When they came to Marah, they could not drink the water of Marah because it was bitter; therefore it was named Marah. And the people murmured against Moses, saying, "What shall we drink?" And he cried to the LORD; and the LORD showed him a tree, and he threw it into the water, and the water became sweet.

There the LORD made for them a statute and an ordinance and there he proved them, saying, "If you will diligently hearken to the voice of the LORD your God, and do that which is right in his eyes, and give heed to his commandments and keep all his statutes, I will put none of the diseases upon you which I put upon the Egyptians; for I am the LORD, your healer." (Exodus 15: 1-26.)

And God spoke all these words, saying,

I am the LORD your God who brought you out of the land of Egypt, out of the house of bondage.

You shall have no other gods before me.

You shall not make yourself a graven image, or any likeness of anything that is in heaven above, or that is in the earth beneath, or that is in the water under the earth; you shall not bow down to them or serve them; for I the LORD your God am a jealous God, visiting the iniquity of the fathers upon the children to the third and the fourth generation of those who hate me, but showing steadfast love to thousands of those who love me and keep my commandments.

You shall not take the name of the LORD your God in vain; for the LORD will not hold him guiltless who takes his name in vain.

Remember the sabbath day, to keep it holy. Six days you shall labor, and do all your work; but the seventh day is a sabbath to the LORD your God; in it you shall not do any work, you, or your son, or your daughter, your manservant, or your maidservant, or your cattle, or the sojourner who is within your gates; for in six days the LORD made heaven and earth, the sea, and all that is in them, and rested the seventh day; therefore the LORD blessed the sabbath day and hallowed it.

Honor your father and your mother, that your days may be long in the land which the LORD your God gives you.

You shall not kill.

You shall not commit adultery.

You shall not steal.

You shall not bear false witness against your neighbor.

You shall not covet your neighbor's house; you shall not covet your neighbor's wife, or his manservant, or his maidservant, or his ox, or his ass, or anything that is your neighbor's. (Exodus 20:1-17; cf. Deuteronomy 5:6-21.)

Naaman, commander of the army of the king of Syria, was a great man with his master and in high favor, because by him the LORD had given victory to Syria. He was a mighty man of valor, but he was a leper. Now the Syrians on one of their raids had carried off a little maid from the land of Israel, and she waited on Naaman's wife. She said to her mistress, "Would that my lord were with the prophet who is in Samaria! He would cure him of his leprosy." So Naaman went in and told his lord, "Thus and so spoke the maiden from the land of Israel." And the king of Syria said, "Go now, and I will send a letter to the king of Israel."

So he went, taking with him ten talents of silver, six thousand shekels of gold, and ten festal garments. And he brought the letter to the king of Israel, which read, "When this letter reaches you, know that I have sent to you Naaman my servant, that you may cure him of his leprosy." And when the king of Israel read the letter, he rent his clothes and said, "Am I god, to kill and to make alive, that this man sends word to me to cure a man of his leprosy? Only consider, and see how he is seeking a quarrel with me."

But when Elisha the man of God heard that the king of Israel had rent his clothes, he sent to the king, saying "Why have you rent your clothes? Let him come now to me, that he may know that there is a prophet in Israel." So Naaman came with his horses and chariots, and halted at the door of Elisha's house. And Elisha sent a messenger to him, saying, "Go and wash in the Jordan seven times, and your flesh shall be restored, and you shall be clean." But Naaman was angry, and went away, saying, "Behold, I thought that he would surely come out to me, and stand, and call on the name of the LORD his God, and wave his hand over the place, and cure the leper. Are not Abana and Pharpar, the rivers of Damascus, better than all the waters of Israel? Could I not wash in them, and be clean?" So he turned and went away in a rage. But his servants came near and said to him, "My father, if the prophet had commanded you to do some great thing, would you not have done it? How much rather, then, when he says to you, 'Wash, and be clean?'" So he went down and dipped himself seven times in the Jordan, according to the word of the man of God; and his flesh was restored like the flesh of a little child, and he was clean.

Then he returned to the man of God, he and all his company, and he came and stood before him; and he said, "Behold, I know that there is no God in all the earth but in Israel; so accept now a present from your servant. But he said, "As the LORD lives, whom I serve, I will receive none." And he urged him to take it, but he refused. Then Naaman said, "If not, I pray you, let there be given to your servant two mules' burden of earth; for henceforth your servant will not offer burnt offering or sacrifice to any god but the LORD. In this matter may the LORD pardon your servant: when my master goes into the house of Rimmon to worship there, leaning on my arm, and I bow myself in the house of Rimmon, when I bow myself in the house of Rimmon, the LORD pardon your servant in this matter." He said to him, "Go in peace." (2 Kings 5:1-19.)

Thus all the work that King Solomon did on the house of the LORD was finished. And Solomon brought in the things which David his father had dedicated, the silver, the gold, and the vessels, and stored them in the treasuries of the house of the LORD. (1 Kings 7:51.)

And King Solomon and all the congregation of Israel, who had assembled before him, were with him before the ark, sacrificing so many sheep and oxen that they could not be counted or numbered. Then the priests brought the ark of the covenant of the LORD to its place, in the inner sanctuary of the house, in the most holy place, underneath the wings of the cherubim. (1 Kings 8:5, 6.)

Then Solomon said,

The LORD has set the sun in the heavens,
but has said that he would dwell in thick darkness.
I have built thee an exalted house,
a place for thee to dwell in for ever.

(1 Kings 8:12, 13.)

Then the king, and all Israel with him, offered sacrifice before the LORD. Solomon offered as peace offerings to the LORD twenty-two thousand oxen and a hundred and twenty thousand sheep. So the king and all the people of Israel dedicated the house of the LORD. (1 Kings 8:62-64.)

Now King Solomon loved many foreign women: the daughter of Pharaoh, and Moabite, Ammonite, Edomite, Sidonian, and Hittite women, from the nations concerning which the LORD had said to the people of Israel, "You shall not enter into marriage with them, neither shall they with you, for surely they will turn away your heart after their gods"; Solomon clung to these in love. He had seven hundred wives, princesses, and three hundred concubines; and his wives turned away his heart. For when Solomon was old his wives turned away his heart after other gods; and his heart was not wholly true to the LORD his God, as was the heart of David his father. For Solomon went after Ashtoreth the goddess of the Sidonians, and after Milcom the abomination of the Ammonites. So Solomon did what was evil in the sight of the LORD, and did not wholly follow the LORD, as David his father had done. Then Solomon built a high place for Chemosh the abomination of Moab, and for Molech the abomination of the Ammonites, on the mountain east of Jerusalem. And so he did for all his foreign wives, who burned incense and sacrificed to their gods. (1 Kings 11:1-8.)

The Eighth Century Prophets: Amos, Micah, Hosea, and Isaiah

I hate, I despise your feasts,
and I take no delight in your solemn assemblies.
Even though you offer me your
burnt offerings and cereal offerings,
I will not accept them,
and the peace offerings of your fatted beasts
I will not look upon.
Take away from me the noise of your songs;
to the melody of your harps I will not listen.
But let justice roll down like waters,
and righteousness like an ever-flowing stream.

(Amos 5:21-24.)

With what shall I come before the LORD,
and bow myself before God on high?
Shall I come before him with burnt offerings,
with calves a year old?
Will the LORD be pleased with thousands of rams,
with ten thousands of rivers of oil?
Shall I give my first-born for my transgression,
the fruit of my body for the sin of my soul?"
He has showed you, O man, what is good;
and what does the LORD require of you
but to do justice, and to love kindness,
and to walk humbly with your God?

(Micah 6:6-8.)

The godly man has perished from the earth,
and there is none upright among men;
they all lie in wait for blood,
and each hunts his brother with a net.
Their hands are upon what is evil, to do it diligently;
the prince and the judge ask for a bribe,
and the great man utters the evil desire of his soul;
thus they weave it together.
The best of them is like a brier,
the most upright of them a thorn hedge.
The day of their watchmen, of their punishment, has come;
now their confusion is at hand.
Put no trust in a neighbor,

have no confidence in a friend;
guard the doors of your mouth
from her who lies in your bosom;
for the son treats the father with contempt,
the daughter rises up against her mother,
the daughter-in-law against her mother-in-law;
a man's enemies are the men of his own house.
But as for me, I will look to the LORD,
I will wait for the God of my salvation;
my God will hear me.

(Micah 7:2-7.)

Who is a God like thee, pardoning iniquity
and passing over transgression
for the remnant of his inheritance?
He does not retain his anger for ever
because he delights in steadfast love.
He will again have compassion upon us,
he will tread our iniquities under foot.
Thou wilt cast all our sins
into the depths of the sea.
Thou wilt show faithfulness to Jacob
and steadfast love to Abraham,
as thou hast sworn to our fathers from the days of old.

(Micah 7:18-20.)

Hear the word of the LORD, O people of Israel;
for the LORD has a controversy with the inhabitants of the land.
There is no faithfulness or kindness,
and no knowledge of God in the land;
there is swearing, lying, killing, stealing, and committing adultery;
they break all bounds and murder follows murder.
Therefore the land mourns,
and all who dwell in it languish,
and also the beasts of the field,
and the birds of the air;
and even the fish of the sea are taken away.
Yet let no one contend,
and let none accuse,
for with you is my contention, O priest.
You shall stumble by day,
the prophet also shall stumble with you by night;
and I will destroy your mother.
My people are destroyed for lack of knowledge;

because you have rejected knowledge,
I reject you from being a priest to me.
And since you have forgotten the law of your God,
I also will forget your children.
The more they increased,
the more they sinned against me;
I will change their glory into shame.
They feed on the sin of my people;
they are greedy for their iniquity.
And it shall be like people, like priest;
I will punish them for their ways,
and requite them for their deeds.
They shall eat, but not be satisfied;
they shall play the harlot, but not multiply;
because they have forsaken the LORD
to cherish harlotry.
Wine and new wine
take away the understanding.
My people inquire of a thing of wood,
and their staff gives them oracles.
For a spirit of harlotry has led them astray.
and they have left their God to play the harlot.
They sacrifice on the tops of the mountains,
and make offerings upon the hills,
under oak, poplar, and terebinth,
because their shade is good.
Therefore your daughters play the harlot,
and your brides commit adultery.
I will not punish your daughters when they play the harlot,
nor your brides when they commit adultery;
for the men themselves go aside with harlots,
and sacrifice with cult prostitutes,
and a people without understanding shall come to ruin.
Though you play the harlot, O Israel,
let not Judah become guilty.

(Hosea 4:1-15.)

I will return again to my place,
until they acknowledge their guilt and seek my face,
and in their distress they seek me, saying,
"Come, let us return to the LORD:
for he has torn, that he may heal us;
he has stricken, and he will bind us up.
After two days he will revive us;

on the third day he will raise us up,
that we may live before him.
Let us know, let us press on to know the LORD; . . .
Your love is like a morning cloud,
like the dew that goes early away. . . .
For I desire steadfast love and not sacrifice,
the knowledge of God, rather than burnt offerings.

(Hosea 5:15; 6:1-3, 4, 6.)

Hear the word of the LORD,
you rulers of Sodom!
Give ear to the teaching of our God,
you people of Gomorrah!
What to me is the multitude of your sacrifices?
says the LORD:
I have had enough of burnt offerings of rams
and the fat of fed beasts;
I do not delight in the blood of bulls,
or of lambs, or of he-goats.
When you come to appear before me,
who requires of you
this trampling of my courts?
Bring no more vain offerings;
incense is an abomination to me.
New moon and sabbath and the calling of assemblies —
I cannot endure iniquity and solemn assembly.
Your new moons and your appointed feasts
my soul hates;
they have become a burden to me,
I am weary of bearing them.
When you spread forth your hands,
I will hide my eyes from you;
even though you make many prayers,
I will not listen;
your hands are full of blood.
Wash yourselves; make yourselves clean;
remove the evil of your doings
from before my eyes;
cease to do evil, learn to do good;
correct oppression;
defend the fatherless,
plead for the widow.

"Come now, let us reason together,"
says the LORD:

(Isaiah 1:10-18.)

The people who walked in darkness
have seen a great light;
those who dwelt in a land of deep darkness,
on them has light shined. . . .
For to us a child is born,
to us a son is given;
and the government will be upon his shoulder,
and his name will be called
Wonderful Counselor, Mighty God,
Everlasting Father, Prince of Peace.

(Isaiah 9:2, 6.)

The Fall of Samaria (722/21 B. C.)

Then the king of Assyria invaded all the land and came to Samaria, and for three years he besieged it. In the ninth year of Hoshea the king of Assyria captured Samaria, and he carried the Israelites away to Assyria, and placed them in Halah, and on the Habor, the river of Gozan, and in the cities of the Medes. (2 Kings 17:5-6.)

King Josiah's Reform (621 B. C.) and Monoyahwism

Judah also did not keep the commandments of the LORD their God, but walked in the customs which Israel had introduced. (2 Kings 17:19.)

Josiah was eight years old when he began to reign, and he reigned thirty-one years in Jerusalem. He did what was right in the eyes of the LORD, and walked in the ways of David his father; and he did not turn aside to the right or to the left. For in the eighth year of his reign, while he was yet a boy, he began to seek the God of David his father; and in the twelfth year he began to purge Judah and Jerusalem of the high places, the Asherim, and the graven and the molten images. And they broke down the alters of the Baals in his presence; and he hewed down the incense altars which stood above them; and he broke in pieces the Asherim and the graven and the molten images, and he made dust of them and strewed it over the graves of those who had sacrificed to them. He also burned the bones of the priests on their altars, and purged Judah and Jerusalem. And in the cities of Manasseh, Ephraim, and Simeon, and as far as Naphtali, in their ruins round about, he broke down the altars, and beat the Asherim and the images into powder, and hewed down all the incense altars throughout all the land of Israel. Then he returned to Jerusalem.

Now in the eighteenth year of his reign, when he had purged the land and the house, he sent Shaphan the son of Azaliah, and Maaseriah the governor of the city, and Joah the son of Joahaz, the recorder, to repair the house of the LORD his God. They came to Hilkiah the high priest and delivered the money that had been brought in to the house of God, which the Levites, the keepers of the threshold, had collected from Manasseh and Ephraim and from all the remnant of Israel and from all Judah and Benjamin and from the inhabitants of Jerusalem. They delivered it to the workmen who had the oversight of the house of the LORD; and the workmen who were working in the house of the LORD gave it for repairing and restoring the house. They gave it to the carpenters and the builders to buy quarried stone, and timber for binders and beams for the buildings which the kings of Judah had let go to ruin. And the men did the work faithfully. Over them were set Jahath and Obadiah the Levites, of the sons of Merari, and Zechariah and Meshullam, of the sons of the Kohathites, to have oversight. The Levites, all who were skillful with instruments of music, were over the burden bearers and directed all who did work in every kind of service; and some of the Levites were scribes, and officials, and gatekeepers.

While they were bringing out the money that had been brought into the house of the LORD, Hilkiah the priest found the book of the law of the LORD given through Moses. Then Hilkiah gave the book to Shaphan. Shaphan brought the book to the king, and further reported to the king, "All that was committed to your servants they are doing. They have emptied out the money that was found in the house of the LORD and have delivered it into the hand of the overseers and the workmen." Then Shaphan the secretary told the king, "Hilkiah the priest has given me a book." And Shaphan read it before the king.

When the king heard the words of the law he rent his clothes. And the king commanded Hilkiah, Ahikam the son of Shaphan, Abdon the son of Micah, Shaphan the secretary, and Asaiah the king's servant, saying, "Go, inquire of the LORD for me and for those who are left in Israel and in Judah, concerning the words of the book that has been found; for great is the wrath of the LORD that is poured out on us, because our fathers have not kept the word of the LORD, to do according to all that is written in this book."

So Hilkiah and those whom the king had sent went to Huldah the prophetess, the wife of Shallum the son of Tokhath, son of Hasrah, keeper of the wardrobe (now she dwelt in Jerusalem in the Second Quarter) and spoke to her to that effect. And she said to them, "Thus says the LORD, the God of Israel: 'Tell the man who sent you to me, Thus says the LORD, Behold, I will bring evil upon this place and upon its inhabitants, all the curses that are written in the book which was read before the king of Judah. Because they have forsaken me and have burned incense to other gods, that they might provoke me to anger with all the works of their hands, therefore my wrath will be poured out upon this place and will not be quenched. But to the king of Judah, who sent you to inquire of the LORD, thus shall you say to him, Thus says the LORD, the God of Israel: Regarding the words which you have heard, because your heart was penitent and you humbled yourself before God when you heard his words against this place and its inhabitants, and you have humbled yourself before me, and have rent your clothes and wept before me, I also have heard you, says the LORD. Behold, I will gather you to your fathers, and you shall be gathered to your grave in peace, and your eyes shall not see all the evil which I will bring upon this place and its inhabitants.'" And they brought back word to the king.

Then the king sent and gathered together all the elders of Judah and Jerusalem. And the king went up to the house of the LORD, with all the men of Judah and the inhabitants of Jerusalem and the priests and the Levites, all the people both great and small; and he read in their hearing all the words of the book of the covenant which had been found in the house of the LORD. And the king stood in his place and made a covenant before the LORD, to walk after the LORD and to keep his commandments and his testimonies and his statutes, with all his heart and all his soul, to perform the words of the covenant that were written in this book. Then he made all who were present in Jerusalem and in Benjamin stand to it. And the inhabitants of Jerusalem did according to the covenant of God, the God of their fathers. And Josiah took away all the abominations from all the territory that belonged to the people of Israel, and made all who were in Israel serve the LORD their God. All his days they did not turn away from following the LORD the God of their fathers. (2 Chronicles 34.)

Josiah kept a passover to the LORD in Jerusalem; and they killed the passover lamb on the fourteenth day of the first month. He appointed the priests to their offices and encouraged them in the service of the house of the LORD. And he said to the Levites who taught all Israel and who were holy to the LORD, "Put the holy ark in the house which Solomon the son of David, king of Israel, built; you need no longer carry it upon your shoulders. Now serve the LORD your God and his people Israel. Prepare yourselves according to your fathers' houses by your divisions, following the directions of Solomon his son. And stand in the holy place according to the groupings of the fathers' houses of your brethren the lay people, and let there be for each a part of a father's house of the Levites. And kill the passover, and sanctify yourselves, and prepare for your brethren, to do according to the word of the LORD by Moses.''

Then Josiah contributed to the lay people, as passover offerings for all that were present, lambs and kids from the flock to the number of thirty thousand, and three thousand bulls; these were from the king's possessions. And his princes contributed willingly to the people, to the priests, and to the Levites. Hilkiah, Zechariah, and Jehiel, the chief officers of the house of God, gave to the priests for the passover offerings two thousand six hundred lambs and kids and three hundred bulls. Conaniah also, and Shemaiah and Nethanel his brothers, and Hashabiah and Jeiel and Jozabad, the chiefs of the Levites, gave to the Levites for the passover offerings five thousand lambs and kids and five hundred bulls.

When the service had been prepared for, the priests stood in their place, and the Levites in their divisions according to the king's command. And they killed the passover lamb, and the priests sprinkled the blood which they received from them while the Levites flayed the victims. And they set aside the burnt offerings that they might distribute them according to the groupings of the fathers' houses of the lay people, to offer to the LORD, as it is written in the book of Moses. And so they did with the bulls. And they roasted the passover lamb with fire according to the ordinance; and they boiled the holy offerings in pots, in caldrons, and in pans, and carried them quickly to all the lay people. And afterward they prepared for themselves and for the priests, because the priests the sons of Aaron were busied in offering the burnt offerings and the fat parts until night; so the Levites prepared for themselves and for the priests the sons of Aaron. The singers, the sons of Asaph, were in their place according to the command of David, and Asaph, and Heman, and Jeduthun the king's seer; and the gatekeepers were at each gate; they did not need to depart from their service, for their brethren the Levites prepared for them.

So all the service of the LORD was prepared that day, to keep the passover and to offer burnt offerings on the altar of the LORD, according to the command of King Josiah. And the people of Israel who were present kept the passover at that time, and the feast of unleavened bread seven days. No passover like it had been kept in Israel since the days of Samuel the prophet; none of the kings of

Israel had kept such a passover as was kept by Josiah, and the priests and the Levites, and all Judah and Israel who were present, and the inhabitants of Jerusalem. In the eighteenth year of the reign of Josiah this passover was kept. (2 Chronicles 35:1-19.)

Jeremiah and Ethical Monotheism

The word that came to Jeremiah from the LORD: "Stand in the gate of the LORD's house, and proclaim there this word, and say, Hear the word of the LORD, all you men of Judah who enter these gates to worship the LORD. Thus says the LORD of hosts, the God of Israel, Amend your ways and your doings, and I will let you dwell in this place. Do not trust in these deceptive words: 'This is the temple of the LORD, the temple of the LORD, the temple of the LORD.'

"For if you truly amend your ways and your doings, if you truly execute justice one with another, if you do not oppress the alien, the fatherless or the widow, or shed innocent blood in this place, and if you do not go after other gods to your own hurt, then I will let you dwell in this place, in the land that I gave of old to your fathers for ever.

"Behold, you trust in deceptive words to no avail. Will you steal, murder, commit adultery, swear falsely, burn incense to Baal, and go after other gods that you have not known, and then come and stand before me in this house, which is called by my name, and say, 'We are delivered!'—only to go on doing all these abominations? Has this house, which is called by my name, become a den of robbers in your eyes? Behold, I myself have seen it, says the LORD. Go now to my place that was in Shiloh, where I made my name dwell at first, and see what I did to it for the wickedness of my people Israel. And now, because you have done all these things, says the LORD, and when I spoke to you persistently you did not listen, and when I called you, you did not answer, therefore I will do to the house which is called by my name, and in which you trust, and to the place which I gave to you and to your fathers, as I did to Shiloh. And I will cast you out of my sight, as I cast out all your kinsmen, all the offspring of Ephraim.

"As for you, do not pray for this people, or lift up cry or prayer for them, and do not intercede with me, for I do not hear you. Do you not see what they are doing in the cities of Judah and in the streets of Jerusalem? The children gather wood, the fathers kindle fire, and the women knead dough, to make cakes for the queen of heaven; and they pour out drink offerings to other gods, to provoke me to anger. Is it I whom they provoke? says the LORD. Is it not themselves, to their own confusion? Therefore thus says the LORD GOD: Behold, my anger and my wrath will be poured out on this place, upon man and beast, upon the trees of the field and the fruit of the ground; it will burn and not be quenched."

Thus says the LORD of hosts, the God of Israel: "Add your burnt offerings to your sacrifices, and eat the flesh. For in the day that I brought them out of the land of Egypt, I did not speak to your fathers or command them concerning burnt offerings and sacrifices. But this command I gave them, 'Obey my voice, and I will be your God, and you shall be my people; and walk in all the way that I command you, that it may be well with you.' But they did not obey or incline their ear, but walked in their own counsels and the stubbornness of their evil hearts, and went backward and not forward. From the day that your fathers came out of the land of Egypt to this day, I have persistently sent all my servants the prophets to them, day after day; yet they did not listen to me, or incline their ear, but stiffened their neck. They did worse than their fathers." (Jeremiah 7:1-26.)

> Every one deceives his neighbor,
> and no one speaks the truth;
> they have taught their tongue to speak lies;
> they commit iniquity and are too weary to repent.
> Heaping oppression upon oppression, and deceit upon deceit,
> they refuse to know me, says the LORD.
> Therefore thus says the LORD of hosts:
> Behold, I will refine them and test them,
> for what else can I do, because of my people? . . .
> I will make Jerusalem a heap of ruins,
> a lair of jackals;
> and I will make the cities of Judah a desolation,
> without inhabitant. . . .

Thus says the LORD: "Let not the wise man glory in his wisdom, let not the mighty man glory in his might, let not the rich man glory in his riches; but let him who glories glory in this, that he understands and knows me, that I am the LORD who practice kindness, justice, and righteousness in the earth; for in these things I delight, says the LORD." (Jeremiah 9:5-7, 11, 23.)

> But the lord is the true God;
> he is the living God and the everlasting King. (Jeremiah 10:10.)

The Exile (598/87, 587/86—538 B.C.), the Problem, and New Prophets

> By the waters of Babylon,
> there we sat down and wept,

when we remembered Zion.
On the willows there
we hung up our lyres.
For there our captors
required of us songs,
and our tormentors, mirth, saying,
"Sing us one of the songs of Zion!"
How shall we sing the LORD's song in a foreign land?

(Psalm 137: 1-4.)

Comfort, comfort my people, says your God.
Speak tenderly to Jerusalem, and cry to her
that her warfare is ended, that her iniquity is pardoned,
that she has received from the LORD'S hand
double for all her sins.

(Isaiah 40:1, 2.)

Have you not known? Have you not heard?
The LORD is the everlasting God,
the Creator of the ends of the earth.
He does not faint or grow weary,
his understanding is unsearchable.

(Isaiah 40:28.)

fear not, for I am with you,
be not dismayed, for I am your God;
I will strengthen you, I will help you,
I will uphold you with my victorious right hand.

(Isaiah 41:10.)

I, I am He
who blots out your transgressions for my own sake,
and I will not remember your sins.

(Isaiah 43:25.)

For your Maker is your husband,
the LORD of hosts is his name,
and the Holy One of Israel is your Redeemer,
the God of the whole earth he is called. . . .
In overflowing wrath for a moment
I hid my face from you,
but with everlasting love I will have compassion on you,
says the LORD, your Redeemer.

(Isaiah 54:5, 8.)

let the wicked forsake his way,
and the unrighteous man his thoughts;
let him return to the LORD, that he may have mercy on him.

(Isaiah 55:7.)

Thus says the LORD:
"Keep justice, and do righteousness,
for soon my salvation will come, and my deliverance be revealed.

(Isaiah 56:1.)

A voice cries:
"In the wilderness prepare the way of the LORD,
make straight in the desert a highway for our God.

(Isaiah 40:3.)

these I will bring to my holy mountain,
and make them joyful in my house of prayer;
their burnt offerings and their sacrifices
will be accepted on my altar;
for my house shall be called a house of prayer
for all peoples.

(Isaiah 56:7.)

The Post-Exilic Period

A record. In the first year of Cyrus the king, Cyrus the king issued a decree: Concerning the house of God at Jerusalem, let the house be rebuilt, the place where sacrifices are offered and burnt offerings are brought; its height shall be sixty cubits and its breadth sixty cubits, with three courses of great stones and one course of timber; let the cost be paid from the royal treasury. And also let the gold and silver vessels of the house of God, which Nebuchadnezzar took out of the temple that is in Jerusalem and brought to Babylon, be restored and brought back to the temple which is in Jerusalem, each to its place; you shall put them in the house of God.

(Ezra 6:3-5.)

And all the people gathered as one man into the square before the Water Gate; and they told Ezra the scribe to bring the book of the law of Moses which the LORD had given to Israel. And Ezra the priest brought the law before the assembly, both men and women and all who could hear with understanding, on the first day of the seventh month. And he read from it facing the square before the Water Gate from early morning until midday, in the presence of the men and the women and those who could understand; and the ears of all the people were attentive to the book of the law.

(Nehemiah 8:1-3.)

Because of all this we make a firm covenant and write it, and our princes, our Levites, and our priests set their seal to it.

(Nehemiah 9:38.)

The rest of the people, the priests, the Levites, the gatekeepers, the singers, the temple servants, and all who have separated themselves from the peoples of the lands to the law of God, their wives, their sons, their daughters, all who have knowledge and understanding, join with their brethren, their nobles, and enter into a curse and an oath to walk in God's law which was given by Moses the servant of God, and to observe and do all the commandments of the LORD our Lord and his ordinances and his statutes.

(Nehemiah 10:28-29.)

Then I replied to them, "The God of heaven will make us prosper, and we his servants will arise and build; but you have no portion or right or memorial in Jerusalem."

(Nehemiah 2:20.)

And the word of the LORD of hosts came to me, saying, "Thus says the LORD of hosts: The fast of the fourth month, and the fast of the fifth, and the fast of the seventh, and the fast of the tenth, shall be to the house of Judah seasons of joy and gladness, and cheerful feasts; therefore love truth and peace.

"Thus says the LORD of hosts: Peoples shall yet come, even the inhabitants of many cities; the inhabitants of one city shall go to another, saying, 'Let us go at once to entreat the favor of the LORD, and to seek the LORD of hosts; I am going.' Many peoples and strong nations shall come to seek the LORD of hosts in Jerusalem, and to entreat the favor of the LORD. Thus says the LORD of hosts: In those days ten men from the nations of every tongue shall take hold of the robe of a Jew, saying, 'Let us go with you, for we have heard that God is with you.'"

(Zechariah 8:18-23.)

Jesus of Nazareth

In the beginning was the Word, and the Word was with God, and the Word was God. He was in the beginning with God; all things were made through him, and without him was not anything made that was made. In him was life, and the life was the light of men. The light shines in the darkness, and the darkness has not overcome it.

(John 1:1-5.)

Jesus said to her, "Woman, believe me, the hour is coming when neither on this mountain nor in Jerusalem will you worship the father. You worship what you do not know; we worship what we know, for salvation is from the Jews. But the hour is coming, and now is, when the true worshipers will worship the Father in spirit and truth, for such the Father seeks to worship him. God is spirit, and those who worship him must worship in spirit and truth."

(John 4:21-24.)

"Teacher, which is the great commandment in the law?" And he said to him, "You shall love the Lord your God with all your heart, and with all your soul, and with all your mind. This is the great and first commandment. And a second is like it, You shall love your neighbor as yourself. On these two commandments depend all the law and the prophets."

(Matthew 22:36-40.)

"Little children, yet a little while I am with you. You will seek me; and as I said to the Jews so now I say to you, 'Where I am going you cannot come.' A new commandment I give to you, that you love one another; even as I have loved you, that you also love one another. By this all men will know that you are my disciples, if you have love for one another."

(John 13:33-35.)

The Sermon on the Plain
(Sermon on the Mount in Matthew 5-7)

And he came down with them and stood on a level place, with a great crowd of his disciples and a great multitude of people from all Judea and Jerusalem and the seacoast of Tyre and Sidon, who came to hear him and to be healed of their diseases; and those who were troubled with unclean spirits were cured. And all the crowd sought to touch him, for power came forth from him and healed them all.

And he lifted up his eyes on his disciples, and said:

> Blessed are you poor, for yours is the kingdom of God.
>
> Blessed are you that hunger now, for you shall be satisfied.
>
> Blessed are you that weep now, for you shall laugh.
>
> Blessed are you when men hate you, and when they exclude you and revile you, and cast out your name as evil, on account of the Son of man! Rejoice in that day, and leap for joy, for behold, your reward is great in heaven; for so their fathers did to the prophets.
>
> But woe to you that are rich, for you have received your consolation.
>
> Woe to you that are full now, for you shall hunger.
>
> Woe to you that laugh now, for you shall mourn and weep.
>
> Woe to you, when all men speak well of you, for so their fathers did to the false prophets.
>
> But I say to you that hear, Love your enemies, do good to those who hate you, bless those who curse you, pray for those who abuse you. To him who strikes you on the cheek, offer the other also; and from him who takes away your cloak do not withhold your coat as well. Give to every one who begs from you; and of him who takes away your goods, do not ask them again. And as you wish that men would do to you, do so to them.
>
> If you love those who love you, what credit is that to you? For even sinners love those who love them. And if you do good to those who do good to you, what credit is that to you? For even sinners do the same. And if you lend to those from whom you hope to receive, what credit is that to you? Even sinners lend to sinners, to receive as much again. But love your enemies, and do good, and lend, expecting nothing in return; and your reward will be great, and you will be sons of the Most High; for he is kind to the ungrateful and the selfish. Be meriful, even as your Father is merciful.
>
> Judge not, and you will not be judged; condemn not, and you will not be condemned; forgive, and you will be forgiven; give, and it will be given to you; good measure, pressed down, shaken together, running over, will be put into your lap. For the measure you give will be the measure you get back.

He also told them a parable:

Can a blind man lead a blind man? Will they not both fall into a pit? A disciple is not above his teacher, but every one when he is fully taught will be like his teacher. Why do you see the speck that is in your brother's eye, but do not notice the log that is in your own eye? Or how can you say to your brother, 'Brother, let me take out the speck that is in your eye,' when you yourself do not see the log that is in your own eye? You hypocrite, first take the log out of your own eye, and then you will see clearly to take out the speck that is in your brother's eye.

For no good tree bears bad fruit, nor again does a bad tree bear good fruit; for each tree is known by its own fruit. For figs are not gathered from thorns, nor are grapes picked from a bramble bush. The good man out of the good treasure of his heart produces good, and the evil man out of his evil treasure produces evil; for out of the abundance of the heart his mouth speaks.

Why do you call me 'Lord, Lord,' and not do what I tell you? Every one who comes to me and hears my words and does them, I will show you what he is like: he is like a man building a house, who dug deep, and laid the foundation upon rock; and when a flood arose, the stream broke against that house, and could not shake it, because it had been well built. But he who hears and does not do them is like a man who built a house on the ground without a foundation; against which the stream broke, and immediately it fell, and the ruin of that house was great.

(Luke 6:17-49.)

". . . For this I was born, and for this I have come into the world, to bear witness to the truth. Every one who is of the truth hears my voice." (John 18:37.)

The Pharisees came and began to argue with him, seeking from him a sign from heaven, to test him. And he sighed deeply in his spirit, and said, "Why does this generation seek a sign? Truly I say to you, no sign shall be given to this generation." (Mark 8:11-12.)

Edith Hamilton, *Witness to the Truth—Christ and His Interpreters*, (New York: W. W. Norton & Company, Inc., The Norton Library N113), pp. 64-65.

Christ was in the direct line of descent from these greatest Hebrews

[Isaiah, Hosea, Amos, Micah, Jeremiah] and their way of convincing men that they spoke God's truth was his way. He showed in a single sentence what he thought about wonder-working as a proof of the truth. In the parable of Dives and Lazarus, when Dives prays Abraham to send Lazarus to his brothers to recall them from their evil ways, Abraham tells him, 'They have Moses and the prophets; let them hear them.' Dives cries out, 'Nay, but if one went to them from the dead, they will repent.' Abraham answers, 'If they hear not Moses and the prophets, neither will they be persuaded though one rose from the dead.' In that one brief sentence Christ dismissed the supernatural as evidence of the truth. No miracle, even the most wonderful, the resurrection of the dead, would mean anything as a guarantee that what the prophets said was true—or that what he himself said was true. Spiritual truth must be its own proof. But he alone in his generation saw that the spiritual cannot be proved by the supernatural.

We have not yet begun to realize his stature. He towers high above magic and all its works. To see him in some degree as he was, to perceive something of his unsurpassable greatness which forever soars beyond our comprehension and yet continually lifts us up toward him, we must strip magic away. Only when it is set aside can we catch a glimpse of Christ himself, attended by his own miracles, the miracle of what he was and the miracle that the world, antagonistic to him, opposed to all he taught, has yet never been able to forget him and let him go. These are the signs and wonders which through all the generations testify of him.

The officers sent to arrest him said, 'Never man spake like this man.' He spoke the truth as no else ever spoke it. What men wanted from him was magic.

Being asked by the Pharisees when the kingdom of God was coming, he answered them, "The kingdom of God is not coming with signs to be observed; nor will they say, 'Lo, here it is!' or 'There!' for behold, the kingdom of God is in the midst of you." (Luke 17:20-21.)

Edith Hamilton, Witness to the Truth, op. cit., pp. 108-109, 120-127.

Luke alone gives Christ's words to the Pharisees who demanded 'when the kingdom of God should come' . . . God's kingdom is of the spirit only. Its coming will not be until men possessing it within shall bring it to pass in the world without. So Luke's authority declared Christ said, and yet in Luke when Christ speaks of it there is a note of urgency absent from Matthew and Mark. 'And he said unto another, Follow me. But he said, Lord, suffer me first to go and bury my father. Jesus said unto him, Let the dead bury their dead: but go thou and preach the kingdom of God. And another also said, Lord, I will follow thee; but let me first go bid them farewell, which are at home at my house. And Jesus said to him, No man, having put his hand to the plough and looking back, is fit for the kingdom of God.' Only one brief sentence in Matthew can match the impression these words give of immediate and overwhelming importance. In Luke alone Christ says the kingdom is not at hand: he 'spake a parable, because he was nigh to Jerusalem [and the cross] and because they thought that the kingdom of God should immediately appear'; and only in Luke is God's kingdom a kingdom of the spirit. Nevertheless, far beyond Matthew and Mark with their conviction that it will be a swift and glorious triumph, Luke stresses the urgent need to work for its coming. It is men's first duty, beside which all other duties count for nothing.

He [John] wrote his gospel to show divinity entering into and abiding in humanity, and individual men able to overcome the world because Christ had lived and died in it and overcome it. . . . Bent though he was on establishing Christ's humanity, he left out of his gospel Mark's account of Gethsemane and Christ's last words on the cross. Both were far too important to be merely passed over. John left them out deliberately. His account of the crucifixion is his own, not like any of the others in any respect. . . . Luke shows Christ's divinity upon the cross, John his humanity. So Christ says, 'I thirst,' and the human suffering is brought home as in none of the others. Last of all he says, 'It is finished.' There could be nothing less dramatic and yet the words are moving far beyond the peacefulness of Luke's 'Father, into thy hands I commend my spirit.' The struggle to open the kingdom of heaven to the suffering world was over. Christ could do no more. It was ended, and he accepted the end. No more than that, no rejoicing, no relief even, but acceptance. 'It is finished.'

It is an extraordinarily realistic account, sober and moderate and restrained as compared with the other three. Yet John would not admit to his gospel that Christ had prayed not to drink of the cup of defeat and death, and that he had felt deserted by God as he died.

. . . he expressed for all men to come the doctrine which is the center of Christianity, the Incarnation, God manifested in man. Years later, in his first epistle, he gave it an even greater expression: 'Beloved, let us love one another: for love is of God; and everyone that loveth is born of God, and knoweth God. He that loveth not knoweth not God; for God is love . . . No man hath seen God at any time. If we love one another, God dwelleth in us . . . God is love; and he that dwelleth in love dwelleth in God, and God in him.' . . .

In the other gospels Christ's greatest discourse is the Sermon on the Mount. It is straight ethical teaching and completely objective. . . .

In John, Christ's greatest discourse is in the three chapters which follow the washing of the disciples' feet directly after the last supper. It is not objective; it is personal, concerned only with Christ's relation to his disciples. 'Let not your heart be troubled: ye believe in God, believe also in me . . . Peace I leave with you, my peace I give unto you. Not as the world giveth, give I unto you . . . Abide in me, and I in you. As the branch cannot bear fruit of itself, except it abide in the vine; no more can ye, except ye abide in me . . . I will see you again and your heart shall rejoice, and your joy no man taketh from you . . . In the world ye shall have tribulation, but be of good cheer; I have overcome the world.'

There is a great difference in matter and tone between these words and the Sermon on the Mount. It is true that the two were spoken under widely different conditions. The Sermon is given by Matthew very early in Christ's life, and Luke agrees as regards the chief part of it. Moreover that time, directly after the temptation, is the natural and logical setting for it. When Christ began to preach, his subject was that men could bring the kingdom of God to pass by doing the will of God. He felt a great confidence in those early days. He knew with absolute certainty that if men would hear him he could teach them how to end the miseries they brought upon and suffered from each other. The way to the kingdom lay open to all who would do the will of God. In the Sermon Christ was telling in detail what God's will called upon men to do. But the discourse in John was spoken when Christ realized that the kingdom of God was not at hand. Defeat was already upon him and the cross was very near. He was leaving the little band who had followed him, and his last words were to tell them that the bond between himself and them would not be broken. Death could not touch it. These words would naturally be marked out from Christ's other talks with his disciples, but the truth is that so far as the personal tone is concerned, they are like all the rest of John's gospel; they are marked out as different only from the other three. There is one passage alone which strikes the note continuous in John, Matthew's 'Come unto me, all ye that labour and are heavy laden, and I will give you rest. Take my yoke upon you, and learn of me; for I am meek and lowly of heart; and ye shall find rest unto your souls. For my yoke is easy and my burden is light.' These words are strange in Matthew. They are of the very essence of Christ's teaching as reported by John.

He was a man greatly gifted. Such men hear, see, think, feel, what others do not. John heard Christ say what the rest of Christ's hearers paid no attention to. Certainly most of his teaching had passed over Peter's head or was forgotten by him. It is much more surprising that the sayings in the Sermon on the Mount made no lasting impression on him than that he dismissed it as visionary talk when Christ spoke about being the light of the world or the true vine. Ideas like that were not within Peter's scope. And on his side John completely disregarded what to the three other evangelists was the substance of Christ's teaching. He left out the Sermon on the Mount, the parables too. In the battle he was fighting for Christ's reality and his close connection with his disciples, ethical teaching was not of instant importance. He mentions the kingdom of God only once. He could not give his mind to it when he who came preaching it was being turned into a fantastic unreality. John thought not of a community devoted to doing God's will, but of every man finding salvation from self in one who was the perfect satisfaction of the longing desire of the heart, the refuge and strength for sinful men, joy in tribulation, light in darkness, security in chaos.

'Whosoever shall do the will of my Father which is in heaven, the same is my brother and sister and mother.' That is Christ's message in the three first gospels. In John it is, 'Abide in me and I in you. As the branch cannot bear fruit of itself, except it abide in the vine; no more can ye, except ye abide in me.' The two are different, but they spring from the same root. The basic attitude to life expressed by each is the same: self-sufficiency ended, self-direction too. The surrender, the abandonment, of self, to God's rule, the three said; to Christ's way, John said, who was the Word of God, expressing in himself God's meaning for all men.

> Where there is no vision, the people perish.
>
> (Proverbs 29:18.)

> And he called to him the multitude with his disciples, and said to them, "If any man would come after me, let him deny himself and take up his cross and follow me. For whosoever would save his life will lose it; and whoever loses his life for my sake and the gospel's will save it. For what does it profit a man, to gain the whole world and forfeit his life?"
>
> (Mark 8:34-36.)

> Now faith is the giving substance to things hoped for, the proving of things not seen.
>
> (Hebrews 11:1.)

St. Paul

I appeal to you therefore, brethren, by the mercies of God, to present your bodies as a living sacrifice, holy and acceptable to God, which is your spiritual worship. Do not be conformed to this world but be transformed by the renewal of your mind, that you may prove what is the will of God, what is good and acceptable and perfect.

For by the grace given to me I bid every one among you not to think of himself more highly than he ought to think, but to think with sober judgment, each according to the measure of faith which God has assigned him. For as in one body we have many members, and all the members do not have the same function, so we, though many, are one body in Christ, and individually members one of another. Having gifts that differ according to the grace given to us, let us use them: if prophecy, in proportion to our faith; if service, in our serving; he who teaches, in his teaching; he who exhorts, in his exhortation; he who contributes, in liberality; he who gives aid, with zeal; he who does acts of mercy, with cheerfulness.

Let love be genuine; hate what is evil, hold fast to what is good; love one another with brotherly affection; outdo one another in showing honor. Never flag in zeal, be aglow with the Spirit, serve the Lord. Rejoice in your hope, be patient in tribulation, be constant in prayer. Contribute to the needs of the saints, practice hospitality.

Bless those who persecute you; bless and do not curse them. Rejoice with those who rejoice, weep with those who weep. Live in harmony with one another; do not be haughty, but associate with the lowly, never be conceited. Repay no one evil for evil, but take thought for what is noble in the sight of all. If possible, so far as it depends upon you, live peaceably with all. Beloved, never avenge yourselves, but leave it to the wrath of God; for it is written, "Vengeance is mine, I will repay, says the Lord." No, "if your enemy is hungry, feed him; if he is thirsty, give him drink; for by so doing you will heap burning coals upon his head." Do not be overcome by evil, but overcome evil with good.

(Romans 12.)

If I speak in the tongues of men and of angels, but have not love, I am a noisy gong or a clanging cymbal. And if I have prophetic powers, and understand all mysteries and all knowledge, and if I have all faith, so as to remove mountains, but have not love, I am nothing. If I give away all I have, and if I deliver my body to be burned, but have not love, I gain nothing.

Love is patient and kind; love is not jealous or boastful; it is not arrogant or rude. Love does not insist on its own way; it is not irritable or resentful; it does not rejoice at wrong, but rejoices in the right. Love bears all things, believes all things, hopes all things, endures all things.

Love never ends; as for prophecy, it will pass away; as for tongues, they will cease; as for knowledge, it will pass away. For our knowledge is imperfect and our prophecy is imperfect; but when the perfect comes, the imperfect will pass away. When I was a child, I spoke like a child, I thought like a child, I reasoned like a child; when I became a man, I gave up childish ways. For now we see in a mirror dimly, but then face to face. Now I know in part; then I shall understand fully, even as I have been fully understood. So faith, hope, love abide, these three; but the greatest of these is love.

(1 Corinthians 13.)

Now while Paul was waiting for them at Athens, his spirit was provoked within him as he saw that the city was full of idols. So he argued in the synagogue with the Jews and the devout persons, and in the market place every day with those who chanced to be there. Some also of the Epicurean and Stoic philosophers met him. And some said, "What would this babbler say?" Others said, "He seems to be a preacher of foreign divinities"—because he preached Jesus and the resurrection. And they took hold of him and brought him to the Are-oṕagus, saying, "May we know what this new teaching is which you present? For you bring some strange things to our ears; we wish to know therefore what these things mean." Now all the Athenians and the foreigners who lived there spent their time in nothing except telling or hearing something new.

So Paul, standing in the middle of the Are-oṕagus, said: "Men of Athens, I perceive that in every way you are very religious. For as I passed along, and observed the objects of your worship, I found also an altar with this inscription, 'To an unknown god.' What therefore you worship as unknown, this I proclaim to you. The God who made the world and everything in it, being Lord of heaven and earth, does not live in shrines made by man, nor is he served by human hands, as though he needed anything, since he himself gives to all men life and breath and everything. And he made from one every nation of men to live on all the face of the earth, having determined allotted periods and the boundaries of their habitation, that they should seek God, in the hope that they might feel after him and find him. Yet he is not far from each one of us, for

'In him we live and move and have our being';
as even some of your poets have said,

'For we are indeed his offspring.'

Being then God's offspring, we ought not to think that the Deity is like gold, or silver, or stone, a representation by the art and imagination of man. The times of ignorance God overlooked, but now he commands all men everywhere to repent, because he has fixed a day on which he will judge the world in righteousness by a man whom he has appointed, and of this he has given assurance to all men by raising him from the dead.''

Now when they heard of the resurrection of the dead, some mocked; but others said, ''We will hear you again about this.'' So Paul went out from among them. But some men joined him and believed, among them Dionýsius the Are-opágite and a woman named Damaris and others with them.

(Acts 17:16-34.)

27
Christianity:
The Counter-Culture
Radoslav A. Tsanoff

Abridged from pp. 145-150 in *The Great Philosophers*, 2d ed., by
Radoslav A. Tsanoff. Copyright, 1953 by Harper & Row, Publishers, Inc.
Copyright © 1964 by Radoslav A. Tsanoff. Reprinted by permission of the
publishers.

The Christianization of the Mediterranean world was a radical revolution
in the history of philosophy which changed the direction of men's
interests and purposes, the emphasis in their thinking and the problems
which engrossed them, their sanctions and methods. The moving spirit
in the early Church was not the classical spirit of critical inquiry. The
writings of the New Testament were not philosophical treatises or
systematic expositions of the nature of things; they were gospels and
epistles, glad tidings of salvation and personal exhortations. The
Christian convert was not a scientific or philosophical inquirer engaged
in investigation or theory or in the pursuit of understanding. He was
a sinner come to the throne of grace in humble hope of salvation. Both
wisdom and virtue, the true insight and the right way of life, were to
him centered in his certainty of redemption through Christ. Christ was
the way, the truth, and the life.

This indifference toward science or philosophical reflection in the
early Church was intensified by its so-called "eschatological" spirit:
its expectation of the imminent end of the world, the return of Christ
to judge the living and the dead. The all-important quest of salvation,
which excluded all naturalistic interests, gained dramatic emphasis by
its alertness to the speedily impending doom. "The fashion of this
world passeth away."[1] We can thus readily understand the initial contrast which the Christian teaching presented to Greek philosophy, and
to classical culture generally. St. Paul's Epistles reveal an attitude of
mutual disregard between the learned Greeks and the early Christians.
Very few of his converts were wise after the flesh, and his preaching
of Christ crucified was foolishness to the gentiles; nonetheless, he never
tired of repeating that the wisdom of this world was foolishness to God,
and devoutly he declared: "We are fools for Christ's sake."[2]

[1] Corinthians 7:31 (American Standard Version).
[2] *Ibid.*, 4:10.

But while proclaiming its divine Gospel of eternal life and the imminent end of the world, the Christian movement was itself in its own time in this world; it was influenced by the civilization which it transformed. St. Paul and the author of the Fourth Gospel show that, even in the first century, the Church included men of intellectual preeminence as well as religious genius. The Gospel that made its initial appeal to the weary and heavy laden gradually united in faith communities more and more representative of the various social and cultural classes. Growing numbers of educated men turned from their classical wisdom to the Christian Gospel of salvation. . . .

The progressive expansion of Christianity among the educated classes brought into the Church the influence of classical ideas. Thinking men did not stop thinking. Accustomed to inquiry, they sought a clear understanding of their new faith. They were sure to reflect upon their new Christian experiences as compared with their former life. The contrast was one of humble piety and worldly sinfulness, but it was also a change in beliefs and ideas. It was a change from the *Nicomachean Ethics* to the Beautitudes, from the myths of Plato to the parables of the Gospel, from Aristotle's statement, "Virtue is a habit of the will,"[4] and the ideal of the godly life as a life of rational contemplation, to the words of Jesus: "Except a man be born again, he cannot see the kingdom of God."[5] But it was also a change from various Greek metaphysics and cosmologies to the doctrines of St. Paul and St. John. The Christian Gospel as a way of life challenged and mastered pagan pride by the divine sublimity of its ideals.

It was in the region of their thinking, in their ideas, that the classical converts to Christianity were bound to be perplexed. From what to what had they been converted? They had perhaps been Stoics or Platonists; how were they now to regard their old doctrines—were they to reject, revise, or to reaffirm them—in the light of their new Christian truths? Instead of the unformulated, burning convictions of the early converts, a new spirit invaded the Church, in which men sought a convincing statement of their beliefs, were embroiled in manifold controversies, and hence imposed the demand for orthodoxy, an acknowledged true Christian doctrine.

In the Sermon on the Mount, Jesus expressed his spiritual principles and values in contrast to the rigid laws of the priestly Jewish tradition. He spiritualized men's relation to God. The Kingdom of God

---

[4] Paraphrased from Aristotle, *Nicomachean Ethics* (trans. F. H. Peters), 10th ed., London, Kegan, Paul, 1906, Bk. II, sec. 1.

[5] John 3:3 (Authorized Version).

was not to be an external theocracy in Jerusalem but a spiritual state: "The kingdom of God is within you."[7] In place of the outward act of religious observance, obedience to God's law and justice toward men, Jesus emphasized love of God and love and brotherhood of all mankind.

The Christianization of the Mediterranean gentile world brought out a different, but equally significant, contrast between Christian and Greek philosophical ideals. The classical outlook on life was secular; the Christian was otherworldly. The Greek pursued an understanding of the nature of things and the harmonious consummation of human powers and capacities. His cardinal virtues—temperance, courage, justice, wisdom—were all expressions of rational human achievement. The Christian virtues were faith, hope, and love. The godly life was seen in humble piety, purity, mercy, and holiness, not seeking any worldly goods or mastery, but aspiring beyond this world and this life to everlasting blessedness in the hereafter. The Christian wisdom was the trusting faith of a child; the Christian temperance was continence and purity from any carnal taint; the Christian justice became loving nonresistance and the return of good for evil; the Christian courage was long-suffering patience, the martyr's firm loyalty unto death.

Though the Christian Gospel appealed mainly to the heart and the will, it was certain eventually to engage also the intellect. A religion that was primarily a devotion to God, a way of life according to God's will, a living hope of salvation by the grace of God in Christ, was bound to become also a doctrine about God, God's self-revelation in Christ, God's relation to the world and to men—a reasoned and formulated theology. In this development, this progressive engagement of the Christian reason, the leadership in the Church was naturally assumed by men of trained reason, and these were minds versed in Greek philosophy. Christian theology and philosophy issued from their endeavors to elaborate and to state systematically many deep but unformulated Christian convictions, and to reason out, consistently with prevailing Christian beliefs, a system of doctrines about nature and human nature which the early tradition of the Church had provided scarcely, if at all.

In the satisfaction of these intellectual needs the church, to be sure, used its Biblical resources and sought a Biblical formulation. But it had become increasingly a gentile Church. Even the interpretation and formulation of its Jewish traditions were being done mostly by minds that thought in Greek and Latin, or by manifold oriental minds with Hellenistic education. This interpenetration of ideas and ways of thought

---

[7] Luke 17:21 (American Standard Version).

became a historical necessity for expanding Christianity. It had to make itself understood by Greco-Roman minds.

Naturally, the various theologians reflected in their Christian doctrines the influence of their respective philosophical beliefs. . . . Even when they used Platonic or Stoic ideas, they did not use them as Platonists or Stoics. Their basic conviction was that the truth to which they had been converted was truth revealed to men by Christ, not merely a human attainment. Their Christian doctrine was to them not just another doctrine, better than others but like them admitting of criticism, revision, and development. It was *the* truth. Their problem was and could be only this: how to understand and to express this truth rightly.

In place of scientific investigation and philosophical inquiry, the Christian emphasized authoritative interpretation of the one and only Christian truth, orthodoxy. Any departure or variation from the one true way was now regarded, not merely as mistaken, but as heresy. This fundamental divine sanction, which Christian theology acknowledged, determined its method and its principles of dogmatic authoritarianism.

The basic character of medieval Christian philosophy is reflected in the history of its development. Its first period covers the formation of orthodoxy by the apologists and by the fathers of the Church; this is called "Patristic" philosophy. It reaches its culmination in the system of St. Augustine in the early fifth century. After the several centuries of intellectual stagnation which followed the fall of Rome, the second period of medieval philosophy begins with the revival of learning; this is called "Scholastic" philosophy. The great schoolmen started with the established principles of orthodoxy and elaborated them into systems of Christian philosophy. The main purpose of the philosophical theologian was and remained to give intellectual statement to his divinely revealed and indubitable Christian convictions. Scholastic philosophy has been called "faith seeking to understand (*fides quaerens intellectum*)."[10]

[10]Etienne Gilson, *The Spirit of Medieval Philosophy* trans. A. H. C. Downes, London, Sheed and Ward, 1936, p. 5.

28
Conflict: Christianity as Seen by Romans

Minicius Felix

Selections from *The Octavius of Minucius Felix, in The Writings of the Fathers down to A.D. 325*, The Rev. Alexander Roberts and James Donaldson (eds.), American Reprint of the Edinburgh Edition, Revised and Chronologically Arranged, with Brief Prefaces and Occasional Notes by A. Cleveland Coxe (Grand Rapids, Michigan: Wm. B. Eerdmans Publishing Company, 1956), IV, Chapters VIII-XIII, pp. 177-179. Used by permission of the publishers.

Chapter VIII. . . . When the men of Athens both expelled Protagoras of Abdera, and in public assembly burnt his writings, because he disputed deliberately rather than profanely concerning the divinity, why is it not a thing to be lamented, that men (for you will bear with my making use pretty freely of the force of the plea that I have undertaken)—that men, I say, of a reprobate, unlawful, and desperate faction, should rage against the gods? who, having gathered together from the lowest dregs the more unskilled, and women, credulous and, by the facility of their sex, yielding, establish a herd of a profane conspiracy, which is leagued together by nightly meetings, and solemn fasts, and inhuman meats—not by any sacred rite, but by that which requires expiation—a people skulking and shunning the light, silent in public, but garrulous in corners. They despise the temples as dead-houses, they reject the gods, they laugh at sacred things; wretched, they pity, if they are allowed, the priests; half-naked themselves, they despise honours and purple robes. Oh, wondrous folly and incredible audacity! they despise present torments, although they fear those which are certain and future; and while they fear to die after death, they do not fear to die for the present: so does a deceitful hope soothe their fear with the solace of a revival.

Chapter IX: "And now, as wickeder things advance more fruitfully, and abandoned manners creep on day by day, those abominable shrines of an impious assembly are maturing themselves throughout the whole world. Assuredly this confederacy ought to be rooted out and execrated. They know one another by secret marks and insignia, and they love one another almost before they know one another. Everywhere also there is mingled among them a certain religion of lust, and they call one another promiscuously brothers and sisters, that even a not unusual debauchery may by the intervention of that sacred name become incestuous: it is thus that their vain and senseless superstition glories in crimes. Nor, concerning these things, would intelligent report speak of things so great and various, and requiring to be prefaced by an apology, unless truth were at the bottom of it. I hear that they adore the head of an ass, that basest of creatures, consecrated by I know not what silly persuasion,—a worthy and appropriate religion for such manners. Some say that they worship the *virilia* of their pontiff and priest, and adore the nature, as it were, of their common parent. I know not whether these things are false; certainly suspicion is applicable to secret and nocturnal rites; and he who explains their ceremonies by reference to a man punished by extreme suffering for his wickedness, and to the deadly wood of the cross, appropriates fitting altars for reprobate and wicked men, that they may worship what they deserve. Now the story about the initiation of young novices is as much to be detested as it is well known. An infant covered over with meal, that it may deceive the unwary, is placed before him who is to be stained with their rites: this infant is slain by the young pupil, who has been urged on as if to harmless blows on the surface of the meal, with dark and secret wounds. Thirstily—O horror!—they lick up its blood; eagerly they divide its limbs. By this victim they are pledged together; with this consciousness of wickedness they are covenanted to mutual silence. Such sacred rites as these are more foul than any sacrileges. And of their banqueting it is well known all men speak of it everywhere; even the speech of our Cirtensian testifies to it. On a solemn day they assemble at the feast, with all their children, sisters, mothers, people of every sex and of every age. There, after much feasting, when the fellowship has grown warm, and the fervour of incestuous lust has grown hot with drunkenness, a dog that has been tied to the chandelier is provoked, by throwing a small piece of offal beyond the length of a line by which he is bound, to rush and spring; and thus the conscious light being overturned and extinguished in the shameless darkness, the connections of abominable lust involve them in the uncertainty of fate. Although not all in fact, yet in consciousness all are alike incestuous, since by the desire of all of them everything is sought for which can happen in the act of each individual.

Chapter X: "I purposely pass over many things, for those that I have mentioned are already too many; and that all these, or the greater part of them, are true, the obscurity of their vile religion declares. For why do they endeavour with such pains to conceal and to cloak whatever they worship, since honourable things always rejoice in publicity, while crimes are kept secret? Why have they no altars, no temples, no acknowledged images? Why do they never speak openly, never congregate freely, unless for the reason that what they adore and conceal is either worthy of punishment, or something to be ashamed of? Moreover, whence or who is he, or where is the *one* God, solitary, desolate, whom no free people, no kingdoms, and not even Roman superstition, have known? The lonely and miserable nationality of the Jews worshipped one God, and one peculiar to itself; but they worshipped him openly, with temples, with altars, with victims, and with ceremonies; and he has so little force or power, that he is enslaved, with his own special nation, to the Roman deities. But the Christians, moreover, what wonders, what monstrosities do they feign!—that he who is their God, whom they can neither show nor behold, inquires diligently into the character of all, the acts of all, and, in fine, into their words and secret thoughts; that he runs about everywhere, and is everywhere present: they make him out to be troublesome, restless, even shamelessly inquisitive, since he is present at everything that is done, wanders in and out in all places, although, being occupied with the whole, he cannot give attention to particulars, nor can he be sufficient for the whole while he is busied with particulars. What! because they threaten conflagration to the whole world, and to the universe itself, with all its stars, are they meditating its destruction?—as if either the eternal order constituted by the divine laws of nature would be disturbed, or the league of all the elements would be broken up, and the heavenly structure dissolved, and that fabric in which it is contained and bound together would be overthrown.

Chapter XI: "And, not content with this wild opinion, they add to it and associate with it old women's fables: they say that they will rise again after death, and ashes, and dust; and with I know not what confidence, they believe by turns in one another's lies: you would think that they had already lived again. It is a double evil and a twofold madness to denounce destruction to the heaven and the stars, which we leave just as we find them, and to promise eternity to ourselves, who are dead and extinct—who, as we are born, so also perish! It is for this cause, doubtless, also that they execrate our funeral piles, and condemn our burials by fire, as if every body, even although it be withdrawn from the flames, were not, nevertheless, resolved into the earth by lapse of years and ages, and as if it mattered not whether wild beasts tore the body to pieces, or seas consumed it, or the ground covered it, or the flames carried it away; since for the carcasses every mode of sepulture is a penalty if they feel it; if they feel it not, in the very quickness of their destruction there is relief. Deceived by this error, they promise to themselves, as being good, a blessed and perpetual life after their death; to others, as being unrighteous, eternal punishment.

Many things occur to me to say in addition, if the limits of my discourse did not hasten me. I have already shown, and take no more pains to prove, that they themselves are unrighteous; although, even if I should allow them to be righteous, yet your agreement also concurs with the opinions of many, that guilt and innocence are attributed by fate. For whatever we do, as some ascribe it to fate, so you refer it to God: thus it is according to your sect to believe that men will, not of their own accord, but as elected to will. Therefore you feign an iniquitous judge, who punishes in men, not their will, but their destiny. Yet I should be glad to be informed whether or no you rise again with bodies; and if so, with what bodies—whether with the same or with renewed bodies? Without a body? Then, as far as I know, there will neither be mind, nor soul, nor life. With the same body? But this has already been previously destroyed. With another body? Then it is a new man who is born, not the former one restored; and yet so long a time has passed away, innumerable ages have flowed by, and what single individual has returned from the dead either by the fate of Protesilaus, with permission to sojourn even for a few hours, or that we might believe it for an example? All such figments of an unhealthy belief, and vain sources of comfort, with which deceiving poets have trifled in the sweetness of their verse, have been disgracefully remoulded by you, believing undoubtingly on your God.

Chapter XII. "Neither do you at least take experience from things present, how the fruitless expectations of vain promise deceive you. Consider, wretched creatures, (from your lot) while you are yet living, what is threatening you after death. Behold, a portion of you—and, as you declare, the larger and better portion—are in want, are cold, are labouring in hard work and hunger; and God suffers it, He feigns; He either is not willing or not able to assist His people; and thus He is either weak or inequitable. Thou, who dreamest over a posthumous immortality, when thou art shaken by danger, when thou art consumed with fever, when thou art torn with pain, dost thou not then acknowledge thy frailty? Poor wretch, art thou unwillingly convinced of thine infirmity, and wilt not confess it? But I omit matters that are common to all alike. Lo, for you there are threats, punishments, tortures, and crosses; and that no longer as objects of adoration, but as tortures to be undergone; fires also, which you both predict and fear. Where is that God who is able to help you when you come to life again, since he cannot help you while you are in this life? Do not the Romans, without any help from your God, govern, reign, have the enjoyment of the whole world, and have dominion over you? But you in the meantime, in suspense and anxiety, are abstaining from respectable enjoyments. You do not visit exhibitions; you have no concern in public displays; you reject the public banquets, and abhor the sacred contests; the meats previously tasted by, and the drinks made a libation of upon, the altars. Thus you stand in dread of the gods whom you deny. You do not wreath your heads with flowers; you do not grace your bodies with odours; you reserve unguents for funeral rites; you even refuse garlands to your sepulchres—pallid, trembling beings, worthy of the pity even of our gods! Thus, wretched as you are, you neither rise again, nor do you live in the meanwhile. Therefore, if you have any wisdom or modesty, cease from prying into the regions of the sky, and the destinies and secrets of the world: it is sufficient to look before your feet, especially for untaught, uncultivated, boorish, rustic people: they who have no capacity for understanding civil matters, are much more denied the ability to discuss divine.

Chapter XIII: "However, if you have a desire to philosophize, let any one of you who is sufficiently great, imitate, if he can, Socrates the prince of wisdom. The answer of that man, whenever he was asked about celestial matters, is well known: 'What is above us is nothing to us.' . . ."

29
The "Counter-Culture": Christian Living
Tertullian

Selections from Tertullian's *Apology*, in the *Ante-Nicene Fathers*, translation of *The Writings of the Fathers down to A.D. 325*, The Rev. Alexander Roberts and James Donaldson (eds.), American Reprint of the Edinburgh Edition, Revised and Chronologically Arranged, with Brief Prefaces and Occasional Notes by A. Cleveland Coxe (Grand Rapids, Michigan: Wm. B. Eerdmans Publishing Company, 1957), III, Chapters II, XXXVIII, XXXIX, pp. 18-20, 45-47. Used by permission of the publisher.

II. . . . When the charges made against us are made against others, they are permitted to make use both of their own lips and of hired pleaders to show their innocence. They have full opportunity of answer and debate; in fact, it is against the law to condemn anybody undefended and unheard. Christians alone are forbidden to say anything in exculpation of themselves, in defence of the truth, to help the judge to a righteous decision; all that is cared about is having what the public hatred demands—the confession of the name, not examination of the charge: while in your ordinary judicial investigations, on a man's confession of the crime of murder, or sacrilege, or incest, or treason, to take the points of which we are accused, you are not content to proceed at once to sentence,—you do not take that step till you thoroughly examine the circumstances of the confession—what is the real character of the deed, how often, where, in what way, when he has done it, who were privy to it, and who actually took part with him in it. Nothing like this is done in our case, though the falsehoods disseminated about us ought to have the same sifting, that it might be found how many murdered children each of us had tasted; how many incests each of us had shrouded in darkness; what cooks, what dogs had been witness of our deeds. Oh, how great the glory of the ruler who should bring to light some Christian who had devoured a hundred infants! But, instead of that, we find that even inquiry in regard to our case is forbidden. For the younger Pliny, when he was ruler of a province, having condemned some Christians to death, and driven some of their steadfastness, being still annoyed by their great numbers, at last sought the advice of Trajan, the reigning emperor, as to what he was to do with the rest, explaining to his master that, except an obstinate disinclination to offer sacrifices, he found in the religious services nothing but meetings at early morning for singing hymns to Christ and God, and sealing home their way of life by a united pledge to be faithful to their religion, forbidding murder, adultery, dishonesty, and other crimes. Upon this Trajan wrote back that Christians were by no means to be sought after; but if they were brought before him, they should be punished. O miserable deliverance, —under the necessities of the case, a self-contradiction! It forbids them to be sought after as innocent, and it commands them to be punished as guilty. It is at once merciful and cruel; it passes by, and it punishes. Why dost thou play a game of evasion upon thyself, O Judgment? If thou condemnest, why dost thou not also inquire. If thou does not inquire, why dost thou not also absolve? . . . Well, you think the Christian a man of every crime, an enemy of the gods, of the emperor, of the laws, of good morals, of all nature; yet you compel him to deny, that you may acquit him, which without his denial you could not do. You play fast and loose with the laws. You wish him to deny his guilt, that you may, even against his will bring him out blameless and free from all guilt in reference to the past! Whence is this strange perversity on your part? How is it you do not reflect that a spontaneous confession is greatly more worthy of credit than a compelled denial; or consider whether, when compelled to deny, a man's denial may not be in good faith, and whether acquitted, he may not, then and there, as soon as the trial is over, laugh at your hostility, a Christian as much as ever? Seeing, then, that in everything you deal differently with us than with other criminals, bent upon the one object of taking from us our name (indeed, it is ours no more if we do what Christians never do), it is made perfectly clear that there is no crime of any kind in the case, but merely a name which a certain system, ever working against the truth, pursues with its enmity, doing this chiefly with the object of securing that men may have no desire to know for certain what they know for certain they are entirely ignorant of. Hence, too, it is that they believe about us things of which they have no proof, and they are disinclined to have them looked into, lest the charges, they would rather take on trust, are all proved to have no foundation, that the name so hostile to that rival power—its crimes presumed, not proved—may be condemned simply on its own confession. So we are put to the torture if we confess, and we are punished if we persevere, and if we deny we are acquitted, because all the contention is about a name. Finally, why do you read out of your tablet-lists that such a man is a Christian? Why not also that he is a murderer? And if a Christian is a murderer, why not guilty, too, of incest, or any other vile thing you believe of us? In our case alone you are either ashamed or unwilling to mention the very names of our crimes. If to be called a "Christian" does not imply any crime, the name is surely very hateful, when that of itself is made a crime.

XXXVIII. . . . as those in whom all ardour in the pursuit of glory and honour is dead, we have no pressing inducement to take part in your public meetings; nor is there aught more entirely foreign to us than affairs of state. We acknowledge one all-embracing commonwealth—the world. We renounce all your spectacles, as strongly as we renounce the matters originating them, which we know were conceived of superstition, when we give up the very things which are the basis of their representations. Among us nothing is ever said, or seen, or heard, which has anything in common with the madness of the circus, the immodesty of the theatre, the atrocities of the arena, the useless exercises of the wrestling-ground. Why do you take offence at us because we differ from you in regard to your pleasures? If we will not partake of your enjoyments, the loss is ours, if there be loss in the case, not yours. We reject what pleases you. You, on the other hand, have no taste for what is our delight. The Epicureans were allowed by you to decide for themselves one true source of pleasure—I mean equanimity; the Christian, on his part, has many such enjoyments—what harm in that?

XXXIX: I shall at once go on, then, to exhibit the peculiarities of the Christian society, that, as I have refuted the evil charged against it, I may point out its positive good. We are a body knit together as such by a common religious profession, by unity of discipline, and by the bond of a common hope. We meet together as an assembly and congregation, that, offering up prayer to God as with united force, we may wrestle with Him in our supplications. This violence God delights in. We pray, too, for the emperors, for their ministers and for all in authority, for the welfare of the world, for the prevalence of peace, for the delay of the final consummation. We assemble to read our sacred writings, if any peculiarity of the times makes either forewarning or reminiscence needful. However it be in that respect, with the sacred words we nourish our faith, we animate our hope, we make our confidence more steadfast; and no less by inculcations of God's precepts we confirm good habits. In the same place also exhortations are made, rebukes and sacred censures are administered. For with a great gravity is the work of judging carried on among us, as befits those who feel assured that they are in the sight of God; and you have the most notable example of judgment to come when any one has sinned so grievously as to require his severance from us in prayer, in the congregation and in all sacred intercourse. The tried men of our elders preside over us, obtaining that honour not by purchase, but by established character. There is no buying and selling of any sort in the things of God. Though we have our treasure-chest, it is not made up of purchase-money, as of a religion that has its price. On the monthly day, if he likes, each puts in a small donation; but only if it be his pleasure, and only if he be able: for there is no compulsion; all is voluntary. These gifts are, as it were, piety's deposit fund. For they are not taken thence and spent on feasts, and drinking-bouts, and eating-houses, but to support and bury poor people, to supply the wants of boys and girls destitute of means and parents, and of old persons confined now to the house; such, too, as have suffered shipwreck; and if there happen to be any in the mines, or banished to the islands, or shut up in the prisons, for nothing but their fidelity to the cause of God's Church, they become the nurslings of their confession. But it is mainly the deeds of a love so noble that lead many to put a brand upon us. *See*, they say, *how they love one another*, for themselves are animated by mutual hatred; how they are ready even to die for one another, for they themselves will sooner put to death. And they are wroth with us, too, because we call each other brethren; for no other reason, as I think, than because among themselves names of consanguinity are assumed in mere pretence of affection. But we are your brethren as well, by the law of our common mother nature, though you are hardly men, because brothers so unkind. At the same time, how much more fittingly they are called and counted brothers who have been led to the knowledge of God as their common Father, who have drunk in one spirit of holiness, who from the same womb of a common ignorance have agonized into the same light of truth! But on this very account, perhaps, we are regarded as having less claim to be held true brothers, that no tragedy makes a noise about our brotherhood, or that the family possessions, which generally destroy brotherhood among you, create fraternal bonds among us. One in mind and soul, we do not hesitate to share our earthly goods with one another. All things are common among us but our wives. We give up our community where it is practised alone by others, who not only take possession of the wives of their friends, but most tolerantly also accommodate their friends with theirs, following the example, I believe, of those wise men of ancient times, the Greek Socrates and the Roman Cato, who shared with their friends the wives whom they had married, it seems for the sake of progeny both to themselves and to others; whether in this acting against their partners' wishes, I am not able to say. Why should they have any care over their chastity, when their husbands so readily bestowed it away? O noble example of Attic wisdom, of Roman gravity—the philosopher and the censor playing pimps! What wonder if that great love of Christians towards one another is desecrated by you! For you abuse also our humble feasts, on the ground that they are extravagant as well as infamously wicked. To us, it seems, applies the saying of Diogenes: "The people of Megara feast as though they were going to die on the morrow; they build as though they were never to die!" But one sees more readily the mote in another's eye than the beam in his own. Why, the very air is soured with the eructations of so many tribes, and *curiae*, and *decuriae*. The Salii cannot have their feast without going into debt; you must get the accountants to tell you what the tents of Hercules and the sacrificial banquets cost; the choicest cook is appointed for the Apaturia, the Dionysia, the Attic mysteries; the smoke from the banquet of Serapis will call out the firemen. Yet about the modest supper-room of the Christians alone a great ado is made. Our feast explains itself by its name. The Greeks call it *agapé*, i. e., affection. Whatever it costs, our outlay in the name of piety is gain, since with the good things of the feast we benefit the needy; not as it is with you, do parasites aspire to the glory of satisfying their licentious propensities, selling themselves for a belly-feast to all disgraceful treatment,—but as it is with God himself, a peculiar respect is shown to the lowly. If the object of our feast be good, in the light of that consider its further regulations. As it is an act of religious service, it permits no vileness or immodesty. The participants, before reclining, taste first of prayer to God. As much is eaten as satisfies the cravings of hunger; as much is drunk as befits the chaste. They say it is enough, as those who remember that even during the night they have to worship God; they talk as those who know that the Lord is one of their auditors. After manual ablution, and the bringing in of lights, each is asked to stand forth and sing, as he can, a hymn to God, either one from the holy Scriptures or one of his own composing, —a proof of the measure of our drinking. As the feast commenced with prayer, so with prayer it is closed. We go from it, not like troops of mischief-doers, nor bands of vagabonds, nor to break out into licentious acts, but to have as much care of our modesty and chastity as if we had been at a school of virtue rather than a banquet. Give the congregation of the Christians its due, and hold it unlawful, if it is like assemblies of the illicit sort: by all means let it be condemned, if any complaint can be validly laid against it, such as lies against secret factions. But who has ever suffered harm from our assemblies? We are in our congregations just what we are when separated from each other; we are as a community what we are individuals; we injure nobody, we trouble nobody. When the upright, when the virtuous meet together, when the pious, when the pure assemble in congregation, you ought not to call that a faction, but a *curia*— [i.e., the court of God].

30
Beliefs and Opinions
in Conflict

Selections from *Address of Tatian to the Greeks*, in *The Ante-Nicene Fathers*, translations of *the Writings of the Fathers down to A.D. 325*, The Rev. Alexander Roberts and James Donaldson (eds.), American Reprint of the Edinburgh Edition, Revised and Chronologically Arranged, with Brief Prefaces and Occasional Notes by A. Cleveland Coxe (Grand Rapids, Michigan: Wm. B. Eerdmans Publishing Company, 1956), II, Chapters II, III, IV, XXI, XXV, XXVI, XXXII, XXXIII, XXXV, pp. 65-66, 74, 75, 76, 78, 79-80. Order of presentation somewhat changed. Used by permission of the publisher.

II
The Vices and Errors of the Philosophers

What noble thing have you produced by your pursuit of philosophy? Who of your most eminent men has been free from vain boasting? Diogenes, who made such a parade of his independence with his tub, was seized with a bowel complaint through eating a raw polypus, and so lost his life by gluttony. Aristippus, walking about in a purple robe, led a profligate life, in accordance with his professed opinions. Plato, a philosopher, was sold by Dionysius for his gormandizing propensities. And Aristotle, who absurdly placed a limit to Providence and made happiness to consist in the things which give pleasure, quite contrary to his duty as a preceptor flattered Alexander, forgetful that he was but a youth; and he, showing how well he had learned the lessons of his master, because his friend would not worship him shut him up and carried him about like a bear or a leopard. He in fact obeyed strictly the precepts of his teacher in displaying manliness and courage by feasting, and transfixing with his spear his intimate and most beloved friend, and then, under a semblance of grief, weeping and starving himself, that he might not incur the hatred of his friends. I could laugh at those also who in the present day adhere to his tenets,—people who say that sublunary things are not under the care of Providence; and so, being nearer the earth than the moon, and below its orbit, they themselves look after what is thus left uncared for; and as for those who have neither beauty, nor wealth, nor bodily strength, nor high birth, they have no happiness, according to Aristotle. Let such men philosophize, for me!

III
Ridicule of the Philosophers

I cannot approve of Heraclitus, who, being self-taught and arrogant, said, "I have explored myself." Nor can I praise him for hiding his poem in the temple of Artemis, in order that it might be published afterwards as a mystery; and those who take an interest in such things say that Euripides the tragic poet came there and read it, and, gradually learning it by heart, carefully handed down to posterity this darkness of Heraclitus. Death, however, demonstrated the stupidity of this man; for, being attacked by dropsy, as he had studied the art of medicine as well as philosophy, he plastered himself with cowdung, which, as it hardened, contracted the flesh of his whole body, so that he was pulled in pieces, and thus died. Then, one cannot listen to Zeno, who declares that at the conflagration the same man will rise again to perform the same actions as before; for instance, Anytus and Miletus to accuse, Busiris to murder his guests, and Hercules to repeat his labours; and in this doctrine of the conflagration he introduces more wicked than just persons—one Socrates and a Hercules, and a few more of the same class, but not many, for the bad will be found far more numerous than the good. And according to him the Deity will manifestly be the author of evil, dwelling in sewers and worms, and in the perpetrators of impiety. The eruptions of fire in Sicily, moreover, confute the empty boasting of Empedocles, in that, though he was no god, he falsely almost gave himself out for one. I laugh, too, at the old wife's talk of Pherecydes, and the doctrine inherited from him by Pythagoras, and that of Plato, an imitation of his, though some think otherwise. And who would give his approval to the cynogamy of Crates, and not rather, repudiating the wild and tumid speech of those who resemble him, turn to the investigation of what truly deserves attention? Wherefore be not led away by the solemn assemblies of philosophers who are no philosophers, who dogmatize one against the other, though each one vents but the crude fancies of the moment. They have, moreover, many collisions among themselves; each one hates the other; they indulge in conflicting opinions, and their arrogance makes them eager for the highest places. It would better become them, moreover, not to pay court to kings unbidden, nor to flatter men at the head of affairs, but to wait till the great ones come to them.

XXV
Boastings and Quarrels of the Philosophers

What great and wonderful things have your philosophers effected? They leave uncovered one of their shoulders; they let their hair grow long;

they cultivate their beards; their nails are like the claws of wild beasts. Though they say that they want nothing, yet, like Proteus (The Cynic Peregrinus is meant), they need a currier for their wallet, and a weaver for their mantle, and a wood-cutter for their staff, and the rich (They need the rich to invite them to banquets), and a cook also for their gluttony. O man competing with the dog (The Cynic), you know not God, and so have turned to the imitation of an irrational animal. You cry out in public with an assumption of authority, and take upon you to avenge your own self; and if you receive nothing, you indulge in abuse, and philosophy is with you the art of getting money. You follow the doctrines of Plato, and a disciple of Epicurus lifts up his voice to oppose you. Again, you wish to be a disciple of Aristotle, and a follower of Democritus rails at you. Pythagoras says that he was Euphorbus, and he is the heir of the doctrine of Pherecydes; but Aristotle impugns the immortality of the soul. You who receive from your predecessors doctrines which clash with one another, you the inharmonious, are fighting against the harmonious. One of you asserts that God is body, but I assert that He is without body; that the world is indestructible, but I say that it is to be destroyed; that a conflagration will take place at various times, but I say that it will come to pass once for all; that Minos and Rhadamanthus are judges, but I say that God Himself is Judge; that the soul alone is endowed with immortality, but I say that the flesh also is endowed with it. What injury do we inflict upon you, O Greeks? Why do you hate those who follow the word of God, as if they were the vilest of mankind? It is not we who eat human flesh—they among you who assert such a thing have been suborned as false witnesses; it is among you that Pelops is made a supper for the gods, although beloved by Poseidon, and Kronos devours his children, and Zeus swallows Metis.

XXVI
Ridicule of the Studies of the Greeks

Cease to make a parade of sayings which you have derived from others, and to deck yourselves like the daw in borrowed plumes. If each state were to take away its contribution to your speech, your fallacies would lose their power. While inquiring what God is, you are ignorant of what is in yourselves; and, while staring all agape at the sky, you stumble into pitfalls. The reading of your books is like walking through a labyrinth, and their readers resemble the cask of the Danaïds. Why do you divide time, saying that one part is past, and another present, and another future? For how can the future be passing when the present exists? As those who are sailing imagine in their ignorance, as the ship is borne along, that the hills are in motion, so you do not know that it is you who are passing along, but that time ὁαιών remains present as long as the Creator wills it to exist. Why am I called to account for uttering my opinions, and why are you in such haste to put them all down? Were not you born in the same manner as ourselves, and placed under the same government of the world? Why say that wisdom is with you alone, who have not another sun, nor other risings of the stars, nor a more distinguished origin, nor a death preferable to that of other men? The grammarians have been the beginning of this idle talk; and you who parcel out wisdom are cut off from the wisdom that is according to truth, and assign the names of the several parts to particular men; and you know not God, but in your fierce contentions destroy one another. And on this account you are all nothing worth. While you arrogate to yourselves the sole right of discussion, you discourse like the blind man with the deaf. Why do you handle the builder's tools without knowing how to build? Why do you busy yourselves with words, while you keep aloof from deeds, puffed up with praise, but cast down by misfortunes? Your modes of acting are contrary to reason, for you make a pompous appearance in public, but hide your teaching in corners. Finding you to be such men as these, we have abandoned you, and no longer concern ourselves with your tenets, but follow the word of God. Why, O man, do you set the letters of the alphabet at war with one another? Why do you, as in a boxing match, make their sounds clash together with your mincing Attic way of speaking, whereas you ought to speak more according to nature? For if you adopt the Attic dialect though not an Athenian, pray why do you not speak like the Dorians? How is it that one appears to you more rugged, the other more pleasant for intercourse?

XXI
Doctrines of the Christians and Greeks Respecting God Compared

We do not act as fools, O Greeks, nor utter idle tales, when we announce that God was born in the form of a man. I call on you who reproach us to compare your mythical accounts with our narrations. Athené, as they say, took the form of Dëiphobus for the sake of Hector, and the unshorn Phoebus for the sake of Admetus fed the trailing-footed oxen, and the spouse of Zeus came as an old woman to Semele. But, while you treat seriously such things, how can you deride us? Your Asclepios died, and he who ravished fifty virgins in one night at Thespiae lost his life by delivering himself to the devouring flame. Prometheus, fastened to Caucasus, suffered punishment for his good deeds to men. According to you, Zeus is envious, and hides the dream from men, wishing their destruction. Wherefore, looking at your own memorials, vouchsafe us your approval, though it were only as dealing in legends similar to your own. We, however, do not deal in folly, but your legends are only idle tales. If you speak of the origin of the gods, you also declare them to be mortal. For what reason is Hera now never pregnant? Has she grown old? or is there no one to give you information? Believe me now, O Greeks, and do not resolve your myths and gods into allegory. If you attempt to do this, the divine nature as held by you is overthrown by your own selves; for, if the demons with you are such as they are said to be, they are worthless as to character; or, if regarded as symbols of the powers of nature, they are not what they are called. But I cannot be persuaded to pay religious homage to the natural elements, nor can I undertake to persuade my neighbour. And Metrodorus of Lampsacus, in his treatise concerning Homer, has argued very foolishly, turning everything into allegory. For he says that neither Hera, nor Athené, nor Zeus are what those persons suppose who consecrate to them sacred enclosures and groves, but parts of nature and certain arrangements of the elements. Hector also, and Achilles, and Agamemnon, and all the Greeks in general, and the Barbarians with Helen and Paris, being of the same nature, you will of course say are introduced merely for the sake of the machinery of the poem, not one of these personages having really existed. But these things we have put forth only for argument's sake; for it is not allowable even to compare our notion of God with those who are wallowing in matter and mud.

IV

The Christians Worship God Alone

. . . Man is to be honoured as a fellow-man; God alone is to be feared, —He who is not visible to human eyes, nor comes within the compass of human art. Only when I am commanded to deny Him, will I not obey, but will rather die than show myself false and ungrateful. Our God did not begin to be in time: He alone is without beginning, and He Himself is the beginning of all things. God is a Spirit, not pervading matter, but the Maker of material spirits, and of the forms that are in matter; He is invisible, impalpable, being Himself the Father of both sensible and invisible things. Him we know from His creation, and apprehend His invisible power by His works. I refuse to adore that workmanship which He has made for our sakes. The sun and moon were made for us: how, then, can I adore my own servants? How can I speak of stocks and stones as gods? For the Spirit that pervades matter is inferior to the more divine spirit; and this, even when assimilated to the soul, is not to be honoured equally with the perfect God. Nor even ought the ineffable God to be presented with gifts; for He who is in want of nothing is not to be misrepresented by us as though He were indigent. But I will set forth our views more distinctly.

XXXII
The Doctrine of the Christians, Is Opposed to Dissensions, and Fitted for All

But with us there is no desire of vainglory, nor do we indulge in a variety of opinions. For having renounced the popular and earthly, and obeying the commands of God, and following the law of the Father of immortality, we reject everything which rests upon human opinion. Not only do the rich among us pursue our philosophy, but the poor enjoy instruction gratuitously; for the things which come from God surpass the requital of worldly gifts. Thus we admit all who desire to hear, even old women and striplings; and, in short, persons of every age are treated by us with respect, but every kind of licentiousness is kept at a distance. And in speaking we do not utter falsehood. It would be an excellent thing if your continuance in unbelief should receive a check; but, however that may be, let our cause remain confirmed by the judgment pronounced by God. Laugh, if you please; but you will have to weep hereafter. Is it not absurd that Nestor, who was slow at cutting his horses' reins owing to his weak and sluggish old age, is, according to you, to be admired for attempting to rival the young men in fighting, while you deride those among us who struggle against old age and occupy themselves with the things pertaining to God? Who would not laugh when you tell us that the Amazons, and Semiramis, and certain other warlike women existed, while you cast reproaches on our maidens? Achilles was a youth, yet is believed to have been very magnanimous; and Neoptolemus was younger, but strong; Philoctetes was weak, but the divinity had need of him against Troy. What sort of man was Thersites? yet he held a command in the army, and, if he had not through doltishness had such an unbridled tongue, he would not have been reproached for being peak-headed and bald. As for those who wish to learn our philosophy, we do not test them by their looks, nor do we judge of those who come to us by their outward appearance; for we argue that there may be strength of mind in all, though they may be weak in body. But your proceedings are full of envy and abundant stupidity.

XXXIII
Vindication of Christian Women

Therefore I have been desirous to prove from the things which are esteemed honourable among you, that our institutions are marked by sober-mindedness, but that yours are in close affinity with madness. You who say that we talk nonsense among women and boys, among maidens and old women, and scoff at us for not being with you, hear what silliness prevails among the Greeks. For their works of art are devoted to worthless objects, while they are held in higher estimation by you than even your gods; and you behave yourselves unbecomingly in what relates to woman. For Lysippus cast a statue of Praxilla, whose poems contain nothing useful, and Menestratus one of Learchis, and Selanion one of Sappho the courtesan, and Naucydes one of Erinna the Lesbian, and Boiscus one of Myrtis, and Cephisodotus one of Myro of Byzantium, and Gomphus one of Praxigoris, and Amphistratus one of Clito. And what shall I say about Anyta, Telesilla, and Mystis? Of the first Euthycrates and Cephisodotus made a statue, and of the second Niceratus, and of the third Aristodotus; Euthycrates made one of Mnesiarchis the Ephesian, Selanion one of Corinna, and Euthycrates one of Thalarchis the Argive. My object in referring to these women is, that you may not regard as something strange what you find among us, and that, comparing the statues which are before your eyes, you may not treat the women with scorn who among us pursue philosophy. This Sappho is a lewd, love-sick female, and sings her own wantonness; but all our women are chaste, and the maidens at their distaffs sing of divine things more nobly than that damsel of yours. Wherefore be ashamed, you who are professed disciples of women yet scoff at those of the sex who hold our doctrine, as well as at the solemn assemblies they frequent. What a noble infant did Glaucippé present to you, who brought forth a prodigy, as is shown by her statue cast by Niceratus, the son of Euctemon the Athenian! But, if Glaucippé brought forth an elephant, was that a reason why she should enjoy public honours? Praxiteles and Herodotus made for you Phryné the courtesan, and Euthycrates cast a brazen statue of Panteuchis, who was pregnant by a whoremonger; and Dinomenes, because Besantis queen of the Paeonians gave birth to a black infant, took pains to preserve her memory by his art. I condemn Pythagoras too, who made a figure of Europa on the bull; and you also, who honour the accuser of Zeus on account of his artistic skill. And I ridicule the skill of Myron, who made a heifer and upon it a Victory because by carrying off the daughter of Agenor it had borne away the prize for adultery and lewdness. The Olynthian Herodotus made statues of Glycera the courtesan and Argeia the harper. Bryaxis made a statue of Pasiphaë; and, by having a memorial of her lewdness, it seems to have been almost your desire that the women of the present time should be like her. A certain Melanippë was a wise woman, and for that reason Lysistratus made her statue. But, forsooth, you will not believe that among us there are wise women!

XXXV
Tatian Speaks as an Eye-Witness

The things which I have thus set before you I have not learned at second hand. I have visited many lands; I have followed rhetoric, like yourselves; I have fallen in with many arts and inventions; and finally, when sojourning in the city of the Romans, I inspected the multiplicity of statues brought thither by you: for I do not attempt, as is the custom with many, to strengthen my own views by the opinions of others, but I wish to give you a distinct account of what I myself have seen and felt. . . .

31
The "Counter-Culture": Family Up-Bringing

Hugh C. Black

St. John Chrysostom (347?-407) and Raising Up an Athlete for Christ

"Stoned on Jesus" youngsters of every generation, "Campus Crusaders for Christ," "Young Life" members, their supporters and their critics, and most of us ponder a crucial question regarding life and its conduct: What does it mean to be a "Christian"? Our particular interpretation determines our belief and opinions and hence the kind of conduct and behavior to which we commit ourselves in living our own way or in criticising others. Important it is, then, that we gain as much understanding as we may be ascertaining what it has meant to those professing to be "Christians." What has the "Christian" outlook meant for the family and what has that perspective on life entailed for members of the family intent on the proper up-bringing of its young members? Some light is afforded by familiarizing ourselves with the thinking of St. John Chrysostom, who lived 347?-407 and expressed himself more fully about these matters in *An Address on Vainglory and the Right Way for Parents to Bring Up Their Children*. [For a good English translation, I recommend the one by M. L. W. Laistner, on pp. 85-122, in his *Christianity and Pagan Culture in the Later Roman Empire*, published from Ithaca, New York, in 1951 by the Cornell University Press.] As I reflect on St. John Chrysostom's beliefs, he seems to say to me something like the following. Here, then, through my modern eyes is his basic view of parental upbringing as he interpreted long ago what it means to be a "Christian." Here are ideas which should incite us to argue and debate what true "Christian" living and upbringing in the family should be!

Chrysostom's outlook on life and family up-bringing is in terms of a battle being fought for the "higher" life of man which requires the family itself in a patriarchal structure to train up each son (preferential treatment over the daughter to be noted by today's advocates of Women's Liberation Movement!) to become "an Athlete for Christ."

In his view it is evident that neither the younger nor the older generation is to question and challenge the "facts of natural society." For example, one is to accept slavery, and the father is to teach the son the difference between slave and freeman. The son in the aristocratic family (with servants) who is destined to govern the household and also the world is to be taught to accept this "status quo." He is to accept the Genesis 9:21-25 story of Noah, Ham, Shem, and Japheth that slavery is the natural order. It is the result of sin, punishment, and penalty for a son insulting his father! Servants, in the order of nature, are of a lower nature than the son of the family who is destined to rule and govern in the affairs of men. If he is "trained" correctly, he will become superior: a leader who has "overcome" the lower habits of slaves who are described as careless, losing or breaking valuable objects, who sometimes appear in life with all the allure of naked women uttering shameful words. In preference, he (the master) may be so trained in time under a patriarchal family structure that he may be inclined to display habits of gentleness, of virtue, of being above common anger and abuse and desire of appetite to show the wisdom of the "kingdom of heaven" against the "fear of hell" and to recognize his fellow-men as brothers deserving of gentle treatment and patience and kindness.

I see this acceptance of the "revealed" side of life, the authoritative, "status quo," unquestioning attitude as revealing what Plato recognized earlier as our great human need: the application of our rational, critical, skeptical natures to our ever upward struggle toward what is "best." The more I read of the "Christian" Chrysostom's view of life and family up-bringing, the more I see the underlying message for our modern eyes: the need for us to be even more (not less) rational than Chrysostom in seeing how even Christians must struggle to overcome vanity, show, and ostentatious pride, what he called "Vainglory"! Chrysostom's view, it seems to me, is yet a far cry from what Jesus of Nazareth intended as the new gospel or message: an ideal for man of love, brotherhood, and humility, and humbleness. As we earlier indicated in our study of Egyptian life of old, this is further testimony to man's ways with ideas in human experience: the many years it takes for man to put into practice the ideals and the best the human experience has revealed about living. By virtue of the hindsight which is now ours, Chrysostom's interpretation of "Christianity" reminds us so much of the Age of the Patriarchs in ancient Hebrew times, of the Puritan days in Colonial America, of the great struggles to free minds from old constraining molds to inaugurate the modern period with new scientific insights, and even of many current styles of life. We begin to understand some of the intense hatreds of minorities for so-called "Christians." Reading Chrysostom, one begins to wonder if Jesus of Nazareth ever lived and thought and contributed his insights to man's peak experiences and offered such resources for the guidance of human lives. As in ancient Egypt, it is as though Akhenaten's insights and monuments had been effectively erased by the Ramses II from the memory of mankind. As with the ancient Hebrews in 621 B. C. with King Josiah's Deuteronomic reforms being compromised into Monoyahwism, so in Chrysostom's interpretation of "Christianity" I seem to see compromises entering in to distort the new message of Jesus. Yet in Chrysostom's particular portrait of life we may yet catch a faint glimmer of the master's sterling insights.

St. John Chrysostom's portrayal of the evil and "wicked spirit" of vainglory strikes me as consistent with the eternal contention and battle between our so human elements. Often life is a contention between lower and higher elements of our nature! Chrysostom is right in seeing the need to resist the temptations and impulses which bring into one's life anarchy, chaos, and confusion. This is the very real lure of the degenerate, the temptation to give way to apathy, to act on impulse of the moment, or to "let go" to the emotion or feeling so insistent on being expressed. But man is capable of something "better." He can cultivate a philosophical disposition and display "the marks of a philosophic mind." He can bring to bear the ordering, tempering, balancing, integrative influence of rational thought and rise from vainglory and selfishness to altruism, to concern for others, to intelligent responsibility in his conduct.

Chrysostom puts this perpetual human condition in terms of a circus spectacular, for he pictures Vainglory as a wild beast in the circus ring "standing over the body of the Church prostrate," "never giving ground nor drawing back." To scare away this wild beast, soldiers of Christ are required. Christian families must raise up athletes for Christ, strong enough to resist the selfish tendencies of our lives and to attain concern for others. All the more difficult is the task for the Christian athlete. For this evil and wicked spirit must be resisted, contended with, and driven away. But it appears to the young man in all the tempting allure of a beautiful harlot in youthful bloom, beckoning with words from a lovely face and a body decked out in soft raiment with all the allure of a perfumed and scented body covered with golden ornaments, encircled by a golden girdle enhancing a head of "curls plaited in the Persian fashion." Lips as sweet as a honeycomb decoy the young man and hide from him the "hideous, fiery, savage spirit" within. No wonder the young man is invaded and his mind driven to frenzy by the temptations of Vainglory. How inclined he is toward the modern view of "letting go." And how appealing to him are the externals when he ought to be concerned with overcoming them and establish the virtues of life: "fair dealing, disdain of money and fame, contempt for what the many think honor," "good place and reputation and honor."

Chrysostom's method for raising up an athlete for Christ is an authoritative, prohibiting, guiding and directing of a youth (as the phrase goes) "fortunate in his birth." For *The Right Way for Parents to Bring Up Their Children* seems to be directed not toward all Christians but only toward the well-born, the aristocrats whose training is so important because it pertains to "the governance of the world." It begins in the patriarchy of the family in constraining and directing the boy toward attaining the virtues through the father as an arbiter who rules through "the fear of Hell and the promise of His Kingdom." The mother takes an active part in exposing him to Scriptural stories teaching lessons of reverence and honor for fathers, the ills of "the greed of the belly," to bear misfortune nobly, to feel kinship with the righteous, and to trust in God. A strict tutor is employed to direct his life and join with the parents in impressing on the "athlete-to-be" (as one does a waxen seal) a reverence for good precepts. The child is not allowed to let his "hair hang down behind, thereby . . . making him look effeminate and like a girl and softening the ruggedness of his sex." Parents discourse to the children "about virginity and sobriety and contempt for wealth and fame" and act as artists in molding the youth. They establish laws which inspire fear and are strong and are to be enforced. These are laws for good order and the general welfare. The child is trained to utter grave and reverent words and to avoid foolish, shameful, common, and worldly words. He is to avoid license, greed, and ambition, and nosiness in the affairs of others. He is sheltered from hearing base and wicked words and from frivolous and old wives' tales. He is to be shielded from base persons and "from a young woman" "as a fire." He is to avoid a crowd of women and forbidden to bathe in their company. Forbidden even to see a woman, he is restricted to speaking only to his mother. He is not permitted money, fine raiment, or soft couches. He is taught to despise luxury. He is "to breathe the air, not to receive sweet odors." The athlete for Christ is to be protected from fragrant scents and herbs and perfumes lest they "penetrate the brain, relax the whole body, and fan into flames the pleasures." His brothers and the servants are encouraged even to be contentious to him, to try, and test him, to try his patience, to cause him to suffer. All of this is discipline for his own good, a part of his training. When one trains to become a wrestler, he must be tried and tested by his companions against whom he contests. So if one is to be a "soldier of God," he must be "trained" by encountering those who make life contentious so that he may suffer and learn to bear up patiently under the tribulations of life—all to the end that he may eventually put on "royal discipline" as his appropriate habit!

Through what appears to modern eyes to be a negative approach of "Thou shalt not's," of censorship, of prohibitions and restraints, somehow a way of firmness is to be established. It begins early and operates through such guardians as the mother, the tutor, and the servants—all of whom maintain a continuous surveillance. But mostly it stems from the family patriarch, the father, and his crucial attitude toward discipline which to me today seems the very embodiment of hypocrisy and negativism in the name of a Christianity which began with Jesus and a positive attitude toward the relationship between persons: of love and respect for the innate dignity and worth of human personality. For I hear Chrysostom proposing this kind of plan of discipline for training the boy. The boy is to be held up to a law—a law that he be fair and courteous, and use no one in despite, that he not swear, and that he not be contentious. If he should break this law, he is to be punished, first with a stern look, next with incisive words, and then with reproachful words. At other times, Chrysostom tells us, he may be won with gentleness and promises. The parent is to avoid a constant resort to blows. He threatens blows but does not strike! [What hypocrisy to the modern eye!] Somehow the boy will gain a fear of blows and never perceive that he will never be struck! Through such means the soldier of God is to be directed and guided toward becoming the kind of person who resists the temptations of desire and feelings and "letting go" to become a disciplined ruler over his household who contributes to the important matter of the "governance of the world"!

Today I live in a time requiring the bridging of gaps, especially those between generations and between minorities. To me a vital requisite for building those bridges has been a wisdom about the true beginning of those relationships between people. I always thought that wisdom came from our "Judeo-Christian" heritage, needed to be balanced by our Graeco-Roman heritage with its emphasis on the rational approach, and must be bulwarked by the developments of our later heritage in science and democracy. I could never understand modern-day skepticism about "Christianity" and its failures because my whole frame of reference for "Christianity" had been what I understood Jesus of Nazareth had taught. Now I am beginning to see in the writings of St. John Chrysostom another view of what "Christianity" has been and meant to some people. Now I am beginning to understand a bit better, and perhaps that is a needed bridge for today's living.

Here, perhaps, is a chance to see one more example of what I have previously called "Man's Ways with Ideas." Earlier when we studied ancient Egyptian civilization, we noted the great leap upward of Akhenaten, whom Breasted called the first individual, the world's first idealist. But his insights came to little or nothing, and that experience causes us to raise the question: Doesn't man really prefer his customary, tempting and alluring supernatural, magical, and mystical approaches to life over the rational, hard, difficult struggle toward ideal being? When we reflect back on the study of the ancient Greeks and Romans, we are tempted to say that man really prefers the way of pleasure and hedonism shown by the Sophists, the orators, and the rhetoricians skilled in the arts of persuasion as against the philosopher's way through critical inquiry to truth. If we should read from Lincoln Steffens, *The Autobiography of Lincoln Steffens* (New York: Harcourt, Brace and Company, 1931), the tremendous story about Christianity in the days he describes on pp. 525-6, 670-1, and 688, would we not be tempted to agree with the man convicted of setting a bomb? He was convinced that the court verdict against him proved that man really prefers the power of dynamite! Man has seemed to prefer his own superiority in class, rule, and money over brotherhood and love. Yet from these shattering realities there still shines through the glimmer of hope and faith and love—these three, of which love is the greatest?

32
The Counter-Culture: Catechumenal Instruction

Hugh C. Black

The Priest and Church between Man and God

We have been following the developing story of "Christianity" in terms of a developing "counter-culture" to paganism. The early Christians were different from others, for they had beliefs which set them apart. In the previous reading we learned from St. John Chrysostom that the family was a main agency for rearing Christian athletes and soldiers of God. The family warned the youth of the dangers to be encountered in the "straight" world of paganism. For example, the Christian youth was not permitted the joys of plays, dramatic performances in the theatre. Instead Chrysostom would enjoin him to fast on Wednesday and Friday and to visit the church and let him often see the head of his church and receive praise "from the bishop's lips." On occasion the father would take the boy in the evening to stand outside the theatre and ridicule the play's spectators when the play was ended, pointing out that the older men have less sense than the young and the young are inflamed by desire. The family was not alone as an agency of warning and instruction for the "set apart" Christians. The growing Christian Church was concerned with the catechetical instruction of the "catechumens" and their instructors. This, as was the case with up-bringing in the family, involved warnings and instruction to those wishing to become Christians.

Gregory of Nyssa composed *The Great Catechism*, his own quite dogmatic position regarding three basic doctrines of the Trinity, the Incarnation, and the sacraments of baptism and the Eucharist. Assuming training in dogmatic theology, it was an aid to instructors of catechumens of good education. Each candidate for baptism had held different religious beliefs depending upon whether he were Jew, Manichaean, pagan, or Gnostic. The Christian teacher could not use the same teaching for all, for the way of the Church was to convince prospective members that their old beliefs were founded on error. So Gregory prepared his instructors to warn the new candidates by censuring the Jews and the pagans and the various heresies so obnoxious to the orthodox Christian (especially Mani and the Manichaeans, who rejected the Old Testament and taught a dualism of a Power of Evil in constant conflict to God the Creator).

Two extant homilies by John Chrysostom and a series of sixteen short allocutions by Theodore of Mopsuestia inform us somewhat about the method of catechetical instruction in Antioch and neighboring bishoprics during the fourth century. Chrysostom attended very little to matters of church doctrine except to point out the significance of the rite of baptism. In characteristic fashion, he dwelt mostly on the kind of character which should distinguish Christians. But Alphonse Mingana's translation of Theodore of Mopsuestia's hitherto lost commentary on the Nicene Creed reveals to us an important part of the story of the development of Christianity. For it tells us more fully the story of priest and Church being put between man and his God and lays a part of the background for the later Protestant Reformation. [Alphonse Mingana's translation of Theodore of Mopsuestia appears in Woodbrooke Studies, V and VI, and available through Trustees of the Woodbrooke Settlement in Birmingham, England, and Messrs. William Heffer and Sons, Cambridge, England, publishers.]

Any convert to Christianity wishing to become a member of the Church accepted its Creed as a statement of its and his belief, thus setting him off from others. Theodore's ten addresses explained the difficult subject of the Nicene Creed in clear and simple language and thus rendered a real service to the Church's program of catechumenal instruction. Moreover, one of his addresses deals with the Lord's prayer, three deal with baptism, and two with the Eucharist—all subjects helpful to the catechumen needing instruction. He was even more helpful in increasing the understanding of the catechumens by introducing similes drawn from everyday life. Laistner, for examples lists the following: "The religious ceremonies of pagans are like the make-believe of a play in the theater. The regeneration of a Christian is like refashioning of damaged pottery. Every body has its shadow, but we cannot identify the shadow alone. The newly baptized is like an infant in swaddling clothes." Thus did Theodore instruct the new members-to-be in religion. Most instructive to us about the Church is the simile from everyday life drawn by Theodore for use with baptismal candidates [Mingana's translation is in Woodbrooke Studies, VI, 33-34]. When a craftsman or workman wishes to enter the house of a powerful, worldly man to contract for work and services, he does not go to the master of the house but rather makes his contract and agreement through the intermediary of the majordomo. So in our religious conduct we are to act in the same way. For Paul has told us that God is so much greater and higher than are we. He is forever invisible and dwells in a light which is ineffable. His house is the Church. His majordomo is the priest, who has been found worthy to preside over the Church. So we are to approach the church's majordomo, profess our faith, and make our contracts and engagements with God through the intermediary of the priest. Only in this way do we become worthy to enter His house and enjoy its sight, its knowledge and its habitation and become enrolled as a citizen in its city!

Through Church, and Creed, and Priest even though it is only the fourth century, we seem already far from Jesus of Nazareth.

How the Catechumens Are to Be Instructed

Selections from *The Apostolical Constitutions*, as quoted in F. V. N. Painter, *Great Pedagogical Essays: Plato to Spencer* (New York: American Book Company, Copyright 1905 by F. V. N. Painter), pp. 153-154.

Let him, therefore, who is to be taught the truth in regard to piety be instructed before his baptism in the knowledge of the unbegotten God, in the understanding of his only begotten Son, in the assured acknowledgement of the Holy Ghost. Let him learn the order of the several parts of the creation, the series of providence, the different dispensations of thy laws. Let him be instructed how the world was made, and why man was appointed to be a citizen therein; let him also know his own nature, of what sort it is; let him be taught how God punished the wicked with water and fire, and did glorify the saints in every generation—I mean Seth, and Enos, and Enoch, and Noah, and Abraham and his posterity, and Melchizedek, and Job, and Moses, and Joshua, and Caleb, and Phineas the priest, and those that were holy in every generation; and how God still took care of and did not reject mankind, but called them from their error and vanity to the acknowledgment of the truth at various seasons, reducing them from bondage and impiety unto liberty and piety, from injustice to righteousness, from death eternal to everlasting life. Let him that offers himself to baptism learn these and the like things during the time that he is a catechumen; and let him who lays his hands upon him adore God, the Lord of the whole world, and thank him for his creation, for his sending Christ his only begotten Son, that he might save man by blotting out his transgressions, and that he might remit ungodliness and sins, and might "purify him from all filthiness of flesh and spirit," and sanctify man according to the good pleasure of his kindness, that he might inspire him with the knowledge of his will, and enlighten the eyes of his heart to consider of his wonderful works, and make known to him the judgments of righteousness, that so he might hate every way of iniquity, and walk in the way of truth, that he might be thought worthy of the laver of regeneration, to the adoption of sons, which is in Christ, that "being planted together in the likeness of the death of Christ," in hopes of a glorious communication, he may be mortified to sin, and may live to God, as to his mind, and word, and deed, and may be numbered together in the book of the living. And after this thanksgiving, let him instruct him in the doctrines concerning our Lord's incarnation, and in those concerning his passion, and resurrection from the dead, and assumption.

33
The "Counter-Culture": Christian Schooling

St. Basil (330-379 A. D.)

Selections from St. Basil, *Address to Young Men on the Right Use of Greek Literature*, translated by Frederick Morgan Padelford, in *Essays on the Study and Use of Poetry by Plutarch and Basil the Great*, Yale Studies in English XV, Albert S. Cook (ed.), (New York: Henry Holt and Company, 1902), pp. 101-119.

Many considerations, young men, prompt me to recommend to you the principles which I deem most desirable, and which I believe will be of use you if you will adopt them. For my time of life, my many-sided training, yea, my adequate experience in those vicissitudes of life which teach their lessons at every turn, have so familiarized me with human affairs, that I am able to map out the safest course for those just starting upon their careers. By nature's common bond I stand in the same relationship to you as your parents, so that I am no whit behind them in my concern for you. Indeed, if I do not misinterpret your feelings, you no longer crave your parents when you come to me. Now if you should receive my words with gladness, you would be in the second class of those who, according to Hesiod, merit praise; if not, I should say nothing disparaging, but no doubt you yourselves would remember the passage in which that poet says: "He is best who, of himself, recognizes what is his duty, and he also is good who follows the course marked out by others, but he who does neither of these things is of no use under the sun." [*Works and Days*, 285 ff.]

Do not be surprised if to you, who go to school every day, and who, through their writings, associate with the learned men of old, I say that out of my own experience I have evolved something more useful. Now this is my counsel, that you should not unqualifiedly give over your minds to these men, as a ship is surrendered to the rudder, to follow whither they list, but that, while receiving whatever of value they have to offer, you yet recognize what it is wise to ignore. Accordingly, from this point on I shall take up and discuss the pagan writings, and how we are to discriminate among them.

II

We Christians, young men, hold that this human life is not a supremely precious thing, nor do we recognize anything as unconditionally a blessing which benefits us in this life only. [See Col. iii. 2: "Set your affections on things above, not on things on the earth."] Neither pride of ancestry, nor bodily strength, nor beauty, nor greatness, nor the esteem of all men, nor kingly authority, nor, indeed, whatever of human affairs may be called great, do we consider worthy of desire, or the possessors of them as objects of envy; but we place our hopes upon the things which are beyond, and in preparation for the life eternal do all things that we do. Accordingly, whatever helps us towards this we say that we must love and follow after with all our might, but those things which have no bearing upon it should be held as naught. But to explain what this life is, and in what way and manner we shall live it, requires more time than is at our command, and more mature hearers than you.

And yet, in saying thus much, perhaps I have made it sufficiently clear to you that if one should estimate and gather together all earthly weal from the creation of the world, he would not find it comparable to the smallest part of the possessions of heaven; rather, that all the precious things in this life fall further short of the least good in the other than the shadow or the dream fails of the reality. Or rather, to avail myself of a still more natural comparison, by as much as the soul is superior to the body in all things, by so much is one of these lives superior to the other. [See *Rep.* X. 614: "And yet, I said, all these things are as nothing, either in number or greatness, in comparison with those other recompenses which await both just and unjust after death, which are more and greater far."]

Into the life eternal the Holy Scriptures lead us, which teach us through divine words. But so long as our immaturity forbids our understanding their deep thought, we exercise our spiritual perceptions upon profane writings, which are not altogether different, and in which we perceive the truth as it were in shadows and in mirrors. Thus we imitate those who perform the exercises of military practice, for they acquire skill in gymnastics and in dancing, and then in battle reap the reward of their training. We must needs believe that the greatest of all battles lies before us, in preparation for which we must do and suffer all things to gain power. Consequently we must be conversant with poets, with historians, with orators, indeed with all men who may further our soul's salvation. Just as dyers prepare the cloth before they apply the dye, be it purple or any other color, so indeed must we also, if we would preserve indelible the idea of the true virtue, become first initiated in the pagan lore, then at length give special heed to the sacred and divine teachings, even as we first accustom ourselves to the sun's reflection in the water, and then become able to turn our eyes upon the very sun itself.

III

If, then, there is any affinity between the two literatures, a knowledge of them should be useful to us in our search for truth; if not, the comparison, by emphasizing the contrast, will be of no small service in strengthening our regard for the better one. With what now may we compare these two kinds of education to obtain a simile? Just as it is the chief mission of the tree to bear its fruit in its season, though at the same time it puts forth for ornament the leaves which quiver on its boughs, even so the real fruit of the soul is truth, yet it is not without advantage for it to embrace the pagan wisdom, as also leaves offer shelter to the fruit, and an appearance not untimely. That Moses, whose name is a synonym for wisdom, severely trained his mind in the learning of the Egyptians, and thus became able to appreciate their deity. Similarly, in later days, the wise Daniel is said to have studied the lore of the Chaldaeans while in Babylon, and after that to have taken up the sacred teachings.

IV

Perhaps it is sufficiently demonstrated that such heathen learning is not unprofitable for the soul; I shall then discuss next the extent to which one may pursue it. To begin with the poets, since their writings are of all degrees of excellence, you should not study all of their poems without omitting a single word. When they recount the words and deeds of good men, you should both love and imitate them, earnestly emulating such conduct. But when they portray base conduct, you must flee from them and stop up your ears, as Odysseus is said to have fled past the song of the sirens, for familiarity with evil writings paves the way for evil deeds. Therefore the soul must be guarded with great care, lest through our love for letters it receive some contamination unawares, as men drink in poison with honey. We shall not praise the poets when they scoff and rail, when they represent fornicators and winebibbers, when they define blissfulness by groaning tables and wanton songs. Least of all shall we listen to them when they tell us of their gods, and especially when they represent them as being many, and not at one among themselves. For, among these gods, at one time brother is at variance with brother, or the father with his children; at another, the children engage in truceless war against their parents. The adulteries of the gods and their amours, and especially those of the one whom they call Zeus, chief of all and most high, things of which one cannot speak, even in connection with brutes, without blushing, we shall leave to the stage.

I have the same words for the historians, and especially when they make up stories for the amusement of their hearers. And certainly we shall not follow the example of the rhetoricians in the art of lying. For neither in the courts of justice nor in other business affairs will falsehood be of any help to us Christians, who, having chosen the straight and true path of life, are forbidden by the gospel to go to law. But on the other hand we shall receive gladly those passages in which they praise virtue or condemn vice. For just as bees know how to extract honey from flowers, which to men are agreeable only for their fragrance and color, even so here also those who look for something more than pleasure and enjoyment in such writers may derive profit for their souls. Now, then, altogether after the manner of bees must we use these writings, for the bees do not visit all the flowers without discrimination, nor indeed do they seek to carry away entire those upon which they light, but rather, having taken so much as is adapted to their needs, they let the rest go. So we, if wise, shall take from heathen books whatever befits us and is allied to the truth, and shall pass over the rest. And just as in culling roses we avoid the thorns, from such writings as these we will gather everything useful, and guard against the noxious. [The general attitude taken here toward selectiveness in reading is Platonic; see, for instance, frequent passages in the *Laws* ii, iii, and vii, and the *Republic* iii.] So, from the very beginning, we must examine each of their teachings, to harmonize it with our ultimate purpose, according to the Doric proverb, "testing each stone by the measuring-line." [St. Gregory Nazianzen cites this proverb in *Letter xxxviii*, and St. John Chrysostom in *Homily xxv*.]

V

Since we must needs attain to the life to come through virtue, our attention is to be chiefly fastened upon those many passages from the poets, from the historians, and especially from the philosophers, in which virtue itself is praised. For it is of no small advantage that virtue become a habit with a youth [Plato frequently touches upon the value of habit in the *Laws* vii, and the *Republic* ii.], for the lessons of youth make a deep impression, because the soul is then plastic, and therefore they are likely to be indelible. If not to incite youth to virtue, pray what meaning may we suppose that Hesiod had in those universally admired lines [*Works and Days*, 285 ff. Plato refers to this same passage in the *Republic* ii. 364.] of which the sentiment is as follows: "Rough is the start and hard, and the way steep, and full of labor and pain, that leads toward virtue. Wherefore, on account of the steepness, it is not granted to every man to set out, nor, to the one having set out, easily to reach the summit. But when he has reached the top, he sees that the way is smooth and fair, easy and light to the foot, and more pleasing

than the other, which leads to wickedness,"—of which the same poet
said that one may find it all around him in great abundance. [*Ibid.*, 287.]
Now it seems to me that he had no other purpose in saying these things
than so to exhort us to virtue, and so to incite us to bravery, that we may
not weaken our efforts before we reach the goal. And certainly if any
other man praises virtue in a like strain, we will receive his words with
pleasure, since our aim is a common one.

Now as I have heard from one skillful in interpreting the mind of
a poet [Libanius, b. at Antioch in 314], all the poetry of Homer is a
praise of virtue, and with him all that is not merely accessory tends to
this end. There is a notable instance of this where Homer first made
the princess reverence the leader of the Cephallenians, though he
appeared naked, shipwrecked, and alone, and then made Odysseus as
completely lack embarrassment, though seen naked and alone, since
virtue served him as a garment. And next he made Odysseus so much
esteemed by the other Phaeacians that, abandoning the luxury in which
they lived, all admired and emulated him, and there was not one of
them who longed for anything else except to be Odysseus, even to the
enduring of shipwreck. The interpreter of the poetic mind argued
that, in this episode, Homer very plainly says: "Be virtue your concern,
O men, which both swims to shore with the shipwrecked man, and
makes him, when he comes naked to the strand, more honored than
the prosperous Phaeacians."

And, indeed, this is the truth, for other possessions belong to the
owner no more than to another, and, as when men are dicing, fall now
to this one, now to that. But virtue is the only possession that is sure,
and that remains with us whether living or dead. Wherefore it seems
to me that Solon had the rich in mind when he said: "We will not
exchange our virtue for their gold, for virtue is an everlasting possession,
while riches are ever changing owners." . . . Also Prodicus, the sophist
of Ceos, whose opinion we must respect, for he is a man not to be
slighted, somewhere in his writings expressed similar ideas about
virtue and vice. I do not remember the exact words, but as far as I
recollect the sentiment, in plain prose it ran somewhat as follows: While
Hercules was yet a youth, being about your age, as he was debating
which path he should choose, the one leading through toil to virtue,
or its easier alternate, two women appeared before him, who proved to
be Virtue and Vice. Though they said not a word, the difference between
them was at once apparent from their mien. The one had arranged
herself to please the eye, while she exhaled charms, and a multitude of
delights swarmed in her train. With such a display, and promising still
more, she sought to allure Hercules to her side. The other, wasted and
squalid, looked fixedly at him, and bespoke quite another thing. For

she promised nothing easy or engaging, but rather infinite toils and hardships, and perils in every land and on every sea. As a reward for these trials, he was to become a god, so our author has it. The latter, Hercules at length followed. [See Xenophon, *Memorabilia* ii, I.22; Cicero, *De Off.* I.32; Chrysostom, *Regnum*; Lucian, *Somnium*.]

VI

Almost all who have written upon the subject of wisdom have more or less, in proportion to their several abilities, extolled virtue in their writings. Such men must one obey, and must try to realize their words in his life. For he, who by his works exemplifies the wisdom which with others is a matter of theory alone, "breathes; all others flutter about like shadows." [*Odys.* X. 495.] I think it is as if a painter should represent some marvel of manly beauty, and the subject should actually be such a man as the artist pictures on the canvas. To praise virtue in public with brilliant words and with long drawn out speeches, while in private preferring pleasures to temperance, and self-interest to justice, finds an analogy on the stage, for the players frequently appear as kings and rulers, though they are neither, nor perhaps even genuinely free men. A musician would hardly put up with a lyre which was out of tune, nor a choregus with a chorus not singing in perfect harmony. But every man is divided against himself who does not make his life conform to his words, but who says with Euripides, "The mouth indeed hath sworn, but the heart knows no oath." [*Hippolytus* 612.] Such a man will seek the appearance of virtue rather than the reality. But to seem to be good when one is not so, is, if we are to respect the opinion of Plato [*Rep.* II, 361.] at all, the very height of injustice.

VII

After this wise, then, are we to receive those words from the pagan authors which contain suggestions of the virtues. But since also the renowned deeds of the men of old either are preserved for us by tradition, or are cherished in the pages of poet or historian, we must not fail to profit by them. . . .

But let us bring our discussion back again to the examples of noble deeds. A certain man once kept striking Socrates, the son of Sophroniscus, in the face, yet he did not resent it, but allowed full play to the ruffian's anger, so that his face was swollen and bruised from the blows. Then when he stopped striking him, Socrates did nothing more than write on his forehead, as an artisan on a statue, who did it, and thus took out his revenge. Since these examples almost coincide with our teachings, I hold that such men are worthy of emulation. For this conduct of Socrates is akin to the precept that to him who smites you upon the one cheek, you shall turn the other also [Matt. v. 39]—thus much may you be avenged. . . . One who has been instructed in the pagan examples will no longer hold the Christian precepts impracticable.

VIIII

But let us return to the same thought with which we started, namely, that we should not accept everything without discrimination, but only what is useful. For it would be shameful should we reject injurious foods, yet should take no thought about the studies which nourish our souls, but as a torrent should sweep along all that came near our path and appropriate it. If the helmsman does not blindly abandon his ship to the winds, but guides it toward the anchorage; if the archer shoots at his mark; if also the metal-worker or the carpenter seeks to produce the objects for which his craft exists, would there be rhyme or reason in our being outclassed by these men, mere artisans as they are, in quick appreciation of our interests? For is there not some end in the artisan's work, is there not a goal in human life, which the one who would not wholly resemble unreasoning animals must keep before him in all his words and deeds? If there were no intelligence sitting at the tiller of our souls, like boats without ballast we should be borne hither and thither through life, without plan or purpose.

An analogy may be found in the athletic contests, or, if you will, in the musical contests; for the contestants prepare themselves by a preliminary training for those events in which wreaths of victory are offered, and no one by training for wrestling or for the pancratium would get ready to play the lyre or the flute. At least Polydamas would not, for before the Olympic games he was wont to bring the rushing chariot to a halt, and thus hardened himself. Then Milo could not be thrust from his smeared shield, but, shoved as he was, clung to it as firmly as statues soldered by lead. In a word, by their training they prepared themselves for the contests. If they had meddled with the airs of Marsyas or of Olympus, the Phrygians, abandoning dust and exercise, would they have won ready laurels or crowns, or would they have escaped being laughed at for their bodily incapacity? On the other hand, certainly Timotheus the musician did not spend his time in the schools for wrestling, for then it would not have been his to excel all in music, he who was so skilled in his art that at his pleasure he could arouse the passions of men by his harsh and vehement strains, and then by gentle ones, quiet and soothe them. By this art, when once he played Phrygian airs on the flute to Alexander, he is said to have incited the general to arms in the midst of feasting, and then, by milder music, to have restored him to his carousing friends. Such power to compass one's end, either in music or in athletic contests, is developed by practice.

I have called to mind the wreaths and the fighters. These men endure hardships beyond number, they use every means to increase their strength, they sweat ceaselessly at their training, they accept many blows from the master, they adopt the mode of life which he prescribes, though it is most unpleasant, and, in a word, they so rule all their conduct that their whole life before the contest is preparatory to it. Then they strip themselves for the arena, and endure all and risk all, to receive the crown of olive, or of parsley, or some other branch, and to be announced by the herald as victor. [See I Cor. ix. 24-27.]

Will it then be possible for us, to whom are held out rewards so wondrous in number and in splendor that tongue can not recount them, while we are fast asleep and leading care-free lives, to make these our own by half-hearted efforts? Surely, were an idle life a very commendable thing, Sardanapalus [Asshurbanipal, King of Assyria, 668-626 B. C.?] would take the first prize, or Margites if you will, whom Homer, if indeed the poem is by Homer, put down as neither a farmer, nor a vine-dresser, nor anything else that is useful. Is there not rather truth in the maxim of Pittacus which says, "It is hard to be good?" For after we have actually endured many hardships, we shall scarcely gain those blessings to which, as said above, nothing in human experience is comparable. Therefore we must not be lightminded, nor exchange our immortal hopes for momentary idleness, lest reproaches come upon us, and judgment befall us, not forsooth here among men, although judgment here is no easy thing for the man of sense to bear, but at the bar of justice, be that under the earth, or wherever else it may happen to be. While he who unintentionally violates his obligations perchance receives some pardon from God, he who designedly chooses a life of wickedness doubtless has a far greater punishment to endure.

IX

"What then are we to do?" perchance some one may ask. What else than to care for the soul, never leaving an idle moment for other things? Accordingly, we ought not to serve the body any more than is absolutely necessary, but we ought to do our best for the soul, releasing it from the bondage of fellowship with the bodily appetites; at the same time we ought to make the body superior to passion. We must provide it with the necessary food, to be sure, but not with delicacies, as those do who seek everywhere for waiters and cooks, and scour both earth and sea, like those bringing tribute to some stern tyrant. This is a despicable business, in which are endured things as unbearable as the torments of hell, where wool is combed into the fire, or water is drawn in a sieve and poured into a perforated jar, and where work is never done. Then to spend more time than is necessary on one's hair and clothes is, in the words of Diogenes, the part of the unfortunate or of the sinful. For what difference does it make to a sensible man whether he is clad in a robe of state or in an inexpensive garment, so long as he is protected from heat and cold? Likewise in other matters we must be governed by necessity, and only give so much care to the body as is beneficial to the soul. For to one who is really a man it is no less a disgrace to be a fop or a pamperer of the body than to be the victim of any other base passion. Indeed, to be very zealous in making the body appear very beautiful is not the mark of a man who knows himself, or who feels the force of the wise maxim: "Not that which is seen is the man," for it requires a higher faculty for any one of us, whoever he may be, to know himself. Now it is harder for the man who is not pure in heart to gain this knowledge than for a blear-eyed person to look upon the sun.

To speak generally and so far as your needs demand, purity of soul embraces these things: to scorn sensual pleasures, to refuse to feast the eyes on the senseless antics of buffoons, or on bodies which goad one to passion, and to close one's ears to songs which corrupt the mind. For passions which are the offspring of servility and baseness are produced by this kind of music. On the other hand, we must employ that class of music which is better in itself and which leads to better things, which David, the sacred psalmist, is said to have used to assuage the madness of the king. . . . Even so great a difference does it make whether one lends his ear to healthy or to vicious music. Therefore you ought to have still less to do with the music of such influence than with other infamous things. Then I am ashamed to forbid you to load the air with all kinds of sweet-smelling perfumes, or to smear yourselves with ointment. Again, what further argument is needed against seeking the gratification of one's appetite than that it compels those who pursue it, like animals, to make of their bellies a god? [See Phil. iii.19.]

In a word, he who would not bury himself in the mire of sensuality must deem the whole body of little worth, or must, as Plato puts it, pay only so much heed to the body as is an aid to wisdom [See *Rep.* iii. 403-412.], or as Paul admonishes somewhere in a similar passage: "Let no one make provision for the flesh, to fulfill the lusts thereof." [Rom. xiii.14.] Wherein is there any difference between those who take pains that the body shall be perfect, but ignore the soul, for the use of which it is designed, and those who are scrupulous about their tools, but neglectful of their trade? On the contrary, one ought to discipline the flesh and hold it under, as a fierce animal is controlled, and to quiet, by the lash of reason, the unrest which it engenders in the soul, and not, by giving full rein to pleasure to disregard the mind, as a charioteer is run away with by unmanageable and frenzied horses. So let us bear in mind the remark of Pythagoras, who, upon learning that one of his followers was growing very fleshy from gymnastics and hearty eating, said to him, "Will you not stop making your imprisonment harder for yourself?" [The plain living of the Pythagoreans is discussed and illustrated in Porphyry, *Life of Pythagoras* 32, 34, and Iamblichus, *Life of Pythagoras* 96, 98.] Then it is said that since Plato foresaw the dangerous influence of the body, he chose an unhealthy part of Athens for his Academy, in order to remove excessive bodily comfort, as one prunes the rank shoots of the vines. Indeed I have even heard physicians say that over-healthiness is dangerous. Since, then, this exaggerated care of the body is harmful to the body itself, and a hindrance to the soul, it is sheer madness to be a slave to the body, and serve it.

If we were minded to disregard attention to the body, we should be in little danger of prizing anything else unduly. For of what use, now, are riches, if one scorns the pleasures of the flesh? I certainly see none, unless, as in the case of the mythological dragons, there is some satisfaction in guarding hidden treasure. . . .

Again, shall we, while manifestly ignoring riches and scorning sensual pleasures, court adulation and fulsome praise, vying with the fox of Archilochus [Poet, ranked by ancients as second only to Homer, flourished 650 B. C.] in cunning and craft? Of a truth there is nothing which the wise man must more guard against than the temptation to live for praise, and to study what pleases the crowd. Rather truth should be made the guide of one's life, so that if one must needs speak against all men, and be in ill-favor and in danger for virtue's sake, he shall not swerve at all from that which he considers right; else how shall we say that he differs from the Egyptian sophist, who at pleasure turned himself into a tree, an animal, fire, water, or anything else? [Proteus; see *Odys.* iv. 455, and Vergil, *Georg.* iv. 386.] Such a man now praises justice to those who esteem it, and now expresses opposite sentiments when he sees that wrong is in good repute; this is the fawner's trick. Just as the polypus is said to take the color of the ground upon which it lies, so he conforms his opinions to those of his associates.

X

To be sure, we shall become more intimately acquainted with these precepts in the sacred writings, but it is incumbent upon us, for the present, to trace, as it were, the silhouette of virtue in the pagan authors. For those who carefully gather the useful from each book are wont, like mighty rivers, to gain accessions on every hand. For the precept of the poet which bids us add little to little [Hesiod, W. and D. 359: "If you are ever adding little to little, soon your store will be great."] must be taken as applying not so much to the accumulation of riches, as of the various branches of learning. In line with this Bias [See Diogenes Laërtius i. 82-88, for this and other of the sayings and doings of Bias] said to his son, who, as he was about to set out for Egypt, was inquiring what course he could pursue to give his father the greatest satisfaction: "Store up means for the journey of old age." By *means* he meant virtue, but he placed too great restrictions upon it, since he limited its usefulness to the earthly life. For if any one mentions the old age of Tithonus [who obtained immortality from the gods, but not eternal youth, and so became a shrunken old man], or of Arganthonius [King of Tartessus in Spain. According to Herodotus (vii. 21) he ascended the throne at the age of forty, and reigned eighty years], or of that Methuselah who is said to have lacked but thirty years of being a millenarian, or even if he reckons the entire period since the creation, I will laugh as at the fancies of a child, since I look forward to that long, undying age, of the extent of which there is no limit for the mind of man to grasp, any more than there is of the life immortal. For the journey of this life eternal I would advise you to husband resources, leaving no stone unturned, as the proverb has it, whence you might derive any aid. From this task we shall not shrink because it is hard and laborious, but, remembering the precept that every man ought to choose the better life, and expecting that association will render it pleasant, we shall busy ourselves with those things that are best. For it is shameful to squander the present, and later to call back the past in anguish, when no more time is given.

In the above treatise I have explained to you some of the things which I deem the most to be desired; of others I shall continue to counsel you so long as life is allowed me. Now as the sick are of three classes, according to the degrees of their sickness, may you not seem to belong to the third, or incurable, class, nor show a spiritual malady like that of their bodies! For those who are slightly indisposed visit physicians in person, and those who are seized by violent sickness call physicians, but those who are suffering from a hopelessly incurable melancholy do not even admit the physicians if they come. May this now not be your plight, as would seem to be the case were you to shun these right counsels!

St. Augustine (354-430 A.D.)

Selections from St. Augustine, *The Works of Aurelius Augustine, Bishop of Hippo* edited by the Rev. Marcus Dods, D. D. Edinburgh, T & T Clark, 38 George Street:
From Vol. XIV, pp. 10-15, 17-18, and 41, 1876, *The Confessions of St. Augustine, Bishop of Hippo*, translated and annotated by J. G. Pilkington: Book I, Ch. VIII, 13; Ch. IX, 14, 15; Ch. X, 16; Ch. XII, 19; Ch. XIV, 23; and Book III, Ch. IV, 7; From Vol. IX, pp. 39-41; 61-63; 74-76, 1873, *On Christian Doctrine; The Enchiridion*, translated by J. F. Shaw: Book II, Ch. VII, 9, 10, and 11; Ch. XXV, 38, 39, and 40; Ch. XXXIX, 58; Ch. XL, 60.

The Confessions

Book I, Chapter VIII
That When a Boy He Learned to Speak, Not by Any Set Method, but from the Acts and Words of His Parents

13. Did I not, then, growing out of the state of infancy, come to boyhood, or rather did it not come to me, and succeed to infancy? Nor did my infancy depart (for whither went it?); and yet it did no longer abide, for I was no longer an infant that could not speak, but a chattering boy. I remember this, and I afterwards observed how I first learned to speak, for my elders did not teach me words in any set method, as they did letters afterwards; but I myself, when I was unable to say all I wished and to whomsoever I desired, by means of the whimperings and broken utterances and various motions of my limbs, which I used to enforce my wishes, repeated the sounds in my memory by the mind, O my God, which Thou gavest me. When they called anything by name, and moved the body towards it while they spoke, I saw and gathered that the thing they wished to point out was called by the name they then uttered; and that they did mean this was made plain by the motion of the body, even by the natural language of all nations expressed by the countenance, glance of the eye, movement of other members, and by the sound of the voice indicating the affections of the mind, as it seeks, possesses, rejects, or avoids. So it was that by frequently hearing words, in duly placed sentences, I gradually gathered what things they were the signs of; and having formed my mouth to the utterance of these signs, I thereby expressed my will. Thus I exchanged with those about me the signs by which we express our

wishes, and advanced deeper into the stormy fellowship of human life, depending the while on the authority of parents, and the beck of elders.

Chapter IX
Concerning the Hatred of Learning, the Love of Play, and the Fear of Being Whipped Noticeable in Boys: and of the Folly of Our Elders and Masters.

14. O my God! what miseries and mockeries did I then experience, when obedience to my teachers was set before me as proper to my boyhood, that I might flourish in this world, and distinguish myself in the science of speech, which should get me honour amongst men, and deceitful riches! After that I was put to school to get learning, of which I (worthless as I was) knew not what use there was; and yet, if slow to learn, I was flogged! For this was deemed praiseworthy by our forefathers; and many before us, passing the same course, had appointed beforehand for us these troublesome ways by which we were compelled to pass, multiplying labour and sorrow upon the sons of Adam. But we found, O Lord, men praying to Thee, and we learned from them to conceive of Thee, according to our ability, to be some Great One, who was able (though not visible to our senses) to hear and help us. For as a boy I began to pray to Thee, my "help" and my "refuge," and in invoking Thee broke the bands of my tongue, and entreated Thee though little, with no little earnestness, that I might not be beaten at school. And when Thou heardedst me not, giving me not over to folly thereby, my elders, yea, and my own parents too, who wished me no ill, laughed at my stripes, my then great and grievous ill.

15. Is there any one, Lord, with so high a spirit, cleaving to Thee with so strong an affection—for even a kind of obtuseness may do that much—but is there, I say, any one who, by cleaving devoutly to Thee, is endowed with so great a courage that he can esteem lightly those racks and hooks, and varied tortures of the same sort, against which, throughout the whole world, men supplicate Thee with great fear, deriding those who most bitterly fear them, just as our parents derided the torments with which our masters punished us when we were boys? For we were no less afraid of our pains, nor did we pray less to Thee to avoid them; and yet we sinned, in writing, or reading, or reflecting upon our lessons less than was required of us. For we wanted not, O Lord, memory or capacity,—of which, by Thy will, we possessed enough for our age,—but we delighted only in play; and we were punished for this by those who were doing the same things themselves. But the idleness of our elders they call business, whilst boys who do the

like are punished by those same elders, and yet neither boys nor men find any pity. For will any one of good sense approve of my being whipped because, as a boy, I played ball, and so was hindered from learning quickly those lessons by means of which, as a man, I should play more unbecomingly? And did he by whom I was beaten do other than this, who, when he was overcome in any little controversy with a co-tutor, was more tormented by anger and envy than I when beaten by a playfellow in a match at ball?

Chapter X
Through a Love of Ball-Playing and Shows, He Neglects His Studies and the Injunctions of His Parents

16. And yet I erred, O Lord God, the Creator and Disposer of all things in Nature,—but of sin the Disposer only,—I erred, O Lord my God, in doing contrary to the wishes of my parents and of those masters; for this learning which they (no matter for what motive) wished me to acquire, I might have put to good account afterwards. For I disobeyed them not because I had chosen a better way, but from a fondness for play, loving the honour of victory in the matches, and to have my ears tickled with lying fables, in order that they might itch the more furiously—the same curiosity beaming more and more in my eyes for the shows and sports of my elders. Yet those who give these entertainments are held in such high repute, that almost all desire the same for their children, whom they are still willing should be beaten, if so be these same games keep them from the studies by which they desire them to arrive at being the givers of them. Look down upon these things, O Lord, with compassion, and deliver us who now call upon Thee; deliver those also who do not call upon Thee, that they may call upon Thee, and that Thou mayest deliver them. . . .

Chapter XII
Being Compelled, He gave his Attention to Learning; but Fully Acknowledges That This Was the Work of God

19. But in this my childhood (which was far less dreaded for me than youth) I had no love of learning, and hated to be forced to it, yet was I forced to it notwithstanding; and this was well done towards me, but I did not well, for I would not have learned had I not been compelled. For no man doth well against his will, even if that which he doth be well. Neither did they who forced me do well, but the good that was done to me came from Thee, my God. For they considered not in what way I should employ what they forced me to learn, unless to satisfy

the inordinate desires of a rich beggary and a shameful glory. But Thou, by whom the very hairs of our heads are numbered, didst use for my good the error of all who pressed me to learn; and my own error in willing not to learn, didst Thou make use of for my punishment—of which I, being so small a boy and so great a sinner, was not unworthy. Thus by the instrumentality of those who did not well didst Thou well for me; and by my own sin didst Thou justly punish me. For it is even as Thou hast appointed, that every inordinate affection should bring its own punishment. . . .

Chapter XIV
Why He Despised Greek Literature, and Easily Learned Latin

23. But why, then, did I dislike Greek learning, which was full of like tales? For Homer also was skilled in inventing similar stories, and is most sweetly vain, yet was he disagreeable to me as a boy. I believe Virgil, indeed, would be the same to Grecian children, if compelled to learn him, as I was Homer. The difficulty, in truth, the difficulty of learning a foreign language mingled as it were with gall all the sweetness of those fabulous Grecian stories. For not a single word of it did I understand, and to make me do so, they vehemently urged me with cruel threatenings and punishments. There was a time also when (as an infant) I knew no Latin; but this I acquired without any fear or tormenting, by merely taking notice, amid the blandishments of my nurses, the jests of those who smiled on me, and the sportiveness of those who toyed with me. I learnt all this, indeed, without being urged by any pressure of punishment, for my own heart urged me to bring forth its own conceptions, which I could not do unless by learning words, not of those who taught me, but of those who talked to me; into whose ears, also, I brought forth whatever I discerned. From this it is sufficiently clear that a free curiosity hath more influence in our learning these things than a necessity full of fear. But this last restrains the overflowings of that freedom, through Thy laws, O God,—Thy laws, from the ferule of the schoolmaster to the trials of the martyr, being effective to mingle for us a salutary bitter, calling us back to Thyself from the pernicious delights which allure us from Thee. . . .

Book III, Chapter IV
In the Nineteenth Year of His Age (His Father Having Died
Two Years before) He Is Led by the Hortensius of Cicero to
"Philosophy," to God, and a Better Mode of Thinking

7: Among such as these, at that unstable period of my life, I studied books of eloquence, wherein I was eager to be eminent from a damnable and inflated purpose, even a delight in human vanity. In the ordinary course of study, I lighted upon a certain book of Cicero, whose language, though not his heart, almost all admire. This book of his contains an exhortation to philosophy, and is called *Hortensius*. This book, in truth, changed my affections, and turned my prayers to Thyself, O Lord, and made me have other hopes and desires. Worthless suddenly became every vain hope to me; and, with an incredible warmth of heart, I yearned for an immortality of wisdom, and began now to arise that I might return to Thee. Not, then, to improve my language—which I appeared to be purchasing with my mother's means, in that my nineteenth year, my father having died two years before—not to improve my language did I have recourse to that book; nor did it persuade me by its style, but its matter. . . .

On Christian Doctrine: The Enchiridion

Book II, Chapter VII
Steps to Wisdom: First, Fear; Second, Piety; Third, Knowledge;
Fourth, Resolution; Fifth, Counsel; Sixth, Purification of Heart;
Seventh, Stop or Termination, Wisdom

9: First of all, then, it is necessary that we should be led by the *fear of God* to seek the knowledge of His will, what He commands us to desire and what to avoid. Now this fear will of necessity excite in us the thought of our mortality and of the death that is before us, and crucify all the motions of pride as if our flesh were nailed to the tree. Next it is necessary to have our hearts subdued by *piety*, and not to run in the face of Holy Scripture, whether when understood it strikes at some of our sins, or, when not understood, we feel as if we could be wiser and give better commands ourselves. We must rather think and believe that whatever is there written, even though it be hidden, is better and truer than anything we could devise by our own wisdom.

10: After these two steps of fear and piety, we come to the third step, *knowledge*, of which I have now undertaken to treat. For in this every earnest student of the Holy Scriptures exercises himself, to find nothing else in them but that God is to be loved for His own sake, and our neighbour for God's sake; and that God is to be loved with all the heart, and with all the soul, and with all the mind, and one's neighbour as one's self—that is, in such a way that all our love for our neighbour, like all our love for ourselves, should have reference to God. And on these two commandments I touched in the previous book when I was treating about things. It is necessary, then, that each man should first of all find in the Scriptures that he, through being entangled in the love of this world—i. e. of temporal things—has been drawn far away from such a love for God and such a love for his neighbour as Scripture enjoins. Then that fear which leads him to think of the judgment of God, and that piety which gives him no option but to believe in and submit to the authority of Scripture, compel him to bewail his condition. For the knowledge of a good hope makes a man not boastful, but sorrowful. And in this frame of mind he implores with unremitting prayers the comfort of the Divine help that he may not be overwhelmed in despair, and so he gradually comes to the fourth step,—that is, *strength* and *resolution*,—in which he hungers and thirsts after righteousness. For in this frame of mind he extricates himself from every form of fatal joy in transitory things, and turning away from these, fixes his affection on things eternal, to wit, the unchangeable Trinity in unity.

11: And when, to the extent of his power, he has gazed upon this object shining from afar, and has felt that owing to the weakness of his sight he cannot endure that matchless light, then in the fifth step—that is, in the *counsel of compassion*—he cleanses his soul, which is violently agitated, and disturbs him with base desires, from the filth it has contracted. And at this stage he exercises himself diligently in the love of his neighbour; and when he has reached the point of loving his enemy, full of hopes and unbroken in strength, he mounts to the sixth step, in which he *purifies the eye itself which can see God* [Matt. v. 8.], so far as God can be seen by those who as far as possible die to this world. For men see Him just so far as they die to this world; and so far as they live to it they see Him not. But yet, although that light may begin to appear clearer, and not only more tolerable, but even more delightful, still it is only through a glass darkly that we are said to see, because we walk by faith, not by sight, while we continue to wander as strangers in this world, even though our conversation be in heaven. [1 Cor. xiii. 12; 2 Cor. v. 7.] And at this stage, too, a man so purges the eye of his affections as not to place his neighbour before, or even in comparison with, the truth, and therefore not himself, because not him whom he loves as himself. Accordingly, that holy man will be so single and so pure in heart, that he will not step aside from the truth, either for the sake of pleasing men or with a view to avoid any of the annoyances which beset this life. Such a son ascends to *wisdom*, which is the seventh and last step, and which he enjoys in peace and tranquillity. For the fear of God is the beginning of wisdom. [Ps. cxi. 10.] From that beginning, then, till we reach wisdom itself, our way is by the steps now described. . . .

Chapter XXV
In Human Institutions Which Are Not Superstitious, There Are Some Things Superfluous and Some Convenient and Necessary

38: But when all these have been cut away and rooted out of the mind of the Christian, we must then look at human institutions which are not superstitious, that is, such as are not set up in association with devils, but by men in association with one another. For all arrangements that are in force among men, because they have agreed among themselves that they should be in force, are human institutions; and of these, some are matters of superfluity and luxury, some of convenience and necessity. For if those signs which the actors make in dancing were of force by nature, and not by the arrangement and agreement of men, the public crier would not in former times have announced to the people of Carthage, while the pantomime was dancing, what it was he meant to express,—a thing still remembered by many old men from whom we have frequently heard it. And we may well believe this, because even now, if any one who is unaccustomed to such follies goes into the theatre, unless some one tells him what these movements mean, he will give his whole attention to them in vain. Yet all men aim at a certain degree of likeness in their choice of signs, that the signs may as far as possible be like the things they signify. But because one thing may resemble another in many ways, such signs are not always of the same significance among men, except when they have mutually agreed upon them.

39: But in regard to pictures and statues, and other works of this kind, which are intended as representations of things, nobody makes a mistake, especially if they are executed by skilled artists, but every one, as soon as he sees the likenesses, recognises the things they are likenesses of. And this whole class are to be reckoned among the superfluous devices of men, unless when it is a matter of importance to inquire in regard to any of them, for what reason, where, when, and by whose authority it was made. Finally, the thousands of fables and fictions, in whose lies men take delight, are human devices, and nothing is to be considered more peculiarly man's own and derived from himself than anything that is false and lying. Among the convenient and necessary arrangements of men with men are to be reckoned whatever differences they choose to make in bodily dress and ornament for the purpose of distinguishing sex or rank; and the countless varieties of signs without which human intercourse either could not be carried on at all, or would be carried on at great inconvenience; and the arrangements as to weights and measures, and the stamping and weighing of coins, which are peculiar to each state and people, and other things of the same kind. Now these, if they were not devices of men, would not be different in different nations, and could not be changed among particular nations at the discretion of their respective soveriegns.

40: This whole class of human arrangements, which are of convenience for the necessary intercourse of life, the Christian is not by any means to neglect, but on the contrary should pay a sufficient degree of attention to them, and keep them in memory.

Chapter XXXIX
To Which of the Above-Mentioned Studies Attention Should Be Given, and in What Spirit

58: Accordingly, I think that it is well to warn studious and able young men, who fear God and are seeking for happiness in life, not to venture heedlessly upon the pursuit of the branches of learning that are in vogue beyond the pale of the Church of Christ, as if these could secure for them the happiness they seek; but soberly and carefully to discriminate among them. And if they find any of those which have been instituted by men varying by reason of the varying pleasure of their founders, and unknown by reason of erroneous conjectures, especially if they involve entering into fellowship with devils by means of leagues and covenants about signs, let these be utterly rejected and held in detestation. Let the young men also withdraw their attention from such institutions of men as are unnecessary and luxurious. But for the sake of the necessities of this life we must not neglect the arrangements of men that enable us to carry on intercourse with those around us. I think, however, there is nothing useful in the other branches of learning that are found among the heathen, except information about objects, either past or present, that relate to the bodily senses, in which are included also the experiments and conclusions of the useful mechanical arts, except also the sciences of reasoning and of number. And in regard to all these we must hold by the maxim, "Not too much of anything"; especially in the case of those which, pertaining as they do to the senses, are subject to the relations of space and time. . . .

Chapter XL
Whatever Has Been Rightly Said by the Heathen, We Must Appropriate to Our Uses

60: Moreover, if those who are called philosophers, and especially the Platonists, have said aught that is true and in harmony with our faith, we are not only not to shrink from it, but to claim it for our own use from those who have unlawful possession of it. For, as the Egyptians had not only the idols and heavy burdens which the people of Israel hated and fled from, but also vessels and ornaments of gold and silver, and garments, which the same people when going out of Egypt appropriated to themselves, designing them for a better use, not doing this on their own authority, but by the command of God, the Egyptians themselves, in their ignorance, providing them with things which they themselves were not making a good use of [Ex. iii. 21, 22, xii. 35, 36]; in the same way all branches of heathen learning have not only false and superstitious fancies and heavy burdens of unnecessary toil, which every one of us, when going out under the leadership of Christ from the fellowship of the heathen, ought to abhor and avoid; but they contain also liberal instruction which is better adapted to the use of the truth, and some most excellent precepts of morality; and some truths in regard even to the worship of the One God are found among them. Now these are, so to speak, their gold and silver, which they did not create themselves, but dug out of the mines of God's providence which are everywhere scattered abroad, and are perversely and unlawfully prostituting to the worship of devils. These, therefore, the Christian, when he separates himself in spirit from the miserable fellowship of these men, ought to take away from them, and to devote to their proper use in preaching the gospel. Their garments, also,—that is, human institutions such as are adapted to that intercourse with men which is indispensable in this life,—we must take and turn to a Christian use. . . .

34
Monasticism

The Rule of St. Benedict

Selections from *The Rule of St. Benedict,* in *Select Historical Documents of the Middle Ages,* translated and edited by Ernest F. Henderson (London: George Bell and Sons, 1896), Prologue (p. 274), chapters 1 (pp. 274-275), 33-34 (p. 289), 38 (pp. 291-292), 42 (p. 294), and 48 (pp. 297-298).

Prologue

. . . we are about to found, therefore, a school for the Lord's service; in the organization of which we trust that we shall ordain nothing severe and nothing burdensome. But even if, the demands of justice dictating it, something a little irksome shall be the result, for the purpose of amending vices or preserving charity;—thou shall not therefore, struck by fear, flee the way of salvation, which can not be entered upon except through a narrow entrance. But as one's way of life and one's faith progresses, the heart becomes broadened, and, with the unutterable sweetness of love, the way of the mandates of the Lord is traversed. Thus, never departing from His guidance, continuing in the monastery in His teaching until death, through patience we are made partakers in Christ's passion, in order that we may merit to be companions in His kingdom.

1: Concerning the Kinds of Monks and Their Manner of Living.

It is manifest that there are four kinds of monks. The cenobites are the first kind; that is, those living in a monastery, serving under a rule or an abbot. Then the second kind is that of the anchorites; that is, the hermits,—those who, not by the new fervour of a conversion but by the long probation of life in a monastery, have learned to fight against the devil, having already been taught by the solace of many. They, having been well prepared in the army of brothers for the solitary fight of the hermit, being secure now without the consolation of another, are able, God helping them, to fight with their own hand or arm against the vices of the flesh or of their thoughts.

But a third very bad kind of monks are the sarabaites, approved by no rule, experience being their teacher, as with the gold which is tried in the furnace. But, softened after the manner of lead, keeping faith with the world by their works, they are known through their tonsure to lie to God. These being shut up by twos or threes, or, indeed, alone, without a shepherd, not in the Lord's but in their own sheep-folds,—their law is the satisfaction of their desires. For whatever they think good or choice, this they call holy; and what they do not wish, this they consider unlawful. But the fourth kind of monks is the kind which is called gyratory. During their whole life they are guests, for three or four days at a time, in the cells of the different monasteries, throughout the various provinces; always wandering and never sta-tionary, given over to the service of their own pleasures and the joys of the palate, and in every way worse than the sarabaites. Concerning the most wretched way of living of all of such monks it is better to be silent than to speak. These things therefore being omitted, let us proceed, with the aid of God, to treat of the best kind, the cenobites. . . .

33: Whether the Monks Should Have Anything of Their Own.

More than any thing else is this special vice to be cut off root and branch from the monastery, that one should presume to give or receive anything without the order of the abbot, or should have anything of his own. He should have absolutely not anything: neither a book, nor tablets, nor a pen—nothing at all.—For indeed it is not allowed to the monks to have their own bodies or wills in their own power. But all things necessary they must expect from the Father of the monastery; nor is it allowable to have anything which the abbot did not give or permit. All things shall be common to all, as it is written: "Let not any man presume or call anything his own." But if any one shall have been discovered delighting in this most evil vice: being warned once and again, if he do not amend, let him be subjected to punishment.

34: Whether All Ought to Receive Necessaries Equally.

As it is written: "It was divided among them singly, according as each had need": whereby we do not say—far from it—that there should be an excepting of persons, but a consideration for infirmities. Wherefore he who needs less, let him thank God and not be dismayed; but he who needs more, let him be humiliated on account of his infirmity, and not exalted on account of the mercy that is shown him. And thus all members will be in peace. Above all, let not the evil of murmuring appear, for any cause, through any word or sign whatever. But, if such a murmurer is discovered, he shall be subjected to stricter discipline. . . .

38: Concerning the Weekly Reader

At the tables of the brothers when they eat the reading should not fail; nor may any one at random dare to take up the book and begin to read there; but he who is about to read for the whole week shall begin his duties on Sunday. And, entering upon his office after mass and communion, he shall ask all to pray for him, that God may avert from him the spirit of elation. And this verse shall be said in the oratory three times by all, he however beginning it: "O Lord open Thou my lips and my mouth shall show forth Thy praise." And thus, having received the benediction, he shall enter upon his duties as reader. And there shall be the greatest silence at table, so that the muttering or the voice of no one shall be heard there, except that of the reader alone. But whatever things are necessary to those eating and drinking, the brothers shall so furnish them to each other in turn, that no one shall need to ask for anything. But if, nevertheless, something is wanted, it shall rather be sought by the employment of some sign than by the voice. Nor shall any one presume there to ask questions concerning the reading or anything else; nor shall an opportunity be given: unless perhaps the prior wishes to say something, briefly, for the purpose of edifying. Moreover the brother who reads for the week shall receive bread and wine before he begins to read, on account of the holy communion, and lest, perchance, it might be injurious for him to sustain a fast. Afterwards, moreover, he shall eat with the weekly cooks and the servitors. The brothers, moreover, shall read or sing not in rotation; but the ones shall do so who will edify their hearers. . . .

42: That After "Completorium" No One Shall Speak

At all times the monks ought to practise silence, but most of all in the nocturnal hours. And thus at all times, whether of fasting or of eating: if it be meal-time, as soon as they have risen from the table, all shall sit together and one shall read selections or lives of the Fathers, or indeed anything which will edify the hearers. But not the Pentateuch or Kings; for, to weak intellects, it will be of no use at that hour to hear this part of Scripture; but they shall be read at other times. But if the days are fast days, when Vespers have been said, after a short interval they shall come to the reading of the selections as we have said; and four or five pages, or as much as the hour permits having been read, they shall all congregate, upon the cessation of the reading. If, by chance, any one is occupied in a task assigned to him, he shall nevertheless approach. All therefore being gathered together, they shall say the completing prayer; and, going out from the "completorium," there shall be no further opportunity for any one to say anything. But if any one be found acting contrary to this rule of silence, he shall be subjected to a very severe punishment. Unless a necessity in the shape of guests should arise, or the abbot, by chance, should give some order. But even this, indeed, he shall do most seriously, with all gravity and moderation. . . .

48: Concerning the Daily Manual Labour

Idleness is the enemy of the soul. And therefore, at fixed times, the brothers ought to be occupied in manual labour; and again, at fixed times, in sacred reading. Therefore we believe that, according to this disposition, both seasons ought to be arranged; so that, from Easter until the Calends of October, going out early, from the first until the fourth hour they shall do what labour may be necessary. Moreover, from the fourth hour until about the sixth, they shall be free for reading. After the meal of the sixth hour, moreover, rising from table, they shall rest in their beds with all silence; or, perchance, he that wishes to read may so read to himself that he do not disturb another. And the nona (the second meal) shall be gone through with more moderately about the middle of the eighth hour; and again they shall work at what is to be done until Vespers. But, if the exigency or poverty of the place demands that they be occupied by themselves in picking fruits, they shall not be dismayed: for then they are truly monks if they live by the labors of their hands; as did also our fathers and the apostles. Let all things be done with moderation, however, on account of the faint-hearted. From the Calends of October, moreover, until the beginning of Lent they shall be free for reading until the second full hour. At the second hour the tertia (morning service) shall be held, and all shall labor at the task which is enjoined upon them until the ninth. The first signal, moreover, of the ninth hour having been given, they shall each one leave off his work; and be ready when the second signal strikes. Moreover after the refection they shall be free for their readings or for psalms. But in the days of Lent, from dawn until the third full hour, they shall be free for their readings; and, until the tenth full hour, they shall do the labour that is enjoined on them. In which days of Lent they shall all receive separate books from the library; which they shall read entirely through in order. These books are to be given out on the first day of Lent. Above all there shall certainly be appointed one or two elders, who shall go round the monastery at the hours in which the brothers are engaged in reading, and see to it that no troublesome brother chance to be found who is open to idleness and trifling, and is not intent on his reading; being not only of no use to

himself, but also stirring up others. If such a one—may it not happen—
be found, he shall be admonished once and a second time. If he do not
amend, he shall be subject under the Rule to such punishment that the
others may have fear. Nor shall brother join brother at unsuitable
hours. Moreover on Sunday all shall engage in reading: excepting those
who are deputed to various duties. But if anyone be so negligent and
lazy that he will not or can not read, some task shall be imposed upon
him which he can do; so that he be not idle. On feeble or delicate
brothers such a labour or art is to be imposed, that they shall neither
be idle, nor shall they be so oppressed by the violence of labour as to
be driven to take flight. Their weakness is to be taken into consideration
by the abbot. . . .

35
Triumph for
the "Counter-Culture"

The Alliance of Church and State:
Precursors of Scholasticism and Universities

Biographical Sketch (by F. V. N. Painter) and selection from Charlemagne's "Capitulary of 787" and selection from Rhabanus Maurus' "Education of the Clergy," (The Seven Liberal Arts) from F. V. N. Painter, *Great Pedagogical Essays from Plato to Spencer* (New York: American Book Company, Copyright 1905 by F. V. N. Painter), pp. 155-157, 159-168. Reprinted by permission of Van Nostrand Reinhold Company.

Charlemagne (742-814)

Biographical Sketch

Charlemagne was king of the Franks from 768 to 814 A.D. On Christmas day, 800, he was crowned by the pope as emperor of the Romans. In spite of his almost incessant wars and his brilliant career as a conqueror, he earnestly sought to promote the material and spiritual welfare of his people. He exhibited a great thirst for knowledge, and was himself a model of diligence in study. He assiduously cultivated his mind by intercourse with learned men; and, to the time of his death, scholarly discussions remained his favorite means of recreation. In addition to his native German he spoke several other languages readily, especially the Latin. He invited to his court from all parts of Europe the most distinguished scholars, of whom Alcuin, of England, is best known. He established a model school at court, and sometimes visited it in person to note the progress of the pupils.

He sought to multiply the educational facilities of his great empire, and even went so far as to contemplate the organization of a popular school system. He endeavored to enlist the interest of the clergy and monks in education, as they were at the time the chief representatives of learning. The monasteries and bishops were urged to improve the schools already existing, and to establish new ones wherever needed. It was to this end that he issued in 787 the following capitulary addressed to the abbot Bangulfus. The translation is that of Mullinger in his "Schools of Charles the Great," and is evidently more literal than elegant.

Capitulary of 787

Charles, by the grace of God, King of the Franks and of the Lombards, and Patrician of the Romans, to Bangulfus, abbot, and to his whole congregation and the faithful committee to his charge:

Be it known to your devotion, pleasing to God, that in conjunction with our faithful we have judged it to be of utility that, in the bishoprics and monasteries committed by Christ's favor to our charge, care should be taken that there shall be not only a regular manner of life and one conformable to holy religion, but also the study of letters, each to teach and learn them according to his ability and the divine assistance. For even as due observance of the rule of the house tends to good morals, so zeal on the part of the teacher and the taught imparts order and grace to sentences; and those who seek to please God by living aright should also not neglect to please him by right speaking. It is written, "By thine own words shalt thou be justified or condemned"; and although right doing be preferable to right speaking, yet must the knowledge of what is right precede right action. Every one, therefore, should strive to understand what it is he would fain accomplish; and this right understanding will be the sooner gained according as the utterances of the tongue are free from error. And if false speaking is to be shunned by all men, especially should it be shunned by those who have elected to be the servants of the truth.

During past years we have often received letters from different monasteries, informing us that at their sacred services the brethren offered up prayers on our behalf; and we have observed that the thoughts contained in these letters, though in themselves most just, were expressed in uncouth language, and while pious devotion dictated the sentiments, the unlettered tongue was unable to express them aright. Hence there has arisen in our minds the fear lest, if the skill to write rightly were thus lacking, so too would the power of rightly comprehending the sacred Scriptures be far less than was fitting; and we all know that though verbal errors be dangerous, errors of the understanding are yet more so. We exhort you, therefore, not only not to neglect the study of letters, but to apply yourselves thereto with perseverance and with that humility which is well pleasing to God; so that you may be able to penetrate with greater ease and certainty the mysteries of the Holy Scriptures. For as these contain images, tropes, and similar figures, it is impossible to doubt that the reader will arrive far more readily at the spiritual sense according as he is the better instructed in learning. Let there, therefore, be chosen for this work men who are both able and willing to learn, and also desirous of instructing others; and let them apply themselves to the work with a zeal equaling the earnestness with which we recommend it to them. It is our wish that you may be what it behooves the soldiers of the Church to be—religious in heart, learned in discourse, pure in act, eloquent in speech; so that all who approach your house, in order to invoke the Divine Master or to behold the excellence of the religious life, may be edified in beholding you, and instructed in hearing you discourse or chant, and may return home rendering thanks to God most high.

Fail not, as thou regardest our favor, to send a copy of this letter to all thy suffragans and to all the monasteries; and let no monk go beyond his monastery to administer justice, or to enter the assemblies and the voting-places. Adieu.

Rhabanus Maurus (b. about 766 A.D.)

Education of the Clergy

> The following selection is translated from "The Education of the Clergy" (*Unterweisung der Geistlichen*) [found in the *Sammlung der bedentendsten pädagogischen Schriften* edited by Schultz, Ganser, and Keller], and is notable for two reasons: (1) It shows us the subordination of education to ecclesiastical ends; and (2) it presents the fullest discussion of the seven liberal arts that has come to us from that period (ninth century).

1. An ecclesiastical education should qualify the sacred office of the ministry for divine service. It is fitting that those who from an exalted station undertake the direction of the life of the Church, should acquire fullness of knowledge, and that they further should strive after rectitude of life and perfection of development. They should not be allowed to remain in ignorance about anything that appears beneficial for their own information or for the instruction of those entrusted to their care. Therefore they should endeavor to grasp and include in their knowledge the following things: An acquaintance with Holy Scripture, the unadulterated truth of history, the derivative modes of speech, the mystical sense of words, the advantages growing out of the separate branches of knowledge, the integrity of life that manifests itself in good morals, delicacy and good taste in oral discourse, penetration in the explanation of doctrine, the different kinds of medicine, and the various forms of disease. Any one to whom all this remains unknown, is not able to care for his own welfare, let alone that of others.

2: The foundation, the content, and the perfection of all wisdom is Holy Scripture, which has taken its origin, from that unchangeable and eternal Wisdom, which streams from the mouth of the Most High, which was begotten before every other creature through the Holy Spirit, which is a light incessantly beaming from the words of Holy Scripture. And when anything else deserves the name of wisdom, it goes back in its origin to this one source of the wisdom of the Church. Every truth, which is discovered by any one, is recognized as true by the truth itself through the mediation of the truth; every good thing, which is in any way traced out, is recognized and determined as good by the good itself; all wisdom, which is brought to light by any one, is found to be wisdom by wisdom itself. And all that is found of truth and wisdom in the books of the philosophers of this world, dare be ascribed to nothing else than just to truth and wisdom; for it was not originally invented by those among whose utterances it is found; it has much rather been recognized as something present from eternity, so far as wisdom and truth, which bring illumination to all with their instruction, have granted the possibility of such recognition.

3: Now the Holy Scriptures, which come to the aid of the weakness of the human will, have, in dependence upon the one perfect language in which under favorable circumstances they might have spread over the whole globe, been widely circulated in the different languages of the translators, in order that they might be known to the nations unto salvation. Those who read them strive for nothing else than to grasp the thought and meaning of those who wrote them, in order thereby to fathom the will of God, at whose bidding and under whose direction, as we believe they were written. But those who read superficially allow themselves to be deceived through the manifold recurring passages, the sense of which is obscure, and the meaning of which is doubtful; they assign to what is read a meaning that does not belong to it; they seek errors where no errors are to be found; they surround themselves with an obscurity, in which they can not find the right path. I have no doubt that this has been so ordered by God's providence that the pride of man may be restrained through spiritual labor; in order that the knowledge of man may be divorced from pride, to which it easily falls a prey, and then loses its value entirely.

4: Above all it is necessary that he, who aims to attain the summit of wisdom, should be converted to the fear of the Lord, in order to know what the divine will bids us strive for and shun. The fear of the Lord fills us with the thought of our mortality and future death. With mortification of the flesh it nails, as it were, the movements of pride to the martyr cross of Christ. Then it is enjoined to be lowly in piety. Therefore we are not to raise any objection to the Holy Scriptures, either when we understand them and feel ourselves smitten by their words, or when we do not understand them, and give ourselves up to the thought that we can understand and grasp something better out of our own minds. We should remember that it is better and more comfortable to truth, to believe what is written, even if the sense remains concealed from us, than to hold that for true which we are able to recognize by our own strength.

5: The first of the liberal arts is grammar, the second rhetoric, the third dialectic, the fourth arithmetic, the fifth geometry, the sixth music, the seventh astronomy.

Grammar takes its name from the written character, as the derivation of the word indicates. The definition of grammar is this: Grammar is the science which teaches us to explain the poets and historians; it is the art which qualifies us to write and speak correctly. Grammar is the source and foundation of the liberal arts. It should be taught in every Christian school, since the art of writing and speaking correctly is attained through it. How could one understand the sense of the spoken word or the meaning of letters and syllables, if one had not learned this before from grammar? How could one know about metrical feet, accent, and verses, if grammar had not given one knowledge of them? How should one learn to know the articulation of discourse, the advantages of figurative language, the laws of word formation, and the correct forms of words, if one had not familiarized himself with the art of grammar?

All the forms of speech, of which secular science makes use in its writings, are found repeatedly employed in the Holy Scriptures. Every one, who reads the sacred Scriptures with care, will discover that our (biblical) authors have used derivative forms of speech in greater and more manifold abundance than would have been supposed and believed. There are in the Scriptures not only examples of all kinds of figurative expressions, but the designations of some of them by name; as, allegory, riddle, parable. A knowledge of these things is proved to be necessary in relation to the interpretation of those passages of Holy Scripture which admit of a twofold sense; an interpretation strictly literal would lead to absurdities. Everywhere we are to consider whether that, which we do not at once understand, is to be apprehended as a figurative expression in some sense. A knowledge of prosody, which is offered in grammar, is not dishonorable, since among the Jews, as St. Jerome testifies, the Psalter resounds sometimes with iambics, sometimes with Alcaics, sometimes chooses sonorous Sapphics, and sometimes even does not disdain catalectic feet. But in Deuteronomy and Isaiah, as in Solomon and Job, as Josephus and Origen have pointed out, there are hexameters and pentameters. Hence this art, though it may be secular, has nothing unworthy in itself; it should rather be learned as thoroughly as possible.

6: According to the statements of teachers, rhetoric is the art of using secular discourse effectively in the circumstances of daily life. From this definition rhetoric seems indeed to have reference merely to secular wisdom. Yet it is not foreign to ecclesiastical instruction. Whatever the preacher and herald of the divine law, in his instruction, brings forward in an eloquent and becoming manner; whatever in his written exposition he knows how to clothe in adequate and impressive language, he owes to his acquaintance with this art. Whoever at the proper time makes himself familiar with this art, and faithfully follows its rules in speaking and writing, needs not count it as something blameworthy. On the contrary, whoever thoroughly learns it so that he acquires the ability to proclaim God's word, performs a good work. Through rhetoric anything is proved true or false. Who would have the courage to maintain that the defenders of truth should stand weaponless in the presence of falsehood, so that those, who dare to represent the false, should know how by their discourse to win the favor and sympathy of the hearers, and that, on the other hand, the friends of truth should not be able to do this; that those should know how to present falsehood briefly, clearly, and with the semblance of truth, and that the patter, on the contrary, should clothe the truth in such an exposition, that listening would become a burden, apprehension of the truth a weariness, and faith in the truth an impossibility?

7: Dialectic is the science of the understanding, which fits us for investigations and definitions, for explanations, and for distinguishing the true from the false. It is the science of sciences. It teaches how to teach others; it teaches learning itself; in it the reason marks and manifests itself according to its nature, efforts, and activities; it alone is capable of knowing; it not only will, but can lead others to knowledge; its conclusions lead us to an apprehension of our being and of our origin; through it we apprehend the origin and activity of the good, of Creator and creature; it teaches us to discover the truth and to unmask falsehood; it teaches us to draw conclusions; it shows us what is valid in argument and what is not; it teaches us to recognize what is contrary to the nature of things; it teaches us to distinguish in controversy the true, the probable, and the wholly false; by means of this science we are able to investigate everything with penetration, to determine its nature with certainty, and to discuss it with circumspection.

Therefore the clergy must understand this excellent art and constantly reflect upon its laws, in order that they may be able keenly to pierce the craftiness of errorists, and to refute their fatal fallacies.

8: Arithmetic is the science of pure extension determinable by number; it is the science of numbers. Writers on secular science assign it, under the head of mathematics, to the first place, because it does not presuppose any of the other departments. Music, geometry, and astronomy, on the contrary, need the help of arithmetic; without it they cannot arise or exist. We should know, however, that the learned Hebrew Josephus, in his work on Antiquities, Chapter VIII. of Book I., makes the statement that Abraham brought arithmetic and astronomy to the Egyptians; but that they as a people of penetrating mind, extensively developed from these germs the other sciences. The holy Fathers were right in advising those eager for knowledge to cultivate arithmetic, because in large measure it turns the mind from fleshly desires, and furthermore awakens the wish to comprehend what with God's help we can merely receive with the heart. Therefore the significance of number is not to be underestimated. Its very great value for an interpretation of many passages of Holy Scripture is manifest to all who exhibit zeal in their investigations. Not without good reason is it said in praise of God, "Thou hast ordained all things by measure, number, and weight." (Book of Wisdom XI. 21.)

But every number, through its peculiar qualities, is so definite that none of the others can be like it. They are all unequal and different. The single numbers are different; the single numbers are limited; but all are infinite.

Those with whom Plato stands in especial honor will not make bold to esteem numbers lightly, as if they were of no consequence for the knowledge of God. He teaches that God made the world out of numbers. And among us the prophet says of God, "He forms the world by number." And in the Gospel the Savior says, "The very hairs of your head are all numbered." . . . Ignorance of numbers leaves many things unintelligible that are expressed in the Holy Scripture in a derivative sense or with a mystical meaning.

9: We now come to the discussion of geometry. It is an exposition of form proceeding from observation; it is also a very common means of demonstration among philosophers, who, to adduce at once the most full-toned evidence, declare that their Jupiter made use of geometry in his works. I do not know indeed whether I should find praise or censure in this declaration of the philosophers, that Jupiter engraved upon the vault of the skies precisely what they themselves draw in the sand of the earth.

When this in a proper manner is transferred to God, the Almighty Creator, this assumption may perhaps come near the truth. If this statement seems admissible, the Holy Trinity makes use of geometry in so far as it bestows manifold forms and images upon the creatures which up to the present day it has called into being, as in its adorable omnipotence it further determines the course of the stars, as it prescribes their course to the planets, and as it assigns to the fixed stars their unalterable position.

For every excellent and well-ordered arrangement can be reduced to the special requirements of this science. . . .

This science found realization also at the building of the tabernacle and temple; the same measuring rod, circles, spheres, hemispheres, quadrangles, and other figures were employed. The knowledge of all this brings to him, who is occupied with it, no small gain for his spiritual culture.

10: Music is the science of time intervals as they are perceived in tones. This science is as eminent as it is useful. He who is a stranger to it is not able to fulfill the duties of an ecclesiastical office in a suitable manner. A proper delivery in reading and a lovely rendering of the Psalms in the church are regulated by a knowledge of this science. Yet it is not only good reading and beautiful psalmody that we owe to music; through it alone do we become capable of celebrating in the most solemn manner every divine service. Music penetrates all the activities of our life, in this sense namely, that we above all carry out the commands of the Creator and bow with a pure heart to his commands; all that we speak, all that makes our hearts beat faster, is shown through the rhythm of music united with the excellence of harmony; for music is the science which teaches us agreeably to change tones in duration and pitch. When we employ ourselves with good pursuits in life, we show ourselves thereby disciples of this art; so long as we do what is wrong, we do not feel ourselves drawn to music. Even heaven and earth, as everything that happens here through the arrangement of the Most High, is nothing but music, as Pythagoras testifies that this world was created by music and can be ruled by it. Even with the Christian religion music is most intimately united; thus it is possible that to him, who does not know even a little music, many things remain closed and hidden.

11: There remains yet astronomy which, as some one has said, is a weighty means of demonstration to the pious, and to the curious a grievous torment. If we seek to investigate it with a pure heart and an ample mind, then it fills us, as the ancients said, with great love for it. For what will it not signify, that we soar in spirit to the sky, that with penetration of mind we analyze that sublime structure, that we, in part at least, fathom with the keenness of our logical faculties what mighty space has enveloped in mystery! The world itself, according to the assumption of some, is said to have the shape of a sphere, in order that in its circumference it may be able to contain the different forms of things. Thus Seneca, in agreement with the philosophers of ancient times, composed a work under the title, "The Shape of the Earth."

Astronomy, of which we now speak, teaches the laws of the stellar world. The stars can take their place or carry out their motion only in the manner established by the Creator, unless by the will of the Creator a miraculous change takes place. Thus we read that Joshua commanded the sun to stand still in Gibeon, that in the days of King Josiah the sun went backward ten degrees, and that at the death of the Lord the sun was darkened for three hours. We call such occurrences miracles (*Wunder*), because they contradict the usual course of things, and therefore excite wonder. . . .

That part of astronomy, which is built up on the investigation of natural phenomena, in order to determine the course of the sun, of the moon, and stars, and to effect a proper reckoning of time, the Christian clergy should seek to learn with the utmost diligence, in order through the knowledge of laws brought to light and through the valid and convincing proof of the given means of evidence, to place themselves in a position, not only to determine the course of past years according to truth and reality, but also for further times to draw confident conclusions, and to fix the time of Easter and all other festivals and holy days, and to announce to the congregation the proper celebration of them.

12: The seven liberal arts of the philosophers, which Christians should learn for their utility and advantage, we have, as I think, sufficiently discussed. We have this yet to add. When those, who are called philosophers, have in their expositions or in their writings, uttered perchance some truth, which agrees with our faith, we should not handle it timidly, but rather take it as from its unlawful possessors and apply it to our own use.

36

Feudalism and the Guild System in Medieval Education

Elmer Harrison Wilds
Kenneth V. Lottich

From *The Foundations of Modern Education*, 4th ed., by Elmer Harrison Wilds and Kenneth V. Lottich, © 1961, 1970 by Holt, Rinehart and Winston, Inc. Reprinted by permission of Holt, Rinehart, and Winston, Inc. "Feudalism as a Type of Medieval Education," pp. 173-179, and "The Guild Approach to Education," pp. 179-182.

Feudalism as a Type of Medieval Education

Out of the decay and demoralization of the later Roman Empire society became as fixed as it had been during the empires of Egypt and Persia. Greek ideas of democracy seemed to vanish, and the Roman concept of universal citizenship became lost. The three classes operative during antiquity again appeared: priests, warriors, and workers. Until the close of the twelfth century in Western Europe, from the Spanish border to northern Sweden, society consisted only of the Christian clergy, the feudal nobility, and the anchored-to-the-land serfs. The end of the Pax Romana and new demands for education provided some necessity for this arrangement, primitive though it may seem.

Both monasticism and scholasticism were direct outgrowths of the ascendancy of the church, whose educational agencies were primarily designed for the training of clergy, regular and secular. Little thought was then given to the education of the lower class. The medieval serf's education was both limited and plain. As in the days prior to Hellenic civilization, the serf learned by direct imitation of his elders the "tilling of the soil, the hewing of wood, and the drawing of water." The simple religious instruction needed for the rites and ceremonies of the church was given by the parish priest.

For the nobility, however, a definite system of education was provided through a new social institution which resulted directly from the needs of medieval feudalism. The age of chivalry dates from about the beginning of the ninth century to the sixteenth, from when feudalism became firmly established to when, under the new national impetus, feudalism began to decay and disintegrate.

To understand chivalry we must first understand its feudal origins. The term *feudalism* itself is not easily explained. One origin considers it a derivative of the Latin *fides* (faith); another traces its descent from the Germanic *fehu* (cattle) for, among the early Teutonic peoples, property was reckoned in terms of cattle. Concerned with both loyalty and property, feudalism has been described as organizing people's relations through the focus of land tenure and binding all, from the king to the lowest serf, together by responsibilities of defense, and mutual service, and sustenance. Since turbulent and unsettled conditions made it practically impossible for the medieval king or lord to rule an extended domain, it served his purpose to divide a portion of his estate among his military retainers, giving each one authority over his holding. In return each retainer covenanted to give military or other aid as was required to his lord. [For a thorough interpretation of the origins and practices of feudalism, see Robert S. Lopez, *The Birth of Europe* (New York: M. Evans and Company, Inc., 1967), pp. 159-169.] Theoretically, feudalism represented a perfect system balanced among its adherents: all for one, and one for all. (Since the serfs went with the land, they were not consulted.)

Such agreements were the genesis of the institution which was general in the ninth century and a powerful political and social force in the eleventh, twelfth, and thirteenth centuries.

The feudal system developed most thoroughly in France, Germany, Italy, England, and Scotland; its cradle was the empire of Charlemagne. Charles, when merely king of the Franks, had determined to build a great Christian empire to include all the Germans; and when he was crowned by the Pope "Emperor of the Romans" (800), he had truly succeeded. Almost every sovereign of the West had become his vassal. Charlemagne's wealth was in land, not in money. So he had paid his loyal war leaders and civil governors in large grants of land and promises of protection; and they had pledged to him their own aid and service and that of their men-at-arms, as had also the nobles he had conquered. His empire had been welded by the bonds of feudalism. The method was not new with Charlemagne; it was a convenience to his Frankish predecessors and to many another landowner. But such an extensive, orderly, and effective use was new, and it established feudalism as the social system of the Middle Ages.

Feudalism developed rapidly in Europe after the breakup of Charlemagne's empire. Because of the weak successors who ruled the divided empire, and because of the inroads of Saracens, Slavs, and Huns, the century after Charlemagne was an age of disorder, and all classes were glad to avail themselves of the protection the system offered. This was especially true of the subordinate classes, for the castles of the feudal nobles provided fortresses against invading lords or bands of marauding brigands. When the kings and princes gave of their lands to feudal lords who in turn granted sections to lesser lords, and so on down, the land so granted was called a fief, or feud; the grantor was called lord, or liege; and the one who received the grant was a vassal, or retainer. The vassal pledged loyalty, military service, and other aid to his lord, and the lord in turn provided his vassal with counsel and protection. The great bulk of the population were serfs, who were bound to the soil and who passed with the land when it changed masters. Thus feudalism was a system of political and economic relationship. Political feudalism centered on the relation of the landlords or nobles to one another and ultimately to the monarch; economic feudalism centered on the relation of the lord to the serfs who toiled in his domain.

The essence of feudalism was service, expressed either in tilling the land or in fighting. Those whose service was of the military type were regarded as of noble character; those whose service consisted of cultivating the soil to which they were tied were deemed of base and common extraction. Thus there developed a warrior class made up of the nobles whose sole excuse for existence seemed that of fighting. The life of the typical lord was absorbed in his castled estate, war, and the chase. But out of this crudely bold life there evolved one of the most interesting of social developments—the system of chivalry. The rules and social usages that accumulated in connection with the life of the nobility constituted chivalry, and the preparation for this life chivalric education. The term *chivalry* comes from the French *cheval* (horse), horsemanship being a basic accomplishment in the system. A noble who had gone through the prescribed training and taken the vows was made a knight; so chivalric education was largely a training for knighthood. [Lopez, pp. 164-165.]

Aims. As a system of education for the nobility, chivalry aimed to teach the best ideals, social and moral, that the Teutons could understand. Chivalry tried to take what good there was in a brutal, selfish, unprincipaled fighting society, and make it over in accordance with the standards of Christianity. It sought a happy blend of barbarian warrior with Christian saint. It taught the protection of the weak, gallantry toward women, honesty in everything. Chivalry provided a definite system of training to inculcate the "rudiments of love, war, and religion." As Messenger states:

> The greatest virtue of the times was courage. The most useful attainment was the ability to fight. The ideals and manner of life practiced and advocated by Christ and his followers could not be comprehended [by most men]. They could under-

stand being heroic. . . . If the courage and the fighting could be put to some good use, the world would be better. This made a good start, and it was the task of chivalry to find some virtues that would harmonize with these. The desire for glory is a powerful motive. . . . Chivalry offered something glorious to fight for. Something particular, tangible, and personal serves as an objective much better than does an abstract principle. Love, war, and religion are more spectacular than labor, thought, and morality. [James F. Messenger, *An Interpretative History of Education* (New York: Thomas Y. Crowell Company, 1931), pp. 78-79.]

The ideals of chivalry were quite different from those of monasticism and scholasticism. Instead of asceticism and intellectualism, chivalry emphasized action. It was a life of high ideals and standards; the true knight was to be devoted to the service of his God, his king, and his lady. Before he could be knighted, he must take (1) the vow of religion, expressing his loyalty to the church; (2) the vow of honor, expressing his loyalty to his feudal superior; (3) the vow of gallantry, expressing his loyalty to his lady. Chivalric education had the essential aim of social discipline, to train the knight to play his part in the faithful observance of the social usages, customs, and ideals approved by his social class. The maxim by which the knight lived was, Act as if the person for whom you have the highest regard were looking on. This produced in the knight courtesy, gallantry, generosity, and good manners—all of which had their refining influence upon society, even if these actions were performed mechanically rather than from the heart.

The ideals of chivalric education are depicted in the lyrics of the troubadours of France, the minnesingers of Germany, and the minstrels of England. Chaucer, Spenser, Scott, and Tennyson have delighted in telling of knightly deeds of courtesy and courage. There was, however, much affectation and superficiality, and Miguel de Cervantes rendered a wholesome service in depicting its exaggerated sentimentality in his delightful but bitter burlesque, *Don Quixote.*

The ideals of chivalry were probably not so effectively realized in England as in an earlier France. Green, in a commentary on the introduction of the tournament in England by Edward I, speaks of "the frivolous unreality of the new chivalry," "the false air of romance," and, in connection with Edward himself, states that "chivalry exerted on him a yet more fatal influence in its narrowing of all sympathy to the noble class, and its exclusion of the peasant and the craftsman from all claim to pity." [J. R. Green, *A Short History of the English People* (London: Macmillan & Co., Ltd., 1929), p. iii.]

Types. Chivalric education was a form of social training. It emphasized manners more than morality, but as a training in social etiquette has probably never been surpassed. It emphasized military training; in fact, it made fighting a profession and devoted a large share of its attention to the development of professional military skills. It placed emphasis upon a phase of education that both monasteries and universities neglected—that of physical training. Religious training was of a rather superficial type: the knight was trained to take part in all the religious rites and ceremonies of the church. There was some literary training, but it was mostly oral and vernacular. Chivalric education was essentially class education and was distinctly aristocratic.

Content. The curriculum was one of activity rather than intellect. The course of study consisted of physical, social, military, and religious activities. At the earlier level the content consisted of health instruction, religious instruction, training in etiquette and obedience to superiors, in playing the harp, singing, chess, and the development of skills in riding, jousting, boxing, and wrestling. Sometimes a little training was given in reading and writing the vernacular. At the higher levels, the curriculum consisted of the Seven Free Arts: (1) jousting, (2) falconing, (3) swimming, (4) horsemanship, (5) boxing, (6) writing and singing verse, and (7) chess. Girls received a thorough training in social etiquette similar to that of boys, but physical and military training was omitted from their instruction. Instead, they were given training in household duties and in such domestic accomplishments as sewing, weaving, and embroidering. Chivalric education for girls differed from convent education in that there was more emphasis upon social and less upon religious and intellectual content.

The most important change fostered by chivalry was the rapid development of vernacular literatures and the practice of them as part of the content of education. By the time of Charlemagne there were two distinct groups of spoken language, the Germanic and the Roman-derived Romance. English, a mixture of Germanic tongues slightly Latinized during the Roman occupation and more so after the Norman Conquest, told its earliest tales of chivalry in the odd conglomeration that we know as Middle English. Similarly, within other Germanic and Romance groups, differing vernaculars developed individually in different localities. The written vernacular practiced in the schools of northern France differed greatly from that of southern France. The Garonne valley from 1100 and 1300 was a land of verse and song, stimulated by chivalry. The singing poets, the troubadours, brought their own hero tales and love ballads to the court at Toulouse and, traveling over Western Europe, helped greatly in the notable ascendancy of the French language. French soon replaced Latin as the language of secular culture of the Middle Ages.

Agencies. The earliest education of the child was in the hands of his mother in the home; later the lords and ladies of the castle of his father's feudal superior were the teachers. The castle, the tournament fields, and the fields of battle, were the schools for the education of the boy; the home and the court were the schools for the girl.

We should not fail to appreciate the importance of the troubadours, minnesingers, and minstrels as agencies of education during the earlier centuries of chivalry. The medieval age was, for the most part, one in which reading was done by few but monks, scholars, and sometimes merchants; travel was slow, difficult, and dangerous; diversions, aside from eating, playing games, hunting, and fighting, were few. Then pass the traveling troubadours! They were the gazetteers, the spreaders of news, the providers of entertainment and amusement. It was their office to bear tidings from castle to castle, to sing the praises of beautiful ladies and gallant knights. They were living magazines, who acquainted the inhabitants of one district with the customs and manners evolving in another—speech, dress, methods of hunting, habits of eating, rules of courtly etiquette; and sometimes they warned of impending danger from jealous rivals or robber bands. Even those troubadours who settled in a particular castle or remained in the castle of their birth exerted appreciable influence in the education of the youth of the estate. And all the while they were circulating the new vernacular, to which each area was contributing and upon which each was drawing.

Organization. From birth until the age of seven, the children of the gentry remained at home where they were given the necessary physical, moral, and religious training by their mothers. At the age of seven, they went to the castle of the feudal overlord. (This custom probably began when the subordinate nobles sent their sons and daughters as hostages or pledges of their fidelity to the overlord.) Orphan children were sent to the castle as wards, because the overlord legally was their guardian. Girls were sent to the court by their parents with the idea of making desirable marriages. Thus the castle became the center of chivalric education.

From seven to fourteen, the boy was a page and attended a noble lady of the court, who directed his education both indoors and out. Between fourteen and twenty-one, the youth was a squire and attended a knight. He still waited upon his lady, with whom he sang, played the harp, and played chess, but his chief duty was to attend upon his lord. Many services were required of him; he served the lord at table, made his bed, groomed his horse, cleaned his armor, carried his shield. He accompanied him in tournaments and actual battle, and thus learned the arts of both peace and war.

At twenty-one his education was complete and he was ready for knighthood. He prepared himself for the ceremony by confession, fasting, and an all-night vigil. Elaborate religious rites were performed; and after promising to be faithful, to protect women and orphans, never to lie or slander, to live in harmony with his equals, and to protect the church, he received the accolade, a slight blow on each shoulder with the flat of the sword; his new sword and spurs were buckled on, and he thus became a knight. [See Sir Edward Strachy, "The Chivalric Inheritance," p. 347, in Grant Uden (Ed.), *A Dictionary of Chivalry* (New York: Thomas Y. Crowell Company, 1968). See also National Geographic Society, *The Age of Chivalry* (Washington, D.C.: The Society, 1969).]

Methods. Since chivalric education was largely the acquisition of skills, the methods used were those of example and practice. Attendance upon his lady and his lord enabled the boy to develop the social behavior and accomplishments of chivalry through imitation. The color and action of court life and the desire for social approval provided motivation for his learning. Ideals were acquired through the songs of love and war, which praised beautiful virtuous ladies and gallant valiant knights, and through the pledges taken in impressive ceremonies. Discipline was maintained through the ideals of obedience and service, though at times these ideals had to be enforced by threats of mortal combat. Pupils learned by doing, were motivated by high ideals, and were restrained and controlled by an adherence to recognized social standards.

The Guild Approach to Education

The late Middle Ages contributed other factors in the development of educational theory: the rise of the middle class, towns, and the organization of the guild system, largely as a result of the Crusades. [For a comprehensive and immensely readable account of this movement see Zoe Oldenbourg, *The Crusades,* trans. by Anne Carter (New York: Pantheon Books, Inc., 1966). Although dealing with only the first three Crusades, Oldenbourg draws a fine picture of the twelfth century, especially the human aspect of society in those changing times.]

Although the Crusades failed to wrest the Holy Land from Muslim control, unexpected results, ultimately disastrous to the system that brought them about, did occur. The insulation of feudal life was broken down, communication between countries was stimulated, new desires were kindled among those who had gone East and those who heard their wondrous tales of a different way of life. The necessity of transporting the armies of the Crusaders resulted in the development of seaport cities as centers of shipping, trade, and banking. Visitors to the East became acquainted with new foods, clothing, and ornamentation; with new luxuries and staples. New desires created new necessities.

As a result, a system of banking, trade, and industry to import, process, and distribute the Eastern commodities was demanded. Towns in which the new commerce and industry were centered became free cities, with feudal immunity and almost total independence from church and king. By purchase, by diplomacy, and even by force such city-states obtained the rights of self-government and so guarded their liberties. "The somber merchant on his mule won in the tilt with the gay knight on horseback."

The burghers, merchant-capitalists, established a new order, a fourth class, distinct from nobles, clergy, and serfs. The needs of this new class were quite different from those of the older classes in medieval society. Consequently, a special type of education was demanded for the burgher's children.

Much of the life of the medieval community was centered on the guild system. Guilds were organizations, or associations, of people engaged in commerce and industry. There were two types: merchant guilds and craft guilds. Merchant guilds were the first to appear and flourished from the twelfth to the fourteenth centuries, especially in England. The members all resided in the same town and were both trade merchants and artisan merchants who dealt in their own manufactures. The local guild usually held a monopoly of the retail trade in its town and exercised the privilege of taxing outsiders who brought in goods for sale.

The craft guilds were associations of manufacturers, artisans, and skilled workers such as weavers, dyers, goldsmiths, or silversmiths. Each craft banded together to maintain and advance the standards of its work. [Lopez, pp. 22, 57, 142-144, 277-278, 280-281, 339. For the details of guild activities, see Robert J. Blackham, *London's Livery Companies* (London: Sampson Low, Marston & Co., Ltd., 1930); Sister Mary A. Mulholland, *Early Guild Records of Toulouse* (New York: Columbia University Press, 1961); and John Edgcumbe Staley, *The Guilds of Florence* (New York: B. Blom, 1967).] Most prominent in the fourteenth and fifteenth centuries, these guilds eventually divided into two organizations: the skilled craftsmen, who were the forerunners of modern trade unions; and the owners of the shops, who formed associations of capitalist employers, which were the forerunners of modern trade associations. Types of education adapted to their needs developed around these guilds.

Aims, Types, and Content. The primary need of this new middle class was for an education of a practical type. Vocational training was necessarily emphasized, for children were to be prepared for the activities of commercial and industrial life. The unique contribution of this movement to education was an emphasis upon a new type of vocational training. The burghers did not want a narrow type of vocational or trade training, which neglected everything else. Elementary instruction in the rudiments of reading and writing the vernacular and in arithmetic was always required as preparation for the industrial and commercial training of the guilds. Masters were obligated to give such instruction to their apprentices and to see that they received adequate religious instruction. Although guild schools were usually taught by priests, these schools were much more secular in spirit and aim than the cathedral, monastic, and parish schools. Usually the intellectual education of the guild class was on the elementary level; yet some guild schools later expanded into Latin schools, such as Merchant Taylors' in London.

Agencies. New types of schools developed in these trading cities for the education of the burgher children. Chantry schools were founded out of bequests made by wealthy merchants or traders, stipulating that special priests be employed to chant masses for the repose of the deceased patrons' souls. Since these special priests had much time at their disposal, many such bequests provided that they devote some time to instruct children of the city in the rudiments of elementary education. Sometimes, through a union of chantry foundations, strong schools were developed in the larger towns. There were 300 chantry schools in England alone at the time of the Reformation.

Burgher schools also arose in the larger cities. These were supported and controlled by the public authorities and were often taught by lay teachers as well as priests. The usual type was the guild school, for the children of craftsmen. These were taught by the same priests who performed religious functions, such as baptism and marriage, for the guild members. Burgher schools usually provided elementary education in the vernacular, which was required as a foundation for the later vocational education given in the guilds themselves.

Organization. The only formally organized education in the guild system was this vocational training. The members of the guilds were divided into three classes: masters, journeymen, and apprentices. The masters alone were entitled to own shops, buy raw materials, and sell the manufactured articles. They bought and sold at prices established by the guild, and their establishments were supervised by the guilds so that inferior goods would not be produced. The beginners were known as apprentices. By the terms of apprenticeship the master furnished the apprentice with a home and taught him the trade. The apprentice was obligated to obey his master and to render him service as long as the apprenticeship lasted; this depended upon the trade to be learned, but usually continued for about seven years. For the apprentice's services the master was obliged to give him only board and lodging.

The second stage, that of journeyman, was more remunerative; the guild candidate now received wages from the master, as well as living quarters; he was not bound to one master, but could travel as he wished. In order to be declared a master the journeyman had to demonstrate his proficiency by constructing a masterpiece, which paralleled the thesis requirement of degree candidates in the medieval university. As soon as the journeyman became a master and amassed sufficient capital, he could set up his own business and employ apprentices and journeymen.

Methods. Nothing was particularly novel in the methods of instruction and training used in guild schools. The chantry, burgher, and trade schools operated much the same as the monastic and parish schools. The methods utilized for apprenticeship were familiar, indeed: example, imitation, and practice. In the burgher schools, dictation, memorization, and catechetical devices were most commonly used, as we shall note in the Latin grammar schools which derived from the burgher and princes' schools. Discipline was no less severe than in other medieval settings, and masters could be quite harsh in the treatment of their pupils.

Before the Reformation, guilds usually appointed members of the clergy to assist in their ecclesiastical training. And as education for work became the usual fare of the common man, some guilds offered a popular program for reading and writing not only for their members' children but also the children of other townspeople. With the addition of Latin to their programs, a few schools even became secondary institutions.

But the significant aspect of this accent on the vocational was that legislation, especially in England, developed to maintain such training programs as social policy, and these provisions found reflection in the education laws of New England and elsewhere. [See Bernard J. Kohlbrenner, "The Catholic Heritage," pp. 103-132, in Richard E. Gross (Ed.), *Heritage of American Education* (Boston: Allyn and Bacon, Inc., 1962).]

37
The Renaissance.
Erasmus (1466-1536)

Selections from William Harrison Woodward, *Desiderius Erasmus Concerning the Aim and Method of Education* (Cambridge: Cambridge University Press, 1904), including selections from *The Treatise of Erasmus De Ratione Studii, that is, Upon the Right Method of Instruction*, 1511, pp. 162-178; from *The Treatise De Pueris statim ac liberaliter instituendis, Addressed* to William, Duke of Cleves, 1529, pp. 179-222; and from *De Conscribendis Epistolis*, 1522, pp. 222-226.

The Treatise of Erasmus
De Ratione Studii, that is
Upon the Right Method
of Instruction,
1511

1: Thought and Expression Form the Two-Fold Material of Instruction. 521 A-B

All knowledge falls into one of two divisions: the knowledge of "truths" and the knowledge of "words": and if the former is first in importance the latter is acquired first in order of time. They are not to be commended who, in their anxiety to increase their store of truths, neglect the necessary art of expressing them. For ideas are only intelligible to us by means of the words which describe them; wherefore defective knowledge of language reacts upon our apprehension of the truths expressed. We often find that no one is so apt to lose himself in verbal arguments as the man who boasts that facts, not words, are the only things that interest him. This goes to prove that true education includes what is *best* in both kinds of knowledge, taught, I must add, under the *best* guidance. For, remembering how difficult it is to eradicate early impressions, we should aim from the first at learning what need never be unlearnt, and that only.

2: Expression Claims the First Place in Point of Time.
Both the Greek and Latin Languages Needful to the Educated Man,
521 B-C

Language thus claims the first place in the order of studies and from the outset should include both Greek and Latin. The argument for this is two-fold. First, that within these two literatures are contained all the knowledge which we recognise as of vital importance to mankind. Secondly, that the natural affinity of the two tongues renders it more profitable to study them side by side than apart. Latin particularly gains by this method. Quintilian advised that a beginning should be made with Greek before systematic work in Latin is taken in hand. Of course he regarded proficiency in both as essential. The elements, therefore, of Greek and Latin should be acquired early, and should a thoroughly skilled master not be available, then—but only then—let the learner fall back upon self-teaching by means of the study of classical masterpieces.

3: The Right Method of Acquiring Grammar Rests Upon
Reading and Not Upon Definitions and Rules. 521 C-522 A

Amongst Greek Grammars that of Theodore Gaza stands admittedly first, next to it I rank that of Constantine Lascaris. Of the old Latin Grammarians Diomedes is the soundest; whilst the *Rudimenta* of Nicholas Perotti strikes me as the most thorough and most comprehensive of modern works. But I must make my conviction clear that, whilst a knowledge of the rules of accidence and syntax is most necessary to every student, still they should be as few, as simple, and as carefully framed as possible. I have no patience with the stupidity of the average teacher of grammar who wastes precious years in hammering rules into children's heads. For it is not by learning rules that we acquire the power of speaking a language, but by daily intercourse with those accustomed to express themselves with exactness and refinement, and by the copious reading of the best authors.

Upon this latter point we do well to choose such works as are not only sound models of style but are instructive by reason of their subject-matter. The Greek prose-writers whom I advise are, in order, Lucian, Demosthenes, Herodotus: the poets, Aristophanes, Homer, Euripides; Menander, if we possessed his works, would take precedence of all three. Amongst Roman writers, in prose and verse, Terence, for pure, terse Latinity has no rival, and his plays are never dull. I see no objection to adding carefully chosen comedies of Plautus. Next, I place Vergil, then Horace; Cicero and Caesar follow closely; and

Sallust after these. These authors provide, in my judgment, sufficient reading to enable the young student to acquire a working knowledge of the two great classical tongues. It is not necessary for this purpose to cover the whole range of ancient literature; we are not to be dubbed "beginners" because we have not yet mastered the whole of the *Fragmenta.*

Some proficiency in expression being thus attained the student devotes his attention to the *content* of the ancient literatures. It is true, of course, that in reading an author for purposes of vocabulary and style the student cannot fail to gather something besides. But I have in my mind much more than this when I speak of studying "contents." For I affirm that with slight qualification the whole of attainable knowledge lies enclosed within the literary monuments of ancient Greece. This great inheritance I will compare to a limpid spring of whose undefiled waters it behooves all who truly thirst to drink and be restored.

4: The Subject-Matter and the Methods Which are Most Suitable to Beginners. 522 A-E.

Before touching upon the order in which the various disciplines should be acquired, and the choice of Masters, I will say something on the instruction of beginners. In reading the authors above mentioned for the purposes of vocabulary, ornament and style, you can have no better guide than Lorenzo Valla. His *Elegantiae* will shew you what to look for and note down in your Latin reading. But do not merely echo his rules; make headings for yourself as well. Refer also to Donatus and Diomedes for syntax. Rules of prosody, and the rudiments of rhetoric, such as the method of direct statement, of proof, of ornament, of expansion, of transition, are important both for the intelligent study of authors and for composition. Such grounding in grammar and in style will enable you to note with precision such matters as these: an unusual word, archaisms, and innovations, ingenuity in handling material, distinction of style, historical or moral instances, proverbial expressions: the note-book being ready to hand to record them. Notes of this kind should not be jotted down at hap-hazard, but carefully devised so as to recall to the mind the pith of what is read.

If it is claimed that Logic should find a place in the course proposed I do not seriously demur; but I refuse to go beyond Aristotle and I prohibit the verbiage of the schools. Do not let us forget that Dialectic is an elusive maiden, a Siren, indeed, in quest of whom a man may easily suffer intellectual shipwreck. Not here is the secret of style to be discovered. That lies in the use of the pen; whatever the form, whether prose or verse, or whatever the theme, write, write, and again write. Supplement writing by learning by heart. Upon this latter question, memory depends at bottom upon three conditions: thorough understanding of the subject, logical ordering of the contents, repetition to ourselves. Without these we can neither retain securely nor reproduce promptly. Read, then, attentively, read over and over again, test your memory vigorously and minutely. Verbal memory may with advantage be aided by ocular impressions; thus, for instance, we can have charts of geographical facts, genealogical trees, large-typed tables of rules of syntax and prosody, which we can hang on the walls. Or again, the scholar may make a practice of copying striking quotations at the top of his exercise books. I have known a proverb inscribed upon a ring, or a cup, sentences worth remembering painted on a door or a window. These are all devices for adding to our intellectual stores, which, trivial as they may seem individually, have a distinct cumulative value.

5: Instruction Generally: Choice of Subjects of Instruction. The Range of Study Necessary to a Well-Read Master. 522 E-523 F.

This brings me to treat of the art of instruction generally, though it seems a mere impertinence in me to handle afresh a subject which has been made so conspicuously his own by the great Quintilian.

As regards the choice of *material*, it is essential that from the outset the child be made acquainted only with the best that is available. This implies that the Master is competent to recognise the best in the mass of erudition open to him, which in turn signifies that he has read far more widely than the range of authors to be taught by him. This applies even to the tutor of beginners. The Master should, therefore, acquaint himself with authors of every type, with a view to contents rather than to style; and the better to classify what he reads he must adopt the system of classifying his matter by means of note-books, upon the plan suggested by me in *De Copia*. As examples of the authors I refer to I put Pliny first, then Macrobius, Aulus Gellius, and, in Greek, Athenaeus. Indeed to lay in a store of ancient wisdom the studious master must go straight to the Greeks: to Plato, Aristotle, Theophrastus and Plotinus; to Origen, Chrysostom, Basil. Of the Latin Fathers, Ambrosius will be found most fertile in classical allusions. Jerome has the greatest command of Holy Scripture. I cannot, however, enumerate the entire extent of reading which a competent knowledge of antiquity demands. I can only indicate a few directions which study ought to take.

For the right understanding of the poets, the *Legends* of Gods and Heroes must be mastered: Homer, Hesiod, Ovid, and the Italian Boccaccio should be read for this. A knowledge of *Geography* is of prime importance, for the study both of ancient poets and of historians. Pomponius Mela makes a useful compendium; Pliny and Ptolemy are learned and elaborate writers; Strabo is something more than a geographer. This subject includes two parts, a knowledge, first, of the names, ancient and modern, of mountains, rivers, cities; secondly, of names of trees, plants, animals, of dress, appliances, precious stones, in which the average writer of today shews a strange ignorance. Here we gain help from the works which have come down to us upon agriculture, architecture, the art of war, cookery, precious stones, and natural history. We can make good use, in the same subject, of etymology (the name "unicorn" is an example). Or again we can trace word-change in names through modern Greek, or Italian and Spanish (Tiber, now "Tevere," is an example). I may say that modern French has wandered too far from its classical mother-speech to be of much help to us in recognising and identifying ancient names.

Material for the study of Archaeology is to be found not only in literary sources, but in ancient coins, inscriptions, and monuments. Astrology—futile as it is in itself—must be understood for the sake of many poetical allusions. Of special importance is the study of History, for its own sake as well as for the reason that it is the key to many references in other writings. Finally, to understand such a poet as Prudentius, the one Christian poet of real literary taste, a knowledge of Sacred History is indispensable.

And indeed we may say that a genuine student ought to grasp the meaning and force of every fact or idea that he meets with in his reading, otherwise their literary treatment through epithet, metaphor, or simile will be to him obscure and confused. There is thus no discipline, no field of study,—whether music, architecture, agriculture or war—which may not prove of use to the teacher in expounding the Poets and Orators of antiquity. "But," you rejoin, "you expect all this of your scholar?" Yes, if he propose to become a teacher; for he thus secures that his own erudition will lighten the toil of acquisition for those under his charge.

6: The Art of Teaching the Rudiments of Language up to the Stage When Composition Is Begun. 523 F-524 C

As regards the methods of the rudiments—that is, of learning to talk and knowing the alphabet—I can add nothing to what Quintilian has laid down. For my own part I advise that when this stage is reached the child begin to hear and imitate the sounds of *Latin* speech. Why should it be more difficult to acquire Roman words or even Greek, rather than the vernacular? No doubt my prescription demands the environment of a cultivated home-circle. But the master may secure even under the conditions of school-life that boys be brought to speak Latin with precision, if patience be shown in encouraging and correcting uncertain efforts, and in insisting upon careful observation of the Teacher's own usage. By degrees devices for increasing fluency may be introduced; as, for instance, a game of forfeits and prizes for faults and corrections, the Master choosing the judges from amongst the top boys. The more common phrases suitable for play, for social life, for meal-times, must be early learned and be apt, and ready to hand.

The time will now have come when the able teacher must select certain of the more necessary rules of accidence and syntax, and state them simply, arrange them in proper order and dictate them for entry in note-books. An author may now be attempted, but of the easiest sort; choose one likely to be helpful in composition and conversation. Through this text the rules just referred to will be driven home, and the examples of syntaclical usages therein contained carefully worked out; all this of course with an eye to the later stages when regular exercises in prose and verse are required.

7: The Importance of the Art of Composition: Its Method Set Out. 524 C-525 C

When this time has arrived care must be taken to propound themes not only worthy in subject but suitable, as being within the range of the boy's interests. For in this way he may acquire not only training in style, but also a certain store of facts and ideas for future use. For example, such a subject as the following would prove attractive: "The rash self-confidence of Marcellus imperilled the fortunes of Rome; they were retrieved by the caution of Fabius." Here we see the underlying sentiment, that reckless counsels hasten towards disaster. Here is another: "Which of the two shewed less wisdom, Crates who cast his gold into the sea, or Midas who cherished it as his supreme good?" Or, "Eloquence too little restrained brought Demosthenes and Cicero to their ruin." One more: "No encomium can exceed the deserts of Codrus, who held that the safety of his subjects claimed even the life of the King himself." But Valerius Maximus will provide you with ample choice of such themes. At first these may be set in the vernacular.

Mythology and fable will also serve your purpose. "Hercules gained immortal fame as the destroyer of monsters." "The Muses delight in the fountain and the grove; they shrink from the crowded haunts of men." "One should not burden a friend with a difficulty which it is a duty to solve ourselves." "All men are conscious of the wallet which hangs in front, but ignore that which they carry behind them." Proverb and moral will suggest such themes as these: "It is not every one's good fortune to visit Corinth." "How far above the type of today was he who counted a man worthy not for his wealth but for his manhood!" "Socrates despises those who live in order to eat; he applauds those who eat in order to live." My book *Adagia* will supply you with instances enough. Other themes may be suggested from the properties of natural objects, such as the attraction of the magnet or the mimicry of the polypus. Similes, also, allegories, sententious sayings, smart turns of expression, will lend themselves to exercises in composition. The Master in the course of his reading will be careful to note instances which present themselves as models suitable for imitation.

The pupil will now have attained a certain facility in speaking and in writing Latin. He will be ready, therefore, to proceed to a more advanced stage in Grammar, which must be learnt by means of rules aptly illustrated by quotations: the rules being expressed as tersely as may be consistent with clearness. I would add that in all that concerns Greek constructions we should do well to allow the guidance of Gaza's grammar.

8: The Methods to Be Pursued in Writing Advanced Exercises in Composition. 525 C-F

But I must repeat that when once the simpler rules of composition, in prose and verse, and the commer figures of speech have been mastered, the whole stress of teaching must be laid upon a close yet wide study of the greater writers. Fortified with this the student can produce *original* work in prose, under the criticism (this is most important) of a thoroughly skilled instructor.

Practice in the pistolary style, both in Greek and Latin, may be gained by writing to an argument propounded in the vernacular. This will come first. Then the whole range of rhetorical prose is open to the student who must gain acquaintance with the different varieties of style; for instance, that demanded in the production of the Fable, or the moral Commonplace, or the short Story, or the Dilemma; the art of expressing an Encomium, or a Denunciation; a Parallel, a Simile, a Description. Another exercise will take the form of paraphrasing poetry into prose and the reverse process. There is also much advantage in attempting the same subject, say an epistle, in two diverse styles. Or one motive may be expressed in four or five different meters. Further, an identical topic may be propounded both for verse and for prose, alike in Latin and in Greek. An affirmation may be set to be proved by three or four differing lines of argument. Perhaps the most useful exercise of all consists in construing from Greek into Latin, practice in which demands diligent attention. For in this exercise we are committed to three distinct operations: first, we have to analyse the construction of the passage in the older tongue: next, we are forced to appreciate carefully the peculiar genius of each language and to note the principles which are common to both: thirdly, in producing an accurate rendering from the Greek we are exercised in moving freely amidst the resources of Roman vocabulary and sentence-structure. So exacting a task claims whatever stimulus, encouragement and skilled aid the master has to offer to the pupil; who will further find inspiration in the reading of model passages of a similar theme to that which he has in hand.

9: Original Composition: Its Variety: The Method of Aiding the Student: Correction of Exercises. 525 F-526 F

It is now time to call for original composition: in which we leave the task of developing a stated theme to the taste and industry of the pupil himself. The right choice of subjects for such exercises is a test of the Master's talent. Suppose an *Epistle* to be required, say of congratulation, or of condolence, or expostulation, or of some other recognised type, the Master should limit himself to indicating certain characteristics of structure or phrasing, common to each variety, and then those which may be specially appropriate to the kind of letter actually proposed. The same method will apply to exercises in *formal Oratory*,—a declamation in praise of Socrates, or in denunciation of Caesar; against reliance on riches, or in favour of Greek Letters; for the married life or against it; against pilgrimages, or in praise of them.

This will lead to the study of the *art* of Oratory as laid down by Cicero and Quintilian. For the subjects proposed as above must be treated in accordance with accepted methods. The master should suggest the number of propositions to be set out on a given theme, of the arguments to be employed, and of the proofs to be adduced in support of each; and the sources from which these may be drawn. This constitutes a kind of skeleton-form of the oration, to be filled in to suit the actual subject selected. Further, the pupil should be led to consider the various methods by which he may adorn his treatment of the argument, such as simile and contrast, parallel cases, moral reflection, adages, anecdotes, parables, and so on; and he should have some guidance in choice of figure and metaphor as aids to ornament in style. In regard to the logical ordering of argument as a whole, the student should be taught to attend to the niceties of exposition,—the exordium, the transition, the peroration; for each of these has its own peculiar excellence, and each, moreover, admits of the merit not only of precision but also of elegance.

Seven or eight exercises of this kind done under careful supervision should be sufficient to enable the pupil to lay out matter for original prose composition without help. Amongst suitable subjects for the purpose are those drawn from legend and ancient history, such as these: "Menelaus before a Trojan assembly claims the restoration of Helen"; "Phalaris presses the priests of Delphi to accept his Brazen Bull as an offering to the god"; "Cicero is warned to reject the offers of Mark Antony." As regards the *correction* of compositions, the Master will note his approval of passages which shew ingenuity in *selection* of material, and in its *treatment,* and in *imitation.* He will censure omission or bad arrangement of matter, exaggerations, carelessness, awkwardness of expression. He will at the same time point out how corrections may be suitably made, and ask for a re-writing of the exercise. Yet, after all, his chief aim will be to stimulate his pupils by calling attention to the progress made by this one or by the other, thus arousing the spirit of emulation in the class.

10: The Best Methods of Procedure in Reading an Author in Class: 526 F 528 C

In reading a classic let the Master avoid the practice, common to inferior teachers, of taking it as the text for universal and irrelevant commentary. Respect the writer, and let it be your rule to rest content with explaining and illustrating his meaning. This would be the method I advise, say, in taking a class through a play of Terence. You begin by offering an appreciation of the author, and state what is necessary concerning his life and surroundings, his talent, and the characteristics of his style. You next consider comedy as an example of a particular form of literature, and its interest for the student: the origin and meaning of the term itself, the varieties of Comedy, and the Terentian prosody. Now you proceed to treat briefly and clearly the argument of the play, taking each situation in due course. Side by side with this you will handle the diction of the writer; noting any conspicuous elegance, or such peculiarities as archaism, novel usage, Graecisms; bringing out anything that is involved or obscure in phrases or sentence-forms; marking, where necessary, derivations and orthography, metaphors and other rhetorical artifices. Parallel passages should next be brought under notice, similarities and contrasts in treatment observed, and direct borrowings traced—no difficult task when we are comparing a Latin poet with his Greek predecessors. The last factor in the lesson consists in the moral applications which it suggests; the story of Orestes and Pylades, or of Tantalus, are obvious examples.

It may be wise in some cases to open the reading of a fresh book by arousing interest in its broader significance. For instance, the Second Eclogue of Vergil must be treated as something more than a purely grammatical or literary exercise. "The essence of friendship," the Master would begin, "lies in similarity. Violently contradictory natures are incapable of mutual affection. The stronger and the more numerous the ties of taste and interest the more durable is the bond." This, amplified by apt adages and wise reflections, of which literature is full, will serve to draw the pupil's thought to the more general aspects of his reading. But it is only a Master of ability, insight and wide culture, to whom such a method is possible. A store of pertinent quotations is the product of careful reading. For instance, in illustration of this particular theme, he will adduce such quotations as this: "cascus cascam ducit: balbus balbum rectius intelligit: semper graculus arridet graculo," and others of the same import. Again, the master will have learnt from his knowledge of men that extreme differences of fortunes or of intellectual tastes do not consist with abiding friendship, that a fool laughs at a man of education, a boor has nothing in common with a courtier. He knows that there is a complete lack of sympathy between the Stoic and the Epicurean, the philosopher and the attorney, the poet and the divine, the orator and the recluse. See, too, what advantage learning gives to the master in enforcing the same theme from tradition and from history. He can refer to Castor and Pollux, to Romulus and Remus, to Cain and Abel. The beautiful myth of Narcissus will, in able hands, prove a parable of striking force. What has more likeness to ourselves than our own reflection? Thus, when one man of learning feels drawn to another, is he not in truth attracted by the reflection of himself? And so of a man of wise temperance, or a man of integrity, conscious of similar excellence in another. Upon such recognition of identical qualities is friendship based,—I mean the frank, open and abiding friendship which alone deserves the name. The Platonic myth of the two types of Aphrodite, the celestial and the profane, may be adduced to prove that true affection can subsist between the good alone. For where excellence is only upon one side, friendship is but a fleeting and insecure thing. Now it is as a parable of unstable friendship that the Master should treat this Eclogue. Alexis is of the town, Corydon a countryman; Corydon a shepherd, Alexis a man of society. Alexis cultivated, young, graceful; Corydon rude, crippled, his youth far behind him. Hence the impossibility of a true friendship. The lesson finally left on the mind of the pupil is that it is the prudent part to choose friends among those whose tastes and characters agree with our own. Such methods of treating a classical story, by forcing attention to the moral to be deduced from it, will serve to counteract any harm which a more literal interpretation might possibly convey. After all, it is what a reader brings to a passage rather than what he finds there which is the real source of mischief.

11: An Introduction to Literary Criticism Is Afforded by Such a Method of Classical Instruction. 528C-529B

Speaking generally, it is advisable to introduce every new book read by indicating its chief characteristics, and then setting out its argument. The characteristics of *Epigram* are aptness and point; of *Tragedy* emotion, the various types of which and their exciting causes must be distinguished. In a great play the argument of each speech, the logical fence of the dialogue, the scene where the action is laid, the period, and the surroundings, call for attention in due order. *Comedy* suggests a different method of introductory treatment: a more familiar setting, lighter, less strenuous emotions, are common to every comedy, though each play will require its own prefactory discussion. In beginning the "Andria," the master will note the contrast of Chremes and Simo, as types of old age, of Pamphilus and Charinus as examples of young men. And so through other plays. The Eclogues of Vergil will be shewn to have their setting in a Golden Age; their ideas, similes, comparisons, are drawn from pastoral life; the emotions depicted are far from complex; the shepherd's delight is in simple melody and the wisdom of maxim and proverb, his reverence is for traditional lore and augury. A historical book, epic or satire, dialogue or fable, will be introduced each in its appropriate way, before the text is touched upon, and the excellence or the defect of the piece emphasised.

Most important is it that the student be brought to learn for himself the true method of such criticism, that he may distinguish good literature from mediocrity. Hence the value of acquaintance with the judgments to be found in the oratorical writings of Cicero and Quintilian; in Sececa and in the old grammarians such as Donatus. Once acquired, this power of insight into the mind of the great writers will lead to a habit of general criticism of character and situation. The student will put such questions to himself as these: Why did Cicero feign to be afraid in his defence of Milo? Why did Vergil depict Turnus as a second hero? But enough to indicate what I mean by literary criticism.

12: Progress in Classical Knowledge Depends upon the Learning and the Skill of the Master. 529 B-530 A

What has been laid down above as the function of the schoolmaster implies, I allow, that he be a person of no slight learning and experience. But, given these qualities, I have no doubt that the class will speedily absorb the kind of knowledge which I have indicated. The first steps may be slow and laborious, but exercise and right instruction make progress certain. I only stipulate that the material selected be of sound classical excellence (nothing mediaeval), and the method skilfully adapted to the growing comprehension; the teacher forcing nothing, but working forward gradually from the broader aspects of his subject to the more minute. Success then is assured. One further counsel, however. The master must not omit to set as an exercise the reproduction of what he has given to the class. It involves time and trouble to the teacher, I know well, but it is essential. A literal reproduction of the matter taught is, of course, not required, but the substance of it presented in the pupil's own way. Personally I disapprove of the practice of taking down a lecture just as it is delivered. For this prevents reliance upon memory which should, as time goes on, need less and less of that external aid which note-taking supplies.

13: Conclusion. 530 A-B

Such weight do I ascribe to right method in instruction—and I include herein choice of material as well as of modes of imparting it—that I undertake by its means to carry forward youths of merely average intelligence to a creditable standard of scholarship, and of conversation also, in Latin and Greek, at an age when, under the common school-master of to-day, the same youths would be just stammering through their Primer. With the foundations thus rightly laid a boy may con-fidently look forward to success in the higher range of learning. He will, when he looks back, admit that the essential condition of his attainment was the care which was devoted to the beginnings of his education.

The Treatise *De Pueris statim ac liberaliter instituendis*, Addressed to William, Duke of Cleves, 1529

*De pueris statim ac liberaliter instituendis libellus; or, The
Argument of Erasmus of Rotterdam, That Children from
Their Earliest Years Be Trained in Virtue and Sound Learning*

1: The Argument at Large: i. 489 A-D

I desire to urge upon you, Illustrious Duke, to take into your early and serious consideration the future nurture and training of the son lately born to you. For, with Chrysippus, I contend that the young child must be led to sound learning whilst his wit is yet unwarped, his age tender, his mind flexible and tenacious. In manhood we remember nothing so well as the truths which we imbibed in our youth. Wherefore I beg you to put aside all idle chatter which would persuade you that this early childhood is unmeet for the discipline and the effort of studies.

The arguments which I shall enlarge upon are the following. First, the beginnings of learning are the work of memory, which in young children is most tenacious. Next, as nature has implanted in us the instinct to seek for knowledge, can we be too early in obeying her behest? Thirdly, there are not a few things which it imports greatly that we should know well, and which we can learn far more readily in our tender years. I speak of the elements of Letters, Grammar, and the fables and stories found in the ancient Poets. Fourthly, since children, as all agree, are fit to acquire manners, why may they not acquire the rudiments of learning? And seeing that they must needs be busy about something, what else can be better approved? For how much wiser to amuse their hours with Letters, than to see them frittered away in aimless trifling!

It is, however, objected, first, that such knowledge as can be thus early got is of slight value. But even so, why despise it, if so be it serve as the foundation for much greater things? For if in early childhood a boy acquire such useful elements he will be free to apply his youth to higher knowledge, to the saving of his time. Moreover, whilst he is thus occupied in sound learning he will perforce be kept from some of the temptations which befall youth, seeing that nothing engages the whole mind more than studies. And this I count a high gain in such times as ours.

Next, it is urged that by such application health may be somewhat endangered. Supposing this to be true, still the compensation is great, for by discipline the mind gains far more in alertness and in vigour than the body is ever likely to lose. Watchfulness, however, will prevent any such risk as is imagined. Also, for this tender age you will employ a teacher who will win and not drive, just as you will choose such subjects as are pleasant and attractive, in which the young mind will find recreation rather than toil.

Furthermore, I bid you remember that a man ignorant of Letters is no man at all, that human life is a fleeting thing, that youth is easily enticed into sin, that early manhood is absorbed by clashing interests, that old age is unproductive, and that few reach it. How then can you allow your child, in whom you yourself live again, to lose even one of those precious years in which he may begin to acquire those means whereby he may elevate his whole life and keep at arm's length temptation and evil?

2: The First Law: Education Must Begin from the Very Earliest Years. 486 D-490 A

I rejoice at your determination that your son shall be early initiated into the arts of true learning and the wisdom of sound philosophy. Herein consists the full duty of fatherhood, the care and guidance of the spirit of him for whose creation you are responsible. And now for my first precept. Do not follow the fashion, which is too common amongst us, of allowing the early years of childhood to pass without fruit of instruction, and of deferring its first steps until the allurements of indulgence have made application more difficult.

3: The Importance of Skilled Control from the Outset. 490 A-491 D

I urge you, therefore, to look even now for a scholar of high character and attainment to whom you may commit the charge of your boy's mind and disposition, leaving to wisely chosen nurses the care of his bodily welfare. By thus dividing control the child will be saved from the mischievous kindnesses and indulgence of foolish serving-women, and of weak relatives, who decry learning as so much poison, and babble about the unfitness of the growing boy for Letters. To such chatter you will turn a deaf ear. For, remembering that the welfare of your son demands not less circumspection from you than a man will gladly bestow upon his horse, his castle, his estate, you will take heed only to the wisest counsel which you can secure, and ponder that with yourself. Consider, in this regard, the care which a boy's mother will lavish upon his bodily frame, how she will take thought should she but faintly suspect in him a tendency to become wry-necked, cross-eyed, crook-backed or splay-footed, or by any mischance prove ill-formed in proportions of his figure. Think, too, how she is apt to busy herself about his milk, his meat, his bath, his exercise, following herein the wise foresight of Galen; will she defer this carefulness until the seventh year? No, from the very day of his birth charge is taken lest mischief hap, and wisely, knowing that a weakly manhood may be thus avoided.

Nay, even before the child be born, how diligent is the wise mother to see that no harm come to herself for her child's sake.

No one blames this as undue or untimely care for the young life. Why then do men neglect that part of our nature, the nobler part, whereby we are rightly called *men*; we bestow, justly, our effort upon the mortal body; yet have we but slight regard for the immortal spirit.

Are other instances needed? Then think of the training of a colt, how early it is begun; or of the work of the husbandman who fashions and trains the sapling to suit his taste or to further the fruitfulness of the tree. This is a task of human skill and purpose; and the sooner these are applied the more sure the result.

4: The Supreme Importance of Education to Human Well-Being, 491 D-492 A

To dumb creatures Mother Nature has given an innate power or instinct, whereby they may in great part attain to their right capacities. But Providence in granting to man alone the privilege of reason has thrown the burden of development of the human being upon training. Well, therefore, has it been said that the first means, the second, and the third means to happiness is right training or education. Sound education is the condition of real wisdom. And if an education which is soundly planned and carefully carried out is the very fount of all human excellence, so, on the other hand, careless and unworthy training is the true source of folly and vice. This *capacity for training* is, indeed, the chief aptitude which has been bestowed upon humanity. Unto the animals nature has given swiftness of foot or of wing, keenness of sight, strength or size of frame, and various weapons of defence. To Man, instead of physical powers, is given a mind apt for training; in this single gift all others are comprised, for him, at least, who turns it to due profit. We see that where native instinct is strong—as in squirrels or bees—capacity for being taught is wanting. Man, lacking instinct, can do little or nothing of innate power; scarce can he eat, or walk, or speak, unless he be guided thereto. How then can we expect that he should become competent to the duties of life unless straight-way and with much diligence he be brought under the discipline of a worthy education? Let me enforce this by the well-known story of Lycurgus, who, to convince the Spartans, brought out two hounds, one of good mettle, but untrained and therefore useless in the field, and the other poorly bred and well-drilled at his work; "Nature," he said, "may be strong, yet Education is more powerful still."

5: Parents Will Not See That in Their Children's Interests Education Matters Most. 492 A-C

Yet we see a father, who bestows no little heed to ensure that his horses and dogs are of the right breed, careless whether his son be properly trained that he may prove an honour to his parents, and helpful to them in their later years, a worthy husband, a brave and useful citizen. Yet for whom does such a father plant and build? for whose behoof does he contrive wealth by land and by sea? For his children, forsooth. But what profit or honour lies in inheriting such things if their possessor has no skill to use them aright? Who will fashion ingeniously a harp for one who has not learnt to play upon it? Or furnish a library for one who knows or cares nothing for books? Why, therefore, heap up riches for one who knows not how to employ them? For note this well: that he who provides for a son who is worthily educated, provides means to virtue: but whoso saves for a child endowed with rude temper and uncultivated wit is but ministering to opportunities of indulgence and mischief. It is the height of folly that one should train the body to be comely, and wholly neglect that excellence of mind which alone can guide it aright. For I hesitate not to affirm that those things which men covet for their sons—health, riches, and repute—are more surely secured by virtue and learning—the gifts of education—than by any other means. True, the highest gifts of all no man can give to another, even to his child; but we can store his mind with that sound wisdom and learning whereby he may attain to the best.

6: Other Parents Neglect the Duty of Education until Too Late. 492 C-493 B

Further, there are those—sometimes men of repute for practical wisdom—who err in deferring education till the stage when the boy finds the rudiments of learning irksome to acquire. Yet these same fathers will be over-anxious for their children's future fortune even before they be born. We hear of astrologers called in: "the child," it is affirmed, "will be a born soldier." "Then let us plan to enter him into the king's service." "He will be the very type of a churchman." "Then let us work for a bishopric or an abbey for him." And this is not thought to be taking care prematurely for a career yet far-distant. Why then refuse to provide not less early that the boy may be worthily prepared to fill it: so that he grow up not only to be a captain of a troop, but a fit and reputable officer of the commonwealth; not merely to be called a bishop, but to be made worthy of his charge? Men seem to me to have regard to nothing less than to that end to which all these other ends are subordinate. Lands, castles, furnishings, dress, servants, all are well cared for, and are of the best: the son of the house alone is left untrained, untaught, ignorant, boorish. A man buys a slave; he may be useless at first, as knowing nothing. Straightway he is tried, and it is quickly found what he can best do, and to that craft he is diligently trained. But the same man will wholly neglect his son's up-bringing. "He will have enough to live upon," he will say. "But *not* enough to live a worthy life," I rejoin. "What need of learning? He will have wealth." "Then the more need of all the guidance that Letters and Philosophy can bestow." How active, for instance, do princes show themselves to get for their sons as large a dominion as they can, whilst no men seem to care less that their heirs should be duly educated to fulfill the responsibility that must fall to them. The saying of Alexander is often quoted: "Were I not Alexander I would be Diogenes." But Plutarch is right in his reflection, that the very fact that he was lord of so great an empire was, had he known it, reason enough for him to desire to be a philosopher as well. How much more does that father give his son who gives him that by which he may *live worthily* than he who merely gives that whereby he may *live!*

7: Reason the True Mark of Man. 493 B-494 A

Now it is the possession of Reason which constitutes a Man. If trees or wild beasts grow, men, believe me, are fashioned. Men in olden time who led their life in forests, driven by the mere needs and desires of their natures, guided by no laws, with no ordering in communities, are to be judged rather as savage beasts than as men. For Reason, the mark of humanity, has no place where all is determined by appetite. It is beyond dispute that a man not instructed through reason in philosophy and sound learning is a creature lower than a brute, seeing that there is no beast more wild or more harmful than a man who is driven hither and thither by ambition, or desire, anger or envy, or lawless temper. Therefore do I conclude that he that provides not that his own son may presently be instructed in the best learning is neither a man nor the son of a man. Would it not be a horror to look upon a human soul clad in the form of a beast, as Circe is fabled to have done by her spells? But is it not worse that a father should see his own image slowly but surely becoming the dwellingplace of a brute's nature? It is said a bear's cub is at birth but an ill-formed lump which by a long process of licking is brought into shape. Nature, in giving you a son, presents you, let me say, a rude, unformed creature, which it is your part to fashion so that it may become indeed a man. If this fashioning be neglected you have but an animal still: if it be contrived earnestly and wisely, you have, I had almost said, what may prove a being not far from a God.

8: Education of Their Children Is a Duty Owed by Parents to the Commonwealth and to God. 494 A-495 A

Straightway from the child's birth it is meet that he should begin to learn the things which properly belong to his well-being. Therefore, bestow especial pains upon his tenderest years, as Vergil teaches. Handle the wax whilst it is soft, mould the clay whilst it is moist, dye the fleece before it gather stains. It is no light task to educate our children aright. Yet think—to lighten the burden—how much comfort and honour parents derive from children well brought up: and reflect how much sorrow is engendered of them that grow up evilly. And further, no man is born to himself, no man is born to idleness. Your children are begotten not to yourself alone, but to your country: not to your country alone, but to God. Paul teaches that women are saved by reason that they bring up their children in the pursuit of virtue. God will straitly charge the parents with their children's faults; therefore, except they bring up their little ones from the very first to live aright, they themselves will share the penalty. For a child rightly educated is a comfort and a joy to his parents, but a foolish child brings upon them shame, it may be poverty, and old age before their time. Nay, I know not a few men of note and place who have lost their sons by lamentable deaths, the results of evil life; some fathers, indeed, which out of many children had scarce one surviving. And this from no other cause than that they have made portions for their sons, but have taken no heed to train them. They are called murderers who kill their new-born children: but such kill kill the mere body. How great, then, is their crime who destroy the soul? For what other thing is the death of the soul than to live in folly and sin? Such fathers do no less wrong to their country, to which, as far as in them lies, they give pestilent citizens. They do, equally, a wrong against God, at whose hands they receive their offspring to bring it up to His service.

9: Vicious Habits in Which Parents Encourage Their Children. 495 B-496 A

But there is an education which is worse than none at all. For how shall we describe those who go about to imbue the tender mind with wickedness, before it be able to know what wickedness is? For example, how can a child grow up to modesty and humility who in his very infancy totters in the purple? He cannot yet sound his letters, but he knows what cramoisie is, and brocade: he craves for dainty dishes and disdainfully pushes away simple food. The tailor contrives some new marvel in cap or tunic; straightway we must dress up the child therein;

we tickle his vanity, and then we wonder that he develops irritation and self-conceit! The serving-women teach him evil words, and for their amusement tempt him to repeat them. He is brought up to sit through long feastings; he hears the noise of jesters, minstrels, and dancers. The guest, nay, his own father, sprawl drunkenly in his presence. And yet you pray that he may grow up honest, temperate, and pure. I would also denounce those who bring up their sons to a love of war. Straight from their mother's arms they are bidden to finger swords and shields, to thrust and strike. With such tastes, already deeply rooted with years, they are handed over to a master, who is blamed for their indifference to worthy interests. If it be urged that parents find some pleasure in this evil precocity of their children, let me ask if any true father will rather that his son pick up gross speech, and copy some shameful act, than hear him, with stammering tongue, utter something worthy and true? Nature has made the first years of our life prone to imitation—though perhaps it is easier to that age to copy evil than good—and with imitativeness she has given also tenacity in retention. Hence the mischief that accrues when mothers are allowed to keep their children in their lap until they are seven years of age: if they want playthings do they not see that monkeys or toy-dogs would serve them just as well? For no one can exaggerate the importance of these years for character, nor the difficulty which such enervating, debasing up-bringing at this stage creates for the teachers who then take over the task. Menander and Paul were perfectly right: such "evil communications corrupt good manners."

10: Savage Nature Teaches the Same Lesson of Care for Early Training of the Young. 496 A-E.

But if neither love nor reason suffice to teach us our duty, let us turn to the example of the brute creation. For mankind has admittedly learned therefrom much useful knowledge. For instance, the hippopotamus has shown us the method of cutting a vein; the ibis the use of the clyster, so much approved by physicians. The stag has taught men that dittany is helpful in drawing out arrows, and that the eating of crabs is an antidote to the poison of spiders. Goats have proved that ivy is a remedy in certain affections. Lizards use dittany against the bite of snakes, their standing foes. From the weasel we learnt the use of rue, from the serpent the use of fennel in affections of the eye. The dragon is our warrant for employing lettuce in sickness. Much more of such knowledge have we derived from dumb animals. Practical arts also have been acquired from them to our great profit. Nay, I might almost say that there is nothing which advantages the life of man of which nature has not shown us some example in wild creatures, to the end that they who have not learnt philosophy and the rational arts may be admonished by them what men may do. Attend, therefore, to that which we may learn from them as to the training of children. We see that every savage creature is not content only to produce its young, but teaches it, and shapes it to fulfill its proper function. A bird is, indeed, created with instinct for flight, but we see how the fledgling is led on and guided in its first attempts by the parent birds. The cat teaches her kittens to watch, to spring, to kill. The stag leads her young in chase, brings them to the leap, shows the methods of escape from pursuit. Authors have recounted to us that the elephant and the dolphin exhibit a veritable art in educating their young ones. So of nightingales—the old bird goes in front, calls back to, and corrects, the young one, which in turn follows and obeys. And I affirm that, as the instinct of the dog is to hunt, of the bird to fly, of the horse to gallop, so the natural bent of man is to philosophy and right conduct. As every creature most readily learns that for which it is created, therefore will Man, with but slight effort, be brought to follow that to which Nature has given him so strong an instinct, viz. excellence, *but on one condition*: that Nature be reinforced by the wise energy of the Educator.

11: The Three Factors in Individual Progress: Nature, Method, Practice. 496 E-497 A.

Can anything be more deplorable than to have to admit that, whilst an unreasoning animal performs by instinct its duty towards its offspring, Man, the creature of Reason, is blind to what he owes to Nature, to parental responsibility, and to God? But I will now consider definitely the three conditions which determine individual progress. They are Nature, Training and Practice. By *Nature,* I mean, partly, innate capacity for being trained, partly, native bent towards excellence. By *Training,* I mean the skilled application of instruction and guidance. By *Practice,* the free exercise on our own part of that activity which has been implanted by Nature and is furthered by Training. Nature without skilled Training must be imperfect, and Practice without the method which Training supplies leads to hopeless confusion.

12: The Error of Those Who Think That Experience Gives All the Education That Men Need. 497 A-F.

They err, therefore, who affirm that wisdom is won by handling affairs and by contact with life, without aid from the teaching of philosophy.

Tell me, can a man run his best in the dark? Or, can a gladiator conquer if he be blindfold? The precepts of philosophy—which is knowledge applied to life—are, as it were, the eyes of the mind, and lighten us to the consciousness of what we may do and may not do. A long and manifold experience is, beyond doubt, of great profit, but only to such as by the wisdom of learning have acquired an intelligent and informed judgment. Besides, philosophy teaches us more in one year than our own individual experience can teach us in thirty, and its teaching carries none of the risks which the method of learning by experience of necessity brings with it. For example, you educate your son to the mystery of medicine. Do you allow him to rely on the method of "experience" in order that he may learn to distinguish between poisons and healing drugs? Or, do you send him to the treatises? It is an unhappy education which teaches the master mariner the rudiments of navigation by shipwrecks: or the Prince the true way of kingship by revolutions, invasions or slaughter. Is it not the wise part to learn beforehand how to avoid mischiefs rather than with the pains of experience to remedy them? Thus Philip of Macedon put his son Alexander to school with Aristotle that he might learn philosophy of him, to the end that when a king he should be saved from doing things which must be repented of. Thus education shews us in brief what we should follow, what avoid; she does not wait till we have suffered the evil results of our mistakes, but warns us in advance against courses which will lead to failure and misery. Let us, therefore, firmly knit up this threefold cord: let Nature be by Training guided to wise ends, let Nature and Training, thus united, be made perfect by right Practice.

When we observe animal life, we notice that each creature learns, first of all, to perform those things which preserve life and to avoid those things which make for pain and destruction. This is true not less of plants, as we can see when we contrast the close-knit tree of the exposed sea-coast and its fellow spreading luxuriantly in warmth and shelter. All living things strive to develop according to their proper nature. What is the proper nature of Man? Surely it is to live the life of Reason, for reason is the peculiar prerogative of man. And what is it that in man makes for pain and destruction? Surely it is Folly, which is life without reason. It is, then, certain that desire for excellence and aversion to folly come readily to man if only his nature, as yet empty of content, be from the outset of life filled with right activities. Yet we hear extravagant complaints "how prone is child-nature to wrong, how hard to win to excellence." But herein men accuse nature unjustly. Parents themselves are to blame in taking little heed for that which the child imbibes in his early years.

13: The Importance of Choosing Aright the Child's First Master: Obstacles Arising from Ignorance, Indifference, Parsimony. 497F-498 E.

I affirm that at the present day three grave mistakes are rife in respect of the first stage of education. Either, there is no education at all: or it is begun too late: or it is entrusted to wrong hands.

With the first of these I have already dealt, and have proved that fathers guilty of this neglect are no fathers at all. And I have shewn that the second error is only less perilous. It remains now to discuss the third. Parents fall into the mistake of making a wrong choice of teacher through ignorance, or rather, perhaps, indifference. A man would not plead that he does not know what kind of man has charge of his stud, or his farm; but he seems content to know nothing about the man who has charge of a far more precious possession, his own son. He will shew much sense in ordering the several duties of his servants. The bailiff, the house-steward, the cook, are chosen with much discretion. The son of the house, on the other hand, is turned over to some dullard or idler, who is regarded as useless for a more serious task. And then people talk about "Nature's fault"!

Or take the case of a father who grudges the pay of a decent tutor, whom he puts off with a lower wage than he gives his groom. Yet the same niggard will spend a fortune upon banquets and wine, upon play, jesters and his mistress. "The cheapest thing going to-day," says the Satirist, "is education." "I pay my cook," said Crates ironically, "four pounds a year; but a philosopher can be hired for about sixpence, and a tutor for three half-pence." So to-day a man stands aghast at the thought of paying for his boy's education a sum which would buy a foal or hire a farm servant. At a single feast and the dicing that follows he will lose two hundred pounds, but he complains of extravagance if his son's education cost him twenty. Frugality? Yes, by all means: but in this matter of all others frugality is no economy; it is another name for madness.

Again, there are those who are ready to consider well the choice of a master, but are ready to select a man merely to oblige a friend. The suitable man is rejected; the incompetent person fixed upon; easy compliance, lacking any sense of responsibility, decides it all. This is the indifference I spoke of; but it is more, it is outrageous folly. For, after all, it is not only a question of the boy himself, but of his parents, his house, nay, of the commonwealth itself to which he will belong.

14: The Nursling. 498 E-499 A.

The child's *nature*, as we have said before, is the primitive endowment with which he is born, which human purpose can do nothing to determine in advance. Still there may be some qualification to this. For instance, it imports much in regard to the child that the father have chosen a wife of sound health and of good stock, with wholesome and virtuous habits. The links that bind together mind and body are so close that it cannot be but that the physical nature affects the spiritual. Again, as the child reflects the disposition of its parents, let them observe moderation in appetites and keep strict guard over themselves that they should be temperate, not given to anger; the father sober, the mother, especially during the months preceding the child's birth, of good conscience and free from anxieties. Further, it will be good for the child that it be nursed by the mother; should necessity arise for a foster-mother, she must be strong and of right disposition. Neglect in this respect may have enduring results for harm, physical and moral. For it is at this period that education truly begins; not, as some would have it, at the seventh year—or the seventeenth!

15: The Tutor and His Relation to the Parents. 499 A-C.

But the most important of the forces that mould the development of the child is the influence of the tutor. In choosing him we cannot show too great diligence, enquire too carefully, or apply too rigorous tests. The right person once secured, we are not to conclude that all is done. Two cautions, indeed, seem necessary. First, that masters, like doctors, must not be changed except for serious cause. The repeated beginnings-afresh are as the weaving and unweaving of Penelope's web. I have known children who have, by the folly of their parents, had as many as a dozen masters before they were as many years of age. Secondly, the responsibility of parents for the education of their children in no way ceases with the appointment of the master. Let the father often visit the schoolroom and note the progress made. Amongst the virtues praised in Aemilius Paulus this is recorded, that as often as his duties to the State allowed he would be present at the lessons of his sons. This was also the custom of Pliny. I speak, however, now of young children: as they grow up it is wiser to remove them somewhat more from their parents' eye.

16: Individuality of the Child; Its Recognition by the Teacher; Its Importance in Determining the Choice of Subjects to Be Taught. 499 c-500 A.

By the *nature* of a man we mean, as a rule, that which is common to Man as such: the characteristic, namely, of being guided by Reason.

But we may mean something less broad than this: the characteristic peculiar to each personality, which we may call *individuality*. Thus one child may shew a native bent to Mathematics, another to Divinity, another to Rhetoric, or Poetry, another to War. So strongly disposed are certain types of mind to certain studies that they cannot be won to others; the very attempt in that direction sets up a positive repulsion. I was once very intimate with a student, who, having attained a high level in Greek and Latin scholarship, and in some other of the liberal arts, was sent by his patron the Archbishop to the University ot study Law. But this discipline he found wholly repugnant to his nature. "I am," he told me, "so averse to the Law that when I force myself to its study I feel as if a sword were being driven through my heart." Minds of that strong determination ought not to be forced against their instinct; it is almost as though we should train a cow to box or a donkey to play the violin.

The Master will be wise to observe such natural inclination, such individuality, in the early stages of child life, since we learn most easily the things which conform to it. It is not, I believe, a vain thing to try and infer from the face and bearing of a boy what disposition he will show. Nature has not omitted to give us marks for our guidance in this respect. Aristotle wrote a work on physiognomy; and Vergil bids us recognise the differences which distinguish one type of cattle from another in regard to the uses to which we may put them. However, I am personally of opinion that where the method is sound, where teaching and practice go hand in hand, any discipline may ordinarily be acquired by the flexible intellect of man. What, indeed, should be beyond his powers when, as we are told, an elephant has been trained to walk a tight-rope?

17: The Effects of Training upon Nature in Human Beings Are Certain and Are Far-Reaching. 500 A-501 A.

Making all allowance, however, for the factor of nature in education, which is, as we said, self-determined, it is not questioned that the other two, Training and Practice, are under human control. Training, or Reason brought to bear upon Nature, implies capacity for learning; practice, readiness to self-exertion. "But," it is asked, "can you begin Education at an age when capacity for learning has not yet developed, and when continuous exertion cannot be expected?" My reply to this is that children are universally taught manners and conduct at the same age; and this implies capacity for effort and for learning. A rudimentary capacity, I admit: but we are only considering rudiments of Letters and of philosophy, or of morals and duty. Animals are trained by degrees according to their powers, and so should children be inured slowly to study. Nature has implanted in the young an ability of their own. It is not for them, I allow, to learn the *Ethics* of Aristotle or the *Epistles* of St. Paul. But if, for instance, you correct their manners at table, they obey and amend; when they go to church they learn to bend the knee and to bear themselves reverently. Such rudiments of modesty and piety the child acquires before he can speak properly, and, thus early learnt, they abide in mind and habit until, as the boy grows older, they form a living part of his higher nature. Notice Nature's teaching. We see how at first the newly-born child knows no difference between his parents and strangers. By degrees he distinguishes his mother, then his father. Respect, obedience, affection follow. From his parents he learns to repress anger and vindictiveness, to make up a quarrel with a kiss; he learns to listen without chattering; to rise in the presence of his elders; to lift his cap as he passes a Calvary. Thus it is established that what is poured into our nature, so to say, in our earliest years becomes an integral part of us. Hence the error, the grave error, of the opinion which maintains that the halting steps of the child avail nothing to the progress of the boy. "It is always best to use the best," even from the very first. For that habit will endure longest which you impart whilst the nature is yet tender, void, and eager to imitate the actions of others. Clay, perhaps, may be sometimes made too moist to retain the mould impressed upon it; but I doubt if there be any period of a child's progress when he is too young to learn. "No age," said Seneca, "is too late for learning." Perhaps. But it is my conviction that no age is too *early*, in respect, that is, of that knowledge which Nature has fittingly prescribed for it. By which I mean, that nature has planted in the youngest child an ape-like instinct of imitation and a delight in activity. From this quality springs his first capacity for learning. Hence as soon as he is born the child may be trained in conduct; and as soon as he can talk he may by virtue of the same imitative instinct be trained in speech and letters. Now note this analogy. As in the nursling action anticipates speech, so throughout life conduct takes the prior place, and learning and the liberal arts must prove themselves her hand-maidens, lest erudition haply work ill rather than good to him who pursues it.

18: The Age at Which Instruction Should Begin to Be Considered.
501 A-C.

The opinion is widely held that children should not be set to learn till they are seven years of age. Hesiod is said to have been the author of this view, but even if that be true, I should not follow him against my own judgment. It is probable, however, that this contention implies no more than this, that the laborious side of studies, such as learning by heart, repetition, long written exercises, should be avoided as far as possible in early education. If figures are to be mentioned at all, we may remember that Chrysippus judges the first *three* years to be the province of the nurse, during which period the child should imbibe right habits and lay the foundations for that edifice of character and learning which will be raised later. And I freely allow that this stage of home education is of profound importance.

19: Right Expression as the Main End of Early Instruction, and Its Importance for Subsequent Progress. 501 C-503 B.

The aim of instruction at the first stage should be to teach children to speak clearly and accurately, a matter in which both parent and nurse share the responsibility. Language, indeed, is not simply an end in itself, as we see when we reflect that through its neglect whole disciplines have been lost, or, at least, corrupted. Think what Theology, Medicine and Law have lost from this cause. Upon the question of early training in expression, Cicero tells us that those famous orators, the Gracchi, owed their distinction largely to Cornelia: "their first school was their mother's knee. Laelia is a similar instance, for she, like Mutia and Licinia, was brought up as a girl in an atmosphere of dignified and refined conversation. We must not forget that besides parents, tutors, serving-women, and playfellows, all have marked influence upon a child's manner of speaking. For it is in speech that the imitative instinct is specially active. We know that a German boy will pick up French unconsciously almost, but most successfully, if only he have opportunity when very young. Now if this be possible in a language which is barbarous and unformed, in which spelling never follows pronunciation, whose sounds are mere noises for which the throat of man was never framed, how much more readily should he learn the tongues of Greece and Rome? Mithridates could administer justice in two-and-twenty dialects and languages: Themistocles, when well advanced in years, learnt Persian in a twelvemonth. To what, then, may not the plastic mind and tongue of a boy attain? For the learning of a language is partly, as we have suggested, a matter of *imitation*; and it is partly a matter of *memory*. It is as instinctive with children to imitate as it is easy for them to remember; while to a man of my age it is difficult to recall exactly a fact read two days ago. How few people do we meet who have been able to learn a new language, especially in respect of accent, in middle life! Cato the elder may be quoted as one of these; but his namesake of Utica is a far more trustworthy pattern for us, as he was the more learned and eloquent of the two, and he was taught Greek from the cradle.

20: The Importance of This Early Training Ought to Lead Parents to Ask Themselves How Far They Can Follow the Example of the Ancients in Becoming Themselves the Instructors of Their Children. 502 B-503 B.

But we may not forget that children are prone to follow the allurement of the senses rather than the rule of reason; to store up in mind what is trivial or bad rather than what is of enduring worth. This fact of human nature sorely puzzled the ancient philosophers, but has its key in the Christian doctrine of Original Sin. True as this explanation is, we are not to forget the part played by faulty training, particularly in the first and most impressionable stage. Wherefore, I bid you recall how Alexander allowed that he had been unable to forget some things which he had learnt, to his hurt, from his tutor in early boyhood; and how the Romans in the days of their prime refused to yield the charge of their sons to any hired person. In those days the parents and other kinsmen taught the growing boy; for instance, it was held the truest honour to the family that as many children as possible of the name should have repute for learning. Nowadays the mark of a noble house seems to consist in exhibiting coats of arms, in giving feasts, in play and sport; and the only service which elders perform for their sons is to provide them with rich marriages. Meantime it is thought natural that as a child he should be left in charge of a man ignorant of learning and of illiberal condition. In old days careful parents trained up a slave specially fit in learning that he might act as a tutor, or they bought one already skilled. But it were wiser that the parents should qualify themselves to this task. If it be objected that time is lacking, I point to the flagrant waste of leisure in play and entertainments, and in the stupid social "duties of our station." He has but lukewarm love for his son who grudges the time for teaching him. I admit that the Romans had the great advantage of a single tongue understood universally; but, in spite of drawbacks in our own day, certain parents of distinction have undertaken the duty of training their own children. Amongst these I name Thomas More. He, although deeply occupied in affairs of the State, devoted his leisure to the instruction of his wife, his son, and his daughters, both in the uprightness of life and in the liberal studies of Greek and Latin. The common tongue of the people may be left to be picked up in the ordinary intercourse of life.

Should, however, neither parent be a suitable instructor to the child, then, I admit, we must secure the services of an able and experienced teacher. But the father should hesitate to take an untried man. In many things, perhaps, negligence may find its pardon; but here the eyes of Argus himself are wanted. There is a proverb that teaches us that in war a general may not make *two* mistakes. In planning his son's education a father dare hardly make *one*.

21: The Objection That Health Is Endangered by Close Application on the Part of the Young Child. 503 B-E.

We have to meet an argument against early training drawn from the superior importance of health. Personally I venture to regard the mental advantages gained as outweighing some slight risks in the matter of physical vigour. We are not concerned with developing athletes, but scholars and men competent to affairs, for whom we desire adequate constitutions indeed, but not the physique of a Milo. I should, certainly, always advise moderation in the amount of mental exertion demanded, but I have little patience with critics who only become anxious about the youthful constitution when education is mooted; but who are indifferent to the far more certain risks of over-feeding, late hours, and unsuitable dressing, which are the common indulgences allowed to children in the classes about whom I am here concerned. In the same way some parents profess alarm lest premature study affect the complexion or figure of their child. This is justifiable to some degree, but we ought not to think too much of such attractions in a boy. Here again evil habits, brawling, and intemperance are far more serious causes of this kind of mischief.

But if the teaching be of a wise sort the danger of harm will be wholly negligible. For the effort required will be but slight, subjects will be few, attractively taught, and adapted to the age and tastes of the scholar. Such study may hardly be distinguished from play, and is a source of enjoyment ot the child.

22: The Disposition of the Teacher. 503 E-504 A.

Seeing, then, that children in the earliest stage must be beguiled and not driven to learning, the first requisite in the Master is a gentle sympathetic manner, the second a knowledge of wise and attractive methods. Possessing these two important qualifications he will be able to win the pupil to find pleasure in his task. It is a hindrance to a boy's progress, which nothing will ever nullify, when the master succeeds in making his pupil hate learning before he is old enough to like it for its own sake. For a boy is often drawn to a subject first for his master's sake, and afterwards for its own. Learning, like many other things, wins our liking for the reason that it is offered to us by one we love. But, on the other hand, there is a type of man of manners so uncouth, of expression so forbidding, of speech so surly, that he repels even when he by no means intends it. Now men of that stamp are wholly unfit to be teachers of children; a man who loves his horse would hardly put such a man to have charge of his stable. Yet there are parents who think such a temper as I have described well adapted to breaking in the young child, thinking, perhaps, that seriousness of that sort betokens a proper gravity. Therein may lie a great error, inasmuch as that demeanour may cloak a depraved nature, which, delighting in tyranny, cows and breaks the spirit of the pupil. *Fear is of no real avail in education*: not even parents can train their children by this motive. Love must be the first influence; followed and completed by a trustful and affectionate respect, which compels obedience far more surely than dread can ever do.

23: The Evil Condition of the Schools, Especially the Private Schools, in the Present Day. 504 A-D.

What shall we say then of the type of school too common at the present time? A boy scarce four years old is sent to school to a master about whose qualifications for the work no one knows anything. Often he is a man of uncouth manners, not always sober; maybe he is an invalid, or crippled, or even mentally deficient. Anyone is good enough to put over the grammar school in popular opinion. Such a man, finding himself clothed with an unlooked for and unaccustomed authority, treats his charges as we should expect. The school is, in effect, a torture chamber; blows and shouts, sobs and howls, fill the air. Then it is wondered that the growing boy hates learning; and that in riper years he hates it still. There are parents who will send their children to learn reading and writing at a dame's school, kept by some incompetent, ill-tempered, perhaps drunken creature. Now as a general principle I should affirm that it is contrary to Nature that men should be placed under the exclusive control of women; for women are not only lacking in the necessary self-control, but when aroused are prone to extreme vindictiveness and cruelty. Nor can I personally, though few agree with me, advise parents to send their sons to school in Monasteries or in the Houses of the Brethren. For, whilst allowing the teaching Brothers to be often good, kindly men, they are usually too narrow and ignorant to be fit to educate children. The monks make a good income out of their schools, which are conducted no one knows how, and are jealously hidden away in the inner recesses of the convent. So I strongly urge: Choose for your boy a *public* school, or keep him at home.

24: Excessive Punishment the Characteristic of Worthless Schools and of Weak Teachers. 504 D-507 E.

A poor master, we are prepared to find, relies almost wholly upon fear of punishment as the motive to work. To frighten an entire class is easier than to teach one boy properly: for the latter is, and always must be, a task as serious as it is honourable. It is equally true of States: the rule which carries the respect and consent of the citizens demands higher qualities in the Prince than does the tyranny of force.

Scotsmen say that they find the French schoolmaster the most thorough-going flogger in Europe: to which the Gaul replies that, if it is true, it is because the Frenchman knows his Scot. Perhaps there is a difference in the method by which the youth of different countries needs to be handled, though for my part I consider it far more a matter of individual than of national temperament. For instance, there are natures which you will rather break than bend by flogging: whilst by kindness and wise stimulus you may do anything with them. I confess that I personally am constituted in this way. Once, my master, with whom I was really on very good terms, a man, too, who had formed a flattering idea of my capacities, conceived a wish to try how far I could stand the test of a very severe discipline. So, watching his opportunity, he charged me with some offence that I had not even dreamt of committing, and thrashed me. Now, that piece of tyranny then and there annihilated in me all further interest in learning, and so dejected, so broken was I, that I gradually fell into a low feverish state. So when my master—no fool and not a bad man at heart, as I have said—realised what he had done, he came forward and admitted his mistake. "I nearly succeeded in ruining his disposition before I had learnt to understand it," he said. But his repentance came too late to alter the consequences, so far as my attitude to him was concerned.

Do schoolmasters consider how many earnest, studious natures have been by treatment of this type—the hangman type—crushed into indifference? Masters who are conscious of their own incompetence are generally the worst floggers. What else, indeed, can they do? They cannot teach, so they beat. By degrees it becomes a positive pleasure to them to torture, especially when they are self-indulgent men, or slothful or cruel by nature.

I know particularly well a certain Churchman of great distinction who selected the masters of his school from amongst the more accomplished wielders of the birch. Flogging, in his educational doctrine, was the prime instrument for "softening and purifying" boys' natures. It was his practice when the mid-day meal was over to order one or other of the boys to be brought out and cruelly thrashed: the innocence or guilt of the boy was not in question. I was present on one occasion when he had before him a lad of about ten years of age, only just admitted to the school. My churchman proceeded to tell us that the boy had been carefully brought up, and had been specially commended to his charge by his mother. A wholly groundless complaint was laid against him. The birch was thereupon handed to the wretched ministrant charged with this duty, who so lost all self-control in his task that the churchman himself had to call halt. The boy swooned away. Then said the divine: "The lad, of course, has done nothing to deserve all this, but it is necessary to curb his spirit by wholesome discipline." But who would dream of training a horse or a slave after this fashion? By patience and kindliness, and not by violence, men tame the lion's whelp and the young elephant. No beast is so wild but that it may be subdued by gentle handling, and none so tame but that cruelty will rouse it to anger.

It is, indeed, the mark of the servile nature to be drilled by fear; why then do we suffer children (whose very name imports free men, "liberi"—those born fit for a "liberal" training—), to be treated as slaves might be? Yet even slaves, who are men like the rest of us, are by wise masters freed from something of their servile state by humane control. Let a father stand towards his son in a more kindly relation than that of a master to his serfs. If we put away tyrants from their thrones, why do we erect a new tyranny for our own sons? Is it not meet that Christian peoples cast forth from their midst the whole doctrine of slavery in all its forms? Paul shews us that a slave is a "dear brother"; and that all Christian believers, whether bond or free, are fellow-servants to one Lord. In speaking of parents as regards their children the Apostle warns them that they "provoke not their children to wrath, but bring them up in the chastening and admonition of the Lord." And what the "chastening" of the Lord Jesus should imply, he may readily perceive who considers with what gentleness, forgiveness, affection, He trained, cherished, and bore with, his own disciples. Contrast with this the story of Auxon, a Roman knight, who for cruelty towards his own son was dragged by the crowd into the Forum, fiercely handled, and with difficulty rescued with his life. I fear that there be many Auxons living still. I could tell you certain stories of wicked cruelty by schoolmasters which it is hard to believe, but for which I vouch my own personal knowledge. In one case in especial, where foul torture was employed, the child, whom I knew,—he was twelve years of age—very nearly died from the ill-usage. He was the innocent victim of some prank played by a school-fellow, who was a favourite with the master, an incompetent and worthless creature, and, therefore, given to violent floggings to enforce his authority. I can only say that hanging the luckless child up by the arms and flogging him as he hung till the brutal master was too tired to go on, was the least disgusting part of the punishment. The Scythians or Phrygians of old were less inhuman. Once more, I cannot forget the rough horse-play which awaited every newly-arrived student at my old College. The brutality of it and the intolerable torments devised by the youthful wits I do not care to particularise. Risks of permanent bodily injury were constantly experienced: and the ceremony ended in a noisy carouse. It was an "initiation," forsooth, into a course of training in the liberal arts: it was naturally well-adapted to turn out the flogging masters whom I have just described. The worst of it was that the authorities winked at the scandal; it was "the tradition," and it was, therefore, "unwise to interfere," and so on. As though the fact that an evil tradition is deep-rooted in the past does not make the stronger call upon sensible men for its abolition. Should not they who pursue the studies we term "liberal" cultivate a type of humour also to match?

25: The Permissible Instruments of Discipline. 507 E-508 D.

Teaching by beating, therefore, is not a liberal education. Nor should the schoolmaster indulge in too strong and too frequent *language* of blame. Medicine constantly repeated loses its force. You may quote against me the old proverb: "He that spareth the rod hateth his own son." Well, perhaps, that my have been true of Jews. But I do not accept it as true for Christians to-day. If we are to "bow the necks" and "chastise," as we are bidden to do, let us see to it that the rod we use is the word of guidance or of rebuke, such as a free man may obey, that our discipline be of kindness and not of vindictiveness. Lycon, the philosopher, sets forward these two spurs to industry: shame, and desire for praise. Shame is the fear of just reproach; by praise a boy is quickened to excel in all he does. Let these, then, be the schoolmaster's weapons to-day. And I can add another: "unwearied pains conquer all things," says the poet. Let us watch, let us encourage, let us press and yet again press, that by learning, by repeating, by diligent listening, the boy may feel himself carried onward towards his goal. Let him learn to respect and to love integrity and knowledge, to hate ignorance and dishonour. Bid him regard those who are lauded for their virtues, be warned by those who are denounced for their ill-doing. Set before him the example of men to whom learning has brought high praise, dignity, repute and position. Warn him of the fate of those who by the neglect of high wisdom have sunk into contempt, poverty, disgrace and evil life. These are your instruments of discipline, my Christian teacher, worthy of your calling and of your flock. But should none of these avail, then, if it must be so, let the rod be used with due regard to self-respect in the manner of it. But I am, at heart, with Quintilian in deprecating flogging under any conditions. If then you ask, "What is to be done with boys who respond to no other spur?" My answer is: "What would you do if an ox or an ass strayed into your school-room?" Turn him out to the plough or the pack-saddle, no doubt. Well, so there are boys good only for the farm and manual toil: send your dunces there for their own good. "Yes," says the master, "but I want my fees." There I cannot help you: your duty is to the boy. But I fear that this matter of profit lies at the root of the whole matter.

26: The Provision of Fit Teachers of Youth Is a National Duty in Which Both Church and State Should Share the Joint Responsibility. 508 D-E.

The ancients drew the ideal of the wise man and of the Orator—types never realised in fact. So it is easier to outline the ideal schoolmaster than to find him in reality. Which brings me to claim it as a duty incumbent on Statesmen and Churchmen alike to provide that there be a due supply of men qualified to educate the youth of the nation. It is a public obligation in no way inferior, say, to the ordering of the army. Vespasian is an example, in that out of his Treasury he maintained Greek and Latin teachers; and the younger Pliny of his private fortune did the same. And if the community be backward in this respect, yet should every head of a household do all that he can to provide for the education of his own.

Now you may rejoin, that men of poor station, whose efforts are absorbed in nurturing their families, can do nothing for them besides. I have nothing to say except this: "We must do as we may, when we cannot do as we would." But the liberality of the rich can be most wisely exercised here, in enabling innate powers to attain their due development by removing the hindrance imposed by poverty.

27: The Qualities Desirable in a Good Master. 508 E-509 B.

Although I have urged the need of gentleness, let it not decline into unwise familiarity towards the pupil; a degree of formal authority must be maintained, such as marked the relation of Sarpedon towards the young Cato, who rendered his master great affection and equal reverence. What would the master do who can only teach by flogging, if he were set up as tutor in a royal household, where no such discipline is for a moment allowed? "Oh," he rejoins, "such pupils are not of the common order." "How then? Are not the children of a citizen men? Do not citizens love their sons no less than kings?" If they be poor men, the more need have they of learning in order to minister to their deficiency; if they be rich, in order to learn to govern their wealth aright. Not a few born in low estate are called to high station, as to Bishoprics. All men do not rise to so great distinction, yet ought all to gain by right education the opportunity of so rising. Now I have said enough of that evil class of schoolmaster which only knows how to beat: but I cannot too seriously deplore that the scandal is in our day so widely spread.

28: The Need of Sympathy in One Who Shall Teach Young Children. 509 B-F.

It is the mark of a good teacher to stand towards his charge somewhat in the relation of a parent: both learning and teaching are made easier thereby. He will also in a sense become a boy again that he may draw his pupil to himself. Though this by no means justifies the choice of the old and infirm as teachers of youth: these indeed have no need to stimulate a childish temper, they are only too truly once more in their second infancy. Rather should the master be in the full vigour of early manhood, able to sympathise naturally with youth, ready to adapt himself to its demands. He will follow in his first instruction the methods of the mother in the earliest training of her nursling. As she prattles baby language, stirs and softens baby food, stoops and guides the tottering steps—so will the master act in things of the mind. Slowly is the transition made to walking alone, or to eating solid food; the tender frame is thus carefully hardened. In exactly the same manner instruction is at first simple, taught by way of play, taught by degrees. The sense of effort is lost in the pleasure of such natural exercise: insensibly the mind becomes equal to harder tasks. Wholly wrong are those masters who expect their little pupils to act as though they were but diminutive adults, who forget the meaning of *youth*, who have no standard of what can be done or be understood except that of their own minds. Such a master will upbraid, exact, punish, as though he were dealing with students as old as himself, and forgets that he was ever himself a child. Pliny warned such a one when he spoke thus to a master: "Remember that your pupil is but a youth still, and that you were once one yourself." But how often does the schoolmaster of to-day prove by his harsh discipline that he wholly forgets this simple truth!

29: What Subjects May Be Most Suitably Chosen for the First Steps in Education. 509 F-510 D.

To treat next of the matter which may be wisely taught the little child. First of all, I give the leading place to practice in spoken language, which it is so great a task for adults to accomplish. As I have already said, this is an exercise of the child's powers of imitation, which it shares with certain birds. As an aid to this study can anything be better adapted to the youthful capacity than the reading of ancient Fables? For they appeal by their romance, they are good for moral lessons, they help vocabulary. There is nothing a boy more readily listens to than an apologue of Aesop, who under cover of pleasant story teaches the youth the very essence of philosophy. You relate, again, how Circe transforms the comrades of Ulysses into swine and other animals. It is a story to rouse interest and, perhaps, amusement; but the lesson is therein driven home that men who will not yield to the guidance of reason, but follow the enticements of the senses, are no more than brute beasts. Could a stoic philosopher preach a graver truth? The poetry styled Bucolic is easy to understand; Comedy is intelligible to boys, and teaches them many deep truths of life in its lighter vein. Then it is time to teach the names of objects—a subject in which even learned men are apt to be uncertain. Lastly, short sentences containing quaint conceits, proverbs, pithy sayings, such as in ancient times were the current coin of philosophy.

But do not forget that children are not seldom seen to show a peculiar bent to particular disciplines, such as Music, Arithmetic or Geography. I have myself known young pupils who, though backward in all that concerned Grammar or Rhetoric, had much facility in these less rigid yet more recondite subjects. Nature, therefore, claims the help of the schoolmaster in carrying forward the special gifts with which she has endowed the child. By following the path which she points out the toil of learning is reduced: whilst on the other hand nothing can be well accomplished *invita Minerva.*

30: Pleasurable Methods Must Be Devised in the First Stages of Teaching. 510 D-511 C.

Progress in learning a language is much furthered if the child be brought up amongst people who are gifted talkers. Descriptions and stories are impressed the better if to good narrative power the teacher or parent can add the help of pictorial illustration. The same method can be more particularly applied to the teaching of natural objects. Names and characteristics of trees, flowers, and animals can be thus learnt: specially is this plan needful where the creature described is wholly unfamiliar to the child, as for instance the rhinoceros, the tragelaphus, the onocrotalus, the Indian ass, and the elephant. A picture is shown, containing an elephant, in combat with a dragon. At once the class shows curiosity. How shall the master proceed? He states the Greek and Latin names for elephant, giving the Latin genitive case as well.

He then points to the trunk, giving the Greek and Latin for it, and the purpose of the organ: he will explain that the elephant breathes as well as feeds by its means. The tusks are next dealt with, the uses and rarity of ivory; if possible he will produce something made of it. The dragon is shown to be of the large Indian species. He states the Greek and Latin equivalents for "dragon," their similarity in form, and their feminines. He will instil the fact that between the dragon and the elephant there is, instinctively and constantly, a ruthless war. If any boy is keen for further knowledge in the subject, the Master will add many other facts concerning the nature and habits of these two great beasts. Boys, too, will generally be attracted by pictures of hunting scenes, through which a wealth of information about trees, plants, birds, and animals may be imparted in a most delightful and yet instructive manner. In choosing subject-matter of this kind it is desirable to take some pains to discuss what is naturally attractive to the youthful mind, and discard what is of too advanced a kind. Remember always that youth is the springtime of life, when harvests are sown and flowers bloom. But autumn is the season for ripe fruits and laden wains. Hence, as only folly will look for purple grapes in May, so no Master who understands his task will demand the tastes and powers of maturity from the growing child. Brightness, attractiveness, these make the only appeals to a boy in the field of learning. Is not this why the ancients fabled the Muses to be comely maidens, given to the song and the dance, and companions to the Graces? It was their doctrine also that excellence in true learning was only to be attained by those who find pleasure in its pursuit; and for this cause the liberal arts were by them called "Humanitas."

Yet there is no reason why in this early stage of education utility should not go hand in hand with delight. On the method which I have here sketched nothing hinders that a boy learn a pretty story from the ancient poets, or a memorable tale from history, just as readily as the stupid and vulgar ballad, or the old wives' fairy rubbish such as most children are steeped in nowadays by nurses and serving women. Who can think without shame of the precious time and energy squandered in listening to ridiculous riddles, stories of dreams, of ghosts, witches, fairies, demons; of foolish tales drawn from popular annals; worthless, nay, mischievous stuff of the kind which is poured into children in their nursery days?

31: The Work of Educating the Young Is a Part of the Service We Owe to God. 511 C-D.

"Granting your contention"—so it may be said—"that we should sweep away this rubbish and place education of the very young on a higher plane, who will consent to stoop to this trying task?" "Well," I reply, "Aristotle, Cheiron, Eli, are examples to my hand. I only ask for the same kind of effort that people are willing to bestow upon training a parrot to talk." What of the pious folk who will make long and dangerous pilgrimages and perform exacting penances to please the Deity? And yet can any duty be more agreeable to God than the right up-bringing of the young? No gloom, no self-mortification, no exhausting effort is demanded in this service: diligence, patience, a cheerful demeanour, will accomplish all. Nay, the very shadow of harsh, exacting toil and compulsion should be banished from the field.

32: Methods of Early Instruction Again Touched upon 511 D-512 E.

Ability to speak is easily learned by use. Next come the arts of reading and writing, where the skill of the teacher can do much to lighten the monotony of learning. Much time is commonly wasted in teaching the child to know his letters and to pronounce words, which could be spent on more important matters to far greater profit. Reading, indeed, should be attacked on methods practised in Roman schools. Letters were made in biscuit form and when learnt were allowed to be eaten. Ivory letters were used, by means of which words were composed by the scholar. And other devices could be employed. In England I heard of a father who taught his boy to aim with bow and arrow at Greek or Roman letters painted on a target; a hit meant a cherry for the archer. This could be carried out as a competition in a class of boys: for as it was, the boy learnt all his letters, their names and sounds, in a few days instead of as many months.

I would not, however, encourage learning by games of chess or dice; nor any devices whose complexity is such that the "aid" costs more to learn than the subject itself. There are machines so intricate that they hinder work rather than shorten it. Amongst the devices I have in mind is the whole class of mnemonic puzzles, put forth merely for their ingenuity, or as a means of making money. Believe me, there is only one sound mnemonic art, and it has three rules: understand, arrange, repeat.

A clever Teacher will utilise the motive of emulation amongst children; for this will often be found effective with boys who will not respond to warnings, to encouragement, or to the offer of rewards. Now the award of the prize must by no means preclude the losers from the chances of proving themselves winners later on: and there may be circumstances under which the master will be wise in granting the first place to one who is not ahead in actual attainment. The due alternation of praise and blame will often provoke keenness. Should you reply that a master may be unwilling to take these pains to adapt his teaching to the youthful mind, I rejoin that, in such case, he is in my judgment unfit for his work.

I allow that the first steps in Latin Grammar are not in themselves attractive to boys. But for this I blame, not a little, the lack of judgment in the master. He should confine his teaching to the things that matter. But as a rule the young beginner is worried, let us say, about the names of the letters, before he knows one of them by sight, or about the case of "Musae," or the tense of "legeris," before he has learnt his accidence. And what beatings are apt to follow failure! Again, a shallow mind will, in order to parade its thin layer of knowledge before the class, import wholly unnecessary difficulty into a lesson; this happens especially in teaching Logic. They are ways by which the rudiments are made harder than they need be. No doubt I shall be told, "I had to learn Latin in this manner when I was a boy; what was good enough for me must do for him."

33: Difficulties Should Be Attacked Patiently. 512 E.-513 A.

My principles of method then are briefly these. First, do not hurry, for learning comes easily when the proper stage is reached. Second, avoid a difficulty which can be safely ignored or at least postponed. Third, when the difficulty *must* be handled, make the boy's approach to it as gradual and as interesting as you can. Lucretius tells us that doctors used to sweeten the rim of the medicine glass with honey. We know that imagination often magnifies a difficulty in life. So in teaching, lead the beginner to face his unfamiliar matter with self-confidence, to attack it slowly but with persistence. We must not under-rate the capacity of youth to respond to suitable demands upon the intelligence. Youth indeed lacks that sheer force which marks the bull, but on the other hand Nature has given it something of the tenacity and industry of the ant. The child, like every other creature, excels in the precise activity which belongs to it. How else could he race about for hours and not be tired? But such exercise is instinctive, it is play to him, there is no sense of toil about it, no compulsion. Follow Nature, therefore, in this, and so far as is possible take from the work of the school all that implies toilsomeness, and strive to give to learning the quality of freedom and of enjoyment. Systematic games must be encouraged as a needful relaxation when boys reach the higher stages of their subject, and can no longer postpone close application and hard work. Such subjects are Greek composition, Latin composition from the Greek, and cosmography. But I would say that no aid to progress is more effectual

than are the boy's reverent affection for his master, his love of learning,
and his ambition to rank with the best.

34: The Argument That the Educational Result Attainable during These Early Years Does Not Justify the Trouble or Expense Involved. 513 A-514 A.

The contention that the time and the outlay involved in this early
education are wasted is unworthy of anyone who realises what true
fatherhood implies. Grant, with Quintilian, that the boy may acquire
in one year after he has passed his fifth birthday as much as he can
during the whole of the previous years, is that a reason for sacrificing
what you admit to be equivalent to the harvest of a twelvemonth? Nor
is the alternative merely that the boy may learn nothing; for he will
undoubtedly be learning that which he must later unlearn. The training
which I propose will serve to interest and occupy the growing child from
the time when he can understand and be understood. The youthful
mind is ever acquiring something—good or evil. The progress made,
slight as it may be, is a saving of labour at a later stage, when the entire
time and energy of the pupil are set free, as Quintilian says, for work
of greater difficulty. Need I repeat what has been said concerning the
aptitude of early childhood to some studies? I cannot, indeed, allow
that it is a trivial gain that a child should win acquaintance with two
languages, and learn to read and write. A merchant is far from despising
the day of small things; he knows that "little" is the necessary beginning
of "much."

Can we, in fact, afford to throw away four years of our children's
lives, when we know that the two hardest things to overtake in this
world are time lost and learning neglected? We can never be said to
begin too soon a task which we can never live to finish: for a man
may cease to learn only when he ceases to live. In all other departments
of life we may succeed in recovering what we have lost by neglect. Time,
however, when once it has flown by—and it flies very quickly—obeys
no summons to return. There is no such miracle as a fountain of
perpetual youth: no physic which can make old men young again. Of
time, then, let us always be sparing; of youthful years most of all,
for this is the best part of man's life, the most profitable, if it be rightly
guarded. No farmer will see his land lying fallow, not even a little
field, but he will sow it with young grasses, or lay it down to pasture,
or use it as a graden. And shall we suffer the best part of our life to pass
without any fruit of wisdom? Land, as we know, when newly ploughed
up must be sown with some crop, lest it bear a harvest of weed. So
the tender mind, unless it be forthwith sown with true instruction, will
harbour evil seeds. The child grows up either to goodness or to

unworthiness: if the latter, there is the hard task of up-rooting. The child has gained no small thing who has escaped evil. See, then, how in various ways it profits that he be early brought up in learning.

35: Examples of the Proficiency of Youth and Its Importance for Later Life. 514 A-E.

But is there need to labour this? How steeped in learning from their very infancy were men of old time! How helpless are their successors to-day! Ovid and Lucan composed not a little of their poetry in their youth: who can now boast the same? Lucan when but six months old was brought to Rome and was soon after placed under the two best taachers of Grammar in the city. For companions he had Bassus and Persius: the former a historian, the latter the famous satirist. No doubt we have here the secret of that notable learning and eloquence, whereby Lucan is distinguished as the typical oratorical poet of ancient Rome. In modern days how rare are examples of similar distinction! Poliziano has celebrated the erudition of Cassandra: and in a letter of elegant Latinity has recorded the genius of the boy Orsini, who at the age of eleven could dictate two Latin letters at once, letters which in composition and scholarly diction struck scholars with admiration. This experiment he on one occasion repeated five times, a feat which some observers ascribed to witchcraft. Well, I will allow this explanation, if by it you mean the "enchantment" that is worked by setting the boy from earliest childhood to work under the example and stimulus of a learned, sincere, and conscientious Master.

By such "enchantments" Alexander of Macedon shewed himself master alike of eloquence and of philosophy; in which indeed he might have attained great distinction had he not been lured away by ambition and by passionate ardour for war. By the same arts Julius Caesar became proficient in oratory and in the mathematical disciplines. Cicero, Vergil, and Horace, not a few of the earlier Emperors, became men of approved learning and of classic style, by reason of the diligent use they were led to make of their early years. For they were taught by their parents from the very nursery the art of refined speech, and were afterwards passed on to masters by whom they were grounded in the liberal arts, in Poetry, rhetoric, History, Antiquity; in Arithmetic; in Geography, and in Philosophy, both moral and political.

36: The Sad Condition of Teaching and of Schools in Modern Days. 514 E-516 A.

What a contrast when we look around to-day! We see boys kept at home in idleness and self-indulgence until they are fourteen or fifteen years of age. They are then sent to some school or other. There, if they are lucky, they gain some touch of Grammar, the simpler inflections, the agreement of noun and adjective. They are then supposed to "know" Latin, and are put on to some terrible text in Logic, which will spoil what little good Latin accidence or syntax they have acquired. My own childhood was tortured by logical subtleties which had no reference to anything that was true in fact or sound in expression. Not a few Masters postponed Grammar to Logic and Metaphysic, but found that they had to revert to the rudiments of Latin when their pupils were fast growing up. Great heavens, what a time was that when with vast pretension the verses of John Garland, eked out with amazing commentary, were dictated to the class, learnt by heart, and said as repetition! When Florista and the Floretus were set as lessons! Alexander de Villa Dei, compared with such a crowd, is worthy of positive commendation. Again, how much time was spent in sophistries and vain mazes of logic! Further, as to the manner of teaching, what confused methods, what needless toil, characterised instruction! How common it was for a master, for mere display, to cram his lesson with irrelevant matter, wise or foolish, but all equally out of place! All this made for needless difficulty; for there is no virtue in *difficulty*, as such, in instruction. And even to-day schoolmasters are not seldom men of no learning at all, or, what is worse, of no character. They have taken to teaching as a means to a life of ease and money-making. If this has been, and is, the true state of education in our schools, no wonder that learning perishes amongst us. The critical years of a boy's life are allowed to run to waste; he acquires the habit, which cannot be cured, of giving but a fraction of his time and thought to serious pursuits, the rest he squanders on vulgar pleasures. The parent looks on and does nothing. And yet we hear talk of the "tender youth," "undeveloped capacity," "meagre results,"—all so many excuses for wicked neglect of the child in his early years!

37: Conclusion. 516 A.

Now I have done. I make my appeal to that practical wisdom which you have always exhibited in affairs. Consider how dear a possession is your son; how many-sided is learning; how exacting its pursuit, and how honourable! Think how instinctive is the child's wish to learn, how plastic his mind, how responsive to judicious training, if only he be entrusted to instructors at once sympathetic and skilled to ease the first steps in knowledge. Let me recall to you the durability of early impressions, made upon the unformed mind, as compared with those acquired in later life. You know also how hard it is to overtake time lost; how wise, in all things, to begin our tasks in season; how great is the power of *persistence* in accumulating what we prize; how fleeting a thing is the life of man, how busy is youth, how inapt for learning is age. In face, then, of all these serious facts you will not suffer, I do not say seven years, but three days even, of your son's life to pass, before you take into earnest consideration his nurture and future education.

From the *De Conscribendis Epistolis*

What follows includes the introduction by William Harrison Woodward and then each of the sections describing *How to Master a Passage from a Classical Author*, omitting the Latin reprinted by Woodward on pp. 223-226.

The following passage forms one of the model letters comprised in the treatise on *Epistolary Composition*. It is inserted here in the original as a good specimen of Erasmian Latin of the later period (1522).

The advice has primary reference to private study, but it is obviously equally applicable to class work. It should be read in conjunction with the section above on *The Method of reading an Author*, and with the *De Ratione Studii*.

Qui Sit Modus Repetendae Lectionis, that is, *How to Master a Passage from a Classical Author. Op. i. 447*

1. It is a mistake to begin by learning the passage by heart.

2. A first reading should aim merely at securing the general sense of the passage.

3. A second reading is concerned with grammatical structure and word-forms.

4. A third reading is devoted to analysis of the rhetorical artifice displayed.

5. A fourth reading notes the uses which the passage admits of for practical, and especially moral, application.

6. The passage thus thoroughly understood will need little effort to commit it to memory, should that be desired.

7. Discussion is useful as aid to establishing or revising your interpretation and your criticisms.

38

The Reformation
Martin Luther (1483-1546)

Selections from Luther's *Letter to the Mayors and Aldermen of All the Cities of Germany in Behalf of Christian Schools* (1524) in F. V. N. Painter, *Great Pedagogical Essays Plato to Spencer* (New York: American Book Company, Copyright 1905 by F. V. N. Painter), pp. 171-186. Reprinted by permission of Van Nostrand Reinhold Company.

First of all, we see how the schools are deteriorating throughout Germany. The universities are becoming weak, the monasteries are declining, and, as Isaiah says, "The grass withereth, the flower fadeth, because the spirit of the Lord bloweth upon it," through the Gospel. For through the word of God the unchristian and sensual character of these institutions is becoming known. And because selfish parents see that they can no longer place their children upon the bounty of monasteries and cathedrals, they refuse to educate them. "Why should we educate our children," they say, "if they are not to become priests, monks, and nuns, and thus earn a support?"

The hollow piety and selfish aims of such persons are sufficiently evident from their own confession. For if they sought anything more than the temporal welfare of their children in monasteries and the priesthood, if they were deeply in earnest to secure the salvation and blessedness of their children, they would not lose interest in education and say, "if the priestly office is abolished, we will not send our children to school." But they would speak after this manner: "If it is true, as the Gospel teaches, that such a calling is dangerous to our children, teach us another way in which they may be pleasing to God and become truly blessed; for we wish to provide not alone for the bodies of our children, but also for their souls." Such would be the language of faithful Christian parents.

It is no wonder that the devil meddles in the matter, and influences groveling hearts to neglect the children and the youth of the country. Who can blame him for it? He is the prince and god of this world, and with extreme displeasure sees the Gospel destroy his nurseries of vice, the monasteries and priesthood, in which he corrupts the young beyond measure, a work upon which his mind is especially bent. How could he consent to a proper training of the young? Truly he would be a fool if he permitted such a thing in his kingdom, and thus consented to its overthrow; which indeed would happen, if the young should escape him, and be brought up to the service of God.

Hence he acted wisely at the time when Christians were educating and bringing up their children in a Christian way. Inasmuch as the youth of the land would have escaped him thus, and inflected an irreparable injury upon his kingdom, he went to work and spread his nets, established such monasteries, schools, and orders, that it was not possible for a boy to escape him without the miraculous intervention of God. But now that he sees his snares exposed through the word of God, he takes an opposite course, and dissuades men from all education whatever. He thus pursues a wise course to maintain his kingdom and win the youth of Germany. And if he secures them, if they grow up under his influence and remain his adherents, who can gain any advantage over him? He retains an easy and peaceful mastery over the world. For any fatal wound to his cause must come through the young who, brought up in the knowledge of God, spread abroad the truth and instruct others.

Yet no one thinks of this dreadful purpose of the devil, which is being worked out so quietly that it escapes observation; and soon the evil will be so far advanced that we can do nothing to prevent it. People fear the Turks, wars, and floods, for in such matters they can see what is injurious or beneficial; but what the devil has in mind no one sees or fears. Yet where we would give a florin to defend ourselves against the Turks, we should give a hundred florins to protect us against ignorance, even if only one boy could be taught to be a truly Christian man; for the good such a man can accomplish is beyond all computation.

Therefore I beg you all, in the name of God and of your neglected youth, not to think of this subject lightly, as many do who do not see what the prince of this world intends. For the right instruction of youth is a matter in which Christ and all the world are concerned. Thereby are we all aided. And consider that great Christian zeal is needed to overcome the silent, secret, and artful machinations of the devil. If we must annually expend large sums on muskets, roads, bridges, dams, and the like, in order that the city may have temporal peace and comfort, why should we not apply as much to our poor, neglected youth, in order that we may have a skilful schoolmaster or two?

It is indeed a sin and shame that we must be aroused and incited to the duty of educating our children and of considering their highest interests, whereas nature itself should move us thereto, and the example of the heathen affords us varied instruction. There is no irrational animal that does not care for and instruct its young in what they should know, except the ostrich, of which God says, "She leaveth her eggs in the earth, and warmeth them in the dust; and is hardened against her young ones, as though they were not hers." And what would it avail if we possessed and performed all else, and became perfect saints, if we neglect that for which we chiefly live, namely, to care for the young? In my judgment there is no other outward offense that in the sight of God so heavily burdens the world, and deserves such heavy chastisement, as the neglect to educate children.

Parents neglect this duty from various causes. In the first place, there are some who are so lacking in piety and uprightness that they would not do it if they could, but, like the ostrich, harden themselves against their own offspring, and do nothing for them. In the second place, the great majority of parents are unqualified for it, and do not understand how children should be brought up and taught. In the third place, even if parents were qualified and willing to do it themselves, yet on account of other employments and household duties, they have no time for it, so that necessity requires us to have teachers for public schools, unless each parent employ a private instructor.

Therefore it will be the duty of the mayors and councils to exercise the greatest care over the young. For since the happiness, honor, and life of the city are committed to their hands, they would be held recreant before God and the world, if they did not day and night, with all their power, seek its welfare and improvement. Now the welfare of a city does not consist alone in great treasures, firm walls, beautiful houses, and munitions of war; indeed, where all these are found, and reckless fools come into power, the city sustains the greater injury. But the highest welfare, safety, and power of a city consist in able, learned, wise, upright, cultivated citizens, who can secure, preserve, and utilize every treasure and advantage.

Since, then, a city must have well-trained people, and since the greatest need, lack, and lament is that such are not to be found, we must not wait till they grow up of themselves; neither can they be hewed out of stones nor cut out of wood; nor will God work miracles, so long as men can attain their object through means within their reach. Therefore we must see to it, and spare no trouble or expense to educate and form them ourselves. For whose fault is it that in all the cities there are at present so few skillful people except the rulers, who have allowed the young to grow up like trees in the forest, and have not cared how they were reared and taught? The growth, consequently, has been so irregular that the forest furnishes no timber for building purposes, but like a useless hedge is good only for fuel.

Yet there must be civil government. For us, then, to permit ignoramuses and blockheads to rule when we can prevent it, is irrational and barbarous. Let us rather make rulers out of swine and wolves, and set them over peoples who are indifferent to the manner in which they are governed. It is barbarous for men to think thus: "We will now rule; and what does it concern us how those fare who shall come after us:" Not over human beings, but over swine and dogs should such people rule, who think only of their own interests and honor in governing. Even if we exercise the greatest care to educate able, learned, and skilled rulers, yet much care and effort are necessary in order to secure prosperity. How can a city prosper, when no effort is made?

But you say again, if we shall and must have schools, what is the use to teach Latin, Greek, Hebrew, and other liberal arts? Is it not enough to teach the Scriptures, which are necessary to salvation, in the mother tongue? To which I answer: I know, alas! that we Germans must always remain irrational brutes, as we are deservedly called by surrounding nations. But I wonder why we do not also say: of what use to us are silk, wine, spices, and other foreign articles, since we ourselves have an abundance of wine, corn, wool, flax, wood, and stone in the German states, not only for our necessities, but also for embellishment and ornament? The languages and other liberal arts, which are not only harmless, but even a greater ornament, benefit, and honor than these things, both for understanding the Holy Scriptures and carrying on the civil government, we are disposed to despise; and the foreign articles which are neither necessary nor useful, and which besides greatly impoverish us, we are unwilling to dispense with. Are we not rightly called German dunces and brutes?

Indeed, if the languages were of no practical benefit, we ought still to feel an interest in them as a wonderful gift of God, with which he has now blessed Germany almost beyond all other lands. We do not find many instances in which Satan has fostered them through the universities and cloisters; on the contrary, these institutions have fiercely inveighed and continue to inveigh against them. For the devil scented the danger that would threaten his kingdom if the languages should be generally studied. But since he could not wholly prevent their cultivation, he aims at least to confine them within such narrow limits that they will of themselves decline and fall into disuse. They are to him no welcome guest, and consequently he shows them scant courtesy in order that they may not remain long. This malicious trick of Satan is perceived by very few.

Therefore, my beloved countrymen, let us open our eyes, thank God for his precious treasure, and take pains to preserve it and to frustrate the design of Satan. For we can not deny that, although the Gospel has come and daily comes through the Holy Spirit, it has come by means of the languages, and through them must increase and be preserved. For when God wished through the apostles to spread the Gospel abroad in all the world, he gave the languages for that purpose; and by means of the Roman empire he made Latin and Greek the language of many lands, that his Gospel might speedily bear fruit far and wide. He has done the same now. For a time no one understood why God had revived the study of the languages; but now we see that it was for the sake of the Gospel, which he wished to bring to light and thereby expose and destroy the reign of Antichrist. For the same reason he gave Greece a prey to the Turks, in order that Greek scholars, driven from home and scattered abroad, might bear the Greek tongue to other countries, and thereby excite an interest in the study of languages.

And let this be kept in mind, that we shall not preserve the Gospel without the languages. The languages are the scabbard in which the word of God is sheathed. They are the casket in which this jewel is enshrined; the cask in which this wine is kept; the chamber in which this food is stored. And, to borrow a figure from the Gospel itself, they are the baskets in which this bread and fish and fragments are preserved. If through neglect we lose the languages (which may God forbid), we shall not only lose the Gospel, but it will finally come to pass that we shall lose also the ability to speak and write either Latin or German.

So much for the utility and necessity of the languages and of Christian schools for our spiritual interests and the salvation of the soul. Let us now consider the body and inquire: though there were no soul, nor heaven, nor hell, but only the civil government, would not this require good schools and learned men more than do our spiritual interests? Hitherto the Papists have taken no interest in civil government, and have conducted the schools so entirely in the interests of the priesthood, that it has become a matter of reproach for a learned man to marry, and he has been forced to hear remarks like this: "Behold, he has become a man of the world, and cares nothing for the clerical state;" just as if the priestly order were alone acceptable to God, and the secular classes, as they are called, belonged to Satan, and were unchristian. But in the sight of God, the former rather belong to Satan, while the despised masses, as happened to the people of Israel in the Babylonian captivity, remain in the land and in right relations with God.

It is not necessary to say here that civil government is a divine institution; of that I have elsewhere said so much, that I hope no one has any doubts on the subject. The question is, how are we to get able and skillful rulers? And here we are put to shame by the heathen who in ancient times, especially the Greeks and Romans, without knowing that civil government is a divine ordinance, yet instructed the boys and girls with such earnestness and industry that, when I think of it, I am ashamed of Christians, and especially of our Germans, who are such blockheads and brutes that they can say: "Pray, what is the use of schools, if one is not to become a priest?" Yet we know, or ought to know, how necessary and useful a thing it is, and how acceptable to God, when a prince, lord, counselor, or other ruler, is well-trained and skillful in discharging, in a Christian way, the functions of his office.

Even if there were no soul, as I have already said, and men did not need schools and the languages for the sake of Christianity and the Scriptures, still, for the establishment of the best schools everywhere, both for boys and girls, this consideration is of itself sufficient, namely, that society, for the maintenance of civil order and the proper regulation of the household, needs accomplished and well-trained men and women. Now such men are to come from boys, and such women from girls; hence it is necessary that boys and girls be properly taught and brought up. As I have before said, the ordinary man is not qualified for this task, and cannot and will not do it. Princes and lords ought to do it; but they spend their time in pleasure—driving, drinking, and folly, and are burdened with the weighty duties of the cellar, kitchen, and bedchamber. And though some would be glad to do it, they must stand in fear of the rest, lest they be taken for fools or heretics. Therefore, honored members of the city councils, this work must remain in your hands; you have more time and opportunity for it than princes and lords.

But each one, you say, may educate and discipline his own sons and daughters. To which I reply: we see indeed how it goes with this teaching and training. And where it is carried to the highest point, and is attended with success, it results in nothing more than that the learners, in some measure, acquire a forced external propriety of manner; in other respects they remain dunces, knowing nothing, and incapable of giving aid or advice. But were they instructed in schools or elsewhere, by thoroughly qualified male or female teachers, who taught the languages, other arts, and history, then the pupils would hear the history and maxims of the world, and see how things went with each city, kingdom, prince, man, and woman; and thus, in a short time, they would be able to comprehend, as in a mirror, the character, life, counsels, undertakings, successes, and failures, of the whole world from the beginning. From this knowledge they could regulate their views, and order their course of life in the fear of God, having become wise in judging what is to be sought and what is to be avoided in this outward life, and capable of advising and directing others. But the training which is given at home is expected to make us wise through our own experience. Before that can take place, he shall die a hundred times, and all through life act injudiciously; for much time is needed to give experience.

Now since the young must leap and jump, or have something to do, because they have a natural desire for it which should not be restrained (for it is not well to check them in everything), why should we not provide for them such schools, and lay before them such studies? By the gracious arrangement of God, children take delight in acquiring knowledge, whether languages, mathematics, or history. And our schools are no longer a hell or purgatory, in which children are tortured over cases and tenses, and in which with much flogging, trembling, anguish, and wretchedness they learn nothing.

If we take so much time and pains to teach our children to play cards, sing, and dance, why should we not take as much time to teach them reading and other branches of knowledge, while they are young and at leisure, are quick at learning, and take delight in it?

As for myself, if I had children and were able, I would have them learn not only the languages and history, but also singing, instrumental music, and the whole course of mathematics. For what is all this but mere child's play, in which the Greeks in former ages trained their children, and by this means became wonderfully skillful people, capable for every undertaking? How I regret that I did not read more poetry and history, and that no one taught me in these branches!

But you say, who can do without his children and bring them up, in this manner, to be young gentlemen? I reply: it is not my idea that we should establish schools as they have been heretofore, where a boy has studied Donatus and Alexander twenty or thirty years, and yet has learned nothing. The world has changed, and things go differently. My idea is that boys should spend an hour or two a day in school, and the rest of the time work at home, learn some trade and do whatever is desired, so that study and work may go on together, while the children are young and can attend to both. They now spend twofold as much time in shooting with crossbows, playing ball, running, and tumbling about.

In like manner, a girl has time to go to school an hour a day, and yet attend to her work at home; for she sleeps, dances, and plays away more than that. The real difficulty is found alone in the absence of an earnest desire to educate the young, and to aid and benefit mankind with accomplished citizens. The devil much prefers blockheads and drones, that men may have more abundant trials and sorrows in the world.

But the brightest pupils, who give promise of becoming accomplished teachers, preachers, and workers, should be kept longer at school, or set apart wholly for study, as we read of the holy martyrs, who brought up St. Agnes, St. Agatha, St. Lucian, and others. For this purpose also the cloisters and cathedral schools were founded, but they have been perverted into another and accursed one. There is great need for such instruction; for the tonsured crowd is rapidly decreasing, and besides, for the most part, the monks are unskilled to teach and rule, since they know nothing but to care for their stomachs, the only thing they have been taught. Hence we must have persons qualified to dispense the word of God and the Sacraments, and to be pastors of the people. But where shall we obtain them, if schools are not established on a more Christian basis, since those hitherto maintained, even if they do not go down, can produce nothing but depraved and dangerous corrupters of youth?

There is consequently an urgent necessity, not only for the sake of the young, but also for the maintenance of Christianity and of civil government, that this matter be immediately and earnestly taken hold of, lest afterwards, although we should gladly attend to it, we shall find it impossible to do so, and be obliged to feel in vain the pangs of remorse forever. For God is now graciously present, and offers his aid. Consider, for example, what great zeal Solomon manifested; for he was so much interested in the young that he took time, in the midst of his imperial duties, to write a book for them called Proverbs. And think how Christ himself took the little children in his arms! How earnestly he commends them to us, and speaks of their guardian angels, in order that he may show us how great a service it is, when we rightly bring them up; on the other hand how his anger kindles, if we offend the little ones, and let them perish.

Therefore, dear Sirs, take to heart this work, which God so urgently requires at your hands, which pertains to your office, which is necessary for the young, and which neither the world nor the Spirit can do without. We have, alas! lived and degenerated long enough in darkness; we have remained German brutes too long. Let us use or reason, that God may observe in us gratitude for his mercies, and that other lands may see that we are human beings, capable both of learning and of teaching, in order that through us, also, the world may be made better.

Finally, this must be taken into consideration by all who earnestly desire to see such schools established and the languages preserved in the German states; that no cost nor pains should be spared to procure good libraries in suitable buildings, especially in the large cities that are able to afford it. For if a knowledge of the Gospel and of every kind of learning is to be preserved, it must be embodied in books, as the prophets and apostles did, as I have already shown. This should be done, not only that our spiritual and civil leaders may have something to read and study, but also that good books may not be lost, and that the arts and languages may be preserved, with which God has graciously favored us.

All the kingdoms that have been distinguished in the world have bestowed care upon this matter, and particularly the Israelites, among whom Moses was the first to begin the work, who commanded them to preserve the book of the law in the ark of God, and put it under the care of the Levites, that any one might procure copies from them. He even commanded the king to make a copy of this book in the hands of the Levites. Among other duties God directed the Levitical priesthood to preserve and attend to the books. Afterwards Joshua increased and improved this library, as did Samuel subsequently, and David, Solomon, Isaiah, and many kings and prophets. Hence have come to us the Holy Scriptures of the Old Testament, which would not otherwise have been collected and preserved, if God had not required such diligence in regard to it.

Has it not been a grievous misfortune that a boy has hitherto been obliged to study twenty years or longer, in order to learn enough miserable Latin to become a priest and to read mass? And whoever has succeeded in this has been called blessed, and blessed the mother that has borne such a child! And yet he has remained a poor ignorant man all through life, and has been of no real service whatever. Everywhere we have had such teachers and masters, who have known nothing themselves, who have been able to teach nothing useful, and who have been ignorant even of the right methods of learning and teaching. How has it come about? No books have been accessible but the senseless trash of the monks and sophists. How could the pupils and teachers differ from the books they studied? A jackdaw does not hatch a dove, nor a fool make a wise man. That is the recompense of our ingratitude, in that we did not use diligence in the formation of libraries, but allowed good books to perish, and bad ones to survive.

But my advice is, not to collect all sorts of books indiscriminately, thinking only of getting a vast number together. I would have discrimination used, because it is not necessary to collect the commentaries of all the jurists, the productions of all the theologians, the discussions of all the philosophsrs, and the sermons of all the monks.

In the first place, a library should contain the Holy Scriptures in Latin, Greek, Hebrew, German, and other languages. Then the best and most ancient commentators in Greek, Hebrew, and Latin.

Secondly, such books as are useful in acquiring the languages, as the poets and orators, without considering whether they are heathen or Christian, Greek or Latin. For it is from such works that grammar must be learned.

Thirdly, books treating of all the arts and sciences.

Lastly, books on jurisprudence and medicine, though here discrimination is necessary.

A prominent place should be given to chronicles and histories, in whatever languages they may be obtained; for they are wonderfully useful in understanding and regulating the course of the world, and in disclosing the marvelous works of God. O how many noble deeds and wise maxims produced on German soil have been forgotten and lost, because no one at the time wrote them down; or if they were written, no one preserved the books: hence we Germans are unknown in other lands, and are called brutes that know only how to fight, eat, and drink. But the Greeks and Romans, and even the Hebrews, have recorded their history with such particularity, that even if a woman or child did anything noteworthy, all the world was obliged to read and know it; but we Germans are always Germans, and will remain Germans.

Since God has so graciously and abundantly provided us with art, scholars, and books, it is time for us to reap the harvest and gather for future use the treasures of these golden years. For it is to be feared (and even now it is beginning to take place), that new and different books will be produced, until at last, through the agency of the devil, the good books which are being printed, will be crowded out by the multitude of ill-considered, senseless, and noxious works.

Therefore, my dear Sirs, I beg you to let my labor bear fruit with you. And though there be some who think me too insignificant to follow my advice, or who look down on me as one condemned by tyrants: still let them consider that I am not seeking my own interest, but that of all Germany. And even if I were a fool, and should hit upon something good, no wise man should think it a disgrace to follow me. And even if I were a Turk and heathen, and it should yet appear that my advice was advantageous, not for myself, but for Christianity, no reasonable person would despise my counsel. Sometimes a fool has given better advice than a whole company of wise men. Moses received instruction from Jethro.

Herewith I commend you all to the grace of God. May he soften your hearts, and kindle therein a deep interest in behalf of the poor, wretched, and neglected youth; and through the blessing of God may you so counsel and aid them as to attain to a happy Christian social order in respect to both body and soul, with all fullness and abounding plenty, to the praise and honor of God the Father, through Jesus Christ our Savior. Amen.

Wittenberg, 1524.

39
Christianity and Problems of the Nineteenth Century

Orestes A. Brownson

Orestes A. Brownson (1803-1876), "Two Articles from *The Princeton Review*, Concerning the Transcendental Philosophy of the Germans, and of Cousin, and its Influence on Opinion in this Country," (Cambridge: John Owen. 1840. 8 vo. pp. 100.), *The Boston Quarterly Review*, III (No. XI, Art. I., July 1840), selections from pp. 265-323: pp. 271-275, 277-280, 322-323, compared with the original materials on microfilm, *American Periodical Series, 1800-1850*, APS 804 Boston Quarterly Review, Reel 380, AS5, A24 mf Reel 380, correcting and following the editing of Perry Miller, *The Transcendentalists: An Anthology* (Cambridge, Massachusetts: Harvard University Press, 1950, 6th printing [Paperback], 1971), pp. 243-246.

[American culture and education cannot be understood fully apart from the Judeo-Christian heritage and its expression in the literature of Puritanism, Calvinism, Deism, Unitarianism, and from Transcendentalism to the present. The following is a sample from the literature of Transcendentalism in which one (Brownson) of two scholars of systematic theology (Theodore Parker and Brownson) replied to Andrews Norton (1786-1853) and the Princeton pundits in the literary war between 1836 and 1841. In answering Norton's accusation of infidelity, Brownson contended that Transcendentalism was a native U.S. movement rather than an importation and describes for us this "profound revolt of the democracy against sacerdotalism."]

. . . The movement is really of American origin, and the prominent actors in it were carried away by it before every they formed any acquaintance with French or German metaphysics; and their attachment to the literature of France and Germany is the effect of their connection with the movement, not the cause.

Moreover, there are no members of the movement party, who would adopt entirely the views of any one of the distinguished foreigners named. We are inquiring for ourselves, and following out the direction of our own minds, but willing to receive aid, let it come from what quarter it may. These distinguished foreigners are not our masters, but our fellow disciples, and we feel under no special obligation to defend their opinions. We have nothing to do with Hegel, or Schelling, or Kant, or Cousin, any further than our own inquiries lead us to approve their speculations. We are aiming at truth, and believe that here, where thought is free, and the philosopher may tell his whole thought without any circumlocution or reticence, we may attain to a purer philosophy than can be found in either France or Germany . . .

The real aim of the Transcendentalist is to ascertain a solid ground for faith in the reality of the spiritual world. Their speculations have reference in the main to the grounds of human knowledge. Can we know anything? If so, how and what? Here is the real question with which they are laboring. Some of them ask this question without any ulterior views, merely for the sake of satisfying their own minds; others ask it for the purpose of legitimating their religious beliefs; others still, that they may obtain a firm foundation for political freedom. This question is, as every philosopher knows, fundamental, and must be answered before we can proceed scientifically in the construction of any system of religion, morals, or politics.

Mr. Norton seems to us to assume the negative of this question . . . Far be it from us, however, to intimate that Mr. Norton consciously and intentionally adopts the skeptical doctrine . . . all we mean is that his language, if taken in its simple and literal sense, must carry him thus far . . . the philosophical system to which he is attached, affords, it is evident, no solid ground to *religious* faith. This system of philosophy, of which Locke is the greatest modern master, recognises in man no power of knowing anything which transcends the senses, except the operations of our own minds. Adopting this system, Berkeley demonstrated but too easily the non-existence of the external world; and Hume, by showing that we can by no power we possess attain legitimately to the idea of cause, opened the door to universal skepticism. Condillac and the French *philosophes*, by taking it up in relation to its account of the origin of human knowledge, struck out of existence all spiritual beings, and of course all religion, and with it all foundation for morals.

It is this fact which has lead our Transcendentalists to reject it. They felt, if that philosophy was to be adopted as the last word of the reason, that faith and reason must forever be irreconcilable, and that no man could be religious but at the expense of his logic. The senses are merely the medium through which we become acquainted with the facts of the external world. They demand in the soul, distinct from themselves, a power to recognise, to perceive the objects they present. Now, if this power be denied, all knowledge must be denied. This power the old philosophy has denied by representing the mind prior to the affection of the senses as a mere blank sheet.

Furthermore, if all our ideas come through the senses, we can have no idea of anything which transcends them. God, all the objects of the spiritual world, in as much as they confessedly are not objects of the senses, must then be absolutely inconceivable. Add, if you will, to the senses reflection, and you do not help the matter. Reflection can add nothing but itself to the materials furnished by the senses, and reasoning can deduce from those materials only what is contained in them. The spiritual is not contained in them, and therefore cannot be deduced from them.

This the Transcendentalists have seen and felt. They have therefore looked into the consciousness, examined human nature anew, to see if they could not find in man the power of recognising and of knowing objects which transcend the reach of the senses. This power they profess to have discovered. They claim for man the power, not of discovering, but of knowing by intuition the spiritual world. According to them objects of religious faith are not merely objects believed on testimony, but objects of science, of which we may have a true inward experience, of which we may have a direct and immediate knowledge, as much so as of the ideas or sensations of our own minds. We may know that God exists as positively, as certainly, as we may know that we feel hunger or thirst, joy or grief . . .

If Mr. Norton be right in representing the truths of religion as matters transcending human knowledge, it follows that we can assert them and believe in them only on the authority of the miraculous being supposed. This being must be miraculously endowed, or else he himself could know no more of the matter than ordinary mortals, and therefore could speak with no more authority. Hence, we are driven to the necessity of declaring miracles the sole evidence possible of Christianity. . . . The whole definition is therefore based on the hypothesis, that it is not the truths of religion themselves that we believe, but the mere fact that they have been miraculously asserted.

The Transcendentalists would define belief in Christianity somewhat differently. They would say, by a belief in Christianity, we mean a belief in the truths, in the reality of the spiritual objects, which Jesus Christ revealed; and now that these truths are revealed, brought to light, we may have a direct perception of them, may know them, and therefore receive them without reference to the authority or endowments of him who first revealed them. While therefore they would not hesitate to acknowledge Jesus as the one who was divinely commissioned to reveal these truths, they would claim for themselves now, in the actual state of Humanity, the ability to perceive them and to know immediately, by intuition, by a mere looking upon them, that they are truths.

Here is the fundamental difference between Mr. Norton and the Transcendentalists, on this question of the evidences of Christianity . . . Mr. Ripley no more than Mr. Norton denies the supernatural origin of Christianity . . . He also admits that the miracles recorded in the New Testament were actually wrought . . . Mr. Norton asserts that we can at best know only the fact, that the teacher is divinely commissioned, from which it is fair to infer the truth of what he taught; Mr. Ripley maintains that we may know by direct perception, by actual experience, the truths themselves, that what the teacher taught is true, without being under the necessity of inferring it from the fact that the teacher was divinely commissioned.

The difference between the two is very great, and the advantages are altogether on Mr. Ripley's side. On Mr. Norton's ground Christianity can be sustained only by means of those historical proofs, that sustain the miracles by which the authority of the teacher is attested. These historical proofs, Mr. Norton himself admits, do not amount to certainty. But this objection he seeks to obviate by contending that certainty is not for such beings as we are . . . On his own hypothesis, the truth of Christianity is not a certainty but a probability. But it is a probability that rests on historical testimony. It can then be a probability only to those who can avail themselves of that testimony. This everybody knows is but a small portion of mankind. His doctrine, then, not only deprives us of all certain evidence of the certain truth of Christianity, but declares that the great mass of mankind are absolutely disinherited by their Maker, placed out of the condition of ever ascertaining for themselves even the probable truth of that which they must believe, or have no assurance of salvation. They are placed entirely at the mercy of the learned few, and the Gospel which was glad tidings to the poor can be glad tidings only to the erudite.

Mr. Ripley's doctrine [George Ripley (1802-1880)], on the contrary, rescues the mass from the power of the learned few, and places the truth of Christianity within the reach of every man. Few only of our race are able to judge of the pretensions of an authorized teacher, to sift the testimony of history, balance probabilities and decide for themselves, whether the miracles recorded in the New Testament were actually wrought or not, or if wrought that they establish the divine authority of the teacher; but all are capable of judging of the doctrine itself, whether it be of God or not. The unlettered ploughman by this is placed, so far as the evidences of his religious faith are concerned, on a level with the most erudite scholar or the profoundest philosopher. Christianity by this is adapted to the masses, and fitted to become an universal religion. Its evidence is simplified, and the necessity of relying on an authorized teacher superseded. It recognises a witness within the soul that testifies for God, and gives us the grounds of a living faith in his being and his providence, in his love and his mercy. It destroys the very foundation of a sacerdotal caste, and saves Humanity from ecclesiastical domination. It paves the way for universal freedom, for every man to become a priest and a king, and gives assurance that the prophets did not merely dream in foretelling the approach of a time, when we shall not "teach every man his neighbor and every man his brother, saying, Know the Lord; for all shall know him from the least to the greatest" . . .

In conclusion, we should say, that we have thus far accepted the name Transcendentalism, although it is not one of our own choosing, nor the one we approve. So far as Transcendentalism is understood to be the recognition in man of the capacity of knowing truth intuitively, or of attaining to a scientific knowledge of an order of existence transcending the reach of the senses, and of which we can have no sensible experience, we are Transcendentalists. But when it is understood to mean, that feeling is to be placed above reaspon, dreaming above reflection, and instinctive intimation above scientific exposition; in a word when it means the substitution of a lawless fancy for an enlightened understanding, as we apprehend it is understood in our neighborhood, by the majority of those who use it as a term of reproach, we must disown it, and deny that we are Transcendentalists.

40
Christianity and Problems of Today

Ronnie Dugger

Selection from Ronnie Dugger, *Dark Star—Hiroshima Reconsidered in the Life of Claude Eatherly of Lincoln Park, Texas* (Cleveland and New York: World Publishing Company, 1967), pp. 244-248.

We are concerned not only with what has happened in [Claude] Eatherly [the World War II pilot who helped A-bomb Hiroshima], we are concerned that what happened to him could happen in our world. In the public square in Sherman, [Texas,] the city where he was questioned on the post office break-ins, there stands a Confederate soldier of gray marble. Musket at rest, he gazes at the national flag on a staff a little way away. The words on the pedestal say, "Sacred to the memory of our Confederate dead: true patriots, they fought for home and country, for the holy principles of self-government—the only true liberty. Their sublime self sacrifices and unsurpassed valor will teach future generations the lesson of high born patriotism, of devotion to duty, of exalted courage, of Southern chivalry." Claude did not waylay Yankees in the thicket or cross muskets with them in the valley, he flew an airplane six miles high and designated for death 200,000 people he had never seen. It was not the old, manly kind of war, killing and being killed with hands and antelope bones and knives and arrows and pistols and rifles and cannons, even with tanks, even with flamethrowers, it was the new kind, cool, mechanical, and distant. Obeying orders to deliver nuclear weapons causes results whose mere quantities are a new species of horror. We are led by Claude's experience to question whether we can go on seeing the world through our respective national lenses without, willy-nilly, committing crimes we cannot atone for. Everything is tainted with this new doubt. Why do Boy Scouts still wear uniforms? What's the connection between a coat hanger and a kendo stick? Is pride murder?

Some who would rather that no one pay any attention to Claude stress that he is an exception, that had he and his life been different, his guilt might not have gathered as it did. True enough; but his guilt is not therefore morally different from the guilt in others who were implicated in mass killing, but who have confined it to shut parts of themselves. It is the same guilt; it is different only dramatically. Reduced, rationalized, modified by the arguments of necessity and the circumstances of each case, still it stays on, stubborn, wary, sullen, a tenacious intruder. The special circumstances of Claude's life seem to sound, plumb lines haphazardly dropped, the features of what Edward Teller calls, with inadvertent irony, "our nuclear future." When—his ethics maimed by his part in random mass killing?—Claude planned to bomb Havana, he augured the corrosion of respect for life in other nations that characterizes world politics. In his pursuit of fun as heedlessness, he enacted the way of life to which we as a people have devolved, making dough and chasing tail while accepting the truth about our own weapons. The selfish parts of him that were satisfied by his conversion to the cause of peace spring from the same instinct of self-preservation that is now the strongest deterrent to nuclear war. Men like Jordan, Tibbets, Sweeney, returned to normal lives in an unbombed and abundant country: therefore, their equability, though typical, misleads us about the future. To what nations will they, and Russian pilots, French, British, Chinese pilots, return, after an all-out nuclear war? Where will they land? If they land, what will they eat? What will they drink? Who will be left to give them medals? To live? Not only one mother but most mothers; not two twisted fetuses, but millions; not 100,000 deaths or 200,000, but 100,000,000, or 200,000,000, or 500,000,000. It has become immoral not to imagine.

Do not some people so angrily debunk Claude precisely because he and his case challenge placing nationality ahead of humanity when that choice must be made? In going along with nuclear warmaking, as Claude did, can we not all of us—Americans, Russians, Frenchmen, Cubans, Englishmen, Chinese, Japanese—become part of mass killing and hurting more horrible by plain quantity than anything the Germans did to the Jews? A young African, a young Mexican, a young Arab, a young Israelite is no less ready to exterminate millions of people than Eatherly was tens of thousands. His story speaks to fervent nationalists everywhere because it helps us understand how men have become willing to do these things.

It is his idea that we should trust each other. Try trust, he says. It seems to be a risky course, considering we don't even trust ourselves. Yet, if anything renewed Claude, trust did. Gowan, Baldwin, the doctors saw his life sympathetically rather than punitively; Mrs. Lunger, Anders, the Hiroshima girls, then the Japanese pacifists said to him, we know; let us hope we can understand each other and work our problems out together. It is possible, is it not, that love works. Sadly surveying the Cold War, Henry Stimson, a key figure in the decision to drop the bomb, wrote to President Truman, "The chief lesson I have learned in a long life is that the only way you can make a man trustworthy is to trust him; and the surest way to make him untrustworthy is to distrust him and show your distrust." Camus was struck by "the fundamental good will of everyone." Schweitzer wrote in 1958, "We cannot continue in this paralyzing mistrust. If we want to work our way out of the desperate situation in which we find ourselves, another spirit must enter into the people. It can only come if the awareness of its necessity suffices to give us strength in its coming. We must presuppose the awareness of this need in all the peoples who have suffered along with us. We must approach them in the spirit that we are human beings, all of us, and that we feel ourselves fitted to feel with each other; to think and to will together in the same way."[1]

Though we cannot return to the times of the pecan-tree bank, do we yet realize, in the daily things we think, that the new weapons have made the world one community of danger? Do Russians, for example, realize that in the first day of all-out war, the United States "could pull the trigger on the equivalent of 16 billion tons of TNT—4,000 times the total dropped in World War II"? Germans, that a single airplane today, manned by a single crew, taking off without to-do from a single airfield, can easily carry seven times the total bombpower dropped on Germany by all of the Allies' almost 1,500,000 sorties in World War II? Latin Americans, that the amount of nuclear power stockpiled in the American arsenal alone is easily more than enough to account for 20,000 pounds of TNT for every man, woman, and child on earth? Chinese, that a single Polaris submarine carries sixteen missiles, each of which is thirty-three times as powerful as the bomb that destroyed Hiroshima? Japanese, that an ordinary 20-megaton hydrogen bomb is one thousand times more powerful that the Hiroshima bomb? Africans, that millions of them could expect to die in an all-out nuclear war whether their countries were party to it or not? Americans, that a 20,000-megaton attack on the United States could kill 95 per cent of them and that each American citizen possesses, proportionately, at least 150 tons of TNT in destructive power? Dr. Teller has said that cobalt bombs' radioactivity could "poison everyone."[2]

We are not nearly as menacing to our next door neighbors as we are to Russians on the other side of the world, nor they to theirs as to us, because the weapons of war have been internationalized, but trust has not.

---

[1] Albert Schweitzer, *Peace or Atomic War?* (1958).
[2] Albert Schweitzer, *op. cit*; *U.S. News and World Report*, October 2, 1961; Oskar Morgenstern, *The Question of National Defense*, Vintage Books; Norman Cousins, *In Place of Folly*, Harper & Brothers, 1961; Associated Press, June 10, 1962; Harrison Brown and James Real, "The Community of Fear," in *A World Without War*, Washington Square Press Inc., 1961; Ralph E. Lapp, "Nuclear War," in John M. Fowler (ed.), *Fallout*, Basic Books, 1960; Edward Teller and Albert L. Latter, *Our Nuclear Future*, Criterion Books, 1958; *Newsweek*, April 10, 1967. .

Yet who could confidently advocate any proposition as something everyone should always adhere to? *Trust*: what if the others destroy you as you love them? *World government*: what if dictators *and* democracies insist on vetoes and bombs? If Claude's story says anything to me for sure, it is only that evil has no nationality, it is personal. Beware of obeying, beware of running with the good fellows who are all around you, for no matter how "close-knit" they are, they may be wrong, they may be set on a work that history will blacken as bestial. Eichmann was probably right when he said he was an ordinary man, with an average character, some good points and many faults. This is the new doubt, too, that an ordinary man, like me, can be a mass murderer and still be a pretty good fellow. Willing to fight in wars, we are just as responsible personally as in refusing to do so; the question has never been whether to be responsible, but what to be responsible for. At some point, whatever the consequences for him, the ordinary man must be ready to confront the crew, the group, the nation itself. There is no strength in numbers.

As long as we could maintain to ourselves that no one was to blame for Hiroshima, that it could not be helped, we felt all right. Occasionally, though, an ordinary person embodies much of the anguish and crisis of his times in the accidents of his own life. It is Claude Eatherly's importance in history (quite a different thing from his personal circumstances) that he, a responsible officer with a significant discretionary role in selecting Hiroshima as the target for extermination, since then has said, "No, wait. I helped do it. I'm responsible." This event in him—however it came to pass, for whatever complex, variously selfish and idealistic reasons— helped us understand that mass killing is subject to personal as well as official blame. Everyone associated with Hiroshima has to answer anew for his part, and everyone associated with the shiny new apparatuses of mass death must more vividly consider whether, in some soon time, in some small circle around a fire of broken boards in a radioactive wasteland, he will have to stand up, turn his back, and say to himself, "I had a choice. I am responsible."

PART FIVE
PRECURSORS
OF THE CONTEMPORARY
IN EDUCATIONAL THEORY

Overview

As the decade of the 1970s opened in the United States, its people pondered such books as *The Greening of America* by Charles A. Reich (Random House, 1970). Little greenery and much of what Reich called "sere, yellow leaf" showed when he took stock of the ways in which we were meeting our obligations as a society in the light of our past, our principles, and our ideals. Some reviewers were pleased with Reich. His book, they said, criticized America in a stock-taking vein reminiscent of Alexis de Tocqueville in the 1830s, of Thoreau in the 1840s and 1850s, and of Walt Whitman in the 1870s; this was very much needed, they said.

But Reich's book struck others differently. Especially did it arouse the indignation of George F. Kennan, who wrote of it: "There is a clear repudiation here of the fundamental principles, political and philosophic, on which not only the governmental system of this country but the entire structure of Western democracy has been erected" (*New York Times*, October 28, 1970). John Kenneth Galbraith reminded Reich that he had not worked out "the economics of the Consciousness III life-style": housing, hospitals, schools, police. These criticisms and Reich's belief that working out these matters was the next step for everyone—both emphasize what is still in controversy. Germane to the 1970s and to such controversies are the readings in Part Five, for they are basic to our understanding of our heritage and the gaining of principles that will help us better to determine what teaching, education, and schooling might be.

In Part Five our quest moves out of the Graeco-Roman and Judeo-Christian backgrounds of our social heritage and enters that period which is the direct precursor of the contemporary in political, philosophical, and educational theory. For understanding our twentieth-century controversies about life and education, there can be no richer materials for study and discussion than these. Within three hundred or so years there accrued to our cultural and social heritage the development of science, the development of democracy, and the industrial revolution. We agree with the writers of the controversial Harvard Report of 1945, *General Education in a Free Society*, and suggest as they did that any adequate account of education must deal with a social heritage which includes these dynamic developments and forces affecting us still.[1]

---

[1] Harvard University, Committee on the Objectives of a General Education in a Free Society, *General Education in a Free Society: Report of the Harvard Committee* (Cambridge, Mass.: Harvard University Press, 1945).

Support for this position comes from the fact that many present-day thinkers have turned to ideas, movements, and developments in this period for clues and suggestions to guide us today. Walter Lippmann is a good example. Before World War II (in 1933-1937) he wrote *The Good Soviety* "in order to define the principles which may guide us in the postwar world."[2] His central theme was "how to reconcile with the comparatively new economy of the division of labor the great and ancient and progressive traditions of liberty embodied in laws which respect the human personality." In that book he affirmed that "the politics, law, and morality of the Western world are an evolution from the religious conviction that all men are persons and that the human person is inviolable." His second basic affirmation was that "the industrial revolution 'which still engages the whole of mankind and poses all the great social issues of the epoch in which we live, arises primarily from the increasing division of labor in ever-widening markets; the machine, the corporation, the concentration of economic control and mass production, are secondary phenomena.'" He argued that "fascism, communism, state socialism, state capitalism, and nineteenth-century laissez-faire individualism [all developments in the period covered by Part Five] are incapable of reconciling the modern economy with our cultural heritage."

Reich and other recent writers could profit from such insights and analyses. Especially fruitful are they to educational theorists. For in this area also Lippmann makes a good example. His 1955 *Essays in the Public Philosophy* was an analysis of men, their ideas, and the developments during the period covered by the readings in Part Five which is relevant to our controversies over education. For his analysis led him to formulate a concept of education quite opposed to the currently popular one—a view from which, we suggest, great benefits might be derived.[3] So do our readings in Part Five feed the fires of educational controversy.

The greatest benefits from study of this period, we maintain, will accrue to the leader who, in the words of Matthew Arnold, sees the men, ideas, and developments "steadily and as a whole." Our suggestion is that the reader can gain his best "overview" of these readings by skipping now to the very last reading in this book, Hugh C. Black's "A Missing Chord in Educational Theory." There, Black suggests, the student of education will find the value of Alexander Meiklejohn's "grand-scale" approach to educational theory. In 1942 in *Education Between Two*

---

[2] Walter Lippmann, *The Good Society* (New York: Grossett & Dunlap, 1943, Grosset's Universal Library, UL-3), p. ix.

[3] Walter Lippmann, *Essays in the Public Philosophy* (New York: The New American Library, 1956, Mentor MP393).

Worlds (2d ed., New York: Harper & Row, 1942), Meiklejohn analyzed the drift from the medieval world to the modern world in terms of schools; perceived a revolution in the procedure for determining what kind of beings human beings should be; sought to understand the intellectual problem underlying the collapse of human learning and teaching as he studied Comenius, Locke, Rousseau, Arnold, and Dewey; and finally formulated a suggestion for its solution. We can profit by reading about Meiklejohn now before approaching these readings.

Our readings in Part Five are arranged into two main groups: (1) those chiefly illustrating a European influence upon developments in the United States—the root ideas of such men as Francis Bacon, John Amos Comenius, John Locke, Jean Jacques Rousseau, Johann Heinrich Pestalozzi, Friedrich Wilhelm Froebel, Johann Friedrich Herbart, and Herbert Spencer; and (2) those pertaining to developments in the United States, the development of a system of common schools, and the continuing controversy over education, as seen in selected writings of Horace Mann, William T. Harris, Francis W. Parker, John Dewey, and William C. Bagley.

Our readings indicating the European influences on American developments begin with Francis Bacon and an emphasis upon induction and scientific method, to indicate the crucial development of science as a part of our cultural heritage. In the beginning of the first chapter we have forsaken Bacon's own writings in favor of James Edwin Creighton's classic, simply-stated account, which has the virtue of placing Bacon's contributions to the inductive method within a broader context—that of the development of logic. Then we go directly to Bacon and introduce our readers to Bacon's account of the idols (of the tribe, den, market, and theatre) that beset the human mind and constitute barriers to the truth even for twentieth-century thinkers. The sample from Bacon indicates possibilities of future earth-shaking developments through science and forecasts ensuing upheavals in lives and thinking. For the new methods and outlooks of science constituted the earliest steps of a progression which would truly "change the world forever,"[4] would shake old beliefs and opinions and arouse new controversies.

John Amos Comenius might perhaps best be understood if he is studied in terms of the contrasts so often argued after his day: medieval vs. modern, science vs. religion, unified vs. dualistic approach to education. He comes at the end of the medieval period and at the dawning of the modern period; yet many of his educational ideas are more "modern" that practices of today. This kindly, keen-minded Moravian bishop suffering travail and hardship was guided and directed by his religious beliefs

---

[4] Sir Richard Livingstone, *Portrait of Socrates* (New York and Oxford: Oxford University Press, 1938), p. v, quoted previously in the Overview to Part Three.

and especially his strong belief in God. He was aware of the New Learning, of developments in science, and took them into account, including in his Pansophic vision provision for the teaching of science. Meiklejohn would have us view Comenius's educational philosophy as a unified approach firmly founded on his religious perspective and belief in God and on his certainty as to what kind of persons education should form. Comenius's approach contrasts with the dualistic approach of John Locke, causing us to ponder the consequences of the choice England made and America followed in basing their educational practices on the dualistic view of Locke rather than the unified approach of Comenius's *The Great Didactic*. As an introduction to Comenius, our sample of readings includes the title page of *The Great Didactic*, the first three paragraphs of the book's "Greeting to the Reader," the table of contents to the entire book, and Chapter XX: "The Method of the Sciences, Specifically."

Most difficult has been the selection of readings to represent John Locke, for he is such a gateway to many developments in many different areas: political theory, philosophy, religion, and education. To make clear our agreement with Meiklejohn on Locke's dualistic approach (in contrast to the unified approach of Comenius), our selections portray Locke's recognition of two kinds of education: education for the poor (represented by his "Proposals for Reform of the Poor Law" [1697]) and education for the gentry (represented by selections from *Some Thoughts Concerning Education*). One of our selections was made on the basis of its shedding light on American controversies over education. Education in the United States, whether in the colonial period, in 1800, in 1900, or in the 1970s, has suffered from deep ideological divisions. We have been split on what doctrines about child nature and education to embrace. In the colonial period (and even much later) Puritan beliefs about man's nature (the view that man was a depraved creature born innately evil) went with an authoritarian, strict-discipline education. In later years at various times educational theorists seem to have swung to the opposite extreme of laissez-faire freedom for the individual, working from the conception that the child is basically good in his nature and that only good can result from releasing him from the constraints of adults, school, and society. American controversy over education has centered on this ideological division, which we came to through European influences— namely, through Rousseau, who was able to formulate his view by studying John Locke, especially the Lockean empirical discovery that there are "No Innate Principles in the Mind." Readers should profit, then, from our selection of that topic from *An Essay Concerning Human Understanding* and also from reading with pure enjoyment as much as we have been able to include from Locke's *Some Thoughts Concerning Education*.

Rousseau, Pestalozzi, Froebel, Herbart, and Spencer should be studied, we suggest, as great European educational reformers, vital in themselves but especially vital in their influence on American education (Pestalozzi's influence was on the common school movement and elementary schooling; Froebel's was on the kindergarten) and their contribution to our ideological debates over education. The selections from Rousseau should be read in the light of Meiklejohn's treatment which Hugh C. Black outlines in the closing reading, "A Missing Chord in Educational Theory." Rousseau, a paradoxical, contradictory thinker, has been called the "Copernicus of modern education" in that he gave us a new concept of education—education as individual development rather than transmission of the social heritage. His ideas influenced Pestalozzi and Froebel and started a line of thinking about education which can be traced in contemporary "Progressive" education and the stance of romantic critics of the public schools in the late 1960s and early 1970s. Herbart represents a different and contrasting line of development, especially as he was interpreted by his disciples. His ideas, brought to the United States about 1900, stimulated much educational controversy, some of which resulted in the publication of such classics in American education as John Dewey's *Interest and Effort in Education* (Boston: Houghton Mifflin Company, 1913).

Spencer merits attention because his writings contribute to the developments in science indicated earlier by Bacon and Comenius and because he was also an educational reformer. To his own question "What knowledge is of most worth?" Spencer answered with the one word "Science." As did John Dewey, Spencer saw the value and usefulness of science. But Spencer emphasized the usefulness of the "what" of science —knowledge—while Dewey, in contrast, seized upon scientific method (the complete act of thought) and emphasized the process of thinking. Spencer, no less than Dewey, reformed education and in time influenced some changes in American schools.

Since Spencer marks the transition in our readings from the European influences to the American developments and bears so heavily on our controversies, it might be well to consider him further as a reformer. Spencer's doctrine that science is the "knowledge of most worth" was extremely repugnant to the educational establishment of his time, where "Latin, Greek, and mathematics had been the staples of education for many generations, and were believed to afford the only suitable preparation for the learned professions, public life, and cultivated society." Further statements by Charles W. Eliot, president of Harvard, writing in 1911, are edifying:

> The profession of teaching has long been characterized by
> certain habitual convictions, which Spencer undertook to shake

rudely, and even to deride. The first of these convictions is that all education, physical, intellectual, and moral, must be authoritative, and need take no account of the natural wishes, tendencies, and motives of the ignorant and undeveloped child. The second dominating conviction is that to teach means to tell, or show, children what they ought to see, believe, and utter. Expositions by the teacher and books are therefore the true means of education. The third and supreme conviction is that the method of education which produced the teacher himself and the contemporary or earlier scholars, authors, and publicists, must be the righteous and sufficient method. Its fruits demonstrate its soundness, and make it sacred. Herbert Spencer, in the essays included in the present volume, assaulted all three of these firm convictions. Accordingly, the ideas on education which he put forth more than fifty years ago have penetrated educational practice very slowly—particularly in England; but they are now coming to prevail in most civilised countries, and they will prevail more and more. Through him, the thoughts on education of Comenius, Montaigne, Locke, Milton, Rousseau, Pestalozzi, and other noted writers on this neglected subject are at last winning their way into practice, with the modifications or adaptations which the immense gains of the human race in knowledge and power since the nineteenth century opened have shown to be wise.[5]

When we turn to education in the United States, the development of a system of common schools, and the continuing controversy over education, little need be added by way of overview. The reading that represents Horace Mann and the establishment of our system of common schools is essential in the light of current threats to the public school system. William T. Harris should be considered a traditionalist in his theory or philosophy of education; he contrasts with Francis W. Parker, a "Progressivist." John Dewey emphasizes the learning-process in his view of education; he contrasts with William C. Bagley, an "Essentialist" who emphasizes the learning-product. With these background readings in mind, the leader of education should be well-equipped to enter the decade of the 1970s, its ideological divisions well understood and the issues basic to educational controversies vividly before him.

---

[5] Introduction to *Herbert Spencer: Essays on Education and Kindred Subjects*, Everyman's Library No. 504 (London: J. M. Dent & Sons Ltd. and New York: Dutton, 1911; reprint ed., 1966), p. viii.

41
Francis Bacon (1561-1626).
Developments in Logic

Induction and Scientific Method

Selections from James Edwin Creighton, *An Introductory Logic*, 4th edition (New York, The Macmillan Company, 1927 printing of 4th edition of 1920), Chapter II, pp. 24-32. Copyright, 1898, 1900, 1909, 1920, by The Macmillan Company. Copyright, 1926, by Katherine Creighton.

Now the part of Aristotle's logic which was best worked out was a theory of proof or demonstration by means of the syllogism. Here he showed clearly the various ways in which different kinds of propositions could be combined as premises to yield valid conclusions, and proved that no conclusion could be drawn from other combinations. This part of the Aristotelian logic has come down to us almost unchanged, . . .

It will be noticed that, in the doctrine of the syllogism, Aristotle was dealing with that kind of reasoning which undertakes to *demonstrate* the truth of some fact, by showing its relation to a general principle which every one admits. In other words, this part of his work may be called the logic of proof or demonstration. Aristotle was at one time of his life a teacher of rhetoric, and he seemed always to have aimed at putting this art of reasoning on a scientific basis. That is, for the rules of thumb and questionable artifices of the Sophists, he wished to substitute general laws and methods of procedure which were based upon a study of the principles and operations of reason. By complying with the rules which he laid down, an argument will necessarily gain the assent of every rational being.

But we do not emply our reason merely in order to demonstrate to ourselves or to others what we already know. We seek to discover new facts and truths by its aid. In other words, we not only wish to prove what is already known, but also to discover new facts, and we need a logic of discover, as well as logic of proof. This distinction between proof and discovery corresponds in general to that between deduction and induction. It is not an absolute distinction, as will appear later, for both processes are constantly employed in conjunction. But, for the present, it may be said that deduction is the process of showing how particular facts follow from some general principle which everybody admits, while Induction shows the methods by which general laws are obtained from an observation of particular facts. Now Aristotle, as we have seen, furnished a very complete theory of Deduction, or method of proof. But he did not treat of Induction, or the method of passing from particular facts to general laws, with anything like the same completeness. Moreover, what he did write on this subject received no attention for many centuries. Aristotle was himself a great scientific observer, and may well be regarded as the father of many of our modern sciences. But, in his logical writings, his main object seems to have been to present a true theory of argumentation, as opposed to the false theories of the Sophists. Science, too, was only in its beginning when Aristotle wrote, and it was impossible for him to foretell the methods of discovery which it has actually employed.

After Aristotle's death (322 B.C.), and after the loss of Athenian independence, there was a great decline of interest in matters of mere theory which had no direct application to the practical affairs of life. The Stoic school did make some slight additions to logical theory, but like their opponents, the Epicureans, they regarded practice, the art of living well, as the supreme wisdom of life. The Romans, who derived their knowledge of Greek philosophy largely from the Stoics, were also interested in the practical advantages of logic, rather than in its theoretical side. It was the possibility of applying the laws of logic to rhetoric and public speaking which especially interested Cicero, who was the first to make Latin paraphrases and adaptations of Greek logic in his rhetorical works.

For more than seven hundred years, during the Middle Ages, the Greek language and literature was almost unknown in Western Europe. During this time, almost the only sources of information regarding logic were Latin translations of Aristotle's *Categories,* and of an Introduction to the same work by Porphyry, who lived 232-303 A.D. Both of these translations were made by Boethius (470-525), who is best known as the author of *The Consolations of Philosophy.* Even when scholars again became acquainted with the original works of Aristotle, in the latter part of the Middle Ages, they did not really understand their true significance. They took the husk, one may say, and neglected the kernel. They adopted the Aristotelian logic as an external and arbitrary set of rules for the guidance of thinking, and neglected entirely the scientific theory upon which these rules were based. A great deal of ingenuity was also shown in subdividing and analyzing all possible kinds of argument, and giving the particular rule for each case. This process of making distinctions was carried so far that scholastic logic became extremely cumbersome and artificial. Its pretensions, however, rapidly increased;

it claimed to furnish a complete instrument of knowledge, and a sure standard for discriminating between truth and falsehood.

It is not very difficult to understand why this set of logical rules seemed so satisfactory to the age of Scholasticism. The men of this period were not greatly interested in new discoveries; they supposed that they were already in possession of everything which was worth knowing. Their only object was to weave this knowledge into a system, to show the connection and interdependence of all its parts, and thus to put it beyond the possibility of attack. And for this purpose the school logic was admirably adapted; it was always possible to bring every case which could arise under one or other of its rules.

There is no doubt that the Aristotelian logic had a real value of its own, and that it exercised a very important influence upon Western civilization, even in the form in which it was taught by the Schoolmen; but there is, of course, nothing complete or final about it. Its main purpose, as we have already seen, was to furnish a method by means of which the knowledge we already possess may be so arranged as to be absolutely convincing. But the centre of intellectual interest has changed since mediaeval times. We are not content merely to exhibit the certainty and demonstrative character of the knowledge which we already have, but we feel that there is a great deal of importance still to be discovered. So that, in modern times, one may say the desire to make discoveries, and so add to the general stock of knowledge, has taken the place of the mediaeval ideal of showing that the traditional doctrines taught by the church are absolutely certain and convincing. And when men became conscious of the importance of gaining new knowledge, and especially knowledge about nature, they at once saw the necessity for a new logic, or doctrine of method, to aid them in the undertaking.

7. Bacon and the Inductive Method

All the great thinkers of the sixteenth and seventeenth centuries saw clearly that the school logic is simply a method of showing the certainty of the knowledge we already possess, and does not aid us at all in making new discoveries. A new method, they all declared, was an absolute necessity. The new point of view was put most clearly and eloquently by the famous Francis Bacon (1561-1626), at one time Lord Chancellor of England. Bacon called his work on logic the *Novum Organum*, thus contrasting it with the *Organon*, or logical treatises of Aristotle. An alternative title of the work is, *True Suggestions for the Interpretation of Nature*. Bacon begins this work by showing the advantages to be gained from a knowledge of nature. It is man's true business, he tells us, to be the minister and interpreter of nature, for it is only by becoming acquainted with the laws of nature that we are ever able to take advantage of them for our own ends. "Knowledge and human power are synonymous, since ignorance of the cause prevents us from taking advantage of the effect." The discovery of the laws of nature, which is therefore of so great practical importance, cannot be left to chance, but must be guided by a scientific method. And it is such a method which Bacon endeavours to supply in the *Novum Organum.*

The method which Bacon proposed seems to us very simple. If we would gain new knowledge regarding nature, he says, and regarding natural laws, we must go to nature herself and observe her ways of acting. Facts about nature cannot be discovered from logical propositions, or from syllogisms; if we would know the law of any class of phenomena, we must observe the particular facts carefully and systematically. It will often be necessary, also, to put pointed questions to nature by such experiments as will force her to give us the information we want. Knowledge, then, must begin with observation of particular facts; and only after we have made a great number of particular observations, and have carefully classified and arranged them, taking account of all the negative cases, are we able to discover in them the general law. No hypotheses or guesses are to be made: but we must wait until the tabulations of the particular phenomena reveal the general 'form' or principle which belongs to them all.

It will be frequently necessary to refer to Bacon's work in what follows. At present, it is sufficient to note that Bacon showed that a knowledge of nature cannot be attained through general propositions and logical arguments, but that it is necessary to begin with the observation of particular facts. He emphasized, also, the importance of systematic observation and carefully planned experiments, and showed that knowledge must begin with facts of perception. This is the method of induction, and Bacon is usually said to have been the founder of the inductive sciences of nature.

Another and quite different method of extending knowledge was proposed by the great Frenchman, Descartes (1596-1650), who took mathematics as the type to which all knowledge should conform. That is, he supposed that the true method of extending knowledge was to begin with general principles, whose truth could not be doubted, and to reason from them to the necessary character of particular facts. Descartes and his followers thought that it was possible to discover certain universal propositions from which all truth could be derived through reason. They thus emphasized Deduction rather than Induction, and reasoning rather than observation and experiment. The spirit of Bacon's teaching was, however, continued in England by John Locke, in the *Essay Concerning Human Understanding* (1690). During the next centuries, philosophical thinkers were divided into two great schools: Rationalists, or those who agreed in the main with Descartes; and Empiricists, or Sensationalists, who followed the teachings of Bacon and Locke.

Although the natural sciences made great advances during the seventeenth and eighteenth centuries, there seems to have been no effort made to analyze and describe the methods which were actually being employed. In England, at least, it seems to have been assumed that all discoveries were made by the use of the rules and methods of Bacon. One of the first writers to attempt to explain the method used by the natural sciences was Sir John Herschel (1792-1871). His work, *Discourse on the Study of Natural Philosophy*, was published in 1832. A little later, and with the same object in view, William Whewell (1794-1866), afterwards Master of Trinity College, Cambridge, undertook his *History of the Inductive Sciences*, which was followed some time after by the *Philosophy of the Inductive Sciences*. The man, however, who did most towards putting the study of logic on a new basis was John Stuart Mill (1806-1873), the first edition of whose *Logic* appeared in 1843. We shall have frequent occasion to refer to this work in future discussions. It is sufficient to say here that Mill continues the empirical tradition of the earlier English writers in his general philosophical position. Mill's book gave a great impulse to the study of logic. Before it was published, writers on the subject had confined their attention almost exclusively to the syllogistic or deductive reasoning. Mill, however, emphasized strongly the importance of induction; indeed, he regarded induction as the only means of arriving at new truth, the syllogism being merely a means of systematizing and arranging what we already know. Though few logicians of the present day adopt this extreme view, the importance of inductive methods of reasoning, and the necessity of studying them, have now become generally recognized. Most modern writers on logic devote a considerable amount of attention to induction. . . .

Barriers to Truth
Francis Bacon's Idols

Selections from Francis Bacon, *Novum Organum: The Great Instauration: Summary of the Second Part, Digested in Aphorisms.—Aphorisms on the Interpretation of Nature and the Empire of Man*, from *The Works*. . . . A New Edition in three volumes . . . by Basil Montagu (Philadelphia: Carey and Hart, 1842), as quoted in Robert U.LICH (ed.), *Three Thousand Years of Educational Wisdom—Selections from Great Documents*, 2d ed. (Cambridge, Massachusetts: Harvard University Press, 1957), pp. 310-311.

38. The idols and false notions which have already preoccupied the human understanding, and are deeply rooted in it, not only to beset men's minds, that they become difficult of access, but, even when access is obtained, will again meet and trouble us in the instauration of the sciences, unless mankind, when forewarned, guard themselves with all possible care against them.

39. Four species of idols beset the human mind: to which (for distinction's sake) we have assigned names: calling the first idols of the tribe; the second idols of the den; the third idols of the market; the fourth idols of the theatre.

40. The formation of notions and axioms on the foundation of true induction, is the only fitting remedy, by which we can ward off and expel these idols. It is, however, of great service to point them out. For the doctrine of idols bears the same relation to the interpretation of nature, as that of confutation of sophisms does to common logic.

41. The idols of the tribe are inherent in human nature, and the very tribe or race of man. For man's sense is falsely asserted to be the standard of things. On the contrary, all the perceptions, both of the senses and the mind, bear reference to man, and not to the universe, and the human mind resembles those uneven mirrors, which impart their own properties to different objects, from which rays are emitted, and distort and disfigure them.

42. The idols of the den are those of each individual. For everybody (in addition to the errors common to the race of man) has his own individual den or cavern, which intercepts and corrupts the light of nature; either from his own peculiar and singular disposition, or from his education and intercourse with others, or from his reading, and the authority acquired by those whom he reverences and admires, or from the different impressions produced on the mind, as it happens to be preoccupied and predisposed, or equable and tranquil, and the like: so that the spirit of man (according to its several dispositions) is variable, confused, and as it were actuated by chance; and Heraclitus said well that men search for knowledge in lesser worlds, and not in the greater or common world.

43. There are also idols formed by the reciprocal intercourse and society of man with man, which we call idols of the market, from the commerce and association of men with each other. For men converse by means of language; but words are formed at the will of the generality; and there arises from a bad and unapt formation of words a wonderful obstruction to the mind. Nor can the definitions and explanations, with which learned men are wont to guard and protect themselves in some instances, afford a complete remedy: words still manifestly force the understanding, throw every thing into confusion, and lead mankind into vain and innumerable controversies and fallacies.

44. Lastly, there are idols which have crept into men's minds from the various dogmas of peculiar systems of philosophy, and also from the perverted rules of demonstration, and these we denominate idols of the theatre. For we regard all the systems of philosophy hitherto received or imagined, as so many plays brought out and performed, creating fictitious and theatrical worlds. Nor do we speak only on the present systems, or of the philosophy and sects of the ancients, since numerous other plays of a similar nature can be still composed and made to agree with each other, the causes of the most opposite errors being generally the same. Nor, again, do we allude merely to general systems, but also to many elements and axioms of sciences, which have become inveterate by tradition, implicit credence, and neglect. We must, however, discuss each species of idols more fully and distinctly, in order to guard the human understanding against them.

42
John Amos Comenius
(1592-1670)
A Unified Approach

Selections from *The Greate Didactic of John Amos Comenius*: Now for the First Time Englished With Introductions, Biographical and Historical, by M. W. Keatinge, B. A., Late Exhibitioneer of Exeter College, Oxford (London, Adam and Charles Black, 1896), title page (front and back), first 3 paragraphs of "Greeting to the Reader," "Subjects of the Chapters," and Chapter XX: "The Method of the Sciences, Specifically," pp. 335-345.

The Method of the Sciences, Specifically

1. We must now collect together the scattered observations that we have made on the proper teaching of the sciences, of the arts, of morality, and of piety. By proper teaching I mean teaching that combines ease, thoroughness, and rapidity.

2. Science, or the knowledge of nature, consists of an internal perception, and needs the same accessories as the external perception of the eye, namely, an object to observe, and light by which to observe it. If these be given, perception will follow. The eye of the inner perception is the mind or the understanding, the object is all that lies within or without our apprehension, while the light is the necessary attention. But, as in the case of external perception a definite procedure is necessary in order to apprehend things as they are, so with internal perception a certain method is necessary if things are to be presented to the mind in such a way that it can grasp them and assimilate them with ease.

3. The youth who wishes to penetrate the mysteries of the sciences must carefully observe four rules:

(i) He must keep the eye of his mind pure.

(ii) He must see that the object be brought near to it.

(iii) He must pay attention.

(iv) He must proceed from one object to another in accordance with a suitable method. For thus he will apprehend everything surely and easily.

4. Over the amount of ability that we possess we have no control, for God has portioned out this mirror of the understanding, this inner eye, according to His will. But it lies in our power to prevent it from growing dusty or dim. By dust, I mean the idle, useless, and empty

416

The Great Didactic

Setting forth

The whole Art of Teaching
all Things to all Men

or

A certain Inducement to found such Schools in all
the Parishes, Towns, and Villages of every
Christian Kingdom, that the entire
Youth of both Sexes, none
being excepted, shall

Quickly, *Pleasantly*, *& Thoroughly*

Become learned in the Sciences, pure in Morals,
trained to Piety, and in this manner
instructed in all things necessary
for the present and for
the future life,

in which, with respect to everything that is suggested,

Its FUNDAMENTAL PRINCIPLES are set forth from the essential
nature of the matter,
Its TRUTH is proved by examples from the several
mechanical arts,
Its ORDER is clearly set forth in years, months, days, and
hours, and, finally,
AN EASY AND SURE METHOD is shown, by which it can
be pleasantly brought into existence.

Let the main object of this, our Didactic, be as follows: To seek and to find a method of instruction, by which teachers may teach less, but learners may learn more; by which schools may.be the scene of less noise, aversion, and useless labour, but of more leisure, enjoyment, and solid progress; and through which the Christian community may have less darkness, perplexity, and dissension, but on the other hand more light, orderliness, peace, and rest.

God be merciful unto us and bless us, and cause his face to shine upon us;
That thy way may be known upon earth, thy saving health among all nations.—Psalm lxvii. 1, 2.

GREETING TO THE READER

[The References are to notes at the end of the book]

1. DIDACTIC signifies the art of teaching. Several men of ability, taking pity on the Sisyphus-labour of schools, have lately endeavoured to find out some such Art, but with unequal skill and unequal success.

2. Some merely wished to give assistance towards learning some language or other with greater ease. Others found ways of imparting this or that science or art with greater speed. Others suggested improvements of various kinds; but almost all proceeded by means of unconnected precepts, gleaned from a superficial experience, that is to say, *a posteriori.*

3. We venture to promise a GREAT DIDACTIC, that is to say, the whole art of teaching all things to all men, and indeed of teaching them with certainty, so that the result cannot fail to follow; further, of teaching them pleasantly, that is to say, without annoyance or aversion on the part of teacher or pupil, but rather with the greatest enjoyment for both; further of teaching them thoroughly, not superficially and showily, but in such a manner as to lead to true knowledge, to gentle morals, and to the deepest piety. Lastly, we wish to prove all this *a priori,* that is to say, from the unalterable nature of the matter itself, drawing off, as from a living source, the constantly flowing runlets, and bringing them together again into one concentrated stream, that we may lay the foundations of the universal art of founding universal schools.

SUBJECTS OF THE CHAPTERS

I. Man is the highest, the most absolute, and the most excellent of things created   177

II. The ultimate end of man is beyond this life   179

III. This life is but a preparation for eternity   184

IV. There are three stages in the preparation for eternity: to know oneself (and with oneself all things) ; to rule oneself; and to direct oneself to God   .   188

V. The seeds of these three (learning, virtue, religion) are naturally implanted in us   192

VI. If a man is to be produced, it is necessary that he be formed by education   .   204

VII. A man can most easily be formed in early youth, and cannot be formed properly except at this age   .   .   .   209

VIII. The young must be educated in common, and for this schools are necessary   .   213

IX. All the young of both sexes should be sent to school   218

X. The instruction given in schools should be universal   222

XI. Hitherto there have been no perfect schools   228

XII. It is possible to reform schools   .   .   233

XIII. The basis of school reform must be exact order in all things   .   .   .   245

XIV. The exact order of instruction must be borrowed from nature .   .   .   250

XV. The basis of the prolongation of life   .   256

XVI. The universal requirements of teaching and of learning; that is to say, a method of teaching and of learning with such certainty that the desired result must of necessity follow . . 263

XVII. The principles of facility in teaching and in learning 279

XVIII. The principles of thoroughness in teaching and in learning . . . 294

XIX. The principles of conciseness and rapidity in teaching 312

XX. The method of the sciences, specifically . 335

XXI. The method of the arts . . . 346

XXII. The method of languages . . 355

XXIII. The method of morals . . . 363

XXIV. The method of instilling piety . . 370

XXV. If we wish to reform schools in accordance with the laws of true Christianity, we must remove from them books written by pagans, or, at any rate, must use them with more caution than hitherto 383

XXVI. Of school discipline 401

XXVII. Of the four-fold division of schools, based on age and acquirements . 407

XXVIII. Sketch of the Mother-School . . 411

XXIX. Sketch of the Vernacular-School . . 418

XXX. Sketch of the Latin-School . . 426

XXXI. Of the University, of travelling students, of the College of Light . . 433

XXXII. Of the universal and perfect order of instruction 439

XXXIII. Of the things requisite before this universal method can be put into practice . 447

occupations of the mind. For our mind is in constant activity, like a continually running mill-stone, and is supplied by its servants, the external senses, with material from every side. But unless the chief inspector, the reason, be continually on the watch, worthless material is supplied, such as chaff, straw, or sand, instead of corn or wheat. Thus it comes to pass that, as in the case of a mill, every corner is filled with dust. This inner mill, therefore, the mind (which is also a mirror) will be kept free from dust, if the young be kept away from worthless occupations and be skilfully trained to like worthy and useful things.

5. In order that the mirror may duly receive the images of the objects, it is necessary that these latter be solid and visible, and be also placed suitably before the eyes. Clouds and similar objects that possess little consistency make but a slight impression on a mirror, while objects that are not present make none at all. Those things, therefore, that are placed before the intelligence of the young, must be real things and not the shadows of things. I repeat, they must be *things*; and by the term I mean determinate, real, and useful things that can make an impression on the senses and on the imagination. But they can only make this impression when brought sufficiently near.

6. From this a golden rule for teachers may be derived. Everything should, as far as is possible, be placed before the senses. Everything visible should be brought before the organ of sight, everything audible before that of hearing. Odours should be placed before the sense of smell, and things that are tastable and tangible before the sense of taste and of touch respectively. If an object can make an impression on several senses at once, it should be brought into contact with several, though with the limitations imposed in the seventh Principle of chap. viii. ["7. (iii) And although there might be parents with leisure to educate their own children, it is nevertheless better that the young should be taught together and in large classes, since better results and more pleasure are to be obtained when one pupil serves as an example and a stimulus for another. For to do what we see others do, to go where others go, to follow those who are ahead of us, and to keep in front of those who are behind us, is the course of action to which we are all most naturally inclined.

It is when the steed has rivals to surpass or leaders to follow,
That he runs his best.

Young children, especially, are always more easily led and ruled by example than by precept. If you give them a precept, it makes but little impression; if you point out that others are doing something, they imitate without being told to do so."]

7. For this there are three cogent reasons. Firstly, the commence-

ment of knowledge must always come from the senses (for the under-standing possesses nothing that it has not first derived from the senses). Surely, then, the beginning of wisdom should consist, not in the mere learning the names of things, but in the actual perception of the things themselves! It is when the thing has been grasped by the senses that language should fulfil its function of explaining it still further.

8. Secondly, the truth and certainty of science depend more on the witness of the senses than on anything else. For things impress them-selves directly on the senses, but on the understanding only mediately and through the senses. This is evident from the fact that belief is at once accorded to knowledge derived from the senses, while an appeal is always made to them from *a priori* reasoning and from the testimony of others. We do not trust a conclusion derived from reasoning unless it can be verified by a display of examples (the trustworthiness of which depends on sensuous perception). No one could have such confidence in the testimony of another person as to disbelieve the experience of his own senses. Science, then, increases in certainty in proportion as it depends on sensuous perception. It follows, therefore, that if we wish to implant a true and certain knowledge of things in our pupils, we must take especial care that everything be learned by means of actual observation and sensuous perception.

9. Thirdly, since the senses are the most trusty servants of the memory, this method of sensuous perception, if universally applied, will lead to the permanent retention of knowledge that has once been acquired. For instance, if I have once tasted sugar, seen a camel, heard a nightingale sing, or been in Rome, and have on each occasion attentively impressed the fact on my memory, the incidents will remain fresh and permanent. We find, accordingly, that children can easily learn Scriptural and secular stories from pictures. Indeed, he who has once seen a rhinoceros (even in a picture) or been present at a certain occurrence, can picture the animal to himself and retain the event in his memory with greater ease than if they had been described to him six hundred times. Hence the saying of Plautus: "An eye-witness is worth more than ten ear-witnesses." Horace also says: "What is entrusted to the fickle ears makes less impression on the mind than things which are actually presented to the eyes and which the spectator stores up for himself."

In the same manner, whoever has once seen a dissection of the human body will understand and remember the relative position of its parts with far greater certainty than if he had read the most exhaustive treatises on anatomy, but had never actually seen a dissection performed. Hence the saying, "Seeing is believing."

10. If the objects themselves cannot be procured, representations of them may be used. Copies or models may be constructed for teaching purposes, and the same principle may be adopted by botanists, geometricians, zoologists, and geographers, who should illustrate their descriptions by engravings of the objects described. The same thing should be done in books on physics and elsewhere. For example, the human body will be well explained by ocular demonstration if the following plan be adopted. A skeleton should be procured (either such an one as is usually kept in universities, or one made of wood), and on this framework should be placed the muscles, sinews, nerves, veins, arteries, as well as the intestines, the lungs, the heart, the diaphragm, and the liver. These should be made of leather and stuffed with wool, and should be of the right size and in the right place, while on each organ should be written its name and its function. If you take the student of medicine to this construction and explain each part to him separately, he will grasp all the details without any effort, and from that time forth will understand the mechanism of his own body. For every branch of knowledge similar constructions (that is to say, images of things which cannot be procured in the original) should be made, and should be kept in the schools ready for use. It is true that expense and labour will be necessary to produce these models, but the result will amply reward the effort.

11. If any be uncertain if all things can be placed before the senses in this way, even things spiritual and things absent (things in heaven, or in hell, or beyond the sea), let him remember that all things have been harmoniously arranged by God in such a manner that the higher in the scale of existence can be represented by the lower, the absent by the present, and the invisible by the visible. This can be seen in the *Macromicrocosmus* of Robert Flutt, in which the origin of the winds, of rain, and of thunder is described in such a way that the reader can visualise it. Nor is there any doubt that even greater concreteness and ease of demonstration than is here displayed might be attained.

12. So much of the presentation of objects to the senses. We must now speak of the light, the absence of which renders the presentation of objects to the eyes useless. This light of the teaching art is attention, and by its means the learner can keep his mind from wandering and can take in everything that is put before him. It is impossible for any man to see an object in the dark, or if his eyes be closed, no matter how near to him it may be; and in the same way, if you talk to one who is not attending, or show him anything, you will make no impression on his senses. This we can observe in the case of those who, while lost in thought, do not notice what is going on before their eyes. He, therefore, who wishes to show anything to another at night

must provide light, and must polish the object so that it shines; and in the same way a master, if he wishes to illumine with knowledge a pupil shrouded in the darkness of ignorance, must first excite his attention, that he may drink in information with a greedy mind. How this can be done we have shown in the 17th chapter, and in the first Principle of the 19th chapter.

13. So much of the light. We will now speak of the mode in which objects must be presented to the senses, if the impression is to be distinct. This can be readily understood if we consider the processes of actual vision. If the object is to be clearly seen it is necessary: (1) that it be placed before the eyes; (2) not far off, but at a reasonable distance; (3) not on one side, but straight before the eyes; (4) and so that the front of the object be not turned away from, but directed towards, the observer; (5) that the eyes first take in the object as a whole; (6) and then proceed to distinguish the parts; (7) inspecting these in order from the beginning to the end; (8) that attention be paid to each and every part; (9) until they are all grasped by means of their essential attributes. If these requisites be properly observed, vision takes place successfully; but if one be neglected its success is only partial.

14. For instance, if any one wish to read a letter that has been sent him by a friend, it is necessary: (1) that it be presented to the eyes (for if it be not seen, how can it be read?); (2) that it be placed at a suitable distance from the eyes (for if it be too far off, the words cannot be distinguished); (3) that it be directly in front of the eyes (for if it be on one side, it will be confusedly seen); (4) that it be turned the right way up (for if a letter or a book be presented to the eyes upside down or on its side, it cannot be read); (5) the general characteristics of the letter, such as the address, the writer, and the date must be seen first (for unless these faces be known, the particular items of the letter cannot be properly understood); (6) then the remainder of the letter must be read, that nothing be omitted (otherwise the contents will not all be known, and perhaps the most important point will be missed); (7) it must be read in the right order (if one sentence be read here and another there, the sense will be confused); (8) each sentence must be mastered before the next is commenced (for if the whole be read hurriedly, some useful point may easily escape the mind); (9) finally, when the whole has been carefully perused, the reader may proceed to distinguish between those points that are necessary and those that are superfluous.

15. These points should be observed by those who teach the sciences, and may be expressed in nine very useful precepts.

(i) Whatever is to be known must be taught.

Unless that which is to be known be placed before a pupil, how is he to acquire a knowledge of it? Therefore let those who teach beware of concealing anything from their pupils, whether of intent, as do the envious and dishonest, or through carelessness, as is the case with those who perform their duties in a perfunctory manner. The two things necessary are honesty and hard work.

16. (ii) Whatever is taught should be taught as being of practical application in every-day life and of some definite use.

That is to say, the pupil should understand that what he learns is not taken out of some Utopia or borrowed from Platonic Ideas, but is one of the facts which surround us, and that a fitting acquaintance with it will be of great service in life. In this way his energy and his accuracy will be increased.

17. (iii) Whatever is taught should be taught straightforwardly, and not in a complicated manner.

This means that we must look straight at objects and not squint, for in that case the eyes do not see that at which they look, but rather distort and confuse it. Objects should be placed before the eyes of the student in their true character, and not shrouded in words, metaphors, or hyperboles. These devices have their use if the object be to exaggerate or to detract from, to praise or to blame what is already known. But when knowledge is being acquired they should be avoided and the facts should be set forth plainly.

18. (iv) Whatever is taught must be taught with reference to its true nature and its origin; that is to say, through its causes.

This method of cognition is the best if the true nature of a fact is to be learned. For if its true nature be not made evident, this is not cognition but error. The true nature of a fact lies in the process that brought it into being. If it appear to contain elements not accounted for by that process, it is evident that there is some misapprehension. Now everything is brought into existence by its causes. Therefore to explain the causes of anything is equivalent to making a true exposition of that thing's nature, in accordance with the principles: "Knowledge consists in having a firm grip of causes," and "Causes are the guides of the understanding." Objects can thus be best, easiest, and most certainly cognised through a knowledge of the processes that produced them. If a man wish to read a letter he holds it as it was written, since it is a difficult thing to read a document that is inverted, or on its side, and in the same way, if a fact be explained by means of the process that gave it birth, it will be easily and surely understood. If, however, the teacher reverse the order of nature, he is certain to confuse the student. Therefore, the method employed in teaching should be based on the method of nature. That which precedes should be taken first, and that which follows last.

19. (v) If anything is to be learned, its general principles must first be explained. Its details may then be considered, and not till then.

The reasons for this have been given in chap. xvi. Principle 6. We give a general notion of an object when we explain it by means of its essential nature and its accidental qualities. The essential nature is unfolded by the questions *what? of what kind? and why?* Under the question *what?* are included the name, the genus, the function, and the end. Under the question *of what kind?* comes the form of the object, or the mode in which it is fitted to its end. Under the question *why?* the efficient or causal force by which an object is made suitable to its end. For example, did I wish to give a student a general notion of a man, I should say: Man is (1) the chief creation of God, and destined for dominion over other creatures; (2) endowed with freedom of choice and action; (3) and on that account provided with the light of reason, that he may direct his choice and his actions with wisdom. This is but a general notion of man, but it goes to the root of the matter and says everything about him that is essential. To these you may, if you like, add some of his accidental qualities, still keeping to generalities, and this must be done by asking the questions: *from what origin? whence? when?* You may then proceed to his parts, the body and the soul. The nature of the body can be demonstrated through the anatomy of its organs; that of the soul by examining the faculties of which it consists. All these points must be taken in their proper order.

20. (vi) All the parts of an object, even the smallest, and without a single exception, must be learned with reference to their order, their position, and their connection with one another.

Nothing exists in vain, and sometimes the strength of the larger parts depends on that of the smallest. Certain it is that in a clock, if one pin be broken or bent, or moved out of its place, the whole machine will stop. Similarly, in a living body, the loss of one organ may cause life to cease, and in a sentence it is often on the smallest words, such as prepositions and conjunctions, that the whole sense depends. Perfect knowledge of an object can therefore only be attained by acquiring a knowledge of the nature and function of each of its parts.

21. (vii) All things must be taught in due succession, and not more than one thing should be taught at one time.

The organ of vision is unable to take in two or three objects at one time (certain it is that he who reads a book cannot look at two pages at once, nay, cannot even see two lines, though they lie quite close together, nor two words, nor two letters, otherwise than successively); and in the same way the mind can only grasp one thing at a time. We should therefore make a distinct break in our progress from one thing to another, that we may not overburden the mind.

22. (viii) We should not leave any subject until it is thoroughly understood.

Nothing can be done in a moment. For every process involves motion, and motion implies successive stages. The pupil should therefore not pass on from any point in a science until he has thoroughly mastered it and is conscious that he has done so. The methods to be employed are emphatic teaching, examination, and iteration, until the desired result is attained. This we have pointed out in chap. xviii. Principle 10.

23. (ix) Stress should be laid on the differences which exist between things, in order that what knowledge of them is acquired may be clear and distinct.

Much meaning lies concealed in that celebrated saying: "He who distinguishes well is a good teacher." For too many facts overwhelm a student, and too great a variety confuses him. Remedies must therefore be applied: in the first case order, by means of which one thing may be taken after another; in the second, a careful consideration of the differences that exist in nature, that it may always be evident in what respects one thing differs from another. This is the only method that can give distinct, clear, and certain knowledge; since the variety and actuality of natural objects depend on their distinctive attributes, as we have hinted in chap. xviii. Principle 6.

24. Now it is impossible that all teachers, when they enter on their profession, should be possessed of the requisite skill, and it is therefore necessary that the sciences which are taught in schools be mapped out in accordance with the foregoing laws. If this be done it will be difficult for any teacher to miss his mark. For, if the laws be rigorously observed, it is beyond question that any man who is once admitted into the royal palace and is allotted a certain space of time can easily and without any trouble master its whole contents, its pictures, statues, carpets, and other ornaments; and just as easy will it be for a youth who is admitted to the theatre of this world to penetrate with his mental vision the secrets of nature, and from that time forward to move among the works of God and of man with his eyes opened.

43
John Locke (1632-1704).
A Dual System

Locke's Proposals for Reform of the Poor Law (1697)

Selections from H. R. Fox Bourne, *The Life of John Locke* (London: Henry S. King & Co., 1876), II, pp. 383-386.

This, rightly considered, shows us what is the true and proper relief of the poor. It consists in finding work for them, and taking care they do not live like drones upon the labour of others. And in order to this end we find the laws made for the relief of the poor were intended; however, by an ignorance of their intention or a neglect of their due execution, they are turned only to the maintenance of people in idleness, without at all examining into the lives, abilities, or industry of those who seek for relief.

In order to the suppression of these idle beggars, the corporations in England have beadles authorised and paid to prevent the breach of the law in that particular; yet, nevertheless, the streets everywhere swarm with beggars, to the increase of idleness, poverty, and villany, and to the shame of Christianity. And, if it should be asked in any town in England, how many of these visible trespassers have been taken up and brought to punishment by those officers this last year, we have reason to think the number would be found to have been very small, because that of beggars swarming in the street is manifestly very great.

But the remedy of this disorder is so well provided by the laws now in force that we can impute the continuance and increase of it to nothing but a general neglect of their execution.

2. Besides the grown people above mentioned, the children of labouring people are an ordinary burden to the parish, and are usually maintained in idleness, so that their labour also is generally lost to the public till they are twelve or fourteen years old.

The most effectual remedy for this that we are able to conceive, and which we therefore humbly propose, is, that, in the fore-mentioned new law to be enacted, it be further provided that working schools be set up in every parish, to which the children of all such as demand relief of the parish, above three and under fourteen years of age, whilst they live at home with their parents, and are not otherwise employed for their livelihood by the allowance of the overseers of the poor, shall be obliged to come.

By this means the mother will be eased of a great part of her trouble in looking after and providing for them at home, and so be at the more liberty to work; the children will be kept in much better order, be better provided for, and from infancy be inured to work, which is of no small consequence to the making of them sober and industrious all their lives after; and the parish will be either eased of this burden or at least of the misuse in the present management of it. For, a great number of children giving a poor man a title to an allowance from the parish, this allowance is given once a week or once a month to the father in money, which he not seldom spends on himself at the alehouse, whilst his children, for whose sake he had it, are left to suffer, or perish under the want of necesaries, unless the charity of neighbours relieve them.

We humbly conceive that a man and his wife in health may be able by their ordinary labour to maintain themselves and two children. More than two children at one time under the age of three years will seldom happen in one family. If therefore all the children above three years old be taken off from their hands those who have never so many, whilst they remain themselves in health, will not need any allowance for them.

We do not suppose that children gf three years old will be able at that age to get their livelihoods at the working school, but we are sure that what is necessary for their relief will more effectually have that use if it be distributed to them in bread at that school than if it be given to their fathers in money. What they have at home from their parents is seldom more than bread and water, and that, many of them, very scantily too. If therefore care be taken that they have each of them their belly-full of bread daily at school, they will be in no danger of famishing, but, on the contrary, they will be healthier and stronger than those who are bred otherwise. Nor will this practice cost the overseers any trouble; for a baker may be agreed with to furnish and bring into the schoolhouse every day the allowance of bread necessary for all the scholars that are there. And to this may be also added, without any trouble, in cold weather, if it be thought needful, a little warm water-gruel; for the same fire that warms the room may be made use of to boil a pot of it.

From this method the children will not only reap the fore-mentioned advantages with far less charge to the parish than what is now done for them, but they will be also thereby the more obliged to come to school and apply themselves to work, because otherwise they will have no victuals, and also the benefit thereby both to themselves and the parish will daily increase; for, the earnings of their labour at school every day increasing, it may reasonably be concluded that, computing all the earnings of a child from three to fourteen years of age, the nourishment and teaching of such a child during that whole time will cost the parish nothing; whereas there is no child now which from its birth is maintained by the parish but, before the age of fourteen, costs the parish 50£ or 60£.

Another advantage also of bringing children thus to a working school is that by this means they may be obliged to come constantly to church every Sunday, along with their schoolmasters or dames, whereby they may be brought into some sense of religion; whereas ordinarily now, in their idle and loose way of breeding up, they are as utter strangers both to religion and morality as they are to industry.

In order therefore to the more effectual carrying on of this work to the advantage of this kingdom, we further humbly propose that these schools be generally for spinning or knitting, or some other part of the woollen manufacture, unless in countries (that is, districts) where the place shall furnish some other materials fitter for the employment of such poor children; in which places the choice of those materials for their employment may be left to the prudence and direction of the guardians of the poor of that hundred. And that the teachers in these schools be paid out of the poor's rate, as can be agreed.

This, though at first setting up it may cost the parish a little, yet we humbly conceive (the earnings of the children abating the charge of their maintenance, and as much work being required of each of them as they are reasonably able to perform) it will quickly pay its own charges with an overplus.

That, where the number of the poor children of any parish is greater than for them all to be employed in one school they be there divided into two, and the boys and girls, if thought convenient, taught and kept to work separately.

That the handicraftsmen in each hundred be bound to take every other of their respective apprentices from amongst the boys in some one of the schools in the said hundred without any money; which boys they may so take at what age they please, to be bound to them till the age of twenty-three years, that so the length of time may more than make amends for the usual sums that are given to handicraftsmen with such apprentices.

That those also in the hundred who keep in their hands land of their own to the value of 25£ per annum, or upwards, or who rent 50£ per annum or upwards, may choose out of the schools of the said hundred what boy each of them pleases, to be his apprentice in husbandry on the same condition.

That whatever boys are not by this means bound out apprentices before they are full fourteen shall, at the Easter meeting of the guardians of each hundred every year, be bound to such gentlemen, yeomen, or farmers within the said hundred as have the greatest number of acres of land in their hands, who shall be obliged to take them for their apprentices till the age of twenty-three, or bind them out at their own cost to some handicraftsmen; provided always that no such gentleman, yeoman, or farmer shall be bound to have two such apprentices at a time.

That grown people also (to take away their pretence of want of work) may come to the said working schools to learn, where work shall accordingly be provided for them.

"That the materials to be employed in these schools and among other the [sic] poor people of the parish be provided by a common stock in each hundred, to be raised out of a certain portion of the poor's rate of each parish as requisite; which stock, we humbly conceive, need be raised but once; for, if rightly managed, it will increase.

The Education of the Gentry

Selections from John Locke, *The Works of John Locke: A New Edition, Corrected, in Ten Volumes* (London: Printed for Thomas Tegg; W. Sharpe and Son; G. Offor; G. and J. Robinson, J. Evans and Co.: Also R. Griffin and Co. Glasgow; and J. Cumming, Dublin, 1823); *An Essay Concerning Human Understanding*, Vol. I, pp. 13, 82-86, 152-152:

Book I, Chapter II
No Innate Principles in the Mind

1. It is an established opinion amongst some men, that there are in the understanding certain innate principles, some primary notions, χοιναι εννοιαι; characters, as it were, stamped upon the mind of man, which the soul receives in its very first being, and brings into the world with it. It would be sufficient to convince unprejudiced readers of the falseness of this supposition, if I should only show (as I hope I shall in the following parts of this discourse) how men, barely by the use of their natural faculties, may attain to all the knowledge they have, without the help of any innate impressions; and may arrive at certainty, without any such original notions or principles. For I imagine any one will easily grant, that it would be impertinent to suppose the ideas of colours innate in a creature, to whom God hath given sight, and a power to receive them by the eyes, from external objects; and no less unreasonable would it be to attribute several truths to the impressions of nature, and innate characters, when we may observe in ourselves faculties, fit to attain as easy and certain knowledge of them as if they were originally imprinted on the mind.

But because a man is not permitted without censure to follow his own thoughts in the search of truth, when they lead him ever so little out of the common road; I shall set down the reasons that made me doubt of the truth of that opinion, as an excuse for my mistake, if I be in one; which I leave to be considered by those, who, with me, dispose themselves to embrace truth wherever they find it. . . .

Book II, Chapter I
Of Ideas in general, and their Original

1. Every man being conscious to himself that he thinks, and that which his mind is applied about, whilst thinking, being the ideas that are there, it is past doubt, that men have in their minds several ideas, such as are those expressed by the words whiteness, hardness, sweetness, thinking, motion, man, elephant, army, drunkenness, and others. It is in the first place then to be inquired, how he comes by them. I know it is a received doctrine, that men have native ideas and original characters stamped upon their minds in their very first being. This opinion I have, at large, examined already; and, I suppose, what I have said, in the foregoing book, will be much more easily admitted, when I have shown whence the understanding may get all the ideas it has, and by what ways and degrees they may come into the mind; for which I shall appeal to every one's own observation and experience.

2. Let us then suppose the mind to be, as we say, white paper, void of all characters, without any ideas; how comes it to be furnished? Whence comes it by that vast store which the busy and boundless fancy of man has painted on it, with an almost endless variety? Whence has it all the materials of reason and knowledge? To this I answer, in one word, from experience: in that all our knowledge is founded, and from that it ultimately derives itself. Our observation employed either about external sensible objects, or about the internal operations of our minds, perceived and reflected on by ourselves, is that which supplies our understandings with all the materials of thinking. These two are the fountains of knowledge, from whence all the ideas we have, or can naturally have, do spring.

3. First, Our senses, conversant about particular sensible objects, do convey into the mind several distinct perceptions of things, according to those various ways wherein those objects do affect them: and thus we come by those ideas we have of yellow, white, heat, cold, soft, hard, bitter, sweet, and all those which we call sensible qualities; which when I say the senses convey into the mind what produces there those perceptions. This great source of most of the ideas we have, depending wholly upon our senses, and derived by them to the understanding, I call SENSATION.

4. Secondly, The other fountain from which experience furnisheth

the understanding with ideas, is the perception of the operations of our own mind within us, as it is employed about the ideas it has got; which operations when the soul comes to reflect on and consider, do furnish the understanding with another set of ideas, which could not be had from things without; and such are perception, thinking, doubting, believing, reasoning, knowing, willing, and all the different actings of our own minds; which we being conscious of and observing in ourselves, do from these receive into our understandings as distinct ideas, as we do from bodies affecting our senses. This source of ideas every man has wholly in himself: and though it be not sense, as having nothing to do with external objects, yet it is very like it, and might properly enough be called internal sense. But as I call the other sensation, so I call this REFLECTION, the ideas it affords being such only as the mind gets by reflecting on its own operations within itself. By reflection, then, in the following part of this discourse, I would be understood to mean that notice which the mind takes of its own operations, and the manner of them; by reason whereof there come to be ideas of these operations in the understanding. These two, I say, viz. external material things, as the objects of sensation; and the operations of our own minds within, as the objects of reflection; are to me the only originals from whence all our ideas take their beginnings. The term operations here I use in a large sense, as comprehending not barely the actions of the mind about its ideas, but some sort of passions arising sometimes from them, such as is the satisfaction or uneasiness arising from any thought.

5. The understanding seems to me not to have the least glimmering of any ideas, which it doth not receive from one of these two. External objects furnish the mind with the ideas of sensible qualities, which are all those different perceptions they produce in us: and the mind furnishes the understanding with ideas of its own operations.

These, when we have taken a full survey of them and their several modes, combinations, and relations, we shall find to contain all our whole stock of ideas; and that we have nothing in our minds which did not come in one of these two ways. Let any one examine his own thoughts, and thoroughly search into his understanding; and then let him tell me, whether all the original ideas he has there are any other than of the objects of his senses, or of the operations of his mind, con- considered as objects of his reflection: and how great a mass of know- ledge soever he imagines to be lodged there, he will, upon taking a strict view, see that he has not any idea in his mind, but what one of these two have imprinted; though perhaps with infinite variety compounded and enlarged by the understanding, as we shall see hereafter.

6. He that attentively considers the state of a child, at his first com- ing into the world, will have little reason to think him stored with plenty

of ideas, that are to be the matter of his future knowledge: it is by degrees he comes to be furnished with them. And though the ideas of obvious and familiar qualities imprint themselves before the memory begins to keep a register of time or order, yet it is often so late before some unusual qualities come in the way, that there are few men that cannot recollect the beginning of their acquaintance with them: and if it were worth while, no doubt a child might be so ordered as to have but a very few even of the ordinary ideas, till he were grown up to a man. But all that are born into the world being surrounded with bodies that perpetually and diversely affect them, variety of ideas, whether care be taken of it or no, are imprinted on the minds of children. Light and colours are busy at hand every where, when the eye is but open; sounds and some tangible qualities fail not to solicit their proper senses, and force an entrance to the mind: but yet, I think, it will be granted easily, that if a child were kept in a place where he never saw any other but black and white till he were a man, he would have no more ideas of scarlet or green, than he that from his childhood never tasted an oyster or a pine-apple has of those particular relishes.

7. Men then come to be furnished with fewer or more simple ideas from without, according as the objects they converse with afford greater or less variety; and from the operations of their minds within, according as they more or less reflect on them. For though he that contemplates the operations of his mind cannot but have plain and clear ideas of them; yet unless he turns his thoughts that way, and considers them attentively, he will no more have clear and distinct ideas of all the operations of his mind, and all that may be observed therein, than he will have all the particular ideas of any landscape, or of the parts and motions of a clock, who will not turn his eyes to it, and with attention heed all the parts of it. The picture or clock may be so placed, that they may come in his way every day; but yet he will have but a confused ideas of all the parts they are made up of, till he applies himself with attention to consider them each in particular.

8. And hence we see the reason, why it is pretty late before most children get ideas of the operations of their own minds; and some have not any very clear or perfect ideas of the greatest part of them all their lives: because though they pass there continually, yet, like floating visions, they make not deep impressions enough to leave in their mind clear, distinct, lasting ideas, till the understanding turns inward upon itself, reflects on its own operations, and makes them the objects of its own contemplation. Children when they come first into it, are surrounded with a world of new things, which, by a constant solicitation of their senses, draw the mind constantly to them, forward to take notice of new, and apt to be delighted with the variety of changing objects.

Thus the first years are usually employed and diverted in looking abroad. Men's business in them is to acquaint themselves with what is to be found without: and so growing up in a constant attention to outward sensations, seldom make any considerable reflection on what passes within them till they come to be of riper years; and some scarce ever at all. . . .

Book II, Chapter XI
Of Discerning, and other Operations of the Mind

15. And thus I have given a short, and, I think, true history of the first beginnings of human knowledge, whence the mind has its first objects, and by what steps it makes its progress to the laying in and storing up those ideas, out of which is to be framed all the knowledge it is capable of; wherein I must appeal to experience and observation, whether I am in the right; the best way to come to truth being to examine things as really they are, and not to conclude they are, as we fancy of ourselves, or have been taught by others to imagine.

16. To deal truly, this is the only way that I can discover, whereby the ideas of things are brought into the understanding: if other men have either innate ideas, or infused principles, they have reason to enjoy them; and if they are sure of it, it is impossible for others to deny them the privilege that they have above their neighbours. I can speak but of what I find in myself, and is agreeable to those notions; which, if we will examine the whole course of men in their several ages, countries, and educations, seem to depend on those foundations which I have laid, and to correspond with this method in all the parts and degrees thereof.

17. I pretend not to teach, but to inquire, and therefore cannot but confess here again, that external and internal sensation are the only passages that I can find of knowledge to the understanding. These alone, as far as I can discover, are the windows by which light is let into this dark room: for methinks the understanding is not much unlike a closet wholly shut from light, with only some little opening left, to let in external visible resemblances, or ideas of things without: would the pictures coming into such a dark room but stay there, and lie so orderly as to be found upon occasion, it would very much resemble the understanding of a man, in reference to all objects of sight, and the ideas of them.

These are my guesses concerning the means whereby the understanding comes to have and retain simple ideas, and the modes of them, with some other operations about them. I proceed now to examine some of these simple ideas, and their modes, a little more particularly.

Some Thoughts Concerning Education, Vol. IX, pp. 6-7, 18-19, 26-28, 36-37, 41-42, 45-48, 53-60, 76, 78-81, 84-86, 128, 187, 190, 193-194.

1. A sound mind in a sound body, is a short but full description of a happy state in this world: he that has these two, has little more to wish for; and he that wants either of them, will be but little the better for any thing else. Men's happiness or misery is most part of their own making. He whose mind directs not wisely, will never take the right way; and he whose body is crazy and feeble, will never be able to advance in it. I confess, there are some men's constitutions of body and mind so vigorous, and well framed by nature, that they need not much assistance from others; but, by the strength of their natural genius, they are, from their cradles, carried towards what is excellent; and, by the privilege of their happy constitutions, are able to do wonders. But examples of this kind are but few; and I think I may say, that, of all the men we meet with, nine parts of ten are what they are, good or evil, useful or not, by their education. It is that which makes the great difference in mankind. The little, or almost insensible, impressions on our tender infancies, have very important and lasting consequences: and there it is, as in the fountains of some rivers, where a gentle application of the hand turns the flexible waters into channels, that make them take quite contrary courses; and by this little direction, given them at first, in the source, they receive different tendencies, and arrive at last at very remote and distant places.

18. . . . The great thing to be minded in education is, what habits you settle: and therefore in this, as all other things, do not begin to make any thing customary, the practice whereof you would not have continue and increase. . . .

30. And thus I have done with what concerns the body and health, which reduces itself to these few and easily observable rules. Plenty of open air, exercise, and sleep; plain diet, no wine or strong drink, and very little or no physic; not too warm and strait clothing; especially the head and feet kept cold, and the feet often used to cold water and exposed to wet.

31. Due care being had to keep the body in strength and vigour, so that it may be able to obey and execute the orders of the mind; the next and principal business is, to set the mind right, that on all occasions it may be disposed to consent to nothing but what may be suitable to the dignity and excellency of a rational creature.

32. If what I have said in the beginning of this discourse be true, as

I do not doubt but it is, viz, that the difference to be found in the manners and abilities of men is owing more to their education than to any thing else; we have reason to conclude, that great care is to be had of the forming children's minds, and giving them that seasoning early, which shall influence their lives always after. For when they do well or ill, the praise or blame will be laid there: and when any thing is done awkwardly, the common saying will pass upon them, that it is suitable to their breeding.

33. As the strength of the body lies chiefly in being able to endure hardships, so also does that of the mind. And the great principle and foundation of all virtue and worth is placed in this, that a man is able to deny himself his own desires, cross his own inclinations, and purely follow what reason directs as best, though the appetite lean the other way.

34. The great mistake I have observed in people's breeding their children has been, that this has not been taken care enough of in its due season; that the mind has not been made obedient to discipline, and pliant to reason, when at first it was most tender, most easy to be bowed. Parents being wisely ordained by nature to love their children, are very apt, if reason watch not that natural affection very warily; are apt, I say, to let it run into fondness. They love their little ones, and it is their duty: but they often with them cherish their faults too. They must not be crossed, forsooth; they must be permitted to have their wills in all things; and they being in their infancies not capable of great vices, their parents think they may safely enough indulge their little irregularities, and make themselves sport with that pretty perverseness, which they think well enough becomes that innocent age. But to a fond parent, that would not have his child corrected for a perverse trick, but excused it, saying it was a small matter; Solon very well replied, "Ay, but custom is a great one."

35. The fondling must be taught to strike, and call names; must have what he cries for, and do what he pleases. Thus parents, by humouring and cockering them when little, corrupt the principles of nature in their children, and wonder afterwards to taste the bitter waters, when they themselves have poisoned the fountain. For when their children are grown up, and these ill habits with them; when they are now too big to be dandled, and their parents can no longer make use of them as playthings; then they complain that the brats are untoward and perverse; then they are offended to see them wilful, and are troubled with those ill humours, which they themselves infused and fomented in them; and then, perhaps too late, would be glad to get out those weeds which their own hands have planted, and which now have taken too deep root to be easily extirpated. For he that has been used to have his will in every thing, as long as he was in coats, why should we think it strange that

he should desire it and contend for it still, when he is in breeches? Indeed, as he grows more towards a man, age shows his faults the more, so that there be few parents then so blind, as not to see them; few so insensible as not to feel the ill effects of their own indulgence. He had the will of his maid before he could speak or go; he had the mastery of his parents ever since he could prattle; and why, now he is grown up, is stronger and wiser than he was then, why now of a sudden must he be restrained and curbed? why must he at seven, fourteen, or twenty years old, lose the privilege which the parent's indulgence, till then, so largely allowed him? Try it in a dog, or a horse, or any other creature, and see whether the ill and resty tricks they have learned when young are easily to be mended when they are knit: and yet none of those creatures are half so wilful and proud, or half so desirous to be masters of themselves and others, as man.

45. That this is so, will be easily allowed, when it is but considered what is to be aimed at, in an ingenuous education; and upon what it turns.

1. He that has not a mastery over his inclinations, he that knows not how to resist the importunity of present pleasure or pain, for the sake of what reason tells him is fit to be done, wants the true principle of virtue and industry; and is in danger of never being good for any thing. This temper, therefore, so contrary to unguided nature, is to be got betimes; and this habit, as the true foundation of future ability and happiness, is to be wrought into the mind, as early as may be, even from the first dawnings of any knowledge or apprehension in children; and so to be confirmed in them, by all the care and ways imaginable, by those who have the oversight of their education.

46. 2. On the other side, if the mind be curbed, and humbled too much in children; if their spirits be abased and broken much, by too strict an hand over them; they lose all their vigour and industry, and are in a worse state than the former. For extravagant young fellows, that have liveliness and spirit, come sometimes to be set right, and so make able and great men: but dejected minds, timorous and tame, and low spirits, are hardly ever to be raised, and very seldom attain to any thing. To avoid the danger that is on either hand is the great art: and he that has found a way how to keep up a child's spirit, easy, active, and free; and yet, at the same time, to restrain him from many things he has a mind to, and to draw him to things that are uneasy to him; he, I say, that knows how to reconcile these seeming contradictions, has, in my opinion, got the true secret of education.

47. The usual lazy and short way by chastisement, and the rod, which is the only instrument of government that tutors generally know,

or ever think of, is the most unfit of any to be used in education; because it tends to both those mischiefs; which, as we have shown, are the Scylla and Charybdis, which, on the one hand or the other, ruin all that miscarry.

56. . . . If you can once get into children a love of credit, and an apprehension of shame and disgrace, you have put into them the true principle, which will constantly work, and incline them to the right. But it will be asked, How shall this be done?

I confess, it does not, at first appearance, want some difficulty; but yet I think it worth our while to seek the ways (and practise them when found) to attain this, which I look on as the great secret of education.

57. First, children (earlier perhaps than we think) are very sensible of praise and commendation. They find a pleasure in being esteemed and valued, especially by their parents, and those whom they depend on. If therefore the father caress and commend them, when they do well; show a cold and neglectful countenance to them upon doing ill; and this accompanied by a like carriage of the mother, and all others that are about them; it will in a little time make them sensible of the difference: and this, if constantly observed, I doubt not but will of itself work more than threats or blows, which lose their force, when once grown common, and are of no use when shame does not attend them; and therefore are to be forborn, and never to be used, but in the case hereafter mentioned, when it is brought to extremity.

58. But, secondly, to make the sense of esteem or disgrace sink the deeper, and be of the more weight, other agreeable or disagreeable things should constantly accompany these different states; not as particular rewards and punishments of this or that particular action, but as necessarily belonging to, and constantly attending one, who by his carriage has brought himself into a state of disgrace of commendation. By which way of treating them, children may as much as possible be brought to conceive, that those that are commended and in esteem for doing well, will necessarily be beloved and cherished by every body, and have all other good things as a consequence of it; and, on the other side, when any one by miscarriage falls into dis-esteem, and cares not to preserve his credit, he will unavoidably fall under neglect and contempt: and, in that state, the want of whatever might satisfy or delight him, will follow. In this way the objects of their desires are made assisting to virtue; when a settled experience from the beginning teaches children, that the things they delight in, belong to, and are to be enjoyed by those only, who are in a state of reputation. If by these means you can come once to shame them out of their faults, (for besides that, I would willingly have no punishment) and make them in love with the pleasure of being well thought on, you may turn them as you please, and they will be in love with all the ways of virtue.

64. And here give me leave to take notice of one thing I think a fault in the ordinary method of education; and that is, the charging of children's memories, upon all occasions, with rules and precepts, which they often do not understand, and are constantly as soon forgot as given. If it be some action you would have done, or done otherwise; whenever they forget, or do it awkwardly, make them do it over and over again, till they are perfect: whereby you will get these two advantages: first, to see whether it be an action they can do, or is fit to be expected of them. For sometimes children are bid to do things, which, upon trial, they are found not able to do; and had need be taught and exercised in, before they are required to do them. But it is much easier for a tutor to command, than to teach. Secondly, another thing got by it will be this, that by repeating the same action, till it be grown habitual in them, the performance will not depend on memory, or reflection, the concomitant of prudence and age, and not of childhood; but will be natural in them. Thus, bowing to a gentleman when he salutes him, and looking in his face when he speaks to him, is by constant use as natural to a well-bred man, as breathing; it requires no thought, no reflection. Having this way cured in your child any fault, it is cured for ever: and thus, one by one, you may weed them out all, and plant what habits you please.

65. I have seen parents so heap rules on their children, that it was impossible for the poor little ones to remember a tenth part of them, much less to observe them. However, they were either by words or blows corrected for the breach of those multiplied and often very impertinent precepts. Whence it naturally followed, that the children minded not what was said to them; when it was evident to them, that no attention they were capable of, was sufficient to preserve them from transgression, and the rebukes which followed it.

Let therefore your rules to your son be as few as is possible, and rather fewer than more than seem absolutely necessary. For if you burden him with many rules, one of these two things must necessarily follow, that either he must be very often punished, which will be of ill consequence, by making punishment too frequent and familiar; or else you must let the transgressions of some of your rules go unpunished, whereby they will of course grow contemptible, and your authority become cheap to him. Make but few laws, but see they be well observed, when once made. Few years require but few laws; and as his age increases, when one rule is by practice well established, you may add another.

66. But pray remember, children are not to be taught by rules, which will be always slipping out of their memories. What you think necessary for them to do, settle in them by an indispensable practice, as often as the occasion returns; and, if it be possible, make occasions. This will beget habits in them, which, being once established, operate of themselves easily and naturally, without the assistance of the memory.

But here let me give two cautions: 1. The one is, that you keep them to the practice of what you would have grow into a habit in them, by kind words and gentle admonitions, rather as minding them of what they forget, than by harsh rebukes and chiding, as if they were wilfully guilty. 2dly, Another thing you are to take care of, is, not to endeavour to settle too many habits at once, lest by a variety you confound them, and so perfect none. When constant custom has made any one thing easy and natural to them, and they practise it without reflections, you may then go on to another.

This method of teaching children by a repeated practice, and the same action done over and over again, under the eye and direction of the tutor, till they have got the habit of doing it well, and not by relying on rules trusted to their memories; has so many advantages, which way soever we consider it, that I cannot but wonder (if ill customs could be wondered at in any thing) how it could possibly be so much neglected. I shall name one more that comes now in my way. By this method we shall see, whether what is required of him be adapted to his capacity, and any way suited to the child's natural genius and constitution: for that too must be considered in a right education. We must not hope wholly to change their original tempers, nor make the gay pensive and grave, nor the melancholy sportive, without spoiling them. God has stamped certain characters upon men's minds, which, like their shapes, may perhaps be a little mended; but can hardly be totally altered and transformed into the contrary.

He therefore, that is about children, should well study their natures and aptitudes, and see, by often trials, what turn they easily take, and what becomes them; observe what their native stock is, how it may be improved, and what it is fit for: he should consider what they want, whether they be capable of having it wrought into them by industry, and incorporated there by practice; and whether it be worth while to endeavour it. For, in many cases, all that we can do, or should aim at, is, to make the best of what nature has given, to prevent the vices and faults to which such a constitution is most inclined, and give it all the advantages it is capable of. Every one's natural genius should be carried as far as it could; but to attempt the putting another upon him, will be but labour in vain; and what is so plaistered on will at best sit but untowardly, and have always hanging to it the ungracefulness of constraint and affectation. . . .

70. Having named company, I am almost ready to throw away my pen, and trouble you no farther on this subject. For since that does more than all precepts, rules, and instructions, methinks it is almost wholly in vain to make a long discourse of other things, and to talk of that almost

to no purpose. For you will be ready to say, "What shall I do with my son? If I keep him always at home, he will be in danger to be my young master; and if I send him abroad, how is it possible to keep him from the contagion of rudeness and vice, which is every where so in fashion? In my house he will perhaps be more innocent, but more ignorant too of the world: wanting there change of company, and being used constantly to the same faces, he will, when he comes abroad, be a sheepish or conceited creature."

I confess, both sides have their inconveniencies. Being abroad, it is true, will make him bolder, and better able to bustle and shift amongst boys of his own age; and the emulation of schoolfellows often puts life and industry into young lads. But til you can find a school, wherein it is possible for the master to look after the manners of his scholars, and can show as great effects of his care of forming their minds to virtue, and their carriage to good breeding, as of forming their tongues to the learned languages; you must confess, that you have a strange value for words, when, preferring the languages of the ancient Greeks and Romans to that which made them such brave men, you think it worth while to hazard your son's innocence and virtue for a little Greek and Latin. For, as for that boldness and spirit which lads get amongst their playfellows at school, it has ordinarily such a mixture of rudeness and an ill-turned confidence, that those misbecoming and disingenuous ways of shifting in the world must be unlearned, and all the tincture washed out again, to make way for better principles, and such manners as make a truly worthy man. He that considers how diametrically opposite the skill of living well, and managing, as a man should do, his affairs in the world, is to that malapertness, tricking, or violence, learnt among schoolboys, will think the faults of a privater education infinitely to be preferred to such improvements; and will take care to preserve his child's innocence and modesty at home, as being nearer of kin, and more in the way of those qualities, which make an useful and able man. Nor does any one find, or so much as suspect, that that retirement and bashfulness, which their daughters are brought up in, makes them less knowing or less able women. Conversation, when they come into the world, soon gives them a becoming assurance; and whatsoever, beyond that, there is of rough and boisterous, may in men be very well spared too: for courage and steadiness, as I take it, lie not in roughness and ill breeding.

Virtue is harder to be got than a knowledge of the world; and, if lost in a young man, is seldom recovered. Sheepishness and ignorance of the world, the faults imputed to a private education, are neither the necessary consequences of being bred at home; nor, if they were, are they incurable evils. Vice is the more stubborn, as well as the more dangerous evil of the two; and therefore, in the first place, to be fenced against. If that sheepish softness, which often enervates those who are bred like fondlings at home, be carefully to be avoided, it is principally so for virtue's sake; for fear lest such a yielding temper should be too susceptible of vicious impressions, and expose the novice too easily to be corrupted. A young man, before he leaves the shelter of his father's house, and the guard of a tutor, should be fortified with resolution, and made acquainted with men, to secure his virtue; lest he should be led into some ruinous course, or fatal precipice, before he is sufficiently acquainted with the dangers of conversation, and has steadiness enough not to yield to every temptation. Were it not for this, a young man's bashfulness and ignorance of the world would not so much need an early care. Conversation would cure it in a great measure; or, if that will not do it early enough, it is only a stronger reason for a good tutor at home. For, if pains be to be taken to give him a manly air and assurance betimes, it is chiefly as a fence to his virtue, when he goes into the world, under his own conduct.

It is preposterous, therefore, to sacrifice his innocency to the attaining of confidence, and some little skill of bustling for himself among others, by his conversation with ill-bred and vicious boys; when the chief use of that sturdiness, and standing upon his own legs, is only for the preservation of his virtue. For if confidence or cunning come once to mix with vice, and support his miscarriages, he is only the surer lost; and you must undo again, and strip him of that he has got from his companions, or give him up to ruin. Boys will unavoidably be taught assurance by conversation with men, when they are brought into it; and that is time enough. Modesty and submission, till then, better fits them for instruction: and therefore there needs not any great care to stock them with confidence beforehand. That which requires most time, pains, and assiduity, is to work into them the principles and practice of virtue and good breeding. This is the seasoning they should be prepared with, so as not easily to be got out again: this they had need to be well provided with. For conversation, when they come into the world, will add to their knowledge and assurance, but be too apt to take from their virtue; which therefore they ought to be plentifully stored with, and have that tincture sunk deep into them.

How they should be fitted for conversation, and entered into the world, when they are ripe for it, we shall consider in another place. But how any one's being put into a mixed herd of unruly boys, and there learning to wrangle at trap, or rook at span-farthing, fits him for civil conversation or business, I do not see. And what qualities are ordinarily to be got from such a troop of playfellows as schools usually assemble together, from parents of all kinds, that a father should so much covet it, is hard to divine. I am sure, he who is able to be at the charge of a tutor at home, may there give his son a more genteel carriage, more manly thoughts, and a sense of what is worthy and becoming, with a greater proficiency in learning into the bargain, and ripen him up sooner into a man, than any at school can do. Not that I blame the schoolmaster in this, or think it to be laid to his charge. The difference is great between two or three pupils in the same house, and three or four-score boys lodged up and down. For, let the master's industry and skill be ever so great, it is impossible he should have 50 or 100 scholars under his eye any longer than they are in the school together: nor can it be expected, that he should instruct them successfully in any thing but their books; the forming of their minds and manners requiring a constant attention and particular application to every single boy; which is impossible in a numerous flock, and would be wholly in vain, (could he have time to study and correct every one's particular defects and wrong inclinations) when the lad was to be left to himself, or the prevailing infection of his fellows, the greatest part of the four-and-twenty hours.

But fathers, observing that fortune is often most successfully courted by bold and bustling men, are glad to see their sons pert and forward betimes; take it for a happy omen that they will be thriving men, and look on the tricks they play their schoolfellows, or learn from them, as a proficiency in the art of living, and making their way through the world. But I must take the liberty to say, that he that lays the foundation of his son's fortune in virtue and good breeding, takes the only sure and warrantable way. And it is not the waggeries or cheats practised among schoolboys, it is not their roughness one to another, nor the welp-laid plots of robbing an orchard together, that makes an able man; but the principles of justice, generosity, and sobriety, joined with observation and industry, qualities which I judge schoolboys do not learn much of one another. And if a young gentleman, bred at home, be not taught more of them than he could learn at school, his father has made a very ill choice of a tutor. Take a boy from the top of a grammar-school, and one of the same age, bred as he should be in his father's family, and bring them into good company together; and then see which of the two will have the more manly carriage, and address himself with the more becoming assurance to strangers. Here I imagine the schoolboy's confidence will either fail or discredit him; and if it be such as fits him only for the conversation of boys, he had better be without it.

Vice, if we may believe the general complaint, ripens so fast now-a-days, and runs up to seed so early in young people, that it is impossible to keep a lad from the spreading contagion, if you will venture him abroad in the herd, and trust to chance, or his own inclination, for the choice of his company at school. By what fate vice has so thriven amongst us these few years past, and by what hands it has been nursed up into so uncontrolled a dominion, I shall leave to others to inquire. I wish that those who complain of the great decay of Christian piety and virtue every where, and of learning and acquired improvements in the gentry of this generation, would consider how to retrieve them in the next. This I am sure, that, if the foundation of it be not laid in the education and principling of the youth, all other endeavours will be in vain. And if the innocence, sobriety, and industry of those who are coming up be not taken care of and preserved, it will be ridiculous to expect, that those who are to succeed next on the stage should abound in that virtue, ability, and learning, which has hitherto made England considerable in the world. I was going to add courage too, though it has been looked on as the natural inheritance of Englishmen. What has been talked of some late actions at sea, of a kind unknown to our ancestors, give me occasion to say, that debauchery sinks the courage of men; and when dissoluteness has eaten out the sense of true honour, bravery seldom stays long after it. And I think it impossible to find an instance of any nation, however renowned for their valour, who ever kept their credit in arms, or made themselves redoubtable amongst their neighbours, after corruption had once broke through, and dissolved the restraint of discipline; and vice was grown to such a head, that it durst show itself barefaced, without being out of countenance.

It is virtue then, direct virtue, which is the hard and valuable part to be aimed at in education; and not a forward pertness, or any little arts of shifting. All other considerations and accomplishments should give way, and be postponed, to this. This is the solid and substantial good, which tutors should not only read lectures, and talk of; but the labour and art of education should furnish the mind with, and fasten there, and never cease till the young man had a true relish of it, and placed his strength, his glory, and his pleasure in it.

The more this advances, the easier way will be made for other accomplishments in their turns. For he that is brought to submit to virtue, will not be refractory, or resty, in any thing that becomes him. And therefore I cannot but prefer breeding of a young gentleman at home in his father's sight, under a good governor, as much the best and safest way to this great and main end of education; when it can be had, and is ordered as it should be. Gentlemen's houses are seldom without variety of company: they should use their sons to all the strange faces that come there, and engage them in conversation with men of parts and breeding, as soon as they are capable of it. And why those, who live in the country, should not take them with them, when they make visits of civility to their neighbours, I know not: this I am sure, a father that breeds his son at home, has the opportunity to have him more in his own company, and there give him what encouragement he thinks fit; and can keep him better from the taint of servants, and the meaner sort of people, than is possible to be done abroad. But what shall be resolved in the case, must in great measure be left to the parents, to be determined by their circumstances and conveniencies. Only I think it the worst sort of good husbandry for a father not to strain himself a little for his son's breeding; which, let his condition be what it will, is the best portion he can leave him. But if, after all, it shall be thought by some that the breeding at home has too little company, and that at ordinary schools not such as it should be for a young gentleman, I think there might be ways found out to avoid the inconveniencies on the one side and the other.

71. Having under consideration how great the influence of company is, and how prone we are all, especially children, to imitation; I must here take the liberty to mind parents of this one thing, viz. that he that will have his son have a respect for him and his orders, must himself have a great reverence for his son. "Maxima debetur pueris reverentia." You must do nothing before him which you would not have him imitate....

90. In all the whole business of education, there is nothing like to be less hearkened to, or harder to be well observed, than what I am now going to say; and that is, that children should, from their first beginning to talk, have some discreet, sober, nay wise person about them, whose care it should be to fashion them aright, and keep them from all ill, especially the infection of bad company. I think this province requires great sobriety, temperance, tenderness, diligence, and discretion; qualities hardly to be found united in persons that are to be had for ordinary salaries, nor easily to be found any where. As to the charge of it, I think it will be the money best laid out that can be about our children; and therefore, thought it may be expensive more than is ordinary, yet it cannot be thought dear. He that at any rate procures his child a good mind, well-principled, tempered to virtue and usefulness, and adorned with civility and good breeding, makes a better purchase for him, than if he had laid out the money for an addition of more earth to his former acres. Spare it in toys and play-games, in silk and ribbons, laces and other useless expenses, as much as you please; but be not sparing in so necessary a part as this. It is not good husbandry to make his fortune rich, and his mind poor....

93. The character of a sober man, and a scholar, is, as I have above observed, what every one expects in a tutor. This generally is thought enough, and is all that parents commonly look for. But when such an one has emptied out, into his pupil, all the Latin and logic he has brought from the university, will that furniture make him a fine gentleman? Or can it be expected, that he should be better bred, better skilled in the

world, better principled in the grounds and foundations of true virtue and generosity, than his young tutor is?

To form a young gentleman, as he should be, it is fit his governor should himself be well-bred, understand the ways of carriage, and measures of civility, in all the variety of persons, times, and places; and keep his pupil, as much as his age requires, constantly to the observation of them. This is an art not to be learnt, nor taught by books: nothing can give it but good company and observation joined together. The tailor may make his clothes modish, and the dancing-master give fashion to his motions; yet neither of these, though they set off well, make a well-bred gentleman: no, though he have learning to boot; which, if not well managed, makes him more impertinent and intolerable in conversation. Breeding is that which sets a gloss upon all his other good qualities, and renders them useful to him, in procuring him the esteem and good will of all that he comes near. Without good breeding, his other accomplishments make him pass but for proud, conceited, vain, or foolish. . . . Good qualities are the substantial riches of the mind; but it is good breeding sets them off: and he that will be acceptable, must give beauty, as well as strength, to his actions. Solidity, or even usefulness, is not enough: a graceful way and fashion, in every thing, is that which gives the ornament and liking. And, in most cases, the manner of doing is of more consequence than the thing done; and upon that depends the satisfaction, or disgust, wherewith it is received. . . . The tutor therefore ought, in the first place, to be well-bred: and a young gentleman, who gets this one qualification from his governor, sets out with great advantage; and will find, that this one accomplishment will more open his way to him, get him more friends, and carry him farther in the world, than all the hard words, or real knowledge, he has got from the liberal arts, or his tutor's learned encyclopaedia; not that those should be neglected, but by no means preferred, or suffered to thrust out the other.

94. Besides being well-bred, the tutor should know the world well; the ways, the humours, the follies, the cheats, the faults of the age he is fallen into, and particularly of the country he lives in. These he should be able to show to his pupil, as he finds him capable; teach him skill in men, and their manners; pull off the mask which their several callings and pretences cover them with; and make his pupil discern what lies at the bottom, under such appearance; that he may not, as unexperienced young men are apt to do, if they are unwarned, take one thing for another, judge by the outside, and give himself up to show, and the insinuation of a fair carriage, or an obliging application. . . . He should accustom him to make, as much as is possible, a true judgment of men by those marks which serve best to show what they are, and give a prospect into their inside; which often shows itself in little things, especially

when they are not in parade, and upon their guard. He should acquaint him with the true state of the world, and dispose him to think no man better or worse, wiser or foolisher, than he really is. Thus, by safe and insensible degrees, he will pass from a boy to a man; which is the most hazardous step in all the whole course of life. . . . I think it of most value to be instilled into a young man, upon all occasions which offer themselves, that, when he comes to launch into the deep himself, he may not be like one at sea without a line, compass, or sea-chart; but may have some notice beforehand of the rocks and shoals, the currents and quicksands, and know a little how to steer, that he sink not, before he get experience. He that thinks not this of more moment to his son, and for which he more needs a governor, than the languages and learned sciences, forgets of how much more use it is to judge right of men, and manage his affairs wisely with them, than to speak Greek and Latin, or argue in mood and figure; or to have his head filled with the abstruse speculations of natural philosophy and metaphysics; nay, than to be well versed in Greek and Roman writers, though that be much better for a gentleman than to be a good peripatetic or Cartesian: because those ancient authors observed and painted mankind well, and give the best light into that kind of knowledge. He that goes into the eastern parts of Asia, will find able and acceptable men, without any of these: but without virtue, knowledge of the world, and civility, an accomplished and valuable man can be found nowhere.

A great part of the learning now in fashion in the schools of Europe, and that goes ordinarily into the round of education, a gentleman may, in a good measure, be unfurnished with, without any great disparagement to himself, or prejudice to his affairs. But prudence and good breeding are, in all the stations and occurrences of life, necessary; and most young men suffer in the want of them, and come rawer, and more awkward, into the world than they should, for this very reason; because these qualities, which are, of all other, the most necessary to be taught, and stand in need of the assistance and help of a teacher, are generally neglected, and thought but a slight, or no part of a tutor's business. Latin and learning make all the noise: and the main stress is laid upon his proficiency in things, a great part whereof belongs not to a gentleman's calling; which is to have the knowledge of a man of business, a carriage suitable to his rank, and to be eminent and useful in his country, according to his station. . . . to initiate his pupil in any part of learning, as far as is necessary for a young man in the ordinary course of his studies, an ordinary skill in the governor is enough. Nor is it requisite that he should be a thorough scholar, or possess in perfection all those sciences, which it is convenient a young gentleman should have a taste of, in some general view, or short system. A gentleman that would

penetrate deeper, must do it by his own genius and undustry afterwards: for nobody ever went far in knowledge, or became eminent in
any of the sciences, by the discipline and constraint of a master.

The great work of a governor is to fashion the carriage, and form
the mind; to settle in his pupil good habits, and the principles of virtue
and wisdom; to give him, by little and little, a view of mankind; and
work him into a love and imitation of what is excellent and praiseworthy; and, in the prosecution of it, to give him vigour, activity, and
industry. The studies which he sets him upon are but, as it were, the
exercises of his faculties, and employment of his time, to keep him from
sauntering and idleness, to teach him application, and accustom him to
take pains, and to give him some little taste of what his own industry
must perfect. For who expects, that under a tutor a young gentleman
should be an accomplished critic, orator, or logician; go to the bottom of
metaphysics, natural philosophy, or mathematics; or be a master in
history or chronology? Though something of each of these is to be taught
him: but it is only to open the door, that he may look in, and, as it were,
begin an acquaintance, but not to dwell there: and a governor would be
much blamed, that should keep his pupil too long, and lead him too far
in most of them. But of good breeding, knowledge of the world, virtue,
industry, and a love of reputation, he cannot have too much: and, if he
have these, he will not long want what he needs or desires of the other.

And, since it cannot be hoped he should have time and strength to
learn all things, most pain should be taken about that which is most
necessary; and that principally looked after which will be of most and
frequentest use to him in the world. . . .

134. That which every gentleman (that takes any care of his education) desires for his son, besides the estate he leaves him, is contained
(I suppose) in these four things, virtue, wisdom, breeding, and learning. . . .

195. . . . To conclude this part, which concerns a young gentleman's studies; his tutor should remember, that his business is not so much
to teach him all that is knowable, as to raise in him a love and esteem
of knowledge; and to put him in the right way of knowing and improving
himself, when he has a mind to it. . . .

Order and constancy are said to make the great difference between
one man and another; this, I am sure, nothing so much clears a learner's
way, helps him so much on in it, and makes him go so easy and so far
in any inquiry, as a good method. His governor should take pains to
make him sensible of this, accustom him to order, and teach him method
in all the applications of his thoughts; show him wherein it lies, and the
advantages of it; acquaint him with the several sorts of it, either from

general to particulars, or from particulars to what is more general; exercise him in both of them; and make him see in what cases each different method is most proper, and to what ends it best serves. . . .

200. These are my present thoughts concerning learning and accomplishments. The great business of all is virtue and wisdom.

Nullum numen abest, si sit prudentia.

Teach him to get a mastery over his inclinations, and submit his appetite to reason. This being obtained, and by a constant practice settled into habit, the hardest part of the task is over. To bring a young man to this, I know nothing which so much contributes, as the love of praise and commendation, which should therefore be instilled into him by all arts imaginable. Make his mind as sensible of credit and shame as may be: and when you have done that, you have put a principle into him, which will influence his actions, when you are not by; to which the fear of a little smart of a rod is not comparable; and which will be the proper stock whereon afterwards to graft the true principles of morality and religion.

201. I have one thing more to add, which as soon as I mention, I shall run the danger of being suspected to have forgot what I am about, and what I have about written concerning education, all tending towards a gentleman's calling, with which a trade seems wholly to be inconsistent. And yet, I cannot forbear to say, I would have him learn a trade, a manual trade; nay, two or three, but one more particularly.

44
Jean Jacques Rousseau (1712-1778). Paradox

The Social Contract

Selections from Jean Jacques Rousseau, *The Social Contract*, An Eighteenth Century Translation Completely Revised, Edited, with an Introduction by Charles Frankel (New York: Hafner Publishing Company, 1947), Book I, Chapters V-VIII, pp. 13-19.

Chapter V
That We Must Always Go Back to a First Convention

Had I granted all which I have refuted, the favourers of despotism would not have found their cause advanced by it. There will always be a great difference between subduing a multitude and governing a society. When unorganized men[1] are successively subjugated by one individual, whatever number there may be of them, they appear to me only as a master and slaves; I cannot regard them as a people and their chief; they are, if you please, an *aggregation*, but they are not as yet an *association*; for there is neither public property, nor a political body, among them. A man may have enslaved half the world, and yet continue only a private individual; his interest is separate from that of others, and confined to himself alone. When such a man falls, his empire remains unconnected and without any bond of union, as an oak dissolves and becomes a mass of ashes when consumed by fire.

"A people," says Grotius, "can give themselves to a king."[2] According to Grotius, then, they are a people before they give themselves to a king. The donation itself is a civil act, and supposes a public consultation. It would therefore be better before we examine the act by which they elected a king, to enquire into that by which they become a

[1] [*des hommes epars.*]

[2] [Grotius (1583-1645), *De jure belli ac pacis* (*The Law of War and Peace*, Bk. I, chap. 3.]

people; for that act, being necessarily anterior to the other, is the true foundation of society.

In fact, if there was no prior convention, where would be—unless the election was unanimous—the obligation which should bind the minority to submit to the choice of the majority? And whence would a hundred men, who wish to submit to a master, derive the right of binding by their votes ten other men who were not disposed to acknowledge any chief? The law which gives the majority of votes the power of deciding for the whole body can only be established by a convention, and proves that there must have been unanimity at one time at least.

Chapter VI
Of the Social Compact

I will suppose that men in the state of nature are arrived at that crisis when the strength of each individual is insufficient to overcome the resistance of the obstacles to his preservation. This primitive state can therefore subsist no longer; and the human race would perish unless it changed its manner of life.

As men cannot create for themselves new forces, but merely unite and direct those which already exist, the only means they can employ for their preservation is to form by aggregation an assemblage of forces that may be able to overcome the resistance, to be put in motion as one body, and to act in concert.

This assemblage of forces must be produced by the concurrence of many; but as the force and the liberty of each man are the chief instruments of his preservation, how can he engage them elsewhere without danger to himself, and without neglecting the care which is due himself? This difficulty, which leads directly to my subject, may be expressed in these words:

"Where shall we find a form of association which will defend and protect with the whole common force the person and the property of each associate, and by which every person, while uniting himself with all, shall obey only himself and remain as free as before?" Such is the fundamental problem of which the Social Contract gives the solution.

The articles of this contract are so unalterably fixed by the nature of the act that the least modification renders them vain and of no effect; so that they are the same everywhere, and are everywhere tacitly understood and admitted, even though they may never have been formally announced; until, the social compact being violated, each individual is restored to his original rights, and resumes his native liberty, while losing the conventional liberty for which he renounced it.

The articles of the social contract will, when clearly understood, be found reducible to this single point: the total alienation of each associate, and all his rights, to the whole community; for, in the first place, as every individual gives himself up entirely, the condition of every person is alike; and being so, it would not be to the interest of any one to render that condition offensive to others.

Nay, more than this, the alienation being made without any reserve, the union is as complete as it can be, and no associate has any further claim to anything: for if any individual retained rights not enjoyed in general by all, as there would be no common superior to decide between him and the public, each person being in some points his own judge, would soon pretend to be so in everything; and thus would the state of nature be continued and the association necessarily become tyrannical or be annihilated.

Finally, each person gives himself to all, and so not to any one individual; and as there is no one associate over whom the same right is not acquired which is ceded to him by others, each gains an equivalent for what he loses, and finds his force increased for preserving that which he possesses.

If, therefore, we exclude from the social compact all that is not essential, we shall find it reduced to the following terms:

Each of us places in common his person and all his power under the supreme direction of the general will; and as one body we all receive each member as an indivisible part of the whole.

From that moment, instead of as many separate persons as there are contracting parties, this act of association produces a moral and collective body, composed of as many members as there are votes in the assembly, which from this act receives its unity, its common self, its life, and its will. This public person, which is thus formed by the union of all other persons, took formerly the name of "city,"[3] and now takes that of "republic" or "body politic." It is called by its members "State" when it is passive, "Sovereign" when in activity, and, whenever it is compared with other bodies of a similar kind, it is denominated "power." The associates take collectively the name of "people," and

---

[3] The true sense of this word is almost entirely lost among the moderns: the name of "city" is now generally used to signify a town, and that of "citizen" applied to a burgess. Men do not seem to know that *houses* make a "town," but that *citizens* make a "city." The Carthaginians once paid dearly for a mistake of this kind. I have never seen it mentioned that the title of *cives* was ever given to the subjects of any prince, not even to the Macedonians formerly, or to the English at present, although they are nearer liberty than any other people. The French alone use the name of "citizen" familiarly to all, because they have no true idea of it, as appears from their dictionaries; and without knowing its meaning they are in

separately, that of "citizens," as participating in the sovereign authority, and of "subjects," because they are subjected to the laws of the State. But these terms are frequently confounded and used one for the other; and it is enough that a man understands how to distinguish them when they are employed in all their precision.

Chapter VII
Of the Sovereign

It appears from this formula that the act of association contains a reciprocal engagement between the public and individuals, and that each individual, contracting, as it were, with himself, is engaged under a double character; that is, as a member of the Sovereign engaging with individuals, and as a member of the State engaged with the Sovereign. But we cannot apply here the maxim of civil right, that no person is bound by any engagement which he makes with himself; for there is a material difference between an obligation to oneself individually, and an obligation to a collective body of which oneself constitutes a part.

It is necessary to observe here that public deliberation, which can bind all the subjects to the Sovereign, in consequence of the doubler character under which the members of that body appear, cannot, for the opposite reason, bind the Sovereign to itself; and consequently that it is against the nature of the body politic for the sovereign power to impose on itself any law which it cannot break. Being able to consider itself as acting under one character only, it is in the situation of an individual forming a contract with himself; and we see therefore that there neither is nor can be any kind of fundamental law obligatory for the body of the people, not even the social contract itself. But this does not mean that this body could not very well engage itself to others in any manner which would not derogate from the contract; for, with respect to what is external to it, it becomes a simple being, an individual. But the body politic, or the Sovereign, which derives its existence from the sacredness of the contract, can never bind itself, even towards outsiders, in anything that would derogate from the original act, such

danger of falling into the crime of lèse majesté, by usurping a title to which they have no just claim. The word "citizen" with them means a virtue, and not a right. Bodin made a very gross mistake, when, in speaking of "citizens" and "burgesses," he mistook the one for the other. M. D'Alembert was better acquainted with the meaning of these terms, and in his article "Genève" he has very properly marked the difference between the four orders of men—indeed I may say five, by including the foreigners—which are found there, and of which two orders only compose the republic. No other French author that I know of has comprehended the true sense of the word "citizen."

as alienating any portion of itself, or submitting to another Sovereign. To violate the contract by which it exists would be to annihilate itself; and that which is nothing can produce nothing.

As soon as this multitude is united in one body, you cannot offend one of its members without attacking the body; much less can you offend the body without incurring the resentment of all the members. Thus duty and interest equally oblige the two contracting parties to lend aid to each other; and the same men must endeavour to unite under this double character all the advantages which attend it.

Further, the Sovereign, being formed only of the individuals who compose it, neither has, nor can have, any interest contrary to theirs; consequently, the sovereign power need give no guarantee to its subjects, because it is impossible that the body should seek to injure all its members; and we shall see presently that it can do no injury to any individual in particular. The Sovereign, by its nature, is always everything it ought to be.

But this is not so with the relation of subjects towards the Sovereign, which, notwithstanding the common interest, has nothing to make them responsible for the performance of their engagements if some means is not found of ensuring their fidelity.

In fact, each individual may, as a man, have a private will,[4] dissimilar or contrary to the general will which he has as a citizen. His own private interest[5] may dictate to him very differently from the common interest; his absolute and naturally independent existence may make him regard what he owes to the common cause as a gratuitous contribution, the omission of which would be less injurious to others than the payment would be burdensome to himself; and considering the moral person which constitutes the State as a creature of the imagination, because it is not a man, he may wish to enjoy the rights of a citizen without being disposed to fulfil the duties of a subject. Such an injustice would in its progress cause the ruin of the body politic.

In order, therefore, to prevent the social compact from becoming an empty formula, it tacitly comprehends the engagement, which alone can give effect to the others—that whoever refuses to obey the general will shall be compelled to it by the whole body: this in fact only forces him to be free; for this is the condition which, by giving each citizen to his country, guarantees his absolute personal independence, a condition which gives motion and effect to the political machine. This alone renders all civil engagements justifiable, and without it they would be absurd, tyrannical, and subject to the most enormous abuses.

4 [volonté particulière.]

5 [intérêt particulier.]

Chapter VIII
Of the Civil State

The passing from the state of nature to the civil state produces in man a very remarkable change, by substituting justice for instinct in his conduct, and giving to his actions a moral character which they lacked before. It is then only that the voice of duty succeeds to physical impulse, and a sense of what is right, to the incitements of appetite. Man, who had till then regarded none but himself, perceives that he must act on other principles, and learns to consult his reason before he listens to his inclinations. Although he is deprived in this new state of many advantages which he enjoyed from nature, he gains in return others so great, his faculties so unfold themselves by being exercised, his ideas are so extended, his sentiments so exalted, and his whole mind so enlarged and refined, that if, by abusing his new condition, he did not sometimes degrade it even below that from which he emerged, he ought to bless continually the happy moment that snatched him forever from it, and transformed him from a circumscribed and stupid animal to an intelligent being and a man.

In order to draw a balance between the advantages and disadvantages attending his new situation, let us state them in such a manner that they may be easily compared. Man loses by the social contract his *natural* liberty, and an unlimited right to all which tempts him, and which he can obtain; in return he acquires *civil* liberty, and proprietorship of all he possesses. That we may not be deceived in the value of these compensations, we must distinguish natural liberty, which knows no bounds but the power of the individual, from civil liberty, which is limited by the general will; and between possession, which is only the effect of force or of the right of the first occupant, from property, which must be founded on a positive title. In addition we might add to the other acquisitions of the civil state that of moral liberty, which alone renders a man master of himself; for it is *slavery* to be under the impulse of mere appetite, and *freedom* to obey a law which we prescribe for ourselves. But I have already said too much on this head, and the philosophical sense of the word "liberty" is not at present my subject.

Emile

Selections from Jean Jacques Rousseau, *Emile*, translated by Barbara Foxley, Everyman's Library 518 (London: J. M. Dent & Sons Ltd.; New York: E. P. Dutton & Co., Inc., 1911), pp. 5-20.

Book I

GOD makes all things good; man meddles with them and they become evil. He forces one soil to yield the products of another, one tree to bear another's fruit. He confuses and confounds time, place, and natural conditions. He mutilates his dog, his horse, and his slave. He destroys and defaces all things; he loves all that is deformed and monstrous; he will have nothing as nature made it, not even man himself, who must learn his paces like a saddlehorse, and be shaped to his master's taste like the trees in his garden.

Yet things would be worse without this education, and mankind cannot be made by halves. Under existing conditions a man left to himself from birth would be more of a monster than the rest. Prejudice, authority, necessity, example, all the social conditions into which we are plunged, would stifle nature in him and put nothing in her place. She would be like a sapling chance sown in the midst of the highway, bent hither and thither and soon crushed by the passers-by.

Tender, anxious mother, I appeal to you. You can remove this young tree from the highway and shield it from the crushing force of social conventions. Tend and water it ere it dies. One day its fruit will reward your care. From the outset raise a wall round your child's soul; another may sketch the plan, you alone should carry it into execution.

Plants are fashioned by cultivation, man by education. If a man were born tall and strong, his size and strength would be of no good to him till he had learnt to use them; they would even harm him by preventing others from coming to his aid; left to himself he would die of want before he knew his needs. We lament the helplessness of infancy; we fail to perceive that the race would have perished had not man begun by being a child.

We are born weak, we need strength; helpless, we need aid; foolish, we need reason. All that we lack at birth, all that we need when we come to man's estate, is the gift of education.

This education comes to us from nature, from men, or from things. The inner growth of our organs and faculties is the education of nature, the use we learn to make of this growth is the education of men, what we gain by our experience of our surroundings is the education of things.

Thus we are each taught by three masters. If their teaching conflicts, the scholar is ill-educated and will never be at peace with himself; if their teaching agrees, he goes straight to his goal, he lives at peace with himself, he is well-educated.

Now of these three factors in education nature is wholly beyond our control, things are only partly in our power; the education of men is the only one controlled by us; and even here our power is largely illusory, for who can hope to direct every word and deed of all with whom the child has to do.

Viewed as an art, the success of education is almost impossible, since the essential conditions of success are beyond our control. Our efforts may bring us within sight of the goal, but fortune must favour us if we are to reach it.

What is this goal? As we have just shown, it is the goal of nature. Since all three modes of education must work together, the two that we can control must follow the lead of that which is beyond our control. Perhaps this word Nature has too vague a meaning. Let us try to define it.

Nature, we are told, is merely habit. What does that mean? Are there not habits formed under compulsion, habits which never stifle nature? Such, for example, are the habits of plants trained horizontally. The plant keeps its artificial shape, but the sap has not changed its course, and any new growth the plant may make will be vertical. It is the same with a man's disposition; while the conditions remain the same, habits, even the least natural of them, hold good; but change the conditions, habits vanish, nature re-asserts herself. Education itself is but habit, for are there not people who forget or lose their education and others who keep it: Whence comes this difference? If the term nature is to be restricted to habits conformable to nature we need say no more.

We are born sensitive and from our birth onwards we are affected in various ways by our environment. As soon as we become conscious of our sensations we tend to seek or shun the things that cause them, at first because they are pleasant or unpleasant, then because they suit us or not, and at last because of judgments formed by means of the ideas of happiness and goodness which reason gives us. These tendencies gain strength and permanence with the growth of reason, but hindered by our habits they are more or less warped by our prejudices. Before this change they are what I call Nature within us.

Everything should therefore be brought into harmony with these natural tendencies, and that might well be if our three modes of education merely differed from one another; but what can be done when they conflict, when instead of training man for himself you try to train him for others? Harmony becomes impossible. Forced to combat either nature or society, you must make your choice between the man and the citizen, you cannot train both.

The smaller social group, firmly united in itself and dwelling apart from others, tends to withdraw itself from the larger society. Every patriot hates foreigners; they are only men, and nothing to him. This defect is inevitable, but of little importance. The great thing is to be kind to our neighbours. Among strangers the Spartan was selfish, grasping, and unjust, but unselfishness, justice, and harmony ruled his home life. Distrust those cosmopolitans who search out remote duties in their books and neglect those that lie nearest. Such philosophers will love the Tartars to avoid loving their neighbour.

The natural man lives for himself; he is the unit, the whole, dependent only on himself and on his like. The citizen is but the numerator of a fraction, whose value depends on its denominator; his value depends upon the whole, that is, on the community. Good social institutions are those best fitted to make a man unnatural, to exchange his independence for dependence, to merge the unit in the group, so that he no longer regards himself as one, but as a part of the whole, and is only conscious of the common life. A citizen of Rome was neither Caius nor Lucius, he was a Roman; he ever loved his country better than his life. The captive Regulus professed himself a Carthaginian; as a foreigner he refused to take his seat in the Senate except at his master's bidding. He scorned the attempt to save his life. He had his will, and returned in triumph to a cruel death. There is no great likeness between Regulus and the men of our own day.

The Spartan Pedaretes presented himself for admission to the council of the Three Hundred and was rejected; he went away rejoicing that there were three hundred Spartans better than himself. I suppose he was in earnest; there is no reason to doubt it. That was a citizen.

A Spartan mother had five sons with the army. A Helot arrived; trembling she asked his news. "Your five sons are slain." "Vile slave, was that what I asked thee?" "We have won the victory." She hastened to the temple to render thanks to the gods. That was a citizen.

He who would preserve the supremacy of natural feelings in social life knows not what he asks. Ever at war with himself, hesitating between his wishes and his duties, he will be neither a man nor a citizen. He will be of no use to himself nor to others. He will be a man of our day, a Frenchman, an Englishman, one of the great middle class.

To be something, to be himself, and always at one with himself, a man must act as he speaks, must know what course he ought to take, and must follow that course with vigour and persistence. When I meet this miracle it will be time enough to decide whether he is a man or a citizen, or how he contrives to be both.

Two conflicting types of educational systems spring from those conflicting aims. One is public and common to many, the other private and domestic.

If you wish to know what is meant by public education, read Plato's *Republic*. Those who merely judge books by their titles take this for a treatise on politics, but it is the finest treatise on education ever written.

In popular estimation the Platonic Institute stands for all that is fanciful and unreal. For my own part I should have thought the system of Lycurgus far more impracticable had he merely committed it to writing. Plato only sought to purge man's heart; Lycurgus turned it from its natural course.

The public institute does not and cannot exist, for there is neither country nor patriot. The very words should be struck out of our language. The reason does not concern us at present, so that though I know it I refrain from stating it.

I do not consider our ridiculous colleges as public institutes, nor do I include under this head a fashionable education, for this education facing two ways at once achieves nothing. It is only fit to turn out hypocrites, always professing to live for others, while thinking of themselves alone. These professions, however, deceive no one, for every one has his share in them; they are so much labour wasted.

Our inner conflicts are caused by these contradictions. Drawn this way by nature and that way by man, compelled to yield to both forces, we make a compromise and reach neither goal. We go through life, struggling and hesitating, and die before we have found peace, useless alike to ourselves and to others.

There remains the education of the home or of nature; but how will a man live with others if he is educated for himself alone? If the twofold aims could be resolved into one by removing the man's self-contradictions, one great obstacle to his happiness would be gone. To judge of this you must see the man full-grown; you must have noted his inclinations, watched his progress, followed his steps; in a word you must really know a natural man. When you have read this work, I think you will have made some progress in this inquiry.

What must be done to train this exceptional man? We can do much, but the chief thing is to prevent anything being done. To sail against the wind we merely follow one tack and another; to keep our position in a stormy sea we must cast anchor. Beware, young pilot, lest your boat slip its cable or drag its anchor before you know it.

In the social order where each has his own place a man must be educated for it. If such a one leave his own station he is fit for nothing else. His education is only useful when fate agrees with his parents' choice; if not, education harms the scholar, if only by the prejudices it has created. In Egypt, where the son was compelled to adopt his father's calling, education had at least a settled aim; where social grades remain fixed, but the men who form them are constantly changing, no one knows whether he is not harming his son by educating him for his own class.

In the natural order men are all equal and their common calling is that of manhood, so that a well-educated man cannot fail to do well in that calling and those related to it. It matters little to me whether my pupil is intended for the army, the church, or the law. Before his parents chose a calling for him nature called him to be a man. Life is the trade I would teach him. When he leaves me, I grant you, he will be neither a magistrate, a soldier, nor a priest; he will be a man. All that becomes a man he will learn as quickly as another. In vain will fate change his station, he will always be in his right place. "Occupavi te, fortuna, atque cepi; omens-que aditus tuos interclusi, ut ad me aspirare non posses." The real object of our study is man and his environment. To my mind those of us who can best endure the good and evil of life are the best educated; hence it follows that true education consists less in precept than in practice. We begin to learn when we begin to live; our education begins with ourselves, our first teacher is our nurse. The ancients used the word "Education" in a different sense, it meant "Nurture." "Educit obstetrix," says Varro, "Educatnutrix, instituit paedagogus, docet magister." Thus, education, discipline, and instruction are three things as different in their purpose as the dame, the usher, and the teacher. But these distinctions are undesirable and the child should only follow one guide.

We must therefore look at the general rather than the particular, and consider our scholar as man in the abstract, man exposed to all the changes and chances of mortal life. If men were born attached to the soil of our country, if one season lasted all the year round, if every man's fortune were so firmly grasped that he could never lose it, then the established method of education would have certain advantages; the child brought up to his own calling would never leave it, he could never have to face the difficulties of any other condition. But when we consider the fleeting nature of human affairs, the restless and uneasy spirit of our times, when every generation overturns the work of its predecessor, can we conceive a more senseless plan than to educate a child as if he would never leave his room, as if he would always have his servants about him? If the wretched creature takes a single step up or down he is lost. This is not teaching him to bear pain; it is training him to feel it.

People think only of preserving their child's life; this is not enough, he must be taught to preserve his own life when he is a man, to bear the buffets of fortune, to brave wealth and poverty, to live at need among the snows of Iceland or on the scorching rocks of Malta. In vain you guard against death; he must needs die; and even if you do not kill him with your precautions, they are mistaken. Teach him to live rather than to avoid death: life is not breath, but action, the use of our senses, our mind, our faculties, every part of ourselves which makes us conscious of our being. Life consists less in length of days than in the keen sense of living. A man may be buried at a hundred and may never have lived at all. He would have fared better had he died young.

Our wisdom is slavish prejudice, our customs consist in control, constraint, compulsion. Civilised man is born and dies a slave. The infant is bound up in swaddling clothes, the corpse is nailed down in his coffin. All his life long man is imprisoned by our institutions.

I am told that many midwives profess to improve the shape of the infant's head by rubbing, and they are allowed to do it. Our heads are not good enough as God made them, they must be moulded outside by the nurse and inside by the philosopher. The Caribs are better off than we are. "The child has hardly left the mother's womb, it has hardly begun to move and stretch its limbs, when it is deprived of its freedom. It is wrapped in swaddling bands, laid down with its head fixed, its legs stretched out, and its arms by its sides; it is wound round with linen and bandages of all sorts so that it cannot move. It is fortunate if it has room to breathe, and it is laid on its side so that water which should flow from its mouth can escape, for it is not free to turn its head on one side for this purpose."

The new-born child requires to stir and stretch his limbs to free them from the stiffness resulting from being curled up so long. His limbs are stretched indeed, but he is not allowed to move them. Even the head is confined by a cap. One would think they were afraid the child should look as if it were alive.

Thus the internal impulses which should lead to growth find an insurmountable obstacle in the way of the necessary movements. The child exhausts his strength in vain struggles, or he gains strength very slowly. He was freer and less constrained in the womb; he has gained nothing by birth.

The inaction, the constraint to which the child's limbs are subjected can only check the circulation of the blood and humours; it can only hinder the child's growth in size and strength, and injure its constitution. Where these absurd precautions are absent, all the men are tall, strong, and well-made. Where children are swaddled, the country swarms with the hump-backed, the lame, the bow-legged, the rickety, and every kind of deformity. In our fear lest the body should become deformed by free movement, we hasten to deform it by putting it in a press. We make our children helpless lest they should hurt themselves.

Is not such a cruel bondage certain to affect both health and temper? Their first feeling is one of pain and suffering; they find every necessary movement hampered; more miserable than a galley slave, in vain they struggle, they become angry, they cry. Their first words you say are tears. That is so. From birth you are always checking them, your first gifts are fetters, your first treatment, torture. Their voice alone is free; why should they not raise it in complaint? They cry because you are hurting them; if you were swaddled you would cry louder still.

What is the origin of this senseless and unnatural custom? Since mothers have despised their first duty and refused to nurse their own children, they have had to be entrusted to hired nurses. Finding themselves the mothers of a stranger's children, without the ties of nature, they have merely tried to save themselves trouble. A child unswaddled would need constant watching; well swaddled it is cast into a corner and its cries are unheeded. So long as the nurse's negligence escapes notice, so long as the nursling does not break its arms or legs, what matter if it dies or becomes a weakling for life. Its limbs are kept safe at the expense of its body, and if anything goes wrong it is not the nurse's fault.

These gentle mothers, having got rid of their babies, devote themselves gaily to the pleasures of the town. Do they know how their children are being treated in the villages? If the nurse is at all busy, the child is hung up on a nail like a bundle of clothes and is left crucified while the nurse goes leisurely about her business. Children have been found in this position purple in the face, their tightly bandaged chest forbade the circulation of the blood, and it went to the head; so the sufferer was considered very quiet because he had not strength to cry. How long a child might survive under such conditions I do not know, but it could not be long. That, I fancy, is one of the chief advantages of swaddling clothes.

It is maintained that unswaddled infants would assume faulty positions and make movements which might injure the proper development of their limbs. That is one of the empty arguments of our false wisdom which has never been confirmed by experience. Out of all the crowds of children who grow up with the full use of their limbs among nations wiser than ourselves, you never find one who hurts himself or maims himself; their movements are too feeble to be dangerous, and when they assume an injurious position, pain warns them to change it.

We have not yet decided to swaddle our kittens and puppies; are they any the worse for this neglect? Children are heavier, I admit, but they are also weaker. They can scarcely move, how could they hurt themselves? If you lay them on their backs, they will lie there till they die, like the turtle, unable to turn itself over.

Not content with having ceased to suckle their children, women no longer wish to do it; with the natural result—motherhood becomes a burden; means are found to avoid it. They will destroy their work to begin it over again, and they thus turn to the injury of the race the charm which was given them for its increase. This practice, with other causes of depopulation, forbodes the coming fate of Europe. Her arts and sciences, her philosophy and morals, will shortly reduce her to a desert. She will be the home of wild beasts, and her inhabitants will hardly have changed for the worse.

I have sometimes watched the tricks of young wives who pretend that they wish to nurse their own children. They take care to be dissuaded from this whim. They contrive that husbands, doctors, and especially mothers should intervene. If a husband should let his wife nurse her own baby it would be the ruin of him; they would make him out a murderer who wanted to be rid of her. A prudent husband must sacrifice paternal affection to domestic peace. Fortunately for you there are women in the country districts more continent than your wives. You are still more fortunate if the time thus gained is not intended for another than yourself.

There can be no doubt about a wife's duty, but, considering the contempt in which it is held, it is doubtful whether it is not just as good for the child to be suckled by a stranger. This is a question for the doctors to settle, and in my opinion they have settled it according to the women's wishes, and for my own part I think it is better that the child should suck the breast of a healthy nurse rather than of a petted mother, if he has any further evil to fear from her who has given him birth.

Ought the question, however, to be considered only from the physiological point of view? Does not the child need a mother's care as much as her milk? Other women, or even other animals, may give him the milk she denies him, but there is no substitute for a mother's love.

The woman who nurses another's child in place of her own is a bad mother; how can she be a good nurse? She may become one in time; use will overcome nature, but the child may perish a hundred times before his nurse has developed a mother's affection for him.

And this affection when developed has its drawbacks, which should make every sensible woman afraid to put her child out to nurse. Is she prepared to divide her mother's rights, or rather to abdicate them in favour of a stranger; to see her child loving another more than herself; to feel that the affection he retains for his own mother is a favour, while his love for his foster-mother is a duty; for is not some affection due where there has been a mother's care?

To remove this difficulty, children are taught to look down on their nurses, to treat them as mere servants. When their task is completed the child is withdrawn or the nurse is dismissed. Her visits to her foster-child are discouraged by a cold reception. After a few years the child never sees her again. The mother expects to take her place, and to repair by her cruelty the results of her own neglect. But she is greatly mistaken; she is making an ungrateful foster-child, not an affectionate son; she is teaching him ingratitude, and she is preparing him to despise at a later day the mother who bore him, as he now despises his nurse.

How emphatically would I speak if it were not so hopeless to keep struggling in vain on behalf of a real reform. More depends on this that you realise. Would you restore all men to their primal duties, begin with the mothers; the results will surprise you. Every evil follows in the train of this first sin; the whole moral order is disturbed, nature is quenched in every breast, the home becomes gloomy, the spectacle of a young family no longer stirs the husband's love and the stranger's reverence. The mother whose children are out of sight wins scanty esteem; there is no home life, the ties of nature are not strengthened by those of habit; fathers, mothers, children, brothers, and sisters cease to exist. They are almost strangers; how should they love one another? Each thinks of himself first. When the home is a gloomy solitude pleasure will be sought elsewhere.

But when mothers deign to nurse their own children, then will be a reform in morals; natural feeling will revive in every heart; there will be no lack of citizens for the state; this first step by itself will restore mutual affection. The charms of home are the best antidote to vice. The noisy play of children, which we thought so trying, becomes a delight; mother and father rely more on each other and grow dearer to one another; the marriage tie is strengthened. In the cheerful home life the mother finds her sweetest duties and the father his pleasantest recreation. Thus the cure of this one evil would work a wide-spread reformation; nature would regain her rights. When women become good mothers, men will be good husbands and fathers.

My words are vain! When we are sick of worldly pleasures we do not return to the pleasures of the home. Women have ceased to be mothers, they do not and will not return to their duty. Could they do it if they would? The contrary custom is firmly established; each would have to overcome the opposition of her neighbours, leagued together against the example which some have never given and others do not desire to follow.

Yet there are still a few young women of good natural disposition who refuse to be the slaves of fashion and rebel against the clamour of other women, who fulfil the sweet task imposed on them by nature. Would that the reward in store for them might draw others to follow their example. My conclusion is based upon plain reason, and upon facts I have never seen disputed; and I venture to promise these worthy mothers the firm and steadfast affection of their husbands and the truly filial love of their children and the respect of all the world. Childbirth will be easy and will leave no ill-results, their health will be strong and vigorous, and they will see their daughters follow their example, and find that example quoted as a pattern to others.

No mother, no child; their duties are reciprocal, and when ill done by the one they will be neglected by the other. The child should love his mother before he knows what he owes her. If the voice of instinct is not strengthened by habit it soon dies, the heart is still-born. From the outset we have strayed from the path of nature.

There is another by-way which may tempt our feet from the path of nature. The mother may lavish excessive care on her child instead of neglecting him; she may make an idol of him; she may develop and increase his weakness to prevent him feeling it; she wards off every painful experience in the hope of withdrawing him from the power of nature, and fails to realise that for every trifling ill from which she preserves him the future holds in store many accidents and dangers, and that it is a cruel kindness to prolong the child's weakness when the grown man must bear fatigue.

Thetis, so the story goes, plunged her son in the waters of Styx to make him invulnerable. The truth of this allegory is apparent. The cruel mothers I speak of do otherwise; they plunge their children into softness, and they are preparing suffering for them, they open the way to every kind of ill, which their children will not fail to experience after they grow up.

Fix your eyes on nature, follow the path traced by her. She keeps children at work, she hardens them by all kinds of difficulties, she soon teaches them the meaning of pain and grief. They cut their teeth and are feverish, sharp colics bring on convulsions, they are choked by fits of coughing and tormented by worms, evil humours corrupt the blood, germs of various kinds ferment in it, causing dangerous eruptions. Sickness and danger play the chief part in infancy. One half of the children who are born die before their eighth year. The child who has overcome hardships has gained strength, and as soon as he can use his life he holds it more securely.

This is nature's law; why contradict it? Do you not see that in your efforts to improve upon her handiwork you are destroying it; her cares are wasted? To do from without what she does within is according to you to increase the danger twofold. On the contrary, it is the way to avert it; experience shows that children delicately nurtured are more likely to die. Provided we do not overdo it, there is less risk in using their strength than in sparing it. Accustom them therefore to the hardships they will have to face; train them to endure extremes of temperature, climate, and condition, hunger, thirst, and weariness. Dip them in the water of Styx. Before bodily habits become fixed you may teach what habits you will without any risk, but once habits are established any change is fraught with peril. A child will bear changes which a man cannot bear, the muscles of the one are soft and flexible, they take whatever direction you give them without any effort; the muscles of the grown man are harder and they only change their accustomed mode of action when subjected to violence. So we can make a child strong without risking his life or health, and even if there were some risk, it should not be taken into consideration. Since human life is full of dangers, can we do better than face them at a time when they can do the least harm?

A child's worth increases with his years. To his personal value must be added the cost of the care bestowed upon him. For himself there is not only loss of life, but the consciousness of death. We must therefore think most of his future in our efforts for his preservation. He must be protected against the ills of youth before he reaches them: for if the value of life increases until the child reaches an age when he can be useful, what madness to spare some suffering in infancy only to multiply his pain when he reaches the age of reason. Is that what our master teaches us?

Man is born to suffer; pain is the means of his preservation. His childhood is happy, knowing only pain of body. These bodily sufferings are much less cruel, much less painful, than other forms of suffering, and they rarely lead to self-destruction. It is not the twinges of gout which make a man kill himself, it is mental suffering that leads to despair. We pity the sufferings of childhood; we should pity ourselves; our worst sorrows are of our own making.

The new-born infant cries, his early days are spent in crying. He is alternately petted and shaken by way of soothing him; sometimes he is threatened, sometimes beaten, to keep him quiet. We do what he wants or we make him do what we want, we submit to his whims or subject him to our own. There is no middle course; he must rule or obey. Thus his earliest ideas are those of the tyrant or the slave. He commands before he can speak, he obeys before he can act, and sometimes he is punished for faults before he is aware of them, or rather before they are committed. Thus early are the seeds of evil passions sown in his young heart. At a later day these are attributed to nature, and when we have taken pains to make him bad we lament his badness.

In this way the child passes six or seven years in the hands of women, the victim of his own caprices or theirs, and after they have taught him all sorts of things, when they have burdened his memory with words he cannot understand, or things which are of no use to him, when nature has been stifled by the passions they have implanted in him, this sham article is sent to a tutor. The tutor completes the development of the germs of artificiality which he finds already well grown, he teaches him everything except self-knowledge and self-control, the arts of life and happiness. When at length this infant slave and tyrant, crammed with knowledge but empty of sense, feeble alike in mind and body, is flung upon the world, and his helplessness, his pride, and his other vices are displayed, we begin to lament the wretchedness and perversity of mankind. We are wrong; this is the creature of our fantasy; the natural man is cast in another mould.

Would you keep him as nature made him? Watch over him from his birth. Take possession of him as soon as he comes into the world and keep him till he is a man; you will never succeed otherwise. The real nurse is the mother and the real teacher is the father. Let them agree in the ordering of their duties as well as in their method, let the child pass from one to the other. He will be better educated by a sensible though ignorant father than by the cleverest master in the world. For zeal will atone for lack of knowledge, rather than knowledge for lack of zeal. But the duties of public and private business! Duty indeed! Does a father's duty come last. It is not surprising that the man whose wife despises the duty of suckling her child should despise its education. There is no more charming picture than that of family life; but when one feature is wanting the whole is marred. If the mother is too delicate to nurse her child, the father will be too busy to teach him. Their children, scattered about in schools, convents, and colleges, will find the home of their affections elsewhere, or rather they will form the habit of caring for nothing. Brothers and sisters will scarcely know each other; when they are together in company they will behave as strangers. When there is no confidence between relations, when the family society ceases to give savour to life, its place is soon usurped by vice. Is there any man so stupid that he cannot see how all this hangs together?

A father has done but a third of his task when he begets children and provides a living for them. He owes men to humanity, citizens to the state. A man who can pay this threefold debt and neglects to do so is guilty, more guilty, perhaps, if he pays it in part than when he neglects it entirely. He has no right to be a father if he cannot fulfil a father's duties. Poverty, pressure of business, mistaken social prejudices, none of these can excuse a man from his duty, which is to support and educate his own children. If a man of any natural feeling neglects these sacred duties he will repent it with bitter tears and will never be comforted.

But what does this rich man do, this father of a family, compelled, so he says, to neglect his children? He pays another man to perform those duties which are his alone. Mercenary man! Do you expect to purchase a second father for your child? Do not deceive yourself; it is not even a master you have hired for him, it is a flunkey, who will soon train such another as himself.

There is much discussion as to the characteristics of a good tutor. My first requirement, and it implies a good many more, is that he should not take up his task for reward. There are callings so great that they cannot be undertaken for money without showing our unfitness for them; such callings are those of the soldier and the teacher.

"But who must train my child?" "I have just told you, you should do it yourself." "I cannot." "You cannot! Then find a friend. I see no other course."

A tutor! What a noble soul! Indeed for the training of a man one must either be a father or more than man. It is this duty you would calmly hand over to a hireling!

The more you think of it the harder you will find it. The tutor must have been trained for his pupil, his servants must have been trained for their master, so that all who come near him may have received the impression which is to be transmitted to him. We must pass from education to education, I know not how far. How can a child be well educated by one who has not been well educated himself?

Can such a one be found? I know not. In this age of degradation who knows the height of virtue to which man's soul may attain? But let us assume that this prodigy has been discovered. We shall learn what he should be from the consideration of his duties. I fancy the father who realises the value of a good tutor will contrive to do without one, for it will be harder to find one than to become such a tutor himself; he need search no further, nature herself having done half the work.

Some one whose rank alone is known to me suggested that I should educate his son. He did me a great honour, no doubt, but far from regretting my refusal, he ought to congratulate himself on my prudence. Had the offer been accepted, and had I been mistaken in my method, there would have been an education ruined; had I succeeded, things would have been worse—his son would have renounced his title and refused to be a prince.

I feel too deeply the importance of a tutor's duties and my own unfitness, ever to accept such a post, whoever offered it, and even the claims of friendship would be only an additional motive for my refusal. Few, I think, will be tempted to make me such an offer when they have read this book, and I beg any one who would do so to spare his pains. I have had enough experience of the task to convince myself of my own unfitness, and my circumstances would make it impossible, even if my talents were such as to fit me for it. I have thought it my duty to make this public declaration to those who apparently refuse to do me the honour of believing in the sincerity of my determination. If I am unable to undertake the more useful task, I will at least venture to attempt the easier one; I will follow the example of my predecessors and take up, not the task, but my pen; and instead of doing the right thing I will try to say it.

I know that in such an undertaking the author, who ranges at will among theoretical systems, utters many fine precepts impossible to practise, and even when he says what is practicable it remains undone for want of details and examples as to its application.

I have therefore decided to take an imaginary pupil, to assume on my own part the age, health, knowledge, and talents required for the work of his education, to guide him from birth to manhood, when he needs no guide but himself. This method seems to me useful for an author who fears lest he may stray from the practical to the visionary; for as soon as he departs from common practice he has only to try his method on his pupil; he will soon know, or the reader will know for him, whether he is following the development of the child and the natural growth of the human heart.

This is what I have tried to do. Lest my book should be unduly bulky, I have been content to state those principles the truth of which is self-evident. But as to the rules which call for proof, I have applied them to Emile or to others, and I have shown, in very great detail, how my theories may be put into practice. Such at least is my plan; the reader must decide whether I have succeeded. At first I have said little about Emile, for my earliest maxims of education, though very different from those generally accepted, are so plain that it is hard for a man of sense to refuse to accept them, but as I advance, my scholar, educated after another fashion than yours, is no longer an ordinary child, he needs a special system. Then he appears upon the scene more frequently, and towards the end I never lose sight of him for a moment, until, whatever he may say, he needs me no longer.

I pass over the qualities required in a good tutor; I take them for granted, and assume that I am endowed with them. As you read this book you will see how generous I have been to myself.

I will only remark that, contrary to the received opinion, a child's tutor should be young, as young indeed as a man may well be who is also wise. Were it possible, he should become a child himself, that he may be the companion of his pupil and win his confidence by sharing his games. Childhood and age have too little in common for the formation of a really firm affection. Children sometimes flatter old men; they never love them.

People seek a tutor who has already educated one pupil. This is too much; one man can only educate one pupil; if two were essential to success, what right would he have to undertake the first? With more experience you may know better what to do, but you are less capable of doing it; once this task has been well done, you will know too much of its difficulties to attempt it a second time—if ill done, the first attempt augurs badly for the second.

It is one thing to follow a young man about for four years, another to be his guide for five-and-twenty. You find a tutor for your son when he is already formed; I want one for him before he is born. Your man may change his pupil every five years; mine will never have but one pupil. You distinguish between the teacher and the tutor. Another piece of folly! Do you make any distinction between the pupil and the scholar? There is only one science for children to learn—the duties of man. This science is one, and whatever Xenophon may say of the education of the Persians, it is indivisible. Besides, I prefer to call the man who has this knowledge master rather than teacher, since it is a question of guidance rather than instruction. He must not give precepts, he must let the scholar find them out for himself.

If the master is to be so carefully chosen, he may well choose his pupil, above all when he proposes to set a pattern for others. This choice cannot depend on the child's genius or character, as I adopt him before he is born, and they are only known when my task is finished. If I had my choice I would take a child of ordinary mind, such as I assume in my pupil. It is ordinary people who have to be educated, and their education alone can serve as a pattern for the education of their fellows. The others find their way alone.

The birthplace is not a matter of indifference in the education of man; it is only in temperate climes that he comes to his full growth. The disadvantages of extremes are easily seen. A man is not planted in one place like a tree, to stay there the rest of his life, and to pass from one extreme to another you must travel twice as far as he who starts half-way.

If the inhabitant of a temperate climate passes in turn through both extremes his advantage is plain, for although he may be changed as much as he who goes from one extreme to the other, he only removes half-way from his natural condition. A Frenchman can live in New Guinea or in Lapland, but a negro cannot live in Tornea or a Samoyed in Benin. It seems also as if the brain were less perfectly organised in the two extremes. Neither the negroes nor the Laps are as wise as Europeans. So if I want my pupil to be a citizen of the world I will choose him in the temperate zone, in France for example, rather than elsewhere.

In the north with its barren soil men devour much food, in the fertile south they eat little. This produces another difference: the one is industrious, the other contemplative. Society shows us, in one and the same spot, a similar difference between rich and poor. The one dwells in a fertile land, the other in a barren land.

The poor man has no need of education. The education of his own station in life is forced upon him, he can have no other; the education received by the rich man from his own station is least fitted for himself and for society. Moreover, a natural education should fit a man for any position. Now it is more unreasonable to train a poor man for wealth than a rich man for poverty, for in proportion to their numbers more rich men are ruined and fewer poor men become rich. Let us choose our scholar among the rich; we shall at least have made another man; the poor may come to manhood without our help.

For the same reason I should not be sorry if Emile came of a good family. He will be another victim snatched from prejudice.

Emile is an orphan. No matter whether he has father or mother, having undertaken their duties I am invested with their rights. He must honour his parents, but he must obey me. That is my first and only condition.

I must add that there is just one other point arising out of this; we must never be separated except by mutual consent. This clause is essential, and I would have tutor and scholar so inseparable that they should regard their fate as one. . . .

But when they consider they must always live together, they must needs love one another, and in this way they really learn to love one another. . . .

This agreement made beforehand assumes a normal birth, a strong, well-made, healthy child. . . .

45
Johann Heinrich Pestalozzi
(1746-1827)

The Conditions against Which Pestalozzi Led a Reform

Selections from an address in Berlin at the celebration of the centennial of the birth of Pestalozzi in 1846 by Adolph Diesterweg, translated in Barnard's *American Journal of Education*, IV, pp. 343-345.

Our present system of common or public schools—that is schools which are open to all children under certain regulations—date from the discovery of printing, in 1436, when books began to be furnished so cheaply that the poor could buy them. Especially after Martin Luther had translated the Bible into German, and the desire to possess and understand that invaluable book became universal, did there also become universal the desire to know how to read. Men sought to learn, not only for the sake of reading the Scriptures, but also to be able to read and sing the Psalms, and to learn the Catechism. For this purpose schools for children were established, which were essentially reading schools. Reading was the first and principal study; next came singing, and then memorizing texts, songs, and the Catechism. At first the ministers taught; but afterward the duty was turned over to the inferior church officers,—the choristers and sextons. Their duties as choristers and sextons were paramount, and as schoolmasters only secondary. The children paid a small monthly fee; no more being thought necessary, since the schoolmaster derived a salary from the church.

Nobody either made or knew how to make great pretensions to educational skill. If the teacher communicated to his scholars the acquirements above mentioned, and kept them in order, he gave satisfaction; and no one thought any thing about separate institutions for school children. There were no school books distinctively so called; the children learned their lessons in the Bible or the Psalter, and read either in the Old or the New Testament.

Each child read by himself; the simultaneous method was not known. One after another stepped up to the table where the master sat. He pointed out one letter at a time, and named it; the child named it after him; he drilled him in recognizing and remembering each. Then they took letter by letter of the words, and by getting acquainted with them in this way, the child gradually learned to read. This was a difficult method for him; a very difficult one. Years usually passed before any facility had been acquired; many did not learn in four years. It was imitative and purely mechanical labor on both sides. To understand what was read was seldom thought of. The syllables were pronounced with equal force, and the reading was without grace or expression.

Where it was possible, but unnaturally and mechanically, learning by heart was practiced. The children drawled out texts of Scripture, Psalms, and the contents of the Catechism from the beginning to end; short questions and long answers alike, all in the same monotonous manner. Anybody with delicate ears who heard the sound once, would remember it all his life long. There are people yet living, who were taught in that unintelligent way, who can corroborate these statements. Of the actual contents of the words whose sounds they had thus barely committed to memory by little and little, the children knew absolutely almost nothing. They learned superficially and understood superficially. Nothing really passed into their minds; at least nothing during their school years.

The instruction in singing was no better. The master sang to them the psalm-tunes over and over, until they could sing them, or rather screech them, after him.

Such was the condition of instruction in our schools during the sixteenth, seventeenth, and two-thirds of the eighteenth centuries; confined to one or two studies, and those taught in the most imperfect and mechanical way.

It was natural that youth endowed, when healthy, with an ever increasing capacity for pleasure in living, should feel the utmost reluctance at attending school. To be employed daily, for three or four hours, or more, in this mechanical toil, was no light task; and it therefore became necessary to force the children to sit still, and study their lessons. During all that time, especially in the seventeenth century, during the fearful Thirty Years' War, and subsequently, as the age was sunk in barbarism, the children of course entered the schools ignorant and untrained. "As the old ones sung, so twittered the young." Stern severity and cruel punishments were the order of the day; and by them the children were kept in order. Parents governed children, too young to attend, by threats of the schoolmaster and the school; and when they went, it was with fear and trembling. The rod, the cane, the raw-hide, were necessary apparatus in each school. The punishments of the teacher exceeded those of a prison. Kneeling on peas, sitting on the shame-bench, standing in the pillory, wearing an ass-cap, standing before the school door in the open street with a label on the back or breast, and other similar devices, were the remedies which the rude men of the age devised. To name a single example of a boy whom all have heard of, of high gifts, and of reputable family,—Dr. Martin Luther reckoned up fifteen or sixteen times that he was whipped upon the back in one forenoon. The learning and training corresponds; the one was strictly a mechanical process; the other, only bodily punishment. What wonder that from such schools there came forth a rude generation; that men and women looked back all their lives to the school as to a dungeon, and to the teacher as a taskmaster, and jailer; that the schoolmaster was of a small repute; that understrappers were selected for school duty and school discipline; that dark, cold kennels were used for schoolrooms; that the school-master's place, especially in the country, was assigned him amongst the servants and the like.

This could not last; it has not, thank God! When and by what efforts of admirable men the change took place, I shall relate a little later on.

Pestalozzi's Ideas.
Selections from His Writings

Selections translated by F. V. N. Painter in his *Great Pedagogical Essays Plato to Spencer* (New York: American Book Company, 1905), pp. 352-355, and reprinted by permission from Van Nostrand Reinhold Company.

Summary by Pestalozzi's biographer Morf

"1. Sense-impression is the foundation of instruction.

"2. Language must be connected with sense-impression.

"3. The time for learning is not the time for judgment and criticism.

"4. In each branch instruction must begin with the simplest elements, and proceed gradually by following the child's developments; that is, by a series of steps which are psychologically connected.

"5. A pause must be made at each stage of the instruction sufficiently long for the child to get the new matter thoroughly into his grasp and under his control.

"6. Teaching must follow the path of development, and not that of dogmatic exposition.

"7. The individuality of the pupil must be sacred for the teacher.

"8. The chief aim of elementary instruction is not to furnish the child with knowledge and talents, but to develop and increase the powers of his mind.

"9. To knowledge must be joined power; to what is known, the ability to turn it to account.

"10. The relations between master and pupil, especially so far as discipline is concerned, must be established and regulated by love.

"11. Instruction must be subordinated to the higher end of education."

Diary, 1774

No education would be worth a jot that resulted in a loss of manliness and lightness of heart. So long as there is joy in the child's face, ardor and enthusiasm in all his games, so long as happiness accompanies most of his impressions, there is nothing to fear. Short moments of self-subjugation quickly followed by new interests and new joys do not dishearten. To see peace and happiness resulting from habits of order and obedience is the true preparation for social life.

Be in no hurry to get on, but make the first step sound before moving; in this way you will avoid confusion and waste. Order, exactness, completion—alas, not thus was my character formed. And in the case of my own child in particular, I am in great danger of being blinded by his quickness, and rapid progress, and, dazzled by the unusual extent of his knowledge, of forgetting how much ignorance lurks behind this apparent development, and how much has yet to be done before we can go farther. Completeness, orderliness, absence of confusion—what important points!

Lead your child out into Nature, teach him on the hilltops and in the valleys. There he will listen better, and the sense of freedom will give him more strength to overcome difficulties. But in these hours of freedom let him be taught by Nature rather than by you. Let him fully realize that she is the real teacher and that you, with your art, do nothing more than walk quietly at her side. Should a bird sing or an insect hum on a leaf, at once stop your talk; bird and insect are teaching him; you may be silent.

I would say to the teacher, Be thoroughly convinced of the immense value of liberty; do not let vanity make you anxious to see your efforts producing premature fruit; let your child be as free as possible, and seek diligently for every means of ensuring his liberty, peace of mind, and good humor. Teach him absolutely nothing by words that you can teach him by the things themselves; let him see for himself, hear, find out, fall, pick himself up, make mistakes; no word, in short, when action is possible. What he can do for himself, let him do it; let him be always occupied, always active, and let the time you leave him to himself represent by far the greatest part of his childhood. You will then see that Nature teaches him better than men.

Selections from Pestalozzi's *The Evening Hour of a Hermit*,1780, as translated by Robert Ulich. Reprinted by permission of the publishers from Robert Ulich, (ed.),*Three Thousand Years of Educational Wisdom*(Cambridge, Massachusetts, Harvard University Press, 1947, 1954) pp. 480-485.

Man who is the same whether in the palace or in a hut, what is he in his innermost nature? Why do not the wise tell us? Why are the greatest of our thinkers not concerned with knowing what their race is? Does a peasant use his ox without knowing it? Does not a shepherd care for the nature of his sheep?

And you who use man and profess that you guard and nurture him, do you care for him as the peasant cares for his ox? Do you tend him as the shepherd tends his sheep? Does your wisdom help you to understand truly your race and is your goodness the goodness of enlightened guardians of the people?

What man is, what his needs are, what elevates and humiliates him, what strengthens and what weakens him ought to be the most important knowledge for the rulers as well as for the humblest.

Mankind feels this need everywhere; everywhere man is struggling upward with pain, labor, and passion. Generations after generations fade away with their lives unfulfilled, and the end of their days tells them that they completed their careers without achieving their goal. Their end is not like the end of ripe fruits which have fulfilled their task before the sleep of the winter.

Why does man seek truth without method and scope? Why does he not search for the necessities of his nature that he may build upon them the enjoyment and happiness of his life? Why does he not seek such truth as gives him peace and enjoyment, which makes him content, which develops his strength, brightens his days and brings blessings upon his years?

Man, driven by his needs can find the road to this truth nowhere but in his own nature.

The nursling, his hunger satisfied, learns in this way what his mother is to him; she develops in him love, the essence of gratitude, before the infant is able to utter the words 'duty' and 'thank'; in the same natural way the son finds his happiness in the duties towards his father who gives him bread and a hearth to warm himself.

Man, if you seek truth in this way of Nature you will find it as you need it according to your station and your career.

Obedience to your nature is essential for your rest and your peace; it is your guiding star in your personal matters; it is the foundation on which your life ought to rest, and it is the spring of your happiness.

Following the path of your nature you cannot make use of all truths. The sphere of knowledge from which man in his individual station can receive happiness is limited; its sphere begins closely around him, around his own self and his nearest relationships, from there his knowledge will expand, and while expanding it must regulate itself according to this firm centre of all the powers of truth.

The pure feeling for truth is formed in limited circles and pure human wisdom rests upon the firm basis of man's knowledge of his closest relationships and upon his maturity in handling his own personal matters.

Power, strong and clear sentiments and a sense for right application is its expression.

Sublime road of Nature, the truth to which thou leadest is power and action and source of culture, enrichment and harmony of humankind.

Yet thou permittest not man to grow hastily and superficially and thy son, o Nature, cannot escape his natural limits, his speech cannot be more than the expression and the result of his knowledge. If men exceed the sequence of thy order, they destroy their inner power and disturb their peace and harmony.

They do so if they immerse themselves in the thousandfold confusion of verbal instruction and opinions, before having trained their minds for truth and wisdom through firsthand knowledge, or if they make sound, speech and words instead of truth derived from reality the basis of their mental development and of the growth of their capacities.

This artificial method of schooling, forging ahead of the free, slow and patient course of Nature and preferring words to things, gives man an artificial polish which conceals his lack of inherent natural power. Such a method can satisfy only times like our century.

The wretched and exhausting pursuit of the mere shadow of truth, the pursuit of tone and sound and words about truth, where no interest inspires and where no application is possible, the direction of all powers of growing youth toward the doctrines of harsh and onesided schoolmasters, the thousandfold arts of juggling words and the latest fashion in teaching, supposed to be the true foundation of human education, all this serves only to lead youth away from the road of Nature.

He, who flutters around all kinds of knowledge and who does

not train himself through steady and firm application, he too loses the road of Nature, the clear, serene and attentive glance, and the quiet and undisturbed sense of deep and true gladness.

Where art thou, Nature, true teacher of man? When also those condemned to travel through the dead and dreary deserts of ignorance, lose their natural simplicity?

Lack of knowledge of your own nature, o man, curbs your wisdom still more than all external restrictions forced upon you. Perversion of the first fundamental relations to your environment, murderous and oppressive power of tyranny, privation of all enjoyments of truth and happiness, unnatural absence of general national enlightenment concerning the fundamental interests and conditions of man, how your heavy shadow darkens the world!

Therefore the desire for full development of the capacities of man, this source of powerful actions and of peaceful enjoyments, is no imaginary impulse and no delusive error.

Realization of our selves, pure force in our nature, thou blessing of our existence, thou art no dream. To seek and strive for thee is the scope and destiny of man and I feel it also as my deepest urge; to search for thee is my innermost wish as well as the aim and destiny of mankind.

Where and how shall I find thee, truth, who art my salvation and who elevates me to the perfection of my nature?

My innermost nature discloses this truth. All men are fundamentally alike and there is only one road which leads to their happiness. Hence the truth which springs from our nature will be the universal truth of all mankind; it will be the truth that will unify the thousands who quarrel over its mere external form.

Hence it is the man with a simple and clear soul whom Nature allows to arrive at true human wisdom, for it is he who applies his knowledge humbly and skillfully and uses all his talents modestly and diligently; whereas the man who destroys this order of Nature and the harmony of his knowledge, will never enjoy the blessings of truth.

Actions which do not conform to the order of our nature undermine our capacity to perceive the truth; they confuse the noble and sublime simplicity of our natural and basic concepts and feelings.

Therefore all human wisdom is founded on the strength of a good and truthful heart and all human happiness on simplicity and purity.

Practice, application and use of power and of wisdom in specific situations and conditions is the proper goal of vocational and class education. But this must always be subordinated to the aim of general education.

Certainly there are chasms between the humble father of a family and a prince, between the poor man toiling for his daily bread and the rich man harassed by still greater anxieties, between the idle dreamers and the genius, whose eagle-flight amazes the world.

Yet if the one on his heights is lacking in pure humanity dark clouds will amass around him; whereas humanity born in the lowest hut will radiate the pure light of human greatness.

Without it the most enlightened laws will be but words about brotherly love in the mouth of unfeeling men.

Man, though your self and the consciousness of your personality and powers is the first object of creative Nature, you do not live for yourself alone. Therefore Nature forms you also for living within human relationships, and it forms you through them.

In proportion as these relationships are close to you, they will educate you for fulfilling your destiny.

The power formed through mastering our nearest relationships is the source of our capacity to master the more remote.

A fatherly spirit makes a good governor—a brotherly spirit a good citizen; both create order at home and in the state.

Man's domestic relationships are the first and foremost ones of Nature.

Man toils in his vocation and bears the burden of communal duties in order to enjoy his home in harmony and peace.

To this peaceful enjoyment man's education for his vocation and for his social rank must be subordinated.

Hence the home is the foundation of a pure and natural education of mankind.

Hence the home is the school of morality and of the state.

Respect first the child in man and then think of him as an apprentice in his vocation.

A healthy childhood benefits the years of apprenticeship and is the foundation of all future happiness.

Whoever departs from this natural order and lays artificial emphasis on class and vocational education, or training for rule or for service, leads man aside from the enjoyment of the most natural blessings to a sea of hidden dangers.

Do you not see, men, do you not feel it, sons of the earth, how their education causes the ruling classes to lose the pith and marrow of their strength? Do you not see it, men, how their departure from the wise order of Nature brings shallowness and misery to them and descends from them to the people? Do you not feel how everywhere men forget the beneficent intimacy of their homes and stream toward the glittering stages of life to brag their learning and to gratify their ambitions?

Erring mankind drifts towards a future of darkness!

God is the nearest relationship of man!

Even though you may deeply enjoy your home, it cannot always give you peace.

Your tender, kind and feeling nature is not strong enough to suffer force and death without God.

The faith in God, the father of your house and the source of your welfare, the faith in God's fatherhood, this faith gives you solace, strength and wisdom which neither force nor death can take from you.

Faith in God is the highest accord of man's feelings; in this faith man the child faces God the father.

From this faith springs the peace of life—from this peace of life springs our security—from our security springs the firm use of our talents, our growth and our wisdom—from wisdom springs all human welfare.

Want of faith is immodesty, feeling ourselves us children of God creates sublime modesty in whatever we are and do.

Pestalozzi and Today

Hugh C. Black, "Pestalozzi and the Education of the Disadvantaged," *The EducationalForum*,XXXIII (No. 4, May 1969): 511-521.

New materials on Pestalozzi suggest again the value to practitioners of the history and philosophy of education. My thesis is that more of us should restudy Pestalozzi, for he can instruct us on the education of the culturally disadvantaged.

What brought me to this thesis was the discovery in Davis, California, of Mary R. Allen's *Personal Recollections of Years Spent in Germany, England, Africa and America*, preserved by her granddaughter, Mrs. James F. Wilson, wife of an Emeritus Professor of the University of California at Davis. The author's true name is Maria Arnold, the ninth child in the family of twelve of John Ramsauer, a close associate of Pestalozzi for the sixteen years from 1800 to 1816— first as a ten-year old student at Burgdorf in 1800, then as a teacher at

Yverdun beginning in 1805, and as private secretary. In 1838 (originally for Diesterweg's *Pedagogical Germany*, with a 2nd edition in 1880) John, or Johann, or Johannes Ramsauer wrote *Short Sketch of my Educational Career, with Special Reference to Pestalozzi and His Institutions*. Most of us know of Ramsauer through Paul Monroe's *Cyclopedia of Education* (V, 105) and brief extracts in English translation from Ramsauer's *Brief Sketch of My Pedagogical Life* which have appeared in such standard sources on Pestalozzi as Russell's *American Journal of Education* (Vol. 7, 1858, pp. 301-304), Hermann Krusi's *Pestalozzi: His Life, Work and Influence* (pp. 50-51, 96-99), and Baron Roger De Guimps' *Pestalozzi: His Aim and Work* (pp. 37, 104-105, 108, 117-118, 127-128, 142, 161, 189, 193-194, and 206). In her *Recollections*[1] Ramsauer's daughter Maria tells us that she could not refrain from stating those incidents in the biography of her father which were closely linked with Pestalozzi. Knowing that "but very few have become acquainted with the epoch in school history erected by him, the sacrifices, sufferings and toils which it cost him to accomplish his purposes for the good of the world," Maria included in her *Recollections* "a few extracts" of Pestalozzi's life as described by her father and other followers "whom he had drawn to himself, inspired with zeal and influenced to unite their strength with his in one common field of labor" (p. 5). The *Recollections* include quotations translated into English from the *Brief Sketch* (some of which are new to most of us) and a moving account of John Ramsauer's death not available elsewhere. The English version of Maria Arnold's *Personal Recollections* is now in the hands of Mrs. Wilson in a beautifully hand-written volume "Copied for the children of my beloved friend Maria" by "B. T." in the year 1881, a xeroxed copy of which is now in the library of the University of California at Davis.

This new source reveals another good reason for Eby, the educational historian, to call Pestalozzi "education's most successful failure."[2] For here is a part of the story of how Pestalozzi experimented with teaching the disadvantaged, tried, suffered, and was successful amidst all his failures—at least, I am suggesting, in the life of John Ramsauer and his family.

Born on May 28, 1794, in Herisau, Canton Appenzell, Switzerland,

---

[1] Page numbers appearing in this paper with quotations not otherwise identified are from the original work by Maria Arnold, who used the penname of Mary R. Allen. The original *Personal Recollections* is now in the possession of Mrs. James F. Wilson of Davis, California.

[2] Frederick Eby, *The Development of Modern Education*, 2d ed. (Englewood Cliffs, N. J.: Prentice-Hall, Inc., 1952), p. 415.

John Ramsauer was not so disadvantaged originally as many of his contemporaries. For, he teels us, his mother was the "owner of a large silk factory and carried an extensive business" (pp. 13-14). But his father died when John was only three years old, and his mother suffered from the bad times which came in 1798 when the great revolution broke out in Switzerland. His diary (through Maria) tells us:

> The French went plundering through the country, Swiss were warring against Swiss, Austrians and Russians were filling the land, fighting against the French. This state of affairs ruined all commerce, put a stop to all kinds of business and caused a great and fearful famine. In the small cantons thousands of children became orphans, therefore the larger and richer cantons sent provisions to the poorer and more unfortunate ones and in 1799 they sent for the poorest children in order to provide for their wants (p. 16).

Ramsauer's entreaties for permission to emigrate finally received approval from his mother (whose other son was soon to die of consumption) when her "necessity became daily greater" (p. 17). On February 4, 1800, with forty-three boys from eight to twelve years of age, John Ramsauer, describing himself as "a homely stout short boy with very red hair plaited behind, short leather-pants and a turned-up hat" began the emigration in "two covered waggons"[3] amidst snow and bitter cold which put him in Burgdorf on February 9. His "disadvantaged" position which he bore very quietly and "without complaining" is pictured for us in these words:

> Sometimes we had to sleep with French soldiers in barns without any supper. Our food when we did get any consisted of potatoes and salt, and we found our rest for the night on a bed of straw (p. 20).

In yet another sense was the young John Ramsauer "disadvantaged," for in his education, he was also destitute. Maria quotes him as saying that "Except religious instructions nothing was done for my education." His father, who died when John was three, had been "a devoted christian"; and his sisters "spent much of their time in reading God's word, the sight of which produced early serious impressions upon my mind." He learned informally. From the conversations to which he listened, "almost invariably about witches, ghosts," he was filled with fear and dread. Fond of stories, he often visited the underground room

---

[3] Cf. "two open carriages" in Baron Roger De Guimps, *Pestalozzi: His Aim and Work,* translated from the edition of 1874 by Margaret Cuthbertson Crombie (Syracuse, N. Y.: C. W. Bardeen, 1889), p. 118.

of the silk factory and was influenced by the stories he heard from the workmen at their looms—their past histories, witch-stories, and from "the Old Eagle" (a former slave in Algiers for more than twenty years) descriptions of the horrors of slavery. From the latter, Ramsauer gained an admiration for his "manner of narrating" and an intense desire "to emigrate and make similar experiences." Since several families lived in his mother's large house and they were visited by a great number of working people daily, he learned from his society. Of formal schooling which began at the age of eight, Ramsauer tells us:

> reading, writing and committing the catechism to memory were our occupations, all the scholars were only governed with the rod, and we had but little respect for the teacher, I had often heard him called a thief, as he had formerly stolen goods from my fathers store and spent a long time of his life in jail (p. 14).

Even though he learned to read, the only secular literature he became acquainted with was "thirty or forty almanachs, which had been preserved from year to year." The remainder of his studies, he tells us, "consisted in looking at the beautiful pictures of a large bible and in committing much of the sacred writings to memory." His most advantageous learning came not from schooling but from his mother's business and his assisting his sisters in selling goods during the absence of his mother. This resulted in his "learning to make reckonings"—an ability from which he profited when he emigrated. After reaching Burgdorf on February 9, 1800, Ramsauer, with sixteen other boys, was led through the woods "for an hour or more" to Schleumen where he was adopted by Mrs. von Werth, "the widow of a nobleman of Bern who lived during the summer-season at her large country-seat in Schleumen." A factor in his adoption was the disclosure (by telling how old her mansion was by reading the date) that he could cipher.

Against this background of poverty came the influence of Henry Pestalozzi. For when the ten-year old John Ramsauer asked to be sent to school, Mrs. von Werth permitted him to attend the only establishment in the neighborhood, the lowest school of which was in Pestalozzi's charge. Maria Arnold describes the first encounter of pupil and teacher in these words:

> When he entered the house, Pestalozzi was in the act of teaching a class, his dress was exceedingly negligent, his motions very quick, his voice loud and rapid. He paced the room with a stick in his hand, explaining figures on the wallpaper. Upon my father's entrance he turned kindly to him,

greeting him with a kiss; this frightened the new comer very much, as he had never been kissed by any one, except his mother, but had often heard of Judas' kiss. Pestalozzi did not speak a word to him for the whole day. Every figure, every hole in the wall-paper we had to describe in simply composed sentences, sometimes repeating Pestalozzi's words. Such as the following:

I   Figure.

II   Red figure, black figure, yellow figure.

III   Round figure, cornered figure, square figure.

IV   Round red figure, black four cornered etc.

V   A round yellow figure next to a round red figure.

A square black figure combined with a round cornered black figure.

In this way the scholars had to express all they saw on paper, pictures etc. No book was used, and of mechanical learning they knew nothing (pp. 27-29).

Also enlightening is this impression of Pestalozzi on the ten-year old boy who became his scholar:

Pestalozzi's language was sometimes so rapid and unintelligible, that on one occasion, when studying natural history and learning about the different species of monkeys, my father half frightened looked at the teacher, at his uncombed hair, long beard, disorderly dress, and almost thought he belonged to the race (p. 29).

Yet, if we may believe Maria Arnold,

The scholars learned to draw and cipher and became in a short time ardently attached to their teacher, whose fervent zeal exercised a deep influence upon my father. These instructions were the first beginnings of reform in school-life, but at that time every one ridiculed the odd reformer (pp. 29-30).

So influenced was John Ramsauer by Pestalozzi that he moved with the other pupils into the castle of Burgdorf in the autumn of 1800 where, according to Maria Arnold,

the institution increased rapidly, teachers were engaged, who, after a proper course of training, were able to assist Pestalozzi in carrying out his ideas. Mockery and ridicule were hushed to silence and were succeeded by esteem and admiration for the head of the institution (p. 31).

Wishing to move to Bern, Mrs. von Werth allowed Ramsauer "to decide for himself" whether he should remain with her, take advantage of her inducements, and attend a large, brilliant school in Bern or cast his lot with Pestalozzi. Maria tells us:

> But the poor boy preferred rather being adopted by Pestalozzi than to become a companion of the rich and indulged city-children, and always in later life looked back with gratitude upon his decision which he felt was directed by God (pp. 31-32).

We appreciate Ramsauer's choice all the more when we realize the great amount of manual labor this decision committed the youngster to. "Not able to pay anything towards the institution," he treaded the large wheel of the well, cleaned the yard and rooms, assisted in the kitchen, and every evening had "to clean eighty pair of boots without a brush" (p. 32). Yet he became interested in mathematics and drawing and soon became the first scholar in both.

Showing off Ramsauer as an example of the fruits of the new system to the thousands of visitors, Pestalozzi would say:

> . . . this is a poor emigrant, who is now learning according to his talents and abilities, he has made astonishing progress in mathematics and drawing in a very short time. . . . This is proof, that amongst the poor and humble are frequently to be found more and higher talents than amongst the rich and favored. But with the former they are very rarely developed, or if so, not according to system (pp. 33-34).

So well did Ramsauer develop that

> . . . not yet eleven years old, Pestalozzi made me the teacher of a large class of boys older than myself. I had good success in preserving order, though corporeal punishment which was then common everywhere, was entirely forbidden by Pestalozzi. But the heavy burden of manual labor continued to rest upon me (pp. 35-36).

On Ramsauer's departure from Pestalozzi in 1816, Niederer could state how Ramsauer "had lived and labored in his spirit, as child, youth, scholar, teacher, and special companion and friend of Pestalozzi" (p. 45). And, by virtue of Pestalozzi's influence, Maria, the ninth child in a family of twelve, could recall later this kind of Ramsauer family life:

> . . . around the table we were not permitted to talk; political news was often read by my father, French was spoken and

topics discussed, which were above our comprehension. The elder children spent the evening hours with our parents, read from the most celebrated authors with them and afterwards conversed freely on what they had read (p. 75).

For a family to become a family "which could talk" was no small achievement in those days. Maria records the fact that one scholarly visitor, after spending a few days with the family and looking back on the experience, wrote Ramsauer: "I can only exclaim: Behold the tabernacle of God among men" (p. 6). She herself gained a better appreciation of the quality of achievement at home when later she lived in England as a governess "with a family of the first rank in society" which, nevertheless, presented to her "a sober and melancoly picture" (p. 6). Quite a contrast—this family life of the Ramsauers—to that of their many contemporaries whom we know, for example, from Pestalozzi's *Leonard and Gertrude!* What an advance over people who lived little better than cattle and who, in one instance we know about, hired as the schoolmaster of their children one who had been taking care of the pigs for the countryside for many years, and when he got too old for that was sent to a miserable cottage to take care of the children.[4] A degraded people generally, "the humble folk" were the victims, so Pestalozzi saw it, of "all the bungling arts" tried in the "word and clapper schools" and never taught to talk.[5]

Thus in the beautiful script of Maria Arnold's *Personal Recollections* we have a heart-warming story of success in educating the disadvantaged. It starts with the ten-year-old John Ramsauer with his bed of straw and his diet of potatoes and salt. It comes to fruition in John Ramsauer, himself a teacher and head of a family described by one of its members later as a family "where parents thought it their highest and sweetest duty to promote day by day the true happiness of their children and prepare their hearts and minds for a useful life" (p. 5). It continues today. For Ramsauer was to teach and influence others, including a later Queen of Greece; and his descendants, including Maria and her grandson Thurman Arnold (attorney-general under FDR), came to the United States, contributed to, and continue to contribute to American life and culture. In between—during the years 1800-1816—stands Pestalozzi and his influence on the culturally disadvantaged of his

---

[4] Eby, *op. cit.,* p. 441.

[5] Johann Heinrich Pestalozzi, *How Gertrude Teaches Her Children,* translated by Lucy E. Holland and Francis C. Turner and edited, with introduction and notes, by Ebenezer Cooke, 5th ed. (Syracuse, N. Y.: C. W. Bardeen, October 1915), "Notes to Letter VII," pp. 234-235.

time. Surely Pestalozzi merits restudy by those who would influence the culturally disadvantaged of our time.

If we should turn to Pestalozzi for guidance today, we would be warned of the complexity of the task of educating the culturally disadvantaged. For example, after exerting his all with the orphans at Stanz, Pestalozzi tells us:

> My success was not immediate. The children were not easily convinced of my love. Their old habits were too strongly fixed, and many were disappointed by the necessary rigour of our lives. . . .[6]

From Pestalozzi's entire career comes the warning: our task is not easy, and we should beware the easy way. Certainly we should not expect some miraculous solution. Hence I am not attempting here to summarize magic formulae I discovered in Pestalozzi. How much would it be worth, for example, to herald two insights we have already discovered in the John Ramsauer part of the Pestalozzi story? The first is that higher talents reside among the poor and humble as well as "amongst the rich and favored," but "they are rarely developed, or if so, not according to system." The second is the usefulness of using the disadvantaged—even eleven-year old John Ramsauer—to teach other disadvantaged youngsters. These insights profit us little, for they are already "in circulation" today. But knowing that Pestalozzi first knew them long ago gives us a better perspective for judging innovations in a decade so enamored of innovations that I have heard my colleagues speak of a "new innovation."

For example I cite the *Teps Newsletter* of November 15, 1966, announcing that "Three New Projects Train Disadvantaged to Teach." In the Bethel (Oregon) Project high school dropouts are being trained as teacher aides and teachers. In the Sausalito (California) Project, "50 students from widely divergent economic levels have begun their first year of teacher education in the Sausalito Schools." And the announcement continues, "Seattle's federally funded *New Careers Project* will recruit, train, and employ disadvantaged adults as paraprofessionals in health, education, welfare, protection, and recreation." Surely these are "new" innovations, for the "innovation" came long ago—in 1801 when Pestalozzi made John Ramsauer into a teacher! My task here is not to cite Pestalozzi's firsts but rather to point out that in the vast ocean of expanding knowledge about the culturally disadvantaged Pestalozzi offers us the possibility of discovering the land which is often not seen for the sea. As Bacon saw it long ago:

[6] J. A. Green, *The Educational Ideas of Pestalozzi*, third impression (London: W. B. Clive, University Tutorial Press, 1911), p. 186.

They are ill discoverers that
Think there is no land, when
They see nothing but sea.[7]

For example, Pestalozzi made clear how important it is, as with any kind of educating, to know the pupils and to have knowledge. We may hear it, as I have, at a statewide teacher education meeting in which a young expert from New York City told us all that we *must* pack up our teacher-preparing programs in colleges and universities and move out into the culturally disadvantaged neighborhoods where the action is. Some have answered this demand by scheduling some meetings and conferences in well-known culturally disadvantaged locales. But that is a far cry from Pestalozzi's ideal: to have real knowledge. For Pestalozzi, if we may believe J. A. Green, had knowledge of the situation of his day:

> Around him he saw, on the one hand, ignorance, poverty, and degradation; on the other, a crowd of insincere politicians whose rhetoric was empty and inconsequent, because it did not spring from a first-hand acquaintance with facts. Words void of real meaning were bandied about from man to man as if they were true coin. For the moment the position seemed hopeless. Here was wretchedness and misery in plenty, and in the face of it, abundance of talk concerning "the rights of man" and other formulae current at the time, high-sounding, but in their use hollow and unreal. What else could be expected when education, from top to bottom, dealt with nothing but words, grammatical or ecclesiastical formulae which did not touch in any way the real lives of those who learned them? Education wrongly conceived was the source of much social mischief; education rightly understood and rightly carried out was the only radical cure.[8]

Pestalozzi knew that the usual efforts toward social amelioration seemed to increase rather than to reduce the evils they were designed to combat. Philanthropic efforts of his day, even as in ours, left men more dependent than ever. Men were not taught to help themselves. "The best service man can render to man," said Pestalozzi, "is to teach him to help himself." "Man as a whole in his inner nature must be

---

[7] Francis Bacon, *Advancement of Learning*, II: VII, 5, as quoted in Walter Lippmann, *Essays in the Public Philosophy* (New York: Little, Brown and Company, 1955).

[8] Green, *op. cit.*, pp. 70-71.

improved if the external circumstances of the poor are to be bettered."[9] Knowing the situation, Pestalozzi concentrated on social reform through "operation uplift," the improvement of the individual person through proper education. From this objective of "The Founder of the Common School Movement" to our own (with all its attendant problems) of educating "all the children of all the people" is not a big jump. Both are grounded in the needs of people and knowledge of those to be educated. Anyone who has read Pestalozzi's classic work *Leonard and Gertrude* stands amazed at the revelation of this idealist's fund of knowledge about people, and especially about the culturally disadvantaged.

> Long years I lived surrounded by more than fifty beggar children. In poverty I shared my bread with them. I lived like a beggar in order to learn how to make beggars live like men.[10]

I suspect his own experiences lie behind this description of a character in *Leonard and Gertrude*:

> He knew his children better in eight days than their parents did in eight years, and employed this knowledge to render deception difficult, and to keep their hearts open before his eyes. He cared for their heads as he did their hearts, demanding that whatever entered them should be plain and clear as the silent moon in the sky. To insure this, he taught them to see and hear with accuracy, and cultivated their powers of attention. Above all, he sought to give them a thorough training in arithmetic; for he was convinced that arithmetic is the natural safeguard against error in the pursuit of truth.[11]

Again, in the same writing does not Pestalozzi reveal to us the essential knowledge of what it is all about?

> Occasionally, however, she would let drop some significant remark which the lieutenant felt went to the root of the whole matter of education. For example, she said to him one day: "You should do for your children what their parents fail to do for them. The reading, writing and arithmetic are not, after all, what they most need; it is all well and good for them to

---

[9] *Ibid.*, p. 69; Introduction to *Views and Experiences*, M, iii, 324.

[10] *How Gertrude Teaches Her Children*, "Notes to Preface and Letter I," p. 213.

[11] J. H. Pestalozzi, *Pestalozzi's Leonard and Gertrude*, translated and abridged by Eva Channing (Boston, Massachusetts: D. C. Heath and Company, 1892), Ch. XXXII, p. 157.

learn something, but the really important thing is for them to *be* something,—for them to become what they are meant to be, and in becoming which they so often have no guidance or help at home."[12]

To become what he is meant to be, to *be* something, to realize his innermost nature as Man "who is the same whether on the throne or in a hut" through the subject-matters of education (such as reading, writing, and arithmetic)—that ideal is Pestalozzi's message to us. Pestalozzi, if I read him correctly, tells us to offer the poor and humble not some special, practical or watered-down curriculum but rather a full diet of education—intellectual, moral, and practical. Mathematics, drawing, geography, reading, writing, languages, literature, singing, history, and surveying—that was the content taught young Ramsauer and the others whom Pestalozzi saw as needing a "complete education" through "public instruction."

Our students see the message in a Sidney Poitier movie "To Sir, with Love" Weights and measures taught in terms of practical use in shopping with mother motivated his students not at all. But the teacher became effective when he threw out all of that and began to give them an ideal of adult life, of what they might *be* as adults. An earlier generation got the same Pestalozzian message from the story of Billie Davis in "I Was a Hobo Kid" which the NEA made into the movie "A Desk for Billie." "Please," she tells the school principal when he tries to give her the special courses for rubber bums (transient, migratory workers) like her, "Let me try English and dramatic art rather than cooking." And in the fall of 1967, at a Yosemite teacher-education conference, a number of "Upward Bound" negroes at Berkeley told the teachers in vivid four-letter words that in their secondary schooling they did not want the "watered-down" and the special. Rather they want the chemistry and the math courses which prepare one for college. They want to advance as much as anyone else. They *as men* rather than *as disadvantaged* need teachers who care and impart the knowledge necessary to their becoming men. As Pestalozzi put it in *The Evening Hour of a Hermit*:

> What man is, what his needs are, what elevates and humiliates him, what strengthens and what weakens him ought to be the most important knowledge for the rulers as well as for the humblest.

This kind of perspective should help us as professional educators concerned with teacher preparation to see our tasks steadily and as a

[12] *Ibid.*,Ch. XXXI, p. 152.

whole amidst the strong, conflicting pressures in our changing world. We recall that only a few short years ago when the Russians launched Sputnik I, educators were told to prepare teachers rich in subject-matter knowledge to teach the college-preparatory and advanced students wasting away in the carnivals that are our schools. We remember Conant recommending for the American high schools his special tracks for the different classes of students, about which Mortimer Adler could write the editors of *Life* and criticize as "undemocratic" or "anti-democratic."

And then came the pressure to switch—so few years later. I witnessed a conference of university people at which a mathematician arose and tried mightily to pass a resolution stating absolutely that education of the culturally disadvantaged is *the* problem of education today. State officials and then school administrators began to exert pressures. The new cry (still with us) is to forget about preparing teachers rich in subject-matter knowledge for middle-class, college preparatory students. Rather we should re-tool completely our teacher preparatory programs and concentrate in our war on poverty on preparing teachers of the culturally disadvantaged.

Against such pressures of the moment Pestalozzi's insights stand as a warning. Having read Rousseau, who was influenced by Plato, Pestalozzi cautions us to exercise the Greek virtues of balance and due emphasis. If I read him correctly, our central concern should be with education (not some all-out emphasis on the special education of the disadvantaged), with teachers (not all-out preparation of teachers of the disadvantaged), and with knowledge about Man (not merely knowledge about the special man, the poor). Teachers, I suggest, should be concerned with the "culturally disadvantaged." But truly that phrase means "all who lack culture," and all teachers must attend to the instructional needs of all students who lack knowledge about life and how it might be lived meaningfully.

Pestalozzi should also be studied because he challenges us to seek more knowledge about education—knowledge of the what and also the how of teaching-learning. Anticipating by a 100 years Jerome Bruner and his emphasis on the structure of knowledge, Pestalozzi stressed such basic elements of knowledge as number, form, and language. He would urge us to extend his search for knowledge of the fundamental elements and ideas of "each branch of teaching" that it might be brought "to a starting point within the reach of the growing powers of the child." In addition he challenges us to go beyond Bruner and recognize something more than the structure of knowledge. Knowledge must be communicated so as to relate to the children themselves and to their lives:

Had I started with the discipline of rules, the severity of external order would not have accomplished my purpose. This would have driven away the children whom I wished to win. I had necessarily first of all to awaken a right feeling within them in order to make them active, attentive, and obedient in matters external. In short, I tried to follow Christ's precept— "Cleanse first that which is within that the outside may be clean also," and, as always has been the case in my experience, the application of this principle brought success.[13]

Pestalozzi, I suggest, can also be read with profit in connection with other contemporary questions. In the past year or two suggestions have been made to the effect that the poor should be removed from their immediate environs and placed in special schools. We should bring to bear on such possibilities *all* knowledge available, such as the CCC experiences of the depression days and the Russian experiences with Boarding Schools during Khrushchev's time of power.[14] Reading Pestalozzi's experiments in *his* different schools may not settle our arguments about such matters, but we can draw inspiration from Pestalozzi's efforts to be everything to the orphans at Stanz:

I had to be all in all to my children. I was from morning to evening practically alone with them. Everything they received, whether for body or mind, came through my hands. Every offer of help, every lesson came from me. My hands were in their hands, and my eyes rested on their eyes. I laughed and cried with them. They were out of the world, they were out of Stanz, they lived entirely with me and I with them. I ate and drank with them. When they were ill I nursed them. I slept in their midst. I was the last to go to bed at night and the first to get up in the morning. At their wish I prayed with them, and even taught them in bed till they fell asleep.[15]

Perhaps in this lies Pestalozzi's greatest lesson to us: to seek as many as we can find of the kind of teachers, like Pestalozzi, of whom their pupils, like Ramsauer, may later write:

The glowing zeal of our beloved guide, his fervent love, his

---

[13] Pestalozzi's account of his work in Stanz which appeared as a letter in *Wochenschrift* in 1807, as quoted in Appendix I to J. A. Green, *op. cit.*, pp. 186-187. See also De Guimps, *op. cit.*, p. 92.

[14] Nancy Ruth Lenoir, "The Soviet Boarding School, 1956-1966," *Journal of Thought*, 3, I: 14-30 (January, 1968).

[15] J. A. Green, *op. cit.*, p. 185.

rare talents, pure benevolence, and the intensity of purpose with which he pursued his plans, drew everyone who lived under his influence towards him and inspired them with admiration and love. He governed without seeming conscious of it. The life of the whole institution was like that of one happy family, the strongest attachment existed between all the members of it and one enjoyed at the same time the rarest and purest pleasures, which acquaintance with nature and art can afford.[16]

The December 9, 1967, issue of *School and Society* reminds us of the twenty-year-old Pestalozzi Children's Village, Switzerland, now under the auspices of UNESCO, "which exists today . . . to give a home to homeless children of many nationalities, and bring them up in an atmosphere of international understanding."[17]   It is named after Pestalozzi, and the present director informs us that "Teaching in the village is based on his life and work." Where is it located? Interestingly enough for those who know the John Ramsauer story, off the usual tourists' beat, in the Alpine foothills south of Lake Constance "in the small Swiss canton of Appenzell." Again, as recently as 1952, the Oxford scholar and educator Sir Richard Livingstone, in summing up his wisdom about education for this age urged us all:

To the injunction, "Teach your pupil to think," I should like to add a further injunction, "Teach your pupil to see and feel."[18]

Long before, Pestalozzi told us to educate the head, the heart, and the hand; and in doing so he used torn wallpaper hanging from the walls of an old castle to teach the John Ramsauers!

[16] Mary R. Allen, *op. cit.*, pp. 37-38.

[17] Arthur Bill, "The Pestalozzi Children's Village," *School and Society*, 95, 2298: 502-503 (December 9, 1967). See also Edwin J. Swineford, "A Professional Pilgrimage in the Footsteps of Henry Pestalozzi," *Phi Delta Kappan*, pp. 347-349 (May, 1961).

[18] Sir Richard Livingstone, *Education and the Spirit of the Age*, (Oxford at the Clarendon Press, 1952), p. 102.

46
Friedrich Wilhelm Froebel
(1782-1852)

Selections from *The Education of Man* (1826) in F. V. N. Painter's *Great Pedagogical Essays Plato to Spencer* (New York: American Book Company, 1905), pp. 372-382. Reprinted by permission of Van Nostrand Reinhold Company.

1. In all things there lives and reigns an eternal law. This all-controlling law is necessarily based on an all-pervading, energetic, living, self-conscious, and hence eternal unity. This Unity is God. All things have come from the divine Unity, from God, and have their origin in the divine Unity, in God alone. God is the sole source of all things. In all things there lives and reigns the divine Unity, God. All things live and have their being in and through the divine Unity, in and through God. All things are only through the divine effluence that lives in them. The divine effluence that lives in each thing is the essence of each thing.

2. It is the destiny and lifework of all things to unfold their essence, hence their divine being, and therefore the divine Unity itself—to reveal God in their external and transient being. It is the special destiny and life-work of man, as an intelligent and rational being, to become fully, vividly, and clearly conscious of his essence, of the divine effluence in him, and therefore, of God; to become fully, vividly, and clearly conscious of his destiny and life-work; and to accomplish this, to render it (his essence) active, to reveal it in his own life with self-determination and freedom. *Education consists in leading man, as a thinking, intelligent being, growing into self-consciousness, to a pure and unsullied, conscious and free representation of the inner law of divine Unity, and in teaching him ways and means thereto.*

3. The knowledge of that eternal law, the insight into its origin, into its essence, into the totality, the connection, and intensity of its effects, the knowledge of life in its totality, constitute *science, the science of life*; and, referred by the self-conscious, thinking, intelligent being to representation and practice through and in himself, this becomes *the science of education*.

The system of directions, derived from the knowledge and study of that law, to guide thinking, intelligent beings in the apprehension of their life-work and in the accomplishment of their destiny, is *the theory of education*. The self-active application of this knowledge in the direct development and cultivation of rational beings toward the attainment of their destiny, is *the practice of education*. The object of education is the realization of a faithful, pure, inviolate, and hence holy life. Knowledge and application, consciousness and realization in life, united in the service of a faithful, pure, and holy life, constitute *the wisdom of life*, pure wisdom.

4. By education, then, the divine essence of man should be unfolded, brought out, lifted into consciousness, and man himself raised into free, conscious obedience to the divine principle that lives in him, and to a free representation of this principle in his life. Education as a whole, by means of instruction and training, should bring to man's consciousness, and render efficient in his life, the fact that man and nature proceed from God and are conditioned by him—that both have their being in God. *Education should lead and guide man to clearness concerning himself and in himself, to peace with nature, and to unity with God*; hence, it should lift him to a knowledge of himself and of mankind, to a knowledge of God and of nature, and to the pure and holy life to which such knowledge leads.

5. Education in instruction and training, originally and in its first principles, should necessarily be *passive, following with due protection, not prescriptive, categorical, or interfering*. Indeed, in its very essence, education should have these characteristics; for the undisturbed operation of the divine Unity is necessarily good—can not be otherwise than good. This necessity implies that the young human being—as it were, still in process of creation—would seek, although still unconsciously, as a product of nature, yet decidedly and surely, that which is in itself best; and, moreover, in a form wholly adapted to his condition, as well as to his disposition, his powers, and means. Thus the duckling hastens to the pond and into the water, while the young chicken scratches the ground, and the young swallow catches its food upon the wing and scarcely ever touches the ground.

6. The prescriptive, interfering education, indeed, can be justified only on two grounds; either because it teaches the clear, living thought, self-evident truth, or because it holds up a life whose ideal value has been established in experience. But, where self-evident, living, absolute truth rules, the eternal principle itself reigns, as it were, and will on this account maintain a passive, following character. For the living thought, the eternal divine principle as such demands and requires free self-activity and self-determination on the part of man, the being created for freedom in the image of God.

7. Again, a life whose ideal value has been perfectly established in experience never aims to serve as model in its form, but only in its essence, in its spirit. It is the greatest mistake to suppose that spiritual, human perfection can serve as model in its form. This accounts for the

common experience that the taking of such external manifestations of perfection as examples, instead of elevating mankind, checks, nay, represses, its development.

8. In good education, in genuine instruction, in true training, necessity should call forth freedom; law, self-determination; external compulsion, inner free-will; external hate, inner love. Where hatred brings forth hatred; law, dishonesty and crime; compulsion, slavery; necessity, serviture; where oppression destroys and debases; where severity and harshness give rise to stubbornness and deceit—all education is abortive. In order to avoid the latter and to secure the former, all prescription should be adapted to the pupil's nature and needs, and secure his coöperation. This is the case when all education in instruction and training, in spite of its necessarily categorical character, bears in all details and ramifications the irrefutable and irresistible impress that the one who makes the demand is himself strictly and unavoidably subject to an eternally ruling law, to an unavoidable eternal necessity, and that, therefore, all despotism is banished.

9. All true education in training and instruction should, therefore, at every moment, in every demand and regulation, be simultaneously double-sided—giving and taking, uniting and dividing, prescribing and following, active and passive, positive yet giving scope, firm and yielding; and the pupil should be similarly conditioned; but between the two, between educator and pupil, between request and obedience, there should invisibly rule a third something, to which educator and pupil are equally subject. The third something is the *right*, and *best*, necessarily conditioned and expressed without arbitrariness in the circumstances. The calm recognition, the clear knowledge, and the serene, cheerful obedience to the rule of this third something is the particular feature that should be constantly and clearly manifest in the bearing and conduct of the educator and teacher, and often firmly and sternly emphasized by him. The child, the pupil, has a very keen feeling, a very clear apprehension, and rarely fails to distinguish whether what the educator, the teacher, or the father says or requests is personal or arbitrary, or whether it is expressed by him as a general law and necessity.

10. The representation of the infinite in the finite, of the eternal in the temporal, of the celestial in the terrestrial, of the divine in and through man, in the life of man by the *nursing* of his originally divine nature, confronts us unmistakably on every side as the only object, the only aim of all education, in all instruction and training. Therefore man should be viewed from this only true standpoint immediately with his appearance on earth; nay, as in the case of Mary, immediately with his annunciation, and he should be thus heeded and nursed while yet invisible, unborn.

11. The debasing illusion that man works, produces, creates only in order to preserve his body, in order to secure food, clothing, and shelter, may have to be endured, but should not be diffused and propagated. Primarily and in truth man works only that his spiritual, divine essence may assume outward form, and that thus he may be enabled to recognize his own spiritual, divine nature and the innermost being of God. Whatever food, clothing, and shelter he obtains thereby comes to him as an insignificant surplus. Therefore Jesus says, "Seek ye first the kingdom of heaven," that is, the realization of the divine spirit in your life and through your life, and whatever else your finite life may require, will be added unto you.

Yet human power should be developed, cultivated, and manifested, not only in inner repose, as religion and religious spirit; not only in outward efficiency, as work and industry; but also—withdrawing upon itself and its own resources—in abstinence, temperance, and frugality. Is it needful to do more than indicate this to a human being not wholly at variance with himself? Where *religion, industry* and *temperance*, the truly undivided trinity, rule in harmony, in true pristine unit, there, indeed, is heaven upon earth—peace, joy, salvation, grace, blessedness.

12. *Play* is the highest phase of child-development—of human development at this period; for *it is self-active representation of the inner—representation of the inner from inner necessity and impulse.* Play is the purest, most spiritual activity of man at this stage, and, at the same time, typical of human life as a whole—of the inner hidden natural life in man and all things. It gives, therefore, joy, freedom, contentment, inner and outer rest, peace with the world. It holds the sources of all that is good. A child that plays thoroughly, with self-active determination, perseveringly until physical fatigue forbids, will surely be a thorough, determined man, capable of self-sacrifice for the promotion of the welfare of himself and others. Is not the most beautiful expression of child-life at this time a playing child?—a child wholly absorbed in his play?—a child that has fallen asleep while so absorbed?

13. The aim and object of parental care, in the domestic and family circle, is to awaken and develop, to quicken all the powers and natural gifts of the child, to enable all the members and organs of man to fulfill the requirements of the child's powers and gifts. The natural mother does all this instinctively, without instruction and direction; but this is not enough; it is needful that she should do it consciously, as a conscious being acting upon another being which is growing into consciousness, and consciously tending toward the continuous development of the human being, in a certain inner living connection.

14. The child—your child, ye fathers—follows you wherever you are, wherever you go, in whatever you do. Do not harshly repel him;

show no impatience about his ever-recurring questions. Every harshly repelling word crushes a bud or shoot of his tree of life. Do not, however, tell him in words much more than he could find himself without your words. For it is, of course, easier to hear the answer from another, perhaps to only half hear and understand it, than it is to seek and discover it himself. To have found one fourth of the answer by his own effort is of more value and importance to the child than it is to half hear and half understand it in the words of another; for this causes mental indolence. Do not, therefore, always answer your children's questions at once and directly; but, as soon as they have gathered sufficient strength and experience, furnish them with the means to find the answers in the sphere of their own knowledge.

15. On the part of parents and educators the period of infancy demands chiefly *fostering care.* During the succeeding period of childhood, which looks upon man predominantly as a unit, and would lead him to unity, *training* prevails. The period of boyhood leads man chiefly to the consideration of particular relationships and individual things, in order to enable him later on to discover their inner unit. The inner tendencies and relationships of individual things and conditions are sought and established.

Such a process constitutes the *school* in the widest sense of the word. The school, then, leads man to a knowledge of external things, and of their nature in accordance with the particular and general laws that lie in them; by the presentation of the external, the individual, the particular, it leads man to a knowledge of the internal, of unity, of the universal. Therefore, on entering the period of boyhood, man becomes at the same time a *school-boy.* With this period school begins for him, be it in the home or out of it, and taught by the father, the members of the family, or a teacher. School, then, means here by no means the school-room, nor school-keeping, but *the conscious communication of knowledge, for a definite purpose and in definite inner connection.*

16. On the other hand, as it has appeared and continues to appear in every aspect, the development and cultivation of man, for the attainment of his destiny and the fulfillment of his mission, constitute an unbroken whole, steadily and continuously progressing, gradually ascending. The feeling of community, awakened in the infant, becomes in the child impulse, inclination; these lead to the formation of the disposition and of the heart, and arouse in the boy his intellect and will. *To give firmness to the will, to quicken it, and to make it pure, strong, and enduring, in a life of pure humanity, is the chief concern, the main object in the guidance of the boy, in instruction and the school.*

17. Will is the mental activity, ever consciously proceeding from a definite point in a definite direction toward a definite object, in harmony

with the man's nature as a whole. This statement contains everything, and indicates all that parent and educator, teacher and school, should be or should give to the boy in example and precept during these years. The starting-point of all mental activity in the boy should be energetic and sound; the source whence it flows, pure, clear, and ever-flowing; the direction, simple, definite; the object, fixed, clear, living and life-giving, elevating, worthy of the effort, worthy of the destiny and mission of man, worthy of his essential nature, and tending to develop it and give it full expression.

Instruction in example and in words, which later on become precept and example, furnishes the means for this. Neither example alone nor words alone will do; not example alone, for it is particular and special, and the word is needed to give to particular individual examples universal applicability; not words alone, for example is needed to interpret and explain the word which is general, spiritual, and of many meanings. But instruction and example alone and in themselves are not sufficient; they must meet a good, pure heart, and this is an outcome of proper educational influences in childhood.

18. In the family the child sees the parents and other members at work, producing, doing something; the same he notices with adults generally in life and in those active interests with which his family is concerned. Consequently the child, at this stage, would like himself to represent what he sees. He would like to represent—and tries to do so—all he sees his parents and other adults do and represent in work, all which he thus sees represented by human power and human skill.

What formerly the *child* did only *for the sake of the activity*, the *boy* now does *for the sake of the result* or *product* of his activity; the child's instinct of activity has in the *boy* become a *formative instinct*, and this occupies the whole outward life, the outward manifestation of boy-life at this period. How cheerfully and eagerly the boy and the girl at this age begin to share the work of father and mother—not the easy work, indeed, but the difficult work, calling for strength and labor!

19. By no means, however, do all the plays and occupations of boys at this age aim at the representation of things; on the contrary, many are predominantly mere practice and trials of strength, and many aim simply at display of strength. Nevertheless, the play of this period always bears a peculiar character, corresponding with its inner life. For, while during the previous period of childhood the aim of play consisted simply in *activity* as such, its aim lies now in a *definite, conscious purpose*; it seeks *representation* as such, or the thing to be represented in the activity. This character is developed more and more in the free boyish games as the boys advance in age.

It is the sense of rare and reliable power, the sense of its increase, both as an individual and as a member of the group, that fills the boy with all-pervading, jubilant joy during these games. It is by no means, however, only the physical power that is fed and strengthened in these games; intellectual and moral power, too, is definitely and steadily gained and brought under control. Indeed, a comparison of the relative gains of the mental and of the physical phases would scarcely yield the palm to the body. Justice, moderation, self-control, truthfulness, loyalty, brotherly love, and, again, strict impartiality—who, when he approaches a group of boys engaged in such games, could fail to catch the fragrance of these delicious blossomings of the heart and mind, and of a firm will; not to mention the beautiful, though perhaps less fragrant blossoms of courage, perseverance, resolution, prudence, together with the severe elimination of indolent indulgence? Whoever would inhale a fresh, quickening breath of life should visit the play-grounds of such boys.

20. The existence of the present teaches man the existence of the past. This, too, which was before he was, he would know. Then there is developed in the boy at this age the desire and craving for tales, for legends, for all kinds of stories, and later on for historical accounts. This craving, especially in its first appearance, is very intense; so much so, that, when others fail to gratify it, the boys seek to gratify it themselves, particularly on days of leisure, and in times when the regular employments of the day are ended.

21. Man is by no means naturally bad, nor has he originally bad or evil qualities and tendencies; unless, indeed, we consider as naturally evil, bad, and faulty the *finite*, the *material*, the *transitory*, the *physical* as such, and the logical consequences of the existing of these phenomena, namely, that man must have the possibility of failure in order to be good and virtuous, that he must be able to make himself a slave in order to be truly free. Yet these things are the necessary concomitants of the manifestation of the eternal in the temporal, of unity in diversity, and follow necessarily from man's destiny to become a conscious, reasonable, and free being.

A suppressed or perverted good quality—a good tendency, only repressed, misunderstood, or misguided—lies originally at the bottom of every shortcoming in man. Hence the only and infallible remedy for counteracting any shortcoming and even wickedness is to find the originally good source, the originally good side of the human being that has been repressed, disturbed, or misled into the shortcoming, and then to foster, build up, and properly guide this good side. Thus the shortcoming will at last disappear, although it may involve a hard struggle *against habit, but not against original depravity* in man; and this is accomplished so much the more rapidly and surely because man himself tends to abandon his shortcomings, for man prefers right to wrong.

47
Johann Friedrich Herbart
(1776-1841)

Selections from Herbart's *Brief Encyclopaedia of Practical Philosophy* (translated by Robert Ulich from *Kurze Encyklopädie der Philosophie aus praktischen Geisichtspuncten entworfen* Johann Friedrich Herbart's Sämmtliche Werke, . . . herausgegeben von G. Hartenstein, Band II, Leipzig, L. Voss, 1850-1852) and his *Science of Education* (as taken by Robert Ulich from "the translation from the German with a biographical introduction by Henry M. and Emmie Felken and a preface by Oscar Browning, published in Boston in 1902, in Heath's Pedagogical Library" and being a revised translation by Robert Ulich "after comparison with the original: *Allgemeine Pädagogik aus dem Zweck der Erziehung abgeleitet*, published in 1806, in Herbart's Sämmtliche Werke, Band X, Leipzig, 1851)," as printed in Robert Ulich (ed.), *Three Thousand Years of Educational Wisdom—Selections from Great Documents*, (Cambridge, Massachusetts: Harvard University Press, 1947, 1954), pp. 508-522.

Brief Encyclopaedia of Practical Philosophy
Chapter XII

On Education. 103. . . . Even for an adult it is not always easy to acquire and maintain a desirable attitude toward the problems of life. All the more one has to refrain from demanding indiscriminatingly that the teacher impart to his pupil the right attitude for the rest of his life. . . .

The simple duty of the teacher at any moment of his work is to preserve his pupil's natural vigor. To create or transform the personality is beyond the teacher's power; but what he can do and what we may demand from him is to ward off dangers from his pupil and to abstain from ill-handling him.

104. To this vigor belongs particularly the natural cheerfulness of youth; but man from his youth onward must voluntarily accept restrictions, particularly as he has to live a communal life. Hence, first: Children must learn to obey. Their natural exuberance must meet enough resistance to avert offense.

Immediately we meet a new difficulty. The easy means for a child not to offend his parents or teachers is concealment and lying!

To cut the knot some teachers assume at once that children always lie if they can. Hence they have to be so closely supervised and watched, and kept so busy from morning to evening that they have no time for trickery. There is some truth in this, but if it is carried out with too much harshness and exactness one may fail in the first fundamental postulate we have set up, that children's vigor must be preserved! For this they need freedom! Those teachers who restrict freedom to such a degree that all the children's actions are calculated to please the observer, educate babies. Such creatures will have to learn how to use their powers when they are grown up,—and in spite of all their endeavors they will remain timid, helpless, and inferior to free personalities, until eventually they will try to compensate in whatever way they can.

Consequently, as such a restricting form of education is dangerous something better must be combined with supervision and occupation.

One says rightly that well bred children have not the heart to deceive their father and mother. Why not? They are used to rely on truth and confidence. This, then becomes the key-note of their lives. Thus we have the third pedagogical postulate. Children must be accustomed to satisfy the need for confidential communication not only among themselves but also in relation to their teacher. Otherwise they will never learn to detest lying. If this attitude is deeply rooted then they will betray occasional lies immediately by showing shame. Only if such conditions prevail the teacher may demand complete sincerity, otherwise this demand only enhances the child's disposition to lie.

105. All this can be summarized in the following words: in spite of a certain severity in your guidance, lead the children into a situation which they like and which invites them to be free and confident.

This is the supreme demand in education; all the rest, whatever one may call it, is only of secondary and tertiary importance; all instruction from the elements of learning to the highest level of scholarship should tend to this. Hence those schools, whose main function is merely teaching and learning cannot be considered as serving education in the deepest sense of the word. They are only of assisting value, and this only for such families as have already fulfilled the educational postulates mentioned above. . . .

It follows that education in order to have a permanent effect must try to use instruction not only for mere information but also for the formation of character.

But the hope which some educators base on instruction has not much more chance to be realized than the hope based on government. It requires a great deal to raise knowledge to the level of erudition: it is a still more difficult task to combine the imparting of knowledge with the formation of character. To achieve this purpose knowledge must be deeply felt and experienced: in other words the mere quantity of knowledge and the logical and practical training in notions, maxims and principles must affect the whole emotional attitude of a person. One may show how instruction has to proceed to produce such an effect. (I have shown this in my *Science of Education*.) The degree of success, however, depends largely on the pupil's individuality.

Only teachers of much experience can imagine how rapidly even carefully implanted and cultivated knowledge vanishes under new conditions. They only can believe how easily new opinions and ambitions emerge and how irresistibly a person is attracted by temptations which appeal to his nature—in spite of all previous precautions. Even superficial experience teaches us that the results of an examination are valid only for the day when it is held. . . . Such facts, however, are easily explained through reference to the continual flow of ideas (apperceptive masses) in our mind. Those, who consider the human soul as a fixed and concrete object, will never understand the mutability of the human character; they will easily resort to false remedies which only aggravate the evil.

106. These facts would reduce to naught the educational value of instruction . . . if we had not to consider an additional factor. Most people are not independent enough to set their own standards; living among their friends and their occupation they need and meet natural leaders whose standards they accept. Thus there emerge in society certain dominant opinions and codes of honor and each individual tries to live up to them, according to his abilities.

Now it is exactly schooling which decides to what level of society an individual belongs. . . . Thus the character of social more than the character of individual life explains the decisive influence and role of knowledge, and the evil or good, confusing or unifying effects of schools and authors.

107. Those, however, who have no true psychological insight, rarely understand anything of education. They may cherish the obsolete opinion that there reside in the human soul certain powers or faculties which have to be trained in one way or another. These people seemingly have in mind gymnastic exercises which strengthen the muscles, for man has only one kind of muscles, Indeed in each single apperceptive mass (mass or group of ideas) are contained so-called fantasy, memory and intelligence, but they are not equally distributed. Rather in one and the same person a certain mass of apperceptions may be of more intellectual, imaginative or of reproductive character; one mass may be penetrated with profound feeling, another with an atmosphere of coolness etc. Therefore what educators call formal discipline (Formelle Bildung) would

be an absurdity if it meant the training of isolated mental faculties which exist only in some people's imagination.[1] But often one mass of ideas supports another one according to the general laws of reproduction.

[After Latin has been taught] the general rule in our schools is to teach French or Greek. This sequence is supposed to be the easiest, since Latin—so one boasts—has already provided the necessary formal discipline. But what would have happened if first French and Greek had been taught and Latin afterwards? Then, so it is said, the formal discipline would have started with French or Greek and then carried over to Latin. And this way, one asserts would have been neither better nor worse than beginning with Latin, since the main purpose is to arouse the mental power. Why then quarrel about the way toward that end? The customary way is the best, simply by virtue of tradition; in a new way one could go astray without need or profit.

This may be true in that the philologist, if forced to begin with another language than Latin, would first have to make some effort to familiarize himself thoroughly with the method of teaching the new language, whereas the method of teaching Latin is already nicely prescribed for every level. But the opinion that it does not matter whether the faculties of the mind are awakened by Greek, French or Latin is a barrier to careful observation. For what is at stake and what must be trained are not abstract powers or faculties but masses of ideas and their gradual formation. . . . The masses of ideas which enter the pupil's mind with French, Latin or Greek are not at all the same. Consequently the sequence with which they are acquired is not unimportant. Rather it is exactly this sequence on which depends the structure and efficacy of the acquired ideas, and that so-called mental power, which is to be aroused, becomes something essentially different if the sequence in the connection of ideas is altered.

A French, a German and an English scholar are three different individuals, who may endeavor a lifetime to become as much alike as is their learning. But they will have to go different ways and will never succeed completely because their mother-tongues and their characteristic modes of thinking were different. . . .

[1] In paragraphs 112 and 113 of the same work Herbart states expressly that the value of the ancient languages cannot be found in the acquisition of formal discipline. Their value lies, according to him, in the preparation for certain professions and particularly in the obligation of our civilization to preserve among the educated adequate awareness of its cultural roots. "No doubt our knowledge would soon lose its foundations and we should lose all criteria of good style in the rhetorical arts if ever the learning of ancient languages should be given up. Furthermore we have to preserve carefully all the historical threads which enable us to trace backward the origin of our culture, otherwise we may lose it."

A German, French or English scholar may debate which one of them may most easily attain that degree of scholarship, which is above all national differences. An impartial judge would tell them that each is in possession of what they are looking for, while he remains in his native country. . . . Certainly such a statement would not deviate from the truth.

108. Another instance of erroneous ideas about formal discipline is the frequent recommendation of mathematics as a special instrument for intellectual training. No wonder that most educators try to attain this end by a shorter method. Why all these figures and formulas if the ancient languages which have to be learned anyway, serve the same purpose? Just study grammar; this will sharpen the intellect even more than mathematics, because as some people believe, they have discovered that even poor intellects can acquire skill in figuring.

But it it is better not to ask whether the grammarians surpass the mathematicians and excel as great statesmen or generals or in other arenas.

Grammatical thinking remains within grammar; and mathematical thinking remains within mathematics; the reasoning within each discipline of thought forms itself in accordance with the discipline. But if grammatical or mathematical notions enter by any chance and even through distant channels into the sphere of activity of a general or a statesman, he will reproduce what he once learnt and it will assist him in his actions.

Hence grammar and mathematics cannot be substituted for one another, but each holds its value in its own sphere. Nor can grammar be used as a pattern for learning logic, though there exists some relationship, consequently also some educational interaction. The same holds true for logic and mathematics. But alas, if somebody who needs logic to master the higher spheres of philosophy relied on his previous studies in grammar and mathematics! Neither grammar, nor mathematics, nor logic makes the metaphysician, although he cannot make any progress without logic and mathematics.

One might better use geography as the example of a science for which training in other branches of learning is useful, for in geography, mathematics, the natural sciences, and history are combined. Unfortunately, geography enjoys least of all the reputation of requiring particular intellectual training, probably because this science, as it is usually taught in our schools, has never effectively combined mathematical, physical and social sciences.

109. If then the teacher cannot put his trust in formal discipline and if the mere bulk of memorized knowledge does not provide individual character and culture, on what can he rely?

First, in regard to subject-matter: synthesis and analysis.

Second, in regard to the pupil: on interest, in so far as it expands and deepens.

1. Synthesis and analysis refer immediately to the sequence of ideas inherent in specific subject-matter.[2]
Whatever is possible must be done to build verbal instruction on a basis of experience, be it natural or artificial. Children who have not seen or observed anything cannot be taught. But after experience is provided it has to be analyzed and conceptualized in order to be fitted for scientific understanding. Thus analysis prepares a great number of associations for all the new notions which afterwards arise from synthesis. The teacher is, from the psychologist's point of view, always on the right track if he considers the texture and the growth of the apperceptive masses occurring during instruction from both the analytical and synthetical point of view, provided his pupils can follow him without exhaustion and without confusion of their ideas from too much pressure.

2. As to interest, it is difficult to make general statements with respect to degrees of deepening. We probably do best to refer to the example of great poets who show the most astounding skill in capturing and increasing the interest of their readers.

On the other hand the expansion of interest can be described and subdivided into [six] different classes, as I have done above.[3]

110. The division of interest into six main classes can be useful to the teacher in the following respects. It can serve him as a criterion as to what and how much he can combine in his instruction in order to keep up the necessary equilibrium of interest. It can serve as a criterion for avoiding the useless and distracting variety of subjects; often the concentration on one subject can better serve the purpose of stimulating and maintaining manifold interests. Finally this division may be particularly useful for judging with some probability whether a pupil can profit from intellectual instruction. Often all classes of interest occurring in expanding instruction are feeble and transitory; in this case they are incapable of producing the necessary intellectual energy. Often just one or the other kind of interest emerges, but in a degree of isolation which characterizes more the onesided artist than a person of well rounded education. But in all cases in which neither curiosity, nor taste, nor patriotism, nor piety can be appealed to and in which neither careful instruction nor impressive presentation nor deliberate discipline show any effect—in such cases the

[2] See *Science of Education*, Book II, Chapters 4 and 5.

[3] In paragraph 83 of the same work Herbart subdivides interest as expressing itself in the acquisition of *knowledge* (empirical, speculative and aesthetic) and in interest as expressing itself in form of *sympathy* (sympathy with the individual; sympathy with the welfare of society; religious feeling of the exposure and dependence of the human race).

teacher is unable to arouse in the pupil that degree of intellectual energy which could give promise for his future conduct. Then of course, the question arises how much there is reason for serious anxiety, and what further resources the teacher has.

In this context, besides man's well known sensuality and its dangers, one has to consider the motives of human conduct as mentioned in the beginning of this book (paragraph 7).[4]

If a person in his youth has failed to develop spontaneous manifold, and culturally rich interests it will show its effect on his later life in that he will be unable to enjoy enriching forms of recreation. But the other motives and modes of life which we have mentioned will still be valid. Industriousness, or a desire for work, is possible as a result of habituation, even without a developed empirical, speculative or aesthetic interest. Relaxation can alternate with work in a blameless, though not particularly commendable way, even if a person shows no outspoken sympathy for individuals, or society, or for religious life. In every-day social routine many a man succeeds who does not set an example but who understands how to keep the middle of the road. Respect for people with superior character, love for their fellows, attachment to their families and finally the severity of service carry many tolerably through their lives, without obvious absence of a good education. Hence, if the teacher has no opportunity for devoting himself to higher tasks, if he is hampered by the feeble disposition of his pupil, there still remains for him to adjust his work to such hopes, though they may not be particularly enchanting. But even for the realization of these hopes certain conditions are necessary which one cannot find or foresee in young men, particularly if they are unprotected by society. But in every case the educated man always appears tolerably refined and has a chance to become current coin, whereas the uneducated offends and repels, and if he falls he will mostly find himself deserted. We all shall agree that avoidance of gross ignorance helps to start and polish a person, though such ignorance cannot be completely avoided even by relatively good instruction which does not meet any interest.

[4] In paragraph 7 Herbart says the conduct of man's life is determined by the following motives:

1. *Occupation:*	2. *Disposition:*	
work	social intercourse	and the
enriching recreation	approval	reverse
relaxation.	love	
3. *Family-relationships:*	4. *Service:*	
the spouse	compulsory	
the parents	paid	
the rest of the family.	honorary.	

111. If on the other hand the teacher succeeds in developing in the pupil manifold interest, then the education becomes a noble task in that it helps mankind to realize the great practical ethical ideas.[5] These ideas will become the more self-evident to the pupil the less it is necessary to teach him merely to swim on the waves of society as was the case with the unsusceptible type. On the other hand it is necessary to combine exact methods of thinking and self-criticism with the enthusiasm which can be imparted to the susceptible pupil by such means as religion and history. Of particular use for such an examining attitude is the capacity of clear ethical discrimination. For by its own nature the human mind is not so well disposed as to apprehend clearly the ideas of justice, equity, perfection and sympathy and to act accordingly. In addition a person with the capacity for inner freedom not rarely abandons traditional ideals and inclines towards eccentric claims and opinions for which, so he thinks, he has to fight and to bring sacrifices in order to carry off the crown of martyrdom. The striving for the unusual and the exceptional is in the spirit of the time, but it does not fit our country. Hence what education has to do is to preserve in talented youth their natural courage and open-mindedness but not to inspire them with burning ambition.

114. Altogether there ought to be more diversity in our schoolsystem than exists today. Each school receives a certain character from its teachers and this is generally desirable. In addition not all children are fitted for the same school.

Some are longing for knowledge to such a degree that they are never satisfied. For them a rich storehouse of intellectual goods is desirable.

Other children need much supervision. For them a school with severe discipline will be best fitted.

Still other children need friendly attachment, it would be a pity if they could not find teachers who understand them.

Some are lazy in scholarly studies, but talented for business; for them a brilliant academic institution is not the right place but only a modest secondary school which does not seek its merits in a high standard of scholarship, but in a steady implanting of useful knowledge.

But especially in the more elementary forms of training uniformity

---

[5] These practical ideas, explained in paragraph 27 are:

Original ideas:	Derived ideas:
inner freedom (Innere Freiheit)	inspired society (Beseel te Gesellschaft)
striving for perfection (Vollkommenheit)	culture (Cultursystem)
sympathy (Wohlwollen)	commonweal (Verwaltungssystem)
justice	lawful government (Rechtgesellschaft)
equity	just reward (Lohnsystem).

is less desirable than variety. For there the diversity of dispositions and needs is extremely great and so far this variety has been not sufficiently explored, nor sufficiently utilized.

General Principles of the Science of Education Psychologically Deduced from Its Aim

Introduction. The aim of all those who educate and demand education is determined by the views they bring to the subject.

The majority of those who teach have entirely neglected to build up a proper view of their work; such a view opens out gradually as the work progresses, and is formed partly by the teacher's individuality, partly by the individuality and environment of the pupil. If the teachers possess originality, they will utilize all that comes to hand to provide stimulus and occupation for the objects of their care; if they have foresight, they exclude all which may be harmful to health, disposition, or manners. Thus a boy grows up, who has tested himself in everything that is not dangerous, who has experience in considering and treating the common things of daily life, and who has developed all the emotions which his environment could arouse in him. If he has really grown up thus, he may be congratulated on the result. But educators complain unceasingly of the harmful influence of surrounding circumstances—of servants, relatives, playmates, the sexual instincts and the university. No wonder that such an education does not always produce a strong character which can bid defiance to unfavorable influences, how could it be otherwise if the meagre mental diet is determined more by chance than by human skill.

Rousseau desired to *harden* his pupil. He defined for himself his own view of the subject, and remained true to it. He follows nature. All the processes of animal development in man are, by means of education, to be assured a free, happy growth from the mother's breast to the marriage bed. To live is the business which he teaches. Yet, he evidently sympathizes with our poet's dictum, "Life is not the highest of all goods," for he sacrifices the whole individual life of the teacher, whom he makes the boy's constant companion. This education costs too dear. The companion's life is in any case worth more than the boy's, even if we go no further than mortality tables; for the probability of being able to live is greater for the man than the child. But is mere existence then, so difficult to man? We thought human *plants* were like the rose; that just as the queen of flowers give the gardener least trouble of all, so human beings thrive in every climate, are nourished by every species of food, learn most easily to accommodate themselves to all circumstances, and to turn everything to advantage. Still it is as difficult for the teacher to educate a "nature man" among cultivated men as it will be later for the pupil to live in the midst of so heterogeneous a society.

How to behave in society, is what *Locke's* pupil will know best. The principal thing for him is conventionality. For fathers who destine their sons for the world, no book of education need be written after Locke; anything added would degenerate into artificiality. Secure at any price a trustworthy man of refined habits, who "himself knows the rules of courtesy and good society with all the varieties arising from difference of persons, times and places, and who will then assiduously direct his pupil as suits his age to the observation of these things."[6]One can say nothing against this. It would be vain to dissuade men of the world from educating their sons to become men of the world. For this desire arises from the impressions of actual life, and is constantly confirmed and increased by new impressions. Preachers, poets, philosophers, may be all unction, all gaiety, all gravity in prose or verse, but one glance at the world around destroys all their effect, and they seem to the men of the world mere actors or visionaries. Why after all should a worldly education not succeed, for with the men of the world, the world is in league.

But I could tell of men who know the world without loving it; who while they will not withdraw their sons from the world, will still less allow them to be lost in it, and who assume that a clear headed person will find in his own consciousness, sympathy, and tastes, the best teachers, to guide him as far into the conventionalities of society as he is willing to go. Such men allow their sons to gain a knowledge of mankind among their comrades; they know that one studies Nature best in Nature, provided the home has already sufficiently sharpened, exercised and directed the power of observation. They desire that their children grow up in the midst of the generation with which they will live. Is this compatible with good education? Perfectly, so long as during the hours of instruction, when the teacher is occupied seriously and systematically with the pupil, such mental activity is pursued as will so arouse the pupil's interest that compared with these hours all boy's play will gradually become trifling, and of little account even to the boy himself.

But such an attitude will never be achieved, if the teacher leaves his pupil for some hours of the day to his natural life and forces him, during other hours, to learn from abstract books. Such an attitude can be created only if natural child-life and learning are interconnected.

---

[6] Locke, *Some Thoughts concerning Education*, par. 93: "To form a young gentleman as he should be, 'tis fit his governor should himself be wellbred, understand the ways of carriage, and measures of civility in all the variety of persons, times, and places, and help his pupil, as much as his age requires, constantly to the observation of them."

Therefore a teacher, inspired by ideals, with the idea of education in all its beauty and greatness, can understand the task of training a boy in the midst of his natural environment to a nobler life, if he has enough intelligence and knowledge to understand and represent natural life and actuality as a fragment of a great whole. He will then say of his own accord, that not he, but the whole power of what humanity has felt, experienced and thought, is the true teacher, to which the boy is entitled, and that the teacher is merely to help him by intelligent interpretation and elevating companionship. Thus to present to youth the whole fund of accumulated experience in a concentrated form is the highest service which mankind can render to its successors, be it as teaching or as warning.

Conventional education [as advocated by Locke] tends to prolong existing evils; whereas a merely natural education [in the sense of Rousseau] would force us to overcome in each pupil evils already overcome by the race. A teacher of limited outlook, who neither knows what is beyond, nor understands how to teach it, will narrow the sphere of teaching and warning to the immediate environment. One ought not to excuse this narrow concept of education by referring to the inefficiency of pedantic teachers, nor to the difficulties of children to grasp things beyond their immediate environment; for pedantry can be avoided and the difficulties don't exist.

How far, however, this may, or may not be true, each man decides from his own experience—I from mine, others from theirs. Only let us all consider the proposition—*each but experiences what he attempts*. A nonogenarian village schoolmaster has the experience of his ninety years dull routine. He may rest on the consciousness of his long toils, but has he also the criticism of his work and his methods? Much that is new has prospered with our modern educators; they have found their reward in the gratitude of men, and they can rejoice over it. But it is another question whether they have a right to determine from their experience for ever all that can be attained by means of education, and all that can be done with children.

I have required scientific knowledge and intelligence from the teacher. . . .

The first, though by no means the only complete science of the teacher, would be a psychology in which all human activities were sketched *a priori*. I think I recognize the possibility as well as the difficulty of such a science. Long will it be before we have it, longer still before we can expect it from teachers. Never, however, can it be a substitute for observation of the pupil; the individual can only be discovered, not deduced. The construction of the pupil on *a priori* principles is therefore a misleading expression in itself, and an empty idea which the science of education cannot handle for a long time.

Book I, Chapter II

I. Is the Aim of Education Single or Manifold? . . . If one considers the nature of education he will recognize that unity of aim is an ideal which cannot be realized, because *the teacher must foresee the future man in the boy. Consequently the teacher must try to envisage the purposes which the pupil will pursue after he has grown up.* It is the teacher's *task to prepare beforehand in his pupil the desirable facility for achieving his goals.* He ought not to stunt the activity of the future man; consequently he ought neither to confine it to single points, nor weaken it by too much diversity. He ought to allow nothing to be lost either in *Intension* or *Extension*, which his pupil might afterwards demand back from him. Great as the difficulties may be, thus much is clear—*since human aims are manifold, the teacher's cares must be manifold also.*

The multiplicity of education can easily be classified under a few categories. The pupil's future aims may be divided into his merely possible aims, which he might perhaps take up at one time or another and pursue to a greater or less degree, and into the *necessary aims* which he could never forgive himself for having neglected. In other words, the aims of education can be subdivided according to aims of *choice* (not of the teacher, nor the boy, but of the future man) and the aims of *morality.* Those two main headings are at once clear to every one who bears in mind the most generally recognized fundamentals of ethics.

II. Many-Sidedness of Interest.—Strength of Moral Character. can the teacher assume responsibility for those aims of the pupil which we designated as *merely possible?*

As these aims will be chosen by the pupil after he has grown up and become independent their factual content is beyond the competence of the teacher, who can seek only to form will and tendencies, and also the demands which the future man will make upon himself. The power, the initiative, and the activity wherewith the future man may meet those demands can be prepared and cultivated by the teacher according to the ideas he has about a mature person. Thus it is not a certain number of separate aims that we, as teachers, ought to have in mind (for how can we foresee them) but the potential activity of the growing man, the quantum of his personal vitality and spontaneity. The greater and more harmonious this quantum, the greater will be the man's maturity and perfection, and the greater the effect of the teacher's care.

Only the flower must not burst its calyx—abundance must not

become weakness through losing direction because of too many distractions. Human society has long found division of labor necessary, that every one may make perfect what he attempts. But the more sub-divided, the greater is that which each later receives from all the rest. Now, since intellectual receptivity rests on affinity of mind, and this on similar activities of mind, it follows that in the higher realm of human achievement, labor ought not to be divided to the point where each man is ignorant of his neighbour's work. Every man must love all activities and be a virtuoso in one. The particular virtuosity is a matter of choice; but manifold receptivity is a matter of education for it grows out of manifold beginnings of a pupil's own efforts. Therefore we call the first part of the educational aim—*many-sidedness of interest*, which must be distinguished from its exaggeration—dabbling in many things. And since no one object of will, nor its direction, interests us more than any other, we must assure a *well-balanced* many-sidedness. We shall thus get at the meaning of the common expression, "harmonious cultivation of all powers." But we must define what we mean when we speak of a "multiplicity and harmony of mental powers."

(2) How can the teacher assume responsibility for the *necessary* aims of the pupil?

Since morality has its place only in the individual's will, founded on right insight, it follows, first, that the work of education is not to develop in the pupil a certain external mode of action, but rather ethical insight with a corresponding will power.

I leave here untouched the metaphysical questions inherent in the problem of the genesis of morality. He who understands how to educate can forget them; he who cannot needs metaphysics before a science of education, and the outcome of his speculations will prove to him whether the idea of education is, or is not, a possible one for him.

I look at life, and find many upon whom morality is a stunted growth, few with whom it is the principle of life itself. Most men possess a character which has not much to do with real goodness, and a plan of life formed only according to their own inclination. They do the good when convenient and they avoid the evil gladly—provided the better leads to the same goal. Moral principles are wearisom to them, because for them nothing follows from these principles except now and then some limitation of their ideas. They rather welcome everything which prevents such limitations; the young rascal, if he sins with some boldness, can be sure of their sympathy, and sure that what is neither ridiculous nor malicious, will be forgiven. If it be the object of moral education to lead the pupil into the rank of these men, we have an easy task; we need only take care that he grows up in the self-consciousness without being teased or insulted, and that he receive certain principles of honor. These principles are easily inculcated because they treat of honor not as a wearisome acquisition, but as a possession given by nature which must be protected and put in force on certain occasions, according to conventional forms. But who will warrant us that the future man will not himself search out the real good, to make it the object of his willing, the aim of his life, the standard of his self-criticism? Who will protect us against the severe judgment which will then overtake us?

48
Herbert Spencer (1820-1903)

What Knowledge
Is of Most Worth?

Ch. I in *Education: Intellectual, Moral, and Physical*, from *Works*, Vol. 6 (New York and London: D. Appleton and Company, 1860, 1910 printing), pp. 1-87. Reprinted by courtesy of Appleton-Century-Crofts.

It has been truly remarked that, in order of time, decoration precedes dress. Among people who submit to great physical suffering that they may have themselves handsomely tattooed, extremes of temperature are borne with but little attempt at mitigation. Humboldt tells us that an Orinoco Indian, though quite regardless of bodily comfort, will yet labour for a fortnight to purchase pigment wherewith to make himself admired; and that the same woman who would not hesitate to leave her hut without a fragment of clothing on, would not dare to commit such a breach of decorum as to go out unpainted. Voyagers uniformly find that coloured beads and trinkets are much more prized by wild tribes than are calicoes or broadcloths. And the anecdotes we have of the ways in which, when shirts and coats are given, they turn them to some ludicrous display, show how completely the idea of ornament predominates over that of use. Nay, there are still more extreme illustrations: witness the fact narrated by Capt. Speke of his African attendants, who strutted about in their goat-skin mantles when the weather was fine, but when it was wet, took them off, folded them up, and went about naked, shivering in the rain! Indeed, the facts of aboriginal life seem to indicate that dress is developed out of decorations. And when we remember that even among ourselves most think more about the fineness of the fabric than its warmth, and more about the cut than the convenience—when we see that the function is still in great measure subordinated to the appearance—we have further reason for inferring such an origin.

It is not a little curious that the like relations hold with the mind. Among mental as among bodily acquisitions, the ornamental comes before the useful. Not only in time past, but almost as much in our own era, that knowledge which conduces to personal well-being has been postponed to that which brings applause. In the Greek schools, music, poetry, rhetoric, and a philosophy which, until Socrates taught, had but little bearing upon action, were the dominant subjects; while knowledge aiding the arts of life had a very subordinate place. And in our own universities and schools at the present moment the like antithesis holds. We are guilty of something like a platitude when we say that throughout his after-career a boy, in nine cases out of ten, applies his Latin and Greek to no practical purposes. The remark is trite that in his shop, or his office, in managing his estate or his family, in playing his part as director of a bank or a railway, he is very little aided by this knowledge he took so many years to acquire—so little, that generally the greater part of it drops out of his memory; and if he occasionally vents a Latin quotation, or alludes to some Greek myth, it is less to throw light on the topic in hand than for the sake of effect. If we inquire what is the real motive for giving boys a classical education, we find it to be simply conformity to public opinion. Men dress their children's minds as they do their bodies, in the prevailing fashion. As the Orinoco Indian puts on his paint before leaving his hut, not with a view to any direct benefit, but because he would be ashamed to be seen without it; so, a boy's drilling in Latin and Greek is insisted on, not because of their intrinsic value, but that he may not be disgraced by being found ignorant of them—that he may have "the education of a gentleman"—the badge marking a certain social position, and bringing a consequent respect.

This parallel is still more clearly displayed in the case of the other sex. In the treatment of both mind and body, the decorative element has continued to predominate in a greater degree among women than among men. Originally, personal adornment occupied the attention of both sexes equally. In these latter days of civilization, however, we see that in the dress of men the regard for appearance has in a considerable degree yielded to the regard for comfort; while in their education the useful has of late been trenching on the ornamental. In neither direction has this change gone so far with women. The wearing of ear-rings, finger-rings, bracelets; the elaborate dressings of the hair; the still occasional use of paint; the immense labour bestowed in making habiliments sufficiently attractive; and the great discomfort that will be submitted to for the sake of conformity; show how greatly, in the attiring of women, the desire of approbation overrides the desire for warmth and convenience. And similarly in their education, the immense preponderance of "accomplishments" proves how here, too, use is subordinated to display. Dancing, deportment, the piano, singing, drawing—what a large space do these occupy! If you ask why Italian and German are learnt, you will find that, under all the sham reasons given, the real reason is, that a knowledge of those tongues is thought ladylike. It is not that the books written in them may be utilized, which they scarcely ever are; but that

Italian and German songs may be sung, and that the extent of attainment may bring whispered admiration. The birth, deaths, and marriages of kings, and other like historic trivialities, are committed to memory, not because of any direct benefits that can possibly result from knowing them; but because society considers them parts of a good education— because the absence of such knowledge may bring the contempt of others. When we have named reading, writing, spelling, grammar, arithmetic, and sewing, we have named about all the things a girl is taught with a view of their direct uses in life; and even some of these have more reference to the good opinion of others than to immediate personal welfare.

Thoroughly to realize the truth that with the mind as with the body the ornamental precedes the useful, it is needful to glance at its rationale. This lies in the fact that, from the far past down even to the present, social needs have subordinated individual needs, and that the chief social need has been the control of individuals. It is not, as we commonly suppose, that there are no governments but those of monarchs, and parliaments, and constituted authorities. These acknowledged governments are supplemented by other unacknowledged ones, that grow up in all circles, in which every man or woman strives to be king or queen or lesser dignitary. To get above some and be reverenced by them, and to propitiate those who are above us, is the universal struggle in which the chief energies of life are expended. By the accumulation of wealth, by style of living, by beauty of dress, by display of knowledge or intellect, each tries to subjugate others; and so aids in weaving that ramified network of restraints by which society is kept in order. It is not the savage chief only, who in formidable war-paint, with scalps at his belt, aims to strike awe into his inferiors; it is not only the belle who, by elaborate toilet, polished manners, and numerous accomplishments, strives to "make conquests;" but the scholar, the historian, the philosopher, use their acquirements to the same end. We are none of us content with quietly unfolding our own individualities to the full in all directions; but have a restless craving to impress our individualities upon others, and in some way subordinate them. And this it is which determines the character of our education. Not what knowledge is of most real worth, is the consideration; but what will bring most applause, honor, respect—what will most conduce to social position and influence—what will be most imposing. As, throughout life, not what we are, but what shall be thought, is the question; so in education, the question is, not the intrinsic value of knowledge, so much as its extrinsic effects on others. And this being our dominant idea, direct utility is scarcely more regarded than by the barbarian when filing his teeth and staining his nails.

If there needs any further evidence of the rude, undeveloped character of our education, we have it in the fact that the comparative worths of different kinds of knowledge have been as yet scarcely even discussed—much less discussed in a methodic way with definite results. Not only is it that no standard of relative values has yet been agreed upon; but the existence of any such standard has not been conceived in any clear manner. And not only is it that the existence of any such standard has not been clearly conceived; but the need for it seems to have been scarcely even felt. Men read books on this topic, and attend lectures on that; decide that their children shall be instructed in these branches of knowledge, and shall not be instructed in those; and all under the guidance of mere custom, or liking, or prejudice; without ever considering the enormous importance of determining in some rational way what things are really most worth learning. It is true that in all circles we have occasional remarks on the importance of this or the other order of information. But whether the degree of its importance justifies the expenditure of the time needed to acquire it; and whether there are not things of more importance to which the time might be better devoted; are queries which, if raised at all, are disposed of quite summarily, according to personal predilections. It is true also, that from time to time, we hear revived the standing controversy respecting the comparative merits of classics and mathematics. Not only, however, is this controversy carried on in an empirical manner, with no reference to an ascertained criterion; but the question at issue is totally insignificant when compared with the general question of which it is part. To suppose that deciding whether a mathematical or a classical education is the best, is deciding what is the proper *curriculum*, is much the same thing as to suppose that the whole of dietetics lies in determining whether or not bread is more nutritive than potatoes!

The question which we content is of such transcendent moment, is, not whether such or such knowledge is of worth, but what is its *relative* worth? When they have named certain advantages which a given course of study has secured them, persons are apt to assume that they have justified themselves: quite forgetting that the adequateness of the advantages is the point to be judged. There is, perhaps, not a subject to which men devote attention that has not *some* value. A year diligently spent in getting up heraldry, would very possibly give a little further insight into ancient manners and morals, and into the origin of names. Any one who should learn the distances between all the towns in England, might, in the course of his life, find one or two of the thousand facts he had acquired of some slight service when arranging a journey. Gathering together all the small gossip of a country, profitless occupation as it would be, might yet occasionally help to establish some useful fact—say, a good example of hereditary transmission. But in these cases, every one would admit that there was no proportion between the required labour and the probable benefit. No one would tolerate the proposal to devote some years of a boy's time to getting such information, at the cost of much more valuable information which he might else have got. And if here the test of relative value is appealed to and held conclusive, then should it be appealed to and held conclusive throughout. Had we time to master all subjects we need not be particular. To quote the old song:—

> Could a man be secure
> That his days would endure
> As of old, for a thousand long years,
> What things might he know!
> What deeds might he do!
> And all without hurry or care.

"But we that have but span-long lives" must ever bear in mind our limited time for acquisition. And remembering how narrowly this time is limited, not only by the shortness of life, but also still more by the business of life, we ought to be especially solicitous to employ what time we have to the greatest advantage. Before devoting years to some subject which fashion or fancy suggests, it is surely wise to weigh with great care the worth of the results, as compared with the worth of various alternative results which the same years might bring if otherwise applied.

In education, then, this is the question of questions, which it is high time we discussed in some methodic way. The first in importance, though the last to be considered, is the problem—how to decide among the conflicting claims of various subjects on our attention. Before there can be a rational *curriculum*, we must settle which things it most concerns us to know; or, to use a word of Bacon's now unfortunately obsolete—we must determine the relative value of knowledges.

To this end, a measure of value is the first requisite. And happily, respecting the true measure of value, as expressed in general terms, there can be no dispute. Every one in contending for the worth of any particular order of information, does so by showing its bearing upon some part of life. In reply to the question, "Of what use is it?" the mathematician, linguist, naturalist, or philosopher, explains the way in which his learning beneficially influences action—saves from evil or secures good—conduces to happiness. When the teacher of writing has pointed out how great an aid writing is to success in business—that is, of the obtainment of sustenance—that is, satisfactory living; he is held to have proved his case. And when the collector of dead facts (say a numismatist) fails to make clear any appreciable effects which these facts can produce on human welfare, he is obliged to admit that they are comparatively value-less. All then, either directly or by implication, appeal to this as the ultimate test.

How to live?—that is the essential question for us. Not how to live in the mere material sense only, but in the widest sense. The general problem which comprehends every special problem is—the right ruling of conduct in all directions under all circumstances. In what way to treat the body; in what way to manage our affairs; in what way to treat the mind; in what way to manage our affairs; in what way to treat the mind; in what way to bring up a family; in what way to behave as a citizen; in what way to utilize all those sources of happiness which nature supplies—how to use all our faculties to the greatest advantage of our-selves and others—how to live completely? And this being the great thing needful for us to learn, is, by consequence, the great thing which education has to teach. To prepare us for complete living is the function which education has to discharge; and the only rational mode of judging of any educational course is, to judge in what degree it discharges such function.

This test, never used in its entirety, but rarely even partially used, and used then in a vague, half conscious way, has to be applied con-sciously, methodically, and throughout all cases. It behoves us to set before ourselves, and ever to keep clearly in view, complete living as the end to be achieved; so that in bringing up our children we may choose subjects and methods of instruction, with deliberate reference to this end. Not only ought we to cease from the mere unthinking adoption of the current fashion in education, which has no better warrant than any other fashion; but we must also rise above that rude, empirical style of judging displayed by those more intelligent people who do bestow some care in overseeing the cultivation of their children's minds. It must not suffice simply to *think* that such or such information will be useful in after life, or that this kind of knowledge is of more practical value than that; but we must seek out some process of estimating their respective values, so that as far as possible we may positively *know* which are most deserving of attention.

Doubtless the task is difficult—perhaps never to be more than approximately achieved. But, considering the vastness of the interests at stake, its difficulty is no reason for pusillanimously passing it by; but rather for devoting every energy to its mastery. And if we only proceed systematically, we may very soon get at results of no small moment.

Our first step must obviously be to classify, in the order of their importance, the leading kinds of activity which constitute human life. They may be naturally arranged into:—1. Those activities which directly minister to self-preservation; 2. Those activities which, by securing the necessaries of life, indirectly minister to self-preservation; 3. Those activities which have for their end the rearing and discipline of offspring; 4. Those activities which are involved in the maintenance of proper social and political relations; 5. Those miscellaneous activities which make up the leisure part of life, devoted to the gratification of the tastes and feelings.

That these stand in something like their true order of subordination, it needs no long consideration to show. The actions and precautions by which, from moment to moment, we secure personal safety, must clearly take precedence of all others. Could there be a man, ignorant as an infant of all surrounding objects and movements, or how to guide himself among them, he would pretty certainly lose his life the first time he went into the street: notwithstanding any amount of learning he might have on other matters. And as entire ignorance in all other directions would be less promptly fatal than entire ignorance in this direction, it must be admitted that knowledge immediately conducive to self-preservation is of primary importance.

That next after direct self-preservation comes the indirect self-preservation which consists in acquiring the means of living, none will question. That a man's industrial functions must be considered before his parental ones, is manifest from the fact that, speaking generally, the discharge of the parental functions is made possible only by the previous discharge of the industrial ones. The power of self-maintenance necessarily preceding the power of maintaining offspring, it follows that knowledge needful for self-maintenance has stronger claims than knowledge needful for family welfare—is second in value to none save knowledge needful for immediate self-preservation.

As the family comes before the State in order of time—as the bringing up of children is possible before the State exists, or when it has ceased to be, whereas the State is rendered possible only by the bringing up of children; it follows that the duties of the parent demand closer attention than those of the citizen. Or, to use a further argument—since the goodness of a society ultimately depends on the nature of its citizens; and since the nature of its citizens is more modifiable by early training than by anything else; we must conclude that the welfare of the family underlies the welfare of society. And hence knowledge directly conducing to the first, must take precedence of knowledge directly conducing to the last.

Those various forms of pleasurable occupation which fill up the leisure left by graver occupations—the enjoyments of music, poetry, painting, &c.—manifestly imply a pre-existing society. Not only is a considerable development of them impossible without a long-established social union; but their very subject-matter consists in great part of social sentiments and sympathies. Not only does society supply the conditions to their growth; but also the ideas and sentiments they express. And, consequently, that part of human conduct which constitutes good citizenship is of more moment than that which goes out in accomplishments or exercise of the tastes; and, in education, preparation for the one must rank before preparation for the other.

Such then, we repeat, is something like the rational order of subordination:—That education which prepares for direct self-preservation; that which prepares for indirect self-preservation; that which prepares for parenthood; that which prepares for citizenship; that which prepares for the miscellaneous refinements of life. We do not mean to say that these divisions are definitely separable. We do not deny that they are intricately entangled with each other in such way that there can be no training for any that is not in some measure a training for all. Nor do we question that of each division there are portions more important than certain portions of the preceding divisions: that, for instance, a man of much skill in business but little other faculty, may fall further below the standard of complete living than one of but moderate power of acquiring money but great judgment as a parent; of that exhaustive information bearing on right social action, joined with entire want of general culture in literature and the fine arts, is less desirable than a more moderate share of the one joined with some of the other. But, after making all qualifications, there still remain these broadly-marked divisions; and it still continues substantially true that these divisions subordinate one another in the foregoing order, because the corresponding divisions of life make one another *possible* in that order.

Of course the ideal of education is—complete preparation in all these divisions. But failing this ideal, as in our phase of civilization every one must do more or less, the aim should be to maintain *a due proportion* between the degrees of preparation in each. Not exhaustive cultivation in any one, supremely important though it may be—not even an exclusive attention to the two, three, or four divisions of greatest importance; but an attention to all,—greatest where the value is greatest, less where the value is less, least where the value is least. For the average man (not to forget the cases in which peculiar aptitude for some one department of knowledge rightly makes that one the bread-winning occupation)—for the average man, we say, the desideratum is, a training that approaches nearest to perfection in the things that have more and more remote bearings on complete living.

In regulating education by this standard, there are some general considerations that should be ever present to us. The worth of any kind of culture, as aiding complete living, may be either necessary or more or less contingent. There is knowledge of intrinsic value; knowledge of quasi-intrinsic value; and knowledge of conventional value. Such facts as that sensations of numbness and tingling commonly precede paralysis, that the resistance of water to a body moving through it varies as the square of the velocity, that chlorine is a disinfectant,—these, and the truths of Science in general, are of intrinsic value: they will bear on human conduct ten thousand years hence as they do now. The extra knowledge of our own language, which is given by an acquaintance with Latin and Greek, may be considered to have a value that is quasi-intrinsic: it must exist for us and for other races whose languages owe much to these sources; but will last only as long as our languages last. While that kind of information which, in our schools, usurps the name History—the mere tissue of names and dates and dead unmeaning events—has a conventional value only: it has not the remotest bearing upon any of our actions; and is of use only for the avoidance of those unpleasant criticisms which current opinion passes upon its absence. Of course, as those facts which concern all mankind throughout all time must be held of greater moment than those which concern only a portion of them during a limited era, and of far greater moment than those which concern only a portion of them during the continuance of a fashion; it follows that in a rational estimate, knowledge of intrinsic worth must, other things equal, take precedence of knowledge that is of quasi-intrinsic or conventional worth.

One further preliminary. Acquirement of every kind has two values —value as *knowledge* and value as *discipline*. Besides its use for guidance in conduct, the acquisition of each order of facts has also its use as mental exercise; and its effects as a preparative for complete living have to be considered under both these heads.

These, then, are the general ideas with which we must set out in discussing a *curriculum*:—Life as divided into several kinds of activity of successively decreasing importance; the worth of each order of facts as regulating these several kinds of activity, intrinsically, quasi-intrinsically, and conventionally; and their regulative influences estimated both as knowledge and discipline.

Happily, that all-important part of education which goes to secure direct self-preservation, is in great part already provided for. Too momentous to be left to our blundering, Nature takes it into her own hands. While yet in its nurse's arms, the infant, by hiding its face and crying at the sight of a stranger, shows the dawning instinct to attain safety by flying from that which is unknown and may be dangerous; and when it can walk, the terror it manifests if an unfamiliar dog comes near, or the screams with which it runs to its mother after any startling sight or sound, shows this instinct further developed. Morever, knowledge subserving direct self-preservation is that which it is chiefly busied in acquiring from hour to hour. How to balance its body; how to control its movements so as to avoid collisions; what objects are hard, and will hurt if struck; what objects are heavy, and injure if they fall on the limbs; which things will bear the weight of the body, and which not; the pains inflicted by fire, by missiles, by sharp instruments—these, and various other pieces of information needful for the avoidance of death or accident, it is ever learning. And when a few years later, the energies go out in running, climbing, and jumping, in games of strength and games of skill, we see in all these actions by which the muscles are developed, the perceptions sharpened, and the judgment quickened, a preparation for the safe conduct of the body among surrounding objects and movements; and for meeting those greater dangers that occasionally occur in the lives of all. Being thus, as we say, so well cared for by Nature, this fundamental education needs comparatively little care from us. What we are chiefly called upon to see, is, that there shall be free scope for gaining this experience, and receiving this discipline,—that there shall be no such thwarting of Nature as that by which stupid schoolmistresses commonly prevent the girls in their charge from the spontaneous physical activities they would indulge in; and so render them comparatively incapable of taking care of themselves in circumstances of peril.

This, however, is by no means all that is comprehended in the education that prepares for direct self-preservation. Besides guarding the body against mechanical damage or destruction, it has to be guarded against injury from other causes—against the disease and death that follow breaches of physiologic law. For complete living it is necessary, not only that sudden annihilation of life shall be warded off; but also that there shall be escaped the incapacities and the slow annihilation which unwise habits entail. As, without health and energy, the industrial, the parental, the social, and all other activities become more or less impossible; it is clear that this secondary kind of direct self-preservation is only less important than the primary kind; and that knowledge tending to secure it should rank very high.

It is true that here, too, guidance is in some measure ready supplied. By our various physical sensations and desires, Nature has insured a tolerable conformity to the chief requirements. Fortunately for us, want of food, great heat, extreme cold, produce promptings too peremptory to be disregarded. And would men habitually obey these and all like promptings when less strong, comparatively few evils would arise. If fatigue of body or brain were in every case followed by desistance; if the oppression produced by a close atmosphere always led to ventilation; if there were no eating without hunger, or drinking without thirst; then would the system be but seldom out of working order. But so profound an ignorance is there of the laws of life, that men do not even know that their sensations are their natural guides, and (when not rendered morbid by long-continued disobedience) their trustworthy guides. So that though, to speak teleologically, Nature has provided efficient safeguards to health, lack of knowledge makes them in a great measure useless.

If any one doubts the importance of an acquaintance with the fundamental principles of physiology as a means to complete living, let him look around and see how many men and women he can find in middle or later life who are thoroughly well. Occasionally only do we meet with an example of vigorous health continued to old age; hourly do we meet with examples of acute disorder, chronic ailment, general debility, premature decrepitude. Scarcely is there one to whom you put the question, who has not, in the course of his life, brought upon himself illnesses which a little knowledge would have saved him from. Here is a case of heart disease consequent on rheumatic fever that followed reckless exposure. There is a case of eyes spoiled for life by overstudy. Yesterday the account was of one whose long-enduring lameness was brought on by continuing, spite of the pain, to use a knee after it had been slightly injured. And to-day we are told of another who has had to lie by for years, because he did not know that the palpitation he suffered from resulted from overtaxed brain. Now we hear of an irremediable injury that followed some silly feat of strength; and, again, of a constitution that has never recovered from the effects of excessive work needlessly undertaken. While on all sides we see the perpetual minor ailments which accompany feebleness. Not to dwell on the natural pain, the weariness, the gloom, the waste of time and money thus entailed, only consider how greatly ill-health hinders the discharge of all duties—makes business often impossible, and always more difficult; produces an irritability fatal to the right management of children; puts the functions of citizenship out of the question; and makes amusement a bore. Is it not clear that the physical sins—partly our forefathers' and partly our own—which produce this ill-health, deduct more from complete living than anything else? and to a great extent make life a failure and a burden instead of a benefaction and a pleasure?

To all which add the fact, that life, besides being thus immensely deteriorated, is also cut short. It is not true, as we commonly suppose, that a disorder or disease from which we have recovered leaves us as before. No disturbance of the normal course of the functions can pass away and leave things exactly as they were. In all cases a permanent damage is done—not immediately appreciable, it may be, but still there; and along with other such items which Nature in her strict account-keeping never drops, will tell against us to the inevitable shortening of our days. Through the accumulation of small injuries it is that constitutions are commonly undermined, and break down, long before their time. And if we call to mind how far the average duration of life falls below the possible duration, we see how immense is the loss. When, to the numerous partial deductions which bad health entails, we add this great final deduction, it results that ordinarily more than one-half of life is thrown away.

Hence, knowledge which subserves direct self-preservation by preventing this loss of health, is of primary importance. We do not contend that possession of such knowledge would by any means wholly remedy the evil. For it is clear that in our present phase of civilization men's necessities often compel them to transgress. And it is further clear that, even in the absence of such compulsion, their inclinations would frequently lead them, spite of their knowledge, to sacrifice future good to present gratification. But we do contend that the right knowledge impressed in the right way would effect much; and we further contend that as the laws of health must be recognised before they can be fully conformed to, the imparting of such knowledge must precede a more rational living—come when that may. We infer that as vigorous health and its accompanying high spirits are larger elements of happiness than any other thing whatever, the teaching how to maintain them is a teaching that yields in moment to no other whatever. And therefore we assert that such a course of physiology as is needful for the comprehension of its general truths, and their bearings on daily conduct, is an all-essential part of a rational education.

Strange that the assertion should need making! Stranger still that it should need defending! Yet are there not a few by whom such a proposition will be received with something approaching to derision. Men who would blush if caught saying Iphigénia instead of Iphigenía, or would resent as an insult any imputation of ignorance respecting the fabled labours of a fabled demi-god, show not the slightest shame in confessing that they do not know where the Eustachian tubes are, what are the actions of the spinal cord, what is the normal rate of pulsation, or how the lungs are inflated. While anxious that their sons should be well up in the superstitions of two thousand years ago, they care not that they should be taught anything about the structure and functions of their own bodies—nay, would even disapprove such instruction. So overwhelming is the influence of established routine! So terribly in our education does the ornamental override the useful!

We need not insist on the value of that knowledge which aids indirect self-preservation by facilitating the gaining of a livelihood. This is admitted by all; and, indeed, by the mass is perhaps too exclusively regarded as the end of education. But while every one is ready to endorse the abstract proposition that instruction fitting youths for the business of life is of high importance, or even to consider it of supreme importance; yet scarcely any inquire what instruction will so fit them. It is true that reading, writing, and arithmetic are taught with an intelligent appreciation of their uses; but when we have said this we have said nearly all. While the great bulk of what else is acquired has no bearing on the industrial activities, an immensity of information that has a direct bearing on the industrial activities is entirely passed over.

For, leaving out only some very small classes, what are all men employed in? They are employed in the production, preparation, and distribution of commodities. And on what does efficiency in the production, preparation, and distribution of commodities depend? It depends on the use of methods fitted to the respective natures of these commodities; it depends on an adequate knowledge of their physical, chemical, or vital properties, as the case may be; that is, it depends on Science. This order of knowledge, which is in great part ignored in our school courses, is the order of knowledge underlying the right performance of all those processes by which civilized life is made possible. Undeniable as is this truth, and thrust upon us as it is at every turn, there seems to be no living consciousness of it: its very familiarity makes it unregarded. To give due weight to our argument, we must, therefore, realize this truth to the reader by a rapid review of the facts.

For all the higher arts of construction, some acquaintance with Mathematics is indispensable. The village carpenter, who, lacking rational instruction, lays out his work by empirical rules learnt in his apprenticeship, equally with the builder of a Britannia Bridge, makes hourly reference to the laws of quantitative relations. The surveyor on whose survey the land is purchased; the architect in designing a mansion to be built on it; the builder in preparing his estimates; his foreman in laying out the foundations; the masons in cutting the stones; and the various artisans who put up the fittings; are all guided by geometrical truths. Railway-making is regulated from beginning to end by mathematics: alike in the preparation of plans and sections; in staking out the line; in the mensuration of cuttings and embankments; in the designing, estimating, and building of bridges, culverts, viaducts, tunnels, stations. And similarly with the harbours, docks, piers, and various engineering and architectural works that fringe the coasts and overspread the face of the country; as well as the mines that run underneath it. Out of geometry, too, as applied to astronomy, the art of navigation has grown; and so by this science, has been made possible that enormous foreign commerce which supports a large part of our population, and supplies us with many necessities and most of our luxuries. And now-a-days even the farmer, for the correct laying out of his drains, has recourse to the level—that is, to geometrical principles. When from those divisions of mathematics which deal with *space*, and *number*, some smattering of which is given in schools, we turn to that other division which deals with *force*, of which even a smattering is scarcely ever given, we meet with another large class of activities which this science presides over. On the application of rational mechanics depends the success of nearly all modern manufacture. The properties of the lever, the wheel and axle, etc., are involved in every machine—every machine is a solidified mechanical theorem; and to machinery in these times we owe nearly all production. Trace the history of the breakfast-roll. The soil out of which it came was drained with machine-made tiles; the surface was turned over by a machine; the seed was put in by a machine; the wheat was reaped, thrashed, and winnowed by machines; by machinery it was ground and bolted; and had the flour been sent to Gosport, it might have been made into biscuits by a machine. Look round the room in which you sit. If modern, probably the bricks in its walls were machine-made; by machinery the flooring was sawn and planed, the mantel-shelf sawn and polished, the paper-hangings made and printed; the veneer on the table, the turned legs of the chairs, the carpet, the curtains, are all products of machinery. And your clothing—plain, figured, or printed—is it not wholly woven, nay, perhaps even sewed, by machinery? And the volume you are reading—are not its leaves fabricated by one machine and covered with these words by another? Add to which that for the means of distribution over both land and sea, we are similarly indebted. And then let it be remembered that according as the principles of mechanics are well or ill used to these ends, comes success or failure—individual and national. The engineer who misapplies his formulae for the strength of materials, builds a bridge that breaks down. The manufacturer whose apparatus is badly devised, cannot compete with another whose apparatus wastes less in friction and inertia. The ship-builder adhering to the old model, is outsailed by one who builds on the mechanically justified wave-line principle. And as the ability of a nation to hold its own against other nations depends on the skilled activity of its units, we see that on such knowledge may turn the national fate. Judge then the worth of mathematics.

Pass next to Physics. Joined with mathematics, it has given us the steam-engine, which does the work of millions of labourers. That section of physics which deals with the laws of heat, has taught us how to economise fuel in our various industries; how to increase the produce of our smelting furnaces by substituting the hot for the cold blast; how to ventilate our mines; how to prevent explosions by using the safety-lamp; and, through the thermometer, how to regulate innumerable processes. That division which has the phenomena of light for its subject, gives eyes to the old and the myopic; aids through the microscope in detecting diseases and adulterations; and by improved lighthouses prevents shipwrecks. Researches in electricity and magnetism have saved incalculable life and property by the compass; have subserved sundry arts by the electrotype; and now, in the telegraph, have supplied us with the agency by which for the future all mercantile transactions will be regulated, political intercourse carried on, and perhaps national quarrels often avoided. While in the details of indoor life, from the improved kitchen-range up to the stereoscope on the drawing-room table, the applications of advanced physics underlie our comforts and gratifications.

Still more numerous are the bearings of Chemistry on those activities by which men obtain the means of living. The bleacher, the dyer, the calicoprinter, are severally occupied in processes that are well or ill done according as they do or do not conform to chemical laws. The economical reduction from their ores of copper, tin, zinc, lead, silver, iron, are in a great measure questions of chemistry. Sugar-refining, gas-making, soap-boiling, gunpowder manufacture, are operations all partly chemical; as are also those by which are preduced glass and porcelain. Whether the distiller's work stops at the alchoholic fermentation or passes into the acetous, is a chemical question on which hangs his profit or loss; and the brewer, if his business is sufficiently large, finds it pays to keep a chemist on his premises. Glance through a work on technology, and it becomes at once apparent that there is now scarcely any process in the arts or manufactures over some part of which chemistry does not preside. And then, lastly, we come to the fact that in these times, agriculture, to be profitably carried on, must have like guidance. The analysis of manures and soils; their adaptations to each other; the use of gypsum or other substance for fixing ammonia; the utilization of coprolites; the production of artificial manures—all these are boons of chemistry which it behoves the farmer to acquaint himself with. Be it in the lucifer match, or in disinfected sewage, or in photographs—in bread made without fermentation, or perfumes extracted from refuse, we may perceive that chemistry affects all our industries; and that, by consequence, knowledge of it concerns every one who is directly or indirectly connected with our industries.

And then the science of life—Biology: does not this, too, bear fundamentally upon these processes of indirect self-preservation? With what we ordinarily call manufactures, it has, indeed, little connexion; but with the all-essential manufacture—that of food—it is inseparably connected. As agriculture must conform its methods to the phenomena of vegetable and animal life, it follows necessarily that the science of these phenomena is the rational basis of agriculture. Various biological truths have indeed been empirically established and acted upon by farmers while yet there has been no conception of them as science: such as that particular manures are suited to particular plants; that crops of certain kinds unfit the soil for other crops; that horses cannot do good work on poor food; that such and such diseases of cattle and sheep are caused by such and such conditions. These, and the everyday knowledge which the agriculturist gains by experiencs respecting the right management of plants and animals, constitute his stock of biological facts; on the largeness of which greatly depends his success. And as these biological facts, scanty, indefinite, rudimentary, though they are, aid him so essentially; judge what must be the value to him of such facts when they become positive, definite, and exhaustive. Indeed, even now we may see the benefits that rational biology is conferring on him. The truth that the production of animal heat implies waste of substance, and that, therefore, preventing loss of heat prevents the need for extra food—a purely theoretical conclusion—now guides the fattening of cattle: it is found that by keeping cattle warm, fodder is saved. Similarly with respect to variety of food. The experiments of physiologists have shown that not only is change of diet beneficial, but that digestion is facilitated by a mixture of ingredients in each meal: both which truths are now influencing cattle-feeding. The discovery that a disorder known as "the staggers," of which many thousands of sheep have died annually, is caused by an entozoon which presses on the brain; and that if the creature is extracted through the softened place in the skull which marks its position, the sheep usually recovers; is another debt which agriculture owes to biology. When we observe the marked contrast between our farming and farming on the Continent, and remember that this contrast is mainly due to the far greater influence science has had upon farming here and there; and when we see how, daily, competition is making the adoption of scientific methods more general and necessary; we shall rightly infer that very soon, agricultural success in England will be impossible without a competent knowledge of animal and vegetable physiology.

Yet one more science have we to note as bearing directly on industrial success—the Science of Society. Without knowing it, men who daily look at the state of the money-market, glance over prices current, discuss the probable crops of corn, cotton, sugar, wool, silk, weigh the chances of war, and from all those data decide on their mercantile operations, are students of social science: empirical and blundering students it may be; but still, students who gain the prizes or are plucked of their profits, according as they do or do not reach the right conclusion. Not only the manufacturer and the merchant must guide their transactions by calculations of supply and demand, based on numerous facts, and tacitly recognising sundry general principles of social action; but even the retailer must do the like: his prosperity very greatly depending upon the correctness of his judgments respecting the future wholesale prices and the future rates of consumption. Manifestly, all who take part in the entangled commercial activities of a community, are vitally interested in understanding the laws according to which those activities vary.

Thus, to all such as are occupied in the production, exchange, or distribution of commodities, acquaintance with science in some of its departments, is of fundamental importance. Whoever is immediately or remotely implicated in any form of industry (and few are not) has a direct interest in understanding something of the mathematical, physical and chemical properties of things; perhaps, also has a direct interest in biology; and certainly has in sociology. Whether he does or does not succeed well in that indirect self-preservation which we call getting a good livelihood, depends in a great degree on his knowledge of one or more of these sciences: not, it may be, a rational knowledge; but still a knowledge, though empirical. For what we call learning a business, really implies learning the science involved in it; though not perhaps under the name of science. And hence a grounding in science is of great importance, both because it prepares for all this, and because rational knowledge has an immense superiority over empirical knowledge. Moreover, not only is it that scientific culture is requisite for each, that he may understand the *how* and the *why* of the things and processes with which he is concerned as maker or distributor; but it is often of much moment that he should understand the *how* and the *why* of various other things and processes. In this age of joint-stock undertakings, nearly every man above the labourer is interested as capitalist in some other occupation than his own; and, as thus interested, his profit or loss often depends on his knowledge of the sciences bearing on this other occupation. Here is a mine, in the sinking of which many shareholders ruined themselves, from not knowing that a certain fossil belonged to the old red sandstone, below which no coal is found. Not many years ago, 20,000£. [20,000 pounds] was lost in the prosecution of a scheme for collecting the alcohol that distils from bread in baking: all which would have been saved to the subscribers, had they known that less than a hundredth part by weight of the flour is changed in fermentation. Numerous attempts have been made to construct electro-magnetic engines, in the hope of superseding steam; but had those who supplied the money, understood the general law of the correlation and equivalence of forces, they might have had better balances at their bankers. Daily are men induced to aid in carrying out inventions which a mere tyro in science could show to be futile. Scarcely a locality but has its history of fortunes thrown away over some impossible project.

And if already the loss from want of science is so frequent and so great, still greater and more frequent will it be to those who hereafter lack science. Just as fast as productive processes become more scientific, which competition will inevitably make them do; and just as fast as joint-stock undertakings spread, which they certainly will; so fast will scientific knowledge grow necessary to every one.

That which our school courses leave almost entirely out, we thus find to be that which most nearly concerns the business of life. All our industries would cease, were it not for that information which men begin to acquire as they best may after their education is said to be finished. And were it not for this information, that has been from age to age accumulated and spread by unofficial means, these industries would never have existed. Had there been no teaching but such as is given in our public schools, England would now be what it was in feudal times. That increasing acquaintance with the laws of phenomena which has through successive ages enabled us to subjugate Nature to our needs, and in these days gives the common labourer comforts which a few centuries ago kings could not purchase, is scarcely in any degree owed to the appointed means of instructing our youth. The vital knowledge—that by which we have grown as a nation to what we are, and which now underlies our whole existence, is a knowledge that has got itself taught in nooks and corners; while the ordained agencies for teaching have been mumbling little else but dead formulas.

We come now to the third great division of human activities—a division for which no preparation whatever is made. If by some strange chance not a vestige of us descended to the remote future save a pile of our school-books or some college examination papers, we may imagine how puzzled an antiquary of the period would be on finding in them no indication that the learners were ever likely to be parents. "This must have been the *curriculum* for their celibates," we may fancy him concluding. "I perceive here an elaborate preparation for many things: especially for reading the books of extinct nations and of co-existing national (from which indeed it seems clear that these people had very little worth reading in their own tongue); but I find no reference whatever to the bringing up of children. They could not have been so absurd as to omit all training for this gravest of responsibilities. Evidently then, this was the school course of one of their monastic orders."

Seriously, is it not an astonishing fact, that though on the treatment of offspring depend their lives or deaths, and their moral welfare or ruin; yet not one word of instruction on the treatment of offspring is ever given to those who will hereafter be parents? Is it not monstrous that the fate of a new generation should be left to the chances of unreasoning custom, impulse, fancy—joined with the suggestions of ignorant nurses and the prejudiced counsel of grandmothers? If a merchant commenced business without any knowledge of arithmetic and book-keeping, we should exclaim at his folly, and look for disastrous consequences. Or if, before studying anatomy, a man set up as a surgical operator, we should wonder at his audacity and pity his patients. But that parents should begin the difficult task of rearing children without ever having biven a thought to the principles—physical, moral, or intellectual—which ought to guide them, excites neither surprise at the actors nor pity for their victims.

To tens of thousands that are killed, add hundreds of thousands that survive with feeble constitutions, and millions that grow up with constitutions not so strong as they should be; and you will have some idea of the curse inflicted on their offspring by parents ignorant of the laws of life. Do but consider for a moment that the regimen to which children are subject is hourly telling upon them to their life-long injury or benefit; and that there are twenty ways of going wrong to one way of going right; and you will get some idea of the enormous mischief that is almost everywhere inflicted by the thoughtless, haphazard system in common use. Is it decided that a boy shall be clothed in some flimsy short dress, and be allowed to go playing about with limbs reddened by cold? The decision will tell on his whole future existence—either in illnesses; or in stunted growth; or in deficient energy; or in a maturity less vigorous than it ought to have been, and consequent hindrances to success and happiness. Are children doomed to a monotonous dietary, or a dietary that is deficient in nutritiveness? Their ultimate physical power and their efficiency as men and women, will inevitably be more or less diminished by it. Are they forbidden vociferous play, or (being too ill-clothed to bear exposure), are they kept in-doors in cold weather? They are certain to fall below that measure of health and strength to which they would else have attained. When sons and daughters grow up sickly and feeble, parents commonly regard the event as a misfortune —as a visitation of Providence. Thinking after the prevalent chaotic fashion, they assume that these evils come without causes; or that the causes are supernatural. Nothing of the kind. In some cases the causes are doubtless inherited; but in most cases foolish regulations are the causes. Very generally parents themselves are responsible for all this pain, this debility, this depression, this misery. They have undertaken to control the lives of their offspring from hour to hour; with cruel carelessness they have neglected to learn anything about these vital processes which they are unceasingly affecting by their commands and prohibitions; in utter ignorance of the simplest physiologic laws, they have been year by year undermining the constitutions of their children; and have so inflicted disease and premature death, not only on them but on their descendants.

Equally great are the ignorance and the consequent injury, when we turn from physical training to moral training. Consider the young mother and her nursery legislation. But a few years ago she was at school, where her memory was crammed with words, and names, and dates, and her reflective faculties scarcely in the slightest degree exercised—where not one idea was given her respecting the methods of dealing with the opening mind of childhood; and where her discipline did not in the least fit her for thinking out methods of her own. The intervening years have been passed in practising music, in fancy-work, in novel-reading, and in party-going: no thought having yet been given to the grave responsibilities of maternity; and scarcely any of that solid intellectual culture obtained which would be some preparation for such responsibilities. And now see her with an unfolding human character committed to her charge—see her profoundly ignorant of the phenomena with which she has to deal, undertaking to do that which can be done but imperfectly even with the aid of the profoundest knowledge. She knows nothing about the nature of the emotions, their order of evolution, their functions, or where use ends and abuse begins. She is under the impression that some of the feelings are wholly bad, which is not true of any one of them; and that others are good, however far they may be carried, which is also not true of any one of them. And then, ignorant as she is of that with which she has to deal, she is equally ignorant of the effects that will be produced on it by this or that treatment. What can be more inevitable than the disastrous results we see hourly arising? Lacking knowledge of mental phenomena, with their causes and consequences, her interference is frequently more mischievous than absolute passivity would have been. This and that kind of action, which are quite normal and beneficial, she perpetually thwarts; and so diminishes the child's happiness and profit, injures its temper and her own, and produces estrangement. Deeds which she thinks it desirable to encourage, she gets performed by threats and bribes, or by exciting a desire for applause: considering little what the inward motive may be, so long as the outward conduct conforms; and thus cultivating hypocrisy, and fear, and selfishness, in place of good feeling. While insisting on truthfulness, she constantly sets an example of untruth, by threatening penalties which she does not inflict. While inculcating self-control, she hourly visits on her little ones angry scoldings for acts that do not call for them. She has not the remotest idea that in the nursery, as in the world, that alone is the truly salutary discipline which visits on all conduct, good and bad, the natural consequences—the consequences, pleasurable or painful, which in the nature of things such conduct tends to bring. Being thus without theoretic guidance, and quite incapable of guiding herself by tracing the mental processes going on in her children, her rule is impulsive, inconsistent, mischeivous, often, in the highest degree; and would indeed be generally ruinous, were it not that the overwhelming tendency of the growing mind to assume the moral type of the race, usually subordinates all minor influences.

And then the culture of the intellect—is not this, too, mismanaged in a similar manner? Grant that the phenomena of intelligence conform to laws; grant that the evolution of intelligence in a child also conforms to laws; and it follows inevitably that education can be rightly guided only by knowledge of these laws. To suppose that you can properly regulate this process of forming and accumulating ideas, without understanding the nature of the process, is absurd. How widely, then, must teaching as it is, differ from teaching as it should be; when hardly any parents, and but few teachers, know anything about psychology. As might be expected, the system is grievously at fault, alike in matter and in manner. While the right class of facts is withheld, the wrong class is forcibly administered in the wrong way and in the wrong order. With that common limited idea of education which confines it to knowledge gained from books, parents thrust primers into the hands of their little ones years too soon, to their great injury. Not recognising the truth that the function of books is supplementary— that they form an indirect means to knowledge when direct means fail—a means of seeing through other men what you cannot see for yourself; they are eager to give second-hand facts in place of first-hand facts. Not perceiving the enormous value of that spontaneous education which goes on in early years—not perceiving that a child's restless observation, instead of being ignored or checked, should be diligently administered to, and made as accurate and complete as possible; they insist on occupying its eyes and thoughts with things that are, for the time being, incomprehensible and repugnant. Possessed by a super- stition which worships the symbols of knowledge instead of the knowledge itself, they do not see that only when his acquaintance with the objects and processes of the household, the streets, and the fields, is becoming tolerably exhaustive—only then should a child be introduced to the new sources of information which books supply: and this, not only because immediate cognition is of far greater value than mediate cognition; but also, because the words contained in books can be rightly interpreted into ideas, only in proportion to the antecedent experience of things. Observe next, that this formal instruction, far too soon commenced, is carried on with but little reference to the laws of mental development. Intellectual progress is of necessity from the concrete to the abstract. But regardless of this, highly abstract subjects, such as grammar, which should come quite late, are begun quite early. Political geography, dead and uninteresting to a child, and which should be an appendage of sociological studies, is commenced betimes; while physical geography, comprehensible and comparatively attractive to a child, is in great part passed over. Nearly every subject dealt with is arranged in abnormal order: definitions, and rules, and principles being put first, instead of being disclosed, as they are in the order of nature, through the study of cases. And then, pervading the whole, is the vicious system of rote learning—a system of sacrificing the spirit to the letter. See the results. What with perceptions unnaturally dulled by early thwarting and a coerced attention to books—what with the mental confusion produced by teaching subjects before they can be understood, and in each of them giving generalizations before the facts of which these are the generalizations—what with making the pupil a mere passive recipient of other's ideas, and not in the least leading him to be an active inquirer or self-instructor—and what with taxing the faculties to excess; there are very few minds that become as efficient as they might be. Examination being once passed, books are laid aside; the greater part of what has been acquired, being unorganized, soon drops out of recollection; what remains is mostly inert—the art of applying knowledge not having been cultivated; and there is but little power either of accurate observation or independent thinking. To all which add, that while much of the information gained is of relatively small value, an immense mass of information of transcendent value is entirely passed over.

Thus we find the facts to be such as might have been inferred *á priori*. The training of children—physical, moral, and intellectual—is dreadfully defective. And in great measure it is so, because parents are devoid of that knowledge by which this training can alone be rightly guided. What is to be expected when one of the most intricate of problems is undertaken by those who have given scarcely a thought to the principles on which its solution depends? For shoemaking or house-building, for the management of a ship or a locomotive-engine, a long apprenticeship is needful. Is it, then, that the unfolding of a human being in body and mind, is so comparatively simple a process, that any one may superintend and regulate it with no preparation whatever? If not—if the process is with one exception more complex than any in Nature, and the task of administering to it one of surpassing difficulty; is it not madness to make no provision for such a task? Better sacrifice accomplishments than omit this all-essential instruction. When a father, acting on false dogmas adopted without examination, has alienated his sons, driven them into rebellion by his harsh treatment, ruined them, and made himself miserable; he might reflect that the study of Ethology would have been worth pursuing, even at the cost of knowing nothing about Aeschylus. When a mother is mourning over a first-born that has sunk under the sequelae of scarlet-fever—when perhaps a candid medical man has confirmed her suspicion that her child would have recovered had not its system been enfeebled by over-study—when she is prostrate under the pangs of combined grief and remorse; it is but a small consolation that she can read Dante in the original.

Thus we see that for regulating the third great division of human activities, a knowledge of the laws of life is the one thing needful. Some acquaintance with the first principles of physiology and the elementary truths of psychology is indispensable for the right bringing up of children. We doubt not that this assertion will by many be read with a smile. That parents in general should be expected to acquire a knowledge of subjects so abstruse, will seem to them an absurdity. And if we proposed that an exhaustive knowledge of these subjects should be obtained by all fathers and mothers, the absurdity would indeed be glaring enough. But we do not. General principles only, accompanied by such detailed illustrations as may be needed to make them understood, would suffice. And these might be readily taught—if not rationally, then dogmatically. Be this as it may, however, here are the indisputable facts:—that the development of children in mind and body rigorously obeys certain laws; that unless these laws are in some degree conformed to by parents, death is inevitable; that unless they are in a great degree conformed to, there must result serious physical and mental defects; and that only when they are completely conformed to, can a perfect maturity be reached. Judge, then, whether all who may one day be parents, should not strive with some anxiety to learn what these laws are.

From the parental functions let us pass now to the functions of the citizen. We have here to inquire what knowledge best fits a man for the discharge of these functions. It cannot be alleged, as in the last case, that the need for knowledge fitting him for these functions is wholly overlooked; for our school courses contain certain studies which, nominally at least, bear upon political and social duties. Of these the only one that occupies a prominent place is History.

But, as already more than once hinted, the historic information commonly given is almost valueless for purposes of guidance. Scarcely any of the facts set down in our school-histories, and very few even of those contained in the more elaborate works written for adults, give any clue to the right principles of political action. The biographies of monarchs (and our children commonly learn little else) throw scarcely any light upon the science of society. Familiarity with court intrigues, plots, usurpations, or the like, and with all the personalities accompanying them, aids very little in elucidating the principles on which national welfare depends. We read of some squabble for power, that it led to a pitched battle; that such and such were the names of the generals and their leading subordinates; that they had each so many thousand infantry and cavalry, and so many cannon; that they arranged their forces in this and that order; that they manoeuvred, attacked, and fell back in certain ways; that at this part of the day such disasters were sustained, and at that such advantages gained; that in one particular movement some leading officer fell, while in another a certain regiment was decimated; that after all the changing fortunes of the fight, the victory was gained by this or that army; and that so many were killed and wounded on each side, and so many captured by the conquerors. And now, out of the accumulated details which make up the narrative, say which it is that helps you in deciding on your conduct as a citizen. Supposing even that you had diligently read, not only "The Fifteen Decisive Battles of the World," but accounts of all other battles that history mentions; how much more judicious would your vote be at the next election? "But these are facts—interesting facts," you say. Without doubt they are facts (such, at least, as are not wholly or partially fictions); and to many they may be interesting facts. But this by no means implies that they are valuable. Factitious or morbid opinion often gives seeming value to things that have scarcely any. A tulipomaniac will not part with a choice bulb for its weight in gold. To another man an ugly piece of cracked old china seems his most desirable possession. And there are those who give high prices for the relics of celebrated murderers. Will it be contended that these tastes are any measures of value in the things that gratify them? If not, then it must be admitted that the liking felt for certain classes of historical facts is no proof of their worth; and that we must test their worth as we test the worth of other facts, by asking to what uses they are applicable. Were some one to tell you that your neighbour's cat kittened yesterday, you would say the information was worthless. Fact though it might be, you would say it was an utterly useless fact—a fact that could in no way influence your actions in life—a fact that would not help you in learning how to live completely. Well, apply the same test to the great mass of historical facts, and you will get the same result. They are facts from which no conclusions can be drawn—

unorganizable facts; and therefore facts which can be of no service in establishing principles of conduct, which is the chief use of facts. Read them, if you like, for amusement; but do not flatter yourself they are instructive.

That which constitutes History, properly so called, is in great part omitted from works on the subject. Only of late years have historians commenced giving us, in any considerable quantity, the truly valuable information. As in past ages the king was everything and the people nothing; so, in past histories the doings of the king fill the entire picture, to which the national life forms but an obscure background. While only now, when the welfare of nations rather than of rulers is becoming the dominant idea, are historians beginning to occupy themselves with the phenomena of social progress. That which it really concerns us to know, is the natural history of society. We want all facts which help us to understand how a nation has grown and organized itself. Among these, let us of course have an account of its government; with as little as may be of gossip about the men who officered it, and as much as possible about the structure, principles, methods, prejudices, corruptions, etc., which it exhibited: and let this account not only include the nature and actions of the central government, but also those of local governments, down to their minutest ramifications. Let us of course also have a parallel description of the ecclesiastical government—its organization, its conduct, its power, its relations to the State: and accompanying this, the ceremonial, creed, and religious ideas—not only those nominally believed, but those really believed and acted upon. Let us at the same time be informed of the control exercised by class over class, as displayed in all social observances—in titles, salutations, and forms of address. Let us know, too, what were all the other customs which regulated the popular life out of doors and in-doors: including whose which concern the relations of the sexes, and the relations of parents to children. The superstitions, also, from the more important myths down to the charms in common use, should be indicated. Next should come a delineation of the industrial system: showing to what extent the division of labour was carried; how trades were regulated, whether by caste, guilds, or otherwise; what was the connection between employers and employed; what were the agencies for distributing commodities, what were the means of communication; what was the circulating medium. Accompanying all which should come an account of the industrial arts technically considered: stating the processes in use, and the quality of the products. Further, the intellectual condition of the nation in its various grades should be depicted: not only with respect to the kind and amount of education, but with respect to the progress made in science, and the prevailing manner of thinking. The degree of aesthetic culture, as displayed in architecture, sculpture, painting, dress, music, poetry, and fiction, should be described. Nor should there be omitted a sketch of the daily lives of the people—their food, their homes, and their amusements. And lastly, to connect the whole, should be exhibited the morals, theoretical and practical, of all classes: as indicated in their laws, habits, proverbs, deeds. All these facts, given with as much brevity as consists with clearness and accuracy, should be so grouped and arranged that they may be comprehended in their *ensemble*; and thus may be contemplated as mutually dependent parts of one great whole. The aim should be so to present them that we may readily trace the *consensus* subsisting among them; with the view of learning what social phenomena co-exist with what others. And then the corresponding delineations of succeeding ages should be so managed as to show us, as clearly as may be, how each belief, institution, custom, and arrangement was modified; and how the *consensus* of preceding structures and functions was developed into the *consensus* of succeeding ones. Such alone is the kind of information respecting past times, which can be of service to the citizen for the regulation of his conduct. The only history that is of practical value, is what may be called Descriptive Sociology. And the highest office which the historian can discharge, is that of narrating the lives of nations, as to furnish materials for a Comparative Sociology; and for the subsequent determination of the ultimate laws to which social phenomena conform.

But now mark, that even supposing an adequate stock of this truly valuable historical knowledge has been acquired, it is of comparatively little use without the key. And the key is to be found only in science. Without an acquaintance with the general truths of biology and psychology, rational interpretation of social phenomena is impossible. Only in proportion as men obtain a certain rude, empirical knowledge of human nature, are they enabled to understand even the simplest facts of social life: as, for instance, the relation between supply and demand. And if not even the most elementary truths of sociology can be reached until some knowledge is obtained of how men generally think, feel, and act under given circumstances; then it is manifest that there can be nothing like a wide comprehension of sociology, unless through a competent knowledge of man in all his faculties, bodily and mental. Consider the matter in the abstract, and this conclusion is self-evident. Thus:—Society is made up of individuals; all that is done in society is done by the combined actions of individuals; and therefore, in individual actions only can be found the solutions of social phenomena. But the actions of individuals depend on the laws of their natures; and their actions cannot be understood until these laws are understood. These laws, however, when reduced to their simplest expression, are found to depend on the laws of body and mind in general. Hence it necessarily follows, that biology and psychology are indispensable as interpreters of sociology. Or, to state the conclusions still more simply:—all social phenomena are phenomena of life—are the most complex manifestations of life—are ultimately dependent on the laws of life—and can be understood only when the laws of life are understood. Thus, then, we see that for the regulation of this fourth division of human activities, we are, as before, dependent on Science. Of the knowledge commonly imparted in educational courses, very little is of any service in guiding a man in his conduct as a citizen. Only a small part of the history he reads is of practical value; and of this small part he is not prepared to make proper use. He commonly lacks not only the materials for, but the very conception of, descriptive sociology; and he also lacks that knowledge of the organic sciences, without which even descriptive sociology can give him but little aid.

And now we come to that remaining division of human life which includes the relaxations, pleasures, and amusements filling leisure hours. After considering what training best fits for self-preservation, for the obtainment of sustenance, for the discharge of parental duties, and for the regulation of social and political conduct; we have now to consider what training best fits for the miscellaneous ends not included in these—for the enjoyments of Nature, of Literature, and of the Fine Arts, in all their forms. Postponing them as we do to things that bear more vitally upon human welfare; and bringing everything, as we have, to the test of actual value; it will perhaps be inferred that we are inclined to slight these less essential things. No greater mistake could be made, however. We yield to none in the value we attach to aesthetic culture and its pleasures. Without painting, sculpture, music, poetry, and the emotions produced by natural beauty of every kind, life would lose half its charm. So far from thinking that the training and gratification of the tastes are unimportant, we believe the time will come when they will occupy a much larger share of human life than now. When the forces of Nature have been fully conquered to man's use—when the means of production have been brought to perfection—when labour has been economized to the highest degree—when education has been so systematized that a preparation for the more essential activities may be made with comparative rapidity—and when, consequently, there is a great increase of spare time; then will the poetry, both of Art and Nature, rightly fill a large space in the minds of all.

But it is one thing to admit that aesthetic culture is in a high degree conducive to human happiness; and another thing to admit that it is a fundamental requisite to human happiness. However important it may be, it must yield precedence to those kinds of culture which bear more directly upon the duties of life. As before hinted, literature and the fine arts are made possible by those activities which make individual and social life possible; and manifestly, that which is made possible, must be postponed to that which makes it possible. A florist cultivates a plant for the sake of its flower; and regards the roots and leaves as of value, chiefly because they are instrumental in producing the flower. But while, as an ultimate product, the flower is the thing to which everything else is subordinate, the florist very well knows that the root and leaves are intrinsically of greater importance; because on them the evolution of the flower depends. He bestows every care in rearing a healthy plant; and knows it would be folly if, in his anxiety to obtain the flower, he were to neglect the plant. Similarly in the case before us. Architecture, sculpture, painting, music, poetry, &c., may be truly called the efflorescence of civilized life. But even supposing them to be of such transcendent worth as to subordinate the civilized life out of which they grow (which can hardly be asserted), it will still be admitted that the production of a healthy civilized life must be the first consideration; and that the knowledge conducing to this must occupy the highest place.

And here we see most distinctly the vice of our educational system. It neglects the plant for the sake of the flower. In anxiety for elegance, it forgets substance. While it gives no knowledge conducive to self-preservation—while of knowledge that facilitates gaining a livelihood it gives but the rudiments, and leaves the greater part to be picked up any how in after life—while for the discharge of parental functions it makes not the slightest provision—and while for the duties of citizenship it prepares by imparting a mass of facts, most of which are irrelevant, and the rest without a key; it is diligent in teaching every thing that adds to refinement, polish, éclat. However fully we may admit that extensive acquaintance with modern languages is a valuable accomplishment, which through reading, conversation, and travel, aids in giving a certain finish; it by no means follows that this result is rightly purchased at the cost of that vitally important knowledge sacrificed to it. Supposing it true that classical education conduces to elegance and correctness of style; it cannot be said that elegance and correctness of style are comparable in importance to a familiarity with the principles that should guide the rearing of children. Grant that the taste may be greatly improved by reading all the poetry written in extinct languages; yet it is not to be inferred that such improvement of taste is equivalent in value to an acquaintance with the laws of health. Accomplishments, the fine arts, *belles-lettres*, and all those things which, as we say, constitute the efflorescence of civilization, should be wholly subordinate to that knowledge and discipline in which civilization rests. *As they occupy the leisure part of life, so should they occupy the leisure part of education.*

Recognising thus the true position of aesthetics, and holding that while the cultivation of them should form a part of education from its commencement, such cultivation should be subsidiary; we have now to inquire what knowledge is of most use to this end—what knowledge best fits for this remaining sphere of activity. To this question the answer is still the same as heretofore. Unexpected as the assertion may be, it is nevertheless true, that the highest Art of every kind is based upon Science—that without Science there can be neither perfect production nor full appreciation. Science, in that limited technical acceptation current in society, may not have been possessed by many artists of high repute; but acute observers as they have been, they have always possessed a stock of those empirical generalizations which constitute science in its lowest phase; and they have habitually fallen far below perfection, partly because their generalizations were comparatively few and inaccurate. That science necessarily underlies the fine arts, becomes manifest, *á priori*, when we remember that art-products are all more or less representative of objective and subjective phenomena; that they can be true only in proportion as they conform to the laws of these phenomena; and that before they can thus conform the artist must know what these laws are. That this *á priori* conclusion tallies with experience we shall soon see.

Youths preparing for the practice of sculpture, have to acquaint themselves with the bones and muscles of the human frame in their distribution, attachments, and movements. This is a portion of science; and it has been found needful to impart it for the prevention of those many errors which sculptors who do not possess it commit. For the prevention of other mistakes, a knowledge of mechanical principles is requisite; and such knowledge not being usually possessed, grave mechanical mistakes are frequently made. Take an instance. For the stability of a figure it is needful that the perpendicular from the centre of gravity—"the line of direction," as it is called—should fall within the base of support; and hence it happens, that when a man assumes the attitude known as "standing at ease," in which one leg is straightened and the other relaxed, the line of direction falls within the foot of the straightened leg. But sculptors unfamiliar with the theory of equilibrium, not uncommonly so represent this attitude, that the line of direction falls midway between the feet. Ignorance of the laws of momentum leads to analogous errors: as witness the admired Discobolus, which, as it is posed, must inevitably fall forward the moment the quoit is delivered.

In painting, the necessity for scientific knowledge, empirical if not rational, is still more conspicuous. In what consists the grotesqueness of Chinese pictures, unless in their utter disregard of the laws of appearances—in their absurd linear perspective, and their want of aerial perspective? In what are the drawings of a child so faulty, if not in a similar absence of truth—an absence arising, in great part, from ignorance of the way in which the aspects of things vary with the conditions? Do but remember the books and lectures by which students are instructed; or consider the criticisms of Ruskin; or look at the doings of the Pre-Raffaelites; and you will see that progress in painting implies increasing knowledge of how effects in Nature are produced. The most diligent observation, if not aided by science, fails to preserve from error. Every painter will indorse the assertion that unless it is known what appearances must exist under given circumstances, they often will not be perceived; and to know what appearances must exist, is, in so far, to understand the science of appearances. From want of science Mr. J. Lewis, careful painter as he is, casts the shadow of a lattice-window in sharply defined lines upon an opposite wall; which he would not have done, had he been familiar with the phenomena of penumbrae. From want of science, Mr. Rosetti, catching sight of a peculiar iridescence displayed by certain hairy surfaces under particular lights (an iridescence caused by the diffraction of light in passing the hairs), commits the error of showing this iridescence on surfaces and in positions where it could not occur.

To say that music, too, has need of scientific aid will seem still more surprising. Yet it is demonstrable that music is but an idealization of the natural language of emotion; and that consequently, music must be good or bad according as it conforms to the laws of this natural language. The various inflections of voice which accompany feelings of different kinds and intensities, have been shown to be the germs out of which music is developed. It has been further shown, that these inflections and cadences are not accidental or arbitrary; but that they are determined by certain general principles of vital action; and that their expressiveness depends on this. Whence it follows that musical phrases and the melodies built of them, can be effective only when they are in harmony with these general principles. It is difficult here properly to illustrate this position. But perhaps it will suffice to instance the swarms of worthless ballads that infest drawing-rooms, as compositions which science would forbid. They sin against science by setting to music ideas that are not emotional enough to prompt musical expression; and they also sin against science by using musical phrases that have no natural relation to the ideas expressed: even where these are emotional. They are bad because they are untrue, and to say they are untrue, is to say they are unscientific.

Even in poetry the same thing holds. Like music, poetry has its root in those natural modes of expression which accompany deep feeling. Its rhythm, its strong and numerous metaphors, its hyperboles, its violent inversions, are simply exaggerations of the traits of excited speech. To be good, therefore, poetry must pay respect to those laws of nervous actions which excited speech obeys. In intensifying and combining the traits of excited speech, it must have due regard to proportion —must not use its appliances without restriction; but, where the ideas are least emotional, must use the forms of poetical expression sparingly; must use them more freely as the emotion rises; and must carry them all to their greatest extent only where the emotion reaches a climax. The entire contravention of these principles results in bombast or doggerel. The insufficient respect for them is seen in didactic poetry. And it is because they are rarely fully obeyed, that we have so much poetry that is inartistic.

Not only is it that the artist, of whatever kind, cannot produce a truthful work without he understands the laws of the phenomena he represents; but it is that he must also understand how the minds of spectators or listeners will be affected by the several peculiarities of his work—a question in psychology. What impression any given art-product generates, manifestly depends upon the mental natures of those to whom it is presented; and as all mental natures have certain general principles in common, there must result certain corresponding general principles on which alone art-products can be successfully framed. These general principles cannot be fully understood and applied, unless the artist sees how they follow from the laws of mind. To ask how the perceptions and feelings of observers will be affected by it. To ask whether drama is well constructed, is to ask whether its situations are so arranged as duly to consult the power of attention of an audience, and duly to avoid over-taxing any one class of feelings. Equally in arranging the leading divisions of a poem or fiction, and in combining the words of a single sentence, the goodness of the effect depends upon the skill with which the mental energies and susceptibilities of the reader are economized. Every artist, in the course of his education and after-life, accumulates a stock of maxims by which his practice is regulated. Trace such maxims to their roots, and you find they inevitably lead you down to psychological principles. And only when the artist rationally understands these psychological principles and their various corollaries, can he work in harmony with them.

We do not for a moment believe that science will make an artist. While we contend that the leading laws both of objective and subjective phenomena must be understood by him, we by no means contend that knowledge of such laws will serve in place of natural perception. Not only the poet, but also the artist of every type, is born, not made. What we assert is, that innate faculty alone will not suffice; but must have the aid of organized knowledge. Intuition will do much, but it will not do all. Only when Genius is married to Science can the highest results be produced.

As we have above asserted, Science is necessary not only for the most successful production, but also for the full appreciation of the fine arts. In what consists the greater ability of a man than of a child to perceive the beauties of a picture; unless it is in his more extended knowledge of those truths in nature or life which the picture renders? How happens the cultivated gentleman to enjoy a fine poem so much more than a boor does; if it is not because his wider acquaintance with objects and actions enables him to see in the poem much that the boor cannot see? And if, as is here so obvious, there must be some familiarity with the things represented, before the representation can be appreciated; then the representation can be completely appreciated, only in proportion as the things represented are completely understood. The fact is, that every additional truth which a work of art expresses, gives an additional pleasure to the percipient mind—a pleasure that is missed by those ignorant of this truth. The more realities an artist indicates in any given amount of work, the more faculties does he appeal to; the more numerous associated ideas does he suggest; the more gratification does he afford. But to receive this gratification the spectator, listener, or reader, must know the realities which the artist has indicated; and to know these realities is to know so much science.

And now let us not overlook the further great fact, that not only does science underlie sculpture, painting, music, poetry, but that science is itself poetic. The current opinion that science and poetry are opposed is a delusion. It is doubtless true that as states of consciousness, cognition and emotion tend to exclude each other. And it is doubtless also true that an extreme activity of the reflective powers tends to deaden the feelings; while an extreme activity of the feelings tends to deaden the reflective powers: in which sense, indeed, all orders of activity are antagonistic to each other. But it is not true that the facts of science are unpoetical; or that the cultivation of science is necessarily unfriendly to the exercise of imagination or the love of the beautiful. On the contrary science opens up realms of poetry where to the unscientific all is a blank. Those engaged in scientific researches constantly show us that they realize not less vividly, but more vividly, than others, the poetry of their subjects. Whoever will dip into Hugh Miller's works on geology, or read Mr. Lewes's "Seaside Studies," will perceive that science excites poetry rather than extinguishes it. And whoever will contemplate the life of Goethe will see that the poet and the man of science can co-exist in equal activity. Is it not, indeed, an absurd and almost a sacrilegious belief that the more a man studies Nature the less he reveres it? Think you that a drop of water, which to the vulgar eye is but a drop of water, loses anything in the eye of the physicist who knows that its elements are held together by a force which, if suddenly liberated, would produce a flash of lightning? Think you that what is carelessly looked upon by the uninitiated as a mere snow-flake, does not suggest higher associations to one who has seen through a microscope the wondrously varied and elegant forms of snow-crystals? Think you that the rounded rock marked with parallel scratches calls up as much poetry in an ignorant mind as in the mind of a geologist, who knows that over this rock a glacier slid a million years ago? The truth is, that those who have never entered upon scientific pursuits know not a tithe of the poetry by which they are surrounded. Whoever has not in youth collected plants and insects, knows not half the halo of interest which lanes and hedge-rows can assume. Whoever has not sought for fossils, has little idea of the poetical associations that surround the places where imbedded treasures were found. Whoever at the seaside has not had a microscope and aquarium, has yet to learn what the highest pleasures of the seaside are. Sad, indeed, is it to see how men occupy themselves with trivialities, and are indifferent to the grandest phenomena—care not to understand the architecture of the Heavens, but are deeply interested in some contemptible controversy about the intrigues of Mary Queen of Scots!—are learnedly critical over a Gceek ode, and pass by without a glance that grand epic written by the finger of God upon the strata of the Earth!

We find, then, that even for this remaining division of human activities, scientific culture is the proper preparation. We find that aesthetics in general are necessarily based upon scientific principles; and can be pursued with complete success only through an acquaintance with these principles. We find that for the criticism and due appreciation of works of art, a knowledge of the constitution of things, or in other words, a knowledge of science, is requisite. And we not only find that science is the handmaid to all forms of art and poetry, but that rightly regarded, science is itself poetic.

Thus far our question has been, the worth of knowledge of this or that kind for purposes of guidance. We have now to judge the relative values of different kinds of knowledge for purposes of discipline. This division of our subject we are obliged to treat with comparative brevity; and happily, no very lengthened treatment of it is needed. Having found what is best for the one end, we have by implication found what is best for the other. We may be quite sure that the acquirement of those classes of facts which are most useful for regulating conduct, involves a mental exercise best fitted for strengthening the faculties. It would be utterly contrary to the beautiful economy of Nature, of one kind of culture were needed for the gaining of information and another kind were needed as a mental gymnastic. Everywhere throughout creation we find faculties developed through the performance of those functions which it is their office to perform; not through the performance of artificial exercises devised to fit them for these functions. The Red Indian acquired the swiftness and agility which make him a successful hunter, by the actual pursuit of animals; and by the miscellaneous activities of his life, he gains a better balancè of physical powers than gymnastics ever give. That skill in tracking enemies and prey which he has reached by long practice, implies a subtlety of perception far exceeding anything produced by artificial training. And similarly throughout. From the Bushman, whose eye, which being habitually employed in identifying distant objects that are to be pursued or fled from, has acquired a quite telescopic range, to the accountant whose daily practice enables him to add up several columns of figures simultaneously, we find that the highest power of a faculty results from the discharge of those duties which the conditions of life require it to discharge. And we may be certain, á priori, that the same law holds throughout education. The education of most value for guidance, must at the same time be the education of most value for discipline. Let us consider the evidence.

One advantage claimed for that devotion to language-learning which forms so prominent a feature in the ordinary curriculum, is, that the memory is thereby strengthened. And it is apparently assumed that this is an advantage peculiar to the study of words. But the truth is, that the sciences afford far wider fields for the exercise of memory. It is no slight task to remember all the facts ascertained respecting our solar system; much more to remember all that is known concerning the structure of our galaxy. The new compounds which chemistry daily accumulates, are so numerous that few, save professors, know the names of them all; and to recollect the atomic constitutions and affinities of all these compounds, is scarcely possible without making chemistry the occupation of life. In the enormous mass of phenomena presented by the Earth's crust, and in the still more enormous mass of phenomena presented by the fossils it contains, there is matter which it takes the geological student years of application to master. In each leading division of physics—sound, heat, light, electricity—the facts are numerous enough to alarm any one proposing to learn them all. And when we pass to the organic sciences, the effort of memory required becomes still greater. In human anatomy alone, the quantity of detail is so great, that the young surgeon has commonly to get it up half-a-dozen times before he can permanently retain it. The number species of plants which botanists distinguish, amounts to some 320,000; while the varied forms of animal life with which the zoologist deals, are estimated at some two million. So vast is the accumulation of facts which men of science have before them, that only by dividing and subdividing their labours can they deal with it. To a complete knowledge of his own division, each adds but a general knowledge of the rest. Surely, then, science, cultivated even to a very moderate extent, affords adequate exercise for memory. To say the very least, it involves quite as good a training for this faculty as language does.

But now mark that while for the training of mere memory, science is as good as, if not better than, language; it has an immense superiority in the kind of memory it cultivates. In the acquirement of language, the connexions of ideas to be established in the mind correspond to facts that are in great measure accidental; whereas, in the acquirement of science, the connexions of ideas to be established in the mind correspond to facts that are mostly necessary. It is true that the relations of words to their meaning is in one sense natural, and that the genesis of these relations may be traced back a certain distance; though very rarely to the beginning; (to which let us add the remark that the laws of this genesis form a branch of mental science—the science of philology.) But since it will not be contended that in the acquisition of languages, as ordinarily carried on, these natural relations between words and their meanings are habitually traced, and the laws regulating them explained; it must be admitted that they are commonly learned as fortuitous relations. On the other hand, the relations which science presents are causal relations; and, when properly taught, are understood as such. Instead of being practically accidental, they are necessary; and as such, give exercise to the reasoning faculties. While language familiarizes with non-rational relations, science familiarizes with rational relations. While the one exercises memory only, the other exercises both memory and understanding.

Observe next that a great superiority of science over language as a means of discipline, is, that it cultivates the judgment. As, in a lecture on mental education delivered at the Royal Institution, Professor Faraday well remarks, the most common intellectual fault is deficiency of judgment. He contends that "society, speaking generally, is not only ignorant as respects education of the judgment, but it is also ignorant of its ignorance." And the cause to which he ascribes this state is want of scientific culture. The truth of his conclusion is obvious. Correct judgment with regard to all surrounding things, events, and consequences, becomes possible only through knowledge of the way in which surrounding phenomena depend on each other. No extent of acquaintance with the meanings of words, can give the power of forming correct inferences respecting causes and effects. The constant habit of drawing conclusions from data, and then of verifying those conclusions by observation and experiment, can alone give the power of judging correctly. And that it necessitates this habit is one of the immense advantages of science.

Not only, however, for intellectual discipline is science the best; but also for moral discipline. The learning of languages tends, if anything, further to increase the already undue respect for authority. Such and such are the meanings of these words, says the teacher or the dictionary. So and so is the rule in this case, says the grammar. By the pupil these dicta are received as unquestionable. His constant attitude of mind is that of submission to dogmatic teaching. And a necessary result is a tendency to accept without inquiry whatever is established. Quite opposite is the attitude of mind generated by the cultivation of science. By science, constant appeal is made to individual reason. Its truths are not accepted upon authority alone; but all are at liberty to test them—nay, in many cases, the pupil is required to think out his own conclusions. Every step in a scientific investigation is submitted to his judgment. He is not asked to admit it without seeing it to be true. And the trust in his own powers thus produced, is further increased by the constancy with which Nature justifies his conclusions when they are correctly drawn. From all which flows that independence which is a most valuable element in character. Nor is this the only moral benefit bequeathed by scientific culture. When carried on, as it should always be, as much as possible under the form of independent research, it exercises perseverance and sincerity. As says Professor Tyndall of inductive inquiry, "it requires patient industry, and an humble and conscientious acceptance of what Nature reveals. The first condition of success is an honest receptivity and a willingness to abandon all preconceived notions, however cherished, if they be found to contradict the truth. Believe me, a self renunciation which has something noble in it, and of which the world never hears, is often enacted in the private experience of the true votary of science."

Lastly we have to assert—and the assertion will, we doubt not, cause extreme surprise—that the discipline of science is superior to that of our ordinary education, because of the *religious* culture that it gives. Of course we do not here use the words scientific and religious in their ordinary limited acceptations; but in their widest and highest acceptations. Doubtless, to the superstitions that pass under the name of religion, science is antagonistic; but not to the essential religion which these superstitions merely hide. Doubtless, too, in much of the science that is current, there is a pervading spirit of irreligion; but not in that true science which has passed beyond the superficial into the profound.

"True science and true religion," says Professor Huxley at the close of a recent course of lectures, "are twin-sisters, and

the separation of either from the other is sure to prove the
death of both. Science prospers exactly in proportion as it is
religious; and religion flourishes in exact proportion to the
scientific depth and firmness of its basis. The great deeds of
philosophers have been less the fruit of their intellect than of
the direction of that intellect by an eminently religious tone
of mind. Truth has yielded herself rather to their patience,
their love, their single-heartedness, and their self-denial, than
to their logical acumen."

So far from science being irreligious, as many think, it is the
neglect of science that is irreligious—it is the refusal to study the
surrounding creation that is irreligious. Take a humble simile. Suppose
a writer were daily saluted with praises couched in superlative language.
Suppose the wisdom, the grandeur, the beauty of his works, were the
constant topic of the eulogies addressed to him. Suppose those who
unceasingly uttered these eulogies on his works were content with
looking at the outsides of them; and had never opened them, much
less tried to understand them. What value should we put upon their
praises? What should we think of their sincerity? Yet comparing small
things to great, such is the conduct of mankind in general, in reference
to the Universe and its Cause. Nay, it is worse. Not only do they
pass by without study, these things which they daily proclaim to be
so wonderful; but very frequently they condemn as mere triflers those
who give time to the observation of Nature—they actually scorn those
who show any active interest in these marvels. We repeat, then, that not
science, but the neglect of science, is irreligious. Devotion to science,
is a tacit worship—a tacit recognition of worth in the things studied;
and by implication in their Cause. It is not a mere lip-homage, but a
homage expressed in actions—not a mere professed respect, but a
respect proved by the sacrifice of time, thought, and labour.

Nor is it thus only that true science is essentially religious. It is
religious, too, inasmuch as it generates a profound respect for, and an
implicit faith in, those uniform laws which underlie all things. By
accumulated experiences the man of science acquires a thorough belief
in the unchanging relations of phenomena—in the invariable connexion of cause and consequence—in the necessity of good or evil
results. Instead of the rewards and punishments of traditional belief,
which men vaguely hope they may gain, or escape, spite of their disobedience; he finds that there are rewards and punishments in the
ordained constitution of things, and that the evil results of disobedience
are inevitable. He sees that the laws to which we must submit are not
only inexorable but beneficent. He sees that in virtue of thase laws, the

process of things is ever towards a greater perfection and a higher happiness. Hence he is led constantly to insist on these laws, and is indignant when men disregard them. And thus does he, by asserting the eternal principles of things and the necessity of conforming to them, prove himself intrinsically religious.

To all which add the further religious aspect of science, that it alone can give us true conceptions of ourselves and our relation to the mysteries of existence. At the same time that it shows us all which can be known, it shows us the limits beyond which we can know nothing. Not by dogmatic assertion does it teach the impossibility of comprehending the ultimate cause of things; but it leads us clearly to recognise this impossibility by bringing us in every direction to boundaries we cannot cross. It realizes to us in a way which nothing else can, the littleness of human intelligence in the face of that which transcends human intelligence. While towards the traditions and authorities of men its attitude may be proud, before the impenetrable veil which hides the Absolute its attitude is humble—a true pride and a true humility. Only the sincere man of science (and by this title we do not mean the mere calculator of distances, or analyser of compounds, or labeller of species; but him who through lower truths seeks higher, and eventually the Highest)—only the genuine man of science, we say, can truly know how utterly beyond, not only human knowledge, but human conception, is the Universal Power of which Nature, and Life, and Thought are manifestations.

We conclude, then, that for discipline, as well as for guidance, science is of chiefest value. In all its effects, learning the meanings of things, is better than learning the meanings of words. Whether for intellectual, moral, or religious training, the study of surrounding phenomena is immensely superior to the study of grammars and lexicons.

Thus to the question with which we set out—What knowledge is of most worth?—the uniform reply is—Science. This is the verdict on all the counts. For direct self-preservation, or the maintenance of life and health, the all-important knowledge is—Science. For that indirect self-preservation which we call gaining a livelihood, the knowledge of greatest value is—Science. For the due discharge of parental functions, the proper guidance is to be found only in—Science. For that interpretation of national life, past and present, without which the citizen cannot rightly regulate his conduct, the indispensable key is—Science. Alike for the most perfect production and highest enjoyment of art in all its forms, the needful preparation is still—Science. And for purposes of discipline—intellectual, moral, religious—the most efficient study is, once more—Science. The question which at first seemed so perplexed, has become, in the course of our inquiry, comparatively simple. We have not to estimate the degrees of importance of different orders of human activity, and different studies as severally fitting us for them; since we find that the study of Science, in its most comprehensive meaning, is the best preparation for all these orders of activity. We have not to decide between the claims of knowledge of great though conventional value, and knowledge of less though intrinsic value; seeing that the knowledge which we find to be of most value in all other respects, is intrinsically most valuable: its worth is not dependent upon opinion, but is as fixed as is the relation of man to the surrounding world. Necessary and eternal as are its truths, all Science concerns all mankind for all time. Equally at present, and in the remotest future, must it be of incalculable importance for the regulation of their conduct, that men should understand the science of life, physical, mental, and social; and that they should understand all other science as a key to the science of life.

And yet the knowledge which is of such transcendent value is that which, in our age of boasted education, receives the least attention. While this which we call civilization could never have arisen had it not been for science; science forms scarcely an appreciable element in what men consider civilized training. Though to the progress of science we owe it, that millions find support where once there was food only for thousands; yet of these millions but a few thousands pay any respect to that which has made their existence possible. Though this increasing knowledge of the properties and relations of things has not only enabled wandering tribes to grow into populous nations, but has given to the countless members of those populous nations comforts and pleasures which their few naked ancestors never even conceived, or could have believed, yet is this kind of knowledge only now receiving a grudging recognition in our highest educational institutions. To the slowly growing acquaintance with the uniform co-existences and sequences of phenomena—to the establishment of invariable laws, we owe our emancipation from the grossest superstitions. But for science we should be still worshipping fetishes; or, with hecatombs of victims, propitiating diabolical deities. And yet this science, which, in place of the most degrading conceptions of things, has given us some insight into the grandeurs of creation, is written against in our theologies and frowned upon from our pulpits.

Paraphrasing an Eastern fable, we may say that in the family of knowledges, Science is the household drudge, who, in obscurity, hides unrecognised perfections. To her has been committed all the work; by her skill, intelligence, and devotion, have all the conveniences and gratifications been obtained; and while ceaselessly occupied ministering to the rest, she has been kept in the background, that her haughty sisters might flaunt their fripperies in the eyes of the world. The parallel holds yet further. For we are fast coming to the *dénouement*, when the positions will be changed; and while these haughty sisters sink into merited neglect, Science, proclaimed as highest alike in worth and beauty, will reign supreme.

49
Horace Mann (1796-1859)

Horace Mann, *The Massachusetts System of Common Schools; Being an Enlarged and Revised Edition of the Tenth Annual Report of the First Secretary of the Massachusetts Board of Education* [Dec. 3, 1846] (No. 37 Congress Street, Boston: Dutton and Wentworth, State Printers, 1849), pp. 7-32.

The Pilgrim Fathers who colonized Massachusetts Bay made a bolder innovation upon all pre-existing policy and usages than the world had ever known since the commencement of the Christian era. They adopted special and costly means to train up the whole body of the people to industry, to intelligence, to virtue, and to independent thought. The first entry in the public record-book of the town of Boston bears the date, "1634, 7th month, day 1." The records of the public meetings for the residue of that year pertain to those obvious necessities that claimed the immediate attention of an infant settlement. But in the transactions of a public meeting, held on the 13th day of April, 1635, the following entry is found: "Likewise it was then generally agreed upon that our brother Philemon Purmont [or Purment] shall be entreated to become scholemaster for the teaching and nourtering of children with us." Mr. Purmont was not expected to render his services gratuitously. Doubtless he received fees from parents; but the same records show that a tract of thirty acres of land, at "Muddy River," was assigned to him; and this grant, two years afterwards, was publicly confirmed. About the same time, an assignment was made of a "garden plott to Mr. Daniel Maude, schoolemaster, upon the condition of building thereon, if neede be." From this time forward, these golden threads are thickly inwoven in the texture of all the public records of Boston.

It is not unworthy of remark, that a word of beautiful significance, which is found in the first record on the subject of schools ever made on this continent, has now fallen wholly out of use. Mr. Purmont was entreated to become a "scholemaster," not merely for the "teaching," but for the "nourtering" of children. If, as is supposed, this word, now obsolete in this connection, implied the disposition and the power, on the part of the teacher, as far as such an object can be accomplished by human instrumentality, to warm into birth, to foster into strength, and to advance into precedence and predominance, all kindly sympathies towards men, all elevated thoughts respecting the duties and the destiny of life, and a supreme reverence for the character and attributes of the Creator, then how many teachers have since been employed, who have not nourished the children committed to their care!

In 1642, the General Court of the colony, by a public act, enjoined upon the municipal authorites the duty of seeing that *every child*, within their respective jurisdictions, should be educated. Nor was the education which they contemplated either narrow or superficial. By the terms of the act, the selectmen of every town were required to "have a vigilant eye over their brethren and neighbors,—to see first that none of them shall suffer so much barbarism in any of their families, as not to endeavor to teach, by themselves or others, their children and apprentices, so much learning as may enable them perfectly to read the English tongue, and [obtain a] knowledge of the capital laws; upon penalty of twenty shillings for each neglect therein."

Such was the idea of "barbarism," entertained by the colonists of Massachusetts Bay more than two centuries ago. Tried by this standard, even at the present day, the regions of civilization became exceedingly narrow; and many a man, who now blindly glories in the name and in the prerogatives of a republican citizen, would, according to the better ideas of the Pilgrim Fathers, be known only as the "barbarian" father of "barbarian" children.

The same act further required that religious instruction should be given to all children; and also, "that all parents and masters do breed and bring up their children and apprentices in some honest, lawful calling, labor, or employment, either in husbandry or some other trade, profitable for themselves and the Commonwealth; if they will not or cannot train them up in learning to fit them for higher employments."

Thus were recognized and embodied, in a public statute, the highest principles of Political Economy and of social well-being;—the universal education of children, and the prevention of drones or non-producers among men.

By the same statute, the selectmen and magistrates were empowered to take children and servants from the custody of those parents and masters, who, "after admonition," "were still negligent of their duty in the particulars above mentioned," and to bind them out to such masters as they should deem worthy to supply the place of the unnatural parent,—boys until the age of twenty-one, and girls until that of eighteen.

The law of 1642 enjoined universal education; but it did not make education *free*, nor did it impose any penalty upon municipal corporations for neglecting to maintain a school. The spirit of the law, however, worked energetically in the hearts of the people; for in Governor Winthrop's Journal (History of New England, vol. 2, p. 215, Savage's edition,) under date of 1645, we find the following: "Divers free schools were erected, as at Roxbury, (for maintenance whereof every inhabitant bound some house or land for a yearly allowance forever,) and at Boston, where they made an order to allow fifty pounds to the master of an house, and thirty pounds to an usher, who should also teach to read and write and cipher, and Indians' children were to be taught freely, and the charge to be by yearly contribution, either by voluntary allowance, or by rate of such as refused, &c., and this order was confirmed by the General Court. Other towns did the like, providing maintenance by several means."

It is probable, however, that some towns, owing to the sparseness of their population and the scantiness of their resources, found all the moneys in their treasury too little to pay the salary of a master; and surrounded by dangers, as they were, from the ferocity of the aborigines and the inclemency of the climate, believed that not an eye could be spared from watching nor a hand from labor, even for so sacred a purpose as that of instruction; and therefore failed to sustain a school for the teaching and "nourtering" of their children. But, in all these privations and disabilities, the government of the colony saw no adequate excuse for neglecting the one thing needful. They saw and felt, that, if "learning were to be buried in the graves of their forefathers, in Church and Commonwealth," then they had escaped from the house of bondage and swam an ocean and braved the terrors of the wilderness, in vain. In the year 1647, therefore, a law was passed making the support of schools compulsory, and education both universal and *Free*.

By this law, every town, containing fifty householders, was required to appoint a teacher, "to teach all such children as shall resort to him to write and read;" and every town, containing one hundred families or householders, was required to "set up a grammar school," whose master should be "able to instruct youth so far as they may be fitted for the university."

The penalty for non-compliance with the above requirements was five pounds per annum. In 1671, the penalty was increased to ten pounds per annum; in 1683, to twenty pounds; and, in 1718, to thirty pounds, for every town containing one hundred and fifty families; and so on, *pro rate*, for towns containing two hundred and fifty or three hundred families. The penalty was increased, from time to time, to correspond with the increasing wealth of the towns. All forfeitures were appropriated to the maintenance of Public Schools.

It is common to say that the act of 1647 *laid the foundation* of our present system of Free Schools. But the truth is, it not only laid the foundation of the present system, but, in some particulars, it laid a far broader foundation than has since been built upon, and reared a far higher superstructure than has since been sustained. Modern times have witnessed great improvements in the methods of instruction and in the motives of discipline; but, in some respects, the ancient foundation has been narrowed, and the ancient superstructure lowered. The term "grammar school," in the old laws, always meant a school where the ancient languages were taught, and where youth could be "fitted for the university." Every town, containing one hundred families or householders, was required to keep such a school. Were such a law in force at the present time, there are not more than twelve towns in the Commonwealth which would be exempt from its requisitions. But the term "grammar school" has wholly lost its original meaning; and the number of towns and cities which are now required by law to maintain a school where the Greek and Latin languages are taught, and where youth can be fitted for college, does not exceed thirty. The contrast between our ancestors and ourselves, in this respect, is most humiliating. Their meanness in wealth was more than compensated by their grandeur of soul.

The institution of a Free School system, on so broad a basis and of such ample proportions, appears still more remarkable, when we consider the period in the world's history, at which it was originated, and the fewness and poverty of the people by whom it was maintained. In 1647, the entire population of the colony of Massachusetts Bay is supposed to have amounted only to twenty-one thousand souls. The scattered and feeble settlements were almost buried in the depths of the forest. The external resources of the people were small, their dwellings humble, and their raiment and subsistence scanty and homely. They had no enriching commerce, and the wonderful forces of nature had not then, as now, become gratuitous producers of every human comfort and luxury. The whole valuation of all the colonial estates, both public and private, would hardly have been equal to the inventory of many a private citizen of the present day. The fierce eye of the savage was nightly seen glaring from the edge of the surrounding wilderness, and no defence or succor, save in their own brave natures, was at hand. Yet it was then, amid all these privations and dangers, that the Pilgrim Fathers conceived the magnificent idea, not only of a Universal, but of a Free education for the whole people. To find the time and the means to reduce this grand conception to practice, they stinted themselves, amid all their poverty, to a still scantier pittance; amid all their toils, they imposed upon themselves still more burdensome labors; and, amid all their perils, they braved still greater dangers. Two divine ideas filled their great hearts,—their duty to God and to posterity. For the one, they built the church; for the other, they opened the school. Religion and Knowledge!—two attributes of the same glorious and eternal truth, and that truth the only one on which immortal or mortal happiness can be securely founded!

It is impossible for us adequately to conceive the boldness of the

measure which aimed at universal education through the establishment
of Free Schools. As a fact, it had no precedent in the world's history;
and, as a theory, it could have been refuted and silenced by a more
formidable array of argument and experience than was ever marshalled
against any other institution of human origin. But time has ratified its
soundness. Two centuries of successful operation now proclaim it
to be as wise as it was courageous, and as beneficent as it was disinterested. Every community in the civilized world awards it the meed
of praise; and states at home, and nations abroad, in the order of their
intelligence, are copying the bright example. What we call the enlightened
nations of Christendom, are approaching, by slow degrees, to the moral
elevation which our ancestors reached at a single bound; and the
tardy convictions of the one, have been assimilating, through a period
of two centuries, to the intuitions of the other.

The establishment of Free Schools was one of those grand mental
and moral experiments whose effects could not be developed and made
manifest in a single generation. But now, according to the manner in
which human life is computed, we are the sixth generation from its
founders; and have we not reason to be grateful, both to God and man,
for its unnumbered blessings! The sincerity of our gratitude must be
tested by our efforts to perpetuate and to improve what they established.
The gratitude of the lips only is an unholy offering.

In surveying our vast country,—the rich savannas of the south
and the almost interminable prairies of the west,—that great valley,
where, if all the nations of Europe were set down together, they could
find ample subsistence,—the ejaculation involuntarily bursts forth,
"Why were they not colonized by men like the Pilgrim Fathers?"—and
as we reflect, how different would have been the fortunes of this
nation, had those states,—already so numerous, and still extending,
circle beyond circle,—been founded by men of high, heroic, puritan
mould; how different in the eye of a righteous Heaven, how different
in the estimation of the wise and good of all contemporary nations, how
different in the fortunes of that vast procession of the generations
which are yet to rise up over all those wide expanses, and to follow
each other to the end of time;—as we reflect upon these things, it
seems almost pious to repine at the ways of Providence; resignation
becomes laborious, and we are forced to choke down our murmurings
at the will of Heaven! Is it the solution of this deep mystery, that our
ancestors did as much in their time, as it is ever given to one generation
of men to accomplish, and have left to us and to our descendants the
completion of the glorious work they began?

The alleged ground upon which the founders of our Free School
system proceeded, when adopting it, did not embrace the whole

argument by which it may be defended and sustained. Their insight was better than their reason. They assumed a ground, indeed, satisfactory and convincing to Protestants; but, at that time, only a small portion of Christendom was Protestant, and even now only a minority of it is so. The very ground on which our Free Schools were founded, therefore, if it were the only one, would have been a reason, with more than half of Christendom, for their immediate abolition.

In later times, and since the achievement of American independence, the universal and ever-repeated argument in favor of Free Schools has been, that the general intelligence which they are capable of diffusing, and which can be imparted by no other human instrumentality, is indispensable to the continuance of a republican government. This argument, it is obvious, assumes, as a *postulatum*, the superiority of a republican over all other forms of government; and, as a people, we religiously believe in the soundness, both of the assumption and of the argument founded upon it. But if this be all, then a sincere monarchist, or a defender of arbitrary power, or a believer in the divine right of kings, would oppose Free Schools, for the identical reasons we offer in their behalf. A perfect demonstration of our doctrine,—that Free Schools are the only basis of republican institutions,—would be the perfection of proof, to his mind, that they should be immediately exterminated.

Admitting, nay, claiming for ourselves, the substantial justness and soundness of the general grounds on which our system was originally established and has since been maintained, yet it is most obvious that, unless some broader and more comprehensive principle can be found, the system of Free Schools will be repudiated by whole nations as impolitic and dangerous; and, even among ourselves, all who deny our premises will, of course, set at nought the conclusions to which they lead.

Again; the expediency of Free Schools is sometimes advocated on grounds of Political Economy. An educated people is always a more industrious and productive people. Knowledge and Abundance sustain to each other the relation of cause and effect. Intelligence is a primary ingredient in the Wealth of Nations. Where this does not stand at the head of the inventory, the items in a nation's valuation will be few, and the sum at the foot of the column insignificant.

The moralist, too, takes up the argument of the economist. He demonstrates that vice and crime are not only prodigals and spendthrifts of their own, but defrauders and plunderers of the means of others; that they would seize upon all the gains of honest industry, and exhaust the bounties of Heaven itself, without satiating their rapacity for new means of indulgence; and that often, in the history of the world, whole generations might have been trained to industry and virtue by the wealth which one enemy to his race has destroyed.

And yet, notwithstanding these views have been presented a thousand times, with irrefutable logic, and with a divine eloquence of truth which it would seem that nothing but combined stolidity and depravity could resist, there is not at the present time, with the exception of the states of New England and a few small communities elsewhere, a country or state in Christendom, which maintains a system of Free Schools for the education of its children. Even in the state of New York, with all its noble endowments, the Schools are not Free.*

I believe that this amazing dereliction from duty, especially in our own country, originates more in the false notions which men entertain *respecting the nature of their right to property* than in any thing else. In the district school meeting, in the town meetings, in legislative halls, every where, the advocates for a more generous education could carry their respective audiences with them in behalf of increased privileges for our children, were it not instinctively foreseen that increased privileges must be followed by increased taxation. Against this obstacle, argument falls dead. The rich man, who has no children, declares that the exaction of a contribution from him, to educate the children of his neighbor, is an invasion of his rights of property. The man who has reared and educated a family of children denounces it as a double tax, when he is called upon to assist in educating the children of others also; or, if he has reared his own children without educating them, he thinks it peculiarly oppressive to be obliged to do for others what he refrained from doing even for himself. Another, having children, but disdaining to educate them with the common mass, withdraws them from the Public School, puts them under what he calls "selecter influences," and then thinks it a grievance to be obliged to support a school which he contemns. Or, if these different parties so far yield to the force of traditionary sentiment and usage, and to the public opinion around them, as to consent to do something for the cause, they soon reach the limit of expense at which their admitted obligation, or their alleged charity, terminates.

It seems not irrelevant, therefore, in this connection, and for the purpose of strengthening the foundation on which our Free School system reposes, to inquire into the nature of a man's right to the property he possesses; and to satisfy ourselves respecting the question, whether any man has such an indefeasible title to his estates, or such

---

* By an act of the New York Legislature, passed at its last session, the question, whether Free Schools shall be established throughout the state, is to be submitted to the decision of the people, to be determined by ballot, at their primary meetings, during the current year.

an absolute ownership of them, as renders it unjust in the government to assess upon him his share of the expenses of educating the children of the community, up to such a point as the nature of the institutions under which he lives, and the well-being of society, require.

I believe in the existence of a great, immortal, immutable principle of Natural Law, or Natural Ethics,—a principle antecedent to all human institutions, and incapable of being abrogated by any ordinances of man,—a principle of divine origin, clearly legible in the ways of Providence as those ways are manifested in the order of nature and in the history of the race,—which proves the *absolute right* to an education of every human being that comes into the world; and which, of course, proves the correlative duty of every government to see that the means of that education are provided for all.

In regard to the application of this principle of natural law,—that is, in regard to the extent of the education to be provided for all, at the public expense,—some differences of opinion may fairly exist, under different political organizations; but under our republican government, it seems clear that the minimum of this education can never be less than such as is sufficient to qualify each citizen for the civil and social duties he will be called to discharge;—such an education as teaches the individual the great laws of bodily health, as qualifies for the fulfilment of parental duties; as is indispensable for the civil functions of a witness or a juror; as is necessary for the voter in municipal and in national affairs; and finally, as is requisite for the faithful and conscientious discharge of all those duties which devolve upon the inheritor of a portion of the sovreignty of this great republic.

The will of God, as conspicuously manifested in the order of nature, and in the relations which he has established among men, founds the *right* of every child that is born into the world, to such a degree of education as will enable him, and, as far as possible, will predispose him, to perform all domestic, social, civil, and moral duties, upon the same clear ground of natural law and equity as it places a child's *right*, upon his first coming into the world, to distend his lungs with a portion of the common air, or to open his eyes to the common light, or to receive that shelter, protection, and nourishment, which are necessary to the continuance of his bodily existence. And so far is it from being a wrong or a hardship to demand of the possessors of property their respective shares for the prosecution of this divinely-ordained work, that they themselves are guilty of the most far-reaching injustice, when they seek to resist or to evade the contribution. The complainers are the wrong-doers. The cry, "Stop thief," comes from the thief himself.

To any one who looks beyond the mere surface of things, it is obvious that the primary and natural elements or ingredients of all property consist in the riches of the soil, in the treasures of the sea, in the light and warmth of the sun, in the fertilizing clouds, and streams, and dews, in the winds, and in the chemical and vegetative agencies of nature. In the majority of cases, all that we call *property*, all that makes up the valuation or inventory of a nation's capital, was prepared at the creation, and was laid up of old in the capacious store-houses of nature. For every unit that a man earns by his own toil or skill, he receives hundreds and thousands, without cost and without recompense, from the All-bountiful Giver. A proud mortal, standing in the midst of his luxuriant wheat-fields or cotton-plantation, may arrogantly call them his own; yet what barren wastes would they be, did not Heaven send down upon them its dews and its rains, its warmth and its light, and sustain, for their growth and ripening, the grateful vicissitude of the seasons! It is said that from eighty to ninety per cent of the very substance of some of the great staples of agriculture are not taken from the earth, but are absorbed from the air; so that these productions may more properly be called fruits of the atmosphere than of the soil. Who prepares this elemental wealth? Who scatters it, like a sower, through all the regions of the atmosphere, and sends the richly-freighted winds, as His messengers, to bear to each leaf in the forest, and to each blade in the cultivated field, the nourishment which their infinitely varied needs demand? Aided by machinery, a single manufacturer performs the labor of hundreds of men. Yet what could he accomplish without the weight of the waters which God causes ceaselessly to flow? or without those gigantic forces which He has given to steam? And how would the commerce of the world be carried on, were it not for those great laws of nature,—of electricity, of condensation, and of rarefaction,—that give birth to the winds, which, in conformity to the will of Heaven, and not in obedience to any power of man, forever traverse the earth, and offer themselves as an uncharted medium for interchanging the products of all the zones? These few references show how vast a proportion of all the wealth which men presumptuously call their own, because they claim to have earned it, is poured into their lap, unasked and unthanked for, by the Being so infinitely gracious in his physical as well as in his moral bestowments.

But for whose subsistence and benefit were these exhaustless treasuries of wealth created? Surely not for any one man, nor for any one generation; but for the subsistence and benefit of the whole race, from the beginning to the end of time. They were not created for Adam alone, nor for Noah alone, nor for the first discoverers or colonists who may have found or have peopled any part of the earth's ample domain. No! They were created for the race, collectively, but to be possessed and enjoyed in succession, as the generations, one after another, should come into existence;—equal rights, with a successive enjoyment of them! If we consider the earth and the fulness thereof as one great habitation or domain, then each generation, subject to certain modifications for the encouragement of industry and frugality,—which modifications it is not necessary here to specify,—has only a life-lease in them. There are certain reasonable regulations, indeed, in regard to the out-going and the in-coming tenants,—regulations which allow to the out-going generations a brief control over their property after they are called upon to leave it, and which also allow the in-coming generations to anticipate a little their full right of possession. But, subject to these regulations, nature ordains a perpetual entail and transfer, from one generation to another, of all property in the great, substantive, enduring elements of wealth;—in the soil; in metals and minerals; in precious stones, and in more precious coal, and iron, and granite; in the waters, and winds, and sun;—and no one man, nor any one generation of men, has any such title to, or ownership in, these ingredients and substantials of all wealth, that his right is invaded when a portion of them is taken for the benefit of posterity.

This great principle of natural law may be illustrated by a reference to some of the unstable elements, in regard to which each individual's right of *property* is strongly qualified in relation to his contemporaries, even while he has the acknowledged right of *possession*. Take the streams of water, or the wind, for an example. A stream, as it descends from its sources to its mouth, is successively the property of all those through whose land it passes. My neighbor, who lives above me, owned it yesterday, while it was passing through his lands; I own it today, while it is descending through mine, and the contiguous proprietor below will own it to-morrow, while it is flowing through his, as it passes onward to the next. But the rights of these successive owners are not absolute and unqualified. They are limited by the rights of those who are entitled to the subsequent possession and use. While a stream is passing through my lands, I may not corrupt it, so that it shall be offensive or valueless to the adjoining proprietor below. I may not stop it in its downward course, nor divert it into any other direction, so that it shall leave his channel dry. I may lawfully use it for various purposes,—for agriculture, as in irrigating lands or watering cattle; for manufactures, as in turning wheels, &c.;—but in all my uses of it, I must pay regard to the rights of my neighbors lower down. So no two proprietors, nor any half-dozen proprietors, by conspiring together, can deprive an owner who lives below them all, of the ultimate right which he has to the use of the stream in its descending course. We see here, therefore, that a man has certain qualified rights,—rights of which he cannot lawfully be divested without his own consent,—in a stream of water, before it reaches the limits of his own estate;—at which latter point, he may, somewhat more emphatically, call it his own. And in this sense, a man who lives at the outlet of a river, on the margin of the ocean, has certain incipient rights in those fountain-sources that well up from the earth at the distance of thousands of miles.

So it is with the ever-moving winds. No man has a *permanent* interest in the breezes that blow by him, and bring healing and refreshment on their wings. Each man has a temporary interest in them. From whatever quarter of the compass they may come, I have a right to use them as they are passing by me; yet that use must always be regulated by the rights of those other participants and co-owners whom they are moving forward to bless. It is not lawful, therefore, for me to corrupt them,—to load them with noxious gases or vapors, by which they will prove valueless or detrimental to him, whoever he may be, towards whom they are moving.

In one respect, indeed, the winds illustrate our relative rights and duties, even better than the streams. In the latter case, the rights are not only successive, but always in the same order of priority,—those of the owner above necessarily preceding those of the owner below; and this order is unchangeable, except by changing the ownership of the land itself to which the rights are appurtenant. In the case of the winds, however, which blow from every quarter of the heavens, I may have the prior right to-day, but, with a change in their direction, my neighbor may have it to-morrow. If, therefore, to-day, when the wind is going from me to him, I should usurp the right to use it to his detriment, to-morrow, when it is coming from him to me, he may inflict retributive usurpation upon me.

The light of the sun, too, is subject to the same benign and equitable regulations. As the waves of this ethereal element pass by me, I have a right to bask in their genial warmth, or to employ their quickening powers. But I have no right, even on my own land, to build up a wall, mountain-high, that shall eclipse the sun to my neighbor's eyes.

Now, all these great principles of natural law, which define and limit the rights of neighbors and contemporaries, are incorporated into, and constitute a part of, the civil law of every civilized people; and they are obvious and simple illustrations of the great proprietary laws by which individuals and generations hold their rights in the solid substance of the globe, in the elements that move over its surface, and in the chemical and vital powers with which it is so marvellously endued (sic). As successive owners on a river's banks have equal rights to the waters that flow through their respective domains, subject only to the modification that the proprietors nearer the stream's source must have precedence in the enjoyment of their rights over those lower down, so the rights of all the generations of mankind to the earth itself, to the streams that fertilize it, to the winds that purify it, to the vital principles that animate it, and to the reviving light, are common rights, though subject to similar modifications in regard to preceding and succeeding generations of men. They did not belong to our ancestors in perpetuity; they do not belong to us in perpetuity; and the right of the next generation in them will be limited and defeasible like ours. As we hold these rights subject to the claims of the next generation, so will they hold them subject to the claims of their immediate successors, and so on to the end of time. And the savage tribes that roam about the head-springs of the Mississippi, have as good a right to ordain what use shall be made of its copious waters, when, in their grand descent across a continent, they shall reach the shores of arts and civilization, as any of our predecessors had, or as we ourselves have, to say what shall be done, *in perpetuity*, with the soil, the waters, the winds, the light, and the invisible agencies of nature, which must be allowed, on all hands, to constitute the indispensable elements of wealth.

Is not the inference irresistible, then, that no man, by whatever means he may have come into possession of his property, has any natural right, any more than he has a moral one, to hold it, or to dispose of it, irrespective of the needs and claims of those, who, in the august procession of the generations, are to be his successors on the stage of existence? Holding his rights subject to their rights, he is bound not to impair the value of their inheritance, either by commission or by omission.

Generation after generation proceeds from the creative energy of God. Each one stops for a brief period upon the earth, resting, as it were, only for a night,—like migratory birds upon their passage,—and then leaving it forever, to others whose existence is as transitory as its own; and the migratory flocks of water-fowl, which sweep across our latitudes in their passage to another clime, have as good a right to make a perpetual appropriation, to their own use, of the lands over which they fly, as any one generation has to arrogate perpetual domination and sovereignty, for its own purposes, over that portion of the earth which it is its fortune to occupy during the brief period of its temporal existence.

Another consideration, bearing upon this arrogant doctrine of absolute ownership or sovereignty, has hardly less force than the one just expounded. We have seen how insignificant a portion of any man's possessions he can claim, in any proper and just sense, *to have earned*; and that, in regard to all the residue, he is only taking his turn in the use of a bounty bestowed, in common, by the Giver of all, upon his ancestors, upon himself, and upon his posterity,—a line of indefinite length, in which he is but a point. But this is not the only deduction to be made from his assumed rights. The *present* wealth of the world has an additional element in it. Much of all that is capable of being earned by man, has been earned by our predecessors, and has come down to us in a solid and enduring form. We have not erected all the houses in which we live; nor constructed all the roads on which we travel; nor built all the ships in which we carry on our commerce with the world. We have not reclaimed from the wilderness all the fields whose harvests we now reap; and if we had no precious metals, or stones, or pearls, but such as we ourselves had dug from the mines, or brought up from the bottom of the ocean, our coffers and our caskets would be empty indeed. But even if this were not so, whence came all the arts and sciences, the discoveries and the inventions, without which, and without a common right to which, the valuation of the property of a whole nation would scarcely equal the inventory of a single man,—without which, indeed, we should now be in a state of barbarism? Whence came a knowledge of agriculture, without which we should have so little to reap; or a knowledge of astronomy, without which we could not traverse the oceans; or a knowledge of chemistry and mechanical philosophy, without which the arts and trades could not exist? Most of all this was found out by those who have gone before us, and some of it has come down to us from a remote antiquity. Surely all these boons and blessings belong as much to posterity as to ourselves. They have not descended to us to be arrested and consumed here, or to be sequestrated from the ages to come. Cato and Archimedes, and Kepler, and Newton, and Franklin, and Arkwright, and Fulton, and all the bright host of benefactors to science and art, did not make or bequeath their discoveries or inventions to benefit any one generation, but to increase the common enjoyments of mankind to the end of time. So of all the great lawgivers and moralists who have improved the civil institutions of the state, who have made it dangerous to be wicked, or,—far better than this,—have made it hateful to be so. Resources developed, property acquired, after all these ages of preparation, after all these facilities and securities, accrue not to the benefit of the possessor only, but to that of the next and of all succeeding generations.

Surely, these considerations limit still more extensively that absolutism of ownership which is so often claimed by the possessors of wealth.

But sometimes, the rich farmer, the opulent manufacturer, or the capitalist, when sorely pressed with his natural and moral obligation to

contribute a portion of his means for the education of the young, replies,
—either in form or in spirit;—"my lands, my machinery, my gold, and
my silver, are mine; may I not do what I will with my own?" There is
one supposable case, and only one, where this argument would have
plausibility. If it were made by an isolated, solitary being,—a being
having no relations to a community around him, having no ancestors
to whom he had been indebted for ninety-nine parts in every hundred
of all he possesses, and expecting to leave no posterity after him,—it
might not be easy to answer it. If there were but one family in this
western hemisphere, and only one in the eastern hemisphere, and
these two families bore no civil and social relations to each other, and
were to be the first and last of the whole race, it might be difficult,
except on very high and almost transcendental grounds, for either one
of them to show good cause why the other should contribute to help
educate children not his own. And, perhaps, the force of the appeal
for such an object, would be still further diminished, if the nearest
neighbor of a single family upon our planet were as far from the earth
as Uranus or Sirius. In self-defence, or in selfishness, one might say to
the other, "What are your fortunes to me? You can neither benefit nor
molest me. Let each of us each keep to his own side of the planetary
spaces." But is this the relation which any man amongst us sustains to
his fellows? In the midst of a populous community to which he is
bound by innumerable ties, having had his own fortune and condition
almost predetermined and foreordained by his predecessors, and being
about to exert upon his successors as commanding an influence as
has been exerted upon himself, the objector can no longer shrink into
his individuality, and disclaim connection and relationship with the
world at large. He cannot deny that there are thousands around him
on whom he acts, and who are continually reäcting upon him. The earth
is much too small, or the race is far too numerous, to allow us to be
hermits; and, therefore, we cannot adopt either the philosophy or the
morals of hermits. All have derived benefits from their ancestors, and
all are bound, as by an oath, to transmit those benefits, even in an
improved condition, to posterity. We may as well attempt to escape
from our own personal identity, as to shake off the threefold relation
which we bear to others,—the relation of an associate with our
contemporaries; of a beneficiary of our ancestors; of a guardian to those
who, in the sublime order of Providence, are to succeed us. Out of these
relations, manifest duties are evolved. The society of which we
necessarily constitute a part, must be preserved; and, in order to
preserve it, we must not look merely to what one individual or family
needs, but to what the whole community needs; not merely to what
one generation needs, but to the wants of a succession of generations.

To draw conclusions without considering these facts, is to leave out the most important part of the premises.

A powerfully corroborating fact remains untouched. Though the earth and the beneficent capabilities with which it is endued, belong in common to the race, yet we find that previous and present possessors have laid their hands upon the whole of it;—have left no part of it unclaimed and unappropriated. They have circumnavigated the globe; they have drawn lines across every habitable portion of it, and have partitioned amongst themselves, not only its whole area, or superficial contents, but have claimed it down to the centre, and up to the concave; —a great inverted pyramid for each proprietor,—so that not an unclaimed rood is left, either in the caverns below, or in the aërial spaces above, where a new adventurer upon existence can take unresisted possession. They have entered into a solemn compact with each other, for the mutual defence of their respective allotments. They have created legislators, and judges, and executive officers, who denounce and inflict penalties even to the taking of life; and they have organized armed bands to repel aggression upon their claims. Indeed, so grasping and rapacious have mankind been, in this particular, that they have taken more than they could use, more than they could perambulate and survey, more than they could see from the top of the mast-head, or from the highest peak of the mountain. There was some limit to their physical power of taking possession, but none to the exorbitancy of their desires. Like robbers, who divide their spoils before they know whether they shall find a victim, men have claimed a continent while still doubtful of its existence, and spread out their title from ocean to ocean, before their most adventurous pioneers had ever seen a shore of the realms they coveted. The whole planet, then, having been appropriated,—there being no waste or open lands, from which the new generations may be supplied as they come into existence,—have not those generations the strongest conceivable claim upon the present occupants for that which is indispensable to their well-being? They have more than a preëmptive, they have a possessory right to some portion of the issues and profits of that general domain, all of which has been thus taken up and appropriated. A denial of this right by the present possessors, is a breach of trust,—a fraudulent misuse of power given, and of confidence implied. On mere principles of political economy, it is folly; on the broader principles of duty and morality, it is embezzlement.

It is not at all in contravention of this view of the subject, that the adult portion of society does take, and must take, upon itself, the control and management of all existing property, until the rising generation has arrived at the age of majority. Nay, one of the objects of their so doing is to preserve the rights of the generation which is still in its minority. Soceity, to this extent, is only a trustee managing an estate for the benefit of a part-owner, or of one who has a reversionary interest in it. This civil regulation, therefore, made necessary even for the benefit of both present and future possessors, is only in further-ance of the great law under consideration.

Coincident, too, with this great law, but in no manner superseding or invalidating it, is that wonderful provision which the Creator has made for the care of offspring, in the affection of their parents. Heaven did not rely merely upon our perceptions of duty towards our children, and our fidelity in its performance. A powerful, all-mastering instinct of love was therefore implanted in the parental, and especially in the maternal breast, to anticipate the idea of duty, and to make duty delightful. Yet the great doctrine, founded upon the will of God, as made known to us in the natural order and relation of things, would still remain the same, through all this beautiful portion of our moral being, whence parental affection springs, were a void and a nonentity. Emphatically would the obligations of society remain the same for all those children who have been bereaved of parents; or who, worse than bereavement, have only monster parents of intemperance, or cupidity, or any other of those forms of vice that seem to suspend or to obliterate the law of love in the parental breast. For these, society is doubly bound to be a parent, and to exercise all that rational care and providence which a wise father would exercise for his own children.

If the previous argument began with sound premises and has been logically conducted, then it has established this position,—that a vast portion of the present wealth of the world either consists in, or has been immediately derived from, those great natural substances and powers of the earth, which were bestowed by the Creator alike on all mankind; or from the discoveries, inventions, labors, and improvements of our ancestors, which were alike designed for the common benefit of all their descendants. The question now arises, *At what time* is this wealth to be transferred from a preceding to a succeeding generation? At what point are the latter to take possession of it, or to derive benefit from it, or at what time are the former to surrender it in their behalf? Is each existing generation, and each individual of an existing genera-tion, to hold fast to his possessions until death relaxes his grasp; or is something of the right to be acknowledged, and something of the benefit to be yielded, beforehand? It seems too obvious for argument, that the latter is the only alternative. If the in-coming generation have no rights until the out-going generation have actually retired, then is every individual that enters the world liable to perish on the day he is born. According to the very constitution of things, each individual must obtain sustenance and succor, as soon as his eyes open in quest of light, or his lungs gasp for the first breath of air. His wants cannot be delayed until he himself can supply them. If the demands of his nature are ever to be answered, they must be answered years before he can make any personal provision for them, either by the performance of any labor, or by any exploits of skill. The infant must be fed before he can earn his bread; he must be clothed before he can prepare garments; he must be protected from the elements before he can erect a dwelling; and it is just as clear that he must be instructed before he can engage or reward a tutor. A course contrary to this, would be the destruction of the young, that we might rob them of their rightful inheritance. Carried to its extreme, it would be the act of Herod, seeking, in a general massacre, the life of one who was supposed to endanger his power. Here, then, the claims of the succeeding generation, not only upon the affection and the care, but upon the *property of* the preceding one, attach. God having given to the second generation as full and complete a right to the incomes and profits of the world, as he has given to the first; and to the third generation as full and complete a right as he has given to the second, and so on while the world stands,—it necessarily follows that children must come into a partial and qualified possession of these rights, by the paramount law of nature, as soon as they are born. No human enactment can abolish or countervail this paramount and supreme law; and all those positive and often arbitrary enactments of the civil code, by which, for the encouragement of industry and frugality, the possessor of property is permitted to control it for a limited period after his decease, must be construed and executed in subservience to this sovereign and irrepealable ordinance of nature.

Nor is this transfer always, or even generally, to be made *in kind*; but according to the needs of the recipient. The recognition of this principle is universal. A guardian or trustee may possess lands, while the ward, or owner under the trust, may need money; or the former may have money, while the latter need raiment or shelter. The form of the estate must be changed, if need be, and adapted to the wants of the receiver.

The claim of a child, then, to a portion of preëxistent property begins with the first breath he draws. The new-born infant must have sustenance, and shelter, and care. If the natural parents are removed, or parental ability fails,—in a word, if parents either cannot or will not supply the infant's wants, then society at large,—the government,—having assumed to itself the ultimate control of all property,—is bound to step in and fill the parent's place. To deny this to any child, would be equivalent to a sentence of death,—a capital execution of the innocent,—at which every soul shudders. It would be a more cruel form of infanticide than any which is practised in China or in Africa.

But to preserve the animal life of a child only, and there to stop, would be,—not the bestowment of a blessing or the performance of a duty,—but the infliction of a fearful curse. A child has interests far higher than those of mere. physical existence. Better that the wants of the natural life should be disregarded, than that the higher interests of the character should be neglected. If a child has any claim to bread to keep him from perishing, he has a far higher claim to knowledge to preserve him from error and its fearful retinue of calamities. If a child has any claim to shelter to protect him from the destroying elements, he has a far higher claim to be rescued from the infamy and perdition of vice and crime.

All moralists agree, nay, all moralists maintain, that a man is as responsible for his omissions as for his commissions;—that he is as guilty of the wrong which he could have prevented, but did not, as for that which his own hand has perpetrated. They, then, who knowingly withhold sustenance from a new-born child, and he dies, are guilty of infanticide. And, by the same reasoning, they who refuse to enlighten the intellect of the rising generation, are guilty of degrading the human race. They who refuse to train up children in the way they should go, are training up incendiaries and madmen to destroy property and life, and to invade and pollute the sanctuaries of society. In a word, if the mind is as real and substantive a part of human existence as the body, then mental attributes, during the periods of infancy and childhood, demand provision at least as imperatively as bodily appetites. The time when these respective obligations attach, corresponds with the periods when the nurture, whether physical or mental, is needed. As the right of sustenance is of equal date with birth, so the right to intellectual and moral training begins at least as early as when children are ordinarily sent to school. At that time, then, by the irrepealable law of nature, every child succeeds to so much more of the property of the community as is necessary for his education. He is to receive this, not in the form of lands, or of gold and silver, but in the form of knowledge and a training to good habits. This is one of the steps in the transfer of property from a present to a succeeding generation. Human sagacity may be at fault in fixing the amount of property to be transferred, or the time when the transfer should be made, to a dollar or to an hour; but certainly, in a republican government, the obligation of the predecessors, and the right of the successors, extend to and embrace the means of such an amount of education as will prepare each individual to perform all the duties which devolve upon him as a man and a citizen. It may go further than this point; certainly, it cannot fall short of it.

Under our political organization, the places and the processes where this transfer is to be provided for, and its amount determined, are the district school meeting, the town meeting, legislative halls, and conventions for establishing or revising the fundamental laws of the state. If it be not done there, society is false to its high trusts; and any community, whether national or state, that ventures to organize a government, or to administer a government already organized, without making provision for the free education of all its children, dares the certain vengeance of Heaven; and, in the squalid forms of poverty and destitution, in the scourges of violence and misrule, in the heart-destroying corruptions of licentiousness and debauchery, and in political profligacy and legalized perfidy,—in all the blended and mutually aggravated crimes of civilization and of barbarism, will be sure to feel the terrible retributions of its delinquency.

I bring my argument on this point, then, to a close; and I present a test of its validity, which, as it seems to me, defies denial or evasion.

In obedience to the laws of God and to the laws of all civilized communities, society is bound to protect the natural life of children; and this natural life cannot be protected without the appropriation and use of a portion of the property which society possesses. We prohibit infanticide under penalty of death. We practice a refinement in this particular. The life of an infant is inviolable even before he is born; and he who feloniously takes it, even before birth, is as subject to the extreme penalty of the law, as though he had struck down manhood in its vigor, or taken away a mother by violence from the sanctuary of home, where she blesses her offspring. But why preserve the natural life of a child, why preserve unborn embroyos of life, if we do not intend to watch over and to protect them, and to expand their subsequent existence into usefulness and happiness? As individuals, or as an organized community, we have no natural right; we can derive no authority or countenance from reason; we can cite no attribute or purpose of the divine nature, for giving birth to any human being, and then inflicting upon that being the curse of ignorance, of poverty, and of vice, with all their attendant calamities. We are brought, then, to this startling but inevitable alternative. The natural life of an infant should be extinguished as soon as it is born, or the means should be provided to save that life from being a curse to its possessor; and, therefore, every state is morally bound to enact a code of laws legalizing and enforcing infacticide, or a code of laws establishing Free Schools!

The three following propositions, then, describe the broad and ever-furing foundation on which the Common School system of Masssachusetts reposes:—

The successive generations of men, taken collectively, constitute one great commonwealth.

The property of this commonwealth is pledged for the education of all its youth, up to such a point as will save them from poverty and vice, and prepare them for the adequate performance of their social and civil duties.

The successive holders of this property are trustees, bound to the faithful execution of their trust, by the most sacred obligations; and embezzlement and pillage from children and descendants have not less of criminality, and have more of meanness, than the same offences. When perpetrated against contemporaries.

50
William T. Harris (1835-1909).
The Conservator

Ninety-nine out of a hundred people in every civilized nation are automata, careful to walk in the prescribed paths, careful to follow prescribed custom. This is the result of substantial education, which, scientifically defined, is the subsumption of the individual under his species. The other educational principle is that of emancipation from this subsumption. This is subordinate, and yet, in our time, we lay more stress upon it than the other.
—William T. Harris, *The Philosophy of Education.*

Already he was exerting a most profound influence upon the teachers and the public-school system of the entire country, and was quoted more frequently and with more approval by educational journals and by public-school teachers than any other American—not even excepting Horace Mann.
—James H. Canfield, 1906.

I

While it was Barnard and Mann who laid the foundations of the American public school system, it was William T. Harris who presided over the rearing of the structure. His most important achievement, however, was to furnish American education with a philosophy which helped the rank and file to adjust their thought and feeling to new actualities without losing the sense of identity with older values and conditions.

When Harris was born in 1835, American nationality had not yet been consolidated; when he died in 1909, no important group seriously challenged it. When he was born, rural America was dominant; when he died, urban and industrial America was in the saddle. When Harris began his educational work, there was still abundant free land, with something approaching, roughly to be sure, economic opportunities for everyone; when he finished his work, the traditional opportunities for the individual were, while still celebrated, in fact very much limited. In

577

1835, most of the intellectual and social leaders of America believed in a personal God, the freedom of the will, and immortality. In 1909, the advance of science had to a considerable extent changed that faith. It was the work of Harris to aid his fellow Americans, and particularly educators, to accept the new order without entirely repudiating the old.

North Killingly, Connecticut, where Harris was born in 1835, was less than a hundred miles from both Boston and Hartford, where Mann and Barnard were then on the threshold of their active educational labors. The parents of Harris were well-to-do farmers, and members of the family were interested in the textile mills which by 1836 made Killingly the most important cotton manufacturing town in Connecticut. Harris was sent to private academies, including the famous Phillips Andover, and in 1835 [sic] entered Yale. He left after two years, not because of the inability of his parents to pay his tuition, but rather because he was dissatisfied with what Yale offered.[1]*

Young Harris had caught the radical virus that had contaminated the solidity and complacency of New England. He became converted to phrenology, mesmerism, and the claims and promises of "natural science," repudiated a good deal of the orthodox Congregationalism with which he had been indoctrinated, and turned his back on the authoritarianism of the classics. While he did not, apparently, interest himself in Fourierism or any radical economic doctrines, he was nevertheless a come-outer. Theodore Parker's writings led him to study German philosophy; and he became, and continued to his death, an ardent student of Kant, Fichte, and above all, of Hegel.[2]

Whether it was the influence of Hegel, whom he discovered after migrating to St. Louis in 1857, or his rapid success as a teacher and administrator in the schools of that city, which sobered his radicalism, one cannot be certain. In any case, the idealism which had been nourished in him by trancendantalism (it was the reading of Bronson Alcott that undermined his faith in phrenology) flourished on the new-found German philosophy, and his opposition to the determinism and empiricism of Spencer became pronounced. The refusal of the editors of *The Atlantic|Monthly* and *The North American Review* to publish a criticism of Spencer led Harris, when but thirty-two years old, to found in St. Louis *The Journal of Speculative Philosophy*, which he continued to edit through twenty-two volumes, and which familiarized many Americans with German idealistic philosophy, as well as with Greek thought, and their applications to aesthetics and the more practical problems of life. The agnostic and deterministic ideas of Spencer were proving popular in many circles, and the doctrines of Darwin were challenging the faith of orthodox Christians. Yet many Americans were

---

* [Footnotes appear at the conclusion of this chapter.]

eagerly seeking for a philosophic justification of faith in God, freedom, and immortality. Harris, by popularizing the absolute idealism of Hegel, provided them with able and authoritarian support for their cherished views.

The Hegelian philosophy which Harris made the basis of all his social and educational thinking[3] possessed the virtue of being thoroughly optimistic and idealistic in character. It infused the world with a divine purpose and endowed the individual with a noble and immortal destiny. At the same time it justified the existing order and authorities by declaring that whatever is, is an inevitable stage in the unfolding of objective reason or the world spirit, and is therefore right. It seemed to lift the individual to a higher plane of self-realization without sacrificing the ideals of self-help and self-activity. At the same time it subordinated the individual to existing social institutions by maintaining that his true, spiritual self, which was constantly in conflict with his natural or physical self, could be realized only by adjusting himself to the divinely appointed environment and institutions that were in actual existence. This doctrine of spiritual self-realization or self-estrangement, as we shall see, was given important applications in the educational and social thought of Harris.

By the use of the dialectic method of resolving antitheses into higher syntheses, Hegelian philosophy also permitted the exploitation of science for social and economic purposes without sacrificing religion and the concerns of the spirit as ultimate values. In short, the right-wing Hegelianism to which Harris subscribed satisfied religious and idealistic aspirations, paid tribute to the cult of individuality and self-help, and at the same time subordinated the mass of individuals to existing institutions, which included the corporation, the city, and the machine, as well as religion and the national state. As we shall see, it also had a good deal to say about socialism and other protests against industrial capitalism.

It would be hard to overemphasize the importance which Harris attached to "spiritual values," both cultural and religious. Reared a Congregationalist, he had flirted for a time during his college days with naturalism and then, until his death, regularly attended the church of his fathers. In his mind philosophy supported the Christian relation; and the church, together with the state, civil society, the family, and the school, was a necessary and beneficent institution. Like its sister institutions, religion enabled the individual to come into harmony and co-operation with human society as a totality and to receive a share of the whole re-enforcing spiritual achievements of the race. As the basis of civilization, religion was a social process by which the intellect, will, and heart of the individual were strengthened. It held conservatively to monogamy and the intergrity of the family; it provided charity for the weaklings of society; above all, it inculcated respect for private property and for law and order.[4]

In Christianity Harris also found a synthesis of the Oriental religions which virtually denied the here and now, individuality, and secondary courses, and the naturalism of Hume, Spencer, and his followers, who virtually dismissed everything except the here and the now, sense experience, and secondary causes. By synthesizing these two extremes, Christianity made room both for ultimate truth, first cause, and God, and for individual self-activity and the affairs of this world. Thus Christianity was an indispensable institution for securing the proper relationship between the individual and the universal, the temporal and the eternal.[5]

Yet Harris did not wish religious instruction to be given in public schools. The principle of religious instruction was authority; that of secular teaching, demonstration and verification. "It is obvious," he remarked, "that these two principles should not be brought into the same school, but separated as widely as possible." Religious instruction should be accompanied by reverence, solemnity, and, preferably, by ritualistic surroundings. In the experience of centuries, Harris thought, the church had admirably learned its technique. Secular instruction in parochial schools often suffered by virtue of carrying over the religious method of authority, memorization, and symbols. Religious instruction in public schools, to meet the varied needs and beliefs of all, had to be denatured into mere Deism.[6]

While the most important of the spiritual values which made up the good life, religion was not the sole one: the higher culture was also fundamental in Harris's *Weltanschauung*. In theory, at least, he had no heart for a culture "belonging to a class that rests like an upper layer upon the mass below, who in turn have to spin and dig for them."[7] Assuming that American industrial civilization provided and would increasingly provide the mass of the people with an opportunity co-operatively to subjugate the elements and win a competence on such easy terms that the greater part of life might be devoted to higher culture, Harris firmly believed that the common man was destined to participate in "the realized intelligence of all mankind."[8]

Elementary education, which must be universal, was to give to each child the tools by which he might participate in the culture of the race—grammar, literature and art, mathematics, geography, and history. These were the "five windows of the soul," which enabled the individual to appreciate the common stock of ideas and cultural values that governed the social organization and civilization of which he was a part. By these "tool subjects" the child was to acquire the instruments for mastering the entire realms of nature and of mind. The vast technological and business developments which provided libraries and newspapers to the masses enabled them to master, independently of teachers and universities, the great cultural treasures of the past, even if they went no farther than the elementary school.[9]

As the utilitarian subjects pressed for an increasing place in the curriculum, Harris, while permitting moderate compromise, insisted on the value of the disciplinary and cultural studies. Although he did not ignore the new emphasis on hygiene and physiology and the demands for better ventilated and better lighted schools, he declared that the great purposes of the school had been and were still realized in dark, ill-aired log schoolhouses, in slum tenements rented for the purpose, and in the shanty school.[10] Emphasis on biological and physiological theory seemed to him an undue surrender to the physical nature of man, which education was primarily responsible for subordinating to the spiritual or true self.[11] The chief object of physical training was to put will into the muscles. But this could be overdone, and Harris always opposed the movement for abandoning the old-fashioned recess, which he believed necessary for relaxation, involving momentary surrender to caprice.[12]

In still other ways Harris defended the cultural and spiritual values in education and in life. Believing that Latin and Greek vocabularies and syntax provided students with the most effective insight into the embryonic period of Western civilization and enabled them better to understand the forms and usages of their intellectual and moral being, he stoutly defended the classics.[13] As superintendent of the St. Louis schools and as the editor of a series of school readers he did a good deal to familiarize American school children with the great literary masterpieces of the past, and he was also an early champion of instruction in art. If he occasionally called attention to the advantage such training would give in the international competition for markets,[14] for the most part he advocated art instruction as a means of cultivating the feelings and curbing the appetites, and of so transcending the beauty of nature as to permit man to realize the divine.[15]

When the manual training movement was launched in the 1880's, Harris minimized its importance and denied that it possessed great intellectual value. His opposition was based in large part on his conviction that sense-training was less valuable than the Pestalozzians thought. "It is a false psychology which says we derive all our knowledge from sense-perception."[16] His view was that school education should develop the power to withdraw from the external world of the senses and to fix attention on forces and principles; it should also open the child's soul to the cultural treasures of the past. He denied that hand labor had any particular moral value, unless it resulted in products for the market place, thereby subordinating the worker for the good of others and in turn enabling him to share in their production.[17] In expressing sympathy for the establishment of manual trade schools for children "unwilling to carry any further their purely cultural studies," Harris, somewhat in the spirit of Dewey, wished these schools to teach not merely the narrow skills and techniques, but the broader aspects of trade—its place in society and its relation to the traditions and needs of civilization.[18] Moreover, students in the trade schools, having acquired the tool subjects in elementary school, might through the newspaper and the public library continue to enrich themselves in cultural and non-technical values.[19] If he overlooked the fact that the newspaper was already in the nineties being transformed into a commercial and even sensational money-making venture, and if he neglected to see that cheap but profitmaking amusements were already commercializing the scant leisure of workingmen, he nevertheless did not intend to condemn them to purely manual, technical, and material values.

The great emphasis that Harris attached to cultural and spiritual values, as well as to religion, made his defense of the machine, of the urbanization of American life, and of industrial capitalism, seem all the more rational and convincing. Indeed he was a pioneer in welcoming the application of science to the affairs of everyday life and in urging the introduction of the sciences into the school curriculum.[20] Recognizing the inevitability of the "machine age," and also aware of some of the contradictions to cultural and spiritual values it implied, Harris resolved the contradictions by the use of the dialectical method and his philosophic presuppositions.

Thus in tracing the development of machine industrialism in England, Harris dwelt on the benefits that the factory system had brought to laborers. "Instead of occasional seasons of work and most inadequate wages on farms, this population obtained in the newly established mills of Manchester and Birmingham a constant employment and remunerative wages,—better dwelling, better food and clothing, and plenty."[21] Actually, of course, the factory system also meant the substitution of wretched urban tenements and frightful slums for rural hovels, child labor under execrable conditions, technological unemployment, suffering during ever recurring crises and depressions—the creation, in short, of an industrial proletariat.

In resolving the contradictions between machine civilization and cultural values, Harris obscured the evils in accentuating the benefits. He never tired of explaining the machine industry, by substituting intelligent direction for brute force and by multiplying the commodities one man could produce, freed the worker from grinding toil and enabled him to share in the products of others. He pictured glowingly the leisure for the pursuit of culture which machine production provided for the laborer.[22]

Harris also emphasized the educational values of machine production. Instead of enslaving the individual, the machine, he contended, actually freed and elevated him. The machine required alertness of mind, versatility, and trained intelligence on the part of its directors; and education must develop these qualities. Harris was not disturbed by the monotonous routine that new machinery was bringing to many former artisans, for he believed that the dull tending of these new instruments of production was a passing phase of industrialism. From the stage that "reduces the human being to a machine" would develop, "by a sort of dialectic necessity," the complete mechanization in which the machine would itself care for all tasks except those demanding intelligence and imagination.[23] Woman, with her alert intellect but weak physique, would particularly benefit from this development, achieving economic independence, freedom for her individuality, and a sense of fulfilling a necessary function in the larger economic order.[24] Harris was not troubled by the specter of technological unemployment, saying that the educated man would easily learn the operation of new machines.[25]

It is noteworthy that Harris sensed in the dominance of the machine certain contradictions to the values of the past which he cherished. These contradictions were, for him, banished by the certainty that the Hegelian process of development and synthesis would eliminate many and that education could dispel others. Education would enable the masses successfully to adjust to the demands of the machine and would teach them to utilize their new leisure by sharing the finest culture of the race. Harris was not impressed by the argument that, so long as the machine was controlled by the owning class and utilized for profits, many of its actual and potential advantages would be offset by such unfortunate consequences as uneven distribution of the increased wealth, commercialized culture for the released leisure of the masses, and overexpansion of industry with subsequent distress for the worker.

Harris was as energetic an apologist for the urbanization of American life as he was for the age of the machine. He believed that the city enabled the laborer to develop greater independence of opinion and action than did the country: both the parent and the employer in the city had to be less patriarchal than in the country.[26] But the city not only marked an important step in the emancipation of the individual; it also stimulated the development of the "directive power which regulates the national industry and prosperity."[27] Harris also rejoiced that the invasion of the daily newspaper into the country elevated its life toward that of city civilization, and hopefully observed that the application of the machine to agriculture, by releasing man power for industry and commerce, would compel the illiterate rural drudge to "climb up or else starve in his attempt to compete with the machine."[28]

In his defense of industrial capitalism Harris was even more confident than in his defense of the machine and the city. Despite his devotion to philosophy and his scant interest in money *per se*—he even refused to have his modest salary as Commissioner of the Bureau of Education raised during his incumbency—Harris was a practical man of affairs. When in 1880 he resigned his position as supertintendent of the St. Louis schools, he was offered the vice-presidency of one of the largest white lead companies in the country.

To this philosopher the industrialist was a builder of civilization. He believed that capitalism was thoroughly in accord with the highest law of existence, altruism, a law which religion, philosophy, and even science, as well as the tradition of the race, confirmed. Wealth, he said, was admirable because it enabled its possessor to grow good and wise and to become more helpful to his fellow men. He praised capitalists for their support of education and rejoiced that higher education, in turn, furnished industrialists with trained experts who stimulated the work of prospecting for natural resources, abroad as well as at home, and who also aided in the accumulation of wealth for the owning class by their work in developing transportation and manufacturing.[29]

Unlike Mann, Harris saw no objection to the accumulation of vast fortunes and rationalized and idealized the formation of trusts and mergers. Far from denouncing captains of industry for the practices involved, he pointed out how higher education could aid in carrying them out. In a lecture to women he favored their study of law so that they might be useful when the welfare of business necessitated the evasion of the anti-trust laws. The "captains of industry," he remarked "depend on higher education to keep themselves out of jail, for great business combinations involve collisions of all kinds with other interests and must adopt legal precautions to avoid civil and criminal liabilities."[30]

Yet these very trusts which Harris accepted and approved in reality submerged the middleman, the small business man. One might have expected Harris, as an individualist, to desire certain restrictions upon this consolidation. But although he admitted that inconvenience and even suffering and injustice might accompany the process, these considerations were dwarfed before the great economies made possible by big business. The savings effected by the elimination of the middle-man enabled the capitalists to apportion "to the producers and consumers their quota of the benefit derived from reducing the expense of the middle term"—and in spite of their immense profits, Harris thought they made such a distribution. In addition, the capitalist's share of the savings permitted him to endow education more richly.[31]

But the defense which this great educational leader made of industrial capitalism was based on even more fundamental convictions. Private ownership of property and its corollary, production for profit, was for him necessary for the participation of the race in the benefits of the invention and productivity of individuals. Through private property and free competition "society gains constantly at the least expense."[32] They were also necessary for the freedom and development of the individual. The discovery of private property Harris described as "the discovery of the possibility of human freedom."[33] The property of the individual is his "'dominium' and he can by its means gain self-respect and self-knowledge."[34] Without this institution Harris thought there could be no freedom of thought or action.

Although he prized highly the function of the captalist class, Harris as an educator, was greatly concerned over the dangers involved in the typical rearing given the offspring of the wealthy. He lamented that well-to-do mothers, eager to play a prominent role in "society," turned over their children to lowbred servants, who frequently spoiled them and thus deprived civilization of the directive ability which he thought such children inherited from their parents. Believing that the kindergarten could salvage these pampered children of the rich, a function he considered of at least equal importance with its power to redeem moral weaklings from homes of poverty and squalor, Harris was a pioneer in its behalf. St. Louis under his superintendency was the first American city to incorporate the kindergarten in the system of public schools.[35]

With the same end in view, Harris wrote President Benjamin Ide Wheeler of the University of California urging him to accept the presidency of Teachers College:

> New York has by far the larger number of the directors of the wealth of the United States. A peculiar problem has arisen in education in recent years through the fact that the children from wealthy families are possessed of unusual directive power and are consequently difficult to manage in ordinary schools. It must be admitted that most of the promising youth from these families are swept away on the tide of dissipation. The New York Teachers College has done more than any other institution to explore new means and methods by which this, a most important class of our population, important because it furnishes nearly all of the directive power to our industries— can save its children for the blessings of society. Turned in directions of selfish pleasure-seeking, the children of the wealthy do more than any other persons to irritate the masses

of the American people and encourage the development of
socialism and lines of political obstruction to the large enterprises of capital in the interest of productive industry . . . In
mentioning the great wealth of the trustees I have hinted that
a phenomenal endowment of this institution is to be expected
when it obtains for itself a universal recognition in the United
States for the higher order of work which it will do.[36]

As a champion of industrial capitalism and the virtues that it
prized, Harris accepted the doctrines of class co.operation and self-
reliance. He sincerely believed that there were no conflicts of interest
between any individual, whether factory worker or tenant farmer, and
his employer or creditor. With equal conviction he upheld the gospel
of self-help and ardently opposed any governmental activity which
would make the individual less likely to take care of himself. "Help
the poor and unfortunate to help themselves, and you elevate them toward
human perfection, and the divine ideal. It is this principle, too, that
makes clear to us what road leads to the surest amelioration of the
evils of poverty and mendicancy. Education is the one sure road to
help the unfortunate. Adopt all the cunning devices that social science
has invented, and you cannot be sure that direct or indirect help of
the poor does not undermine their self-respect and weaken their
independence."[37] Thus Harris subscribed to the middle-class doctrine set
forth by Franklin and cherished by President Hoover as "rugged
individualism."

While it was the common thing for American educational leaders
in this period to condemn organized opposition to capitalism, Harris
went a good deal farther than his colleagues. Again and again he
elaborated detailed refutations of all the criticisms of capitalism then
current. Not on one, but on many occasions, Harris pleaded persuasively
with his listeners or readers to have no faith in the teachings of Karl
Marx and Henry George. His benevolence, his kindliness, his shrewdness,
must have made his unquestionably skillful attacks on those doctrines
all the more effective. In his papers and addresses which were designed
to refute what he regarded as subversive economic doctrines, Harris
displayed an impressive knowledge of statistics.[38] While he was aware
of some of their pitfalls, he himself did not always avoid them.

In attacking Henry George, Harris put his finger on some of the
weak spots in the doctrine of the single tax. He pointed out that George
made no distinction between land used for agriculture and for building
sites and that his tax would actually fall with greatest severity upon
the farming population. But the conclusion he himself drew from the
distinction between urban and rural lands has scarcely been confirmed
by subsequent events. Rapid transportation, Harris declared, would

prevent city land prices from soaring by bringing them in competition with the cheap building lot carved out of the near-by country farm.

The educator also took Henry George to task for overemphasizing the amount of revenue which could be derived from ground rents. He estimated on the basis of the census of 1880 that the income in rent from privately owned land, calculated at 4 per cent, would provide but two cents revenue a day per inhabitant of the country, or $8 a year. If this pittance were added to the income of each individual, he observed, it would scarcely bring leisure or luxury to the masses who were struggling with poverty. Private property in land held no power to rob capital or labor. Furthermore, Harris insisted that, contrary to the doctrine of *Progress and Poverty*, capital actually frees labor from the tyranny of land, for under industrial capitalism other forms of wealth become a greater proportion of the total wealth.[39]

Turning his attention to Marx, Harris insisted that he likewise ignored the evidence of statistics which disproved the contention that the poor were becoming poorer and more numerous and the rish, richer and fewer. However valid the evidence Harris marshaled to show that the average wage of laborers was increasing and that a greater number of families were gaining middle-class and moderately wealthy incomes, it did not meet the Socialist argument that the increasing wealth of the owning class was, relatively as well as actually, greater than the added earnings of the proletarian class.[40] Harris ridiculed the desirability of an even division of the national income, which he considered the primary aim of Marxian economics, by estimating that it would give all workers only $34.80 a month and by asserting that every laborer who earned more at the present time had no ground for complaint but rather must be considered on the side of the "bloated bondholders."[41] With his convictions concerning private property,[42] he ignored the possibility of an increase in the total national income of a socialist state.

In his efforts to refute the teachings of Marx, Harris contended that the author of *Capital* did not understand that the largest cost to the consumer lay in the collection and distribution of commodities—the function of the market. He insisted that the capitalist accumulated his wealth, not by grinding the poor, but by virtue of the fact that he or his forefathers possessed the habit of thrift or had developed methods for reducing the cost of producing or distributing goods. The captain of industry, Harris maintained, earned far more for society than he accumulated for his own profit—the savings made by big business were, in effect, socialized. He went so far as to assert that capital took only one-tenth of what it saved by virtue of its services in increasing the efficiency of the market: the other nine-tenths were distributed to producers and consumers.[43]

In using the argument of the market as the chief means of refuting Marx, Harris seemed to assume that large-scale production, cost-saving devices, and the world market would exist only under capitalism. Moreover, he did not refute the central thesis of Marx, the theory of surplus value—the argument that capitalists gained profits by the productivity of a labor day much longer than was necessary to produce an equivalent of what the worker was paid and the cost of materials and equipment. For him capitalism was sufficiently exonerated from all charges of exploitation by showing that savings had been effected during its reign.

To buttress his defense of capitalism, Harris tackled the problem of unemployment. In an article published in *The Forum* in 1898 he clearly stated the problem of technological unemployment and raised the question as to whether there could be work enough for all. Admitting that the bare necessities of life might, as the result of new labor-saving machinery, be increased beyond the needs of the community, he contended that it was impossible to overproduce in the sphere of creature comforts and luxuries. He insisted that the entire surplus of laborers released by the application of machinery could be taken up in the manufacture of comforts and in the production of cultural services for everyone. This, of course, is the argument of "the new capitalism," so frequently heard in the 1920's, and apparently so shaken by the events of 1929 and its aftermath.

Harris thought that the readjustment of vocations could be easily accomplished if workers were intelligent. He would not have admitted that the industrial scrap heap was due in any sense to the profit motive of manufacturers. He ascribed it merely to the lack of intelligence and education on the part of workers: with a "knowledge of the rudiments" they should be able to re-adapt themselves in new luxury industries, the products of which they and their fellow workers were to consume. Harris believed that the vocations providing for the protection and comfort of the masses, medicine, insurance, teaching, art, drama, science, literature and religion, could expand indefinitely, and that with increased education workers displaced by the invention of machinery could find places for themselves in the professions designed to administer to the protection and comfort of society.[44]

The deep-rooted antagonism which Harris felt toward socialism can be understood only in the light of the philosophy of social evolution which he derived from Hegel. According to this philosophy, the whole process of history had been the emancipation of the individual from the group. Over a long period of time the civil community, the state, and the church had so developed as to give ever larger scope to the individual. Church had been separated from state, and the individual had acquired religious freedom. The development of the Anglo-Saxon system of local government and *laissez faire* removed obstacles to the free action of the individual. Socialism, which Harris thought of as a primitive economic form flourishing in the early medieval community and guild, restricted the free action of the individual. It sought to help him, not by the removal of such obstacles as hindered his self-activity, but by so arranging matters that he might share equally in the products of the social whole without reference to his producing power. It would put a premium on weakness and incompetency at the expense of the able and the thrifty. Socialism would destroy the precious gain to the sacredness and development of personality that private property had brought, and would revert to the primitive and Oriental subordination of the individual to the group. It would, in short, turn the hands of the clock backward."[45]

Harris not only defended capitalism against its critics, but explicitly pointed out how education might serve more effectively the established order. In greeting the National Education Association in 1894, when the country was in the throes of labor "disorders," he observed that the school provided the people with training in those habits of regularity, silence, and industry which would "preserve and save our civil order." In the public school, the center of discipline, the pupil learned "first of all to respect the rights of organised industry,"[46] In the kindergarten the child of the slum, the weakling of society, learned self-respect, moral ideals, industry, and perseverance—the means, in short, of conquering natural obstacles.[47]

It was, however, to higher education that Harris especially looked for the training which would counteract economic heresies. Although he did not realistically face the question of the relationship of the economic status of the family to the problem of selection for higher education, he did hope that more and more young Americans would enter college. To promote this end he favored an adjustment between the public high school and the higher institutions of learning so that private school training would not be necessary in order to meet college entrance requirements.[48] While the elementary and secondary schools were to fit the pupil for participation in the cultural heritage and the social cooperation of the race, higher education was to provide a critical and comparative evaluation of human knowledge. Through the insight gained by such training, Harris believed the college student would learn "at once to suspect all mere *isms* and one-sided tendencies like socialism and anarchy and anything that has the form of a universal panacea."[49]

College graduates, being acquainted with the relation of the many branches of human learning to the conduct of life, would become the spiritual monitors of society: they would recognize the deep foundations of existing institutions and check the extravagances of less educated people who took a fragmentary view and were swept by specious arguments for radical reform into the ranks of the agitators.[50]

Anxious to extend to adults the methods and point of view of higher learning, Harris warmly supported the movement for university extension. In referring to its origin in England, he observed that "there is no movement . . . which has worked for the perpetuation of the power of the upper classes . . . as has this movement of university extension." Since demagogism increased in proportion to the neglect of the lower stratum of society by the highest, he contended that enlightened selfishness dictated the support of extension work in this country. In view of the demagogic and sensational appeals of the popular newspapers, it was all the more necessary to equip the masses with the ability to resist such appeals. Just as the earlier educators had advocated the free common school to preserve the established order, Harris championed university extension as a double safeguard.[51]

In his relations with educational administrators and with teachers Harris likewise gave evidence of his fundamentally capitalistic bias. He advised superintendents that in their relations with school boards they would find "the conservative business man" their best support in dealing with the members who might be classified as cranks, reformers, and demagogues.[52] Harris regarded the teachers as the most conservative group in society with the single exception of the clergy.[53] He offered with confidence the comfort of the capitalist to those who were dissatisfied with their salaries of $400 or $500 a year. The teacher must remember that her lot depended in large measure on her own efforts, that her position would be bettered if she improved her technique, her general culture, and her skill. As in industry, so in the teaching profession, the best from the lowest ranks were certain to rise if they had ability. He did not mention the influence of politics, religion, personal charm, and the "school machines." With the advance of civilization and the increase of productive wealth, he reassured his listeners, the status of the profession in general would improve. Meantime teachers might take comfort in the knowledge that in view of the industrial progress of the country and the "economic law law of increased values of vocations that have for their object the protection of culture," the future outlook for teachers' salaries was bright.[54]

II

The school child who did not learn from his teacher any of the ideas about capitalism and socialism with which the addresses of Harris in educational meetings and his papers in professional periodicals acquainted her was shielded from susceptibility to radicalism by the educational methods that he popularized. It is true that by insisting on the cardinal importance of the five traditional school subjects, literature and art, history, geography, mathematics, and grammar, Harris tended to keep such utilitarian matters as manual training from occupying an important rôle in the curriculum; and his halfhearted support of trade schools did not promote the training of a large number of skilled workers to enhance the profits of industry.

Yet in other respects Harris did influence the schools in such a way as to make them serviceable to the established order. Frankly maintaining that an important purpose of education was to train the child to respect authority, he opposed the Pestalozzian concept of self-government in the schools, a concept that Parker, Dewey, and their followers were beginning to emphasize. "The school pupil simply gets used to established order and expects it and obeys it as a habit. He will maintain it as a sort of instinct in after life, whether he has ever learned the theory of it or not." Instruction in the reasons for good behavior Harris considered less important than forming "habits of punctuality, silence, and industry."[55]

While this great conservator sometimes paid qualified tribute to educational reformers, he opposed the adoption of "fads" and kept the schools fairly rigid in the lock-step scheme of organization, method, and point of view. He was one of the most sturdy champions of the textbook method of teaching, which he felt was peculiarly well adapted to the needs of American children.[56] He believed that the Herbartian emphasis on interest as the motive force in teaching went too far and frequently became a mere craze for novelty. Forgetting that interests were good, bad, and indifferent, and should be furthered or repressed in accordance with what the child was to become rather than with what he desired at the moment, the Herbartians, Harris thought, failed to appreciate the value of discipline.[57]

By opposing the doctrine of interest with its applications of education through sense-perception and vocationalism and self-government in schools, and by emphasizing the value of discipline, will-training, textbook methods, and traditional subject matter, Harris, in the opinion of many, retarded the adjustment of the American school system to the needs of a true democracy.

Yet it would be unfair to Harris to overemphasize his rôle as a conservator of older and more authoritarian educational methods and values. If he hesitated to recommend that teachers study "the new psychology" for fear that it would negate ethical and religious convictions, he admitted that it might aid in determining the best length of study and recitation periods and in preventing fatigue.[58] If he stood for authority, discipline, and the lock step, he was too much an individualist to favor the mechanization of the child; and he advocated the short-interval system by which the brighter and quicker students were more rapidly promoted and the duller ones given more frequent chances and new incentives.[59]

Harris opposed overthorough methods of instruction, which, he held, might tend to produce arrested development in the child who must not, during his long period of infancy and helplessness, be inured to any habit or fixed form that would interfere with his ethical and spiritual development. In the spirit of *Gestalt* psychology he insisted that "the absorption of the gaze upon adjustments within the machine prevents us from seeing the machine as a whole . . . The habit of parsing every sentence that one reads may prevent one from enjoying a sonnet of Wordsworth."[60] The discipline and authority for which he stood was intended to be rational in character and to enable the individual *freely* to subscribe to the law of the social whole in order fully to realize his true, spiritual self. Yet in the hands of the average teacher the principles for which Harris tood doubtless encouraged discipline in the ordinary sense, rather than spiritual freedom and self-realization under the law. Certainly the educational values and methods he promoted tended to encourage, not independent thought, but devotion to the existing order.

III

Harris was no less ardent a champion of American nationalism and imperialism than he was of industrial capitalism. As a Hegelian, he believed that the national state was the greatest of human institutions, necessary for civilization and for the realization of true individualism. Only through the state could the individual be free to absorb the benefits of civilization. Since the individual *freely* accepted the sovereignty of the state in order to secure true freedom, there could be no conflict between the interests of one and the other.

As an adherent of the Hegelian interpretation of history—in 1908 he was able to say he had read the great German's *Philosophy of History* seventeen times—Harris loved to dwell on the peculiar mission of the Hebrews, the Greeks, the Romans, the Anglo-Saxons, and their American offspring. The Hebrews gave the race the realization of a monotheistic God, personal immortality, and divine will; the Greeks, individuality and beauty; the Romans, law, organization, contract, and private proeerty; the Anglo-Saxons, local self-government, which still further emancipated the individual from authority; and the Americans carried on the process by providing the individual with an even greater freedom in local self-government, in public education, and in industry.[61]

Such enthusiastic nationalism committed the public school to the task of educating for the American state. "We educate the future citizens of the United States, not the future citizens of Prussia, France, of England, of China, or of Japan." This fundamental fact, Harris believed, must condition instruction in citizenship. Our school system, by fitting the individual for the new industrial age, offered the rest of the world an object lesson. Yet his national ideal was essentially a competitive one; Harris held that we could not compete industrially with the other nations of the world unless our children were so educated in common schools that they would, to the full extent of their capacity, utilize and improve machinery.[62]

Since the history of a nation was a commentary on its political principle—in our case, self-government, self-help, co-operative individualism—the teaching of history must emphasize that political principle. It must also show how that principle becomes entwined in all other spheres, social, aesthetic, religious, and "world-historical." Americans must be taught through history what our national ideals are and what they mean. While Harris in 1870 thought that the teaching of our history should include only the period ending with the formation of the Constitution,[63] he recommended, in the Report of the Committee of Fifteen (1895,) the inclusion of the Civil War. The pupil, however, was to be taught to examine each event in history in the light of "all contemporary events and to study its relation to all that has preceded it."[64] In addition, Harris thought that the study of history should train the child to discriminate between important and unimportant facts, to appreciate the ethical aspects of history, and understand the method of historical investigation.

While Harris regarded America as the culmination of the historical process which transferred government from one person to the mass of the citizens, and while he took pride in the free activity which *laissez-faire* American democracy provided for its people, he opposed the experiment of self-government through "the school city" and the notion that the child might learn civic functions by performing them.[65] The school should rest content with instilling a knowledge of the Constitution, our early history, and our great national heroes; and with providing the child with such character training as would lead him to choose the rational in preference to the irrational, to respect authority, to discipline his self-activity and to subordinate himself in voluntary co-operation with the social group for the realization of a higher and truly authentic freedom. The nationalism for which Harris stood did not lead him to favor the teaching of the patriotism expressed in the slogan, "My country, right or wrong." Patriotic sentiment, like all sentiment, could not be formally cultivated; it must, like the root of a plant, be well grounded. The teacher must encourage it, not by appeals to blind passion and to sentiment, but to reason.[66]

The philosophy of history to which Harris subscribed also prevented him from advocating the Americanization of the immigrant by steam-roller methods. As superintendent of the St. Louis schools he upheld the teaching of German, pointing out that when an immigrant population broke suddenly with its past, there was apt to be a great loss in the stability of individual character. With an Hegelian respect for the ethos of each people Harris believed that the presence of our immigrant population promoted tolerance, mutual respect, and a high degree of personal liberty.[67] At the same time he warned against carrying the idea that America was an asylum for the oppressed of Europe so far as to make our country another Botany Bay.[68] As we shall see, he also regarded the immigrant as chiefly responsible for political corruption.

That his attitude toward nationalism did not prevent him from desiring education to aid in the process of promoting solidarity is plain when one considers the attitude of Harris toward the Indian and the Negro. Education, he thought, might well enable the Indian to skip over the stages of the village community (socialsim) and feudalism (subordination) and quickly realize our present and higher stage of industrial nationalism. By introducing him to the printed page the school could provide the Indian with the ideals of Christianity and of civil society, which would permit him to secure the greatest possible freedom in the social whole.[69] For the Negro, he thoroughly approved industrial training, which would give discipline and habits of regularity, obedience, self-control, co-operation, and industry. "The Negro must teach himself to become a capitalist." But in addition to industrial training, the Negro must be given a cultural education which not only would fit him for the professions but would also introduce him to the roots of our civilization and enable him to become integrated in our national life.[70]

No American, perhaps, endeavored with greater success than Harris to put on a high and idealistic plane the imperialism on which we embarked at the end of the Spanish-American War. Expansion was held to be inevitable; it was, moreover, our duty to take a hand in the work of dividing outlying regions in order to show that we could govern backward peoples for their own benefit. It was, in short, our historical mission to help these races toward self-government. Unlike European imperialists, we would, by universal education, elevate these primitive folk into our superior industrial civilization. If we failed to lift these less advanced peoples to self-government, then our ideal would be threatened by sheer overweight of numbers in an essentially undemocratic world. We must teach the Filipinos and Puerto Ricans how to command their physical environment, how to participate in the cultural achievements of the race, and how to further both. To that end we must help not one class of these islanders, but all classes, for the highest ideal of civilization demanded for the lower classes participation in all that was "good and reasonable" and increased self-activity or individuality.[71]

Just as our capitalists were helping the poor of the slums by building better tenements at cheaper rents, just as they were aiding the farmer by constructing railroads to lower freight rates, so, declared Harris, they would extend similar blessings to our newly acquired territories. There was no word of the profits they might make, no hint of anything but the most altruistic behavior and motives. Blind to the arguments which Bryan and other anti-imperialists were making, Harris assumed that our capitalists would emancipate these backward peoples from unproductive methods, give them ownership of the land, and provide them with access to our cultural civilization.[72]

Harris realized that imperialism thrust new responsibilities on his countrymen and that education could not be indifferent to them. He welcomed the training that Oxford would provide, through the Rhodes scholarships, to our young men who might become administrators in our possessions and who would advance our new influence in the councils of the world.[73] "The new era is one of great portent to American statesmen. All legislation must be hereafter scrutinized in view of its influence on our foreign relations."[74] Our people must be prepared for the responsibilities of a closer union with Europe. We must study foreign literature to understand the basis of foreign opinion and foreign psychology; we must more adequately prepare our young men for the diplomatic service. Our elementary education, however, was not to be altered even in view of the change involved in the emergence of the United States as a world power.

IV

However ardent a champion of industrial capitalism, nationalism, and imperialism Harris was, he was too intelligent to be blind to all the evils within the existing order. Recognizing the prevalence of political corruption, he ascribed it not to the determination of railroads, manufacturers, and corporations to have legal immunity for their profit-making activities and legal assistance in worsting their rivals and "getting ahead," but rather to the presence of unlettered immigrants. Not being sufficiently strong in self-respect, the result of poverty and illiteracy under a monarchical government abroad, the ignorant immigrant failed to resist pecuniary offers for his vote. The temptation offered by this "lowest political stratum" was too great for the unscrupulous politician, who, as Harris explained, frequently grew up in a home where poverty and want dwarfed self-respect. When the immigrant was educated in political conscience, all would come out well. In the meantime, the higher classes must suffer "*because* the lower *are* the lower."[75] Thus Harris placed the major responsibility for political corruption upon the immigrant and only in a very qualified and left-handed way admitted that some guilt might be laid at the door of native sons or American conditions.

The slum with its squalor, degeneration, poverty, and crime was, in the eyes of Harris, the rendezvous of the "moral weaklings of society." The remedy was not charity, which could only further undermine self-respect and weaken what shreds of independence these poor wretches had left. The remedy rather was education—education which would teach these people to curb their appetites and cultivate self-respect, thrift, and decency. The kindergarten would help; the trade school would contribute to that end; instruction in domestic science would aid in stopping "the propagation of pauperism by preventing the transmission of unthrifty habits from parents to children."[76] Again and again Harris declared that it was "to the educational systems of large cities, and to them alone, that we look for the invention of more powerful and effective means to break the chain of heredity between the adult criminal and the criminal offspring, so as to eradicate the slum in the future."[77] Thus Harris continued one of the main arguments of pre-Civil War educators.

In spite of the *laissez-faire* attitude to which Hegelianism committed him, Harris was willing to lend his influence to certain reforms.[78] An early advocate of co-education, he desired women to enjoy not only the highest cultural type of learning but professional training as well. At the twenty-fifth anniversary of Smith College Harris declared that the progress of science, the conquest of nature by means of invention, the elimination of brute strength as a result of mechanical operations, and the achievements of women in higher education assured them of securing their share in the division of labor and in political control.[79]

Harris also thoroughly approved the movement for instruction in temperance in the schools, which he believed furnished a permanent and active means for disseminating correct views regarding the effects of alcohol on the human body. "It may be said that this movement is the most effective one ever devised by the friends of temperance to abate a great evil, perhaps the greatest evil abroad in the land."[80]

Toward the effort to eliminate international war from modern civilization Harris maintained a very interesting attitude. In an address before a peace society in St. Louis in 1873 he recognized war as a divinely appointed institution by which mankind ascended into a higher consciousness of rational principles; it would disappear only when civilization had discovered and realized other methods of attaining to this all-essential knowledge. As an Hegelian, Harris emphasized the inevitability of conflicts whenever a new and deeper idea emerged.[81]

Years later, in preparing an address for the Lake Mohonk Conference on Arbitration, Harris found a strikingly large number of legitimate causes for war.[82] As long as war was necessary, the individual must submit to the will of the social whole. But the time would come, and education would hasten the day, when each people would so participate in the thought of other nations that war would be obsolete.[83] In assuming that war was caused merely by a lack of understanding, a conflict of ideas, Harris, like the more ardent pacifists of the period, overlooked the economic conflicts out of which misunderstandings arose. Although he was opposed to a war with Spain until the very eve of its declaration, he accepted it with enthusiasm and cloaked it with noble and inspiring idealism.[84]

The conservatism of Harris is the more striking because he realized that he lived in an age of transition. He even went so far as to declare that in view of such rapid changes in industry and in social conditions, it was "indispensable that the individual shall be educated into the power to adapt himself to his circumstances, the power to readjust himself in the case of emergencies." But for that purpose he regarded industry, courteous behavior, and mastery of the tools of thought as the essential requisites; no important changes in the school were necessary.[85]

Realizing that the school was a product of civilization and integrated with all the forces of society, Harris thought that it was less important in the educative process than the family, the church, the civil community, and the state.[86] Unlike Mann and Dewey, he did not expect that the school could contribute substantially to the creation of a new order, even had he thought one desirable. As an Hegelian, he believed that improvement would take place in any case and by necessity; that the school was an agent, not for guiding the change, but for preserving the values of the past and adjusting the individual to society.

Harris held that education, in its function of adjusting the individual to the social whole in order that he might realize his true ethical self, should be founded on sociology, "the science of a combination of men into social wholes."[87] The Hegelian found it easy to solve the conflict between the individual and society: education, which includes not only the school but the family, the church, the civil community, and the state, places the child's hands "in the hands of the great social whole, and thus he is led toward his fruition." In past ages and in the Orient the individual had existed solely for the social whole, and the result had been slavery. Freedom is the state in which the individual contributes to society his infinitesimal product and in return participates in what the social whole produces. Education gives the individual freedom by enabling him to use the whole as his instrument.

In thus emphasizing both individuality and social obligation Harris served well the dominant forces in the America of his day. On the one hand, he preserved and, at least in theory, elevated and spiritualized the American tradition of individualism; and on the other, he reconciled it with the new forces of modernism in Christianity, nationalism, imperialism, social stratification, and industrial capitalism.

However great or however little was the influence of Harris upon American life, one is impressed by the weight his name carried in educational circles.[88] His influence can be explained by the fact that he was a representative social philosopher. In spite of the technical character of Hegelianism, it was in many ways admirably suited to the requirements of the American scene. Without sacrificing the old American ideals of self-help and *laissez-faire* it seemed to lift the individual to a higher plane. Charged with idealism and optimism, it at the same time justified the existing order by declaring that whatever is, is right. It rationalized the victory of nationalism, imperialism, and industrial capitalism by insisting that true individualism could be realized only by subordinating the individual to existing institutions. It confirmed class arrangements but obscured them by idealizing class collaboration for the realization of an ethical and spiritual whole.

Who can say how far the reluctance of Americans to experiment seriously with social control, to abandon traditional *laissez-faire* individualism in spite of its patent contradiction by harsh facts, was related to the skill and plausibility with which Harris told two generations of Americans what they already believed, and what they wanted to believe? Who can estimate the influence of Harris in standardizing the school system, enveloping it with spiritual purposes, housing it in ivory towers, and excluding from its curriculum and its methods everything that did not confirm the existing economic and social structure?

Footnotes

[1] Henry Sabin, "Reminiscences of William Torrey Harris," *Journal of Education*, Vol. LXXI (May 5, 1910), pp. 483-484; William T. Harris, "How I Was Educated," *The Forum*, Vol. I (Aug., 1886), pp. 552-561.

[2] Harris to S. S. McClure, Sept. 7, 1887, Harris Mss, No. 863: "Books That Have Helped Me," *The Forum*, Vol. III (April, 1887), pp. 142-451.

[3] For a brief discussion of Harris's philosophy see John S. Roberts, *William T. Harris, A Critical Study of His Educational and Related Philosophic Views* (Washington, D. C., 1924).

[4] Wm. T. Harris, "Social Culture in the Form of Education and Religion," *Ed. Rev.*, Vol. XXIX (Jan., 1905), pp. 18-37.

[5] *Ibid.*

[6] Wm. T. Harris, "Religious Instruction in the Public Schools," *Independent*, Vol. LV (Aug. 6, 1903), pp. 1841-1843.

[7] A *Statement of the Theory of Education in the United States by Many Leading Educators* (Washington, D. C., 1874), p. 34.

[8] — *Ibid.*, p. 35.

[9] Wm. T. Harris, *What Shall We Study?* Reprint from *Journal of Education*, St. Louis, Vol. II (Sept., 1869), pp. 1-3.

[10] Wm. T. Harris, *The Danger of Using Biological Analogies in Reasoning on Educational Subjects* (Bloomington, Ill., 1902).

[11] *Annual Report of the St. Louis Public Schools*, 19th, 1872-1873, p. 110.

[12] "Observations on Physical Training in and out of School," in Harris Mss; Wm. T. Harris, *Recess (Popular Education Document*, No. 20, St. Louis, 1884), p. 8.

[13] "On the Function of the Study of Latin and Greek in Education," address, Sept. 4, 1884, in Harris Mss; Wm. T. Harris, "A Brief for Latin," *Ed. Rev.*, Vol. XVII (April, 1899), pp. 313-316.

[14] Wm. T. Harris, *Compulsory Education in Relation to Crime and Social Morals* (Washington, 1885), p. 13.

[15] Wm. T. Harris, "The Aesthetic Element in Education," N. E. A., *Proceedings*, 1897, pp. 330-338; "The Study of Art and Literature in the Schools." *Report of the Commissioner of Education*, 1898-1899, Vol. I, pp. 687-706.

[16] *Education*, Vol. IX (May, 1889), p. 580.

[17] *The Forum*, Vol. IV (Feb., 1888), p. 580.

[18] Wm. T. Harris, "The Intellectual Value of Tool Work," *Scientific American*, supplement, No. 1598 (Aug. 18, 1906).

[19] Wm. T. Harris, "The Printing Press as an Instrument of Education," *Education*, Vol. I (March, 1881), pp. 371-383; "What Shall the Public Schools Teach?" *Forum*, Vol. IV (Feb., 1888), pp. 573-581.

[20] *St. Louis Report*, 17th, 1870-1871, p. 173.

[21] *Education*, Vol. V (May, 1885), p. 444.

[22] N. E. A., *Proceedings*, 1898, p. 124; *Atlantic Monthly*, Vol. LXIX (June, 1892), p. 731; *The Educational Journal of Virginia*, Vol. XXII (Nov., 1891), pp. 519-523.

[23] Wm. T. Harris, "Co-education of the Sexes," *Report of the Commissioner of Education*, 1900-1901, Vol. II, pp. 1241-1247; N. E. A., *Proceedings*, 1898, pp. 124-125; *The Arena*, Vol. XVII (Feb., 1897), pp. 355-356; *St. Louis Report*, 19th, 1872-1873, p. 130.

[24] Wm. T. Harris, "The Relation of Woman to the Trades and Professions," *Ed. Rev.*, Vol. XX (Oct., 1900), pp. 217-229; "Co-education of the Sexes," *loc. cit.*

[25] Wm. T. Harris, *Do the Public Schools Educate Children Beyond the Position Which They Must Occupy in Life?* (New Haven, 1882), pp. 34-35.

[26] *Atlantic Monthly*, Vol. LXIX (June, 1892), p. 726; N. E. A., *Proceedings*, 1890, pp. 485-486.

[27] Address at the dedication of a new building for public school management on the fiftieth anniversary of the Board of Education of New York City, Harris Mss, No. 712.

[28] Speech at New Orleans, Dec. 28, 1898, Harris Mss.

[29] "What Captains of Industry Owe the Higher Education," clipping, *The Patriot*, Jackson, Mich., Oct. 20, 1901, Harris Mss, No. 754. In an interview in the *Brooklyn Daily Eagle*, Aug. 16, 1899, Harris sought to refute the statement of Collis P. Huntington, the great railway magnate, that the average American boy was over-educated. *Ibid.*, No. 726. See also *Report of the Commissioner of Education*, 1902, Vol. I., pp. 951-952.

[30] Wm. T. Harris, "Why Women Should Study Law," *Ohio Educational Monthly* Vol. L (July 1901), pp. 289-292. For a eulogy of the corporation see *Do the Public Schools Educate Children Beyond the Position Which They Must Occupy in Life?* p. 37.

[31] *Report of the Commissioner of Education*, 1902, Vol. I, pp. 949-951; Harris to Lucia Ames, Dec. 20, 1895, Harris Mss, No. 380.

[32] Wm. T. Harris, *The Right of Property and the Ownership of Land*, read before the National Social Science Association, Sept. 10, 1886 (Boston, 1887), p. 148.

[33] *Ibid.*, p. 146.

[34] *The Forum*, Vol. VIII (Oct., 1889), p. 205.

[35] Wm. T. Harris, "The Kindergarten as a Preparation for the Highest Civilization," *Atlantic Educational Journal*, Vol. VII (July-Aug., 1903), pp. 35-36; *Report of the Commissioner of Education*, 1896-97, Vol. I, p. 903.

[36] Harris to Wheeler, Aug. 23, 1897, Harris Mss, No. 855.

[37] *Education*, Vol. IX (Dec., 1888), p. 215.

[38] Wm. T. Harris, "Statistics vs. Socialism," *The Forum*, Vol. XXIV (Oct. 1897), pp. 186-199; "The Tenth Census from an Educational Point of View," Department of Superintendence, N. E. A., *Proceedings*, 1880 (Bureau of Education, *Circular of Information*, No. 2, 1880), pp. 61-67; "The Statistical Data Required to Settle the Great Economic Questions of the Day," Harris Mss, No. 558.

[39] W. T. Harris, "Henry George's Mistake About Land," *The Forum*, Vol. III (July, 1887), pp. 435-441.

[40] *Ibid.* See also "Edward Bellamy's Vision," *The Forum*, Vol. VIII (Oct., 1889), pp. 199-208, and "Statistics versus Socialism," *ibid.*, declared that as capital increases it draws a smaller proportion from the product as its share while labor gets a larger proportional amount. *The Forum*, Vol. III, p. 204.

[41] *The Forum*, Vol. III, p. 441.

[42] *Ante.*

[43] *Report of the Commissioner of Education* (1902), Vol. I, pp. 950-952.

[44] Wm. T. Harris, "Is There Work Enough for All?" *The Forum*, Vol. XXV (April, 1898), pp. 224-236.

[45] Wm. T. Harris, "The Definition of Social Science and the Classification of the Topics Belonging to Its Several Provinces," *Journal of Social Science*, Vol. XXII (June, 1887), pp. 1-7; "English and German: A Study in the Philosophy of History," *Andover Review*, Vol. VI (Dec., 1886), pp. 590-607; *The Forum*, Vol. VIII, pp. 199-208.

[46] N. E. A., *Proceedings*, 1894, p. 59. For the opposition of Harris to the demands of organized labor in the Bureau of Engraving see *Education*, Vol. XIX (Feb., 1899), p. 378.

[47] Wm. T. Harris, "The Kindergarten as a Preparation for the Highest Civilization," *Atlantic Educational Journal*, Vol. VI (July-Aug., 1903), pp. 35-36.

[48] N. E. A., *Proceedings*, 1891, p. 141; *Report of the Commissioner of Education*, 1893-1894, Vol. I, pp. 618-619.

[49] *Education*, Vol. XVII (June, 1897), p. 583.

[50] Wm. T. Harris, "The Use of the Higher Education," *Ed. Rev.*, Vol. XVI (Sept., 1898), pp. 147-161.

[51] Wm. T. Harris, "The Place of University Extension in American Education,"

Report of the Commissioner of Education, 1891-1892, Vol. II, pp. 743-751; N. E. A., *Proceedings*, 1894, pp. 133-134.

[52] *Ed. Rev.*, Vol. III (Feb., 1892), p. 169.

[53] *Education*, Vol. XII (Dec., 1891), p. 194.

[54] Wm. T. Harris, "The Future of Teachers' Salaries," *Independent*, Vol. LIX (Aug. 3, 1905), pp. 255-258.

[55] *Education*, Vol. XII (Dec., 1891), pp. 196-197. See also "The Isolation of the School: Its Educational Function," *Independent*, Vol. LIII (Aug. 1, 1901), pp. 1782-1786; "The Relation of School Discipline to Moral Education," *The Third Yearbook of the National Herbartian Society*, 1897, pp. 58-72.

[56] In fairness to Harris it should be said that he recognized some of the abuses of the textbook and did not favor mere memorization of facts. N. E. A., *Proceedings*, 1880, p. 108; 1898, pp. 127-128.

[57] Wm. T. Harris, "Herbart's Doctrine of Interest," *Ed. Rev.*, Vol. X (June, 1895), pp. 71-80; *North American Review*, Vol. CLX (May, 1895), p. 542; N. E. A., *Proceedings*, 1910, p. 193.

[58] Wm. T. Harris, "Fruitful Lines of Investigation in Psychology," Vol. I (Jan., 1891), pp. 8-14; "The Old Psychology versus the New," *Report of the Commissioner of Education*, 1893-1894, Vol. I, pp. 433-437.

[59] Wm. T. Harris, "The Pendulum of School Reform," *Education*, Vol. VIII (Feb., 1888), pp. 347-350; *St. Louis Report*, 20th, 1873-1874, p. 121; N. E. A., *Proceedings*, 1900, p. 336.

[60] Wm. T. Harris, "The Study of Arrested Development in Children as Produced by Injudicious School Methods," *Education*, Vol. XX (April, 1900), pp. 453-466.

[61] Wm. T. Harris, "The Philosophic Aspects of History," *Papers of the American Historical Association*, Vol. V (1891), pp. 247-254; Preface to Thomas Davidson, *The Education of the Greek People* (New York, 1903), pp. v-viii; *The Arena*, Vol. XVII (Feb., 1897), p. 354; N. E. A., *Proceedings*, 1891, p. 72, "The Practical Lessons of History," Harris Mxx, No. 804.

[62] N. E. A., *Proceedings*, 1910, p. 191; *Education*, Vol. V (May, 1885), p. 448.

[63] *St. Louis Report*, 18th, 1871-1872, p. 152; "What the American Youth Can Learn from the History of His Own Country," Harris Mss, No. 885.

[64] *St. Louis Report*, 16th, 1869-1870, p. 169.

[65] Wm. T. Harris, "The School City," *School Bulletin*, Vol. XXXII (March, 1906), pp. 113-114.

[66] *Newark Evening News*, May 2, 1890, Harris Mss, No. 787.

[67] *St. Louis Report*, 20th, 1893, p. 171.

[68] "Immigration and Rural Problems," Address before the American Defense Association, Philadelphia, Dec., 1890, Harris Mss, No. 855.

[69] *Proceedings of the 13th annual meeting of the Lake Mohonk Conference of the Indian*, 1895, pp. 33-38; N. E. A., *Proceedings*, 1902, p. 876; "A Definition of Civilization," *Report of the Commissioner of Education*, 1904, Vol. I, pp. 1129-1139.

[70] Wm. T. Harris, "The Education of the Negro," *Atlantic Monthly*, Vol. LXIX (June, 1892), pp. 720-736; "Normal School Training for the Negro," Harris, Mss, No. 866. Harris supported the Blair Educational Bill, Harris to J. R. Preston, 1889, Harris Mss, No. 519.

[71] N. E. A., *Proceedings*, 1898, pp. 49-51; "An Educational Policy for Our New Possessions," *ibid.*, 1899, pp. 69-79.

[72] *Ibid.*, 1899, pp. 75-76.

[73] *Report of the Commissioner of Education*, 1902, Vol. I, p. 959.

[74] *Ed. Rev.*, Vol. XVI (Sept., 1898), p. 205.

[75] *North American Review*, Vol. CXXXIII (Sept., 1881), pp. 219-221. Harris

recognized, however, that the political education of the adult immigrant was not a responsibility primarily of the public school.

[76] Address, Home Congress, Boston, Oct. 5, 1896, Harris Mss, No. 614; Remarks in *A Memorial of the Life and Services of John D. Philbrick*, pp. 59-61.

[77] Address, Public School Society Centenary, April 5, 1905, Harris Mss, No. 773; "Education to regenerate the Slums," *Brooklyn Eagle*, Dec. 30, 1900, *ibid.*, No. 728; "The Old Philanthropy and the New," address at Lake Mohonk, Oct. 9, 1895, Harris Mss, No. 375.

[78] For a somewhat facetious paper on reformers see his address before the Missouri State Teachers Association, April 8, 1868, Harris Mss, No. 3.

[79] "The Relation of Women to the Trades and Professions," Smith College Anniversary, 1900, Harris Mss, No. 719; Address at the Women's Educational Association, Boston, April 18, 1872, *ibid.*; *St. Louis Report*, 16th, 1869-1770, pp. 18 *et seq.*

[80] *Pall Mall Gazette*, May 14, 1894, Harris Mss, No. 219-334; *Report of the Commissioner of Education*, 1900-1901, pp. xli-xliii.

[81] "On the Significance of Peace," *The Western*, Sept., 1873, Harris Mss, No. 800.

[82] "Sketch on the Justifications of War," *ibid.*, No. 788.

[83] *Ed. Rev.*, Vol. XXVII (March, 1904), p. 269; *Harper's New Monthly Magazine*, Vol. XC (April, 1895), p. 790; N. E. A., *Proceedings*, 1891, p. 73.

[84] Paper read at the Southern Education Association at New Orleans, Dec. 28, 1898, Harris Mss: Harris to J. L. M. Curry, April, 1898, Curry Papers.

[85] *Education*, Vol. XII (Dec., 1891), p. 197; Harris, in *A Memorial of the Life and Services of John D. Philbrick*, pp. 60-61.

[86] *North American Review*, Vol. CXXXIII (Sept., 1881), p. 216.

[87] N. E. A., *Proceedings*, 1896, p. 196.

[88] The importance of Harris can in part be estimated by the character of the tributes that have been made to his influence by such educators as Ella Flagg Young, Nicholas Murray Butler, William Maxwell, James M. Greenwood, W. S. Sutton, Frank A. Fitzpatrick, George P. Brown, A. E. Winship, and James H. Canfield. For evidence of the influence of Harris see *Outlook*, Vol. XCIII (Nov. 20, 1909), pp. 611-612; *The Nation*, Vol. LXXXIII (July 5, 1906), pp. 8-9; G. Stanley Hall, *Life and Confessions of a Psychologist* (New York, 1923), pp. 496-497; *Journal of Education*, Vol. XLI (Feb. 21, 1895); *ibid.*, Vol. LXX (Dec. 16, 1907), p. 1881; *Ed. Rev.*, Vol. XXXIX (March, 1910), pp. 229-308; *ibid.* (Jan., 1910), pp. 1-12; *ibid.* (Feb., 1910), pp. 120-143; *ibid.*, Vol. XL (Sept., 1910), pp. 173-183; N. E. A., *Proceedings*, 1910, pp. 185-198; *Education*, Vol. XXX (Dec., 1909), p. 247. Canfield observed that Harris was more frequently quoted and approved by educational journals than any other American educator, not excepting Horace Mann, and that he was one of the best loved as well as the most widely known and influential educators "in this or any other country." *American Review of Reviews*, Vol. XXXIV (Aug., 1906), pp. 164-166. The influence of Harris on the curriculum, through the Report of the Committee of Fifteen, his work on other important committees of the N. E. A., his impressive contributions to educational literature, his widely read reports while superintendent of the St. Louis school system, 1869-1880, and his work as Commissioner of Education, 1889-1906, was great. For additional evidence of the influence of Harris see Roberts, *William Torrey Harris*, Chaps. XI-XII. Henry Ridgley Evans, *A List of the Writings of William Torrey Harris* (Washington, 1908) contains 479 titles but is not complete. The National Education Association is the repository of the manuscripts of Harris.

51
Francis W. Parker (1837-1902)

Notes of Talks on Teaching, Given by Francis W. Parker, at the Martha's Vineyard Summer Institute, July 17 to August 19, 1882, Reported by Lelia E. Patridge (New York: E. L. Kellogg & Co., 1882), Talk XXV. "Moral Training," pp. 166-182.

No matter how much educators may differ, in regard to the means and methods of teaching, upon one point, there is substantial agreement; vis. that the end and aim of all education, is the development of character. There is also, little or no difference of opinion, in regard to the elements that form the common ideal of character. Love of truth, justice, and mercy; benevolence, humility, energy, patience, and perseverance, are recognized the world over, as some of the essentials that should govern human action. True character, is recognized and felt, by all classes and conditions of society; though they may be incapable of its analysis. Just as the lower types of intellect, feel the power of the few masterpieces of art, without knowing its source.

All the knowledge and skill of an individual, all he thinks, knows, and does, is manifested in his character. Character is the summation of all these manifestations. Character, is the expression of all that is in the mind; and it may be analyzed into habits. A habit, is the tendency and desire to do that which we have repeatedly done before. A habit then, consists in doing, the primary foundation of which, is to be found in the possibilities for action that lie latent in the mind of the new-born child. The environment of the child, determines the kind, quality, and direction of its mental action. Education adapts the environment, by limiting it to those circumstances which lead the mind to act in the right manner, and in the right direction. The mother and teacher, be it through ignorance or knowledge, determine the doing of the child. The true teacher, leads the child to do that which ought to be done. The famous principle of Comenius: "Things that have to be done, should be learned by doing them," includes in its category, the whole truth that should govern every parent and teacher in building the character of a child. Everything that may determine action, be it religious precepts, moral maxims, the best influences, or whatever of good may be brought to bear upon the child, find their limitations in what they inspire, and stimulate the child to do.

The opinion prevails among many teachers, that intellectual development, is, by its nature, separate and distinct from moral training. Of all the evils in our schools, this terrible mistake is productive of the greatest. The powers of the mind, determine by their limitations, all human action. There is no neutral ground. Every thing done, has a moral, or immoral tendency. That is, doing, forms by repetition, a habit, and habits make up character. Let no one think that I am trenching on religious or theological grounds. I simply repeat what I have said before; the greatest truths of religion, the highest forms of morality, nature and art with all their beauty, can do no more than stimulate, inspire, direct, and fix mental action. This action may be right, or wrong. If right, it leads upward to all that is good, true, and beautiful. If wrong, it leads down to falsehood, wickedness, and sin. No teacher should say, "I train the intellect," and leave moral and spiritual teaching to others. Every act of the teacher, his manner, attitude, character, all that he does, or says, all that he calls upon his pupils to do or say, develops in a degree, moral or immoral tendencies. I am aware that this is a very strong statement. I may not be able to prove it, entirely to your satisfaction, but I believe it with all my heart, and will try to give you reasons for the faith that is in me.

First, and foremost of the habits to be acquired, is that of self-control, and to self-control, we shall all agree, every act in educating the child should lead. The vices that ruin mankind, are the baneful fruitage of the lack of self-control; and generous, humanity-loving people, spend millions to mitigate the evils arising from this lack. An ounce of prevention is worth a ton of cure! One dollar, spent for Kindergartens, will do more in the cause of temperance, than thousands for reform schools, or Washingtonian homes. The mind is controlled by three causes. First, by the will of another. Second, by one's own desire, whether right or wrong. Third, by reason; i. e., that a course of action is knowingly right, and therefore must be taken. As I said, in the talk upon school government, the mother and teacher *must* be the will of the child, until the child's reason, or knowledge of right, leads it to do right acts. Otherwise, its own unreasoning desire will govern the will from the first. I have known many a child, tired and jaded by the care of controlling its parents, which control began, when it first cried for a light, and *got* it; and continued, up to the time that it came under the influence of the sweet strong will of a kind-hearted teacher; I have known such children, to act as though a great burden was rolled from their little shoulders, as they sat and worked, at last in perfect peace, and quietness; but alas, only to go home and resume the reins of government! The child finds true happiness alone, under the dominion of a firm, steady, reasonable will outside of himself.

But there is a dangerous and delicate point, beyond which, the will of the parent or teacher must not be carried. The moment a child can act from a dictate of his own reason, that tells him something is right, the superimposed will of the parent should give way to the child's own volition. The law, that we learn to do by doing, comes in here with full force. The importance of training the will by developing the knowledge of right, cannot be overrated. The knowledge of right, comes from leading the mind to discover the truth. The truth is of no use, unless it is expressed in action. The opportunities for this action, at home, and in school, are innumerable. These opportunities should be seized upon, and used, by the mother or teacher, as means of training self-control. I cannot repeat often enough, the great truth, that we learn to do by doing. If a child be selfish, he has acquired the habit by selfish acts. The wrong tendency may, it is true, be inborn, but the habit, is acquired by selfish doing. A bad habit can be cured, only, by repetitions of good acts, directly opposed to it. Thus, a selfish child, may be given many opportunities to perform benevolent, and generous acts. Cruelty, may be turned into loving-kindness and mercy, in the same way. In the school, we find all the primary elements of society, but lacking the conventionalities of the grown-up world; and here, the child acts out his nature, freely. The eager, searching eye of the teacher, fixed upon the good of the child's soul, rather than the quantity of knowledge to be gained; sees through the mass of her little ones, into the weakness of each individual. The order, the writing, the reading, the number lessons, the playground, all furnish countless occasions, where the child may be led to act in the right way, from right motives. Selfishness may be turned to benevolence, cruelty to love, deceit to honesty, sullenness to cheerfulness, conceit to humility, and obstinacy to compliance, by the careful leading of the child's heart to the right emotion. But, in this work, the most responsible of all human undertakings, we cannot afford to experiment; there is one indispensable requirement,—*the teacher must know the child, and its nature.*

The true method of teaching, is the exact adaptation of the subject taught, or means of growth, to the learning mind. The mind can best grow, in only one way. If the adaptation of the subject to the mind is wrong, the action of the mind is impaired, and weakened, by ineffectual attempts to grasp it; and then the will of the teacher is obliged to come in, with artificial stimulants—to unhealthy mental action. Under such conditions, real essential happiness, that must come from the child's right emotions, is wanting; and the subject becomes in itself, an object of dislike and disgust to the child. Such teaching, I hold, must be, of its very nature, immoral. On the other hand, when the mind is in the full tide of healthy normal action, when it loves what it does, and does what it loves, the leading power of the teacher, in right directions, is enhanced to an incalculable degree. If the teacher knows the child, and her heart lies close to the child's heart, every motion of his mental and moral pulse, every desire to do wrong or right, will always be felt by her. However much the teacher may desire to help the child, however strong her own moral or religious feelings may be, wrong methods, and misapplied teaching, stand as formidable barriers between herself and the child. Many a father, who would have given his life for his boy, simply because he did not understand his child's nature, has failed in his method of training, and driven the boy to ruin. The will of a parent, may deprive the child of the use of his reason so long, that when the controlling will is removed, the child finds himself weak, and helpless; a prey to any stronger will that may chose to master him.

Primary education consists, as I have said, in training the power of attention. The attractiveness of the object attended to, controls the will. The desire to attend, is thus aroused, making it possible for the mind to exert more and more power in such acts, until the reason comes in to govern the will, enabling the mind to concentrate itself whenever required. The boy who is trained to solve a difficult problem, by a long and labored struggle with the thought, stimulated only, by the desire that comes from former successes to gain a new victory, has a will trained by reason in a high degree. You may say that this boy, notwithstanding his power in one direction, might perform immoral acts; and you are right. The energy generated in one direction, if it be not broadened and deepened in all other right ways, may be fatal to the welfare of the possessor. Lead and train a child to do one good thing thoroughly, through love of doing, and you have a central force of moral power, that can be turned into all doing.

Let us look for a moment on the other side of this question. God has so created the mind, that healthy moral, mental, and physical exercise, produces pleasure; this truth, I believe, cannot be gainsaid. If the work be not adapted to the grasp of the pupil, this pleasurable stimulant is lacking, and artificial stiumulants must be used. I have discussed, in a former talk, the use of fear in governing children. I need but appeal to all those, into whose heads knowledge has been driven by the terror of punishment, to obtain the strongest testimony, that such a course invariably disgusts children with learning, and defeats the ends it seeks to promote. The ubiquitous croaker now arises, with his single, ever reiterated poser: "Webster, Clay, Sumner, and all our greatest, were educated in the old ways, why require better methods when we can point to such results as these?" My dear sir; you can count, it is true, a few saved and successful men and women, but is your power of calculation great enough, to count the failures, the lost? It is time for us, teachers, to call a halt! All about us are men and women, who find themselves, to-day, crippled, for want of that power which their school-training should have given them. You feel the same lack, and so do I. Now, these men and women, have risen up, and are demanding better things for their children. We have but to look, to see the handwriting on the wall,—"Thou are weighed in the balances, and art found wanting."

The other artificial stimulant, is the hope of reward, in the shape of merits, per cents, prizes;—glittering empty baubles; sugar-coated but bitter pills! I have not time to point out, in detail, the immoral influences of these false stimulants. I will allude to one, and that is, the common tendency in examinations to appropriate other's earnings. How common this is, you all know, from primary school to college. Ponies, cuffs, hidden slips of paper, sly glances at books, promptings, and the thousand and one means to present stolen results; all testify to the prevalence of this evil. This is nothing more nor less than systematic training in habits of dishonesty. I have no doubt, that many of the frauds and defalcations, so sommon at present in this country, may be traced directly back to the well-meant, but dishonest training in the school-room.

Truth should govern the will, and the great work of the teacher is, to guide the child in his discoveries of truth. The habit of searching, finding, and using the truth, then, is one of the first importance. Truth sets the child free, and leads him to the source of all truth. The highest freedom is obedience to God. The learning of words, and pages of the text-books, without the privilege of verifying the facts and generalizations there given, weakens the reasoning power, that should be developed for the purpose of controlling the will. I do not here refer to religious truths, but to the habit of seeking and prizing the truth, wherever found in the branches taught in our common schools. If this habit is formed there, it will be carried into the affairs of politics, and society. For instance; a man so trained, will vote, not because he happens to belong to a party, or because he believes the *ipse dixit* of a leader; but because, through force of habit, he will discover from all the sources of information that lie in his power, what the truth really is, and exercise his right to vote accordingly. "Put that you would have the State, into the school," is an old German maxim. Americans must learn to apply this saying, in a vigorous way, or our, politics, from their downward tendency, will reach, in no far distant day, their lowest level.

There are two factors in education;—thought, and expression. Most teaching, is the training of the skill to express thought, with little or no regard to the thought itself. Precision, is an indispensable mode of training skill in writing, drawing, position, and accurate ways of acting; but, when the training of precision is made the main motive of school-work; when the ways a child sits, places his feet, holds his hands, stares at a book, stands up, marches, utters a sentence, etc. are the be all and end all in the teacher's plan of work; then, precision invades the sacred realm of thought evolution, and the mind's power to act, is crushed and crippled. I have seen schools of this description, where the results would be grand, if the systematic clock-work-like operations were performed with puppets, instead of living human beings. Such training, educates the willing followers of demagogues; prompt to march when the commanding boss gives the word.

Conceit, is another outgrowth of this quantity ideal. The spectacle is a common one, of a young man, the model of his class, persistent and alert, possessed of a powerful verbal memory, which enables him to cram page after page of the textbook, distancing all competitors, carrying off all the class honors, and finally; armed with his sheepskin, [his Alma Mater's gracious indorsement of his wonderful attainments] confidently stepping out into the world, never questioning but that he will conquer in the new life, as easily as he did in the old. But the first spear-thrust of reality, shivers his panoply of empty words, and leaves him defenceless, before the rigorous demands of an uncompromising world. "The long perspective of our life i s truth, and not a show;" and I hold that sort of teaching, in the highest degree immoral, which crams the heads of our children, with the unusable pages of text-books, and then leads them to suppose that they are gaining real knowledge. By making quantity our ideal, we develop and foster conceit; and conceit is one of the most formidable barriers to true knowledge.

Inspire them to seek earnestly for the truth, and develop in them, one of the greatest of all human virtues—humility. "The meek shall inherit the earth," said the Great Teacher. He alone is really learning, who feels the immensity of the truth, and realizes that all he knows, or can know, in this world, is but as a drop to the great ocean of truth, that stretches boundless and fathomless into eternity. The teacher, above all others, should constantly be adding to his store of knowledge; and he who imagines that he has no more to learn in the art of teaching, is fit only, to take his small place among other fossils.

Primary education consists, as I have repeatedly tried to show, in the development of the power of attention; and it will be plain to all, that the selection of the objects of thought and attention, is a matter of the highest importance. The things presented must be pure, good, and beautiful, for that to which we attend, comes into the heart, and forms the basis of all our thinking and imagination; "Out of the heart the mouth speaketh." Where shall we look for the highest source of the good, the true, and the beautiful? To the thoughts of God in nature. The study of nature, is the best and highest foundation for morality, and a preparation for the revealed truth, that comes to the child later in life. Compare the drill upon hieroglyphics, empty words, and meaningless forms, to the observation of trees, flowers, animals, and the forms of earth. The one stimulates thought, and fills the mind with ideas of beauty; the other crowds the mind with useless, ugly forms; that cannot, from their very nature, stimulate it to renewed action. A child's mind, filled with that which is pure, and good, has no room for wickedness and sin. The study of the natural sciences, is one of the best means of bringing about this result. Did you ever observe the character of a boy who early fell in love with nature, and who spent his spare hours with plants, or animals, seeking for their haunts, watching their habits, and making collections for preservation? Such boys, so far as I have known, are genuinely good. They have neither the time, nor the inclination, for evil doing. The study of the thoughts of God in nature, lling the mind, as it does, with things of beauty, prepares the imagination for clear and strong conceptions of the higher and spiritual life.

Let no one misunderstand me, or imagine for a moment, that I mean to limit moral training to these subjects. Far from it. I am only trying to show, how all these things may be used in developing true character. Children learn very much by imitation. The teacher, whether good or bad, leaves his everlasting imprint on every child under his care. He can conceal nothing from the intuitional power of the child. Whatever you are, becomes immortal through the souls of your pupils. The precepts of a true teacher, have immense weight; but the example has a still greater.

A fact very much bemoaned and bewailed in these times, is, that children love to read trashy literature; that they read Dime Novels, sensational newspapers, and stories like, The Robber of the Bloody Gulch; or The Red Handed Pirate of the Spanish Main. This unwholesome, and vicious tendency, is almost wholly caused, I believe, by the neglect of school authorities to furnish a generous supply of pure, interesting literature, to the schools under their charge. I know a superintendent of schools, who often waxes eloquent over the vices engendered by such reading. I once visited his schools, and found his pupils learning to spell column after column, and page after page of words, one-tenth of which, they probably never would use in their lives. I satisfied myself that these poor victims hardly knew the meaning of one word, the forms of which they were struggling over. The money expended for those spelling-books, would have purchased a rich supply of excellent reading; and the time thrown away in conning that fearful book, if used in reading the best literature, would have rendered unnecessary some of that superintendent's eloquent, and pathetic periods, in regard to the miseries caused by reading sensational works. An entire year of the little child's life, is generally given to the reading of one book, not much thicker than my little finger. Let a child read a selection twice or three times, and he knows every word by heart. He can read his lesson with the book upside down, after that. I once tested one of the best schools in this country. The pupils read very well indeed, I asked them to close their books; and as soon as they understood what I wanted, they repeated every word, verbatim, with great gusto, simply by my reading one word, anywhere in the book. They knew that book from beginning to end; and yet, following the course of study, they must repeat those words, over and over again, for five long months! We are paying millions of dollars, in this country, for such worse than stupid and useless repetitions. A class will read a Primary Reader, through, in a very short time. The cost of a dozen different series of books [bought by the school authorities] is not so great as the price paid, by the children, for the Readers of a single series. Every school can, and should have a good library, made of sets of different books, embracing; the best Readers; works on natural history adapted to children, such as, Prang's little boosk, "Little Folks in Feathers and Fur," "Life and Her Children," and "The Fairyland of Science;" primary geographies, like "Our World," and Guyot's "Introduction;" histories; books of travel; poetry; and the best fiction. In my experience, it is the easiest of all problems, to lead children to read, and to love to read, the very best literature. If the hours devoted to the spelling-book; to useless repetitions of words already learned; were spent in the perusal of the best books, children would never feel the necessity for the trash they read, whose baneful influence is immeasurable.

In my talk upon School Government, I said, that the end and aim of school education, is to train a child to work, to work systematically, to love work, and to put his brains into work. The clearest expression of thought, is expression in the concrete. Working with the hands, is one great means of primary development. It is also one of the very best means of moral training. From the first, every child has an intense desire to express his thought in some other way, than in language. Froebel discovered this, and founded the Kindergarten. No one can deny, that true Kindergarten training is moral training. Ideas and thoughts come into the mind, demanding expression. The use of that which is expressed, to the child, is the means it gives him, to compare his thought, with its concrete expression. The expression of the form made, compared with the ideal, stimulates to further trials. In making and building, is found the best means of training attention.

I wish to make a sharp distinction here, between *real work*, and *drudgery*. Real work is done on real things, producing tangible results, results that are seen and felt. Real work is adapted at every step to the child's power to do. Every struggle brings success, and makes better work possible. Drudgery, on the other hand, is the forced action of the mind, upon that which is beyond mental grasp; upon words that cannot be apprehended, upon lessons not understood. Drudgery, consists, mainly of the monotonous use of the verbal memory. There is no variety; not a bush or shrub along the pathway. This is the kind of study that produces ill-health. It is the straining of the mind upon disliked subjects, with the single motive, to gain applause, rewards, and diplomas. Thousands, of nervous, earnest, faithful girls, spurred on by unwise parents, yearly lose their lives, or become hopeless invalids, in this costly and useless struggle. Real work, stimulates every activity of mind and body. It furnishes the variety, so necessary to interest, and is like true physical development, that exercises every muscle and strengthens the whole man. Real work is always interesting, like real play. No matter how earnest the striving may be, it is followed by a glow of genuine pleasurable emotion.

There is great outcry against our schools and colleges, caused by the suspicion that they educate children to be above manual labor. This suspicion is founded upon fact, I am sorry to say; but the statement of the fact is not correct. Children are educated *below* manual labor. The vague, meaningless things they learn, are not adapted to real work; no effectual habits of labor are formed by rote-learning. The student's desire is too often, when he leaves school or college, to get a living by means of empty words. The world has little or no use for such rubbish. That man should gain his bread by the sweat of his brow, is a curse changed to the highest possible blessing. The clergyman, the lawyer, the physician, the teacher, need the benefit of an early training in manual labor, quite as much as the man who is to labor with his hands all his life. Manual labor is the foundation of clear thinking, sound imagination, and good health. There should be no real difference between the methods of our common schools, and the methods of training in manual labor schools. A great mistake has been made in separating them. All school work should be real work. We learn to do by doing. "Satan finds some mischief still, for idle hands to do." The direct influence of real work is, to absorb the attention in the things to be done; leaving no room in the consciousness for idleness, and its consequent vices. Out of real work, the child develops a motive, that directs his life work. Doing work thoroughly, has a great moral influence. One piece of work well done, one subject well mastered, makes the mind far stronger and better, than a smattering of all the branches taught in our schools. School work, and manual labor, have been for a long time divorced; I predict that the time is fast coming, when they will be joined in indissoluble bonds. The time too, is coming, when ministers will urge upon their hearers, the great importance of manual labor, as a means of spiritual growth. At no distant date, industrial rooms will become an indispensable part of every good school; the work of the head, and skill of the hand, will be joined in class-room, and workshop, into one comprehensive method of developing harmoniously the powers of body, mind, and soul. If you would develop morality in the child, train him to work.

In all that I have said, and whatever mistakes I have made, either in thought or expression, I have had but one motive in my heart, and that is, that the dear children of our common country, may receive at our hands, a development of intellectual, moral, and spiritual power, that will enable them to fight life's battle, to be thoughtful conscientious citizens, and prepare them for all that may come thereafter. Whatever we would have our pupils, we must be ourselves.

52
John Dewey (1859-1952)

The Basis:
A New Scientific Formulation of the Nature of Experience Based upon Biology and A Change in Psychology

Selections from John Dewey, *Reconstruction in Philosophy* (New York: Henry Holt and Company, 1920), pp. 84-87. Enlarged edition copyright 1948 by Beacon Press. Reprinted by permission of Beacon Press.

. . . We are only just now commencing to appreciate how completely exploded is the psychology that dominated philosophy throughout the eighteenth and nineteenth centuries. According to this theory, mental life originated in sensations which are separately and passively received, and which are formed, through laws of retention and association, into a mosaic of images, perceptions, and conceptions. The senses were regarded as gateways or avenues of knowledge. Except in combining atomic sensations, the mind was wholly passive and acquiescent in knowing. Volition, action, emotion, and desire follow in the wake of sensations and images. The intellectual or cognitive factor comes first and emotional and volitional life is only a consequent conjunction of ideas with sensations of pleasure and pain.

The effect of the development of biology has been to reverse the picture. Wherever there is life, there is behavior, activity. In order that life may persist, this activity has to be both continuous and adapted to the environment. This adaptive adjustment, moreover, is not wholly passive; is not a mere matter of the moulding of the organism by the environment. Even a clam acts upon the environment and modifies it to some extent. It selects materials for food and for the shell that protects it. It does something to the environment as well as has something done to itself. There is no such thing in a living creature as mere conformity to conditions, though parasitic forms may approach this limit. In the interests of the maintenance of life there is transformation of some elements in the surrounding medium. The higher the form of life, the more important is the active reconstruction of the medium. This increased control may be illustrated by the contrast of savage with civilized man. Suppose the two are living in a wilderness. With the savage there is the maximum of accommodation to given conditions; the minimum of what we may call hitting back. The savage takes things "as they are," and by using caves and roots and occasional pools leads a meagre and precarious existence. The civilized man goes to distant mountains and dams streams. He builds reservoirs, digs channels, and conducts the waters to what had been a desert. He searches the world to find plants and animals that will thrive. He takes native plants and by selection and cross-fertilization improves them. He introduces machinery to till the soil and care for the harvest. By such means he may succeed in making the wilderness blossom like the rose.

Such transformation scenes are so familiar that we overlook their meaning. We forget that the inherent power of life is illustrated in them. Note what a change this point of view entails in the traditional notions of experience. Experience becomes an affair primarily of doing. The organism does not stand about, Micawber-like, waiting for something to turn up. It does not wait passive and inert for something to impress itself upon it from without. The organism acts in accordance with its own structure, simple or complex, upon its surroundings. As a consequence the changes produced in the environment react upon the organism and its activities. The living creature undergoes, suffers, the consequences of its own behavior. This close connection between doing and suffering or undergoing forms what we call experience. Disconnected doing and disconnected suffering are neither of them experiences. Suppose fire encroaches upon a man when he is asleep. Part of his body is burned away. The burn does not perceptibly result from what he has done. There is nothing which in any instructive way can be named experience. Or again there is a series of mere activities, like twitchings of muscles in a spasm. The movements amount to nothing; they have no consequences for life. Or, if they have, these consequences are not connected with prior doing. There is no experience, no learning, no cumulative process. But suppose a busy infant puts his finger in the fire; the doing is random, aimless, without intention or reflection. But something happens in consequence. The child undergoes heat, he suffers pain. The doing and undergoing, the reaching and the burn, are connected. One comes to suggest and mean the other. Then there is experience in a vital and significant sense.

Certain important implications for philosophy follow. In the first place, the interaction of organism and environment, resulting in some adaptation which secures utilization of the latter, is the primary fact, the basic category. Knowledge is relegated to a derived position, secondary in origin, even if its importance, when once it is established, is overshadowing. Knowledge is not something separate and self-sufficing, but is involved in the process by which life is sustained and evolved. The senses lose their place as gateways of knowing to take their rightful place as stimuli to action.

The Core of Dewey's Way of Thinking

Selections from Edwin A. Burtt, "The Core of Dewey's Way of Thinking," *The Journal of Philosophy*, LVII (No. 13, June 23, 1960), pp. 402-407, *passim.*

[Originally a neo-Hegelian, Dewey abandoned this philosophical view-point after publication of his text on *Psychology* in 1886 and a struggle to a new unity of thinking in the next decade. The shift is evident in his *Outline of Ethics* in 1891 and definitely established in his moral philosophy with his syllabus on *The Study of Ethics* in 1897.] What remained after that date was the task of his whole career—to clarify the bearing of the new orientation, first on logic and on educational theory, and then through these disciplines on every other branch of philosophy. What was it that happened in those decisive years of the late 1880's and early 1890's?

I suppose the crucial thing that happened was something in his own experience . . . that issued in clarified commitment to a democratic and dynamic ideal of life and society. What this meant, in his conception of it, was a vision of man's social relationships so organized and energized that the goods gradually approved as such in human experience are rendered secure and made available to all. In this process every achievement gained would serve as a foundation on which aspiration toward and realization of further goods is always expected—goods that earlier could not even be imagined as possible. Dewey became more and more sure that philosophy arises and fills its proper function in the setting of this human quest. . . .

. . . Human experience is a progressive reconstruction of ends as well as a selection of means for the realization of ends already accepted, and the vital task of moral philosophy is to provide a method by which men may guide their reflection in performing this two-fold task.

. . . The general assumption of previous philosophies had been that moral theory is the product of a detached thinker who contemplates the scene of ethical action and its problems from the outside. As a man he is of course involved in them; as a philosopher he views them *sub specie aeternitatis*, for only thus can he achieve a philosophic perspective. Dewey is now convinced that this notion is not only unrealistic but perverts the very nature of ethical theory. Genuine reflection about moral problems, whether specific or general, is a stage in the development of moral practice. That is, as any moral act emerges into full expression in the experience of the actor, it passes through a stage at which reflection is needed. The actor is puzzled as to what he should do; he pauses to consider. The value of such reflection is that it anticipates the consequences of various courses of action and thus guides the act that is taking form toward its true fulfillment. In the paper mentioned Dewey states this contention in the words: "Theory is the cross-section of a given stage of action in order to know the conduct that should be." And he defines certain basic ethical concepts, such as the concept 'ought,' in terms of this position; as the actor analyzes the facts of the situation, "that to which intelligence sees it [the act] moving is the 'ought to be'."

By the time Dewey wrote his syllabus on the *Study of Ethics* a few years later he had worked out a complete system of moral philosophy on this foundation. All the major concepts in which his position is characteristically expressed in later books appear in this syllabus, and so far as I can see have already gained the meaning which they have in his subsequent writing. Moral ideals, for example, are explicitly conceived as filling an essentially "instrumental" role in resolving this or that specific moral problem. And knowledge of the situation in which the problem occurs is "experimental" in the same basic sense in which scientific knowledge is experimental. The general criterion of rightness and wrongness which applies to any moral situation is "found in the fact that some acts tend to narrow the self, to introduce friction into it, to weaken its power, and in various ways to *disintegrate* it, while other acts tend to expand, invigorate, harmonize, and in general to organize the self." [*The Study of Ethics*, Ann Arbor, 1897, p. 22.] He assumes here, as always, that a self which accepts the guidance of intelligence and thus provides a sound moral criterion is a socialized self—that is, one which fulfills itself in the social relationships of family, school, neighborhood, vocation, and the human community as a whole.

The main idea which called for further elaboration in the years immediately following—prior to Dewey's publications in the field of logic just after the turn of the century—is that what in these writings he had shown to be true of ethical thinking is true of thinking in general—in fact, that in a vital sense all thinking is ethical thinking. His logical theory consisted in the application of this idea to the distinctive problems arising in that field, and his later work in each of the other branches of philosophy consisted basically in its application to them. The essence of this idea—already clearly implied in *The Study of Ethics*—may be expressed as follows. Thinking always fills an instrumental and experimental role within the larger activity that we call human conduct. By its very nature it plays a mediating function in situations where the primary impulses and formed habits which ordinarily determine our action are inadequate to do so. In such situations we do not know what we want to do or should do; we are in a state of hesitation, which on the intellectual side is experienced as doubt. The function of thinking is to resolve that doubt—to guide us in discovering what to do. If successful, it enables us to regain our lost unity and assurance, and permits renewed action guided by the conclusions reached. The reflection has experimentally transformed "ideas as hypotheses" into "warranted assertions."

. . . Dewey belongs to that line of philosophers who may be called philosopher-moralists. . . . whose distinctive feature is that they caught a vision of ultimate ethical value whose realized expression in all branches of philosophy—so these thinkers believe—would give them their true fulfillment. . . . What becomes the key to Dewey's way of thinking when it is approached from this standpoint? I think the answer is clear and simple. The central principle is that of *responsibility* —not, of course, in the limited meaning this word has in the philosophy of law or even in traditional moral philosophy with its separate field of problems, but in the meaning it might convey when applied by a reflective moralist to all philosophical issues. And what would that meaning be in Dewey's case? Well, somewhere around 1890, when the forces above described were finding their way to a unity in his mind, the idea must have dawned that *all human action, including thinking as an important part of action, has consequences; and that the vital difference which men in general and philosophers especially are concerned about is whether responsibility for those consequences is accepted or not.* The consequences, whether or not we wish it to be so, are involved in every act; the act is performed and its consequences brought into being by the actor; therefore he cannot escape responsibility for them. But nothing is easier or more tempting than to try to escape it. Under pressure of instinctive urges and formed habits he drives ahead in action, blind to what the consequences will be; and even when he consciously foresees them, narrowed vision and biased selection are very easy—he anticipates only those consequences fastened upon by the fearful emotion, the strong demand, or the self-centered desire of the moment. All the evils of human life that might be avoided, all the missed goods of human aspiration, are due, Dewey was sure, to this failure. The true role of philosophy arises from recognition of this fact. In *The Study of Ethics* of 1897 occurs this illuminating passage:

> . . . Every bad man is (in the substantial sense) irresponsible; he cannot be counted upon in action, he is not certain, reliable, trustworthy. He does not respond to his duties, to his functions. . . . Irresponsibility is but another name for his lack of unity, of integrity; being divided within himself, he is unstable, we can never be sure of him, he is not sure of himself. . . . He is *capable* of foreseeing consequences, and of having these foreseen consequences influence or modify his conduct. The person who fails in one respect or other of these factors is insane, imbecile or morally immature, and is not responsible.

And again: "We are responsible for our deeds because they are ourselves. . . . I am myself, I am conscious of myself in my deeds, I am responsible, name not three facts, but one fact."

. . . The major task of human life is to develop power of intelligent foresight of consequences in every kind of situation; the essential task of philosophy is to clarify the conditions that such foresight involves, so that men will understand what it means to be responsible in every phase of life and how that responsibility must be carried out. . . .

Criteria for Determining an Educative Experience: Continuity and Interaction

Selections from Hugh C. Black, "The Learning-Product and the Learning-Process Theories of Education: An Attempted Synthesis," Dissertation, University of Texas, 1949, pp. 179-191, an adaptation of John Dewey, *Experience and Education* (New York: The Macmillan Company), 1938, pp. 23-52.

[In the 1916 *Democracy and Education* an ideal of growth was posited under the definition of education as a constant reorganizing or reconstructing of experience "which adds to the meaning of experience, and which increases ability to direct the course of subsequent experience" (pp. 89-90). This conception of education is a mediated view in contrast to two extremes of "Progressivism" (unfolding of latent powers from within) and "Conservatism" (formation from without). It recognizes the importance of education in the development of children and youth and also in that of the future society in which they will live and participate. Its distinctive point of view is to emphasize the role of education in contributing to people who exhibit intelligent behavior in contrast to capricious or routine behavior. The essence of education comes down to the quality of the experiences involved. Some education involves experiences in which the maintenance of established custom is the measure of value. This leads to routine acts and behavior, a one-sided, isolated uniform way of acting. Some education involves experiences which lead to capricious behavior in which one does not care what happens and just lets himself go. In these experiences one fails to think and thereby perceive the connections between what one does and what happens as a result. Thus one fails to anticipate the consequences of his behavior and actions. This is to fail in responsibility. But we are capable of something better by way of education and experiences. We have the promise of educative rather than mis-educative experiences. Amid our controversies over education we would profit from delineating that kind of education which may be made our instrument for realizing the better hopes of men. Hence we turn to particular kinds of experiences: educative ones, those involving continuity and interaction.]

Continuity is the first of two proposed criteria for discriminating among experiences to determine which are educative.

Basic to this principle is the fact that our biological organisms form habits. We have experiences; that is, we act and undergo the consequences. Something is taken up from this which modifies the person and affects the quality of subsequent experiences. In this way we form our habits, emotional and intellectual attitudes, basic sensitivities, tendencies and dispositions toward behavior. Our continuing experiences determine the kind of persons we become.

There is some kind of continuity in every experience, for every experience affects for better or worse the attitudes which help decide the quality of further experiences. It does this by setting up certain preferences or aversions and by making it easier or harder to act for this or that end. Too, each experience influences in some degree the objective conditions under which further experiences are had. Consider, for example, the person who decides to become a teacher. His choice determines to some extent the environment in which he will act in the future. He thereby renders himself more sensitive and responsive to stimuli which pertain to the teacher, and he becomes relatively immune to those things about him which would be stimuli to the lawyer, physician, or stockbroker.

While the principle of continuity applies in some way in every case, the quality of the present experience influences the way in which the principle applies. Herein lies the basis for discriminating between an educative and mis-educative experience. Every experience is a moving force. One can judge its value only on the ground of what it moves toward and into. Notice the way in which the principle of continuity applies in the case of the spoilt child. When the child is overindulged, the experience has continuity. That is to say, it sets up an attitude which operates in his future experiences. But notice the way in which continuity operates. The spoilt child henceforth seeks the kind of situation which enables him to do what he feels like doing at the time. He avoids and is comparatively incompetent in situations requiring effort and perseverance. Thus in this case the principle of continuity operates so as to leave the individual arrested on a low plane of development. It operates in a way which limits later capacity for growth. How differently continuity works in an experience which arouses curiosity, strengthens initiative, and sets up desires and purposes that are sufficiently intense to carry a person over dead places in the future. Hence an experience may be judged to be educative or mis-educative only on the ground of what it moves toward and into.

The second chief principle for interpreting an experience in its educational function and force is interaction. This principle recognizes two factors in experience—objective and internal conditions. Internal conditions refer to the individual; objective conditions refer to the environment, to objects and other persons. Any normal experience is constituted by the interplay of these two sets of conditions. These two sets of conditions taken together, or in their interaction, form a situation. To say that individuals live in a world is to say that they live in a series of situations. This means that interaction is going on between an individual and objects and other persons. The terms situation and interaction are inseparable.

What characterizes an experience is the transaction taking place between the individual and his environment. The environment may consist of people with whom the individual is talking and also include the topic or event talked about. The situation may include the rocking-horse with which the child is playing. Or it may include the materials of an experiment the scientist is performing. A further illustration of what is meant by "environment" is the book the person is reading. The England, Africa, ancient Greece, or any imaginary region about which he is reading (or even any castles in the air he may construct in his fancy) is truly a part of the environment, of the transaction and inter-action. For these are examples of conditions which may interact with the individual's personal needs, desires, and purposes to create the resulting experience.

The principle of interaction assigns equal rights to both factors in experience: objective and internal conditions. One condition should not be subordinated to the other. An illustration may make clearer what is meant. An infant has certain internal conditions—that is, needs for food, rest, and activity. But there are also certain objective conditions which the parent must so arrange and order that a particular kind of interaction with these immediate internal states may be brought about. In this way the infant's experience of food, sleep, and activity occurs. When objective conditions are subordinated to what goes on within the infant, the result may be that the parent feeds the baby at any time when the baby is cross or irritable instead of having a program of regular hours of feeding and sleeping. The wise mother, however, recognizes the needs of the infant and takes them into account. But she does not do so in a way which dispenses with her own responsibility for regulating the objective conditions under which the needs are satisfied. When she assigns equal rights to objective conditions as to internal conditions, she draws upon her own past experiences and those of experts for the light that they shed upon what experiences are in general most conducive to the normal development of infants. This indicates that the parent has responsibility for arranging the conditions under which the infant's experience of food and sleep occurs. It indicates also that the responsibility is fulfilled by utilizing the funded experience of the past. The point is that interaction assigns equal rights to the objective and internal conditions of experience.

Notice should be taken that the two principles of continuity and interaction are not separate from each other. They intercept, unite, and form the longitudinal and lateral aspects of experience. Individuals live in a world—in a series of situations in which interaction is going on between the individual and objects and other persons. Although different situations succeed one another, something—because of the principle of continuity—is carried over from the earlier situations to the later ones. What he has learned in one situation becomes an instrument of understanding and dealing effectively with the situations which follow. Thus, as he passes from one situation to another, his world or environment expands or contracts. He finds himself living in a different part or aspect of one and the same world rather than in another world. This process goes on as long as life and learning continue. The course of experience becomes disorderly and the world becomes divided when the individual factor that enters into making an experience is split, when personality is divided. When this splitting up reaches a certain point and few of the parts and aspects of a world do not hang together for a person, that person is called insane. But we are capable of something better. We can construct and so relate the objects of our world as to integrate our successive experiences and achieve fully integrated personality.

The conclusion thus reached is that continuity and interaction are the two criteria of experience. In their union with each other they provide the measure of the educative significance and value of an experience. It remains to show the educational applications of these criteria—applications which may increase the meaning of the conclusion.

It has been said that the value of an experience can be judged only on the ground of what it moves toward and into. The implication for education is clear. It means that the business of the educator is to see in what direction an experience is heading and to judge and direct it on the ground of what it is moving into. For the adult as educator has a greater maturity of experience which places him in a position to evaluate each experience of the young in a way in which the immature student cannot do. The educator should use his greater insight to help organize the conditions of the experience of the immature. He should, however, exercise the wisdom of his own wider experience without imposing a merely external control. He may do so by being alert to see what attitudes and habitual tendencies are being created, by being able to judge what attitudes are actually conducive to continued growth and what are detrimental, and by having that sympathetic understanding of individuals as individuals which gives him an idea of what is actually going on in the minds of the students. Such is not an easy task. On the other side, there is also a danger. Experience should not be treated as though it were something going on exclusively inside an individual's body and mind. Of course, experience does go on inside a person; for it influences the formation of attitudes of desire and purpose. This, however, is not the whole story. For every experience has an active side which changes in some degree the objective conditions under which experiences are had. To treat experience as though it were something going on exclusively inside an individual is to ignore several facts. It is to ignore the fact that the individual lives from birth to death in a world of persons and things which in large measure is what it is because of what has been done and transmitted from previous human activities. It is to ignore the fact that experience does not occur in a vacuum. It is to ignore the fact that there are sources outside an individual which give rise to experience and that experience is fed from these springs. These so often ignored facts indicate the second way in which the educator can direct the experience of the young without engaging in imposition. Educators should be aware of the general principle of the shaping of actual experience by environing conditions. They should also recognize in the concrete what surroundings are conducive to having experiences that lead to growth. And, above all, they should know how to utilize the physical and social surroundings that exist so as to extract from them all that they have to contribute to building up experiences that are worth while. The teacher should become intimately acquainted with the conditions of the local community—physical, historical, economic, occupational—in order to utilize them as educational resources.

Another educational implication is that the immediate and direct concern of an educator is with the situations in which interaction takes place. There are two factors which enter into any situation. One is the pupil, who is what he is at that given time. The other factor is objective conditions. It is the latter which the educator can regulate to some extent. Objective conditions include what is done by the educator and the way in which it is done. It includes the words spoken and the tone of voice in which they are spoken. It includes equipment, books, apparatus, toys, games played, and the materials with which a pupil interacts. Most important of all, it includes the total social set-up of the situations in which the pupil is engaged. This power of the educator to regulate the objective conditions, to influence directly the experience of the pupil, and thereby to influence the education obtained by the pupil places a responsibility upon the educator. It becomes his duty to determine that environment which will interact with the existing capacities and needs of the pupil to create a worth-while experience. This carries with it the responsibility of understanding the needs and capacities of the pupils who are learning at a given time. Certain materials and methods which have proved effective with others in the past will not necessarily function in generating an educative experience in a particular pupil at a particular time. It is not true that some subjects and methods and acquaintance with certain facts and truths possess educational value in and of themselves. They must be adapted to the needs and capacities of the pupils. In order to have educational value, they must function in generating an educative experience in the particular pupil.

The principle of continuity in its educational application has another meaning. It means that the future has to be taken into account at every stage of the educational process. This does not mean that by acquiring certain skills and by learning certain subjects which might be needed later, pupils are as a matter of course made ready for the needs and circumstances of the future. This conception of preparation is treacherous. But we may conceive and define education in terms of growth, continuity, and the reconstruction or reorganization of experience. The essential meaning of such education is to provide those experiences which will prepare the individual for later experiences of a deeper and more expansive quality. This desirable effect is not achieved by requiring the pupil to acquire a certain amount of arithmetic, geography, and history which are taught and studied because they may be useful at some later date. Neither will the acquisition of skills in reading and figuring automatically constitute preparation for their right and effective use under conditions very unlike those in which they were acquired. To believe this is to hold an erroneous view of preparation; it is to defeat the very aim and purpose of preparation. One reason is that the subject-matter is learned in isolation and stowed away in a water-tight compartment. When exactly the same conditions recur as those under which it was acquired, it may also recur and be available. But when conditions in actual life vary somewhat from the original conditions, the learning acquired as a pupil may not be available for the adult to use. It may still be stowed away in the special compartment where it was learned. Another reason for the failure of this conception of preparation is the tendency to stress only the particular thing that the pupil is studying at the time and to overlook collateral learnings. Collateral learnings in the way of formation of enduring attitudes, of likes and dislikes, may be more important than the particular lesson. In fact, these attitudes are fundamentally what count in the future. Consider, for example, the important attitude of desire to go on learning. If impetus in this direction is weakened instead of strengthened, the pupil not only lacks preparation but he is robbed of native capacities which otherwise would enable him to cope with the circumstances of his future life. This, then, is the fallacy of the theory that makes preparation the controlling end. It omits or shuts out the very conditions by which a pupil can be prepared for his future. It sacrifices the present to a remote and more or less unknown future. On the other hand, an educator may react from this extreme to its opposite and equally erroneous extreme. He may infer that it does not make much difference what the present experience is as long as it is enjoyed. This is false because it has already been shown that the educator is responsible for the kind of present experiences the young undergo.

In the educational scheme, what, then, is the true meaning of preparation? It means that a person, young or old, gets out of his present experience all that there is in it for him at the time in which he has it. Since we live only at the time we live, we can be prepared for living in the future only by extracting the full meaning from each present experience. This means that attentive care must be devoted to the conditions which give each present experience a worth-while meaning. The educator who has achieved maturity and best sees the connection between the pupil's present and future is responsible for an ever-present process. He is responsible for instituting the conditions for the kind of present experience which has a favorable effect upon the future.

What is Educationally Vital: The Formation of a Disciplined Logical Ability to Think

Selections from John Dewey, *How We Think*, 1st ed. (Boston: D. C. Heath & Co., Publishers, 1910), Chapter 6, pp. 68-78. Cf. 2nd edition, 1933, pp. 91-101. Reprinted by permission of the publishers.

Chapter Six
The Analysis of a Complete Act of Thought

. . . In this chapter we shall make an analysis of the process of thinking into its steps or elementary constituents, basing the analysis upon descriptions of a number of extremely simple, but genuine, cases of reflective experience.[1]

A Simple Case of Practical Deliberation. 1. "The other day when I was down town on 16th Street a clock caught my eye. I saw that the hands pointed to 12:20. This suggested that I had an engagement at 124th Street, at one o'clock. I reasoned that as it had taken me an hour to come down on a surface car, I should probably be twenty minutes late if I returned the same way. I might save twenty minutes by a subway express. But was there a station near? If not, I might lose more than twenty minutes in looking for one. Then I thought of the elevated, and I saw there was such a line within two blocks. But where was the station? If it were several blocks above or below the street I was on, I should lose time instead of gaining it. My mind went back to the subway express as quicker than the elevated; furthermore, I remembered that it went nearer than the elevated to the part of 124th Street I wished to reach, so that time would be saved at the end of the journey. I concluded in favor of the subway, and reached my destination by one o'clock."

A Simple Case of Reflection upon an Observation. 2. "Projecting nearly horizontally from the upper deck of the ferryboat on which I daily cross the river, is a long white pole, bearing a gilded ball at its tip. It suggested a flagpole when I first saw it; its color, shape, and gilded ball agreed with this idea, and these reasons seemed to justify me in this belief. But soon difficulties presented themselves. The pole

---

[1] These are taken, almost verbatim, from the class papers of students.

was nearly horizontal, an unusual position for a flagpole; in the next place, there was no pulley, ring, or cord by which to attach a flag; finally, there were elsewhere two vertical staffs from which flags were occasionally flown. It seemed probable that the pole was not there for flag-flying.

I then tried to imagine all possible purposes of such a pole, and to consider for which of these it was best suited: (a) Possibly it was an ornament. But as all the ferryboats and even the tugboats carried like poles, this hypothesis was rejected. (b) Possibly it was the terminal of a wireless telegraph. But the same considerations made this improbable. Besides, the more natural place for such a terminal would be the highest part of the boat, on top of the pilot house. (c) Its purpose might be to point out the direction in which the boat is moving.

"In support of this conclusion, I discovered that the pole was lower than the pilot house, so that the steersman could easily see it. Moreover, the tip was enough higher than the base, so that, from the pilot's position, it must appear to project far out in front of the boat. Moreover, the pilot being near the front of the boat, he would need some such guide as to its direction. Tugboats would also need poles for such a purpose. This hypothesis was so much more probable than the others that I accepted it. I formed the conclusion that the pole was set up for the purpose of showing the pilot the direction in which the boat pointed, to enable him to steer correctly."

A Simple Case of Reflection Involving Experiment. 3. "In washing tumblers in hot soapsuds and placing them mouth downward on a plate, bubbles appeared on the outside of the mouth of the tumblers and then went inside. Why? The presence of bubbles suggests air, which I note must come from inside the tumbler. I see that the soapy water on the plate prevents escape of the air save as it may be caught in bubbles. But why should air leave the tumbler? There was no substance entering to force it out. It must have expanded. It expands by increase of heat or by decrease of pressure, or by both. Could the air have become heated after the tumbler was taken from the hot suds? Clearly not the air that was already entangled in the water. If heated air was the cause, cold air must have entered in transferring the tumblers from the suds to the plate. I test to see if this supposition is true by taking several more tumblers out. Some I shake so as to make sure of entrapping cold air in them. Some I take out holding mouth downward in order to prevent cold air from entering. Bubbles appear on the outside of every one of the former and on none of the latter. I must be right in my inference. Air from the outside must have been expanded by the heat of the tumbler, which explains the appearance of the bubbles on the outside.

"But why do they then go inside? Cold contracts. The tumbler cooled and also the air inside it. Tension was removed, and hence bubbles appeared inside. To be sure of this, I test by placing a cup of ice on the tumbler while the bubbles are still forming outside. They soon reverse."

The Three Cases Form a Series. These three cases have been purposely selected so as to form a series from the more rudimentary to more complicated cases of reflection. The first illustrates the kind of thinking done by every one during the day's business, in which neither the data, nor the ways of dealing with them, take one outside the limits of everyday experience. The last furnishes a case in which neither problem nor mode of solution would have been likely to occur except to one with some prior scientific training. The second case forms a natural transition; its materials lie well within the bounds of everyday, unspecialized experience; but the problem, instead of being directly involved in the person's business, arises indirectly out of his activity, and accordingly appeals to a somewhat theoretic and impartial interest. We shall deal, in a later chapter, with the evolution of abstract thinking out of that which is relatively practical and direct; here we are concerned only with the common elements found in all the types.

Five Distinct Steps in Reflection. Upon examination, each instance reveals, more or less clearly, five logically distinct steps: (i) a felt difficulty; (ii) its location and definition; (iii) suggestion of possible solution; (iv) development by reasoning of the bearings of the suggestion; (v) further observation and experiment leading to its acceptance or rejection; that is, the conclusion of belief or disbelief.

1. *The occurrence of a difficulty.* 1. The first and second steps frequently fuse into one. The difficulty may be felt with sufficient definiteness as to set the mind at once speculating upon its probable solution, or an undefined uneasiness and shock may come first, leading only later to definite attempt to find out what is the matter. Whether the two steps are distinct or blended, there is the factor emphasized in our original account of reflection—*viz.* the perplexity or problem. In the first of the three cases cited, the difficulty resides in the conflict between conditions at hand and a desired and intended result, between an end and the means for reaching it. The purpose of keeping an engagement at a certain time, and the existing hour taken in connection with the location, are not congruous. The object of thinking is to introduce congruity between the two. The given conditions cannot themselves be altered; time will not go backward nor will the distance between 16th Street and 124th Street shorten itself. The problem is *the discovery of intervening terms which when inserted between the remoter end and the given means will harmonize them with each other.*

In the second case, the difficulty experienced is the incompatibility of a suggested and (temporarily) accepted belief that the pole is a flagpole, with certain other facts. Suppose we symbolize the qualities that suggest *flagpole* by the letters a, b, c; those that oppose this suggestion by the letters p, q, r. There is, of course, nothing inconsistent in the qualities themselves; but in pulling the mind to different and incongruous conclusions they conflict—hence the problem. Here the object is the discovery of some object (O), of which a, b, c, and p, q, r, may all be appropriate traits—just as, in our first case, it is to discover a course of action which will combine existing conditions and a remoter result in a single whole. The method of solution is also the same: discovery of intermediate qualities (the position of the pilot house, of the pole, the need of an index to the boat's direction) symbolized by d, g, l, o, which bind together otherwise incompatible traits.

In the third case, an observer trained to the idea of natural laws or uniformities finds something odd or exceptional in the behavior of the bubbles. The problem is to reduce the apparent anomalies to instances of well-established laws. Here the method of solution is also to seek for intermediary terms which will connect, by regular linkage, the seemingly extraordinary movements of the bubbles with the conditions known to follow from processes supposed to be operative.

2. *Definition of the difficulty.* 2. As already noted, the first two steps, the feeling of a discrepancy, or difficulty, and the acts of observation that serve to define the character of the difficulty may, in a given instance, telescope together. In cases of striking novelty or unusual perplexity, the difficulty, however, is likely to present itself at first as a shock, as emotional disturbance, as a more or less vague feeling of the unexpected, of something queer, strange, funny, or disconcerting. In such instances, there are necessary observations deliberately calculated to bring to light just what is the trouble, or to make clear the specific character of the problem. In large measure, the existence or non-existence of this step makes the difference between reflection proper, or safeguarded *critical* inference and uncontrolled thinking. Where sufficient pains to locate the difficulty are not taken, suggestions for its resolution must be more or less random. Imagine a doctor called in to prescribe for a patient. The patient tells him some things that are wrong; his experienced eye, at a glance, takes in other signs of a certain disease. But if he permits the suggestion of this special disease to take possession prematurely of his mind, to become an accepted conclusion, his scientific thinking is by that much cut short. A large part of his technique, as a skilled practitioner, is to prevent the acceptance of the first suggestions that arise; even, indeed, to postpone the occurrence of any very definite suggestion till the trouble—the nature of the problem—has been thoroughly explored. In the case of a

physician this proceeding is known as diagnosis, but a similar inspection is required in every novel and complicated situation to prevent rushing to a conclusion. The essence of critical thinking is suspended judgment; and the essence of this suspense is inquiry to determine the nature of the problem before proceeding to attempts at its solution. This, more than any other thing, transforms mere inference into tested inference, suggested conclusions into proof.

3. *Occurrence of a suggested explanation or possible solution.* The third factor is suggestion. The situation in which the perplexity occurs calls up something not present to the senses: the present location, the thought of subway or elevated train; the stick before the eyes, the idea of a flagpole, an ornament, an apparatus for wireless telegraphy; the soap bubbles, the law of expansion of bodies through heat and of their contraction through cold. (a) Suggestion is the very heart of inference; it involves going from what is present to something absent. Hence, it is more or less speculative, adventurous. Since inference goes beyond what is actually present, it involves a leap, a jump, the propriety of which cannot be absolutely warranted in advance, no matter what precautions be taken. Its control is indirect, on the one hand, involving the formation of habits of mind which are at once enterprising and cautious; and on the other hand, involving the selection and arrangement of the particular facts upon perception of which suggestion issues. (b) The suggested conclusion so far as it is not accepted but only tentatively entertained constitutes an idea. Synonyms for this are *supposition, conjecture, guess, hypothesis,* and (in elaborate cases) *theory.* Since suspended belief, or the postponement of a final conclusion pending further evidence, depends partly upon the presence of rival conjectures as to the best course to pursue or the probable explanation to favor, *cultivation of a variety of alternative suggestions* is an important factor in good thinking.

4. *The rational elaboration of an idea.* 4. The process of developing the bearings—or, as they are more technically termed, the *implications* —of any idea with respect to any problem, is termed *reasoning.*[2] As an idea is inferred from given facts, so reasoning sets out from an idea. The *idea* of elevated road is developed into the idea of difficulty of locating station, length of time occupied on the journey, distance of station at the other end from place to be reached. In the second case, the implication of a flagpole is seen to be a vertical position; of a wire-

---

[2] This term is sometimes extended to denote the entire reflective process—just as *inference* (which in the sense of *test* is best reserved for the third step) is sometimes used in the same broad sense. But *reasoning* (or *ratiocination*) seems to be peculiarly adapted to express what the older writers called the "notional" or "dialectic" process of developing the meaning of a given idea.

less apparatus, location on a high part of the ship and, moreover, absence from every casual tugboat; while the idea of index to direction in which the boat moves, when developed, is found to cover all the details of the case.

Reasoning has the same effect upon a suggested solution as more intimate and extensive observation has upon the original problem. Acceptance of the suggestion in its first form is prevented by looking into it more thoroughly. Conjectures that seem plausible at first sight are often found unfit or even absurd when their full consequences are traced out. Even when reasoning out the bearings of a supposition does not lead to rejection, it develops the idea into a form in which it is more apposite to the problem. Only when, for example, the conjecture that a pole was an index-pole had been thought out into its bearings could its particular applicability to the case in hand be judged. Suggestions at first seemingly remote and wild are frequently so transformed by being elaborated into what follows from them as to become apt and fruitful. The development of an idea through reasoning helps at least to supply the intervening or intermediate terms that link together into a consistent whole apparently discrepant extremes (*ante*, p. 72).

5. *Corroboration of an idea and formation of a concluding belief.* 5. The concluding and conclusive step is some kind of *experimental corroboration* or verification, of the conjectural idea. Reasoning shows that *if* the idea be adopted, certain consequences follow. So far the conclusion is hypothetical or conditional. If we look and find present all the conditions demanded by the theory, and if we find the characteristic traits called for by rival alternatives to be lacking, the tendency to believe, to accept, is almost irresistible. Sometimes direct observation furnishes corroboration, as in the case of the pole on the boat. In other cases, as in that of the bubbles, experiment is required; that is, *conditions are deliberately arranged in accord with the requirements of an idea or hypothesis to see if the results theoretically indicated by the idea actually occur.* If it is found that the experimental results agree with the theoretical, or rationally deduced, results, and if there is reason to believe that *only* the conditions in question would yield such results, the confirmation is so strong as to induce a conclusion—at least until contrary facts shall indicate the advisability of its revision.

Thinking Comes between Observations at the Beginning and at the End. Observation exists at the beginning and again at the end of the process: at the beginning, to determine more definitely and precisely the nature of the difficulty to be dealt with; at the end, to test the value of some hypothetically entertained conclusion. Between those two termini of observation, we find the more distinctively *mental* aspects of the entire thought-cycle: (i) inference, the suggestion of an explanation or solution; and (ii) reasoning, the development of the bearings and implications of the suggestion. Reasoning requires some experimental observation to confirm it, while experiment can be economically and fruitfully conducted only on the basis of an idea that has been tentatively developed by reasoning.

The Trained Mind, One that Judges the Extent of Each Step Advisable in a Given Situation. The disciplined, or logically trained, mind—the aim of the educative process—is the mind able to judge how far each of these steps needs to be carried in any particular situation. No cast-iron rules can be laid down. Each case has to be dealt with as it arises, on the basis of its importance and of the context in which it occurs. To take too much pains in one case is as foolish—as illogical—as to take too little in another. At one extreme, almost any conclusion that insures prompt and unified action may be better than any long delayed conclusion; while at the other, decision may have to be postponed for a long period—perhaps for a lifetime. The trained mind is the one that best grasps the degree of observation, forming of ideas, reasoning, and experimental testing required in any special case, and that profits the most, in future thinking, by mistakes made in the past. What is important is that the mind should be sensitive to problems and skilled in methods of attack and solution.

53

The Continuing Controversy over Education

William C. Bagley

William C. Bagley "An Essentialist's Platform for the Advancement of American Education," *Educational Administration and Supervision*, XXIV (No. 4, April, 1938): 241-256.

Prefactory Note

The first three sections of this paper were prepared by the writer for discussion by a small group which met at Atlantic City on February 26, 1938, and which adopted the name, The Essentialist Committee for the Advancement of American Education. An unauthorized release to the press including a few statements from this paper gave rise to rather wide publicity and led to somewhat fiery denunciations by prominent leaders in American educational theory. For this reason the first three sections are here published essentially as they were first presented. The article is published on the sole responsibility of the writer, and not as an official pronouncement of the Committee, although the members of the Committee are in substantial agreement with the position here taken and have suggested only minor changes, almost all of which have been made in revising the original draft. The Managing Editor of Educational Administration and Supervision has kindly agreed to publish further articles dealing with the same problem. It is hoped that other members of the Committee will make contributions. The Committee includes in addition to the writer: Dr. M. Demiashkevich; Dr. Walter H. Ryle; Dr. M. L. Shane; Mr. F. Alden Shaw, *Chairman and Organizer*; Dr. Louis Shores; Dr. Guy M. Whipple.

I. The Situation

In spite of its vast extent and its heavy cost to society, public education in the United States is in many ways appallingly weak and ineffective. For the sake of brevity only a few outstanding evidences of this weakness will be set forth here:

1. Age for age, the average pupil of our elementary schools does not meet the standards of achievement in the fundamentals of education that are attained in the elementary schools of many other countries. In

so far as English-speaking countries are concerned, this statement can be and has been substantiated by the scores made in the elementary schools of these countries on American achievement tests, the norms of which represent the average scores of large, unselected groups of American pupils. In the most extended investigation[1] of this type, the differences revealed are so wide as to justify no other inference than that American elementary-school achievement is far below what it could be and what it should be.

2. Similar comparisons relative to secondary education cannot be made because the secondary schools of practically all other countries are not intended for "all the children of all the people" as are our high schools. It is generally agreed among competent students of the problem that our average 18-year-old high-school graduate is scholastically far behind the average 18-year-old graduates of the secondary schools of many other countries. This difference has been recognized in the practice of admitting the latter to junior-year standing in many American colleges. But even granting that secondary education elsewhere is in general selective, there is abundant evidence that in our laudable efforts to send everyone to and through high school standards have been unnecessarily lowered. Both the bright and the slow pupils are handicapped by weaknesses in the fundamentals that all except those hopelessly subnormal are able to master. Within the past decade the effectiveness of high-school instruction has been weakened by increasing disabilities in so basic an accomplishment as reading. It is scarcely too much to say, indeed, that increasing proportions of pupils in the junior and senior high schools are essentially illiterate. Failures in such high-school studies as mathematics and natural science are in many cases traceable to the fact that pupils cannot read effectively. Classes in "remedial" reading are now necessary on the secondary level to bring pupils to a standard of literacy that primary- and intermediate-grade instruction could and should have insured. Equally lamentable weak-

---

[1] The study here referred to was published by the University of London Press in 1934 for the Scottish Council for Research in Education. (MacGregor, G.: *Achievement Tests in the Primary Schools: A Comparative Study with American Tests in Fife.*) child in the County of Fife—about seven thousand in all. Even mentally defective children were included. While the findings are somewhat difficult to evaluate because Scottish children enter school at five rather than six, the conclusion stated in the text is clearly justified. The use of achievement tests in Canadian schools tells a similar story, for example in the province-wide survey of the schools of British Columbia conducted by Professor Peter Sandiford. One of the writer's colleagues who has constructed many tests reports that when he has included significant numbers of Canadian pupils in "standardizing" the tests, the norms have been raised to a point where the tests could not be used equitably with American pupils.

nesses in basic arithmetic are reported. And it is now taken for granted by high-school teachers of Latin and modern languages that one of their chief duties is to teach their pupils the rudiments of English grammar.

3. In other and not at all exclusively scholastic accomplishments, American education is relatively ineffective. A recent study suggests that juvenile delinquency may be correlated in many cases with these reading disabilities which we contend are almost always unnecessary and easily avoidable by appropriate elementary education. And while no causal relationship is claimed, it is well to know that during the one hundred years in which universal elementary education has been increasingly the policy of all civilized countries, ours is apparently the only country in which the expansion of the universal school has not been paralleled by a significant and in some cases a remarkable decrease in the ratios of serious crime.

II. The Causes: A. General Economic and Social Factors

4. American education has been confronted with uniquely difficult and complicated problems which have arisen from a rapid growth in population; from a constantly advancing frontier; from the increase in national wealth; from the arrival year after year and decade after decade of millions of immigrants of widely diverse national origins; from the complex social and political situations involved in racial differences; from the profound changes brought about by the transition from a predominantly agricultural to a predominantly industrial civilization; from the growth of cities; from an ever-increasing mobility of the population; and from a multitude of other factors which have operated here with a force unprecedented in history and unparalleled in any other part of the world.

The American public school has met some of these problems with a notable measure of success. Of outstanding significance is the fact that among the states which by any test would be rated as the most advanced in civilization are those which have had the heaviest burden of immigration from backward countries to assimilate. And it should be said that, in general, the states that have had the most substantial (but not necessarily the most "Progressive") school systems have by far the lowest ratios of serious crime. In a notable degree, too, these same states, many of which do not rank high in *per capita* wealth, are those that have been least dependent upon the federal government for "relief" during the depression years. Beyond all this, the schools can claim a very high degree of definitely measurable success for their programs of physical development and health education.

5. The upward expansion of mass-education first to the secondary

and now to the college level, which is probably the chief cause of our educational ineffectiveness, has been an outcome, not alone of a pervasive faith in education, to the realization of which the material wealth of the country was fairly adequate, but also and perhaps more fundamentally of economic factors. Power-driven machinery, while in many cases reducing occupational opportunities on the purely routine levels, quite as markedly opened new occupational opportunities in types of work that could not be done by machinery; work that involved deliberation and judgment; work for which a broad foundation in general education as well as specialized technical and vocational training was advantageous and often essential. That increasing numbers of young persons should seek the advantages of an extended education has been inevitable. Fortunately the wealth of the country has enabled the people of many sections to meet this demand. In opening the high schools and colleges to ever-increasing numbers, however, it was just as inevitable that scholastic standards should be relaxed, and when such a need arises it is only natural that those responsible for the administration of education should welcome any theory or philosophy which justifies or rationalizes such a policy—any theory of education which can make a virtue of necessity. Under such a condition, it is easy to understand why the relaxation of standards has been carried far beyond the actual needs of the case.

III. The Causes: B. Educational Theories that Are Essentially Enfeebling

6. Throughout the long history of education—and organized education is practically as old as civilization—two opposing theories have been in evidence. Although over-simplification is always dangerous, one with this caution may contrast these two theories of education by certain conflicting concepts summed up in pairing such opposites as "individual vs. society," "freedom vs. discipline," "interest vs. effort," "play vs. work,"—or to use more recently current expressions, "immediate needs vs. remote goals," "personal experience vs. race experience," "psychological organization vs. logical organization," "pupil-initiative vs. teacher-initiative." The fundamental dualism suggested by these terms has persisted over the centuries. It came out sharply in Greek education during the Age of the Sophists. It was reflected in the educational changes brought about by the Italian Renaissance. It appeared in the 17th Century in a definite school of educational theory the adherents of which even at that time styled themselves the "Progressives." It was explicit in the successive educational reforms proposed by Rousseau, Pestalozzi, Froebel, and Herbart. In American education it was reflected in the theories advocated and practiced by Bronson Alcott, in the work

of Horace Mann, and later in the work of E. A. Sheldon and Francis W. Parker; while the present outstanding leader, John Dewey, first came into prominence during the last decade of the 19th Century in an effort to resolve the dualism through an integration expressed in the title of his classic essay, now called "Interest and Effort in Education."

7. Under the necessity which confronted American education of rationalizing the loosening of standards and the relaxation of rigor if mass-education were to be expanded upward, the theories which emphasized interest, freedom, immediate needs, personal experience, psychological organization, and pupil-initiative, and which in so doing tended to discredit and even condemn their opposites—effort, discipline, remote goals, race-experience, logical sequence, and teacher-initiative —naturally made a powerful appeal. Over more than a generation these theories have increasingly influenced the lower schools.[2] They find specific expression today in a variety of definite movements so numerous that even the more outstanding can here be listed.

(a) *The complete abandonment in many school systems of rigorous standards of scholastic achievement as a condition of promotion from grade to grade, and the passing of all pupils "on schedule."* This policy which found a strong initial support thirty years ago in the studies of "retardation and elimination" has of late been given even a wider appeal by the teachings of mental hygiene regarding the possible effects of failure in disintegrating personality. The problem is extremely complicated as a later reference to it will show, but the movement has already resulted in at least one very important change. Instead of having "overage" pupils piling up in the intermediate grades, we now have "overgraded" pupils handicapped in the work of the junior and senior high schools by their lack of thorough training in the fundamentals already referred to.

---

[2] Dr. H. C. Morrison (*School and Commonwealth*, Chicago, 1937, p. 11) states that an educational philosophy embodying such theories has been gradually taking form in American education during the past fifty or sixty years. The present writer has publicly called attention for more than thirty years to manifestations of this influence, and to its weakening tendencies. His charges, with evidence supporting them, are matters of published record, duly documented. They have been frequently denounced, but never answered. In addition to published articles, the following books by the present writer make references to the problem: *The Educative Process*, 1905; *Classroom Management*, 1907; *School Discipline*, 1914; *Determinism in Education*, 1925; *Education, Crime, and Social Progress*, 1932; *Education and Emergent Man*, 1934. The theories were influencing the schools long before the terms "activity program," "integrated curriculum," "child-centered school," and the like came into vogue or had even been coined. It should be noted, too, that these theories have had no comparable recognition in the school systems of other countries except the Soviet Union, where after twelve years of consistent application they were abandoned in 1933 as hopelessly weak and ineffective.

(b) *The disparagement of system and sequence in learning and a dogmatic denial of any value in, even of any possibility of learning through, the logical, chronological, and causal relationships of learning materials.* This has led to an enthronement of the doctrine of incidental learning. Only as one becomes acquainted with facts and principles through applying them to vital problems that appeal to one as worth solving at the moment (so the theory holds) can one truly learn such facts and principles. And on the side of skills—such as the fundamental arts of language, measurement, and computation—mastery as far as possible should await an occasion when one of them is needed. As someone has said in effect, "These things are only tools, and when a workman needs a tool he goes to the shop and gets it." And yet this theory that "mind will not learn what is alien to its fundamental vital purposes," Thorndike has pronounced on the basis of extended experimentation, "to be attractive and plausible but definitely false."[3] The disparagement of systematic and sequential learning has also been criticized in no uncertain terms by John Dewey.[4]

(c) *The wide vogue of the so-called "activity movement."* This is an outgrowth of the so-called "project-method" which in its turn was an effort to find, or to encourage the learner to find, problems or vital purposes in the solution of which desirable learnings could be effected. The activity movement and the resulting "activity programs" and "activity curricula," like the project-method, have an important place —a central function in the primary school, and a very useful supplementary function on all educational levels. The tendency to make them a substitute for systematic and sequential learning and to go even further and regard activity as a sufficient end in itself irrespective of whether or not anything is learned through the activity is another matter. It is, however, an intriguing proposal. As one enthusiastic activist said, "Let us not use activities as pegs on which to hang subject-matter." If the schools only provide an abundance of "rich experiences" for the learner, it seems, other things will miraculously take care of themselves. This is not at all absurd if one accepts the premises; it is a thoroughly consistent result of the theory of incidental learning carried to its logical conclusion.

(d) *The discrediting of the exact and exacting studies.* The most significant barrier to opening the high schools to the masses was at the outset the practically universal requirement of Latin, algebra, and geometry in the secondary program. Perhaps inherently and certainly as commonly taught, the difficulties in mastering these subjects were quite beyond a large proportion of pupils. At the same time the practical

[3] Thorndike, E. L.: *Adult Interests.* New York, 1935, p. 52.
[4] Especially in an article in *The New Era* referred to below.

value of the subjects was difficult to defend. Their central place in the curriculum, however, was believed to be justified in a high degree by the mental discipline that their mastery involved. Anything that would tend to discredit this justification was seized upon by those responsible for the upward expansion of mass-education. Most fortunately for their purposes there appeared just at the turn of the century the report of the first careful psychological experiments testing the validity of the theory of mental discipline. These really classic experiments of Thorndike and Woodworth were followed by a long series of similar investigations that aimed to determine in how far learnings acquired in one subject were, or could be, applied in other situations. The results in general indicated that such a "transfer" was far from inevitable and in some cases either quite negative or so slight as to bring the whole theory into question.

The proponents of the universal high school and of other educational movements that were impeded by the requirement of subjects inherently difficult to the average mind were not slow to capitalize these experimental findings. As is natural under conditions of this sort, the evidence was generalized to a far greater extent than the experiments warranted, and with far-reaching results in school practice. Although the absolute number enrolled in Latin classes has increased, only a small proportion of pupils graduating from the high schools during the past ten years have even been exposed to Latin. Increasing proportions, too, are quite innocent of any training in elementary mathematics beyond the increasingly ineffective modicum of arithmetic acquired in the elementary schools. But the important fact is that there has been a growing practice of discouraging even competent learners from undertaking the studies that are exact though exacting; hence the upward expansion of mass-education, while sincerely a democratic movement, is not guarding itself against the potentially most fatal pitfall of democracy. It has deliberately adopted the easy policy of leveling-down rather than facing resolutely the difficult task of leveling-up—and upon the possibility of leveling-up the future of democracy indisputably depends. As John Dewey has contended, the older curriculum of classics and mathematics does have a unique value to those competent to its mastery—a value for which the so-called reform movements have not as yet, in his judgment, provided a substitute.[5]

[5] "Development . . . is a continuous process, and continuity signifies consecutiveness of action. Here was the strong point of traditional education at its best. . . . The subject-matter of the classics and mathematics involved of necessity, for those who mastered it, a consecutive and orderly development along definite lines. Here lies, perhaps, the greatest problem of the newer efforts in education." Dewey, J.: "The Need of a Philosophy of Education." The New era, London, November, 1934, pp. 214f.

(e) *An increasingly heavy emphasis upon the "social studies."* While the exact and exacting studies were in effect being discredited, the primrose path of least resistance was opened ever wider in the field known as the social studies. The argument here is plausible and appealing. "Education for citizenship" is a ringing slogan with limitless potentialities, especially in an age when high-sounding shibboleths, easily formulated, can masquerade as fundamental premises and postulates wrought through the agony of hard thinking.

Obviously no fundamental premise in educational thinking could fail to recognize the importance of a firm foundation in the history of human institutions, or of an acquaintance with present and pressing social problems especially in the light of their genesis, or of an acquaintance with such principles of economics, sociology, and political science as have been well established.

But just as obviously the social sciences, so called, are not in the same class with the natural sciences. Their generalizations permit trustworthy predictions only in a few cases and then only in a slight degree. When the human element enters, uncertainty enters—else the world could have anticipated and adjusted itself to Hitler and Mussolini and Stalin and the military oligarchy of Japan and would not be standing dazed and impotent as it stands today. And while to expect an educational pabulum of social studies in the lower schools essentially to overcome this inherent limitation of the social sciences is an alluring prospect, it is to expect nothing less than a miracle. It is, indeed, just as sensible as would be a brave and desperate effort to incite immature minds to square the circle.

(f) *Using the lower schools to establish a new social order.* The proposal definitely and deliberately to indoctrinate immature learners in the interest of a specific social order and one that involves wide departures from that which prevails in our country is to be questioned, if for no other reasons, upon the grounds set forth in the preceding paragraphs. With the growing ineffectiveness of the lower schools in failing to lay adequate foundations in fundamental and established learnings of unquestioned permanence and value, such efforts would necessarily be superficial in the last degree. It would be an extreme case of building what may be characterized for the sake of argument as a perfectly splendid edifice on shifting sands—in this case, quicksands would be the more appropriate metaphor. And here we might well study certain peoples that have actually achieved a social order which is pointed to by our idealists as exemplifying in many ways the realization of their dreams. Reference is made, of course, to such countries as Sweden, Denmark, Norway, and New Zealand. An outstanding fact of fundamental significance is that these countries have *not* achieved these laudable results by emasculating their educational systems. Their peoples indeed would stand aghast at the very suggestion.

(g) *The "curriculum-revision" movement and its vagaries.* The various reform proposals just discussed have culminated in the general movement known as curriculum-revision which has dominated the lower schools for nearly twenty years. A primary emphasis has been the alleged need of building the programs of instruction around the local community. As long ago as 1933 more than 30,000 different curricula were on file in the curriculum-laboratory of Teachers College, Columbia University. Most of these had been prepared during the preceding decade by committees of teachers in local school systems throughout the country. Sometimes the committees were personally directed by a "curriculum-expert"; in practically all cases a rapidly developing theory evolved by these specialists guided the work. In so far as we can learn, this theory has never explicitly recognized that the state or the nation has a stake in the content of school instruction. The need of common elements in the basic culture of all people, especially in a democracy, has in effect been denied. Furthermore, with the American people the most mobile in the world, with stability of residence over the period of school attendance the exception and not the rule in many sections of the country, and with a significantly higher average of school failure among pupils whose parents move from place to place than among those who remain in the same community, the curriculum theorists have been totally insensitive to the need of a certain measure of uniformity in school requirements and in the grade-placement of crucial topics. In addition to all this, the clear tendency of the curriculum-revision movement has been to minimize basic learnings, to magnify the superficial, to belittle sequence and system, and otherwise to aggrevate the weakness and ineffectiveness of the lower schools.

IV. *The Problem and the Platform*

8. It is particularly unfortunate that American education should be unnecessarily weak at a time when the situation both at home and abroad is critical in the last degree.

The American people are facing an economic problem which both in nature and in magnitude is without an even remotely similar precedent in all history. In the richest country in the world, two thirds of the world's unemployment is now concentrated. In the midst of potential abundance, the cogs in the wheels of production, distribution, exchange, and consumption have lamentably failed to mesh.

It is the indicated and imminent task of the present dominant generation to solve this problem under whatever expert guidance at the hands of the economist and the social engineer it may find and accept. The student of education must cooperate with all other citizens in this task. It is his own specific duty, however, to consider the problems in his field that are bound to arise in the changes that seem now to be inevitable, regardless of the form which the solution of the present desperate economic situation may take—this with one exception, for if in desperation the American people discard democracy and yield to a dictator the sincere student of education will have no function and consequently no duty. The yes-man and the rubberstamp will take his place. He will be a luxury without a purpose; and the dictators have standardized a simple but effective technique for liquidating luxuries of this sort.

9. We shall assume, however, that "it can't happen here" and that, whatever may be the new economic and social order, the political order based upon representative government and the Bill of Rights will persist. Hence a primary function of American education will be to safeguard and strengthen these ideals of American democracy, with especial emphasis upon freedom of speech, freedom of the press, freedom of assembly, and freedom of religion. It is clear enough now that whenever any one of these is permitted to collapse, the whole democratic structure will topple like a house of cards. These, then, are among the first essentials in the platform of the Essentialist.

10. Democracy is now distinctly on trial. It is under criticism and suspicion. Every weakness will be watched for and welcomed by its enemies. Inevitably the future will bring competition if not clashes and conflicts with the now militantly anti-democratic peoples. Democratic societies cannot survive either competition or conflict with totalitarian states unless there is a democratic discipline that will give strength and solidarity to the democratic purpose and ideal. If the theory of democracy finds no place for discipline, then, the theory will have before long only historical significance. French education, much closer to the danger, has recognized this imperative need. Still unswerving in fidelity to the ideals of democracy, and still giving its first emphasis to clarity of thought and independence in individual thinking as the time-honored objectives of French education, it recognizes no less the fundamental importance of social solidarity in the defense of democracy.[6]

American educational theory long since dropped the term "discipline" from its vocabulary. Today its most vocal and influential spokesmen enthrone the right even of the immature learner to choose

---

[6] See the concluding paragraphs of Bouglé, C.: "The French Conception of 'Culture Générale,'" a series of lectures at Teachers College, Columbia University, April, 1938. To be published by the Teachers College Bureau of Publications.

what he shall learn. They condemn as "authoritarian" all learning tasks that are imposed by the teacher. They deny any value in the systematic and sequential mastery of the lessons that the race has learned at so great a cost. They condone and rationalize the refusal of the learner to attack a task that does not interest him. In effect they open wide the lines of least resistance and least effort. Obedience they stigmatize as a sign of weakness. All this they advocate in the magic names of "democracy" and "freedom."

Now, obviously, the freedom of the immature to choose what they shall learn is of negligible consequence compared with their later freedom from the want, fear, fraud, superstition, and error which may fetter the ignorant as cruelly as the chains of the slave-driver—and the price of this freedom is systematic and sustained effort often devoted to the mastery of materials the significance of which must at the time be taken on faith.

11. This problem is far more than merely personal or individual in its reference. A democratic society has a vital, collective stake in the informed intelligence of every individual citizen. That a literate electorate is absolutely indispensable not only to its welfare but to its very survival is clearly demonstrated by the sorry fate that so speedily overtook every unschooled and illiterate democracy founded as a result of the War that was to "Make the world safe for democracy."

And literacy in this sense means, of course, far more than the mere ability to translate printed letters into spoken words; it means the development and expansion of ideas; it means the basis for intelligent understanding and for the collective thought and judgment which are the essence of democratic institutions. These needs are so fundamental to an effective democracy that it would be folly to leave them to the whim or caprice of either learner or teacher.

Among the essentials of the Essentialist, then, is a recognition of the right of the immature learner to guidance and direction when these are needed either for his individual welfare or for the welfare and progress of the democratic group. The responsibility of the mature for the instruction and control of the immature is the biological meaning of the extended period of human immaturity and necessary dependence. It took the human race untold ages to recognize this responsibility. It is literally true that until this recognition dawned man remained a savage. Primitive societies, as numerous students have observed (and their testimony seems to be unanimous), pamper and indulge their young. Freedom of children from control, guidance, and discipline is with them a rule so nearly universal that its only brief but significant exception during the nearly universal savage ceremonies marking the adolescent onset of maturity is regarded as the first faint beginning of consciously directed human education.

It would be futile to deny that control and discipline may be stupid and brutal and used for unworthy ends. It would be futile to deny the need for the development of self-discipline and for the relaxation of external discipline with the growth of volitional maturity. But all this does not alter the fundamental truth that freedom must go hand in hand with responsibility, and that responsible freedom is always a conquest, never a gift.

12. An effective democracy demands a community of culture. Educationally this means that each generation be placed in possession of a common core of ideas, meanings, understandings, and ideals representing the most precious elements of the human heritage.

There can be little question as to the essentials. It is by no means a mere accident that the arts of recording, computing, and measuring have been among the first concerns of organized education. They are basic social arts. Every civilized society has been founded upon these arts, and when these arts have been lost, civilization has invariably and inevitably collapsed. Egypt, Asia Minor, and Mesopotamia are strewn with the ruins of civilizations that forgot how to read and write. Contemporary civilization, for the first time in history has attempted to insure its continuance by making these arts in so far as possible the prerogative of all.

Nor is it at all accidental that a knowledge of the world that lies beyond one's immediate experience has been among the recognized essentials of universal education, and that at least a speaking acquaintance with man's past and especially with the story of one's own country was early provided for in the program of the universal school. Widening the space horizon and extending the time perspective are essential if the citizen is to be protected from the fallacies of the local and the immediate.

Investigation, invention, and creative art have added to the heritage and the list of recognized essentials has been extended and will be further extended. Health instruction and the inculcation of health practices are now basic phrases of the work of the lower schools. The elements of natural science have their place. Neither the fine arts nor the industrial arts are neglected.

We repeat that there can be little question as to the essentials of universal education. As Charles A. Beard has so well said: "While education constantly touches the practical affairs of the hour and day, and responds to political and economic exigencies, it has its own treasures heavy with the thought and sacrifice of the centuries. It possesses a heritage of knowledge and heroic examples—accepted values stamped with the seal of permanence."[7]

13. A specific program of studies including these essentials should be the heart of a democratic system of education. In a country like ours with its highly mobile population there should be an agreement as to the order and grade-placement of subjects and especially of crucial topics.[8] There is no valid reason for the extreme localism that has come to characterize American education. There is no valid reason for the failure of the American elementary school to lay as firm a foundation in the fundamentals of education as do the elementary schools of other democracies. It is especially regrettable that contemporary educational theory should in effect condone and rationalize scamped work by ridiculing such traits as thoroughness, accuracy, persistence, and the ideal of good workmanship for its own sake. One may be very sure that democracy schooled to the easy way will have short shrift in competition or conflict with any social order dominated by objectives which, however reprehensible, are clear-cut and appealing, and are consequently embraced even by disfranchised masses.

14. Generally speaking, the recognized essentials should be taught as such through a systematic program of studies and activities for the carrying out of which the teachers should be responsible. Informal learning through experiences initiated by the learners is important, and abundant opportunities should be provided for such experiences through-out the range of organized education. Beyond the primary grades, however, where as we have said it may well predominate, informal learning should be regarded as supplementary rather than central.

15. Failure in school is unpleasant and the repetition of a grade is costly and often not very effective. On the other hand, the lack of a stimulus that will keep the learner to his task is a serious injustice both to him and to the democratic group which, we repeat, has a fundamental stake in his effective education. Too severe a stigma has undoubtedly been placed upon school failure by implying that it is symptomatic of permanent weakness. By no means is this always the case. No less a genius than Pasteur did so poorly in his first year at the Higher Normal School of Paris that he had to go home for further preparation. One of the outstanding scientists of the present century had a hard time in meeting the requirements of the secondary school,

---

[7] *The Unique Function of Education in American Democracy.* Washington: The Educational Policies Commission of the National Education Association, 1937, p. 71.

[8] Fortunately the National Society for the Study of Education is sponsoring a *Yearbook* dealing with this problem. This will be published in 1939.

failing, it is said, in the most elementary work of the field in which he later became world-famous. The list could be extended almost indefinitely.

Obviously not all learners can progress at the same rate. Some will go very, very slowly. Others will have trouble in getting started but will progress rapidly when they overcome the initial handicaps. Let us not stigmatize failure as we have done in the past. On the other hand, if education abandons rigorous standards and consequently provides no effective stimulus to the effort that learning requires, many persons will pass through twelve years of schooling only to find themselves in a world in which ignorance and lack of fundamental training are increasingly heavy handicaps. This in an all too literal sense is to throw the baby out with the bath.

16. The transition from a predominantly rural to a predominantly urban life has laid increasing burdens upon American education. For four decades or more we have been told that the school must provide opportunities for types of education that the normal bringing-up of children once provided on the farm and in the home. Manual training and the household arts were among the first responses to this demand. The parallel development of physical training with its later ramifications into various forms of health education are traceable in part to the same causes. Playgrounds, gymnasiums, and swimming pools are material expressions of the effort to meet these recognized needs. School and college athletics are lusty by-products representing in a very real sense the importance of finding a substitute for the vigorous physical work that once devolved of necessity upon the great majority of young people.

With the profound changes in the conditions of life already in progress, and with their clearly predictable extension and intensification in the immediate future, analogous substitutes must be sought for other educative experiences which the simpler conditions of life naturally and normally provided. Bread-winning employment is now postponed for vast numbers of young people. Willy-nilly they must remain dependent upon society, whether in attendance at school or college, or in such highly important educational enterprises as the Civilian Conservation Corps, or in "made work" of one variety or another.

The analogy of our civilization with the older civilizations based upon slavery is in no sense far-fetched. It has, indeed, a profound significance. Our slaves, it is true, are mechanical and not human. They are power-driven and increasingly they are being automatically controlled. They can do much more economically than human slaves the heavy work and the routine work. In some tasks they can perceive distinctions far too fine to be detected by the human senses, and they can respond far more quickly and far more accurately and dependably than can human nerves and muscles. Fortunately they can neither feel nor suffer, and so the grossest evils of the old slave civilizations are avoided. The fact remains, however, that the perils to those who are the supposed beneficiaries of a slave civilization are in no significant degree changed, whether the slaves be men or robots. Every slave civilization has within it the seeds of degeneration, decay, and ultimate extinction. Struggle and competition, selection and rejection, have often been cruel, but in both biological and social evolution they have been primary factors of progress. In societies that have lifted themselves above the plane of the brute and the savage, a most powerful steadying and civilizing force has been the ideal of personal economic responsibility for one's own survival and for one's old age and the care of one's dependents.

Generally speaking, then, "social security," like responsible freedom, has been a conquest, not a gift. Making it a gift involves some definite dangers. In our own country, few families have long survived the social security that comes through inherited wealth. "Three generations from shirt-sleeves to shirt-sleeves" has usually told the story. But this rule has had its exceptions. Here, as in some other countries, social security has, with occasional families, remained secure over a much longer time—but under the condition that each generation has been rigorously disciplined to its responsibilities and made clearly aware of the pitfalls that await the spendthrift and the idler. These exceptions, and especially those among them that have exemplified the development in each generation of a vigorous and highly sensitized social conscience, warrant the hope that an economy of abundance with social security for all may be so organized that our machine-slave civilization can escape that fate of the slave civilizations that have gone before. Herein lies an educational problem of the first magnitude which our educational theorists seem not even dimly to have sensed—so busy have they been in condemning out of hand the economic system which has made possible an economy of abundance based upon a machine-slave civilization.

A clear and primary duty of organized education at the present time is to recognize the fundamental character of the changes that are already taking place, and to search diligently for means of counteracting their dangers. Let us repeat that an educational theory to meet these needs must be strong, virile, and positive not feeble, effeminate, and vague. The theories that have increasingly dominated American education during the past generation are at basis distinctly of the latter type. The Essentialists have recognized and still recognize the contributions of real value that these theories have made to educational practice. They believe, however, that these positive elements can be preserved in an educational theory which finds its basis in the necessary dependence of the immature upon the mature for guidance, instruction, and discipline. This dependence is inherent in human nature. "What has been ordained among the prehistoric protozoa," said Huxley, "cannot be altered by act of Parliament"—nor, we may add, by the wishful thinking of educational theorists, however sincere their motives. "Authoritarianism" is an ugly word. But when those who detest it carry their laudable rebellion against certain of its implications so far as to reject the authority of plain facts, their arguments, while well adapted perhaps to the generation of heat, become lamentably lacking in light.

PART SIX
THE CONTEMPORARY
SCENE
WILL WE MAKE IT?

Overview

All that has gone before comes down to this: our times, our issues, our discussions, the contemporary scene. As Alfred North Whitehead so clearly perceived, what is past is foreground for the present and future. As Edith Hamilton saw it, there is an "ever-present past." Our intention has been to present from the wisdom of the past that part which will help us focus on problems of life and education in the present. Our underlying thesis or assumption has been that there is a discipline of knowledge called the history and philosophy and foundations of education. So much of this knowledge of the racial experience, represented in Parts Two, Three, Four, and Five, *is* relevant and helpful to us as we meet the problems of life and education—the basic, perennial questions we raised in Part One, which each generation must answer as best it can. So we end where we started: with the challenge to engage in educational discussions, to think through the problems of aims and purposes and objectives, of curriculum, of method, and of all the other manifold problems of the school and society, including financial problems.

When we come to the contemporary scene and current arguments, our quest for wisdom encounters new elements. So much is at stake today. Our answers and what we do will—for good or ill—vitally affect us, our loved ones, and our society—not the ancient Greeks, ancient Romans, or early Christians. Moreover, our discussions and leadership today must take place under the hovering cloud of possible nuclear destruction of all possibilities. Our very survival hangs in the balance, and we wonder, "Will we make it?" Whatever answers we agree upon, whatever action we can bring to bear, must be terribly relevant to our lives today and to this crucial question of our making it. Ours is an urgent, seemingly overwhelming challenge.

Out of the past to help us comes Bacon's insight in *The Advancement of Learning* (1605). "They are ill discoverers," he wrote, "that think there is no land when they see nothing but sea." What follows here in Part Six will surely bring us in contact with enough of the "seas" of our contemporary life to stagger us. But just as surely, some of our previous readings and some we shall encounter here will afford us touchstones of land underlying the seas or bridges derived from the racial experience of living and educating.

For the discovery of touchstones and bridges we recommend study of the philosophy of education. "A Four-Fold Classification of Educational Theories," our first reading, should help us clarify and understand the positions and debates which have characterized twentieth-century battles over the schools. This reading represents a rather traditional approach to the philosophy of education, reminding us of Plato's ideal beings who analyze, classify, and synthesize ideas to make right judgments of what ought to be. Its value may be judged by applying it to the 1970 Argüelles-Grene controversy in higher education, covered in Chapter 63, and seeing the underlying pattern of our continuing debates. That reading ties in with the concluding readings by Seckinger and Black and with events in the schools.

But the philosophy of education has its own problems. In American education not much attention has been given to this representative approach of the few to educational philosophy.[1] Linguistic analysis and existentialism have been "where the action is" and dominate the field. Our second reading, an analysis by Jonas F. Soltis entitled "Analysis and Anomalies in Philosophy of Education," provides a perspective for considering the alternative approach of linguistic and conceptual analysis. M. I. Berger's "Existential Criticism in Educational Theory: A Subjective View of a Serious Business" presents existential thought and the important figures of that alternative in philosophy of education.

Whichever approach we may prefer for reaching our philosophy of education, we must solve our educational problems in terms of our understanding of the deeper issues of life. Most challenging to us is the perennial problem of learning how to live together without compounding our vices and, as Reinhold Niebuhr put it, "covering each other with mud and with blood."[2] Edwin A. Burtt argues that we are challenged to find an all-embracing orientation to life and the universe which will avoid the errors of past thinkers. He proposes that the most promising way is to form a philosophy of man. That need is brought home to us in the next reading. For in 1968, at the time of the third of a series of assassinations which shocked contemporary Americans as nothing else had, Arthur Schlesinger, Jr., in his "Existential Politics and the Cult of Violence," posed the question of our time for educators and teachers: "What sort of people are we, we Americans?" Events of recent years, he reminds us, "must at last compel us to look searchingly at ourselves and our society before hatred and violence rush us on to more evil and finally tear our nation apart." As opposed to a "letting-go," individualistic, laissez-faire, "existential," anarchic approach,

---

[1] See Hugh C. Black, "Educational Philosophy and Theory in the United States—A Commentary," *Educational Theory*, 20, No. 1 (Winter 1970): 73-82, in the light of the concluding chapters of E. H. Wilds and Kenneth V. Lottich, *Foundations of Modern Education*, 4th ed. (New York: Holt, Rinehart and Winston, 1970), which correctly describe developments in terms of these controversies.

[2] "Man and Society: The Art of Living Together," in *Moral Man and Immoral Society* (New York: Charles Scribner's Sons, 1932), Ch. I, pp. 1-22.

Schlesinger stresses a need for self-knowledge, self-control, civility, and the life of reason and decency that forms the best of our Western tradition—so reminiscent of Plato's appeal to Athenians of the fifth century B.C.

How difficult the achievement of that ideal will be for us is made clear in the next reading, in which Hans J. Morgenthau lists the great issues of the 1970s: "the militarization of American life, the Vietnam war, race conflicts, poverty, the decay of the cities, the destruction of the natural environment." They are, he says, "not susceptible to rational solutions within the existing system of power relations." When he identifies the single overriding issue as the distribution of power in American society, he stresses the relevancy of the ideas advanced by Meiklejohn as disclosed by Black in the very last reading "A Missing Chord in Educational Theory." Our school problems are related to larger issues in society and life. The readings in this section of Part Six force upon us the challenge of living today with Burtt presenting the problem of our recovering an inclusive view of life and the universe, Schlesinger the problem of violence, and Morgenthau the problem of the political state.

Next our readings turn to more specific problems of education and the challenge to solve this vast array of crucial educational problems —problems in school finance (Joseph M. Cronin's "School Finance in the Seventies: The Prospect for Reform"), in school curriculum (Arthur W. Foshay, "How Fare the Disciplines?"), with the disadvantaged (Robert J. Havighurst, "Curriculum for the Disadvantaged"), and in higher education (the José Argüelles-Marjorie Grene articles in *Main Currents in Modern Thought*). Finally we are challenged about what we do in schools as Seckinger outlines our tasks in "Freedom and Responsibility in Education" and "Initiative in Learning." We conclude with "A Missing Chord in Educational Theory," discussed previously, and with the plea to move beyond impulse, irrationalism, and the analysis of words. In the best spirit of our Western tradition, let us synthesize and thrust beyond where we are now, in pursuit of the good.

54
Synthesis Based on Analysis?

Hugh C. Black

A Four-Fold Classification
of Educational Theories

Hugh C. Black, "A Four-Fold Classification of Educational Theories,"
Educational Theory, XVI (No. 3, July 1966), pp. 281-291.

The "either-or" reality characterizes so very much of human life and experience. Especially does this seem so in the areas of inquiry which immediately concern us here: those of philosophy, philosophy of education, the theory and practice of education, and the educational controversies of our day. If philosophy of education (at the very least) means the search for wisdom about education, then our tasks as philosophers of education involve us in a distinct discipline relating philosophy and education meaningfully in a period characterized by confusion and conflict.

Tackling the confusing, conflicting problems of educational theory and practice, the philosopher of education who approaches this complex task by way of philosophy brings with him a frame of reference perhaps useful in our time. For his contacts with "either-or" in philosophy may suggest a helpful approach in education.

Certainly in that branch of philosophy called logic, he has dealt with "either-or" at least in "disjunctive" propositions in argument. Moreover, his study of ethics has challenged him with a host of alternatives in that area of philosophy where matters of judgment, of choice, of preferences are critical. "Absolutism *or* relativity in morals," "a skeptical approach *or* a constructive way to relativity in morals," "egoism *or* altruism"—such alternatives of "either-or" stand as samples in this area of human experience and thought. But none is so vital and crucial to us today as the moral situation itself—either for the individual or the society facing the roadblock of decision and choice in which alternative courses of action (oftentimes in the form of "either-or") must be evaluated and weighed. R. A. Tsanoff, the Idealist historian of philosophy and long-time student of morality, phrases it so well in this statement in his *Ethics* (rev. ed., New York, Harper & Bros., 1955, p. 128) which approaches a metaphysical view of reality and the human experience:

> Our life course is not a neutral level but a concourse and contest of ennobling and degrading tendencies, achievement and debacle, an urge and a drag, the gleam of the ideal and the lure of the degenerate. At the crossroad of decision, our choice may point towards fruition, harmony and self-fulfillment, or to backwash and retrogression. The slope on which we are moving is an upward but also a downward slope; our every act and word and thought are either uplifting or degrading us, and through us uplifting or degrading others.

And I need not cite for any true student of John Dewey the reality of "either-or to that philosopher who grappled over a long life-time with the problems of men and education in a democratic society!

The "either-or" approach and the taking into account of extremes is as vividly real in education today as it is in philosophy. Whether it be a Whitehead earlier or a person in West Germany commenting in 1958 on the alternatives to be considered following the launching of Sputnik I in the fall of 1957, the alternative of "education or destruction" strikes in our ears a note of poignant reality and concern. And in January, 1965, (as this is written) when our President delivers his message on the State of the Union, educators must hear the ring of alternatives: "This *or* that," "this *or* that," as striking a vivid note of reality in both education and life.

Especially do we encounter "either-or" in our controversies over education and its specifics today. "Are the Public Schools Doing Their Job? asked *The Saturday Evening Post* of September 21, 1957. "No," replied John Keats in his article. "Yes," came the alternative reply by Herbert L. Brown, Jr. These articles were later included in such compilations as Scott, Hill, and Burns' *The Great Debate—Our Schools in Crisis*. Thus the battle over education as it becomes a part of the literature of our day is put in terms of extremes. "Is European Education Better?"—the title of another article in the controversy—received an answer which was typically oversimplified in terms of extremes of black-or-white, good-or-bad. And so with the *U.S. News & World Report* symposium on U. S. schools today in its issue of June 7, 1957, which phrased it: "Are We Less Or Better Educated Than 50 Years Ago?" in reporting on "The Battle Over Teaching Methods." Arthur Bestor had told the public in the issue of November 30, 1956, that we are less educated than 50 years ago. The later symposium presented the resounding "We are NOT less educated than 50 years ago!" of six educators who replied to Bestor. Beginning with our century and continuing to the present, the battle of alternatives in education continues to be our concern. "Academician *or* educationist" and "subject-matter *or* method" beat in upon us in ever increasing, rather than decreasing, tempo. No wonder, then, confusion about education reigns supreme, and we suffer: pupils, parents, teachers, educators, and our society—all. The challenge is to our profession, now as it has been for years. Strikingly, the challenge comes in the form of a familiar alternative: "fish or cut-bait!"

Listen to these statements:

> Our practical education bristles with contradiction. Even a superficial survey of prevailing practice and principles in education shows them often running at cross-purposes. Learning to read in the first grade illustrates this. . . . Such contradictory practices and theories prevail all through our educational system and leave young teachers in a quandary. More reflective study of these difficulties reveals deeper-lying oppositions which are so fundamental as to constitute the knotty problems for thinkers and experts in education. . . . This diversity or contrariety of opinions among theorists and practical educators leads many people easily to the conclusion that there are few settled standards in education, no real pedagogical science, and that our well-meant efforts to train teachers are not founded on broad basal principles, but are of the nature of devices and accommodations to practical needs. . . . Such wide variety of opinions and lack of agreement on fundamental issues are not only discouraging, but, to some extent, demoralizing, to the rank and file of teachers. Even principals and superintendents are disconcerted by these opposing claims which throw a hesitating uncertainty into a teacher's actions. In recent times this confusion of tongues has been increased by new elements of discord. The present unusually conflicting and chaotic state of our course of study and of our school doctrine and practice is due to rapid and radical changes, to numerous importations of new materials and new ideas, which have been rapidly accumulated, but are not yet organized into a consistent plan. Our aims and our theories are now undergoing the process of reconstruction and reformation: practice, in trying to keep up with these swift changes, takes on a variety of inconsistent forms. There has been a recasting of old methods and an evolution of the new.

I submit that these statements describe very well our confusion and status in 1965. But actually the words were published long ago: in 1914—fifty-one years ago! They were written by a professional educator in whom we can take pride: Charles A. McMurry. They appear in his book entitled: *Conflicting Principles in Teaching—and How to Adjust Them* (Boston: Houghton Mifflin Company, 1914), pp. 4-8.

The real tragedy, as I see it, is that the professional educators, including the philosophers of education, in these intervening years have seemingly done so little to get us beyond the confusions and conflicts of 1914—and of today. It may be that the 1920's and 1930's needed to be devoted to the conflict. It may well be that I. L. Kandel was right in deploring (in "Controversy Ended," *Educational Forum*, XXII (January, 1958), pp. 175-181) the energies and time spent by concerned educators who were forced to drop their main business of thinking through the central problems of education to wage the war of "Traditionalism vs. Progressivism." It may be that, further, World War II delayed our getting ahead in education. (Witness, for example, the unfamiliarity of school people with Henry C. Morrison's *The Curriculum of the Common School* which appeared in the war year of 1944 and which, I suggest, if put into practice, may have saved us from some of the sharp arrows of criticism of the 1950's and 1960's from the Bestors, Conants, and Rickovers.) We may debate Kandel's contention that education got off the track about the turn of the century. But I think we must agree that the much-battered car of education drastically needs to be put on the right track today.

This entire symposium, and this paper as a part of it, is devoted to the belief that a fruitful step in the right direction possibly lies in continuing the work of the few in philosophy of education to classify the theories of education; bring understanding of, and wisdom about, the confusions and chaos; and lead an advance. After many years of distractions and concerns with subsidiary matters, this approach is the direct-line inheritor of a rich tradition of insights in professional education. Perhaps it began with Charles A. McMurry's insight of 1914 (in the book cited) when he recognized:

> Whatever fundamental principles we may have are at least obscured and covered up by these controversies. The opponents and critics of a science of education discover in such disagreements and conflicts of opinion a direct support of their hostile criticisms. Now if we can clear the field of all unnecessary controversies, we may be able to rescue our main educational doctrines from discredit and thus secure a more generally acknowledged basis for educational science. (p. 7.)

A similar move was made by John Dewey in his classic *Experience and*

Education (New York: Macmillan, 1938) when (on pp. 1-6) he outlined the main alternatives between Traditionalism and Progressivisim. His capable opponent, I. L. Kandel, made a similar contribution in his notable work *Conflicting Theories of Education* (New York: Macmillan, 1938, pp. 20-26). In 1939 in his first edition of *Modern Philosophies of Education*, John S. Brubacher concluded his survey with Chapter XIV entitled "Systematic Philosophies of Education" in which he summarized the educational theories under two categories: "progressive education" and "traditionalists" or "essentialists." Similarly, but using more categories, Brameld (in his 1950 *Patterns of Educational Philosophy*) included in his classificatory scheme "Essentialism" and "Progressivism." Their work has been continued and enlarged, and they have been joined by the other participants represented here. Most of us are indebted especially to John P. Wynne for his efforts to focus attention again upon this important line of development in philosophy of education. His paper entitled "Subject-Matter Content of Philosophy of Education" appearing in *Proceedings of the Twentieth Annual Meeting of the Philosophy of Education Society* (1964, pp. 44-51) brought to our attention several new approaches which he called "the historical approach, the experience framework, the mediation of extremes, the levels of reflection, and the open-closed framework."

Wynne termed my particular classificatory scheme the "mediation of extremes" approach. Whatever the most appropriate name may be, my fourfold classificatory scheme is intended to serve certain purposes and is characterized by a distinct approach, both purposes and approach being rooted in realities of our time, life, and discipline. Sharing some common elements with the other schemes, it may be distinct in that it encompasses the other approaches.

Emphasizing the close relationship between educational theory and practices, the four-fold classification should meet some of the crucial needs of the present situation in education. It may, then, serve several purposes. First, it may afford help to students of education and practitioners by offering an orienting guide useful in understanding and assessing the present controversies and in bringing order out of the chaos and confusion. Second, such an orientation to theories of education seems indispensable and necessary in making intelligent judgments about educational practice. Third, the classification system may well serve the needs of theorists grappling with the complex problem of achieving new theories in another decade of crisis in American education. For several years now, more and more recognition has been given to inadequacies of and deficiencies in the older, conflicting accounts of education. Too long has the battle over American education been fought and refought in the same old terms: those of oversimplification, over-generalization, black-or-white, either-or, and extremes. This new approach may suggest a mediation of such extremes, resulting in a synthesis which gives a more adequate and truer account of what education is. However that may be, imperative seems to be the need to get beyond the present level of conflict and argument and arrive at new theories carrying the arguments to a new and, hopefully, a higher level.

I suggest that we approach the problems of educational theory and practice as philosophers capitalizing on rich insights from that discipline as we apply them to our own. The "either-or" reality about which I spoke in detail at the beginning of this paper offers much help. Let us turn to good account the fundamental dualism in educational theory running from ancient times to the present. From the time of the Sophists in 5th-century B.C. Greece, as Bagley so well pointed out in 1938 (William C. Bagley, "An Essentialist's Platform for the Advancement of American Education;" *Educational Administration and Supervision,* XXIV (April, 1938), pp. 241-256), educational theories (and the accompanying controversies and practices) have often emphasized *either* "interest, freedom, immediate needs, personal experience, psychological organization, and pupil-initiative," *or* "effort, discipline, remote goals, race-experience, logical sequence, and teacher-initiative." But instead of carrying on the aged battle by emphasizing one set of these concepts and condemning the opposite, let us set them up as boundary marks useful in orienting and guiding us through the often baffling controversies which beset us. I label these extreme views as "Traditionalism" and "Progressivism" and define what I mean by each in both theory and practice. Again profiting from philosophy, we may recognize that in education, as in the moral life, an intelligent approach may reveal alternatives perhaps more tenable and "better" than the extremes recognized so quickly. Here knowledge is needed, the kind and clue to its attainment being suggested by a philosopher and educator of old: Plato. For Plato suggested to us the ideal of conceptual knowledge which can be attained by analyzing conflicting opinions, by defining and classifying concepts to arrive at generalizations which bring order out of chaos. If thereby we arrive at logical constructs, certainly we begin with and ground them in the realities of existence. Witness how Plato's system of philosophy arose from his grappling with the complex educational problems of a rapidly changing socio-economic period. So we extend our inquiry by analyzing the particular philosophies and theories of education of specific men whose lives and writings are a part of the history of education. We may begin with the present and go backward in time to Rousseau and Herbart, or we may start with them and arrive at present writers. Either way, our analysis leads us to two main types of educational theory, two differing alternative accounts of what education is which stand somewhere between the extreme alternatives of "Traditionalism" and "Progressivism." Following the insight of J. Alvis Lynch, who first used the terms at The Rice Institute in Houston in the late 1930's, we label these two further accounts of education as "The Learning-Product Theory" and "The Learning-Process Theory." We then have a four-fold classificatory scheme which may help us meet our needs of orientation and guidance. But again philosophy comes to our aid in meeting our remaining needs. For we need an account of education which sees education steadily and as a whole, synthesizing, drawing together the several aspects varyingly emphasized in the older accounts. The four-fold classification may, then, constitute a springboard for a new, integrated view of education, yielding significant judgments for educational practices. The discipline of philosophy is our model in this endeavor, for it suggests the value of the synoptic view. Moreover, the "both-and" approach I suggest in preference to the usual "either-or" you will recognize as coming from a philosopher: John Dewey.

Using the above approach, I suggest a four-fold classification of educational theories which may be summarized in the chart. This might be considered a scale of educational theories consisting of a line upon which one marks four points of orientation. Two points should be located near the outer limits of the line to indicate the two extreme contrasting views of education. The other two points should be located near the center (one on each side) to indicate the two contrasting less extreme, "more tenable" theories of education. At each point of orientation a name is given to each basic view as suggested above: at the extreme right, "Traditionalism"; at the less extreme right point, "The Learning-Product Theory"; at the extreme left, "Progressivism"; and at the less extreme left point, "The Learning-Process Theory." Aimed at being an orienting guide to theories of education, the chart allows the user, if he wishes, places "to hang" variations he may discover according to their differing emphases on the main aspects of education. He may encounter some views of education which may be considered as more extreme than "Traditionalism" and "Progressivism" as defined here. If so, they may be placed beyond our outer limits on the chart. As advances are made and new syntheses achieved, some views may have to be put above the line and the chart extended upward in dialectic progression à la Hegel and the traditional diagram of thesis, antithesis, and synthesis.

In further explanation of the chart as now advanced, I turn to the two extreme viewpoints which characterize the outer limits of our

A CLASSIFICATION OF THEORIES OF EDUCATION   Hugh C. Black

Theory   Practice

	X	X	X	X
	Extreme Progressivism	Learning-Process Theory (Dewey)	Learning-Product Theory (Morrison)	Extreme Traditionalism

Extreme Progressivism

1. Education as individual development (the young become educated by interacting with the environment and in the process gaining their own experience, knowledge, and skills).

2. Education as a development from within based on natural endowment (unfolding of natural powers and abilities).

Learning-Process Theory (Dewey)

Emphasizes:
Education as individual development

Education as process, method

Takes into account:
Education as transmission of social heritage

Personality as product of education

Learning-Product Theory (Morrison)

Emphasizes:
Education as transmission of social heritage

Personality as product of education

Takes into account:
Education as individual development

Education as process, method

Extreme Traditionalism

1. Education as transmission of the social heritage from the older generation to the younger generation (the direct handing on to the young of the ideas, beliefs, standards, rules of conduct, and culture of the older generation).

2. Education as a formation from without ("a process of overcoming natural inclination and substituting in its place habits acquired under external pressure").

insights, ideas as to how to live, values, culture, social heritage-organized bodies of knowledge in possession of the elders and in books

To members of the younger generation

Transmitted by Teacher

Produces

Man living in Society env.

Individual Child interacts with environment } Meets Problems } Solves Them } Gains knowledge becomes Educated

Environment

3. Education is life. Objective: Make the most of present life.

4. Minimize importance of books and of teachers. Emphasize activity, doing, pupil-planning, self-expression.

5. The child: outgoing, vigorous, enthusiastic, even boisterous.

6. Discipline: mild.

7. Child-centered school.

3. Education is preparation for life. Objective: Preparation for future life by acquiring organized bodies of knowledge.

4. Reliance upon textbooks and depositories of the social heritage and upon teachers as instruments for transmission of social heritage. Acquisition of isolated skills and techniques by drill.

5. The child: in-going, receptive, passive, docile, obedient.

6. Discipline: strict.

7. Teacher and subject-matter centered school.

Theory

Practice

orienting guide. Here we must define "Traditionalism" and "Progressivism" to state what we mean by them in both educational theory and practice. These definitions offer little which is startlingly new; for analysis of the perennial discussions reveals that the antagonists waging the battle over education when our schools are in crisis really do put it all in the nutshell of extreme alternatives. And better scholars than I have summarized these extremes of "either-or": namely, Kandel and Dewey in 1938 in the works previously cited and Brubacher in 1939. Moreover, the traditional labels are retained because they are familiar terms frequently used in the literature of philosophy of education in our own day as well as in the immediate past.

"Traditionalism" appears on the right side of the chart. In theory, it is defined as that philosophy, view, or theory of education which emphasizes exclusively the concept of education as the transmission of the social heritage from the older to the younger generation. The "Traditionalist" conceives of education as being primarily a formation from without, or, as Dewey expressed it, "a process of overcoming natural inclination and substituting in its place habits acquired under external pressure" (*Experience and Education*, p. 1). This view, account, or theory of education has implications for practices in schools. Likewise, witnessing the practices in schools, one may readily identify the underlying view or account of education. These practices have been so well delineated in the sources mentioned and have become so customary in school-lore that I need merely to summarize the main, contrasting points. Since they appear in the chart, I shall not repeat them here.

In contrast, "Progressivism" appears on the left extreme of the chart. In theory, it is defined as that philosophy, view, or theory of education which emphasizes exclusively the concept of education as individual development. Taking their cue from that "Copernicus of Modern Education" Rousseau, the "Progressivists" maintain that education is a development from within based on natural endowment. This theoretical view contrasts with that of Traditionalism as we have defined it. The educational practices that follow as implications also contrast and are summarized on the chart for ready grasp and convenience.

Next we turn to the center areas of our four-fold classificatory scheme. Here our concern is with less extreme conceptions of education to which I have applied the terms: "Learning-Product Theory" and "Learning-Process Theory" after Lynch. To my way of thinking, these two types of educational theory are more tenable than either of the two extreme theories. If their basic concepts are put into school practice, we would more likely achieve better products than those from Traditionalist or Progressive schools. But more than this, they are more tenable theories because they give a more adequate account of what education really is. However that may be, they are two further approaches to education in both theory and practice.

Since the proposed classificatory scheme is intended to be expressed in chart form for easy grasp by students, we shall modify our procedure in this area of the chart or scale. We shall limit ourselves to placing on the chart a general statement about each class of educational theory, the name of one representative of the whole class, and a statement of the contrasting points of emphasis of each. Hence we are unable to list contrasting practices implied by each theory as we did with Traditionalism and Progressivism. But the student should know that each of our "more tenable" theories has implications for practices in schools. Moreover, he should be encouraged to study those sources which indicate the detailed, contrasting practices. For example, to understand fully the "Learning-Product Theory" as represented by Henry C. Morrison, he should study Morrison's *The Curriculum of the Common School* and *The Practice of Teaching in the Secondary School* as well as *Basic Principles in Education*. Similarly he should study all of Dewey's *Democracy and Education* as well as those parts stating Dewey's theory of education.

The "Learning-Product Theory," at the less extreme position on the right of our scale of educational theories, is that view of the nature of education which has its source in the educational theory of Herbart and its development in the writings of the German Herbartians and of such American writers as Charles DeGarmo, Charles and Frank McMurry, S. C. Parker, Charles H. Judd, and Henry C. Morrison. This theory of education opposes Traditionalism; yet, when carried to its extreme limit, the learning-product theory becomes that of Traditionalism. It also opposes Progressivism and contrasts directly with the learning-process theory. The writings of the late Henry C. Morrison best exemplify the "Learning-Product Theory of Education."

Morrison does not commit the error of Traditionalism and Progressivism in giving an exclusive emphasis to one aspect of education only. He emphasizes the concept of education as the transmission of the social heritage, but he does not do so to the same extent as extreme Traditionalists. He takes into account but does not emphasize the concept of education as individual development, the concept emphasized exclusively by extreme Progressivists. Especially to be noted is the fact that Morrison's account of education includes—and emphasizes—an additional aspect of education: the product of education. According to Morrison, personality is the product of education; and, contrary to Dewey, he spells out its structure. Each learning mastered by the pupil (from "learning-units" taught under systematic procedures) results in a product, a new attitude of understanding or appreciation, a new ability, or a skill which is expressed as an accretion to personality. This product of education and the concept of education as transmission of the social heritage are the two aspects of education Morrison emphasizes. But he does take into account individual development and the process or method of education.

The "Learning-Process Theory," at the less extreme position on the left in our scale, is that view of education which has its source in Rousseau, Pestalozzi, and Froebel and its development in such writers as William James, G. Stanley Hall, John Dewey, and Boyd H. Bode. When carried to its extreme limit, the learning-process theory becomes that of Progressivism. It opposes Traditionalism and contrasts directly with the learning-product theory. The most complete and representative statement of the learning-process theory is that of John Dewey.

Dewey, as Morrison, does not commit the error of Traditionalism and Progressivism in giving an exclusive emphasis to one aspect of education alone. Dewey emphasizes the conception of education as individual development, but he does not do so to the same extent as extreme Progressivists. He takes into account, but does not emphasize, as Morrison does, education as the transmission of the social heritage, the concept which Traditionalists emphasize exclusively. Furthermore, Dewey, as Morrison, brings from the penumbra of educational theory into bright light an additional aspect of education. But it is a different one: the concept of education as a process. Dewey contrasts with Morrison in this emphasis upon the process of education, the method of educating. Dewey's main concern is with the *way* in which the young come into likemindedness with the older generation, with communicat*ing*, direct*ing*, and grow*ing*. But he does take into account the concept of education as transmission of the social heritage, and his theory implies (although he does not spell out its structure, as does Morrison) personality as the product of education.

This four-fold classificatory scheme thus recognizes four aspects of education and distinguishes the four classes of educational theories according to differences in emphasis. Four concepts—education as transmission of the social heritage, education as individual development, education as a product, and education as a process—are the differentiating factors.

The suggested scheme of classification should help students and practitioners in that orientation to theories of education so necessary before making judgments about educational practices. Several specific examples may make clearer the use of the scheme in gaining orientation. These examples should lead the reader to the point of making his own interpretation of current writers on education and placing them appropriately on our scale for orientation. Thus will be made easier the task of getting one's bearings on the Bestors, Rickovers, and Conants of our day.

If we turn to articles in periodicals, the January, 1958, issue of *The Educational Forum* affords two examples. I. L. Kandel's article "Controversy Ended" expressed the belief that the old battle between the Traditionalists and Progressivists would end after the launching of the first Sputnik on October 4, 1957. By virtue of our four-fold classificatory chart, the reader should be better able to assess Kandel's statements because he would recognize that Kandel is writing from the "Learning-Product Theory" point of view. He would probably judge that a Progressivist would not agree. Actually this is the case, for a few pages later appears Samuel Tenebaum's article "The Case for Progressive Education" which in fact continues the old, old battle. Even without the title, a few pages of reading should lead the reader who is aware of our chart to identify Tenenbaum as a "Progressivist" on the scale.

The Kandel illustration points up a difference between this suggested classificatory scheme and some of the others. Whereas several of the other classifications use the terms "Traditionalism" and "Essentialism" interchangeably, I have assigned a specific meaning to "Traditionalism" and restricted the term "Essentialism" to the specific movement by Bagley, Kandel, Demiaschevich, and others arising about February, 1938. These writers are not "Traditionalists" as defined here but members of the class termed "Learning-Product Theory." I believe this does more justice to their positions and is more accurate historically.

If we turn to books rather than articles in professional journals, several other examples of the use of my classificatory scale come to mind. Going back to the end of World War II, we find the important *Education for ALL American Youth* by the influential Educational Policies Commission and the Report of the Harvard Committee on General Education in a Free Society, *General Education in a Free Society*. Applying the scale, the student or practitioner may readily identify the first on our scale as "Learning-Process" tending toward "Progressivism" in its view of education. The second book expresses the "Learning-Product" theory of education. Also to be placed in the "Learning-Product" category are the books on education by Sir Richard Livingstone, a British writer from whom Americans would profit. Harry S. Broudy's *Building a Philosophy of Education*, written by a Classical Realist, and J. Donald Butler's *Four Philosophies of Education and Religion*, written by an Idealist, would nevertheless express a similar view of education when compared with writings on the other side of the scale. Both books would be classified as expressing the "Learning-

Product" view of education. For contrasting views of education, we may turn to several books which may be identified as on the left side of our scale in their orientation. John P. Wynne's writings are "Learning-Process" and a direct-line continuation of John Dewey. Ernest Bayles' *Democratic Educational Theory* may be identified as one variant of the Dewey "Learning-Process Theory." On the chart somewhere between "The Learning-Process Theory" and "Progressivism" I would place such "social consensus" and "group dynamics" writers as Raup, Stanley, Smith, Thomas, and Benne. Harold Rugg's views would be classified as a departure from Dewey most appropriately placed close to or within our category of "Progressivism." Emphasizing method and approach rather than content and substance, the "Linguistic Analysis" writers would appear somewhere on the left side of our scale depending upon the interpretation of the work of the specific individual. Such a recent book as Hullfish and Smith's *Reflective Thinking: The Method of Education* would be placed in a similar area on our chart.

In addition to furnishing an orienting guide useful to students and practitioners baffled by the confusion, conflicts, controversies, and chaos in the battle over education, the four-fold classification may lead to a much-needed deeper understanding of education and even to further wisdom about educational theory and practice. The person who uses the scale should certainly come to see that extreme "either-or" theories and practices are inadequate and fail to do justice to "education." Two-fold classifications must give way to broader classifications which bring into the picture more adequate accounts of education than the extreme views. If such recognition leads to "more tenable" theories of education, we may come to see the further problem of justifying one of the differing emphases over the other. We may hope, then, that some philosopher of education will advance a new account of education that goes beyond present accounts to relate in an integrated whole the main aspects of education. My own articles in *Educational Theory* ("A Way Out of Educational Confusion," 4 (April, 1954): 113-119, and "Practical Implications of a Theory of Education," 4 (October, 1954): 263-268) have suggested one possibility. Others may do better.

Philosophers of education have the opportunity of leading an advance by evolving new theories and philosophies of education which synthesize the older conflicting theories of education and give even better accounts of education. Hopefully, we should at least raise the controversy to a higher level; but if we do, the suggested four-fold classification may still serve us well. Two examples of recent attempts at syntheses come to mind. Theodore Brameld's *Toward a Reconstructed Philosophy of Education* (1956) is one such attempt which was declared at that time not to be yet a fully developed philosophy of education.

Another is Frank C. Wegener's *The Organic Philosophy of Education* (1957). If their works raise the controversy to a new level, our classification helps us get our bearings. For Brameld's "Reconstructionism," as I interpret it, may be placed on our scale somewhere on the left side between the "Learning-Process Theory" and "Progressivism"; Wegener's view of education, on the right side of our scale with the "Learning-Product Theory." Again the argument is joined, but at another level. But our four-fold classificatory scheme of educational theories helps us see the argument "steadily and as a whole."

55
Linguistic Analysis?

Jonas F. Soltis

Analysis and Anomalies in Philosophy of Education

Jonas F. Soltis, "Analysis and Anomalies in Philosophy of Education," *Educational Philosophy and Theory*, 3 (No. 2, October 1971): 37-50. Reprinted by permission from L. M. Brown, editor, *Educational Philosophy and Theory*.

In this essay I would like to make use of some of the ideas and terminology developed by Thomas S. Kuhn in his book, *The Structure of Scientific Revolutions*,[1]* in order to provide a perspective from which to view linguistic and conceptual analysis in philosophy of education. This is not to imply that I accept without question the major thesis of Kuhn's work as he attempts to explain radical shifts in the metaphysics and epistemology of natural sciences. These theses contain separate and important philosophical issues worthy of closer scrutiny in their own right.[2] Rather, I will utilize selectively only those aspects of Kuhn's work which are descriptive of the symptoms of change and the social psychology of change as they provide the basis for an admittedly impressionistic, incomplete and thinly documented historical sketch of contemporary philosophy of education.

Readers of Kuhn will recall that his general model for displaying the dominant feature in the state of the science before, during, and after a period of change is built upon the key ideas of "paradigm," "normal science," "anomalies," "crisis" and "paradigm shift."[3] A paradigm for Kuhn is a model provided by a single achievement or a set of works of such magnitude and impact in a field of study that they set the problems and ground rules for future inquiry in that field. In science, the work of a Newton or a Darwin exemplifies the Kuhnian concept of paradigm in that such works not only solve some troublesome old problems in the field, but also provide fertile avenues for new inquiry of a different

* References appear at the conclusion of this chapter.

type. The actual investigations undertaken by following the model of the new paradigm is what Kuhn calls the activity of normal science. If the paradigm maker can be seen as a creator of a new way to approach old problems, the normal inquirer then may be viewed as a dedicated "puzzle solver," one who utilizes his ingenuity and skill not to create a new mode of inquiry, but to apply the methods of the paradigm to problems which fit its mould.

However, in the normal course of extending the use of the paradigm to solve more and more problems, anomalies may arise. Anomalies are of two basic sorts. On the one hand, there may be increasing recognition of a major problem or set of problems which resist the methods of normal solution dictated by the paradigm. On the other, in the course of pursuing normal puzzle-solving activities, unexpected results may occur which eventually may force a re-evaluation of the paradigm as supplying the best or proper methods for inquiry. If either or both these sorts of anomalies occur, they may precipitate what Kuhn calls a "crisis state" in which the old paradigm comes under close scrutiny and attack by the vanguards of an emerging new paradigm. If such a new paradigm emerges and seems to offer a way out of the impasse created by the anomalies and the old paradigm, this can produce what Kuhn calls a "paradigm shift." Such a paradigm shift brings with it a new set of appropriate puzzles, a new set of rules for solving them and a new period of less disruptive normal inquiry. The cycle is thus completed.

Of necessity, there is much omitted from the brief summary sketch above, but once again readers of Kuhn may recall his frequent references to textbooks and to the role they play as indicators of change in a field and as instruments for initiating new generations of students into the accepted paradigm for normal inquiry. By taking a rough sample of texts in philosophy of education written from the analytical point of view, an account of the emergence and acceptance of the paradigm of linguistic analysis in philosophy of education can be sketched with sufficient resolution to permit extrapolations to possible future directions for this mode of inquiry.

If we take the state of the field of philosophy of education in the '20's, '30's and '40's, to be analogous to a state of "normal science,"[4] we can view it as operating within a paradigm which sets as legitimate problems for the field, the definition of education in terms of some broad world view, the discernment of the aims of education from such a point of view and the recommendation of procedures and teaching methods to attain these aims which are deemed to be most desirable.

The most apparent anomaly during this period was lack of agreement between theorists about the proper definition, aims and procedures for education without any clear criteria available for choice between competing theories. During the same period, the so-called analytic revolution in general philosophy had begun to gain a solid foothold in England and was gaining adherents in American universities. In his introduction to what is now recognized as the first analytic textbook in the field, written in 1942, C. D. Hardie pointed clearly at the anomaly of disagreement among educational theorists:

> If two educational theorists disagree I think it should be made clear whether the disagreement is factual or verbal or due to some emotional conflict. If this is to be done it is necessary always to state each theory in the clearest possible way so that no ambiguity may be allowed to flourish undiscovered.[5]

Needless to say, the first formal questioning of the adequacy of the paradigm of normal inquiry into the aims and methods of education had little impact. In fact, fifteen years later, D. J. O'Connor was led to remark in his Preface to *An Introduction to the Philosophy of Education* that "the viewpoint (of my book) is that of contemporary 'philosophical analysis' (and) indeed, the only previous attempt of the kind so far as I am aware, is Professor C. D. Hardie's excellent little book *Truth and Fallacy in Educational Theory* published in 1942 and now out of print."[6]

O'Connor went on to attack more directly the older paradigm by arguing that:

> Most would agree that the traditional philosophers prom- ised more than they were able to deliver and that their claim to interpret the universe on a grand scale must be rejected for just the same reasons that the claims of alchemists, astrologers, or magicians are now rejected (p. 17).[7]

It is one thing to question a dominant paradigm as did Hardie, but quite another to directly attack and attempt to overthrow it as did O'Connor. Indeed, another British-trained analytic philosopher, R. S. Peters, dared to question one of the most fundamental assumptions of the paradigm of normal philosophy of education when he asked, "Must an educator have an Aim?"[8] In the late '50's and early '60's, many of the symptoms of Kuhn's concept of crisis state were apparent. Most readers of this paper lived through that period and will recall both the spate of papers at philosophy of education conventions directed at the question—what is philosophy of education—and the acrimonious debates between those who saw promise in analytic techniques and those who felt threatened by the way in which these techniques seemed to relegate their work to the derogatory realms of vagueness, meaninglessness and "metaphysics." But more often these were real and "deep debates over legitimate methods, problems and standards of solution (of the sort that occurs during) periods when paradigms are first under attack and then subject to change."[9]

In the American Philosophy of Education Society, the fight for and final establishment of a permanent place on the programme for Analysis as a "special interest group" was bitterly contested behind the scenes but finally carried the day. In Kuhn's psychological terms, many philosophers of education quite clearly felt that they were being forced to make not only a choice between two competing paradigms, but a more fundamental one between two "incompatible modes of community life."[10]

Some, I am sure, also felt quite threatened, assuming that if the analytical paradigm was adopted as the new paradigm they might be one of Kuhn's dinosaurs belonging to an older school which gradually disappears. "In part, their disappearance is caused by their members' conversion to the new paradigm. But there are always some men who cling to one or another of the older views and they are simply read out of the profession, which thereafter ignores their work."[11]

In retrospect, of course, these very human fears and reactions were unnecessary while the more serious debates were more valuable. The two paradigms seem quite compatible now. But there is no denying the reality of the social psychological symptoms of the crisis state (as suggested in Kuhn's description of the social psychology of paradigm change) during this period in the recent history of philosophy of education in the English speaking world.

Once again, however, we should look to the textbooks that were produced during the period to see how they provided for the initiation of students into the new paradigm and were also used in an attempt at conversion of those already practising in the field. Just one year after O'Connor's book had appeared, Israel Scheffler prefaced his anthology, *Philosophy and Education*, with these words:

> It is hoped that the book will . . . contribute toward the establishment of closer relations between "general" philosophy and the philosophy of education; relations which would enrich the former by diversifying the scope of its methods and which would strengthen the latter by bringing its foundations under intensive new cultivation.[12]

Two things are important to notice here. First, Scheffler is making it clear that this book is not just another work operating within the old paradigm of settling questions about the aim and methods of educating. Instead, (note his title) it is trying to persuade philosophers of education to be *philosophers* (in the new paradigm sense of the analytical philosophers). Second, it is an anthology, not a single man's treatment of topics in education, but rather a collection of papers "intended to illustrate and to stimulate the application of newer philosophical approaches to education."[13] That is, it presents models of the analytical paradigm . . . models from which to learn tacitly the rules of procedure for analytic inquiry, the types of problems amenable to the new paradigm and the proper stance or attitude of the competent practitioner of philosophical analysis.

Other anthologies of the same sort follow Scheffler's model of presenting a vehicle for initiation into the new paradigm. In 1961, B. O. Smith and R. Ennis produced *Language and Concepts in Education*,[14] and in 1965, Reginald Archambault followed with an all-British Scheffler type anthology called *Philosophical Analysis and Education*.[15] Both of these, like the Scheffler volume, take pains in the introduction to point to the perceived anomalies of the traditional paradigm of philosophy of education, such as conflicting theories and doctrines, lack of connection with general philosophy, failure to deliver what was promised for educational practice, etc. And Archambault continues the style of attack launched by O'Connor when he says:

> I spoke earlier of the need to clear the stables. This is particularly pressing in educational theory, for the eclecticism and broad, synthetic treatments have spawned vagueness, ambiguity, pseudo-problems and pseudo-explanations, vacuous principles and impractical prescriptions. These are characteristic of writings in the philosophy of education.[16]

These volumes also try to persuade the community to "clean the stables," to re-examine educational concepts from a fresh vantage point. But their major function as texts is to provide models for imitation and initiation into the analytic paradigm. As such they even reflect the "piecemeal" attack strategy of the analytic philosopher. They are collections of separate and distinct analyses of seemingly unconnected topics generally belonging to the broad field of education but not at all arranged or even suggestive of a comprehensive, systematic approach. How well the initiation and conversion processes worked in a short time might be suggested by a few words drawn from Scheffler's introduction to the second edition of *Philosophy and Education*:

> There is now a recognizable and growing corpus of writings dealing relatively directly with educational matters in the spirit of (philosophical analysis) . . . The old walls are crumbling . . . The lesson has been learned.[17]

How well Scheffler felt the "lesson has been learned" can also be judged from the remarks in the introduction of his two non-anthology texts for educational philosophy, *The Language of Education* (1960),[18] and *The Conditions of Knowledge* (1965).[19] In the earlier volume Scheffler takes pain to make clear what analysis is about and how it differs from the older mode of inquiry into the history of philosophical ideas and thinkers associated with the traditional paradigm. But even here he is not on the attack or pointing to anomalies as much as he is trying to explicate analysis persuasively. In *Conditions of Knowledge*, however, not only are attacks on the old paradigm missing in the introduction, but also there is not even any attempt to justify or persuade one of the value of the analytic mode of inquiry which follows. The validity of this mode is taken to be a recognized and accomplished fact. From Scheffler's vantage point the lesson had been learned and there was no longer need for attack, persuasion, or apology.

Of course, attacks, pointing to the old anomalies and apologies still appear in more recent texts, but the authors of these are not unaware that there is a large segment of the philosophy of education population for whom such now ritualistic remarks are unnecessary. In Kuhn's terms I think it would be fair to say that a paradigm shift in philosophy of education has occurred and that there is a significant number of philosophers of education for whom "normal" inquiry into problems in philosophy of education is done *via* the rules and procedures set by the analytic paradigm. The shift has not been total, of course, but the paradigm of analysis occupies a recognized and legitimate sector of the field.

In a review of my book, *An Introduction to the Analysis of Educational Concepts*,[20] Michael Parsons makes these points quite succinctly:

> O'Connor thought that conceptual analysis was the whole of what was legitimate as philosophy of education. Mr. Soltis does not and consequently offers an introduction to part of the field and not the whole . . . Again, he is clear, as some of the writers using the positional approach still are not, that conceptual analysis is not another option that may be preferred to pragmatism. Consequently there is no need for aggressive debate between analysts and, for example, Realists . . . (This) reflects, I think, a shift in the interests and ideas in the profession as a whole in the last ten years. It leaves Soltis free to discuss analytically some concepts used in thinking about education which O'Connor did not do . . . It surveys some of the better work in this vein from the last ten years . . . In this way, too, it marks progress in the field, *for O'Connor had nothing to review.*[21]

If this sketch of the immediate past has any validity, it can now be used as a basis from which to project some ideas about the possible directions which might be taken by philosophers of education occupying that sector of the field dominated by the analytic paradigm. Clearly, it seems highly probable that the literature flowing from the pens of those in pursuit of conceptual and linguistic problems which fit the normal patterns of the analytic paradigm will continue. The language of education is still full of analytic-type puzzles waiting to be solved and new languages, slogan systems and theories appear with sufficient regularity to keep the "normal" analytic philosopher of education active for many years. By the same token it would seem that there will be less and less need for formal defences of the analytic paradigm or even for claims that it is *the* only legitimate mode of inquiry into philosophical problems in education. The pursuit of converts will become unnecessary because post-revolutionary texts will continue to be produced and new students will be inducted into the paradigm without any sense of the battles that raged over its acceptance only a short time ago. They will view other standard approaches as different or perhaps even irrelevant, but not as threatening.

Moreover, given a large enough group of initiates, they probably will tend to write "brief articles addressed only to professional colleagues, the men whose knowledge of a shared paradigm can be assumed and who prove to be the only ones able to read the papers addressed to them."[22]

But all this is to predict what is very easy to predict given Kuhn's description of the normal pursuit of problems after a paradigm shift. The course of continued normal analytic inquiry seems fairly clear and firmly set. But what about those grand Marxian-Kuhnian forces which suggest that a paradigm contains within itself the seeds of its own destruction in the form of emerging anomalies and the precipitation of crises? Here we have the basis for projections of another sort less easily predicted exactly and more subject to the sensibilities of individuals in their perceptions of and tolerance for, anomalies. In what follows, I shall make such a speculative projection for the analytic paradigm from the only vantage point I have, my own. I grant that others may view the scene differently, or may see different anomalies from those I do, or even may see no anomalies at all, in current analytic practice. But I shall try to substantiate my claims for the existence of certain present anomalies in the field through argument and example thereby suggesting what I take to be important problems which most likely will alter the future direction of the field.

As I reflect on the last ten years of analytic work on the language and concepts of education, two major anomalies stand out in my mind.

The first is internal to the analytic paradigm itself in that careful, cumulative and persistent use of analytic techniques to clarify the concept of learning has brought with it disturbing results which run counter to the expectations of those who believe in the power of the paradigm to make clear, precise and distinct "fuzzy" categories. The second, in a sense, is external to the paradigm in that previous educational questions concerning values and social issues persist as major philosophical problems in education, but seem to be resistant to the strategies of analysis. In what remains of this paper, I would like to sketch in more detail the nature of these anomalies and suggest what bearing they may have on the future direction of analysis in philosophy of education.

In recent years, philosophers of education with an analytic bent have frequently examined various aspects of the concept of learning and one of the major results of these investigations has been a fairly general consensus with respect to the identification of three or four basic types of learning. One major type, often called "propositional" or learning *that*, refers to those things which are learned in the form of assertions such as, "Columbus discovered America." The learning of procedures, or skills (learning *how* to), on the other hand, has been distinguished from the learning of propositions by noting the need for practice in acquiring such learning products as the ability to swim, to play the piano, or to perform brain surgery. Moreover, it has been argued that to successfully learn all the relevant propositions describing the activity of a skill like swimming is no guarantee that one will be able to swim upon entering the water for the first time.

Although these two basic types of learning products cover the wide range of things we ordinarily think of as knowledge of such things as facts and skills, analytic philosophers have been forced to recognize a third type of learning outcome variously called a "disposition," "propensity," or "tendency" (learning *to*) which clearly is more than learning what to do and how to do it; it is acquiring the *tendency* to act in certain ways under certain circumstances. Thus, although one might have learned that honesty is the best policy and know how to be honest in a variety of situations, unless he has also acquired the disposition to be honest, he may not act honestly at all. Knowledge of rules and how to apply them is no guarantee that one will act in accord with them.

Finally, it is generally recognized that there are states of "attainment" *via* learning such as appreciation and understanding which seem to reach beyond the three types of learning outcomes described above even though any one or combination of all may be essential prerequisites to attaining such states. Surely one can learn a poem, but fail to appreciate it, or, indeed, in some cases, fail to understand it; and it is this stubborn fact of the everyday world of learning outcomes which often pull up short of understanding and appreciation even though some learning has occurred that has led many contemporary analytic philosophers to recognize "attainments" as a separate learning category.

Now, while I cannot and would not deny the logic and usefulness of these distinctions in many theoretical and pedagogical contexts, I must admit to a growing dissatisfaction with this analytic schema when it is taken to be genuinely descriptive of the types of things possible for humans to learn. Three things bother me most about this schema and point to its general anomalous status. First, there is a static quality about it which belies the more dynamic aspects of human learning which anyone can sense in his own experience with things he has learned. The distinctness and hence separateness of the analytic types fails to give a sense of the amalgam of things which are part and parcel of both the processes and products of human learning. Second, there is no suggestion of the ways in which different learnings may combine, be related to one another, or, indeed, of what may be common to each type so that one fails to see any generic sense of learning emerging from the analytic classification. Finally, I find the schema lacking any consideration of a concept of mind which seems to be essential to a philosophically and pedagogically useful description of human learning.

In a way, it is strange that a mode of investigation with these types of learning could be launched by Gilbert Ryle's distinction between "knowing how" and "knowing that" in a book called *Concept of Mind*[23] and reach a point totally lacking any explicit rendering of a sophisticated theory of mind. The only recent work of a semi-analytic sort which implicitly recognizes the anomalies I point to above and tries to deal with them is Donald Arnstine's *Philosophy of Education: Learning and Schooling*.[24] There, Arnstine tries to put the various types of learning distinguished by analysts under the general umbrella concept of "disposition," making all learning the acquisition or modification of some disposition. His work is very suggestive and at least squarely faces the anomalies of the situation, but it fails I think, mainly because of its inadequate development of a clear, useful and logically consistent concept of mind and because of the ambiguity built into his treatment of his key concept of "disposition," which at one time refers to one property of mind among many others (p. 122) and at another is equivalent to mind itself (p. 135) and though claimed to be distinguishable from attitudes (p. 30 and p. 37) is treated as an attitude (p. 125 *et alia*).[25]

While it is easy enough to convey a personal sense of self-felt discomfort over the results of analytic efforts to deal adequately with the concept of learning and thus suggest that these efforts to date result in anomalies, it is another thing to show more technically and in more detail just how the persistent and thorough use of analysis produces a specific anomaly. Without realizing it at the time, however, I did just this two years ago in my discussion of Scheffler's very thorough analysis of "knowing that."[26] There, like Scheffler and others familiar with the cumulative results of analysis of the concepts of learning and knowing, I accepted the distinctions between propositions, procedures, dispositions and attainments as sound and correct. These had become clear-cut distinctions and if any of them could be called the clearest and best isolated at all, it seemed to be the propositional sense of learning or knowing "that." But as Scheffler skilfully penetrated further into what he called the "strong" sense of knowing "that" which demanded that the conditions of truth, belief and evidence be met, it seemed to me that a strange thing had happened.

As I explicated Scheffler's analytic treatment of the evidence condition with which I had found no "logical" or "analytic" fault, I was forced to point out:

> . . . where this fuller examination of Scheffler's treatment of the evidence condition has taken us from a concentrated examination of the logical nature of knowing *that*, we have come (with Scheffler and in terms of his own analysis) to talk of knowing *how* to pattern data to constitute a proof. Gathering evidence, supporting our assertions, producing arguments, etc., all seems to involve the use of some complex skills. Thus knowing that in the strong sense seems to involve knowing *how*! Moreover, "seeing the point," "appreciating the force of an argument," or "understanding a proof" all seem to go beyond propositional and procedural knowledge altogether to what Scheffler has called "attainments"—attaining a state of appreciation or understanding; states which "outstrip knowing in range."[27]

In simple terms, I had come upon a rather striking anomaly. Years of analytic work had clearly isolated the propositional sense of learning and knowing from all others and yet through normal analysis came the unexpected and anomalous result of finding some of these and other different types of knowing and learning absolutely essential to propositional knowing. Surely one could find reason to question the paradigm given such a result. But at the time I merely followed the above quoted paragraph with a half-hearted warning that perhaps in practice one shouldn't take theoretical analysis too literally and that perhaps more analysis was needed to rectify this "paradoxical" situation. In Kuhn's terms, I was acting the part of the normal inquirer by not questioning the paradigm, but rather suggesting that continued normal inquiry would probably straighten everything out.

The upshot of all this is to reinforce my contention that one of the major anomalies in the current analytic approach to philosophy of education is to be found in analytic treatments of the concept of learning. This is to suggest that within the continual stream of projected normal inquiry *via* analysis, there may arise a significant challenge to the paradigm because of the inadequacy of its treatment of that most central educational concept, learning. I have no crystal ball, but I would expect philosophers of education who become impatient with the anomaly to try to find some more acceptable answers or different ways to ask the questions by turning to the general area of philosophy of mind, or in the style of Piaget, to the pursuit of a philosophical-empirical study of "genetic epistemology." Will a crisis occur and will a new paradigm emerge or will the analytic paradigm be sufficient to the task? I have no way of knowing, but if a crisis and paradigm shift were to come in analysis, I would expect that the anomalies in analytic treatments of learning could prove to be one of the most fertile spawning grounds for revolution.

Now it is time to turn to the second, more amorphous anomaly, which I described above as being in a sense external to the analytic paradigm and involving questions of value and social issues which are resistant to the methods of analysis. In Kuhn's terms, a paradigm not only sets the methods acceptable for the solution of problems, but also defines the kinds of questions which the followers of a paradigm are permitted to ask. Now clearly, the realms of axiology and social philosophy are not out of bounds for the practitioners of normal analysis, but it should be equally clear that certain kinds of philosophical questions within those realms are illegitimate from the analytic point of view. One can ask for clarification of the idea of equality of opportunity, but one cannot ask if the schools *should* provide the equality of opportunity. The same is true for such concepts as social purpose, relevance, social morality, humaneness, etc.

Indeed, the lesson has been learned well! One could imagine the chanted recitation of a tacit decalogue by contemporary analytic philosophers of education which goes, "We are the normal analytic philosophers of education and shall allow no false claimants to a superior knowledge of the Good within our ranks. Remember to keep holy the principle of neutrality. Honour the counter example. Do not prescribe nor make value judgements, etc. . . ."

Admittedly the caricature is drawn with a heavy hand, but only to display the full import of the anomalous situation which confronts the sensitive normal inquirer in the realm of pressing social and educational issues of value. To paraphrase Kuhn, when a paradigm fails to be able to address itself to the problems deemed most important or urgent to the community in which one lives and works, a state of paradigm crisis may ensue. There is no denying the sense of urgency felt in the contemporary educational world for answers to fundamental questions of value and social principle. One could speculate that during the period of paradigm shift to analysis in the late '50's and early '60's, no such "value crisis" was upon us. Students were docile and willing to "be educated" so that they could then take their place in a booming society of technological progress. Tacitly, the aims of education were pretty well agreed upon by educators and their disputes, if I may paraphrase R. S. Peters, reflected not so much what they thought education was directed at, but how they thought it best to get students there. Quite clearly the contemporary educational scene has shifted radically.

But once again, all this is merely to suggest an anomalous situation created by external pressures upon the paradigm which are not totally of its own making. I think, however, that there is another task one could take to show that even without the violent accidents of our time, this anomaly of value crisis is integral to the analytic paradigm itself whenever it is applied to education. I think this can be demonstrated by selectively sketching some of the thoughts of R. S. Peters, who, I believe, has been struggling valiantly with this anomaly throughout his career as an educational philosopher. In his inaugural lecture on appointment to the chair of philosophy of education at the University of London Institute of Education in 1964, he makes clear his analytic stance by remarking that he considers himself "a very mundane fellow whose eyes are more likely to be fixed on the brass tacks on or under the teacher's desk than on the Form of the Good."[28]

Nonetheless, he goes on to sketch one of his earliest forms of his analysis of the concept of education which demands "the intentional bringing about of a desirable state"[29] and "that 'to be educated' implies . . . caring about what's worthwhile . . ."[30] He is criticized in a review concerning certain analytic points about confusion of task and achievement senses of the term education and the related ideas of teaching and learning,[31] but is not treated harshly on the grounds that he is taking on value questions outside the "box" prescribed by the analytic paradigm. Peters follows with his book, *Ethics and Education,* in which he reworks the analysis of the concept of education paying due attention to the task-achievement distinction and concludes:

    (i)   that 'education' implies the transmission of what is worth-while to those who become committed to it;

    (ii) that 'education' must involve knowledge and understanding and some kind of cognitive perspective which is not inert;

(iii) that 'education' at least rules out some procedures of transmission, on the grounds that they lack wittingness and
voluntariness on the part of the learner.[32]

This analysis is attacked in normal analytic fashion as being
prescriptive because while claiming to be neutral, it qualifies as valuable
that knowledge which is not *inert* and gives specific *grounds* for determining the *value* of how knowledge should be transmitted.[33]

At almost the same time that this attack is launched, Peters is
busy preparing a paper entitled "Education and the Educated Man: Some
Further Reflections," which was recently read at the British Philosophy
of Education Society Meetings. In it he again wrestles with the fundamental problem set by his clear notion that education *is* and, in fact,
must be, concerned with the valuable and the worthwhile, but he is
still beset by the non-prescriptive limits of the analytic paradigm within
which he works. I shall not summarize his "further reflections" here,
but merely quote his last line, "my claim is that this fresh attempt at the
analysis of the concept of 'education' (and the 'educated man') does
something to present in a more specific way the tasks that lie ahead
which are of central importance not just for the philosophy of education,
but for ethical theory in general." These "tasks," unless I misunderstand
him, are in reality substantive issues of traditional ethical theory concerning certain aspects of the good and their justifications as they relate
to the ideal of "an educated man." In a word, I think Peters has come
to tacitly recognize the anomaly of which I speak and certainly has
asked and may even be prepared to try to carefully answer questions
which seem to be disallowed by the analytic paradigm.

Although admittedly brief, this treatment of Peters' concern with
the value dimension of education provides a way to indicate more
specifically the internal tension of this second major anomaly which
I've identified. What this suggests to me is that while one may find it
much easier to utilize the general philosophical analytic paradigm in
epistemoloyg, metaphysics, aesthetics and even ethics, in education it
is much more difficult to do so because a large part of the everyday
business of educating is imbued with the unavoidable task of making
decisions of value or acting upon assumed valuations. Certainly, clarification of the issues at hand can be helpful, but that is not yet to offer a
solution to the fundamental value considerations necessary to the task
(except covertly in some instances when neutral-looking analyses carry
with them implicit valuations).[34]

It would seem, then, that the analytic paradigm has another "soft
spot," the anomaly of value issues which may effect crisis and a paradigm

shift if normal inquiry into this sphere is unable either to satisfy the external demands or to relieve the internal tensions. It seems probable that the challenge to the analytic paradigm may come from new forms of inquiry into ethics or social philosophy. What shape these new forms might take if indeed they emerge at all is impossible to predict. But one thing seems certain and that is that if they come forth, they will *claim* to be able to deal adequately with the sorts of value issues which have been set aside and made out of bounds by analytic philosophers as well as by contemporary "normal" behavioural and social scientists. It is even conceivable that a new paradigm sufficient to the task may come from the social and behavioural scientists themselves rather than from that sector of the philosophical community which has more recently turned its back on questions of value.[35]

In this essay I have tried to sketch the state of the field of the analytic sector of philosophy of education as I see it presently and as I am able to project its possible directions for the immediate future. It may well be that there will be no crises within the analytic paradigm and that the persistent use of normal analytic methods will dissolve the anomalies I've pointed out. If, however, new paradigms do arise to meet the challenges of these anomalies, I think it is possible to make one last projection. It seems possible to me that a hybrid paradigm might develop and be called "analytic-pragmatics." This may be more wish than guess because it seems to me that unless philosophy of education is to have some consequence for educational practice, it will be an intolerably sterile field of study. But more to the point: in both of the general anomalies I've described, it is the analyst's inattention to the consequences of the results of his "normal" inquiry for educational practice which force the anomalies upon him. The consequence of the analyses of learning is failure to match any ordinary or technical theories of learning and the consequences of eliminating direct value considerations proscribes what is impossible to proscribe in the real world of educating. Thus, one could expect that if anything could remedy this situation, it would be an "analytic-pragmatics" which provides due regard both for careful theorizing and for the consequences and potential use of that theorizing tested in the real world.

For whatever insights I have about analysis, I am most indebted to the suggestive description of change in the field of study provided by Thomas S. Kuhn. Even if my strained analogy breaks down, I still think that a legitimate claim can be made that there is much work which needs to be done in theory of mind, learning, value theory and social philosophy if educational philosophers are to meet the challenges of the future.

References

[1] Kuhn, Thomas S., *The Structure of Scientific Revolutions*, The University of Chicago Press, 1962.

[2] Indeed, Israel Scheffler does just this when, in his recent work *Science and Subjectivity*, Bobbs-Merrill, Indianapolis, 1967, he takes Kuhn to task for claiming that "paradigm change in science is not generally subject to deliberation and critical assessment" (p. 89). See chapter 4, pp. 67-89.

[3] Kuhn, *op. cit.*, passim. I have omitted reference to Kuhn's "preparadigm stage" because I will not treat philosophy of education as a field in such a state. Certainly the analogue between Kuhn's view of the pre-paradigm stage as one of competing schools, lack of a satisfactory paradigm, etc., and the state of philosophy of education in the immediate past and present seems most appropriate. But for the purposes of this essay, it will be more useful to settle for the less accurate but more suggestive analogue of philosophy of education prior to the advent of analysis as a field with a dominant accepted paradigm pursuing a mode of "normal inquiry."

[4] See footnote 3, *supra*.

[5] Hardie, C. D., *Truth and Fallacy in Educational Theory*, American edition, Teachers College, Columbia University, 1962, p. xix.

[6] O'Connor, D. J., *An Introduction to the Philosophy of Education*, Routledge and Kegan Paul, London, 1957, p. v. Perhaps O'Connor was unaware of Israel Scheffler's seminal article in the *Harvard Educational Review*, XXIV (Fall, 1954), pp. 223-230. "Toward an Analytic Philosophy of Education," and the symposium sponsored by the *Harvard Educational Review* entitled "The Aims and Content of Philosophy of Education," XXVI (Spring, 1956).

[7] *Ibid.*, pp. 4, 17.

[8] Peters, R. S., *Authority, Responsibility and Education*, George Allen and Unwin, London, 1959, Chap. 7, "Must an Educator Have an Aim?" pp. 83-95. The chapter is based on talks delivered mainly on the Home Service and Third Programme of the BBC, between April, 1956 and January, 1959.

[9] Kuhn, *op. cit.*, p. 48.

[10] *Ibid.*, p. 93.

[11] *Ibid.*, pp. 18-19.

[12] Scheffler, I., editor, *Philosophy and Education*, First edition, Allyn and Bacon, Boston, 1958, p. v.

[13] *Ibid.*, p. 1.

[14] Smith, B. O. and Ennis, R. H., editors, *Language and Concepts in Education*, Rand McNally, Chicago, 1961.

[15] Archambault, R. D., *Philosophical Analysis and Education*, The Humanities Press, 1965.

[16] *Ibid.*, p. 8.

[17] Scheffler, I., editor, *Philosophy and Education*, Second edition, Allyn and Bacon, Boston, 1966, pp. 12-13.

[18] Scheffler, I., *The Language of Education*, Charles C. Thomas, Springfield, Illinois, 1960.

[19] Scheffler, I., *The Conditions of Knowledge*, Scott, Foresman, Chicago, 1965.

[20] Soltis, J. F., *An Introduction to the Analysis of Educational Concepts*, Addison-Wesley, Reading, Mass., 1968.

21 Parsons, M., "Review Article," Educational Theory, IXX, 1969, p. 102.

22 Kuhn, op. cit., p. 20.

23 Ryle, G., The Concept of Mind, Hutchinson, London, 1949.

24 Arnstine, D., Philosophy of Education: Learning and Schooling, Harper and Row, New York, 1967.

25 Ibid. Obviously, a critical sentence should not be taken as an adequate critique of a very thoughtful work such as Arnstine's, but this is not the place to carry this discussion further. Of more import are the undeniable facts that Arnstine implicitly recognizes the anomalies I suggest and seriously attempts to resolve them.

26 Soltis, J. F., An Introduction to the Analysis of Educational Concepts, Addison-Wesley, Reading, Mass., 1968, pp. 44-48. (See especially the footnote on page 48 where I thought the point of my argument was to indicate that "Scheffler does not seem to recognize this paradox of talking about a 'strong' sense of knowing whose elements 'outstrip knowing in range.'") Scheffler's original analysis is to be found in his Conditions of Knowledge, op. cit.

27 Soltis, op. cit., pp. 47-48. All phrases in single quotes are from Scheffler's Conditions of Knowledge.

28 Peters, R. S., Education as Initiation, Evans Brothers, London, 1964, p. 8.

29 Ibid., p. 15.

30 Ibid., p. 25.

31 Soltis, J. F., "Education as Initiation," in Studies in Philosophy of Education: Reviews and Rejoinders, Vol. 5, No. 1, 1966-1967, pp. 189-190.

32 Peters, R. S., Ethics and Education, Scott, Foresman, Palo Alto, 1967, Ch. I. Peters goes on to examine analytically and argue rationally for a number of important ethical principles such as justice, equality, freedom, etc. Here Peters attempts to merge a neutral analysis of the concept of education with a substantive argument for certain ethical principles trying to bridge the anomalous gap.

33 Soltis, J. F., "On Defining Education: An Apology," Philosophy of Education 1969: Proceedings of the 25th Annual Meeting of The Philosophy of Education Society, D. Arnstine (ed.), Studies in Philosophy of Education, 1969, pp. 172-176.

34 Scheffler has been frequently charged with being prescriptive in offering the rational model of teaching as a neutral analysis of the concept of teaching. I for one must admit that I accept his model not because of the propriety and correctness of the analysis, but because I value its commitment to rationality in pedagogical practice.

35 It may even be that some conjoint concern over what the social sciences have to offer and what the philosopher of education reads as problems of value will lead the way. Indeed, Ira S. Steinberg in Educational Myths and Realities, Addison-Wesley, Reading, Mass., 1968 seems to attempt just such a project to a limited degree and with only relative success, but nonetheless, thereby provides a modest prototype for such philosophizing.

56
Existentialism?

M. I. Berger

Existential Criticism
in Educational Theory:
A Subjective View
of a Serious Business

M. I. Berger, "Existential Criticism in Educational Theory: A Subjective View of a Serious Business," *Proceedings of the Nineteenth Annual Meeting of the Philosophy of Education Society, Sir Francis Drake Hotel, San Francisco, California, April 7-10, 1963*, edited by Martin Levit (Lawrence, Kansas, Ernest E. Bayles, University of Kansas, 1963), pp. 93-98.

My paper concerns existential thought. I will try to describe the prominent features of this attitude, particularly its view of the modern world, and show how it is employable as a critical technique in contemporary educational practice and theory.

Transcending all differences among those presenting existential ideas (and I admit the impertinence in trying to do this) I would say that all existential thinkers believe there is an unbridgeable gap between our personal, subjective existence and our objective knowledge of ourselves and the world. This difference between the self-conscious individual and the world, between man's immediate and man's cognitive experience, between persons and objects, points to the vital existential assertion that "existence" cannot be circumscribed by reason; that, indeed, "existence" refers to precisely that which is inaccessible to reason. Accordingly, the truth of human existence cannot objectively be established. Karl Jaspers states the thesis in *Reason and Existence*:

> The rational is not thinkable without its other, the nonrational, and it never appears in reality without it. The only question is, in what form the other appears, how it remains in spite of all, and how it is to be grasped.

It is appropriate for philosophizing to strive to absorb the non-rational and counter-rational, to form it through reason, to change it into a form of reason, indeed, finally to show it as identical with reason; all Being should become law and order.

But both the defiant will and honest mind turn against this. They recognize and assert the unconquerable non-rational.[1]

Existentialism attempts to preserve the tension between human existence and human knowledge. It believes that recognizing this tension, this paradox, yields insight into authentic human existence. Paradox, ambiguity, absurdity, irony, these are the *leitmotifs* of existential literature that echo the character of man's nature. The task is to describe the enigma of man's existence without violating any part of life: to avoid, in the description, either dissection or murder. Such a task involves explaining and yet not explaining, speaking and yet not speaking. Man's existence must be expressed in this indirect manner because existence is such that it cannot be forced; its truth cannot be objectively established. That is why the most important things men have to say to one another cannot quite be said. That is why the best expressions of existential thought are found in literature rather than philosophy.

Before we can go any further with this analysis a necessary philosophical explanation must be made. At the level of common understanding the preceding paragraphs, if not entirely acceptable, are at least comprehensible. Every human being has sensed the difference between himself as a "self" and the world of objects and others about him. Moreover men know, even though they may not be able to express the knowledge, that their "humanity" sharply sets them off from the physical world. Finally, all men know what it means to be abused as an individual, that is, to be treated as an object. But if such descriptions are appreciated in the popular world, they may be considered meaningless in the disciplined philosophical world where words are carefully analyzed. What is meant by saying there is an "unbridgeable gap between our personal, subjective existence and our objective knowledge of ourselves and the world"? Does it mean that we gain knowledge of our "selves" in a different way from the way we learn about the external world? If so, what is this other method: intuition, introspection, or perhaps just plain mysticism? If "existence" is inaccessible to reason, to what is it accessible? If "existence" cannot be described, by what sign is it known? In a word, how can a philosopher dare to speak about that which he admits cannot be spoken?

---

[1]Karl Jaspers, *Reason and Existenz,*(New York: The Noonday Press, 1956), p. 19.

Such unrelenting questioning reveals the charm of Anglo-American analytic thought. Analysis forces philosophy to be honest: philosophy cannot hide its confusion in nonsensical utterances. And unquestionably this is what existentialism often tries to do.

Moreover, the freewheeling use of such powerful words as "reason," "experience," "sense," and "self" is unpardonable. But it is one thing to accuse a philosophy of using language loosely; it is quite another to say that it is meaningless. For it may very well be that the insights of existential thought, though obscurely expressed, are yet reasonable. In any case, if existentialism is to remain in philosophy it must become clearer or else remove itself to another discipline where the emotive value of existential utterances can be accepted freely.

Despite the obvious defects in existentialism the attitude proves valuable as a method of social criticism—an activity most other modern philosophies have avoided. All existential thinkers sense the deformity of their age. All feel that with the advent of the modern age something went rotten. I think that from an existential viewpoint no word better describes modern decadence than "seriousness." In the following analysis I mean to use "seriousness" to characterize those things which, according to existentialism, have gone wrong.

"I am the only one in our serious age who is not serious," wrote Kierkegaard. If Kierkegaard's age, over a hundred years ago, was serious, how much more serious is our own? A serious age experiences a radical upheaval of all its values and yet refuses to admit its own tragic condition. It is an age of objective madness where men try to resurrect those traditions and beliefs that are lost forever. In a serious age men, unable to admit the subjectivity of all values, unable to accept responsibility for their lives, retreat into a world where the order of things is absolute. Existentialism describes such retreats as self-deception, bad faith and inauthentic existence.

In a serious age human existence is simplified and objectified. Though there is no one description of man which all can accept, there is the faith that the "true" nature of man will soon be found: statistics, measurement, experimentation—these are the tools which will dig out the necessary truth. If truth is not at hand, it soon will be because progress is inevitable. A serious age believes it can capture human existence with a single metaphysical or methodological stroke when ironically it was just such self-deception that brought the age to its crisis.

A serious age produces two kinds of men: those who worship the time and those who criticize it. The critics are also the innovators who, because they realize that all standards and values have been destroyed, painstakingly work out their own standards. Thus a serious age produces a James Joyce and a D. H. Lawrence, but it also bans their books.

In a serious age normality becomes pathological and the "sick" say truer things than the "healthy." The paradigmatic existential figure is Dostoevsky's underground man—a creature who lives apart from society. In a jeering, venomous monologue the underground man attacks the materialistic and scientific assumptions of his time. He hopes for the destruction of all that western civilization has stood for: progress, reason, logic and order.[2] Is this merely the study of a mad man or is there another intention in this anti-rational assault by Dostoevsky? For the existentialist the "Notes from Underground" are a challenge: to see if we can transcend the sterile limits of deceitful reality, break away from the rigid categories of health and sickness, good and evil, and in that breaking away to see the vast possibilities of existence in others and in ourselves. This is not a plea for either irrationalism or insanity. It is an attempt to see the absurdity of existence and the impossibility of reducing existence to a pure, reasoned description. In the moment of such recognition categories fall away and men are neither healthy nor sick; they are men.

Kierkegaard continually admonishes his readers to remember that they are so intimately involved in the objective world that they cannot be content to regard the truth objectively, disinterestedly. "It is impossible to exist without passion," he says. Pedagogy today lacks passion because it ignores the existence of man, *qua* man. Education, reflecting the age, has become a dispassionate, serious business. It has to be so since the school has serious tasks: producing scientists, making citizens, adjusting individuals to an ever-changing world. The situation is irreversible—seriousness is the inevitable consequence of progress. The real danger is that with enough progress men may come to believe that the only way to live is "seriously." Other-directed personalities, organization men and mass men are creatures who live solely by the standards of their serious world; they work for a large cause without ever coming to know themselves or their freedom. If the education of men becomes dominated by the overriding demands of politics, society, or culture, seriousness will ensue.

We cannot eliminate politics, or society or culture; but we can come to recognize the tragedy that follows. To live in a world with other men means to admit the necessity of forces which will treat men as objects rather than as individuals. The danger is that these necessary evils may be transformed into virtues. This is precisely what threatens education today. Unfortunately we must have larger schools and we must have administrators and they must, for the sake of efficiency, often deal with pupils and teachers as statistical abstractions. Granted that

---

[2] Fyodor Dostoevsky, "Notes from Underground," *The Short Novels of Dostoevsky*, (New York: Dial Press, 1945), pp. 127-222.

such practices are necessary; but how many school officials are sensitive to the tragedy of their own profession? On the contrary the administrator takes pride in the efficiency with which he runs a plant and looks forward to even greater efficiency. New types of tests, the increased sophistication of I.B.M. cards, more accurate devices for predicting the future performance of a student—these are the bright promise of future education.

The administrators of our schools are not the only ones who are culpable. The most esteemed educators are serious. Consider James B. Conant. Here is a reasonable man who writes clearly, precisely, intelligently. Yet what is there about his recent books that disturb the sensitive mind? In *Slums and Suburbs* he says that after visiting city slums he ". . . grows impatient with both critics and defenders of public education who ignore the realities of school situations to engage in fruitless debate about educational philosophy, purposes, and the like."[3] What *are* the realities of the situation? For Mr. Conant they are the evidence found in percentages, surveys, the *status quo*, and general trends. There is no better way to describe him: he is a serious man. However, behind that seriousness is a lack of passion that only an efficiency expert could exhibit. It is not just that there is nothing new in what Mr. Conant says; the greater transgression is that there is nothing courageous about the way he says it.

Consider one instance of Mr. Conant's social engineering that shows why his view is repugnant to an existential view of things: his analysis of the American Negro and American Education. Stated simply it is the popular notion of "uplifting" the Negro, albeit within the framework of Yankee liberalism. Mr. Conant does not discuss the possibility that the liberation of the Negro might depend more on the moral and psychological improvement of the whites than the enlightenment of the blacks. The graver oversight, however, and here Mr. Conant's seriousness is betrayed, is his failure to remind the reader that the anguish of being a Negro in America will not be ameliorated merely by giving Negroes better jobs or equal educational opportunity. Even the "successful" Negro remains an outsider in America. Because Mr. Conant was interested in the Negro as a social force, he forgot the man. Studying the Negro as a "social force" and witnessing the existence of the Negro as a human being is the difference between what Mr. Conant has written in *Slums and Suburbs* and what James Baldwin, an American Negro, wrote in *The New Yorker* on November 17, 1962.[4] It is the difference between the objective report of an inspector-general

[3] James B. Conant, *Slums and Suburbs*, (New York: McGraw-Hill Book Co., 1961), p. 21.

[4] James Baldwin, "Letter From a Region In My Mind," *The New Yorker*, November 17, 1962, pp. 59-144.

and the impassioned confession of an individual. It is the difference between *Dasein* which for Jaspers and Heidegger represents what is commonplace in human existence and *Existenz*, that which is breathtaking.

Kafka wrote in his notebooks that he wanted to exaggerate situations until everything became clear. Admittedly, the attack upon Mr. Conant is exaggerated; yet it remains a valid criticism. And if Mr. Conant, a reasonable man, and for all his seriousness one who has strengthened American public education, is culpable, how much more vulnerable are other educators and educational traditions?

Yet one must admit there is a weakness in such existential criticism. Even this brief attempt at an existential view of matters reveals the over-riding negativism of this attitude. Because existentialism is obsessed with the inwardness of personal existence it has been forced to ask the question, "What does it mean to exist as an individual?" In seeking an answer existentialists have certainly succeeded in showing what it means *not* to exist as an individual. But, as one writer aptly posed the problem, "It is one thing to describe man's anguish and despair, it is quite another to provide philosophical and psychological analysis of those feelings and suggest a solution which does not merely dismiss the protest as adolescent and mistaken."[5] Here we arrive at the crux of existential philosophizing. Does existentialism offer a solution? Or is it a mere negative view of the world that can do little else than protest? I think the question is still open. Croce denounced existentialism as a thing which encumbers the world of the spirit. He described the philosophy as "overstimulated, poisonous, perverse, a kind of swelling of the groin."[6] Critics, agreeing with Croce, argue that existential philosophy inevitably sinks in its own sea of nihilistic despair. On the other hand men have leaped from existentialism into every kind of faith and philosophical system. Some philosophers once skeptical of the movement now see signs of something positive. Marjorie Grene, a penetrating critic of existentialism, called the philosophy at one time a new expression of an old despair; later she called it " a floating philosophy, like autumn leaves unable to take hold again upon the parent branch." More recently, however, she began to see hope in Tillich's existential theology expressed as a "courage to be."[7] I believe

---

[5] Hazel Barnes, *The Literature of Possibility*, (Lincoln, Nebraska: University of Nebraska Press, 1959), p. 4.

[6] Guido DeRuggiero, *Existentialism*, (New York: Social Science Publishers, 1948), p. 28.

[7] Marjorie Grene, *Introduction to Existentialism* (first published as *Dreadful Freedom*), Phoenix Books, University of Chicago Press, 1948; also "The German Existentialists," *Chicago Review*, Summer 1959, Vol. 13, No. 2, pp. 49-58.

that the most promising extension of existential thought points toward a humanistic ethic in which self-realization is linked with some kind of social commitment. Hazel Barnes in her splendid book, *The Literature of Possibility*,[8] sees just such a humanistic existentialism in three French writers: Jean Paul Sartre, Simon de Beauvoir and Albert Camus.

Lionel Trilling has observed that the function of literature, through all its mutations, has been to make us aware of the particularity of selves and the high authority of the self in its quarrel with its society and its culture. Perhaps existentialism is nothing more than the instinct of humanistic literature made explicit.[9] Everett Knight speaks of existentialism as literature considered as philosophy,[10] Thomas Hanna writes of the lyrical existentialists[11] and Hans Meyerhoff asserts that all varieties of existentialism are literary types of philosophy.[12] But whatever existentialism is and whatever direction it may finally take it has already proved its service to humanity. To have disturbed a serious world—that is enough of a contribution.

[8] Hazel Barnes, *op. cit.*

[9] Lionel Trilling, *Freud and the Crisis of Our Culture*, (Boston: The Beacon Press, 1955), p. 33.

[10] Everett W. Knight, *Literature Considered as Philosophy*, (New York: The Macmillan Co., 1958); also "Literature and the Objective Society," *Chicago Review*, Summer 1959, Vol. 13, No. 2, pp. 19-26.

[11] Thomas Hanna, *The Lyrical Existentialists*, (New York: Atheneum, 1962).

[12] Hans Meyerhoff, *Time in Literature*, (Berkeley, California: The University of California Press, 1960); also "The Return to the Concrete," *Chicago Review*, Summer 1959, Vol. 13, No. 2, pp. 27-38.

57

The Problem of Recovering an Inclusive View of Life and the Universe

Edwin A. Burtt

The Philosophy of Man as an All-Embracing Philosophy

Edwin A. Burtt, "The Philosophy of Man as All-Embracing Philosophy," *The Philosophical Forum*, II (No. 2 New Series, Winter 1970-1971): 159-171.

The greatest challenge to philosophers today in our part of the world is the challenge to recover an inclusive view of life and the universe—an all-embracing orientation. But it must be so envisioned as to avoid the errors that thinkers in the past who sought such a view have fallen into.

Their fundamental error, as modern philosophers more and more realize, arose from a basic presupposition characteristic of ancient and mediaeval metaphysics—that a final explanation of reality can be achieved. During that long period the almost universal belief was that science and philosophy form an organic whole, science consisting of the detailed truths that can be established in any area of nature's doings while philosophy establishes the unifying principles that provide the foundation and capstone for the structure. This belief reigned without serious challenge for many centuries, and only gradually has it weakened during the modern period. But it has weakened, and now hardly any influential thinker regards it as possible to realize a sound philosophy of wholeness in that form.

How can it most plausibly be realized?

I

I propose the hypothesis that the most promising way to seek an inclusive orientation is in the form of a philosophy of man, however implausible that hypothesis may sound at first. It can be argued for by several lines of thought, each of which would have to be followed in considerable detail if it is to be clarified and rendered persuasive. In a discussion paper there is room to develop only a single approach. I am restricting myself therefore to a historical approach—more precisely, an approach by way of examining some revealing features in the evolution of Western philosophy. Elsewhere I hope to follow other lines of thought that can be equally illuminating.

Let us begin by considering the broad nature of the transition from mediaeval to modern conceptions of the task of philosophy. The change that stands out most provocatively is the change to concentration on the problems of "method" as contrasted with concentration on the forms of "being" or—as we would now be likely to say—on the structure of reality. This change implicitly involves a reference to the thinker who is exemplifying this or that method. Instead of assuming that the forms of being will be unambiguously revealed to any mind seeking to grasp them, the assumption now is that the right method—that is, the proper way to approach those forms if they are to be grasped aright—must first be securely established.

But in the early period of modern philosophy this shift to an emphasis on method was not very radical; the vital role of the thinker did not stand out clearly. Descartes and Spinoza were convinced that the essential change needed was simply to realize that the proper method is that of the mathematicians. Once it is seen that the structure of being is not teleological (as Platonic and Aristotelian thought had believed) but mathematical, the truth about the universe will be discovered and given systematic articulation. In other respects the ancient and mediaeval orientation underwent no revolutionary change. And for a time this compromise appeared satisfactory. When, however, we pass from the rationalists to the empiricists the radical implication of insisting that a methodological must precede an ontological approach is sharply revealed.

The empiricists realize clearly that their concern is not directly with being but with "experience" of being. And experience of being is man's experience; to understand it requires that one recognize all the conditions which make it what it is, including the conditions that have to be located in man's way of perceiving the world and of interpreting what he perceives. Again, however, this empirical conception of method did not at once reveal the drastic consequences that were involved. Locke and Berkeley retained many of the presuppositions of preceding thinkers, especially the presupposition that since the universe is the creation of God we can be sure that it has the structure which expresses His purpose in creating it.

With Hume the revolutionary implications of this methodological approach come out fully; and it is rather astonishing that few volumes on the history of philosophy seem to realize their radical force. A comprehensive treatment of philosophical problems takes with him the form of a *Treatise of Human Nature*. And it is important to see how this conception is worked out in detail. For Hume the problems involved in a study of method become problems as to how man's understanding operates when it deals with such basic categories as space, time, causality, existence, and self; the problems involved in a study of the "passions" become problems concerning man's emotional nature; and the problems of moral philosophy become problems about the factors revealed in man's judgment of virtue and vice. Hume's basic presupposition is that what the philosopher needs to understand, in the last analysis, is why people think the way they do in the areas of metaphysics, religion, moral experience, science, and everywhere else. The drastic challenge that he posed to his contemporaries and successors lies in this idea.

It is true that when Hume wrote his *Enquiries* a decade or more later, this orientation underwent a superficial change, which is reflected in the titles of those books. But I see no evidence of any change in his fundamental conception of philosophy. The interesting differences that appear when one compares the *Enquiries* with the *Treatise* are due in part to an altered conviction on specific problems and in part, as he himself frankly said in his autobiography, to his disappointment at the literary failure of the *Treatise* and his wish to rewrite its themes in such a way that wider attention to them would be won.

Kant's "critical philosophy" is especially instructive in our present setting. When a student of Kant becomes absorbed in the complex and difficult system that he develops it is easy to lose sight of his over-all approach and the conception of the philosopher's task it expresses. The three great questions of philosophy according to him are these: What can I know? What ought I to do? and, For what may I hope? Now the "I" in these questions is of course not Immanuel Kant, but man—all men, man in general. The change from traditional metaphysics thus reflected is vividly shown in Kant's conviction that his epistemology is a "Copernican revolution"; instead of assuming that in knowledge the human mind conforms to objects as given, a thinker should assume that in their knowable structure objects conform to the human mind. The bearing of this revolution on a philosophy of man is somewhat obscured by his confident belief that the objectivity of knowledge requires the assumption of a universal mind or transcendental consciousness, whose forms and categories can be grasped in their absolute nature and thus provide a final solution of the perennial problems about knowledge. It is intriguing to speculate on what this Copernican revolution would have become had Kant recognized the variations from individual to individual, from culture to culture, and from age to age in the way a truth-seeking mind works.

Hegel's main significance, I would suggest, consists in his desperate and skillful attempt to turn a philosophy of man into a philosophy of the universe as the latter had been traditionally envisioned. He sought, in effect, to sketch the cosmic picture that results when the historical development of the human mind is taken as a valid clue to the evolution of reality. The basic weakness in his system is that, like Kant, he assumes to be absolute and final a description of the structure of mind that is actually relative and transitory.

II

When one surveys the history of Western philosophy during the century and a half since Hegel, in the perspective now guiding us, two influential and persistent trends appear. One is the trend that culminates in the analytic philosophy so prominent today in England and America. To it we shall soon return. The other is the trend exemplified in several philosophies which superficially look quite different, namely existentialism, Marxism, and pragmatism. But they are not as different as they look, because each of them concentrates on man's quest to find and fulfill himself—each in its own way proposes to make a philosophy of man into an all-embracing philosophy. We shall glance at them from this angle.

The existential philosopher is concerned with this quest when man is taken as an individual. It is his struggle to realize himself under the impact of surrounding forces that the philosopher needs primarily to understand. That struggle, with its emotional involvements as well as its intellectual perplexities, provides the setting in which from an existentialist standpoint all philosophical problems can be best considered.

Marxism is the widely appealing philosophy which is concerned with this quest of man when taken as a social being. For it, all problems are dealt with wisely only when they are seen in the perspective of social history. In our day this means a perspective emphasizing the struggle to end the exploitation of man by man and to realize the classless society of the future. Philosophical ideas willy nilly reflect the place of the one who holds them in this evolving process. Students of Jean-Paul Sartre's philosophy must have found his recent writings—especially the *Critique of Dialectical Reason*—most instructive. From a position in which his social philosophy was subordinate to his existentialism, he has now passed to a position in which Marxism is fundamental and existentialism fills a subordinate role in it.

As for pragmatism, it is a fascinating philosophy when approached in this setting. It clearly represents a systematic attempt to develop a comprehensive orientation in the form of a philosophy of man. The experience which constitutes inclusive reality for the pragmatists is the dynamic experience of man. What then is the major difference between the form this orientation took in James and the form it took in Dewey? That difference might be described by saying that in James the experience of man as an individual is dominant, while in Dewey it is the experience of man in society, confronting inescapable social problems that have not yet been satisfactorily solved.

When the history of philosophy is surveyed in this fashion, I submit that what stands out vividly is a gradual trend from the assumption that the philosopher can grasp the structure of reality as it is apart from man toward the realization that what he is building is always a philosophy of man—man interacting with other realities, of course, but with the ultimate questions about that process leading for their answer to characteristics in man. The natural assumption encouraged by such a survey is that this trend will continue—that significant progress in the future will consist in its further development, freeing our present understanding of man from whatever weaknesses haunt it and realizing more and more fully a wiser understanding.

III

And now the time has come to fill the yawning gap that you must have been feeling. How about analytic philosophy? It is one of the major philosophical trends of the last hundred years, and through earlier history its basic presuppositions have been influential at various times and with important thinkers.

I admit at once that the conception of philosophy consciously held by analytic thinkers is very different from the conception implied by the phrase "philosophy of man". In fact, the latter is vehemently rejected as a sad perversion of philosophy by all analysts with whom I am acquainted. They insist that every taint of what they would call "subjectivity" should be left behind, not explicitly accepted. But it may be that this rejection is plausible only as long as certain fundamental questions are not raised—questions that a philosopher eager to understand cannot help sooner or later raising. It could even be that when those questions are faced, in an unflinching concern for truth, analytic philosophy itself becomes an obvious and instructive example of the philosophy of man. How so?

Let us reflect on three facts revealed by the evolution of analytic philosophy since the turn of the century, and the questions they naturally suggest.

Consider first the fact that the method of analysis, as it has been employed by its champions, is an approach to philosophy which is not universally persuasive and shows no sign of becoming so. Hence we need to ask: Why should one adopt that way of philosophizing instead of any of the alternative ways championed by other philosophical movements? When I have asked this question of an analytic philosopher, the only answer offered me is that he is unable to see how alternative ways accomplish anything, while the analytic method does solve the problems he wants to see solved. But such an answer may reveal limitations in him, which, in the interest of fruitful discussion with his philosophical colleagues, he needs to recognize. When they are recognized he will probably continue to be absorbed in the same kind of problem but he will realize that the appeal of his method, and the philosophy thus developed, reflect particular values that he has chosen but which other philosophers will not necessarily choose. What his philosophy primarily brings to light is then something in him rather than something in the subject matter he is analyzing. That subject matter is there of course, and he is interacting with it. But when we seek to understand his way of interacting with it, can we escape from the necessity to answer in terms of factors at work in him?

Consider, second, a trend now clearly shown in the progress of analytic philosophy over several decades. At first, formal logic provided the basic instrument of analysis for its champions. At present, however, the basic instrument of analysis is the structure of language rather than logic as the latter has been conceived in the past. This is an instructive change. In fact, some analytic philosophers are worried about it, and their worry has been shown in an interesting reinterpretation of the word "logic." The concept of "logical analysis" has been broadened at their hands, so that they construe it as essentially identical with "linguistic analysis." This means that they now describe as "logical" certain factors which, in terms of traditional notions of formal necessity, would be regarded as conventional rather than logical. The change is quite obvious in the conception of logic developed by the "ordinary language" philosophers; it includes what they have called "rules of the correct use" of this or that expression.

What does this significant reinterpretation reveal? Surely, among other things, it reveals a recognition of the fact that language is intrinsically a medium of communication between men while logical form can be plausibly regarded, and has often been regarded, as the structure of reality apart from man. For this reason an adequate linguistic analysis finds that it must take account of all the conditioning factors in men that are at work whenever they communicate successfully, whereas logic can ignore those factors.

Consider, third, the impressive and startling succession of schools that have appeared in the evolution of analytic philosophy during the last two-thirds of a century. The schools that especially stand out are the analytic realism of Russell and his contemporaries fifty years or more ago, the logical positivism prominent in the 1920's and 1930's, and the analysis of ordinary language that has captivated most analytic philosophers since 1940. Each of these schools has been confident that it authentically exemplifies the method that analytic philosophy ought to follow. But there are major differences between them. What explains those interesting differences? So far as I am aware, during the course of this evolution no new empirical facts have been discovered which the later schools take into account but not the earlier ones, and there has been no new insight into logical form requiring the later schools to diverge from their predecessors.* Their differences then must be due to something else. What is it?

I submit that when these differences are examined they turn out to rest on the criteria by which the analytic philosopher decides what is essential to an acceptable analysis. He is usually unconscious of those criteria, but they fill this crucial role nonetheless. Certain criteria, we find, are common to all three of the analytic schools, e.g., the assumption of an ultimate difference between fact and form and the assumption of a pluralistic atomism, both in the empirical world and in the language by which it is properly described. But certain criteria vary from one analytic school to another, and these variations are especially instructive. For the positivists an acceptable analysis must presuppose the "verifiability" theory of meaning, and hence requires metaphysical statements to be meaningless; it also presupposes that an ideal scientific language can be set up in which any meaningful assertion may be expressed. For the ordinary language philosophers an acceptable analysis must reject both of these presuppositions, assuming instead that the already established uses of language in any area of experience are philosophically justified as they stand; those uses need only to be clearly exhibited in their contrast with misleading uses into which philosophers have been tempted.

How are we to understand these partly parallel, partly divergent conceptions of what constitutes an acceptable analysis? What do they reflect? These questions call insistently for an answer.

I see no plausible answer other than this: They reflect partly identical and partly different valuations—that is, underlying convictions as to what is philosophically important. The criteria shared in common reflect

---

* Each later school has had its own *theory* of logic, e.g., the theory of many positivists that logical form is essentially tautologous. But these theories have so far as I know brought no reconstruction of formal systems.

a common commitment to the values achieved by the method of analysis; the divergent criteria reflect values on which these analytic schools disagree. Think for example of the radical difference between positivism and the ordinary language philosophy. The former prizes the value of scientific exactitude so highly that it wants to see what it calls the "language of science" employed in every statement purporting to be true. The positivist therefore selects the facts about language and the theory of logic which support this valuation, passing blithely over the facts and theories which fail to support it. The ordinary language philosopher prizes the rich variety of linguistic uses that crop up, when one is open to see them in the endless nuances of human speech as it is employed in this or that set of circumstances. He is sure that philosophy can profit by all these varied uses in their bearing on its perennial problems. He therefore selects the facts about language and defends the theory of logic which support this dominant valuation, likewise passing over the historical and linguistic considerations which fail to harmonize with his controlling aim.

So obvious does this explanation seem to me that I venture to predict that when the next analytic school emerges and becomes widely influential, it too will illustrate this explanation. It will replace the values dominating the ordinary language orientation by some newly appealing value which has its own implications as to the features essential in an acceptable analysis. That is, I predict that this will happen unless, by that time, there is a widespread realization of the limitations of this whole way of philosophizing. In that case we would expect the succession of analytic fads to come to an end and that the new linguistic techniques will play a subordinate role in whatever philosophical movements arise.

IV

The conclusion toward which all these considerations point is, is it not, that every philosophy turns out inevitably to be a philosophy of man when its basic presuppositions are brought to light and compared with the presuppositions of other ways of thinking? If we persist in raising Hume's and Kant's questions, we find that any philosophical orientation tells us more about the thinker who champions it than it does about anything outside him. Of course he is in an environing universe, hence such an orientation always offers itself as an interpretation of that universe. But the universe thus interpreted is not the same thing as "external reality." What do philosophical systems reveal about external reality other than that it tolerates them more or less cheerfully? It tolerates more cheerfully the systems that are meticulously honest and responsible than it does those that are not so honest and responsible. In every case, however, a philosophical orientation reveals a great deal about the men who hold it, especially the framework of thought they take for granted and the dominant valuation that framework reflects.

To put my hypothesis in provocative psychological terms, every philosophy arises by projecting some emotionally potent valuation on the subject matter with which the philosopher is concerned. Without such a projection philosophizing would never take place. And the tremendous importance of recognizing this truth is that when it is recognized philosophers can begin to understand the process and to guide it constructively. When it is not recognized, their controlling valuation and basic presuppositions change from time to time, but they do so accidentally and fitfully—that is, under the impact of forces within and without that are not understood and therefore cannot be guided intelligently.

V

But if one accepts this conclusion does he thereby accept the distressing idea that philosophy must be unscientific? That further conclusion might easily seem to follow. So I must meet as best I can this serious objection, and I believe that it can be met completely. Science itself is an excellent example of the principles above described rather than an exception to them. When the same fundamental questions are raised about it that have just been raised about philosophical schools and movements, I am confident that this reassuring truth becomes apparent.

Look carefully at the crucial fact that science has a history—not merely in the trivial sense that it reveals a succession of discoveries which add to our knowledge, but in the very important sense that it reveals a succession of theories about what science essentially is and about the form its observations and explanations should take. These theories vary from culture to culture and (though slowly) from age to age in the same culture. Is there not every reason to expect that such variations will continue in the future as they have continued in the past? Always, of course, the scientist seeks some regular order in the objects and events that make up the world investigated; were this not the case we would not use the word "science" to refer to his product. But also it is always an order that man with his perceptive organs is able to notice and with his mental faculties to delineate. It cannot help being a human order in this vital sense. What a natural order would be like apart from or independent of our ways of observing and explaining it, we have no means of guessing.

The most instructive lesson that emerges as in this setting one surveys the history of Western thought is that at any given time science presupposed the special kind of order that needs to be emphasized if it is to realize the values dominant among thinkers at that time. Ponder the broad difference that stands out when the conception of science generally taken for granted in ancient and mediaeval times is compared with the modern conception. Ancient and mediaeval thinkers, almost without exception so far as I know, took it for granted that science and metaphysics form a single body of knowledge whose structure was indicated in my introduction. It was believed that through the unifying metaphysical principles that body of knowledge can become a final explanation of the universe and all that it contains.

If we ask what dominant valuation was reflected in these presuppositions, a very plausible answer is that it was man's longing for security in a very insecure universe. When everything that happens is explained by a cognitive system thus constructed, thinkers feel that they are achieving intellectual security through the demonstrated and potentially complete knowledge which is established, and that achievement is the intellectual aspect of the urgent emotional security they seek.

Modern thinkers have become more ambitious and self-confident. In contrast with the ancient and mediaeval orientation they have gained the conviction that by verified knowledge, organized in a different pattern, men can increasingly control toward their chosen ends the processes going on in the world. Instead of security, ever-growing mastery is the dominant value of modern science, and its representatives presuppose the kind of order in nature that makes possible the fullest realization of this value.

What kind of order is thus presupposed? The answer I am sure is simple and obvious. It may not seem so at first sight, because almost everyone takes it unqualifiedly for granted. Instead of an order grounded in metaphysical principles that are supposedly eternal, it is a network of causal relations so conceived that thinkers can predict the future effects of causes now at work and can make them serve desirable ends wherever the conditions necessary to those ends are within their power. The basic presupposition of modern science is, in short, that the pervasive order that needs to be uncovered is an order permitting accurate prediction and increasing control on the part of man as he interacts with the environing world.

If this answer is sound, our expectation would be that when man has realized as much of these values as he feels to be needed, another transformation will take place comparable to the historical transformation from ancient to modern science, as a result of which thinkers will presuppose a new kind of orderly structure in nature. It will be so conceived that knowledge of it can serve whatever human value becomes dominant in that epoch which has not yet dawned. It may be that thus far only a small fraction of the patterns of order that might provide a model for scientific knowledge have been taken as a basis for man's quest to understand his world. Perhaps some of the possible models will take seriously conceptions of order that have appeared in other cultures than those sharing the heritage of Western civilization. At any rate, I see no justification in the history of science for expecting that the currently dominant values with their distinctive presuppositions will remain dominant forever.

The objection might be raised that this interpretation does not square with the objectivity of scientific knowledge. I have answered that objection implicitly, but an explicit comment is needed. The crucial point is that objectivity does not imply externality. To elucidate this point, for truth to be objective requires that it be external to the individual mind, but not to the total quest of man for reliable and shared understanding. When thinkers transcend subjectivity—which in the pursuit of truth is surely necessary—they do not leave human ways of perceiving and explaining behind. They leave behind ways that vary from person to person and group to group in favor of ways leading to results that can be dependably verified by anyone who understands the question to which they are the solution. The scientist knows that his conclusions are sound, not when he has jumped out of human experience into something else but when he has reached a result that is agreed upon by his scientific colleagues who also seek a dependable solution.

If I have fallen into no drastic mistake, science then is itself an enlightening example of the principles central to a philosophy of man. The sciences do not tell us what the world apart from man is like. They guide us in discovering what the world is like when it is approached in terms of presuppositions reflecting some human value that has come to exercise pervasive influence in this or that epoch of history. The path to understanding, here as elsewhere in the presence of important ways of observing and thinking, is not the futile attempt to look at external reality but to look at man as he interacts with other realities. The fundamental questions that call for an answer in this search for understanding lead inescapably to factors in man—factors especially revealed when he adopts a set of basic presuppositions and when he later revises them. The decisive reason for any such revision is always that his previously ruling value has lost its force and is being replaced by a new value. Of course the scientist, in his quest as scientist, does not ask these questions. But my contention is that the philosopher, in his quest as philosopher, cannot avoid asking them.

VI

One more query should be raised. Would anything important be left out when we try to make a philosophy of man coextensive with philosophy at large? If it would, the enterprise has failed and the resulting orientation is inadequate.

I do not see that anything is left out when a philosophy of man is given the comprehensive form that it can be given and naturally would be given. There would obviously be a place for metaphysics, for moral and social philosophy, for logic, for philosophy of science; by the same token there would be a place for esthetics, for metatheology, and for every other branch of philosophy. All these words or phrases refer to human ways of thinking about some area of human experience. To make continued progress in each of them philosophers have to concentrate their attention on the appropriate subject matter, as at any given time it takes form. But what that progress always reveals, when it is critically scrutinized in the search for ultimate understanding, is some further illumination about man, in dynamic interaction with his fellows and with the rest of the universe.

58
The Problem of Violence

Arthur Schlesinger, Jr.

Existential Politics
and the Cult of Violence

Arthur Schlesinger, Jr., "Existential Politics and the Cult of Violence," a slightly shortened version of the address delivered by the holder of the Albert Schweitzer Chair in the Humanities at the City University of New York at the CUNY commencement on June 5, 1968 (the day Senator Robert Kennedy died) as it appeared (with the author's permission; copyright 1968 by Harper's Magazine Inc.) in *Phi Delta Kappan*, XL (No. 1, September 1968): 9-15. A longer version of the argument is to be found in Ch. 1, *The Crisis of Confidence* (Boston: Houghton, Mifflin, 1969).

The world today is asking a terrible question—a question which every citizen of this republic should be putting to himself: What sort of people are we, we Americans?

And the answer which much of the world is bound to return is that we are today the most frightening people on this planet.

We are a frightening people because for three years we have been devastating a small country on the other side of the world in a war which bears no rational relationship to our national security or our national interest.

We are a frightening people because we have already in this decade murdered the two of our citizens who stood preeminently before the world as the embodiments of American idealism—and because last night we tried to murder a third.

We are a frightening people because the atrocities we commit trouble so little our official self-righteousness, our invincible conviction of our moral infallibility.

The ghastly things we do to our own people, the ghastly things we do to other people—these must at last compel us to look searchingly at ourselves and our society before hatred and violence rush us on to more evil and finally tear our nation apart.

We can not take the easy course and blame everyone but ourselves for the things we do.

We can not blame the epidemic of murder at home on deranged and solitary individuals separate from the rest of us. For these individuals are plainly weak and suggestible men, stamped by our society with a birthright of hatred and a compulsion toward violence.

We can not blame our epidemic of murder abroad on the wickedness of those who will not conform to our views of how they should behave and how they should live. For the zeal with which we have pursued an irrational war—a war which makes no sense in the traditional terms of foreign policy—suggests the internal impulses of hatred and violence demanding outlet and shaping our foreign policy to their ends.

We must recognize that the evil is in us, that it springs from some dark, intolerable tension in our history and our institutions. It is almost as if a primal curse had been fixed on our nation, perhaps when we first began the practice of killing and enslaving those whom we deemed our inferiors because their skin was another color. We are a violent people with a violent history, and the instinct for violence has seeped into the bloodstream of our national life.

We are also, at our best, a generous and idealistic people. Our great leaders—Lincoln most of all—have perceived both the instinct for hatred and violence and the moral necessity of transcending hatred and violence if we are going to have any sort of rational and decent society. They have realized how fragile the membranes of civilization are, stretched so thin over a nation so disparate in its composition, so tense in its interior relationships, so cunningly enmeshed in underground fears and antagonisms, so entrapped by history in the ethos of violence.

Now, as our nation grows more centralized, our energy more concentrated, our inner tensions more desperate, our frustrations in our own land and in the world more embittered, we can no longer regard hatred and violence as accidents and aberrations, as nightmares which will pass away when we awake. We must see them as organic in our national past; we must confront them; we must uncover the roots of hatred and violence and, through self-knowledge, move toward self-control. And we must exert every effort in the meantime to protect and strengthen the membranes of civility against the impulses of destruction.

In this effort, I would suggest, a special responsibility lies on our intellectual community. For one can expect primitive emotions on the part of those who roughly occupy the right wing of our national politics. But the intellectual community should be the particular custodian of the life of reason. It should be the particular champion of discipline and restraint. It should be the particular enemy of hatred and violence.

Little is more dismaying than the way in which some, a few, in the intellectual community have rejected the life of reason, have succumbed to the national susceptibility for hatred and violence, have, indeed, begun themselves to exalt hatred and violence as if primitivism in emotion constituted a higher morality.

I do not suggest that such intellectuals are responsible for the atrocities committed at home and abroad. I do suggest that they have contributed to the atmosphere in which hatred and violence are not only tolerated but prized. I do suggest that they are reinforcing the assault on civility and hastening the decomposition of the American social process.

Some wonder, no doubt, whether that social process is worth saving. But the alternative to process is anarchy, where those who dispose of the means of violence win out; and the intellectual community has never disposed of the means of violence. Our process, with all its defects, is a process of change—a process of peaceful change—on which all decency and rationality depend.

Let me make it clear that I am not talking about the student uprisings of recent weeks. I have no question that on balance the world stands to gain from student protest. No doubt such protest has on occasion led to excess. But it is already a shameful state of affairs when excess proves the only way of attracting the attention of complacent administrations and indifferent faculties to the problems and perplexities of the coming generation.

The cause of student insurgency vary from college to college, and from country to country. It would seem likely that the primary incitement in our own nation has been the war in Vietnam—a war which has tempted our government into its course of appalling and insensate destruction, a war which, through the draft, has demanded that young Americans kill and die where they can see no rational relationship between personal sacrifice and national interest. But the cause is also more than the Vietnam war. For that war has come for many to prefigure a larger incomprehensibility, a larger absurdity, even a larger wickedness, in our official society. For some it has come to seem, not an aberration, but the inevitable result of the irremediable corruption of the American system.

I cannot share the belief that there was something foreordained and ineluctable about the war in Vietnam—that the nature of American society would have compelled any set of men in Washington to pursue the same course of folly. This really seems determinist nonsense. One can still understand, though, why the contradictions of our society weigh so heavily on the young—the contradictions between the righteousness of a Secretary of State and the ruthlessness of a B-52; between the notion that violence is fine against simple folk ten thousand miles away and shocking against injustice in our own land; between the equality demanded by our constitutional structure and the equality denied by our social structure; even between the accepted habits of one generation and the emerging habits of the next, as when a parent tipsy on his fourth martini begins a tirade against marijuana.

The very weight of these contradictions produced a rush of despair about libertarian democracy itself. By libertarian democracy I mean simply the system in which the rule of the majority at any given time rests on the guarantee of the right of minorities to convert themselves into new majorities. Such a system assumes political action to be in its essence a rational process—that is, a deliberate choice of means to achieve desired ends. As a rational process, libertarian democracy requires the widest possible freedom of discussion and debate; and this implies, of course, a considerable indulgence of wrongheadedness and imbecility along the way.

This has been the American theory, as laid down, for example, in the Constitution and the Bill of Rights. And, in the course of our national history, libertarian democracy has led to many useful results. It has also led to many frustrations. It has left problems unsolved, wrongs unredressed, and sinners unpunished. It cannot be relied upon to produce rapid and conclusive change. The very insistence on reasonableness and due process has seemed at times a pretext for inaction and therefore a mask for injustice. This has been particularly the case in recent years. From the moment we started bombing North Vietnam in February, 1965, our government appeared rigidly and sanctimoniously unresponsive to reasoned criticism of its course. Increasingly persuaded that change was impossible within the constitutional order, people started to turn to civil disobedience, emotional agitation, and even violent protest. A sense began to arise that libertarian democracy itself was impotent in the new world of economic, military, and intellectual corporatism. One saw a growing conviction, especially among the young, that party politics were a facade and a fake. One saw a growing cynicism about democratic institutions, a growing defection from the democratic process. In due course, the spreading sense of the impotence of libertarian democracy generated a creed systematically and candidly opposed to libertarian democracy.

The new creed has two parts. The first part is an attempt to clear away what its theorists regard as the noxious rubbish of the Bill of Rights. The new creed thus perceives the First Amendment as the keystone, not of liberty, but of a wicked apparatus of tolerance employed by an oppressive social order to resist basic change. I do not wish to do this new doctrine an injustice, so I will state in the words of its leading advocate—that is, Herbert Marcuse—the belief that it is *necessary* and *right*, as a matter of principle, to suppress views with which one disagrees and to howl down those who utter such views.

Marcuse begins with the proposition that contemporary society, in his idiom, is defined by "the passing of the historical forces which, at the preceding stage of society, seemed to represent the possibility of new forms of existence." In other words, contemporary society has absorbed and abolished the historic means of social revolution. It has learned the secret of "containing social change—qualitative change which would establish essentially different institutions, a new direction of the productive process, new modes of human existence."

The strategy by which contemporary society achieves these results, Marcuse argues, is through a system of indoctrination and manipulation made possible by an ingenious and despicable combination of welfarism and tolerance. Capitalism, in short, buys off potential opponents by offering a measure of apparent economic security and personal freedom. Marcuse regards this as a terrible state of affairs. As he sees it, any improvement in the condition of the powerless and the oppressed only plays into the hands of the rulers—and is therefore to be regretted. And the evil device of tolerance renders "the traditional ways and means of protest ineffective—perhaps even dangerous because they preserve the illusion of popular sovereignty."

Tolerance is evil because it dissipates the force of protest. It is also evil because it permits the promulgation of evil ideas. Therefore, Marcuse suggests, the way to revive the possibilities of social change is to strike at the root of the evil. He is candid about his repudiation of the Bill of Rights.

> The traditional criterion of clear and present danger seems no longer adequate to a stage where the whole society is in the situation of the theater audience when somebody cries: 'fire.' . . . The whole post-fascist period is one of clear and present danger. Consequently, true pacification requires the withdrawal of tolerance before the deed, at the stage of communication in word, print, and picture. . . . Certain things cannot be said, certain ideas cannot be expressed, certain policies cannot be proposed, certain behavior cannot be permitted without making tolerance an instrument for the continuation of servitude."

And he is specific about what he would forbid. His program, as he states it,

> would include the withdrawal of toleration of speech and assembly from groups and movements which promote aggressive policies, armament, chauvinism, discrimination on the grounds of race and religion, or which oppose the extension of public services, medical care, etc. Moreover, the restoration of freedom of thought may necessitate new and rigid restrictions on teachings and practices in the educational institutions.

Marcuse's call for the forcible suppression of false ideas is, I have suggested, only the first part of the new creed. Nor is such an assault on the Bill of Rights new, even for radicals. The Stalinists of the Thirties, for example, had no compunction in arguing in much the same way that civil freedom should be denied those who resist the Stalinist truth. What particularly distinguishes the New Left of the Sixties from previous American radicalisms is the second part of its creed—and here not the summons to revolution, which again is familiar, but the refusal to state revolutionary goals except in the most abstract and empty language. To put it more precisely, what distinguishes the New Left is not only its unwillingness to define what it aims for after the revolution but its belief that such reticence is a virtue.

In its positive side, the new creed becomes, so to speak, a kind of existentialism in politics—a primitive kind, no doubt, but still rooted in some manner in the existential perception that man dwells in an absurd universe and defines himself through his choices. In extreme cases, this perception may lead to *voyages au bout de la nuit*: As Nietzsche said, "Nihilism represents the ultimate logical conclusion of our great values and ideals—because we must experience nihilism before we can find out what value these 'values' really had." In its serious form, existentialism can lead to an immense and intense sense of individual responsibility as every man realizes that only he can provide his own escape from the enveloping nothingness around him. In its vulgar form, however, with which we are dealing here, existential politics becomes the notion that we must feel and act before we think; it is the illusion that the experience of feeling and action will produce the insight and the policy.

Existential politics in this form springs much more from Sorel than from Kierkegaard. Sorel, you will recall, drew a distinction between myths, which, he said, were "not descriptions of things, but expressions of a determination to act," and utopias, which were intellectual products, the work of theorists who "seek to establish a model to which they can compare existing society." Sorel regarded utopias—that is, rational programs—as contemptible. The myth must be the basis of action; the myth would produce the revolution, which would then produce its own program; and "the myth," Sorel emphasized, "must be judged as a means of acting on the present; any attempt to discuss how far it can be taken literally as future history is devoid of sense." So, in the footsteps of Sorel, the New Leftists believe in the omnipotence of the deed and the irrelevance of the goal. The political process is no longer seen as the deliberate choice of means to move toward a desired end. Where libertarian democracy had ideally demanded means consistent with the end, and where the Stalinist left of the Thirties contended that the end justified the means, the New Left propounds a different doctrine: that the means create the end.

Let us not ignore the attractions of the existential approach. After all, there are many absurdities in our world. Our country has never undertaken any thing more absurd in its history than the Vietnam war. After all, a man does make himself by his decisions. After all, our conventional liberalism is to a discouraging degree a liberalism of promises and excuses. After all, social renewal can only come from personal commitment.

All these things help explain, I think, the appeal of the new creed. Yet this creed contains so much in the way of fakery and fallacy—to put it bluntly, it is so preposterous and so depraved—that I do not see how it can be long entertained by any serious democrat.

Let us look first at the negative part: the demand for the forcible suppression of false ideas. This immediately raises a self-evident question: How is one to tell which ideas are amissible and which are to be suppressed? "In the interplay of theory and practice," Marcuse replies, "true and false solutions become distinguishable. . . . Freedom is liberation, a specific historical process in theory and practice, and as such it has its right and wrong, its truth and falsehood." But who is to make this determination? What agency is the repository of final judgment on truth and falsehood? Here, alas, Marcuse lets us down, except to introduce hopelessly vague standards, as, for example, that "what is *not* conducive to a free and rational society, what impedes and distorts the possibilities of its creation" should be forbidden; in the end, he places his confidence in what he mystically calls "the democratic educational dictatorship of free men."

This is not very satisfactory; so let us pursue the question a step further. I suppose that the new creed does not expect to make such judgments through a man. But, if not through a man, these judgments must be made through a mechanism, which means through men. Such a mechanism would plainly have to have an extraordinary degree of power. What assurance can there ever be that this power would be used disinterestedly—that is, for the good and the true, should there ever be a means of defining the good and the true—rather than in the interests of the men operating the mechanism? What will this mechanism become—what have such mechanisms ever become—but a means for the suppression of all criticism of the manipulators of the mechanism? So the mechanism, in the end, rests on an assumption of human infallibility.

But the assumption of human infallibility has never been justified in the long and varied history of mankind. It implies the rule of those whom Mr. Dooley long ago defined as men who do what they think "th' Lord wud do if He only knew the facts in th' case"—and Mr. Dooley was defining a fanatic. Jefferson in his First Inaugural made a relevant comment:

> Sometimes it is said that man cannot be trusted with the government of himself. Can he, then, be trusted with the government of others? Or have we found angels in the form of kings to govern him? Let history answer this question.

History has answered the question: Man has never found angels in the form of kings, or even of philosopher-kings, to govern him. And, if he should, "the unfortunate thing," Pascal said, "is that he who would act the angel acts the brute."

Not only do men who claim infallibility in politics do far more evil than good, but the systematic suppression of supposedly false ideas would deeply constrict and impoverish human knowledge and understanding. "There is no error so crooked," Tupper said, "but it hath in it some lines of truth." Or, as Norman Mailer recently put it, "Sometimes a profound idea is buried in a particularly ugly notion." Human creativity takes a marvelous and sinister diversity of forms. How dare anyone assume the right to censor and deny the unlimited freedom of human expression? "I tolerate with the utmost latitude the right of others to differ from me in opinion without imputing to them criminality," wrote Jefferson. "I know too well the weakness and uncertainty of human reason to wonder at its different result."

The demand for the forcible suppression of "false" ideas would be an enormously effective way of calling a halt to human progress. Nor does the other half of the new creed make any more sense: that is, the conviction that one should feel and act first and think later, that the means create the end. The kind of action supremely required to strike through the mask of official society, we are told, is violence. Without violence, official society, in its present sophisticated condition, will calmly co-opt and emasculate the opposition. Only violence will force official society to drop the amiable mask of tolerance and reveal its inner viciousness. More than this, violence becomes a means of social and individual redemption. As Franz Fanon has written, "Violence is a cleaning force. It frees the native from his inferiority complex and from his despair and inaction; it makes him fearless and restores his self-respect. . . . Violence alone, violence committed by the people, violence organized and educated by its leaders, makes it possible for the masses to understand social truths."

This is hardly, of course, a new doctrine. Others in this century have propagated the cult of the deed. It was, after all, Mussolini who used to distinguish between "a violence that liberates and a violence

that enslaves . . . a violence that is moral and a violence that is immoral."
And it was Hitler who wrote, "The very first essential for success is a
perpetually constant and regular employment of violence." It is perfectly obvious why Mussolini and Hitler favored violence: It is because
violence, by abolishing the procedures and civilities of society, opens
the way for those who are most successful in the use of force. I do not
know about the situation in developing countries; there violence in
certain contexts may have the benign effects claimed by Fanon. But
surely little is more pathetic than the view that violence in American
society will benefit the left. A limited amount of violence may stimulate
the process of democratic change; but, if the left, through the cult of
the deed, helps create an atmosphere which destroys the process of
democracy itself, the only beneficiaries will be those on the right.

The new creed, with its dismissal of free discussion and its conviction that violence will mystically generate policy and program, represents an assault on rationality in politics—an assault based on the
ultimate proposition that rights and wrongs in public affairs are so
absolute and so easily ascertainable that opposition can be legitimately
destroyed. This assault on the Bill of Rights and on libertarian democracy is in my judgment wrong, because no one is infallible. It is stupid,
because the beneficiaries of this view will not be the idealists of the
left but the brutalists of the right. It is dangerous because it represents
a reversion to and rationalization of the strain of hatred and violence in
our own national tradition: the politics of lynch law against the politics
of Lincoln. It is a vote for the worst against the best in our political ethos.

The new creed above all overlooks the fact of human frailty. "Men
are not flattered," wrote Lincoln, "by being shown that there has been
a difference of purpose between the Almighty and them." Yet men are
not gods. That is why absolutism always fails in human society. Democracy requires consent—it insists, that is, that a majority of the electorate
be persuaded that one course is preferable to another. If men or
mechanisms were infallible, there would be no need for persuasion. But,
because they are not, the discipline of consent is indispensable to civilized society. The discipline of consent means that policies must triumph
not through divine right or through a "democratic educational dictatorship" but through making sense to a majority of the people; and the
condition of bringing a majority along is the best guarantee that
policies relate, not to personal fantasy or personal power, but to the
greatest good of the greatest number.

This discussion of the new creed may seem irrelevant to the pragmatic insurgencies of our society. And, indeed, so long as these insurgencies remain pragmatic—that is, related to specific issues and specific
injustices—they represent a desperately needed pressure against the

established complacencies of a self-righteous nation. Yet the new creed exists; it has received serious, if not convincing, formulation; it has won support because of the spreading sense in recent years of the impotence of libertarian democracy; and it has created among some of the young a mystical passion for revolutionary upheaval.

I have said that the new creed will only weaken democracy against its enemies. I would say further that it underestimates the power of rational democracy—that is, the power of the people, in one way or another, to modify the system and alter its course. We have had, I noted earlier, a season of despair about our democracy. But those whom despair led on to desperation underestimated the capacity of public opinion eventually to catch on to what is happening, even in fairly controlled and manipulated societies, and to demand a change in things. This has happened even in authoritarian states, like France. It has happened even in Communist states, like Czechoslovakia. And it has happened in our own country.

Here the democratic process has turned out to be more effective than its critics had supposed. The rebellion against libertarian democracy gathered momentum, we have noted, because of the obstinate and righteous determination of our government to pursue a policy of military escalation in Vietnam. Yet in the last six months the democratic process, working in its own inscrutable way, has forced the President to abandon—for a moment, at least—the escalation policy; it has forced him to begin serious peace talks; it has forced him to withdraw from the presidential contest. These are not inconsiderable accomplishments.

I do not contend that the process works swiftly. Obviously, if President Johnson had given his March 31 speech a year earlier, many Americans and Vietnamese now dead might be alive; and the evidence against the escalation policy was just as strong on March 31, 1967, as it was on March 31, 1968. Nor do I contend that the process works surely. There is no guarantee against the re-escalation of the war. Nor is there any guarantee, given the irresponsibility of the romantic left, against the election of a President committed to continue the persons and policies against which the rebellion began. Nor, alas, is there any guarantee against the resurgence of violence, bloodshed, and murder. Yet, with all its tardiness and inconclusiveness, democracy in America continues to show a certain vitality and efficacy. "The sober, second thought of the people," as Martin Van Buren said years ago, "is never wrong, and always efficient." At any rate, it is wiser in the long run than the certitudes of the absolutists.

Nietzsche once wrote, "Gaze not too deeply into the abyss, lest the abyss gaze into you." Those who claim to be bearers of absolute truth are men who have gazed too deeply into the abyss. They have committed what Hawthorne called the Unpardonable Sin—the sin of self pride, which destroys discrimination, enslaves people, breeds fanaticism and violence, and concludes in madness and catastrophe. It is sad when the derelicts of our society surrender to the Unpardonable Sin; it is despicable when our intellectuals exemplify it. Let us strike out against the concrete and particular evils of our time. But let us not yield to that awful despair which dissolves all distinctions in thought and action and rushes us on to the politics of apocalypse. In the long run, any sane society must rest on freedom and reason. If we abandon this, we abandon everything.

If we are to survive as a nation, we must resist our inbred impulse to violence, not capitulate to it, not celebrate it. We must resist our inbred impulse to intolerance. We must resist our inbred impulse to absolutism. As we identify these impulses, as we strive against them wherever they appear—whether in the gutter press or in the abstractions of intellectuals—we create a chance of defying the winds of unreason. But we cannot suppose that this problem will solve itself. We must, indeed, define ourselves by our choices, but do so by making the choices which respect human reason and human dignity—the choices which acknowledge and nourish the human capacity for mutual respect and affection.

When Martin Luther King was murdered, Robert Kennedy broke the news of his death to a black audience on a street corner in Indianapolis. He said:

In this difficult day, in this difficult time for the United States, it is perhaps well to ask what kind of a nation we are and what direction we want to move in. For those of you who are black . . . you can be filled with bitterness, with hatred, and a desire for revenge. We can move in that direction as a country, in great polarization—black people amongst black, white people amongst white, filled with hatred toward one another.

Or we can make an effort, as Martin Luther King did, to understand and to comprehend, and to replace that violence, that stain of bloodshed that has spread across our land, with an effort to understand with compassion and love. . . . I had a member of my family killed, but he was killed by a white man. But we have to make an effort in the United States, we have to make an effort to understand. . . . What we need . . . is not division; what we need . . . is not hatred; what we need . . . is not violence or lawlessness, but love and wisdom, and compassion toward one another, and feeling of justice towards those who still suffer within our country, whether they be white or they be black.

Robert Kennedy concluded with a quotation from Aeschylus: "In our sleep, pain which cannot forget falls drop by drop upon the heart until, in our own despair, against our will, comes wisdom through the awful grace of God."

59
The Problem of
the Political State

Hans J. Morgenthau
Reflections on
the End of the Republic

Hans J. Morgenthau, "Reflections on the End of the Republic," *The New York Review of Books*, XV (No. 5, September 24, 1970): 38-41. Reprinted with permission *The New York Review of Books*. Copyright © 1970 New York Review, Inc.

Rereading now the essays I have written for this and other papers in the Sixties, I am struck by the activistic, almost rationalistic, mood that permeates them. One only needed, or so it seemed, to call the President's attention to the probable consequences of certain policies and show him the alternatives and their probable consequences, and he would choose a policy most likely to serve the national interest. I remember with wry amusement my strenuous and ultimately successful efforts in 1965 to bring my views on the Vietnam war to the attention of President Johnson—efforts undertaken in the naive assumption that if power were only made to see the truth, it would follow that lead. President Johnson's political reaction to this kind of responsible criticism is a matter of public record. His personal reaction was a systematic attempt, making full use of the informal powers of his office, to discredit and silence the voice of the dissenter. In that latter undertaking, he had the voluntary and sometimes enthusiastic assistance of eminent academic and institutional (for instance, Freedom House) supporters of his policy.

If one must admit the failure of these essays, in so far as they had an immediate political purpose, to influence political action, one cannot help noticing that the experience of their futility is not a private, personal matter but that it coincides with a collective experience of futility that pits American youth not only against American politics and society but against the modern world itself. And that American revolt, in turn, is but a national manifestation of a world-wide revulsion against the world as it is. The student revolt, expressing itself positively in attempts at creating a new culture and negatively in aimless destructiveness and revolutionary tantrums, has its most profound roots in the seeming meaninglessness of life as it is led throughout the world and, more particularly, in the United States. What does a man live for? What is his purpose in life? What is the meaning of death, which appears to wipe out that life as though it had never existed? What, in short, is the truth about the human condition?

Man has always had to ask such questions, and in the past religion, reason, and science have endeavored to lay his questioning to rest. Yet the different systems of truth provided by these three methods of comprehending man and his world have tended to cancel each other out. Religion did not pass the test of reason, science discredited the metaphysical systems engendered by reason and has given us mastery over a monstrous world that needs religion and reason to give it meaning. That world is doubly monstrous because it sacrifices human ends to technological means, as well as the needs of the many to the enrichment and power of the few, and thereby diminishes the stature of man and threatens his very existence.

The universities have provided us with that mastery over nature, but they have been unable to give it meaning and harness it to human purposes. They claim to be dedicated to the disinterested search for truth about man, society, and the universe. But they have transformed themselves, through the very dynamics of their undertakings, into gigantic and indispensable service stations for the powers-that-be, both private and public. They serve society but do not sit in judgment on it. The student who enters the university with those questions about man and the universe on his lips finds himself in the presence of an institution that, to paraphrase Tolstoy, is like a deaf man answering questions nobody has asked. The university pretends to be the mouthpiece of the truth, the whole truth, and nothing but the truth. But in actuality, in so far as what it presents as the truth is really true, it is largely irrelevant to what concerns man, young and old, and much of what it presents as truth is either not truth at all or truth only by accident, arrived at because it furnishes the powers-that-be with ideological rationalizations and justifications for the *status quo*.

When the student turns from the university as the pretended source of truth and experiences it as one social institution among many, he comes face to face with another gap between pretense and reality. Social institutions pretend to serve the individual, and the university even pretends to do so *in loco parentis*. However, for whatever services they render, they exact a price, which, in turn, impairs or even negates the services themselves. Social institutions, in the measure that they are mechanized and bureaucratized, diminish the individual, who must rely upon others rather than himself for the satisfaction of his wants, from the necessities of life to his spiritual and philosophic longings. What he once controlled himself others now control, and in the measure that they do, they diminish his freedom.

Thus, modern society suffers from a profound ambivalence. It pretends to take care of needs that formerly the individual had to struggle to take care of himself, and to a high degree it lives up to that pretense. Yet the institution that takes care of man's needs also has the power to withhold that care. If it does, the individual's needs are left without care, in so far as he has no alternative means to satisfy them through his own individual efforts; and the sphere in which such individual efforts can be effective has been reduced by the mechanization and bureaucratization of social institutions below the minimum necessary for the satisfaction of the individual's elemental needs. In a word, the individual, to a high and unprecedented degree, is at the mercy of the institutions established for the purpose of meeting his needs.

When the student turns to the economic sphere, he faces a contradiction between the objective conditions conducive to an economy of abundance and economic practices carried over from the traditional economy of scarcity. On the one hand, he is surrounded and well-nigh engulfed by the hedonism of the *status quo* as the prevailing economic attitude, the *status quo* being synonymous with the continuing increase of material wealth enjoyed by a substantial majority of the people. An ever greater national product, ever higher personal incomes, ever more extensive social benefits, ever more amenities of life, an ever greater variety of novelties, and change for its own sake of the cogs and bolts of a hardly moving social machine—such are the goals in which the purpose of America seems to exhaust itself. As I pointed out in 1960 in *The Purpose of American Politics,*

> The unrestrained and self-sufficient hedonism of contemporary society has brought in its wake what must be called a society of waste. For where the productivity of the nation feeds, as it were, upon itself and does not serve as a means to transcendent ends that select and assign the goods to be produced, waste necessarily ensues. Production, engendered by the needs of life and carried forward by the desire to make life easier, more attractive, and more nearly complete, becomes like a cancerous growth, multiplying and creating with elaborate and costly artificiality demands that can be called rational only in view of the goal of producing more and more goods.

This system of production is irrational because it rejects human needs and genuine desires as determining factors, replacing them with quantity of production for its own sake. . . . This system of production is irrational not only because it performs no positive economic or other social function, but also because it is wasteful of the resources of the nation. . . . This waste is a result of artificially induced competition and obsolescence. Essentially identical products compete with one another for a greater share of the market. They are essentially identical because the needs they serve are identical and must in the nature of things be satisfied by identical products. Competition among products of this kind can be justified neither in terms of price nor of quality, since both are essentially identical.

The enormous, wasteful proliferation of virtually identical products for competitive purposes, sometimes even within the same company, calls for the artificial creation and ever renewed and increased stimulation of demand. These wants are created, stimulated, and satisfied by artificial or imaginary obsolescence, advertising, and marketing. These efforts, as wasteful as the proliferation of products of which they are the inevitable result, add nothing to the substance of the product but serve exclusively the purpose of selling a maximum quantity of the product to people who would otherwise feel no need for it.

Not only American youth is repelled by this conspicuous irrationality. At a conference on "Culture and Society" held in Belgrade in the winter of 1969, one participant expressed dismay at a similar prospect for his society: "If the social development is not directed energetically toward a radical change of the social role and importance of the intellectual and cultural factors, I doubt whether it will be possible to achieve on our soil anything more important than a belated, Balkan variant of modern technological-consumer civilization."

In America that intellectual dismay becomes moral outrage. For while the orgy of wasteful production and distribution devours the resources of the nation, society appears to be unable to relieve hunger and stamp out poverty. While in 1967 the Bureau of the Census classified more than 25 million Americans as poor and hence in want of proper food, farmers are allowed to burn potatoes in order to get higher prices and the government pays farmers for not producing. As school lunches for the poor tend to be perverted into subsidies for middle-class children (See Robert Sherrill, "Why Can't We Just Give Them Food?" *The New York Times Magazine,* March 22, 1970, pp. 29, 91-103.) and farmers, so the agricultural support program tends to make the rich farmer richer and leave the poor farmer poor (See William Robbins, "Farm Policy Helps Make the Rural Rich Richer," *The New York Times*, April 5, 1970, pp. 1, 56.). The regulatory agencies intended to protect the consumer have become the protectors of the economic forces they were created to regulate. The traditional liberal remedies have turned out to be not only unsuccessful but irrelevant to the issues at hand.

These experiences of a gap between pretense and performance culminate in the political sphere. The student has been told that his is a government of the people, by the people, for the people. Yet three basic experiences contradict that statement. First, the experience of the bureaucratization and mechanization of social life and the consistent diminution of the human person, to which we have referred before, is particularly pronounced in the political sphere. For the very political relationship—that is, one man imposing his will upon another—of necessity diminishes the latter's stature as a person. Yet contemporary political relationships are marked by an unprecedented discrepancy in power between the wielder of power and its object. That power over-whelms the individual not only by its irresistibility, but also, because of its mechanized and bureaucratized nature, by its unfathomable anonymity. He lives in something approaching a Kafkaesque world, insignificant and at the mercy of unchallengeable and invisible forces.

Furthermore, the student not only feels helpless in the face of the powers-that-be but also appears incapable of influencing them. Students have demonstrated for freedom of speech in totalitarian countries; they have demonstrated against the Vietnam war and in support of racial justice in the United States and elsewhere. But what has been the result of all their demonstrations? Totalitarian governments still allow freedom of speech only to the rulers, the Vietnam war is still going on, and racial justice is still a postulate rather than a fact.

This experience of futility is powerfully reinforced and made definitive by a third factor: the lack of a workable alternative to the dominant philosophy, regime, and policies. That is as true of the Soviet Union as it is of France, as true of Japan as it is of the United States. What difference does it make for whom one votes when the policies of different persons and parties are virtually interchangeable?

Take the classic case of the 1964 Presidential elections. Most of us thought that it was as clear-cut a case of two different personalities, two different political philosophies, and two different political programs as one could wish. But those who voted for the loser were pleasantly surprised to find that his political program, at least on the international scene, was in good measure executed by the victor who had opposed that political program in the election campaign. As Senator Goldwater put it in the fall of 1969, when asked how he felt about President Johnson's executing his program: "Well, he did it after he had read my speeches."

While we used to stress the opportunities over the dangers, we now put the emphasis the other way around. For it should by now have become obvious that the great issues of our day—the militarization of American life, the Vietnam war, race conflicts, poverty, the decay of the cities, the destruction of the natural environment—are not susceptible to rational solutions within the existing system of power relations.

The militarization of American life is rooted in three factors, of which only one, the first, is susceptible to rational argument: the assumption that the same modes of thought and action which since the beginning of history have been applied to conventional weapons are also applicable to nuclear ones; a demonological conception of the world in which the United States is pitted in ineluctable conflict against other nations of incalculable power and infinite cunning; and social interests that have economic and political stakes in the continuation of policies derived from these factors.

Our involvement in the Vietnam war is similarly justified by this demonological conception of the world, which assigns to the United States the mission to defend the "Free World" against aggression and subversion from the Communist conspiracy. The strangeness to each other of the races is an existential psychological fact, transformed into acute antagonism and conflict by prejudice (which within limits is susceptible to rational refutation), concern for relative social status, and economic interests. Poverty on a large scale, like the decay of the cities and the ruination of the natural environment, is a result not of accidental misfortunes but of social and economic policies in whose continuation powerful social groups have a vested interest.

To the degree that these issues have been created and maintained in their unsolved state by powerful social groups, any approach toward reform that leaves the relative distribution of power intact will at best mitigate the social ills or at worst convey to the victims the soothing appearance of remedial action while confirming the *status quo*. In brief, the overriding single issue, of which all the others are but specific manifestations, is the distribution of power in American society, and that distribution has in its determining essentials survived all reform movements, from Populism through the Progressive Movement, Theodore Roosevelt's Square Deal, Woodrow Wilson's New Freedom, Franklin D. Roosevelt's New Deal, and Harry Truman's Fair Deal to John F. Kennedy's New Frontier, Lyndon B. Johnson's Great Society, and the contemporary antiwar movements.

These movements have achieved much by changing the relations of the government to different social groups as well as the conditions of the social groups themselves. But when it comes to the over-all distribution of power in American society, they all appear in retrospect as essentially futile attempts at accomplishing through rational and moderate reform what can be accomplished only by a radical shift of power and priorities, either through the disintegration of the existing power structure or through revolution.

Thus the world into which the student is born, and into which he is supposed to fit himself to find his life's fulfillment, must appear to him as a world of make-believe, a gigantic hoax where nothing is as it appears to be and upon which what he feels, thinks, aspires to, and does has no effect except to provide inducement for harassment and repression. All the while, that meaningless and unbending world carries on under the shadow of an atomic cloud, which, if present trends continue, is likely to make an end to all of us. The real possibility of atomic destruction under present conditions compounds in the long run the senselessness of human existence that the practices of society bring home every day. The reaction of the activist youth has been threefold. It attacks universities as the weakest and most easily accessible outpost of the "establishment." It challenges the "establishment" at its fringes, as in the draft and the windows, furniture, and offices of public and corporate buildings. It tries to create a new culture in which man will come into his own, satisfying his emotions and expanding his consciousness.

However, while the destruction of the university is easy—a couple of hundred determined students can do it—it is also irrelevant to the distribution of power in society. One can even assert that in so far as the university has been faithful to its mission to speak truth to power, it has been a thorn in the side of the powers-that-be. Thus the destruction of the university may for a fleeting moment satisfy the emotions of the destroyers, but it performs no useful political or social function. The same conclusion applies to challenging the "establishment" at its fringes. The fringes are expendable and easily repaired. The demonstrated futility, so far as taking effective power is concerned, of the attacks upon the university and upon the fringes of the "establishment" by the very same token reveals for all to see the "establishment's" unchallengeable power.

It is a different matter with respect to the attempts at creating a subculture different from, and opposed to, the prevailing culture. If such a subculture were able to impose a new system of values and new modes of thought and action upon the material conditions of society, it would indeed thereby create a new society. Yet what many of the proponents of a subculture seem to seek is not to make rational and humane use of those material conditions but either to destroy them or to escape from them. In so far as they do the latter—returning to a state of nature both physical and emotional—they may at best save themselves as individuals. But they do nothing—except set an example for some—for society at large.

Thus far we have spoken of what youth can do to society. However, given the weakness in both the power and purpose of youth, it is much more important to ask, in view of its unchallengeable power, what society may do to youth and the rest of us. Society has essentially two choices: It can face the issues its own dynamics have created by perverting and faulting its original purpose of equality in freedom, to which it is still rhetorically committed, and thereby renew itself; or it can try to maintain the *status quo* with all means at its disposal, even at the expense of its original purpose. The preservation of the existing system then becomes the ultimate purpose.

There can be no doubt, in view of the record, that American society has chosen the latter alternative. Regardless of the libertarian and reformatory rhetoric, its policies, both at home and abroad, have served the defense of the *status quo*. Abroad, the United States has become the antirevolutionary power par excellence, because our fear of Communism has smothered our rational insight into the inevitability of radical change in the Third World. Our interventions in Vietnam and the Dominican Republic are monuments to that fear. At home, our commitment to making all Americans equal in freedom has been at war with our fear of change and our conformist subservience to those in power.

Our commitment to the American purpose of equality in freedom has won a battle in enforcing the rights of the black Americans at least in certain respects, a step forward that appears rather big as compared with the conditions of twenty years ago and rather insignificant as compared with the present conditions of the blacks in education, employment, and housing. What the change in the status of the blacks amounts to is the willingness of the ruling forces to co-opt blacks in such numbers and such conditions as not to endanger the over-all distribution of power within American society. When those who hold power in the United States perceive, rightly or wrongly, that the danger point is being approached, they call a halt to change and man the bastions of the *status quo*. Thus they sacrifice the purpose of America to the preservation of the existing power relations, which they will allow to be exposed to minor adjustments but not to radical transformation.

The extent of the repression in store for the dissenters will depend upon the subjective estimate of the seriousness the leaders in Washington and throughout the country place upon the threat to their power. In view of the thus far marginal nature of the threat, society will need only resort to marginally totalitarian methods. The dissenters will people our prisons, our graveyards, our Bohemias or—as utter cynics—our positions of power. The latter will not be unlike the Marxist-Leninists of the Soviet Union: They will mouth a litany of slogans in which they not only do not believe but which they despise. Such a society can carry on for a while, like a body without a soul, but sooner or later it must either recover its soul—that is, the purpose that has given it life—or disintegrate from within. Perhaps, then, a new society, with a new purpose, will be built upon the ruins of the old; or perhaps nothing will be left but ruins for later generations to behold.

60
Problems of Finance

Joseph M. Cronin
School Finance in the Seventies: The Prospect for Reform

Joseph M. Cronin, "School Finance in the Seventies: The Prospect for Reform," *Phi Delta Kappan*, LI (No. 3, November 1969): 117, 122. Guest Editorial, Special Issue on School Finance.

Youngstown, Ohio, taxpayers allowed their public schools to remain closed from Thanksgiving, 1968, to January, 1969. The Philadelphia Board of Education thought it might run out of funds. School systems from Chicago to St. Albans, Vermont, worried about school deficits for which no relief was in sight. For example, neither the governor of Illinois nor Mayor Richard Daley could produce the 10 million dollars needed to balance the current Chicago school budget. Everyone's funds were "already committed."

Money was only one of the problems in the nation's impoverished rural backwaters, working-class suburbs, and blighted industrial centers. If the buildings weren't old, then the teachers and administrators were burdened with the task of helping highly mobile school populations. If the curriculum was inadequate or "irrelevant," then the staff lacked the materials or the subsidized summer periods in which to select or prepare more appropriate programs.

As the nation moved toward the 1970's, legislators and school boards strained to find new sources of revenue. Maybe a tax on universities and church properties would help? Maybe the federal government would send post-Vietnam "peace dividends" to the states, the cities, and thence to school systems?

Simultaneously, a small but sturdy band of school system spokesmen revealed that they had given up on their state legislatures. In the late 1960's no fewer than seven groups took to court their charges that state school aid formulas shortchanged their children, in effect denying them the "equal protection" guaranteed by the Constitution. Although reformers since Ellwood P. Cubberley early in the century showed legislators formulas by which to equalize educational grants, contemporary scholars such as Alan K. Campbell pointed out that many suburban systems with hefty state subsidies could spend one and one-half times what central cities could afford per student.

Meanwhile, both the Congress and the executive branch issued appeals for evidence of educational productivity. Their call for cost/benefit studies took the form of requests for budgetary program analyses and for estimates of anticipated performance for each new program presented to them. In the late 1960's two very different men, Robert Kennedy and Lyndon Johnson, had insisted on the need for educational evaluation as a concomitant of federal financing. The U. S. Office of Education and Bureau of Budget officials under the Nixon Administration were not expected to repudiate that position.

Still another set of critics called for competitive schools or school systems. Blacks frustrated with city schools set up their own free schools; one group persuaded the Massachusetts legislature to pay for an experimental school largely for ghetto youth and housed initially in the Boston Museum of Science. White liberals stressed that parents should have choices, that especially the poor should be given tuition grants to search for an effective learning center for each child. Milton Friedman's tuition voucher plan appealed to another group which believed that the "free market" principle ought to be applied to social services such as schools.

Each approach had flaws. The U. S. Supreme Court, willing to tender "one man, one vote" and warn the poor of their rights under arrest, declined to find merit in the first set of school board suits which charged the states with denying children "equal protection" under the law. Of course other landmark decisions, including *Brown v. Board of Education*, represented reversals of previous judgments. The search for adequate measures of educational attainment lagged behind the desire to assess what education was worth; nor was it clear that the kinds of incentives used to build space or missile systems would yield as much productivity as budgeteers hoped—witness the criticism of the Job Corps centers, many of which had contracts with performance criteria specified and results rewarded. And it was not assured that the poor would make as rational a choice in selecting schools as, say, the upper-middle class. Teacher unions could even use competitive school systems to bid up still further, beyond what is now possible between neighboring school systems, the rising level of teacher salaries. No cost savings here —rather, an attempt to break up a monopoly. Presumably the Office of Economic Opportunity, restyled an innovative agency under the Nixon banner, might finance a prototype "parallel system" scheme, much as welfare work incentive pay was tested out in advance of presidential advocacy.

Economics has been dubbed the dismal science; some prospects in the economics of education are indeed dismal for taxpayers. The possibility of federal tax-sharing for the mid-1970's will be debated at a time when teacher collective bargaining forces an immediate search for upwards of a billion dollars for schools alone by 1972. The impact of the negotiated New York teachers' contract will be not only to thrust minimum and maximum salaries higher in other metropolitan areas, but to propel teachers to the top step faster—the new top in New York City being the eighth year of service. Estimated costs of educational services may exceed $50 billion a year before 1980.

Nor is it clear that traditional norms of equality will suffice; to lift a poor city child to literacy and beyond may cost twice as much as the $1,000 to $1,500 about to be spent on suburban children. So much of the evidence now points to the need for a higher minimum income for the family new to a city. So much of what passes for success in school depends also on adequate nutrition and on early diagnosis and correction of medical problems. These prerequisites to educability also require the outlay of large sums of money.

While public school people fight for funds, so will parochial school advocates—and convincingly. A 1969 Gallup Poll shows a strong trend of opinion supporting private and church-related schooling. Legislators have learned that the latter schools are willing to secularize much of the curriculum and accept difficult assignments in fighting poverty and social disorganization.

Michael Usdan and others observe that in a few states the competition between the schools and higher education has already grown tense. Legislators express their reluctance to increase appropriations for services whose leaders and supporters fight each other for funds and fail to agree on priorities.

Our forebears might not have embraced the goal of free, public, universal education had they known what it would cost. The cost requires not only dollars but an increasing proportion of the adult work force. Only in America, Paul Goodman points out, have citizens agreed that all students should go to school so long and to comprehensive high schools, some rather less comprehensive than others. The 1970's will test our continued interest in sustaining a state monopoly financed rather well, but rather inequitably. The challenges will come in the form of court challenges, calls for parent choices and control, and requests for cost/effectiveness evidence not now used to justify increased expenditures.

Education articles in this special issue of the *Kappan* were solicited to illuminate the kinds of arguments advanced in the next round of struggles to finance the schools of the 1970's.

61
Problems of Curriculum

Arthur W. Foshay

How Fare the Disciplines?

Arthur W. Foshay , "How Fare the Disciplines?" *Phi Delta Kappan*, LI (No. 7, March 1970): 349-352. William Van Til, guest editor for this special issue entitled "Curriculum for the 1970's," prefaces Foshay's article: "A researcher and curriculum theorist, Mr. Foshay brought the disciplines proposal' for curriculum development before the Association for Supervision and Curriculum Development in his 1961 presidential address titled 'A Modest Proposal.' Here he reexamines the advantages and limitations of the disciplines idea in light of our experience with the reconstruction of some disciplines in the 1960's and the pressing need for a new curriculum in the 1970's."

The idea that the structure, or logic, of each of the scholarly disciplines offers a way of learning the discipline itself was "in the air" during the latter part of the Fifties, and was stated vividly by Jerome Bruner in his *The Process of Education* in 1960. Here, we will call this idea the "disciplines proposal." Bruner's book was surely the most influential bit of educational writing of its time. While the proposal is not very clearly explained in the book, it communicated a fresh insight to a large number of people.

The war between the Progressives and the subject matter specialists had been going on for more than two generations. Within the National Education Association, the departments in the various subject matter fields and the departments dealing with the school as a whole (such as the Association for Supervision and Curriculum Development, the Department of Elementary School Principals and the National Association of Secondary School Principals) had drifted out of contact with each other. Each group—the generalists and the specialists—patronized the other and indicted it on the one hand for being fuzzy and on the other for being too narrowly subject-centered. Bruner's proposal offered a welcome way out of the impasse that had developed. If we could take subject matter as something becoming, instead of as something given, a ground for negotiation would be immediately apparent.

In these pages, I want to discuss what has become of the disciplines proposal since its wide promulgation in 1960, to indicate some of its built-in limitations and possibilities, and to offer certain suggestions for its future.

If anyone had asked the Progressives how they thought subject matter should be learned, they would, as good Deweyites, have responded that all subject matter had to conform to the same general laws of reasoning, and that subject matter ought to be pursued in an active, not passive, way. Of course, the subject matter specialists had the same thing in mind. It is entirely possible that what confused the issue between the generalists and the specialists in the years between 1920 and 1955 was their interpretation of Dewey's notion of the complete act of thought. I myself was present at a highly dramatic faculty seminar at Ohio State in 1956 when a bacteriologist pointed out to one of our principal Deweyites that the complete act of thought did not describe the way he conducted inquiry in his own discipline—that, specifically, it failed to take into account the problem of unknown variables operating in his experiments, and that bacteriologists had long since incorporated a way of dealing with unknown variables into the basic log of their inquiry.

This was a shocker. The discussion foundered on this rock because, in the last analysis, it called into question the whole core curriculum. The seminar took the position that the function of teaching any given subject matter was to help students to learn how the members of the discipline thought—how they conducted inquiry. Similar discussions must have been going on all around the country. It was because of an audience that had been created by these discussions that Bruner's pronouncement struck fire so quickly.

The idea that the function of instruction is to develop in the student's mind several modes of inquiry is one of the very rare new ideas to have taken root in instruction. The idea has no important background in the tradition of elementary and secondary school instruction. While it probably had occurred to many people at many times, to my knowledge no group had ever coalesced around it before 1960. In the degree that it had any currency, it was found in certain projects within subject matter fields. Harold Fawcett had approached it in the Thirties with a project on mathematics instruction for the Progressive Education Association. No doubt many science teachers had used the idea without naming it during the preceding decades. But the grand tradition of education is not in science and mathematics, both of which are comparatively modern subjects in the curriculum. The grand tradition is in literature, history, geography. The disciplines proposal never had any currency in these fields.

The innovations in instruction of the Progressive era were either technical (like the "unit of work") or policy-oriented (like the "life problems" of the core curriculum). The function of the social studies program during the Twenties, Thirties, and Forties was to teach children how to identify and solve problems, using Dewey's complete act of thought as the means. It was this thrust that separated the Progressives from the subject matter groups.

But if one could take a subject matter as a mode of inquiry, then many of the problems that separated the groups would disappear. One could have an active learner, for he would be actively inquiring. One could have an inquiry-centered strategy which was enough like the "problem-centered" strategy to be recognizable. More important, the approach through inquiry promised a student who would be equipped to persevere in the subject matter he was learning. The older approach to subject matter, whatever its virtues, did not take perseverance as one of its stated objectives. It was, basically, statically conceived. The idea was to make mastery palatable and "meaningful"—but the palatability and meaningfulness were to be found through ingenious applications of subject matter to real external life, thus demonstrating its utility. They were not to be found by equipping a student so that he could carry on inquiry independently within the subject matter field. On the other hand, the core curriculum was intended precisely to make the student able to carry on independent inquiry concerning social problems.

The disciplines proposal had developed first in the physics project (PSSC) under Gerrold Zacharias. It was his group which, having found that updating the existing physics curriculum resulted in an impossible load of subject matter, cut through the problem with the notion that the function of instruction in physics was not to teach subject matter directly, but to teach it indirectly. Indirect teaching refers to the teaching of styles and methods of thought, as against teaching the myriad of facts that such thought deals with. Not surprisingly, the idea spread rapidly through the several science curriculum projects supported by the National Science Foundation after 1955. This same basic idea also appeared in the new mathematics programs then under development. It appeared in chemistry and biology almost at once.

There has been a substantial evolution of the idea in mathematics and science from that day to this. The new mathematics is said to be in its third generation now. The PSSC program has been followed by Harvard Project Physics and others. There were at least two prominent chemistry programs, each somewhat differently conceived, and three notable versions of biology.

Interestingly enough, the idea has not fared nearly so well in curriculum projects in other fields, such as literature and history. A distinction perhaps has to be made between fields of knowledge in which inquiry is central and other fields in which something like interpretation is central. One can have disciplined interpretation as well as disciplined inquiry, of course. However, the tradition of disciplined inquiry in literature has had two distinct branches, the historical and the critical; and literary scholars have not traditionally been concerned with the question of the structure of their discipline. In the case of history, although historiography has existed for a long time, writing in the field of historiography has not been nearly so central to historians as has been the writing of history itself. Only recently has a series of books been published to deal with the nature of history as a field of speculation and thought. Perhaps this is why the curriculum projects of the early Sixties in these two fields have not been so concerned with their areas as modes of inquiry as have mathematics and science.

Instruction in foreign language has an independent history that goes back to World War II and the widespread acceptance of the methods of the Army Language Schools. More recently, under the influence of Noam Chomsky, some beginnings are being made to bring contemporary linguistic science to bear on the approach to instruction in this field. Unfortunately, only beginnings are showing; the field is one of the last to respond to this change in the curriculum climate.

The disciplines proposal has suffered the fate of many ideas in education. That is, it has been trivialized, attacked as nothing more than the old enemy, subject-centeredness; it has been misapplied, equated with its opposite (i. e., the complete act of thought), thrown into contrast with creativity (as if there were no such thing as creative inquiry), and so on. We shall not concern ourselves here with this aspect of what has become of the idea. All educational ideas have to survive such pathologies. Rather, let us consider what the built-in advantages and limitations of the idea have turned out to be.

Primary among the advantages of the disciplines proposal is the fact that students are offered subject matter as if it were reasonable. So much of what is offered in school is not reasonable—it is a set of arbitrary codes to be learned, or a set of arbitrary statements to be given back upon demand or recalled when needed—that it is a relief to have subject matter thought of by students as something they can derive out of their own logical processes.

Teachers have wanted students to "understand" subject matter for as long as there have been teachers. We have not had an adequate operational definition of "understanding." The disciplines proposal offers one such. To understand is to be able to give reasons. To inquire is to develop reasons that adequately explain phenomena. The two, understanding and inquiry, finally match each other. The promise of the disciplines proposal is the promise of understanding itself.

Moreover, if pursued in sufficient depth, the approach through the disciplines offers a fresh and enriched view of the nature of general education. At the bottom of every discipline we teach, one may say, is general education. At the bottom, that is, not at the top. A superficial acquaintance with science or mathematics consists only of knowledge of technique. The conceptual material is somewhat deeper. But at the conceptual level the vocabulary of the learned fields turns out to be the intellectual vocabulary of general education. The fundamental concepts of the fields we teach in the lower schools have very wide applicability. *Inverse ratio,* for example, taken from mathematics, can be applied to all sorts of non-mathematical phenomena. There is probably an inverse ratio between the degree of selectivity of the school system and the breadth of knowledge held by the general population in the country. The idea that the more of one thing one has, the less of another, can be learned (it probably is learned) in elementary mathematics. With only slight help, children can see its general value. The notions of *fact, legend,* and *myth,* all from the field of history, have the same general applicability. The notions of *relative motion, the properties of objects, interaction,* and *systems* all arise in one of the better new elementary science programs. I have seen children using this vocabulary in non-science applications, yet with great precision and insight.

The fact that general education has a vocabulary has not been widely recognized. Part of the promise of the disciplines proposal is that the minds of children can be furnished with such a vocabulary, and that the possibility of a real general education is thereby enhanced.

What are the limitations of the disciplines idea? Does it, indeed, have any limitations? There are those who would say that there are none. But there are some.

First, the disciplines proposal begs the question of the integration of knowledge. We must recognize that the integrity of the fields of inquiry—the disciplines—must be preserved if they are to be learned. But this immediately makes it impossible in theory to combine disciplines into multi-disciplines for instruction. The subjects have to be taught separately, each in its own way, according to its own logic. To do otherwise is to relapse back into Dewey's complete act of thought, and to resume the old confusions. But to teach subjects separately leaves the problem of integration of knowledge to the student himself to carry out, more or less unaided.

Second, the disciplines proposal does not deal directly with the relationship between education and life—what we call "relevance." One of the oldest questions in education is how education is to be related to real life. The disciplines proposal deals with this question only in terms of the applications of separate fields of knowledge. It does not deal, of itself, with the kinds of life problems the core curriculum used to be concerned with, problems which do not come packaged in disciplines. One could study physics thoroughly and gain very little insight into problems of racial injustice or crime. One could study history—yes, even history—and gain little knowledge of real importance about the problems of poverty in Appalachia, or the nature of the poverty syndrome in our big urban ghettos. To the degree that we allow the school curriculum to be dominated by the disciplines proposal, we fail to offer students the opportunity to become more than superficially acquainted with great public problems.

Third, the disciplines proposal failed to take into account the nature of and need for teacher education. While all of the early science and mathematics programs provided teacher training, the training was brief, suited primarily to those who already had some knowledge of the discipline itself, and not suitable for pre-service education. There was no solid, or even recognizable, conception of teacher education operating in those early projects.

Fourth, the projects as originally conceived did not seek to deal realistically with all the children in the schools. The projects were conceived as suitable primarily for the college-bound, and indeed were mainly intended to improve the education of the college-bound. The 60 percent or so of the population that has no intention of pursuing education beyond high school was simply not taken into account in the early disciplines projects.

Of more fundamental importance is the fact that the disciplines proposal itself is a strictly rational affair. It is naive to assume that all of the problems of the world can be solved by rational men being reasonable with one another. They simply are not. To portray the major fields of knowledge as if they were sufficient is to tell a big lie. The disciplines proposal can be accused of having accidentally committed this grievous error. Man is much more than rational.

The most popular of the criticisms of the disciplines proposal is the lack of relevance of the curricula as developed to anything but further work in the selected disciplines. The projects were too exclusively committed to perseveration as a goal. During the years ahead, it is likely that increasingly sophisticated attempts will be made to show how conceptual knowledge of the kind developed in the disciplines does indeed apply to real problems in the world.

The questions of the integration of knowledge and the relevance of knowledge to the real world will not be denied. They demand a response from the school curriculum, one way or another. If the discipline-oriented curricula cannot respond effectively to these questions, then other responses will be found. It is predictable that we will reinvent the core curriculum, perhaps with some modifications, that a substantial incursion into the regular school day will be made by what were formerly thought of as co-curricular activities, and that students will increasingly refuse to undertake the discipline-oriented subjects. This last has already happened in the case of the physics program, the enrollment having dropped 10 percent during the last 10 years.

We must recognize that the assumptions of values upon which the disciplines proposal is based have come under radical examination during the past few years. Some people reject out of hand the proposal that we improve the present work-oriented system. "If we are foolishly willing to agree that experts are those whose role is legitimized by the fact that the technocratic system needs them in order to avoid falling apart at the seams, then of course the technocratic status quo generates its own internal justification: The technocracy is legitimized because it enjoys the approval of experts; the experts are legitimized because there could be no technocracy without them. . . . Thus, if we probe the technocracy in search of the peculiar power it holds over us, we arrive at the myth of objective consciousness. There is but one way of gaining access to reality—so the myth holds—and this is to cultivate a state of consciousness cleansed of all subjective distortion, all personal involvement. What flows from this state of consciousness qualifies as knowledge, and nothing else does." The above is quoted from a disturbing book, *The Making of a Counter Culture*, by Theodore Roszak (Garden City, N. Y.: Doubleday, Anchor Books, 1969, pp. 207-08). It is in the cool, objective, logic-oriented quality of the disciplines proposal that the sensitive and aware young radicals find their greatest challenge. They demand precisely that knowledge be hot, involved, and personal. They would believe the account of scientific inquiry contained in the *Double Helix* before they would believe the account contained in the technical reports on DNA. It is personal knowledge they want, not objective consciousness.

It seems unlikely, given these limitations, that the disciplines proposal of the early Sixties will survive intact into the Seventies. The science and mathematics programs that have emerged out of this period are without doubt more engaging than their predecessors, more respectful of the students' intellectual attainments, less arbitrary, and more sensible. They are also more intellectual in character than the programs that preceded them. It is the quality of this very intellectuality that probably will have to change during the next decade, if the programs are to survive.

I do not mean to propose here that if these challenges are not met, we will go back to what we were doing before. I doubt that we would want to. But we could easily enter into a chaotic period, during which the nature of knowledge would come under fundamental reexamination. What is called for is a change in the spirit of the discipline-oriented curricula and a development of new curricula in the social sciences and in the arts that have something like the power and reach of those in the sciences and mathematics. This latter change is not yet happening in anything like the necessary volume or with the necessary determination.

It is precisely in the social sciences and in the arts that it is easiest to see the connection between education and life. If schooling is to be required to respond to the demand that it be "relevant"—and it seems clear that it has to respond to just such a demand—then the social sciences and the arts would seem to be the curriculum areas in which our efforts should be concentrated in the short run.

Over the long run, it is quite possible that some new version of what a school is and ought to become will be developed. The task is mind-boggling. Without sacrificing the intellectual quality (but at the same time changing its spirit) of the best of the new curricula, we have to find ways of allowing the real problems of the external world to come under searching examination in school. Our secondary school students are rapidly, it appears to me, challenging the concept of adolescence itself. They want to see themselves as participants in the world they live in, not as apprentices for it. They want the world to be in the school and the school in the world.

We cannot meet that requirement satisfactorily by going back to the "problem-centered" curriculum of a generation ago. We have to develop some new synthesis of what is real in the world with what is conceptual, and, as teachers, make all of this suitable for young people who know neither the reality nor the conceptual frameworks.

How fare the disciplines? To me they seem to have become a prologue for a new kind of curriculum theory, a new kind of curriculum organization, a new kind of conception of the meaning of instruction that is likely to come to some sort of fruition during the decade ahead.

62
Problems of the Disadvantaged

Robert J. Havighurst
Curriculum
for the Disadvantaged

Robert J. Havighurst, "Curriculum for the Disadvantaged," *Phi Delta Kappan*, LI (No. 7, March 1970): 371-373. William Van Til, guest editor for this special issue entitled "Curriculum for the 1970's," prefaces Havighurst's article: "An experienced student of human development, Mr. Havighurst is an active participant in controversies concerning the work of the schools in relation to disadvantaged people. He predicts changes in the social setting of the Seventies which could eliminate the need for a special curriculum for the disadvantaged child (except for a pre-school system), reorientation of teachers to rewards and an orderly classroom regime, and relatively small adaptations to fit specific knowledge deficiencies and self-image needs."

In writing usefully about school programs which will be valid for the coming decade in the education of the economically disadvantaged, it is important to look ahead at the shape of things to come, and to avoid being turned to stone by the backward look at the ways of the past.

What is the probable social setting in the 1970's for children of the poorest 20 percent of the American population? With considerable assurance we can predict the following:

1. Increased real income and greater stability of that income. Some reform of the welfare system is sure to come very soon to provide a basic family allowance for every poor family. It will operate to keep fathers and mothers together with their children.

2. Higher educational level of low-income parents. The increase in grade-level attainment since the war is reflected in the young adults whose children are now beginning to enter school. Lower-income parents will be better able to appreciate the school experience of their children, to read to them, etc.

3. Pre-school education for at least one year before the age of five. An improved and amplified Head Start program is now ready for widespread use, and teachers trained in one of several programs proven successful will be available in increasing numbers. These

successful programs are raising the I. Q. level of disadvantaged children by an average of 10 to 15 points and keeping this gain for three years, at least. In another year or two, we will know whether these children retain their improved learning ability up to the third- or fourth-grade level. If they do, we will be able to employ a curriculum for the intermediate grades which is based on the assumption of very little reading retardation of children in inner-city schools.

4. Improved methods of working in primary grades with disadvantaged children. This is part of the situation we have just described. Once a child from a disadvantaged family has been aided substantially by a pre-school program, he will continue to be aided by primary school teaching that gears in with his Head Start experience.

5. Slowly decreasing racial and economic segregation by race and income which was set in the 1950's and supported by public housing practices will only slowly be overcome by the forces now at work to produce integration in the central city and the suburbs. While we may expect substantial change in the direction of integration, it will not affect large proportions of disadvantaged children during the decade immediately ahead.

6. A gradually decreasing gap in material style of life and in social attitudes and values between the middle class and the disadvantaged lower-class group. Though the gap will continue throughout the decade, it will become less noticeable. The "subculture of poverty" which dominates the life style of many poor families today will lose much of its grasp.

To some readers this may appear to be an overoptimistic view of the immediate future, but it seems essentially realistic to me. It is far better for the schools to "tune up" to the future than to prepare for a disappearing past.

The goal of education for all children, rich or poor, from literate or illiterate families, is the same if it is expressed in general terms. This is to help the child become a competent and happy person, now and in the future, in a democratic, productive, and increasingly urban society. There is no distinction here between social classes. It does not make sense in this society to talk about "turning a lower-class child into a middle-class child" as though this were a good or a bad thing to do. There are common goals of competence and happiness in a productive and socially integrated society. Children will differ individually, because of social group differences, in their progress toward these goals. The school's mission is to help all children move toward these common goals.

There are two important questions to be answered with respect to the curriculum for economically disadvantaged children. One has to do with *methods* of teaching, the other with *content* of the curriculum.

Methods for the Disadvantaged

There is a growing body of data on the relation of reward to learning among children which supports the following propositions.*

1. There are differences among socioeconomic groups and ethnic subcultures in the reward systems they teach and use with their children. External rewards (material, or intangible—such as praise) and punishments are to be contrasted with internal (superego and ego) rewards and punishments.

2. In general, external rewards (material or intangible) have greater positive value for disadvantaged or failing children.

3. Appropriate teaching methods can help a child evolve from the external to the internal reward system.

Thus a system of deliberate external rewards (material things like toys, gold stars, edibles) and praise should be employed with disadvantaged pupils.

A Child-Originated Curriculum?

When children do not learn well in school, we naturally ask ourselves whether there is something wrong with the curriculum or the way it is presented to the pupil. There are two contrasting answers to this question. One is that we adults are imposing a limited, rigid curriculum on children and putting their minds in a straitjacket. The other is that we do not present the curriculum in such a way that the child can understand what he is doing and where he is going.

The first view has had considerable play during the last few years, in a revival of the child-centered curriculum movement which was popular in the 1920's and 1930's. Among its persuasive presenters are John Holt and George Dennison, authors of books recently published. Holt, in his book, *How Children Learn*,[1] says, "Only a few children in school ever become good at learning in the way we try to make them learn. Most of them get humiliated, frightened, and discouraged. They use their minds, not to learn, but to get out of doing the things we tell them to do—to make them learn. In the short run, these strategies seem to work. They make it possible for many children to get through their schooling even though they learn very little. But in the long run these strategies are self-limiting and self-defeating, and destroy both character and intelligence. The children who use such strategies are prevented by them from growing into more than limited versions of

* These propositions are developed more fully in my article on "Minority Sub-cultures and the Law of Effect," *American Psychologist*, 1970 (in press).

[1] John Holt, *How Children Learn*. New York: Pitman Publishing Company, 1967.

the human beings they might have become. This is the real failure that takes place in school; hardly any children escape. . . . What is essential is to realize that children learn independently, not in bunches; that they learn out of interest and curiosity, not to please or appease the adults in power; and that they ought to be in control of their own learning, deciding for themselves what they want to learn and how they want to learn it."

As expounded by Holt, this proposition seems to apply more to middle-class children than to the economically disadvantaged group. However, Herbert Kohl's *36 Children*[2] appears to present much the same kind of case, based on experience in a Harlem ghetto school.

Kohl describes how he worked for a year with a class of 36 Negro slum children who were below average in academic skills. He did get results. There is no reason to doubt this. His method of encouraging them to write about their fears, their hates, and their likes, about the bad and good things they experienced in their homes and streets, loosened their pens and their tongues, added to their vocabulary, and got them interested in school.

What Kohl appears to have done was to attach school learning to the impulses of the children. By helping them to talk and write about the things that were most impelling in their daily lives, he made school relevant to them. To put this into psychodynamic terms, Kohl was marshaling the forces of the id on behalf of learning, just as Holt proposes to do. But Holt talks in "safe" middle-class terms about children's curiosity and interests, while Kohl faces the slum realities of children's fears and hates.

But how far can a system based on children's felt needs go? How far can a slum child (or a middle-class child) go toward mastery of arithmetic, of English sentence style, of knowledge of science and history, if he is motivated only by his drive to express his feelings or to satisfy his curiosity, or possibly also by his desire to please his friendly and permissive teacher?

We do not know how far this kind of reward will carry a child's learning. We might guess that it would carry children up to about the seventh-grade level. Therefore, we should ask Kohl and others of this school of thought to prove that their methods will carry children to the eighth-grade level. No such claims appear to have been substantiated, except in the case of socially advantaged children, such as those attending A. S. Neill's school at Summerhill, England. And some observers of this school argue that it can only work with children who have a strong British middle-class superego, and can profit from teaming

---

[2] Herbert Kohl, *36 Children*. New York: New America Library, 1967.

their somewhat starved id with the superego in the pursuit of learning.

The contrasting view of curriculum calls for more rather than less adult-created structure than the pupil generally gets today, but a structure which is carefully fitted to the student's present knowledge and to his motives. It aims to achieve "a real dialectic of authority and empathy in the classroom," which Donald Barr, headmaster of the Dalton School, called for in his criticism of Holt's position.[3]

The essential element is the pupil's perception of the connection between what he does in the classroom or in his school work and a result which he wants. When this condition is met, the pupil's ego can come into action to guide his effort and reward his success.

Programmed learning is an example, where it is used skillfully. The pupil accepts an assignment to learn a particular lesson or set of facts, and he is informed immediately of every successful step he takes toward this goal.

According to this view, the pupil must accept the notion that he has hard work to do which will require effort on his part in order to achieve the goal that he sees clearly.

Another example is the Mastery Program which Benjamin Bloom has helped to work out in schools in Puerto Rico, a program now ready for general use. The work assignments are divided into relatively small units with frequent tests for mastery. The pupil works for the mastery of his assignment and keeps on working until he has demonstrated mastery. No matter how slow he is, compared with the rest of his class, he achieves mastery before going on to the next assignment. Bloom has found that the slow pupils move along much more rapidly than he had expected. Not only do pupils learn more effectively, they also come to enjoy learning. Bloom says, "The clearest evidence of affective outcomes is the reported interest the student develops for the subject he has mastered. He begins to 'like' the subject and to desire more of it. To do well in a subject opens up further avenues for exploration of the subject. Conversely, to do poorly in a subject closes an area for further study. The student desires some control over his environment, and mastery of a subject gives him some feeling of control over a part of his environment. Interest in a subject is both a result of mastery of the subject [and] a cause of mastery."

The successful innovative programs for high-school-age students

---

[3] Donald Barr, "The Works of John Holt," *The New York Times Book Review*, Special Education Book Supplement, September 14, 1969.

[4] Benjamin S. Bloom, "Learning for Mastery," *Administrator's Notebook*, April, 1968 (Midwest Administration Center, University of Chicago). See also B. S. Bloom, J. T. Hastings, and G. Madaus, *Formative and Summative Evaluation of Student Learning*, New York: McGraw-Hill, 1970.

also contain this element of motivation toward a clearly understood goal. For example, the storefront academies that give high school dropouts a chance to prepare for the G. E. D. test and high school diploma equivalency probably are successful because they work with young people who have become convinced that they need more education; they see clearly the connection between their study in the storefront academy and the achievement of this goal.

The Upward Bound and High Potential programs for disadvantaged high school and college youth, where they are successful, seem to combine the element of motivation to succeed with a clearly outlined program of study for a summer or a semester. Such programs can be seen as a long step forward by the student.

Emphases for the Disadvantaged

The argument to this point has been as follows: Economically disadvantaged children have difficulty in the school system for two reasons:

1. Their family environment limits their perceptual, conceptual, and linguistic experience in their early years, thus preparing them poorly for school. But this family factor is improving, due to the reduction of poverty and the increasing level of education among low-income parents.

2. Teaching methods in the schools have not been well-adapted to the learning styles of economically disadvantaged children. But recent research has shown the way to improved methods of teaching these children.

This line of reasoning suggests that there is no special need for a special curriculum for the disadvantaged child.

Still, there are certain topics and subject areas that might well be given special stress in a school that serves disadvantaged children and youth. These have one or the other of two kinds of value:

1. *To meet specific deficiencies in the life of the child.*—For example, it is well established that the diet of children in poor families is very likely to be inadequate, partly because the family lacks money to pay for essential foods and partly because the child and his family lack knowledge about nutrition. Therefore it would seem wise to put special emphasis on the study of nutrition at two levels of the school— the third-or fourth-grade level, with simple and clear rules about diet, and the ninth-or tenth-grade level, with science-based information about nutrition.

2. *To meet self-image needs in the child and adolescent.*—Several disadvantaged minority groups have been given shabby treatment in American history and literature, which gets into the school curriculum

and tends to undermine the self-esteem of children of these groups when they meet this material in front of their classmates. Three groups have suffered the most from this kind of experience—Negroes, American Indians, and Mexican-Americans.

For the sake of all American youth, the study of these minority groups should be more accurate, truth-based, and positive.

For the sake of minority group members whose forefathers are presented as inferior, cruel, savage, or servile, and who are themselves subject to discrimination in contemporary society, there may be some value in special readings and projects which give them a more positive picture of the past and present status of their own ethnic group.

Conclusion

Thus my conclusions concerning the education of the economically disadvantaged are:

1. We need a pre-school program of at least one year's duration aimed at improving the cognitive and language development of disadvantaged children.

2. Elementary school teachers need to learn more effective methods of rewarding disadvantaged children for effort and achievement in school.

3. Elementary school teachers need to create and maintain an orderly classroom regime in which pupils are convinced that they will be rewarded in the future for consistent effort today.

4. A relatively small adaptation of the ordinary school curriculum should be made to fit specific knowledge deficiencies and self-image needs of disadvantaged children and youth.

63
Controversy in Higher Education

José Argüelles, "The Believe-In—An Aquarian Age Ritual," *Main Currents in Modern Thought*, 26 (No. 5, May-June 1970): 140-145. Marjorie Grene, "Believe-In—What?—A Reply to José Argüelles," *Main Currents in Modern Thought*, 27 (No. 1, September-October 1970): 24-26. José A. Argüelles, "Towards a New University Model—A Response to Professor Grene," *Main Currents in Modern Thought*, 27 (No. 1, September-October 1970): 26-28.

José A. Argüelles
The Believe-In— An Aquarian Age Ritual

I
Knowledge, Information, Transmission and the Purpose of Education

A common idea with regard to higher education—to education in general—developed in the technological age is that its primary purpose is the transmission of knowledge. The advent of computers, however, has made it clear that although there is a definite phenomenon known as information which can be quantified, stored and retrieved, this does not necessarily constitute knowledge. In terms of education, transmission of knowledge has generally come to be the transmission of information. This has been particularly the case to an increasing degree in correspondence to what has come to be called the knowledge (actually, information) explosion: the more data that has been created, the more it has become necessary to create new "fields" or subject-matter areas to purvey this "new" information, the more it has become the teacher's role merely to purvey, or, at best, to acquaint the student with this ever-proliferating data. Historically, this process has been congruent with the technological revolutions of the past two hundred years. Indeed, our external technology is especially well-suited for the creation of new information, and the modelling of our mental processes along technological lines has made us peculiarly susceptible to the belief that the transmission of information is synonymous with the transmission of knowledge.

Yet, although we have been ingenious enough to create the computer to handle the massive amounts of information now at our disposal, we have still to realize a basic impact of the computer upon our traditional educational processes: it has made them obsolete. Indeed, as long as we view the teacher as a purveyor of information and the student as a receptacle of this information (information which can be spewed up at will at what are called final exams), then we are preparing ourselves for evolutionary obsolescence, for we are, in so doing, only duplicating very poorly the function of the computer. Obviously the time has come to re-align the goals of education, and this, of necessity, must call forth radical but organic alternatives to what we are now doing. If the computer has come to fulfill the function of the transmission of knowledge (as information), then the function of the teacher must be realized as that of the agent of the knowledge on transmission, that is, the teacher must more and more assume the role of catalyst of new, or *awakening*, experience. However, since "awakening" implies a degree of conscious realization of what *is* (as contrasted with an unawakened state, impervious to actualities), such an experience has to include the evocation of *inner depth*, and the consequent release of energy and passage to other states of being or consciousness which the experience of inner depth implies.

This new role should not be that difficult to realize, much less to actualize. Relieved more and more of the burden of being a mere conveyor of information, the teacher may turn to the spectacle of his own and the student's experience as beings involved in a swiftly transforming world, and begin to relate to this world of change in a way that is creative and equally transforming. For if the goals and structure of the educational process change radically, obviously the structure of society as a whole must change accordingly. The direction of education and society will (and must), with the teacher in the role of agent of transmission of experimental knowledge, become organically integrative: the teacher will assume more the role of *guide*, the knowledge "taught" will be self-knowledge, the goal will be the integrated self, able to operate on the various planes of consciousness, rather than just the one plane for which present-day technical education prepares the student.

In actuality, this process of integrative education should begin at birth. Krippner[1] cites the example of the present day residents of the

---

[1] Stanley Krippner and Don Fersh, "Paranormal Experience Among Members of American Contra-Cultural Groups," Maimonides Medical Center, Brooklyn, N. Y., 1970, p. 8.

Libre commune in Colorado who chant a child from birth into life, preferably out in the open beneath the sun or moon. But for most, the commune is but an exotic and isolated experience, and the turn towards an integrative educational experience does not come until much later in life,—say as a teenager or college student,—and therefore when this turn comes, it is usually in the form of a shock, such as an LSD experience. In view of this, the universities (and where possible, the high schools) must become the launching pads of the New Education.[2] The teachers of these institutions must soon realize the great impetus towards an integrative experience which is felt by the young who have been experimenting with drugs and/or various forms of mystical behavior, which in almost all cases accentuate introspective and group tendencies. If the universities are to perform their function as catalysts of knowledge and change, rather than to be the fabricators of masses of unrelated information useful only to government and industry, they must lend themselves to the possibilities being experienced by the youth.

This situation is all the more acute given the ecological imperative, and the way in which the universities contribute to the social and economic forces which perpetuate the ecological aggravations besetting the globe. The crucial point is that the turn must begin in a critical self-examination, for much that is passed off as curriculum or subject-matter, as well as methodology by which knowledge is transmitted, is quite irrelevant, because the over-specialization so characteristic of higher education means a loss of contact with ever-changing reality. This is further complicated by the vested interest in these over-specialized subject-matter areas due to the extreme particularity of higher academic disciplines. Finally, there is the blindness of unquestioning allegiance to traditional modes of perception and methodological organization, which may well present the greatest obstacle to positive change. Yet the leap must be made, for, in a sense, we have written, read and calculated ourselves into a corner, and there is little further we can go by the methods of literacy and reason until we integrate what we have gained by this process (the crux of our educational and social mores since the Renaissance) with other means of transmitting knowledge.

Though Marshal McLuhan has recently made us aware of the dilemma caused by our dependence upon literate, linear models of

---

[2] I take my phrase from Alice A. Bailey's *Education in the New Age*, (N. Y., Lueis Press, 1954). This is perhaps the most pragmatic of the Bailey books and presents a clear and concise outline of operations for transiting from the present into the New Age. It is of interest that for Alice Bailey the three major sciences of the Aquarian Age are: (1) the Science of the Antahkarana--integration of the personality, at-one-ment; (2) Science of Meditation; (3) the Science of Service. Also emphasized is the significance of the formation of groups and group consciousness.

perception, the late Tibetan scholar, W. Y. Evans-Wentz, offers an equally incisive critique as well as certain alternatives to the basic limitations of literacy (knowledge through reason):

> It is not commonly recognized among Occidentals that there are methods of imparting culture other than through literacy, which according to the *Gurus*, is the least efficient of all. Four methods are employed in the Orient: (1) through telepathy or psychic osmosis; (2) through abstract symbols, such as *mudras* made by the various members of the body, and *mandalas* inscribed on the earth or painted on paper, cloth or wood; and also through concrete symbols, which may be geometrical forms, images of living animals and their effigies, the celestial bodies and magically produced forms; (3) through sound, as in music or audibly expressed *mantras*, or spoken words which are often whispered into the ears of the neophyte in initiations; (4) through written words, setting forth the secret doctrines, usually in symbolical and very abstruse technical and metaphorical style. The first method is the highest, the fourth is the lowest method of imparting the Higher Learning.[3]

There is a certain irony to Evans-Wentz' statement, considering that the American universities view themselves as institutes of higher learning, yet at best only specialize in the category of literacy. But other factors must be entertained, for we are not Orientals, and our situation is not that of pre-electrical Tibet but of high electrical age America—not that ultimately Evans-Wentz' critique is inapplicable. But we must first begin with where we are, and where we are is at an evolutionary juncture between a period in the evolution of consciousness which has been dominated by the primacy of analytical intelligence—rationalism, the one-by-one analysis of phenomena—that aspect of consciousness which functions multidimensionally, grasping phenomena as a simultaneity of corresponding features. Conjunct with the appearance of a predominantly intuitive consciousness is the tendency towards the formation of groups whose mode of operation is organic; this is only natural, since the tendency of integrated individual consciousness functioning intuitively is towards a greater expansiveness. Our planetary heredity dictates but one route to a more unified and expanded consciousness: through the creation of organic group consciousness, the integrated union of a number of individual centers of consciousness acting synchronistically. Thus, in the most advanced industrial societies we witness

---

[3] W. Y. Evans-Wentz, *Tibetan Book of the Great Liberation* (London, Oxford Univ. Press, 1954), p. 24.

the re-emergence of a kind of tribalism, which is in reality the impulse towards the new group consciousness.

But so far, the groups have been forming in a haphazard manner and generally without any social sanction; in fact, there is a tendency to view the groups as an anti-social, "drop-out" phenomenon, and at worst, as an actual threat to the existing social fabric. A more just view would be to see in them models for new social structures. Accordingly, it would be wise to orient our educational procedures in a like direction, so that the individual integration and consequent formation of group consciousness may be as rapid, orderly and widespread as possible. Only when consciousness has been re-structured and re-oriented to regulate and understand itself without external coercion or threat will a true basis for coming to terms with the swiftly deteriorating global situation—the ecological crisis—be possible.

The practical question is, how to begin effecting this change-over, how to change from the product orientation which produces x-million graduates every year to the process orientation of creating truly inner-directed, on-going, self-sustaining group organisms? Three factors are necessary for the new education: (1) a proper estimation of the existing global situation, including appropriate technical know-how for correct-ing it, making, of course, whatever possible use of computers and computer technology; (2) the re-introduction of "esoteric" knowledge and systems which have always been the key to self-knowledge, for self-knowledge is today the key to our survival; (3) a proper under-standing of ritual as organic process and binding medium in the creation of group consciousness.

II
On Creating a Ritual

The nature of the situation determines the nature of the resolution to the *problem* which any situation presents. Although my situation as a teacher has its idiosyncratic aspects, yet, because the situation itself is the norm in institutions of higher learning today, I believe that the resolution/process upon which I have embarked may be adapted according to the capacities and exigencies of other learning situations.

Let me first begin with a few basic observations with regard to the stumbling blocks to an effective learning experience. These are, first, a curriculum geared to the specialized mentality of graduate school problem-solving, with little sense of coherence outside the elaborately in-grown technical frame of reference which characterizes almost all areas of knowledge and which makes them "professional," and, second, the grade/product oriented mentality which is a stable feature of all learning experiences from grade one through the Ph. D., the net effect of which tends to deaden the sense of spontaneity on the part of student or teacher. Thus, higher learning itself tends to become a situation in which large masses of information are meant to be memorized in an atmosphere of heightened and often bewildering competitiveness; this is no surprise considering the goals and demands of our technological society. Finally, the information to be memorized is generally lacking in coherent relation to the student's experience as a whole; thus the synapse to creativity has been closed. One thing which the entire educational process has overlooked is that creativity is a basic, bio-organic urge—and by creativity, I simply mean the ability to act spontaneously in any given situation.

Such, at least, was my assessment of the higher learning situation after some three years of teaching. Personally, something had to give, and since the initiative for real change was not to be immediately expected from above, I had to take the situation into my own hands and risk change at the class-room level in my own "subject-matter" area. With regard to curriculum, I replaced what seemed to me the rather empty title "History of Modern Painting," with the "Developmental History of Media and Visual Perception;" if nothing else, this broke down the rote, linear conception of artistic development. In any case, what struck me as important was not that x derived his style from y who got it from z, but that certain events were manifestations of some aspect of consciousness which altered the totality of consciousness at a given moment, and that the very way in which we sense, see and experience the world is a result of our having taken at one point these alterations of consciousness and then *fixed* them so that they then became the stable data by which we interpret our experience. The aim, of course, in presenting the data of art history in this way is simply to expand the awareness of the student by making him examine his own perceptual processes, and realize the extent to which he is responsible for the creation of his own reality—for if this awareness is not acquired, the alternative is that reality is created for us. We then remain the pawns of a massive life-game perpetuated by machines with the level of mentality necessary for their maintenance. With more than wit did McLuhan declare that man is the sex organ of the machine.

However, I discovered that the development of a teaching technique to expand the awareness of the student was severely limited by the final examination syndrome which continued to dictate a competitive and therefore uncreative mode of thought and unspontaneous path of action. At the end of the spring quarter, 1969, I decided, after much inner struggle, that the only solution was for the student to write or do his own examination. The results were encouraging and produced a most creative response—poems, essays, autobiographical revelations, paintings and so forth—leaving me simply the burden of "grading" these efforts,—which quickly made me realize that you can grade a computer, but not a creative act.

Thus, by the beginning of the Autumn quarter, 1969, and faced with a class of 180 students, I had to discover some way of breaking down the built-in impersonality of such large classes and of making the learning experience unique and relevant for everyone in that classroom. Clear that my main role was transmitting knowledge-as-immediate-experience, rather than the impersonal imparting of information, I realized that the first necessity was to create the right situation, an environment of trust. Too often teacher and student are separated by formalities and conventions which deny the other's humanness. To overcome this, I have openly shared my feelings with my students, encouraging them to do likewise, with each other as well as with me. The creation of a community of trust probably does more to dispel the obstacles of fear, prejudice and ignorance, and hence to promote and facilitate real learning, than any other teaching aid. In a state of trust and faith, all things are possible. This is a truth we all gradually came to learn and to act upon; thus, as a class we slowly become a group, evolving our own sense of identity and creative potential.

Yet, despite the growing sense of trust between myself and the students, heightened by impromptu sessions of dream and thought sharing, all of which tended to bring the class to a convergence point, there still remained the problem of the final examination. By this time it was towards Hallowe'en. In class we had been focussing on Blake and Goya and the incipient effects of the new technological age—the rise of what Roszak[4] describes as "objective consciousness," as opposed

---

[4] Theodore Roszak, *The Making of a Counter-Culture* (New York, Doubleday, 1969). Of particular interest is the chapter entitled, "The Myth of Objective Consciousness," pp. 203-238. How long have we labored under the myth of particularizing, objective consciousness? Over two and one half centuries ago, Thomas Traherne wrote:

> Nevertheless some things were defective too (at Oxford under the Commonwealth). There was never a tutor that did professly teach Felicity, though that be the mistress of all the other sciences. Nor did any of us study these things but as *aliens*, which we ought to have studied as our own enjoyments. We studied to inform our knowledge, but knew not for what end we studied. And for lack of aiming at a certain end, we erred in the manner.
>
> "He knoweth nothing as he ought to know, who thinks he knoweth anything without seeing its place and the manner how it relateth to God, angels and men, and to all the creatures in earth, heaven and hell, time and eternity." Quoted in Aldous Huxley, *The Perennial Philosophy* (N. Y., Harper & Row, 1945) p. 110.

to a consciousness of the integrated whole which Blake, in particular, so powerfully epitomizes. With all of this in mind, and with a sense of wanting each student to follow his own impulses, I happened to hear on the local "Underground" radio station a song, I believe by Buffy Saint-Marie, with the evocative and repeated chorus, "Believe in magic." That gave me the answer to the problem of the exam: it would be a true initiation rite in the form of a Believe-In, with the idea that everyone would have a chance to work out and express what he believed in. On Hallowe'en this idea was presented to the class. Yet one matter was somewhat unclear; we did not wish this to be a chaotic event, and 180 people acting out what each believed in seemed in itself an invitation to anarchy. All along I had had the vague idea of breaking the class into groups—but how and according to what rationale or logic evaded me, until my wife came up with the idea of creating zodiacal groups, which students would join according to their natal sign. This further proposal was met with delight and enthusiasm. There seemed to be no doubt that as a collective unit we were entering the New Age.

What happened during the month of November was nothing short of a miracle: the students began learning from each other. Certainly, in terms of out-of-class activity, I suspect the students devoted more time and enthusiastic effort to this final exam than to almost any other final exam of their lives. However, having entered on new ground there were some problems. There were lingering competitive instincts; many had the idea that each group was to come up with a project designed either to suit me as authoritarian teacher-figure, or to compete with other groups. To deal with this contingency I adopted for myself the role of Nobodaddy (from Blake, of course) which seemed to handle the authority problem by rendering it personal yet distinct. Secondly, in order to neutralize competitiveness and put the group happenings on a level of unmotivated feeling and good will, I made it a point to attend at least one meeting of each of the zodiacal groups. These meetings were intimate gatherings, in which the sharing of feelings was emphasized through group meditations, with all of us sitting in a circle, holding hands, and concentrating on the groups as an organized unified whole.

Slowly it came to be understood that more important than creating an end-product—which is the staple of technological, competitive consciousness—was the creation of a sense of organic wholeness and interdependence. From this, in turn, arose an implicit trust that the right process or activity would evolve of its own accord. Thus, the groups tended to concentrate on coming together and spending time together: weekends at beaches or in the mountains. As one boy put it, "If we can't get ourselves together here and now as students while we have a chance, how can we expect the leaders of the world to do as much?" The students learned that whatever happens to them is ultimately their own responsibility, and that in the end they can depend on no one but themselves to lead them to their own truths and realizations. Moreover, they gained a growing awareness of the critical state of the planet, which increased their sense of brotherhood.

As the group consciousness intensified, it became clear to most of the members of the class that the highest things to know or realize— love, giving, creating, and right living—are not necessarily classifiable data, and, indeed, that the most significant aspects of the entire biological cycle are elusive to definition, since by nature they are ever-changing processes. It appeared that the best acknowledgment of the basics of existence is their celebration: education as a revelatory and celebratory process. Together—students and teacher—we began to understand the magical efficacy and biological necessity of ritual, for this was the spectacle that unfolded at the final examination on Friday, December 12th.

The scene was the Campus Coffee House, an informal rendezvous near the center of the campus. The time of the exam was set for the hours of three to eight. The groups, many wearing costumes and bearing astrological banners of their own design, met just in front of the Coffee House, while monitors, as well as my wife and myself, performed the task of obtaining grades; this was done by each student openly announcing to his group what his self-assigned grade was. Once this exercise was completed, the groups proceeded into the Coffee House. Over the entrance to the main meeting rooms was draped a large sheet upon which was written FINAL EXAM IN PROGRESS. The true irony of the situation was revealed when several students who were not in the class asked if they could participate in the final exam; several of these were admitted, but only after they had been initiated by the group of their corresponding natal signs.

Once the groups were all assembled, they were silenced by music, then addressed briefly on the aim of the final exam: to observe trust, fellowship, mutual harmony and love. Then, a chant began, *Ha Ya Griva Hulu Hulu Hum Pai*! which was built up into a circle dance, the climax of which immediately touched off the Aries group, followed almost instantaneously by the other groups; a collective rhythm was created and sustained for the next two-and-one-half hours. Spontaneous music and chanting broke out everywhere, and everyone danced. Magical painted stones appeared, faces were painted, beads and necklaces were exchanged, bread was broken, water was passed in cups from hand to hand; in a room to the side the walls had been covered with aluminum foil and a large six-foot high piece of foam rubber all but covered the floor, while at the back of the room a strange fire-and-water process sculpture slowly consumed itself; at the entrance to this room Tarot readings were being given. Everything flowed and wove together; individual identities melted and merged, and throughout, the rhythm built up in joyous surges. The climax was reached when the entire group joined in a peace dance, everyone chanting, *Peace, Peace, Peace.* The transfiguration had taken place. From within ourselves as a collectivity, from our own rhythm and our own joy we had created something more than ourselves—we had created the experience of UNITY.

As if in acknowledgement of this experience, the Peace Dance dissolved, and the word went out that there would be a procession to a small lake at the southern edge of the campus. Within minutes the Coffee House was cleared out; at the head of the procession which wended its way through a soft rain was an altar constructed of styrofoam, decorated with streamers, medallions, incense and candles and bearing various religious inscriptions. At the lake this altar was deposited in the water and set aflame; it blazed for almost half an hour, slowly sinking before the mute assembly. Then began the slow silent procession back to the Coffee House. It was now after seven; for over four hours the final exam had followed its ritual course and then spent itself. But in the process, something had happened, something new had been born. Perhaps more than anything was the sense of energy released, accompanied by the collective realization of untapped resources, of potentials for creative responses hitherto undreamed of—all permeated by a sense of communal love. Personally, as a result of the experience, I feel I have more understanding of the nature and power of the Whirling Dervish cults which originated with the Sufi mystic Jallaludin Rumi, or of the early Christian love-Agape rites. As one student put it, the Aquarian Age finally arrived—on a college campus during a final exam.

III
Towards a New Civilization

The history of modern art—a fable of visual transformation—is wrought with the energy of men with but one aim: the transformation of society. This is not a mere manipulation of various social conventions, but a process of de- and re-education. Our civilization is not so much evolved as it is involved, and the problem is to break the bonds of that hypnotic self-involvement, or, at least, to reveal the imprisoning and self-destructive nature of those bonds (as is rapidly becoming evident in the recent manifestations of eco-catastrophes) in order that a new civilization may evolve. To achieve this goal—and few will deny its necessity—many conventions must be relinquished, many educational disciplines must merge their methods and, often, yield their (arbitrary) distinctiveness to the exigencies of the total situation. Thus, in my case, I have attempted a merger between the disciplines of history, art and psychology, along with a shift in teaching emphasis from the transmission of information to the catalysis of new experience—the knowledge of transmission itself. The educational goal I have set is that it is not what a man does for a living that counts, but how he lives.

Obviously, the danger in rapid educational shifts is that masses of people will be released from the authoritarian archetype, thus setting the stage for widespread anarchy. Herein lies the significance of the institution of group experiences and the role of ritual in furthering the cohesiveness of group energies. The group obviously acts as a counter-measure to individual anarchy. In reality, there is no group anarchy; although there are mobs or masses, these are not groups: groups are determined by the full realization of the law of inter-dependence. Ritual and group formations go hand in hand. Ritual can be taken as a model in the human world of the ordering process that is inherent in nature; group ritual reveals in a condensed, symbolic form/process the structure of interdependence and change which underlies all phenomena. In drawing individual minds together in this realization, ritual is also an instrument of consciousness. Hence, groups further the purpose of nature, thereby revealing that man is nature in process, and that the law of nature is harmony, not resistance. Harmony accepts, resistance demands, and the purpose of man as agent of planetary consciousness is not to plunder, but to preserve and nurture what he has been given. In this respect, the civilization that we have thus far devised resists our true fate, the creation of universal harmony.

I believe that in the experiences I have embarked upon there lies the possibility for an educational process which will lead more directly to the creation of the basis for a new civilization. In this process, priority is given to an understanding of the individual personality, functioning as an organic whole within a larger set of interdependent organic systems. We must now go beyond the analysis of parts as distinct from one another and realize the whole, and the whole can never be understood without taking into full account the personality which is doing the analysis. For in the end, the world is not outside of ourselves, something to be statistically verified and put on a shelf, but a continuum within which we are the creators of that which we seek to know. Therefore, if we truly seek to know, it can only be within the context of Self-Knowledge, attuned to the everchanging spectrum of events and manifestations evolving towards a greater realization of the harmony which is perpetually at one with itself. In the words of Sri Aurobindo, "When we have passed beyond knowings, then we shall have Knowledge. Reason was the helper; Reason is the bar. . . . Transform reason into ordered intuition; let all thyself be light. This is the goal."[5]

Marjorie Grene
Believe-In—What?—
A Reply to José Argüelles

In the torrent of materials urging a "New Education" with which we are being inundated, José Argüelles's paper has at least the merit of being relatively short. One feels, therefore, that one might be able to take hold somewhere of its contents and hazard a reply. I have an interest, admittedly a vested interest, but also, I believe, an objective interest, in maintaining and, if possible,[1] improving the quality of education. Dr. Argüelles and his allies (who, alas, are many) will of course allege that I mean by "education" that dreadful "purveying of information" which they so deplore. They will see me and my fellow traditionalists (who are fast becoming a silent minority) as among the "fabricators of masses of unrelated information useful only to government and industry." That is ridiculous. A university is an educational institution, not in the sense that it turns out polymaths, let alone polymaths "useful only to government and industry," but in the sense that it gives, or should give, students an academic environment in which they may, if they are able and willing, come to enlarge and enrich their imaginations through contact with, and initiation into, the great scientific and humane disciplines of our culture. In terms of this aim—and it is an ancient, but not therefore mistaken aim—no committed teacher has ever seen himself "as purveyor of information and the student as a receptacle of this information." On the contrary, he has always seen himself as being, or as trying to be (for like all

---

[5] Sri Aurobindo, *Thoughts and Glimpses* (Pondicherry, India, 1964), p. 3.

[1] I say "if possible" not because I think we are perfect, far from it, but because financial-political pressures on the one hand and the pressure of prophets like Dr. Argüelles on the other are making it increasingly difficult for us to implement improvements.

significant human goals, the goal of the teacher is not easily or automatically or frequently realized) "the agent of knowledge on transmission," a "catalyst," even of "new, or *awakening* experience," as Dr. Argüelles urges. To constitute an education, however, such experience must be intellectual. It is the awakening of *intellectual* passions and their embodiment in the detailed mastery of particular disciplines to which higher education has been and ought to be devoted.

Dr. Argülles's concept of "education," on the contrary, is radically anti-intellectual. Since it entails, therefore, the rejection of clarity or precision as an ideal of discourse, it is correspondingly difficult to criticize. Entering into his "argument" is like walking into quicksand. And any reply to it (if one can "reply" to a congeries of non-sequiturs, false dichotomies, pieces of empty verbiage[2] and mouthings of popular polysyllables[3]) will at once be set aside as another act of subservience not only to that strange aim of academics, "literacy," but even to that alleged bugbear of our civilization, "logic."[4] But let me try, for the sake of those who have not yet lost, or would like to regain, a foothold on terra firma, to examine a few of Dr. Argüelles's absurdities.

He starts, as I have already indicated, from a false dichotomy. The teacher, when he is really teaching, is not "purveying information"; he is acting as a "catalyst," but as a catalyst assisting in intellectual growth. This possibility, which is, in my view, the *raison d'etre* of higher education, Dr. Argüelles does not recognize as existing at all. *Either* one hands out dead and disconnected information *or* one encourages in the "student" an immediate, intuitive experience—of what? Of himself. Now of course it is true that education cannot be detached from the growth and maturation of the person whose education it is. But the teacher as "agent of knowledge" is by no means to be equated, as Dr. Argüelles seeks to equate him, with the agent of self-knowledge in and of itself. It is precisely the fostering of *disinterested*ness, the enouragement of young people's understanding of, and devotion of themselves to, ends and values and subject-matters more far-reaching than their own individual appetites and aversions, that education seeks to realize. Here we have instead, as we have had recurrently from

---

[2] E.g., Dr. Argüelles substitutes "Developmental History of Media and Visual Perception" for "History of Art," the latter a discipline with articulate and rigorous methods and a great tradition of great minds, the former a piece of gibberish as illuminating as most MacLuhanesque slogans.

[3] "Ecological," "irrelevant," "creativity," "group-consciousness," etc.

[4] For an excellent critique of the current depreciation of "logic" by the revolutionaries of the immediate, see Alasdair MacIntyre's *Herbert Marcuse*, New York: Viking, 1970.

Descartes to the drug culture, that over-abstract alternative: pure meaningless exteriority or pure self-contained interiority, the *en soi* or the *pour-soi*, the two null-points of modern philosophy. Kierkegaard anticipated them in a note in his *Journals*: on the one hand tautologies presiding over empty data (what was to become 20th century positivism), on the other his own *cri de coeur*, "Subjectivity is Truth." What an impoverished, what a false picture of human life it is!

From this over-abstract disjunction, next, Dr. Argüelles proceeds to draw an equally untenable inference. From such withdrawals from a meaningless out-there as drug experience or "mysticism," Dr. Argüelles elicits—as sensitivity addicts often do—the experience of the commune. An "integrative" experience of self (how "integrated" when wholly immediate and undisciplined?) turns into an experience of community. Both Kierkegaard and Sartre saw the impossibility of this equation on the basis of that very *en soi-pour soi* dichotomy which Dr. Argüelles so enthusiastically adopts. The way to truer community, like the way to all great goods, is difficult, devious and full of dangers; it is certainly not one simple step, as Dr. Argüelles suggests, from "truly inner-directed" consciousnesses to "self-sustaining group organisms."

In his adjuration to us to add to "the methods of literacy and reason" "other means of transmitting knowledge," moreover, Dr. Argüelles confuses means and ends. In stressing new means of trans-mission of knowledge, he takes those means as ends and loses, so far as one can see, the knowledge to be transmitted entirely from view. He ends up, simply, with "the knowledge of transmission itself." What has his new "teaching" method or his famous final examination to do with the knowledge he had, as a teacher of art history, been delegated to transmit? That it has nothing to do with it, he himself proudly boasts: "The aim, of course, in presenting the data (?) of art history in this way is simply to expand the awareness of the student by making him examine *his own perceptual processes* [my italics], and realize the extent to which he is responsible for the creation of his own reality." Further: ". . . my main role was transmitting knowledge-as-immediate-experience, rather than the impersonal imparting of information." That false dichotomy again! The second, admittedly, is bad university teaching; the first, however, is not teaching at all, it is a pure and simple fraud. I regret its predominance in our society at large in the "sensitivity" "counter-culture," in the encounter group fad, in all the pseudo-therapies that proliferate around us. But whatever its popularity, it has no place whatsoever in a university curriculum. It is corrosive for growth, whether individual or social, destructive of any means for planned or concerted action, productive only of a swamp of confusion and boredom, a short way to an ersatz Nirvana.

Dr. Arguelles's lament over our literacy (would there were more of it!) gives him the occasion, further, to reiterate and aggravate the false dichotomy from which he had set out. We now have "the primacy of analytical intelligence" versus "creativity, . . . the ability to act spontaneously in any given situation." Thus we have built up to another insidious overabstraction: the equation of all learning, all scholarship, all rationality with technology and with its depersonalizing effects on our industrialized and commercialized society. In this common plaint against "our technological age," at least five things are wrongly identified with one another: the deplorable by-products of technological efficiency,[5] the deplorable uses to which technology has purposely been put, technology itself (that is, the total of engineering know-how, which has been to a great extent an ingenious application of scientific knowledge, but sometimes also of inventiveness distinct from science), science (a complexity interlocking multiplicity of disciplines through which in the past three or four centuries in particular men have come to understand various aspects of the natural world), a mistaken philosophy of science which equates that kind of disciplined yet innovative understanding with pure "objectivity," thus neglecting its necessary root in the impassioned search of scientists—who are also people—for an immense variety of particular truths about particular areas of the real world, and still another mistaken philosophy of science which equates science with engineering, the quest for knowledge with the quest for practical techniques. (Dr. Argüelles clearly adopts this last error himself, not only for science, but for art: "This history of modern art is . . . wrought with the energy of men with but one aim: the transformation of society.")

This is not the place to argue these distinctions; but with one much-quoted source for their denial, which Dr. Argüelles also quotes, I would like to take issue here. That is Chapter VII of Roszak's *Making of a Counter-Culture*, which purports to outline the "myth of objective consciousness" on which our society is said to rest.[6] In that chapter Roszak cites Michael Polanyi's *Personal Knowledge* as a critique of science on which he has heavily relied. Polanyi's critique, however, is not of science but of scien*tism*, not of scientific objectivity, but of "objectivism": of the kind of "logical reconstruction" of science which cuts out from it the heuristic passion of the scientist himself as well as his rootedness in the intellectual and institutional traditions of his particular branch of science. Were science what Roszak and his followers believe it to be, it would never have come into existence nor

[5] What Dean Kenneth Tollett of Houston aptly calls "technological fallout."

[6] Theodore Roszak, *The Making of a Counter-Culture*, Garden City: Doubleday, 1969.

could it have survived. Nor, as Polanyi clearly expains,[7] is the logical structure of scientific search identifiable with the very different structure of engineering or invention. Our self-appointed "new educators" would throw overboard all these distinctions, essential as they are to the understanding of our intellectual history, and therefore, since we are willy nilly products of that history, to the self-understanding they so joyously claim to seek.

Dr. Argüelles's theory of instant rituals—about as good a surrogate for the real thing, I should imagine, as instant coffee for the genuine article—I am not professionally competent to judge. But, finally, a minor point. Dr. Argüelles of course abhors grades—those imperfect tags by which we do at least roughly distinguish the attainments of some students from those of others (not "competitively," I may say, unless one is so barbarous as to grade "on a curve"), yet his procedure seems to me, while academically indefensible, also, relative to our old-fashioned methods, inhumane. In his case each student announced "openly to his group" the grade he thought he deserved. This reminds me of an account I once read of the Russian equivalent of our progressive education: its defender explained that instead of the wicked punishments we used to inflict in the West, the erring scholar was simply made to stand before the class in expiation of his error. Our grades are at least a private matter between student and teacher (and alas, the registrarial computer), not proclaimed publicly by the student himself or others to his peers.

In short, there is nothing to be celebrated about Dr. Argüelles's alleged reform, and there is a very great deal to be deplored.

José A. Argüelles
Towards a New University Model—
A Response to Professor Grene

Professor Marjorie Grene's position, as I understand it, is that the university is an institution constituted fundamentally for intellectual

---

[7] Michael Polanyi, *Personal Knowledge*, Chicago: University of Chicago Press, 1958, Torchbook edition 1962, Ch. 6, sec. 8.

purposes, and that the sole instrument for reaching truth in this kind of institution is by way of reason. My position, reduced to its essentials, is that the university system should be expanded to include other approaches to truth as well, most notably by way of intuition or revelation and its attendant disciplines.

I would also like to state that the conclusions, declarations and speculations that I have made concerning my educational experiment were the results of my own inner promptings, and that in no way did I wish to imply an inherent "rightness" or "superiority" of these views at the expense of the validity of any other set of views or systems. I might further add that the Believe-In, the experiment itself, was sufficient—to both the students involved as well as myself—in making its point with regard to the possibilities of approaching the higher education learning experience through the use of intuitive methods. My efforts since then have focussed more and more on the integration of self-discovery techniques with the body of knowledge (in this case, the History of Modern Art), in such a way that a more inclusive understanding may be arrived at. Since in many respects the more recent History of Modern Art may be viewed as a mirror reflecting the turmoil of a changing time, I do not find this approach inappropriate. Such an approach approximates the idea set by Dane Rudhyar, that education, broadly speaking, *"is a process according to which a particular man and his mentalemotional-physical activities are being attuned to the needs and the aspirations for progressive changes of his society."*[1]

My ideal, therefore, is not to destroy any system, particularly the University, but rather to see that all systems and methods be either integrated or transformed. Nor has it been my intention to dichotomize, and if it seems that I lean on one pole more than another, that is merely enthusiasm, and a sense of urgency, and not a declaration of the absoluteness of any one method or attitude over another. I do not believe in dichotomies or dualistic absolutes. Though I recognize polarities, each set of polarities is a whole, the one cannot exist without the other. It is the resolution of the polarities that is important; it is the finding of a place appropriate to *all* of the aspects and attributes of life that is of significance if there is to be a state of Harmony. Thus, my aim is not to set one force against another, but to find the means by which the various forces may exist and contribute productively to a larger, more inclusive whole.

In any case, the *real* issue remains: how are we to deal with the

[1] Dane Rudhyar, *The Planetarization of Consciousness*, Servire, Waasenaar, The Netherlands, 1970, p. 232.

crisis that is rending the fabric not only of our universities, but of our society and even of our entire civilization? I do not feel it is too sweeping to include civilization in the crisis since it is the universities that have traditionally been the fountainhead of our civilization; when the universities experience difficulties, as is now so apparent, that only means that the *dis-ease* has finally reached the head or the brain of the body proper. No responsible person involved in higher education is unaware of the crisis, and indeed, however it is interpreted, it is the most crucial issue on the campuses today, an issue that cuts across the whole complex of forces and institutions which comprise the modern university. Thus, the question arises: what is the function of the university in our present society, and what is the nature of the educational process needed to survive and even make the most of the current crisis?

In answering this for myself, I have certainly not meant to be anti-intellectual, nor anti-Western, much less pro-Eastern, but rather, inclusive and synthesizing with a view towards the integration of the various values and aspects of the human experience. For instance, because I say that one cannot educate simply the intellect alone, I do not mean that the intellect is bad, wrong or inferior. But I do feel there is more to the higher educational experience than training the intellect and cultivating the faculty of reason. I am also aware that many rationalists and intellectuals tend to believe that if there is not reason, then there can only be unreason, and what is not reason is generally considered a negative, and unfortunately even mystical, phenomenon. And though the rationalists may admit that the applications of their methods have not brought altogether happy results, the solution is difficult, for at least part of the problem is our immersion in the very methods of reason. Thus, though we have the tools to enhance our lives, too often we seem to lack the judgment by which these tools can be beneficially and wisely applied. A civilization rich in power but lacking in wisdom is in great danger, indeed.

I am not suggesting at all the elimination of the method of reason —that would be throwing out the baby with the bathwater—but first, recognition and acceptance of its limitations. This should be followed by integration of the rational/intellectual faculty with the other faculties, according to Jung, of sensation, feeling and intuition. Otherwise, the intellect—cerebration—will be to man what physical size was to the dinosaur. In this process, socially and historically, the university has become the bulwark of the intellect. As might be expected in a predominantly rational culture, education has come to be identified or associated almost exclusively with intellectual develop-ment, much to the detriment of the human faculties, and thus contributing to the dangerously one-sided attitude. This is all the more complex because the problem is engrained in our very customs and processes of consciousness. Awareness of this problem has surfaced, as in Maslow's, *The Psychology of Science*, or Kuhn's, *The Nature of Scientific Revolutions*, which seriously begin to question the intellectual assumptions we have been operating upon, not so much to destroy what has come to be, as to expand our field of vision. It is also well to note historically that the primacy of empirical truth as manifest in the rise of modern science in the Seventeenth and Eighteenth centuries was accompanied by a zealous driving out of the temples of learning nearly all the methods of arriving at the truth by way of intuition or revelation. The time has come to restore the balance, to make the university universal, for our survival is at stake.

For this reason, it is not surprising that unrest is sweeping our universities, the "brains" of our civilization. Many are there who thirst for a richer diet; others are there who should not be there as the university is so constituted. S. I. Hayakawa brought out this last point in a speech at Boulder, Colorado, this past summer by indicating that the present university situation is only aggravated by the fact that "parents push many middle class and upper middle class children into college even though they don't know what they want to study."[2] It is for people like these that the university has become a meaningless place. To an institution that has been traditionally consecrated as the domain of the intellect, this is difficult to absorb, yet this is the actuality of the situation.

Though it may be folly to envision a reorganization of higher education without a corresponding plan for social reorganization, in the interest of providing a base for further reflection, I put forth the following vision for a reconstitution of the structure of the higher educational process:

1. At the center, an Information Core comprising libraries, computers, data processing centers, etc. Philological and historical research might also be located here, as well as other research facilities relying strongly on the use of the computer and statistical methods.

2. The Research Ring, comprising research centers, science laboratories, would be an intellectual base, a la Princeton's Institute for Advanced Studies. Students here would work more on an apprenticeship basis, acquiring particular skills.

---

[2] S. I. Hayakawa, quoted in AP news release, July 22, 1970. It should be pointed out that Hayakawa suggested a break between high school and college to provide young people with an opportunity for work experience or participation in national service. He also proposed that universities require students to spell out their goals before being admitted.

3. Institute of Intuitional Studies: Here the majority of the youth would initially spend time, essentially orienting themselves in studies emphasizing creative expression, self-knowledge and techniques for the development of judgment and intuitive abilities. By self-knowledge I mean the ability of the individual to place himself within the spectrum of the social and cultural situation as well as having the opportunity in so doing to express himself and thereby discover the extent of his limits and abilities. Students might have selective access to the Research Ring and free access to the Information Core. It should be pointed out that development of intuitive abilities must demand as much discipline as the empirical techniques. Furthermore, training here might well be in conjunction with training in some empirical science, the main point being that with a firm base in intuitive abilities a person might be better able to apply wisely his empirical knowledge.

4. The Institute of Applied Change: This outer circuit would supply a base for those—teachers and students alike—oriented to social change; it would be the place where the university-head would intermesh with the body of society proper.

In this vision, which I realize is nothing more than a tentative sketch, much of what is now the traditional, intellectually oriented university would remain constituted at the Core and Research Ring. Much of what we now call graduate studies would occur there, with an emphasis on advanced empirical research and technical studies. The outer two rings would deal essentially with the youth, and would be concerned with interrelating self-knowledge techniques and appropriate study in fields of particular interest, with an end to proper application of means or skills. However, there would be a two-way flow between the intellectual/informational centers and the intuitional/applicative ones. Thus, should a student in the Intuitional Institution show a particular interest requiring further empirical training he would be admitted to study with the corresponding teacher in one of the inner rings. Or conversely, should a student already in one of the inner rings show an inclination for intuitive or applicative endeavors with regard to his professed empirical skills, he would do further work under a corresponding teacher in one of the outer rings. Teachers in the inner rings would naturally be more akin to researchers and technicians as we now conceive of them; those in the outer rings would be as much guidance counsellors as practitioners of a given skill or craft.

Whether or not such an approach to education is the university's concern is, I feel, begging the question. The fact of the matter is that our society has no adequate way of dealing with the large mass of intelligent young people of post-high school age other than channeling them into the technical-intellectual institution of the present-day college and university system. Certainly for some of this group this is fitting and proper, but for a majority it is not necessarily the best answer that can be given them. True, many of these muddle through or get by, some even with excellent grades, but that does not mean that they have received a satisfactory education. To emphasize this, I need only point out the growing disaffection and disenchantment of the college youth, not to mention that of the growing numbers who have or are in the process of "dropping out." Perhaps the university should not deal with this problem—but then who will?

That this is a situation affecting all institutions of higher learning and not just the large land grant "multiversities" is underlined by the following statement by Kingman Brewster, Jr., President of Yale University, and with which I shall conclude these reflections:

> I do think we should be more forthcoming in our admission of the weaknesses and contradictions in our university inheritance. We should recognize and admit that the university is not for all people, nor for most people at all times of their lives. It is not even the only or, for many, even the best circumstance for learning. Action, too, has its claim as a teacher of wisdom. Capacity can be extended and enlarged by doing as well as by thinking.
>
> We must even admit that reason is not the only clue to truth. Intuition and creative imagination have their role in perception as well as in expression, in learning as well as in life. Not all that is perceived can be analyzed, let alone weighed or measured. Not all that is worth expressing can be "programmed." Not all that is "true" can be proved by objective evidence.
>
> We should admit all this. We should leave room for—we should positively encourage—intuition, imagination, and the affirmation of revealed truth, even within the academy. We can acknowledge all these things, but we must continue to assert that impetuous action, conscious oversimplification, refusal to doubt, and the rejection of reason are enemies of the university.[3]

[3] Kingman Brewster, Jr., "The Real Enemies of the University," quoted in the *University of California News,* vol. 45, no. 52, June 23, 1970.

64
What Shall the Schools Do?

Donald S. Seckinger

Freedom and Responsibility in Education

The terms freedom and responsibility can be made to mean different things to different people. Educational philosophers often have sought to make terms such as these meaningful, in order to clarify educational discourse. Propagandists of education, however, whether attacking or apologizing for the schools, treat freedom and responsibility as slogans, meaningless in theory and irrelevant in practice.

This is not to say that educational propaganda is worthless. The schools are dependent on many publics for support and, moreover, are particularly vulnerable to the pressures of special interest groups and the demagoguery of all manner of critics. Propaganda from within education serves to mobilize its friends and neutralize unfounded attacks or severe cutbacks in school programs. This function of educational propaganda often is buttressed by the defense of schools in terms of actual cash value, and there is no doubt that education is an investment in future productivity.

Educational propaganda, nevertheless, does have its limitations, and these appear all too clearly when arguments about the schools shift from cash values to the aims and content of instructional programs. It is at this point that propagandists and philosophers part company, and here that many educators, unfortunately, settle for the slogans, rather than the meanings, of freedom and responsibility.

Slogans usually are safe from public criticism, but meanings often are controversial. Consider the following: "Freedom must be earned by those mature enough to understand and accept the responsibilities it involves. The schools will teach controversial issues, but only at the appropriate level of maturity and understanding." This would be perfectly acceptable propaganda for most school systems. It enables the schools to affirm their faith that, *all in good time*, the students in their charge will be inducted into the responsibilities of citizenship.

In the meantime, what are the schools doing to develop individual initiative and responsibility? Most often, the school program involves the organization and transmission of information, which then is fed back to the teacher through recitations, examinations, and performances of one sort or another. It is an open question as to how much is retained, but one suspects that a great deal is forgotten, even as the process is repeated in a variety of guises up through the systems of schooling.

Freedom, in this situation, is the freedom to learn the informational cues of grade getting, by which the teacher reveals what he expects, and to learn the codes of conduct enforced by the peer group. The individual's responsibility to himself is blurred in this situation, as his judgments must stand public scrutiny and verification in the eyes of teacher and classmates.

This is the price exacted of teachers and students in schools where socially acceptable propaganda suffices for individual decision. The school is a training ground for occupational and social skills, and the development of the individual is seen in terms of learning the roles appropriate to these skills. All protestations to the contrary, the individual is treated as an object in a social system.

In the light of protestations and slogans about freedom and responsibility, there is a curious relationship between propaganda and philosophy in education. Frequently, educators look on propaganda as a useful tool for blunting criticism, enlisting support, and getting on with the job of keeping school. Philosophy, in contrast, is viewed as an impractical, visionary enterprise, far removed from everyday learning situations with real students in real schools.

Yet, it is the propaganda of education which treats the individual as an object by abstracting him into a typical learner. Genuine philosophizing in education, on the contrary, insists on dealing with concrete, and often paradoxical, ethical and moral situations faced by real human beings, and with obligations of schools to face these situations.

The propagandist follows the conventional wisdom; he is frightened at the idea of taking risks with ideas. The philosopher demands the human right to make mistakes for the sake of discovering what it is to be human, to be responsible for making one's own judgments. The learner may have to break with the conventional wisdom to find himself, to experience commitment, to march to the beat of his own distant drummer.

Not surprisingly, programs of instruction based on the propaganda of education are geared to the same safe averages and norms, the same social expectations, as is the propaganda itself. These programs must stress the comfortable and the conformable. They must purvey knowledge which is prepackaged and procedures where the getting of this knowledge, as a commodity to be stored and fed back to the school on demand, are spelled out. Rewards and punishments also are spelled out, and skillful teachers are encouraged to exploit social pressures in the name of individual freedom.

This freedom to conform to intellectual cues and social expectations is, of course, no freedom at all; it is coercion, packaged in the benevolent rationale of education as socialization, framed in the lofty rhetoric of education for excellence. Responsibility is not to the society through the self, but through a social situation which presumes to define the self, to treat it as a classifiable item of social data.

Freedom in education demands occasions for learning. These occasions require teachers who are open to the intellectual risks involved in sharing discoveries in knowledge with their students. Freedom involves students in the uncoerced appropriation of knowledge that may lead on to self-discovery and the awareness that one is responsible for his own decisions.

We live in a time of social unrest and social progress, of technological achievement which sees us poised between unprecedented material well-being and a new age of incredible barbarism and suffering. In such a time, the desire for escape is understandable, but there is no escape.

For the educator, there is no tuning out of society, whatever its imperfections, nor is there any really comfortable retreat from freedom in the conformities of educational propaganda. There is only the facing of freedom, the responsibility to answer for oneself, and the obligation we have as educators to provide the occasions wherein others may seek their own commitments to themselves and to the world.

Donald S. Seckinger
Initiative in Learning

Donald S. Seckinger, "Initiative in Learning," *School & Society*, 98 (No. 2322, January 1970): 24-25.

Initiative, an inescapable condition of citizen participation and civilized living in society as a whole, is essential in any authentic learning situation. If "freedom involves students in the uncoerced appropriation of knowledge,"[1] it also demands that students take personal responsibility in the pursuit and verification of knowledge to their own satisfaction.

This does not mean that student opinions constitute a law unto themselves. Initiative in learning carries the student obligation to relate in defensible ways to existing bodies of knowledge. It requires self-discipline in following difficult lines of reasoning and in searching out valid sources of evidence. Initiative for the student leads not only to the pleasures of discovery, but also to the painful recognition of one's own errors and inadequacies.

The teacher's role in this process is an extremely difficult one, calling for understanding and sensitivity in the face of human frailty, along with a tough-minded sense of intellectual and moral standards. It is all too easy for the teacher to compromise the hard but rewarding experiences of teaching-learning and settle for the mechanics of telling-reciting.

In telling-reciting, which is a superficial parody of teaching-learning, there is no genuine appropriation of knowledge by either students or teachers. Teachers tell and students memorize for retrieval. Students do not learn from their teachers and teachers do not learn from their students. There is no dialogue, no sharing of the process of discovery. Instead of encouraging individual initiative in the working through of arguments, emphasis is placed on closure and predigested conclusions, on fixed and final generalizations.

Teachers who are aware of this problem know that imitation is the worst form of flattery. A teacher does not want disciples. In the words of Kneller, "When one sees one's own ideas quoted verbatim, one's heart should sink. . . ."[2]

And yet, there are many temptations and strong pressures which move us away from the risks and complexities of teaching-learning toward the simplistic solutions of telling-reciting. As teachers, we seek to make knowledge more appealing and end by catering to the whims of current intellectual fashion; or we try to firm up standards and end by submitting ourselves and our students to standardization.

Then there are the social pressures. Today, more than ever, the schools are being forced to program heavier and heavier dosages of information through their courses of instruction. There is an unhealthy emphasis on quantitative measurement of teachers and students alike,

---

[1] Donald S. Seckinger, "Freedom and Responsibility in Education, *Schools & Society*, 96: 279, Summer, 1968.

[2] George F. Kneller, *Existentialism and Education* (New York: Philosophical Library, 1958), p. 116.

reflecting the treatment of persons as objects in contemporary society.

The students themselves present the greatest challenge of all. Many of them have grown accustomed to telling-reciting. They want to be told what to do and when and how to do it, or at least this is the way it appears. But do students really want to be told what to learn? Have they not separated out the doings and the recitings of formal education from genuine learning already? In that case, we might say that students want to be told how to play the game of telling-reciting, as the price of admission to the games people play in adult society.

To the problem of the skeptical students must be added the dilemma of the credulous, those who seek some form of authority in a confusing world. For these students, the words of Scheffler apply, and, as teachers, we would do well to take note of them. "The person engaged in teaching does not merely want to bring about belief, but to bring it about through the exercise of free rational judgment by the student. This is what distinguishes teaching from propaganda. . . ."[3]

The paradox of our times is the ease with which both young people and adults move from skepticism to credulity, from doubt and fear of established social patterns to a craving for ideological conformity. The lesson so many of us have yet to learn is that we can not escape the trials of modern civilization through specious simplicities. There is no substitute for hard, disciplined, reasoned thought in the life of the individual and in society. And the prerequisite of reason, in school as in society, is initiative in learning.

Hugh C. Black
A Missing Chord
in Educational Theory

Footnotes appear at the end of the chapter.

In 1942, during World War II, Alexander Meiklejohn clearly saw in the collapse of human learning and teaching that "The crucial, the decisive problem of our culture is that of the nature and functions, the powers and limitations, of the political state."[1] He phrased it then for us today: "We must see, therefore, how, in the field of teaching, the

[3] Israel Scheffler, *Conditions of Knowledge* (Glenview, Ill.: Scott, Foresman, 1965), p. 11.

conflict between democracy and despotism, between reason and violence, has forced itself upon us."[2] In the 1970s, as in the 1940s, disparities of life continue to give us intolerable burdens, as wars threaten to inundate us, as the gap between generations separates us, as families, cities, states, and schools and colleges fall apart. Our society seems to resound to the clamor of self-seeking interest groups pursuing power approaches to life and to education. The educational publicists of our day issue war cries emphasizing the individual and his rights and his freedoms "from" authority while others in our society strike the chord of "law and order" in extreme form. We all suffer. If we are to have a better education, we must, I suggest, have a better conception of politics, of what we should achieve through a better conception of the state, and of what men may accomplish when they work together rather than against each other. Educational philosophy will be more relevant if we bring to bear upon these critical needs that knowledge which gives understanding of how we got this way and which synthesizes and puts together in patterns which might bring order out of our chaos and confusion. That grand-scale approach in educational theory has not blessed our field in recent years. We need to hear once again this lost chord in educational theory.

To illustrate my suggestion, I recommend Meiklejohn's *Education Between Two Worlds* of 1942, used by Joseph Tussman in his 1969 *Experiment at Berkeley*.[3] Just as most of our college students busily setting up their experimental college courses are ignorant of Meiklejohn's *The Experimental College* of 1932,[4] so I believe we can profit from being reminded of insights appearing in a book published during the distractions of the past hot war. My purpose in this paper is to present enough of that book as might suggest the value of Meiklejohn's "grand-scale" approach to educational theory.

In *Education Between Two Worlds* Meiklejohn attempts to help mankind understand the intellectual problem underlying the collapse of human learning and teaching, and he also offers suggestions for its solution. He studies the schools in the Anglo-Saxon democracies of the last three centuries, which represent what he terms a "Protestant-capitalist civilization." What he perceives is a drift from the medieval world to the modern world, a shift constituting a revolution in the procedure "for determining what kind of beings human beings shall be."[5] In the medieval world the church, as no other institution, knew what life should be, had the authority to use those beliefs and values for the concrete guidance and control of human behavior, and taught men and women how to live. The modern world has experienced the change from religious to political teaching: "It is government, national, provincial, or local, which has control of teaching."[6] Between two worlds—

"one dead,/The other powerless to be born," as Matthew Arnold expressed it in *The Grand Chartreuse*—we wander today in the face of terrifying problems of what, if any, values and convictions we have out of which we may make a scheme of teaching. In a changed society which doubts its own beliefs, what shall "our young people learn to think and be and do? . . . Shall our education express our tradition or our criticism of that tradition, our customs or the intelligence which summons those customs to appraisal and to acceptance or rejection?"[7] Can we have a liberal social order in which both customs and intelligence hold sway? The crucial problem of our contemporary culture is the relation between government and intelligence. "What, then, is the state? Does it speak for reason? Or is it primarily an agency of force, of violence?"[8]

For me, a part of the attraction of Meiklejohn's book lies in his analysis of the attitudes and ideas of five powerful thinkers. Most of us have studied and taught separately Comenius, Locke, Arnold, Rousseau, and Dewey. But Meiklejohn studies them in relationship to this modern problem and puts it all together in a pattern which edifies and guides us. John Amos Comenius expresses in its early Protestant form the Christian view of what schools are and do. John Locke displays "all the self-contradictory social tendencies which have dominated the Protestant-capitalist era."[9] Two hundred years after Locke, Matthew Arnold tells Meiklejohn "in stinging, desperate words, the futility into which Protestant teaching has fallen, as he sees it in the schools and the culture of England and the United States."[10] Jean Jacques Rousseau "combines, as no one else since Plato has done, the study of society and the study of education. Better than anyone else he seems to me to lead the way into the consideration of 'modern' problems."[11] This leads Meiklejohn to an evaluation of John Dewey "to see whether or not he and his colleagues have solved the problem which Rousseau stated." Meiklejohn concludes "that the pragmatic attempt has failed at its most essential point. It is significant chiefly because it is so faithfully representative of the inner failure and collapse of the civilization for which it speaks. If that is true, then we must try to go beyond pragmatism."[12] Taking his cue from Rousseau's *The Social Contract*, Meiklejohn proceeds then to suggest "the direction in which our social and education theory and practice should now proceed."[13] That is what this exciting study is about. From it I have tried to select those parts which give us understanding of where we are today and what we must do.

Our enlightenment begins with the year 1642 and "one of the momentous decisions of modern history" which opened up "the Great Divide in social and educational theory." That was the year England's

Long Parliament failed to act to grant funds and assign buildings for Comenius' Pansophic Institute, an association of research scholars to undertake the unification of the new learning. England was standing at the crossroads deciding what should be the moral and intellectual presuppositions "underlying the great career of industry and commerce upon which she was preparing to enter."[14] Blindly, Meiklejohn feels, she chose as her pattern of culture, of learning and teaching the way of Locke and his *Thoughts Concerning Education*. That was the way of disorganic theory, of multiplicity, of aristocracy. Available were the insights of Comenius and the other way of *The Great Didactic*—the way of organic theory, of unity, of democracy. Of the consequences, Meiklejohn conjectures:

> I do not mean that, single-handed, he could have lashed into submission the wild beasts soon to be let loose by the new competitive industry. But I do mean that his single-minded insight might have saved England, and so England's imitators, from something of the duplicity of mind and of motive which has cursed the rise and growth of modern industry. What would it have meant for the shaping of a new civilization if the boys and girls of England had had the same education, if the children of yeomen, workmen, merchants, and nobles had attended the same schools, if to all of them had been given the same unified scheme of teaching, if that teaching had had organic connection with the life of the society of which they were members! If those conditions had been met England might have had some better understanding of what she was doing. She might have escaped that frightful division of her character into the low cunning of the market place on the one side and the high idealism of her 'better nature' on the other. If she had kept or won her spiritual unity, the world might have been saved from something of the brutality, the aggressive exploitation of the weak by the strong, which we call Capitalism. The simple-minded old Czech bishop believed something. And he knew how to teach it. If he had been given his chance he might have profoundly influenced the modern world.[15]

Today we seek to understand the dilemmas of our society whether it be the old one of racial inequalities in a "Christian" society or the latest one of the women's liberation movement. We swallow whole such schemes as Conant's three-track plan for the American high school, struggle with segregated schools, institute a variety of parallel programs in our colleges, add to our already plentiful smorgasborg of courses in an elective system a rash of "experimental college" courses,

and somehow wonder why we experience the trauma of lack of understanding between the generations and between groups in our society.
In such matters Meiklejohn, I maintain, helps us.

Meiklejohn enlarges our vision by calling our attention to the
origins of our dilemmas in the acceptance of Locke's educational ideas
in *Some Thoughts Concerning Education* (1693) and his memorandum
of 1697 on the reform of the Poor Law. Locke thus had two plans for
the education of the young people of England, and that tended to
break down the social unity of the educational program. In his plan
for tutoring the young gentleman of the aristocratic class, Locke put
learning in a secondary position and emphasized "good breeding,
knowledge of the world [how to win friends and influence people, or
getting along well with others], virtue, industry, and a love of reputation."
It matters little what subjects he is to study. He is to sample each of
many which might be useful to him but only to the extent of the tutor
opening the door to each. The tutor, says Locke, should not "keep his
pupil too long and lead him too far." Serious study as a primary activity
of the human individual is not in Locke's prescription. A third emphasis
in Locke is his seeing learning as a hodge-podge collection of scattered
information directed largely toward occupational interests. History,
law, and politics, for example, are to be studied for their practical
usefulness to the politician or the industrialist. Opposed to this is
the Comenius, who gives us an alternative account—the view England
failed to act on. Comenius saw man's first concern to be the kind of
learning which leads to lives of virtue and piety. Man's normal business
is that kind of learning which results in one's so knowing the world
in accuracy, comprehensiveness, and well-unified understanding as to
be a person intelligent in living. Meiklejohn helps us see the larger
picture when he paints the contrast:

> Comenius and Locke believed in the same God and read
> the same Bible. They had also both accepted the New Learning
> of Europe. [But their teaching plans at every point are different.]
> For Comenius, mankind is one fellowship, one society, bound
> together by the common purpose of using intelligence for the
> making of a common life. For Locke, mankind falls apart into
> groups, classes, sets, factions, nations, individuals, which,
> seeking each its own ends inevitably tend to plunge into hatred
> and strife, one against another.[16]

We have followed in practice the wrong view, that of Locke rather than
that of Comenius. Matthew Arnold felt the despair of the results when
he wrote in *Culture and Anarchy*: "The great middle class, the kernel
of the nation, entered the prison of Puritanism and had the key turned
upon its spirit there for two hundred years."[17] Locke it was who spoke

for that Puritan individualism. Whereas Comenius had said, "I believe in God; therefore. . ."; Locke had said, "I believe in God; but . . ." That "but" brought into play forces which affect us today; for we are still influenced by a theory of the individual, of society, of government, and of education which set men to follow their own individual ways rather than to work together in brotherhood to find bonds of common purpose, of mutual understanding. Such is Meiklejohn's message.

That brings us to the problem: What is the relationship between the state and the rights of the individual? Meiklejohn enlightens us in showing the differences between Locke and Rousseau by relating them both to Comenius when he writes:

> The Czech bishop had no doubt that both the state and the individual were created by God. That was the medieval point of view. The English public servant takes half the step from this medievalism to modernism. Locke's theory is that the individual was made by God but that the state was made by man. Rousseau takes the full stride into modern thought. Both men and the state are made by men. Civilization, whether in its individual or its social phases, is a human achievement.[18]

On this problem we have in Locke and Rousseau two differing social theories which make a terrific difference. Locke gives a biblical, theological interpretation of man in a rhetorical "state of nature." In it God endows man with "natural rights" to freedom, equality, property, justice, and the like. At this stage, men have little concern for the rights of others; for they pursue their own self-interests, they plunder and kill, they take what they can get. Then by mutual consent, of necessity and as a merely prudential rather than a moral matter, men give to government authority over themselves and their possessions. Man, not God, establishes the political state as a secondary social phenomenon to "secure" his "natural rights" received from God. Such "mental jugglery" as this, believes Meiklejohn, has enabled the Anglo-Saxon world all these years "to combine righteousness in morals with success in business."[19] In complete antithesis, Rousseau sees that man is a political animal, that Locke's "natural rights" are nonsense, and that government is primary. The political state creates "rights" and "wrongs," for they have no meaning apart from it. "The state," Meiklejohn interprets Rousseau as saying, "is the creator of mankind. It makes civilization, makes culture, makes human beings. To paraphrase Comenius we may say that 'only by becoming a citizen does one become a man.' Human rights are whatever the changing activities of organized living require of human reason that they should be. . . . Human rights are political."[20] When conflict occurs between the individual and government, Locke's theory tips the balance in favor of the dictates of the individual's own will over the concerted political judgments of our fellow human beings. Rousseau's theory allows them to meet on equal terms, for both the rights of the individual and the authority of the state derive from the same stock: man rather than God. Rousseau's theory allows us to see that "The only freedom which can be justified . . . is not freedom 'from' the state. It is freedom 'in' and 'by' the state. The only rights men have are those which citizenship in a political society confers upon them."[21]

Rousseau's social and political theory makes available to us a life-line to better education. As Meiklejohn puts it:

> Our American individualism has been far too simple, far too childlike a theory of human experience to account for the facts. As we teach a young person it is not enough to teach him to 'be himself.' We must teach him to 'be himself in an organized society.' To comprehend the mingling of individual freedom and social authority which that statement intends is the intellectual task of modern education. It is that task to which Rousseau has summoned us.[22]

Rousseau is more helpful to Meiklejohn than John Dewey's philosophizing about the general theory of education and society. For Meiklejohn finds the ideas of pragmatism fully as negative as Dewey and his colleagues' war cries against Victorianism and the old theological absolutism. Meiklejohn finds in Dewey a disorganic theory which leaves us with an education in which pupils are free to pursue the interests of each according to individual likes and dislikes. Lacking any "critical intelligence" or "objective, disinterested judgment" in terms of which we may criticize and judge pupil interests, teaching fails to cultivate what is "good" as determined by the community. A great deal more is demanded, especially in the face of advancements in learning which accelerated with the publication of Darwin's *Origin of Species* in the year John Dewey was born and at a time when Matthew Arnold was thirty-seven and in despair over a religion which buried itself in its literal interpretation of the Bible, its authoritarian dogmas, and its Puritan individualism for which Locke had been the spokesman.

The old belief was that morality and intelligence come from God. What happens to our civilization when its underlying structure (belief in God) is destroyed and religion is disintegrating? Rousseau helps Meiklejohn by suggesting the possibility that "we moderns can create a nontheological civilization which can carry on the work of morality and intelligence."[23] He does so by having declared that morality and intelligence are political and the state is the maker and maintainer of freedom and justice, of equality and intelligence, of industry and ownership. In education this means to Meiklejohn teaching

> pupils to participate, not in an intelligence which makes and controls the universe but in an intelligence which men are inventing as they seek to create meaning and value in an otherwise meaningless world. . . . If individuals or groups are to find support, consolation, co-operation, they can find them only by standing together, by uniting with one another. The state, which takes charge of education, can have value and efficacy only as an agency of that attempt at human unity.[24]

Behind that lies Meiklejohn's belief in a human basis for a new building, for a reconstruction of the old building. "It may be," he says, "that underlying all our standards of conduct and opinion we can find, in human nature itself, a warrant quite as adequate, more adequate than that which the belief in God had given. There may be human 'reasons' for truth and freedom, justice and generosity, which can well replace the divine 'reasons' which have previously been given."[25]

Believing that the myths about God's existence in themselves constitute supremely important knowledge about mankind, Meiklejohn searches underneath the myths of our faith to find the truths from which the myths drew their meaning and power. What he discovers is what we have described as other than, higher than ourselves: the brotherhood of man, the ideal that we are "all members of a single family, tied together by the bonds of common purpose, of mutual understanding."[26] "Men are brothers only as they become so by their own moral and intellectual achievements. The life of fellowship is an ideal, a goal, toward which men may strive."[27] ". . . human insight has described life to be such that it cannot be lived rightly or intelligently unless men deal with one another as if they were brothers."[28] Here lies the basis for an answer to the educational question: What kind of intelligence do we wish to inculcate—the friendly wisdom of persons co-operating in a common cause, or the cleverness and calculating self-interest of individuals, each of whom is, in the last resort, seeking his own advantage?[29] That men should be brothers Meiklejohn offers us as a principle which goes beyond Dewey and pragmatism; it is a principle of critical intelligence, a working criterion both in the moral and intellectual fields. It affords society a measure, a standard by which it may appraise its behavior and that of its members. It affords a basis for educational theory and practice, a goal toward which our schools and colleges may direct their activities and in relation to which our teaching may be criticized.

Along with this ideal, we must have a proper theory of the state in which can be combined the freedom of the individual with the authority, the organic unity, of the state, and this be related to education. Meiklejohn finds his solution in the "Christian" tradition as given a secular statement in Rousseau's *The Social Contract*. He looks for an organic theory (which he finds in Rousseau) in preference to a disorganic theory such as in Locke or Dewey. For he seeks an explanation of social action in terms of a striving for order and coherence, a seeking to create unity of idea and purpose in the midst of a vast multiplicity of interests and influences. Rousseau's organic theory fits, for it means, as applied to education, that "a pupil should be taught, not as an isolated individual, but as a member of a fellowship, a state. He should learn to be sensitive, generous, intelligent, active, in his relations with his fellows. He will find his life, not by being apart from them, but by being one with them."[30] *The Social Contract* presents the state as "a form of association which will defend and protect with the whole common force the person and goods of each associate and in which each, while uniting himself with all, may still obey himself alone; and remain as free as before."[31] It is illustrated in our Bill of Rights, a public rather than a private document, whose validity and authority "are to be found, not in the separate demands of independent individuals, each fighting for his own rights and interests, but in the concerted wisdom and action of a political community."[43] The state, as a concerted endeavor of all in a common life expressing a general will, an identity of purpose, exists "to ensure the blessings of liberty to our posterity." In it we give ourselves and our possessions "without reserve," and thereby we find our own persons, our own rights and good, protected by the full force of the community. This asserts in secular terms what the "Christian" tradition maintained in the old doctrine: "whosoever will lose his life for my sake will find it." This theory says that "each of us, in a well organized society, yields to the state all that he is, all that he has, and that, in doing so, each of us becomes a free person. . . . And, further, as we share in the common will, the common devotion to the common welfare, each of us finds himself 'obeying himself alone, and thus as free as he was before.' "[33]

The state in this sense, and as the agency of education, makes possible for civilized man what was not possible for him in a "state of nature." At that lower level without political institutions, life would be lived at the level of physical impulse and appetite. Justice and morality would be absent. But when man passes into a politically organized society and the "civil state," then the higher levels of living become possible:

Man 'consults his reason' instead of merely 'listening to his inclinations.' The license of 'natural liberty' is lost. But, in its place, men gain in the order of 'civil liberty.' As a substitute for the 'possession of goods,' which are gained and held only 'by force' or by 'the right of the first occupier,' the citizens of a civil state are guaranteed 'proprietorship,' founded on 'a positive title.' From control by the impulses of appetite, which is slavery, men rise to that obedience to law which is 'moral liberty,' the liberty which, by mutual agreement, we create for ourselves. In a word 'Although in this state, he deprives himself of some advantages he got from nature, he gains in return others so great, his faculties are so stimulated and developed, his ideas so extended, his feelings so ennobled, and his whole soul so uplifted, that, did not the abuses of this new condition often degrade him below that which he left, he would be bound to bless continually the happy moment which took him from it forever, and, instead of a stupid and unimaginative animal, made him an intelligent being and a man.[34]

Teaching, then, is concerned with the institutions of property, morality, law, justice, freedom, duty, intelligence, and reason which are "human," not "natural," and which grow as human society grows, which are "made and remade as organized groups of human beings fashion and refashion their relations, one to another."[35]

From here in 1942 Meiklejohn went on to make his suggestions for us under the conception of the state as not a mechanical collocation of individuals and groups but an "ordered, moralized, intellectualized, civilized fellowship," the agency of education. We need, I suggest, to be reminded again of such insights as these:

> We cannot teach world fellowship unless we believe in it, unless we put it into action by the creation of a political organization which shall take charge of the fortunes and the virtues of humanity. . . . Education is, and must be, an activity carried on by a social group. It is initiation into an existing 'pattern of culture.' And as such, it depends upon the support and the authority of the group to which both the pattern and the pupil belong.[36]

> Every human being, young or old, should be taught, first of all, to be a citizen of the world, a member of the human fellowship. All other lessons are derivates of that primary lesson.[37]

> If we are to have an effective human fellowship, the pupils in every corner of the earth will have the same basic lessons to learn. They need to know each other. They must become aware of the humanity of which they are members.

They must become acquainted with that whole human undertaking which we sum up under the phrase 'the attempt at
civilization.' Only by having that common knowledge, can they
become reasonable in their relations to one another. 'The
proper study of mankind is Man.'[38]

We elders are caught in fear, in habit, in custom, in prejudice, in prudence, in common sense. It is we, therefore, who
resist the education or re-education which we need. If we are to
have the moral and intellectual reconstruction which are implied in the making of a world-state, the prime essential is an
adequate process of adult education. Our minds will have to
be refashioned. And we ourselves must do it. There is no one
else to teach us. We, members of a common humanity, acting together as one sovereign people, must teach ourselves to
do and to be what our common citizenship offers us to do and
be. We must learn to so know and care for all our fellow men
that we can participate with them in the one common cause.
That task of human self-education our generation is called upon
to begin. But it will be only a beginning. The road to reasonableness goes on and on.[39]

Humanity is reasonable as well as unreasonable. It is the
struggle between these two which defines the course of education. We know what teaching is only as we see and feel what
the free spirit of man is trying to do and to be.[40]

Footnotes

[1] Alexander Meiklejohn, *Education Between Two Worlds*, 2d ed. (New York:
Harper & Bros., 1942), p. 3.

[2] *Ibid.*, pp. 3-4.

[3] Joseph Tussmann, *Experiment at Berkeley*, (New York: Oxford University
Press, 1969).

[4] Alexander Meiklejohn, *The Experimental College*, (New York: Harper &
Bros., 1932).

[5] Meiklejohn, *Education Between Two Worlds*, p. 4.

[6] *Ibid.*, p. 3.

[7] *Ibid.*, p. 109.

[8] *Ibid.*, pp. 10-11.

[9] *Ibid.*, p. 11.

[10] *Ibid.*

[11] *Ibid.*, p. 12.

[12] *Ibid.*

[13] *Ibid.*

[14] *Ibid.*, p. 24.

[15] *Ibid.*, pp. 24-25.

[16] *Ibid.*, pp. 33-34.
[17] Matthew Arnold, *Culture and Anarchy*, p. 143.
[18] Meiklejohn, *Education Between Two Worlds*, p. 79.
[19] *Ibid.*, p. 83.
[20] *Ibid.*, pp. 81-82.
[21] *Ibid.*, p. 84.
[22] *Ibid.*, p. 95.
[23] *Ibid.*, p. 85.
[24] *Ibid.*, p. 200.
[25] *Ibid.*, p. 202.
[26] *Ibid.*, p. 207.
[27] *Ibid.*, p. 206.
[28] *Ibid.*, p. 204.
[29] *Ibid.*, p. 205.
[30] *Ibid.*, p. 213.
[31] *Ibid.*, p. 215.
[32] *Ibid.*, p. 217.
[33] *Ibid.*, pp. 215-216.
[34] *Ibid.*, pp. 219-220.
[35] *Ibid.*, p. 220.
[36] *Ibid.*, p. 288.
[37] *Ibid.*, p. 286.
[38] *Ibid.*, p. 287.
[39] *Ibid.*, p. 289.
[40] *Ibid.*, p. 291.

Index of Names

Abraham, 234-236, 257, 294, 325
Achilles, 95-97, 99, 100-101, 282-283
Adams, John, 30
Adler, Mortimer, 493
Aemilius Paulus, 362
Aeschylus, 539, 714
Aesop, 374
Agamemnon, 96, 102, 153, 282
Agatha, St., 388
Agnes, St., 388
Akhenaten, 73-75, 288, 291
Alcott, Bronson, 578, 635
Aldred, Cyril, 72-73
Alexander de Villa Dei, 380, 388
Alexander (the Great), 200, 278, 356, 360, 366, 379
Allen, Mary R., 482-484, 486, 488, 495
Ambrose, St., 343
Amos, 241-242, 257
Anaxagoras, 226
Anthony, Mark, 221, 348
Anytus, 124-125, 279
Archambault, Reginald, 672
Archilochus, 305
Archimedes, 569
Argüelles, José A., 652-653, 743-758
Aristeides, 131
Aristippus, 227, 278
Aristophanes, 89, 199, 341
Aristotle, 82, 88, 163-179, 200, 265, 278, 280, 342-343, 360, 363-364, 376, 409-411, 692
Arkwright, Richard, 569
Arnold, Maria. See Allen, Mary R.
Arnold, Matthew, 404-405, 770, 773, 775
Arnold, Thurman, 488
Arnstine, Donald, 676
Athenaeus, 343
Atia, 187
Augustine, St., 267, 307-315
Aurelia, 186
Aurobindo, Sr., 754
Auxon, 370

Bacon, Sir Francis, 405, 407, 409, 411-415, 651
Bagley, William C., 405, 408, 632-647, 659, 665
Bailey, Alice A., 745
Baldwin, James, 688
Bangulfus, 322
Barnard, Henry, 577-578
Barnes, Hazel, 689-690
Barr, Donald, 740
Barr, Stringfellow, 81, 95-103
Basil, St., 296, 343
Bayles, Ernest, 666, 684
Beard, Charles A., 68, 643-644
Beauvoir, Simon de, 690

Benedict, St., 316-320
Benne, Kenneth D., 666
Berger, M. I., 652, 684-690
Berkeley, William, 393, 692
Bestor, Arthur, 655-657, 665
Bill, Arthur, 495
Black, Hugh C., 68-77, 133, 286, 292, 404-407, 482, 652-667, 769-779
Blackham, Robert J., 337
Blake, William, 749-750
Bloom, Benjamin, 740
Boccaccio, 344
Bode, Boyd, 664
Boethius, 410
Bougle, C., 641
Bourne, H. R. Fox, 429
Brameld, Theodore, 658, 666
Breasted, James H., 69, 71, 73, 291
Brewster, Kingman, Jr., 763
Bridgman, Laura, 49
Broudy, Harry S., 665
Brown, Herbert L., Jr., 655
Brown, M. L., 668
Brownston, Orestes A., 233, 392-396
Brubacher, John S., 658-662
Bruner, Jerome, 493, 728, 729
Bryan, William J., 595
Bryce, James, 182, 184
Burtt, Edwin A., 615-618, 652, 691-702
Butler, Donald J., 665

Caesar, Julius, 186, 189, 211, 341, 347
Calvus, 221
Campbell, Alan K., 725
Camus, Albert, 399, 690
Canfield, James H., 577
Carter, Anne, 336
Cato, Marcus, 186, 218, 276, 365, 569
Cephalus, 134
Cervantes, Miguel de, 333
Channing, Eva, 491
Channing, George, 26
Channing, William E., 38
Charlemagne, 321-322
Charles, M. R., 46
Chase, Stuart, 54-55
Chastain, Herb, 14
Chaucer, 333
Chomsky, Noam, 731
Christ, 79-80, 232, 254-261, 264-266, 286-291, 294-295, 316, 494, 499, 608
Chrysippus, 197, 199, 208, 221, 350, 365
Chrysostom, St. John, 286-293, 299, 301, 343
Cicero, Marcus Tullius, 93, 186, 191-195, 220-221, 223, 226, 301, 311, 345, 347-348, 350, 365, 379, 410
Clay, Henry, 606
Cleanthes, 221

Collingswood, L. G., 69
Columbus, 88
Comenius, John Amos, 405-408, 416-428, 603, 770-773
Comstock, Anthony, 19
Conant, James B., 493, 657, 665, 688-689, 772
Condillac, 393
Cook, Albert S., 296
Cooke, Ebenezer, 488
Copernicus, 88, 693
Cornelia, 183, 186, 365
Cornford, Francis M., 159-160
Cotta, 193
Cousin, Victor, 392
Crassus, Lucius, 186, 192, 223
Crates, 345, 361
Creighton, James Edwin, 405, 409-413
Croce, Benedict, 689
Crombie, Margaret C., 484
Cronin, Joseph M., 653, 724-727
Cubberley, Ellwood P., 725
Curti, Merle, 577, 602
Cyrus (the Great), 252

Daley, Richard, 724
Daniel, 298
Darwin, Charles, 88, 578, 668, 775
David, 241, 245, 247-248, 304, 390
Davis, Billie, 492
Davis, Calvin O., 22
D'Alembert, 455
DeGarmo, Charles, 663
DeGuimps, Roger, 483-484, 494
DeLaguna, Grace, 49
Demiashkevich, Michael, 632, 665
Demosthenes, 89, 94, 220, 226, 341, 345
Dennison, George, 738
DeRuggiero, Guido, 689
Descartes, Rene, 412-413, 449, 692, 756
Desroches-Noblecourt, Christiane, 73
Dewey, John, 49, 231-232, 405, 407-408, 582, 591, 597, 613-631, 636-638, 655, 657, 660-664, 666, 695, 729, 730-731, 770, 774-776
Diogenes, 278, 304, 356
Diomedes, 341-342
Diesterweg, Adolph, 474
Dods, Marcus, 307
Donaldson, James, 268, 273, 278
Donatus, 342, 350, 388
Dostoevsky, Fyodor, 687
Dugger, Ronnie, 233, 397-400   ·

Eatherly, Claude, 397-398, 400
Eby, Frederick, 72, 483
Edward I, 333
Eichmann, Adolf, 400
Eliot, Charles W., 407
Elisha, 239
Emile, 457-473
Empedocles the Greek, 210
Ennis, R., 672
Epicurus, 227, 280

Erasmus, Desiderius, 233, 340-381
Eratosthenes, 199
Euripides, 90, 279, 301, 341
Evans-Wentz, W. Y., 746-747
Evenus, 123
Everett, Edward, 21, 22-26, 32-33
Ezra, 252

Fabius, 345
Fanon, Franz, 710
Farnsworth, Dana, 18
Fawcett, Harold, 729
Felix, Minicius, 268, 272
Fellini, Frederico, 2, 5-8
Fersh, Don, 744
Fichte, Johann Gottlieb, 578
Finney, Ross L., 2, 9-10
Flutt, Robert, 424
Forbes, Clarence A., 180
Foshay, Arthur W., 653, 728-735
Foxley, Barbara, 457
Frankel, Charles, 452
Franklin, Benjamin, 569, 586
Freud, Sigmund, 57
Froebel, Friedrich Wilhelm, 405, 407, 496-502, 635, 664
Fulton, Robert, 569
Fyfe, W. Hamilton, 186

Galbraith, John Kenneth, 403
Galen, 354
Gallup, George, 726
Gardner, John, 17
Garland, John, 380
Gaza, Theodore of, 341, 346
Gellius, Aulus, 343
George, Henry, 586-587
Gildersleeve, Basil L., 87
Gilson, Etienne, 267
Glaucon, 140, 143, 148, 150, 152
Goethe, Wolfgang, 548
Goldwater, Barry, 719-720
Goodman, Paul, 726
Goodsell, 184-185
Gorgias, 82, 123
Goya, Francisco Jose de, 749
Green, J. A., 489-491
Green, J. R., 333
Green, T. H., 69
Gregory of Nyssa, 292-293
Grene, Marjorie, 652-653, 689-690, 743, 754-758
Gross, Richard E., 339
Grotius, Hugo, 452

Hall, G. Stanley, 664
Hall, Mosiah, 181-185
Hamilton, Edith, 43, 76-77, 80, 86-94, 256-257, 651
Hanna, Thomas, 690
Hardie, C. D., 670
Harley, G. W., 46
Harris, William T., 405-408, 577-598
Hart, C. W. M., 45

Hartenstein, G., 503
Hastings, J. T., 740
Havighurst, Robert J., 653, 736-742
Hayakawa, S. I., 761
Heidegger, Martin, 689
Hegel, G. F. W., 392, 578-579, 583, 588,
    592, 594, 596, 615, 660, 694
Henderson, Ernest F., 316
Heraclitus, 279, 414
Herbart, Johann Friedrich, 405, 407,
    503-516, 591, 635, 660
Herod (King of Israel), 573
Herodotus, 306, 341
Hershel, Sir John, 413
Hertzel, Leo J., 83
Hesiod, 199, 296, 299, 306, 344, 364
Hilkiah, 246
Hippias, 82, 123
Hitler, Adolf, 65, 711
Hobhouse, L. T., 69
Holland, Lucy E., 488
Holmes, Henry W., 9
Holt, John, 738-739, 740
Homer, 93, 95, 98, 115, 147, 168, 211,
    218, 282, 300, 303, 305, 310, 341, 344
Hoover, Herbert, 586
Horace, 341, 379, 423
Hosea, 241, 243-244, 257
Hullfish, Gordon, 666
Humboldt, Alexander, 517
Hume, David, 393, 580, 693, 698
Huxley, Aldous, 749
Huxley, Thomas, 552-553, 647

Iamblichus, 305
Irwin, William A., 76
Isaiah, 241, 245, 251-252, 257, 325, 382
Isocrates, 82, 120

Jaeger, 78
James, D. G., 48
James, William, 50, 87, 664, 695
Jason, 96
Jaspers, Karl, 684-685, 689
Jay, John, 31
Jefferson, Thomas, 29, 31, 710
Jeremiah, 250, 257
Jerome, St., 185, 343
John, St., 231, 254, 258-259
Johnson, Haynes, 11-15
Johnson, Lyndon, 712, 715, 720, 725
Josephus, 325, 327
Joshua, 294, 329, 389-390
Josiah, 245, 247-249, 329
Jowett, Benjamin, 137-138, 140-141, 160
Joyce, James, 686
Judd, Charles H., 663

Kafka, Franz, 689, 719
Kandel, Isaac L., 657-658, 662, 665
Kant, Immanuel, 392, 578, 693-694, 698
Keatinge, M. W., 416
Keats, John, 655
Keller, Helen, 49
Kennan, George F., 403

Kennedy, John F., 720
Kennedy, Robert, 703, 713-714, 725
Kepler, Johannes, 569
Kerr, Clark, 19
Khrushchev, Nikita, 65, 494
Kierkegaard, Sören, 686, 708, 756
King, Martin Luther, 713
Kirk, Claude, 12
Kneller, George F., 767
Knight, Everett, 690
Kohl, Herbert, 739
Kohlbrenner, Bernard J., 339
Kopkind, Andrew, 43, 67
Krippner, Stanley, 744-745
Krusi, Hermann, 483
Kuhn, Thomas S., 668-674, 677-678, 681,
    761

Laistner, M. L. W., 293
Lamar, Mirabeau Buonaparte, 28-29
Langer, Susanne, 42, 48-60
Lascaris, Constantine, 341
Lawrence, D. H., 686
Lazarus, Emma, 31-32
Lenoir, Nancy Ruth, 494
Levit, Martin, 684
Lewes, 548
Lewis, J., 546
Libanus, 300
Lincoln, Abraham, 88, 704, 711
Lippmann, Walter, 404-405, 490
Livingstone, Sir Richard, 79, 133, 231,
    405, 495, 665
Locke, John, 393, 405-406, 408, 412-413,
    429-451, 512-513, 692, 770-776
Lopez, Robert S., 331, 337
Lorimer, Frank, 49, 53
Lottich, Kenneth V., 330-339, 652
Lucan, 379
Lucian, St., 341, 388
Lucretius, 210, 377
Luke, St., 256-258
Luther, Martin, 233, 382-391, 474-475
Lycon, 124, 371
Lycurgus, 104-105, 107, 109, 112, 355,
    461
Lynch, J. Alvis, 660

Macrobius, 343
MacGregor, G., 633
Madaus, G., 740
Madison, James, 30
Mailer, Norman, 710
Mann, Horace, 405, 408, 557-575,
    577-578, 584, 597, 636
Mark, St., 256-257, 260
Marcellus, 345
Marcuse, Herbert, 706-709, 755
Marx, Karl, 586-588, 674, 694, 723
Matthew, St., 254, 258-259
Maude, Daniel, 557
McLuhan, Marshall, 745, 748, 755
McMurry, Charles A., 657, 663
McMurry, Frank, 663
Mead, Margaret, 45

Meiklejohn, Alexander, 404-407, 653,
    769-778
Mela, Pomponius, 344
Meletus, 123-125, 279
Menander, 341, 358
Menelaus, 348
Menen, Aubrey, 72-73
Meno, 121-122
Messenger, James F., 332-333
Meyerhoff, Hans, 690
Micah, 241-242, 257
Mill, John Stuart, 413
Miller, Hugh, 548
Miller, Perry, 233
Milo, 176, 302, 350, 367
Milton, John, 26, 408
Mingana, Alphonse, 9, 293
Mithridates, 365
Monroe, James, 30
Monroe, Paul, 483
Montagu, Basil, 413
Montaigne, Michael E. de, 408
More, Thomas, 366
Morgenstern, Oskar, 399
Morgenthau, Hans J., 653, 715-723
Morrison, Henry C., 636, 657, 661,
    663-664
Moses, 236-237, 248, 252, 257, 294, 298
Mulholland, Mary A., Sr., 337
Murray, Gilbert, 91
Mussolini, Benito, 711

Naaman, 238-239
Nazianzen, St. Gregory, 299
Nebuchadnezzar, 252
Nehemiah, 253
Neill, A. S., 739
Nettleship, Richard Lewis, 134, 137-139,
    141
Newton, Sir Isaac, 569, 668
Niebuhr, Reinhold, 652
Nietzsche, Friedrich Wilhelm, 708, 712
Nixon, Richard M., 725-726
Noah, 234, 287, 294
Norton, Andrew S., 392-395

O'Conner, D. J., 670-673
Odysseus (or Ulysses), 95-103, 298, 300
Oldenbourg, Zoe, 336
Origen, 325, 343
Orsini, 379
Ovid, 344, 379

Padelford, Frederick Morgan, 296
Painter, F. V. N., 294-295, 321, 382, 476,
    496
Parker, Francis Wayland, 405, 408, 591,
    603-612, 636
Parker, S. C., 663
Parker, Theodore, 392, 578
Parsons, Michael, 673
Partridge, Lelia E., 603
Pascal, Blaise, 710
Pasteur, Louis, 644
Paul, St., 232, 261-264, 294, 304, 351,

358, 364
Pedaretes, 460
Pericles, 89, 92-93, 107, 113-118, 226
Perotti, Nicholas, 341
Pestalozzi, Johann Heinrich, 405, 407-408,
    474-495, 581, 635, 664
Peter, St., 260
Peters, R. S., 679-680
Phalaris, 348
Philip (of Macedon), 200, 360
Piaget, Jean, 678
Pindar, 110
Pitkin, Walter B., 54
Plato, 82, 88, 90-91, 94, 107, 118-119,
    121-141, 162, 164, 173, 214, 226,
    278-299, 305, 325, 343, 426, 461, 493,
    651, 653, 659, 692
Plautus, 341, 423
Pliny, 343-344, 362, 372
Plotinus, 343
Plutarch, 81, 104-112, 356
Poitier, Sidney, 492
Polanyi, Michael, 757-758
Polemarchus, 134
Porphyry, 305, 410
Posetti, 546
Post, L. A., 159
Prodicus (of Ceos), 82, 123, 300
Protagoras, 82, 118, 268
Proteus, 281, 305
Prudentius, 344
Ptolemy, 344
Purmont, Philemon, 557
Pythagoras, 221, 279-280, 284, 305, 328

Quintilianus, Marcus Fabius (Quintilian),
    195-228, 341, 343-344, 347, 350, 371
    378

Rameses II (Egypt), 73, 75, 288
Ramsauer, John, 482-489, 495
Raup, Bruce, 666
Regulus, 228, 460
Reich, Charles A., 403-404
Rhabanus Maurus, 323
Richet, Charles, 54
Richie, A. D., 49
Rickover, Hyman S., 657, 665
Rignano, Eugenio, 50
Ripley, George, 394-395
Robbins, William, 719
Roberts, Alexander, 268, 273, 278
Roosevelt, Franklin D., 720
Roosevelt, Theodore, 720
Roszak, Theodore, 734, 749, 757-758
Rousseau, Jean-Jacques, 405-408, 452-473,
    493, 511, 635, 660, 662, 664, 770-771,
    773-776
Rudhyar, Dane, 759
Rugg, Harold O., 666
Ruskin, John, 546
Russell, Bertrand, 49, 697
Russell, William, 483
Ryle, Gilbert, 676
Ryle, Walter H., 632

Sandiford, Peter, 633
Santayana, George, 94
Sardanapalus, 164, 303
Sartre, Jean-Paul, 690, 694, 756
Scheffler, Israel, 671-673, 677, 768
Schelling, Friedrich Wilhelm von, 392
Schlesinger, Arthur, Jr., 652-653, 703-714
Schweitzer, Albert, 399
Scott, Sir Walter, 26, 333
Seckinger, Donald S., 41-42, 44-47,
　　652-653, 764-768
Seneca, 328, 350, 364
Shakespeare, William, 26
Shane, M. L., 632
Shaw, F. Alden, 632
Sheldon, Edward A., 636
Sherrill, Robert, 718
Shores, Louis, 632
Shorey, Paul, 160
Smail, William M., 195
Smith, B. Othanel, 666, 672
Socrates, 82, 86, 119, 121-134, 276, 279,
　　301-302, 347, 518
Solomon, 231, 240-241, 247-248, 325,
　　389-390
Solon, 300, 438
Soltis, Jonas F., 652, 668-683
Sophocles, 86
Sorel, Georges, 708
Speke, John H., 517
Spencer, Herbert, 405, 407-408, 517-556,
　　578, 580
Spenser, Edmund, 333
Spinoza, Baruch, 692
Staley, John Edgcumbe, 337
Stalin, Joseph V., 708
Stanley, William O., 666
Steffens, Lincoln, 291
Stevenson, Robert Louis, 87
Stimson, Henry, 398
Strabo, 344
Strachy, Sir Edward, 336
Sulpicius, 193
Sumner, Charles, 606
Swineford, Edwin J., 495

Tacitus, Publius Cornelius, 186-190
Tatian, 278-285
Taylor, John Wilson, 180
Teller, Edward, 398-399
Tenebaum, Samuel, 665
Tennyson, Lord Alfred, 333
Terence, 341
Terpander, 110
Tertullian, 273-277
Theaetetus, 128-132
Themistocles, 365
Theodore of Gaza, 341, 346
Theodore of Mopsuestia, 293
Theophrastus, 343
Thomas, Lawrence, 666
Thoreau, Henry D., 403
Thorndike, Edward L., 637-638
Thrasymachus, 134

Thucydides, 93, 113-118
Tillich, Paul, 689
Timotheus, 217, 302
Tocqueville, Alexis de, 403
Tollett, Kenneth, 757
Tolstoy, Leo, 716
Toynbee, Arnold, 3, 34-37, 40, 80, 84-85
Traherne, Thomas, 749
Trilling, Lionel, 690
Troland, Leonard, 52
Truman, Harry S., 398, 720
Tsanoff, Radoslav A., 232, 264, 654-655
Tuchman, Barbara W., 16-20, 42
Turner, Francis C., 488
Turnus, 350
Tussmann, Joseph, 779
Tut-ankh-Amun, 74
Tyndall, 552

Uden, Grant, 336
Ulich, Robert, 413, 478, 503
Ulysses. See Odysseus
Usdan, Michael, 726

Valerius Maximus, 345
Valla, Lorenzo, 342
Van Buren, Martin, 712
Van Til, William, 728, 736
Varro, 210, 462
Vecchio, Frank, 14-15
Vecchio, Mary, 11-15
Vespasian, 372
Virgil (or Vergil), 211, 222, 305, 310, 341,
　　349-550, 363, 379
Vitello, Philip, 14
Von Werth, Mrs., 485, 487

Ward, Barbara, 43, 61-66
Washington, George, 27-28
Webster, Daniel, 606
Wegener, Frank C., 667
Welldon, E. C., 163
Wheeler, Benjamin Ide, 585
Whewell, William, 413
Whipple, Guy M., 632
Whitehead, Alfred North, 70, 651
Whitman, Walt, 403
Wilds, Elmer Harrison, 330-339, 652
William, Duke of Cleves, 352
Wilson, Mrs. James F., 482-483
Wilson, Woodrow, 720
Winthrop, John, 558
Woodward, William H., 340, 381
Woodworth, William, 638
Wordsworth, William, 592
Wynne, John P., 658, 666

Xenophon, 301, 472

Zacharias, Gerrold, 730
Zechariah, 253
Zeno, 221, 279